T3-BOQ-248

COMPARATIVE POLITICS 92/93

Tenth Edition

Editor

Christian Soe
California State University, Long Beach

Christian Soe was born in Denmark, studied in Canada and the United States, and received his doctoral degree in political science from the Free University in Berlin. He is a political science professor at California State University, Long Beach. Dr. Soe teaches a wide range of courses in comparative politics and contemporary political theory, and actively participates in professional symposiums in the United States and abroad. He founded and continues to direct the Pacific Workshop on German Affairs, and his research deals primarily with developments in contemporary German politics. As an observer of the first free election in East Germany in March 1990, he gathered fresh data on the reemergence of political pluralism in that part of the country. In November and December 1990 he returned as an observer of the first Bundestag election after Germany's unification.

At present Dr. Soe is writing a short study of the Free Democratic Party in the enlarged Federal Republic, and is co-editor of a planned book, *The Germans and Their Neighbors,* that will examine foreign reactions to the emergence of a larger and more powerful Germany.

Annual **E**ditions
A Library of Information from the Public Press

Cover illustration by Mike Eagle

The Dushkin Publishing Group, Inc.
Sluice Dock, Guilford, Connecticut 06437

The Annual Editions Series

Annual Editions is a series of over 55 volumes designed to provide the reader with convenient, low-cost access to a wide range of current, carefully selected articles from some of the most important magazines, newspapers, and journals published today. Annual Editions are updated on an annual basis through a continuous monitoring of over 300 periodical sources. All Annual Editions have a number of features designed to make them particularly useful, including topic guides, annotated tables of contents, unit overviews, and indexes. For the teacher using Annual Editions in the classroom, an Instructor's Resource Guide with test questions is available for each volume.

VOLUMES AVAILABLE

Africa
Aging
American Government
American History, Pre-Civil War
American History, Post-Civil War
Anthropology
Biology
Business and Management
Business Ethics
Canadian Politics
China
Commonwealth of Independent States and Central/Eastern Europe (Soviet Union)
Comparative Politics
Computers in Education
Computers in Business
Computers in Society
Criminal Justice
Drugs, Society, and Behavior
Early Childhood Education
Economics
Educating Exceptional Children
Education
Educational Psychology
Environment
Geography
Global Issues
Health
Human Development
Human Resources
Human Sexuality

International Business
Japan
Latin America
Life Management
Macroeconomics
Management
Marketing
Marriage and Family
Microeconomics
Middle East and the Islamic World
Money and Banking
Nutrition
Personal Growth and Behavior
Physical Anthropology
Psychology
Public Administration
Race and Ethnic Relations
Social Problems
Sociology
State and Local Government
Third World
Urban Society
Violence and Terrorism
Western Civilization, Pre-Reformation
Western Civilization, Post-Reformation
Western Europe
World History, Pre-Modern
World History, Modern
World Politics

Library of Congress Cataloging in Publication Data
Main entry under title: Annual Editions: Comparative Politics. 1992/93.
    1. World politics—Periodicals. 2. Politics, Practical—Periodicals. I. Soe, Christian, comp.
II. Title: Comparative Politics.
ISBN 1-56134-081-2   909'.05   83-647654

© 1992 by The Dushkin Publishing Group, Inc. Annual Editions ® is a Registered Trademark of The Dushkin Publishing Group, Inc.

Copyright © 1992 by The Dushkin Publishing Group, Inc., Guilford, Connecticut 06437

All rights reserved. No part of this book may be reproduced, stored, or transmitted by any means—mechanical, electronic, or otherwise—without written permission from the publisher.

Tenth Edition

Manufactured by The Banta Company, Harrisonburg, Virginia 22801

Editors/Advisory Board

EDITOR

Christian Soe
California State University
Long Beach

ADVISORY BOARD

Mark Bartholomew
University of Maine
Farmington

Louis Cantori
University of Maryland
Baltimore

Leonard Cardenas
Southwest Texas State University

Parris Chang
Pennsylvania State University
University Park

Maureen A. Covell
Simon Frasier University

Robert L. Delorme
California State University
Long Beach

John Echeverri-Gent
University of Virginia

Richard S. Flickinger
Wittenberg University

E. Gene Frankland
Ball State University

Ronald Inglehart
University of Michigan

Karl H. Kahrs
California State University
Fullerton

Aline Kuntz
University of New Hampshire

Gregory Mahler
University of Mississippi

Anthony M. Messina
Tufts University

Joyce Marie Mushaben
University of Missouri
St. Louis

Helen Purkitt
United States Naval Academy

Martin Slann
Clemson University

Frederick Swan
Livingstone College

Joel D. Wolfe
University of Cincinnati

Rodger Yeager
West Virginia University

Eleanor E. Zeff
Iowa State University

Charles Ziegler
University of Louisville

Members of the Advisory Board are instrumental in the final selection of articles for each edition of Annual Editions. Their review of articles for content, level, currentness, and appropriateness provides critical direction to the editor and staff. We think you'll find their careful consideration well reflected in this volume.

STAFF

Ian A. Nielsen, Publisher
Brenda S. Filley, Production Manager
Roberta Monaco, Editor
Addie Raucci, Administrative Editor
Cheryl Greenleaf, Permissions Editor
Diane Barker, Editorial Assistant
Lisa Holmes-Doebrick, Administrative Coordinator
Charles Vitelli, Designer
Shawn Callahan, Graphics
Meredith Scheld, Graphics
Steve Shumaker, Graphics
Libra A. Cusack, Typesetting Supervisor
Juliana Arbo, Typesetter

To the Reader

In publishing ANNUAL EDITIONS we recognize the enormous role played by the magazines, newspapers, and journals of the *public press* in providing current, first-rate educational information in a broad spectrum of interest areas. Within the articles, the best scientists, practitioners, researchers, and commentators draw issues into new perspective as accepted theories and viewpoints are called into account by new events, recent discoveries change old facts, and fresh debate breaks out over important controversies.

Many of the articles resulting from this enormous editorial effort are appropriate for students, researchers, and professionals seeking accurate, current material to help bridge the gap between principles and theories and the real world. These articles, however, become more useful for study when those of lasting value are carefully *collected, organized, indexed,* and *reproduced* in a *low-cost format,* which provides easy and permanent access when the material is needed. That is the role played by *Annual Editions.* Under the direction of each volume's *Editor,* who is an expert in the subject area, and with the guidance of an *Advisory Board,* we seek each year to provide in each *ANNUAL EDITION* a current, well-balanced, carefully selected collection of the best of the public press for your study and enjoyment. We think you'll find this volume useful, and we hope you'll take a moment to let us know what you think.

This collection of readings brings together many recent articles to help you understand the politics of distant, foreign lands. You will soon discover that studying politics from a comparative perspective not only opens up a fascinating world beyond our borders, it also leads to greater insights into yourself and your social and political situation.

The articles in unit one cover Great Britain, Germany, France, and Japan in a serial manner. Each of these modern societies has developed its own governmental institutions, defined its own political agenda, and found its own dynamic balance of continuity and change. Nevertheless, as the readings of unit two show, it is possible to point to some common denominators to make useful cross-national comparisons among these and other representative democracies. Unit three goes one step further by discussing the impact of two major changes that are rapidly transforming the political map of Europe—the growth of the European Community (EC) and the collapse of communism in much of Central and Eastern Europe.

The continuing political importance of Europe has been underscored by these two developments. While the integration of the European Community has been a process of several decades, it accelerated markedly in the latter part of the 1980s with the passage and implementation of the Single Europe Act. By contrast, there was little advance warning of the recent upheaval that has weakened or toppled the Communist regimes imposed in the countries of Central and Eastern Europe after World War II. The result is nothing less than a major revolution, as these nations attempt to replace one-party rule and socialist state planning with multiparty democracy and market economics.

Unit four looks at developing so-called Third World countries in Latin America and Africa; China and India are also discussed in this section. The diversity of these countries in their struggle to overcome traditional obstacles to development is the emphasis of these articles. Unit five considers some of the major trends, issues, and prospects of political development. The lasting impact of the trend toward democratic rule is yet to be assessed, and just how it will be affected by capitalism and the momentum of traditional ethnic identity are considered.

There has rarely been so interesting and important a time for the study of comparative politics as now. We can already see that the political earthquake of 1989–1990 has altered the political landscape with consequences that will be felt and studied for many years to come. But even in a time of such major political transformation, there are important patterns of continuity as well. We must be careful to look for both as we seek to gain a comparative understanding of the politics of other countries and peoples.

This is the tenth edition of *Annual Editions: Comparative Politics.* It includes many new articles that reflect the changes discussed above. The basic format has also been adjusted to take into account the revolutionary developments that have created a post–cold war world.

I am grateful to members of the advisory board and The Dushkin Publishing Group as well as to many readers who have made useful comments on past selections and suggested new ones. My own students also keep me posted on concerns and needs that this anthology must address. Susan B. Mason, who recently received her master's degree in political science at my university, has been a superb research assistant over the past few years. I ask you all to help me improve future editions of this anthology by keeping me informed of your reactions and suggestions for change. Please complete and return the article rating form in the back of the book.

Christian Soe
Editor

Contents

Unit 1

Pluralist Democracies: Country Overviews

Nineteen selections examine the current state of politics in Great Britain, Germany, France, and Japan.

The concepts in bold italics are developed in the article. For further expansion please refer to the Topic Guide and the Index.

Unit 2

Pluralist Democracies: Factors in the Political Process

Eleven selections examine the functioning of Western European democracies with regard to political ideas and participation, the role of women in politics, and the institutional framework of representative government.

The concepts in bold italics are developed in the article. For further expansion please refer to the Topic Guide and the Index.

Unit 3

Europe — West, Center, and East: The Politics of Integration, Transformation, and Distintegration

Twelve selections examine the European continent, the politics of integration, post-Communist Central and Eastern Europe, and Russia and the other post-Soviet Republics.

The concepts in bold italics are developed in the article. For further expansion please refer to the Topic Guide and the Index.

Unit 4

The Third World: Diversity in Development

Ten selections review Third World economic and political development in Latin America, Africa, China, and India.

The concepts in bold italics are developed in the article. For further expansion please refer to the Topic Guide and the Index.

The concepts in bold italics are developed in the article. For further expansion please refer to the Topic Guide and the Index.

Unit 5

Comparative Politics: Some Major Trends, Issues, and Prospects

Seven selections discuss the rise of democracy, how capitalism impacts on political development, and the political assertion of group identity in contemporary politics.

The concepts in bold italics are developed in the article. For further expansion please refer to the Topic Guide and the Index.

Topic Guide

This topic guide suggests how the selections in this book relate to topics of traditional concern to students and professionals involved with the study of comparative politics. It is very useful in locating articles that relate to each other for reading and research. The guide is arranged alphabetically according to topic. Articles may, of course, treat topics that do not appear in the topic guide. In turn, entries in the topic guide do not necessarily constitute a comprehensive listing of all the contents of each selection.

Pluralist Democracies: Country Overviews

- **Great Britain (Articles 1–6)**
- **Germany (Articles 7–11)**
- **France (Articles 12–15)**
- **Japan (Articles 16–19)**

The United Kingdom, Germany, France, and Italy rank among the most prominent industrial societies in Western Europe. Although their modern political histories differ sharply, they have all become stable pluralist democracies with competitive party systems and representative governments. Japan is far less pluralist in sociocultural terms, but it occupies a similar position of primacy among the few industrial democracies in Asia.

In this and the following two units, the articles covering the political systems of Great Britain, Germany, France, and Japan are presented in separate country studies. Each of these modern societies has developed its own set of governmental institutions, defined its own political agenda, and found its own dynamic balance of continuity and change.

Great Britain was for most of this century regarded as a model of parliamentary government and majoritarian party politics, or what became known as "the Westminster model" of rule. In the 1970s, however, the country became better known for its chronic governing problems. Some observers spoke about the British sickness or *Englanditis,* a condition characterized by such problems as economic stagnation, social malaise, political polarization, and a general incapacity of the elected government to deal effectively with such a malady.

By the mid-1980s Great Britain began to pull considerably ahead of other West European countries in its annual economic growth rates. This apparent economic turnabout was associated with the rule of then–prime minister Margaret Thatcher, who had come to power in May of 1979, and who had introduced a drastic change in economic and social policy for the country. She portrayed herself as a conviction politician, determined to introduce a strong dose of economic discipline by encouraging private enterprise and reducing the role of government, in contrast to the compromising consensus politics of her Labour and Conservative predecessors.

Thus the worries about ungovernability, which had dominated discussions about British politics in the 1970s, gave way in the 1980s to quite different questions about the consequences of Thatcher's economic and social policies. The debate also shifted to new concerns about the government's efforts to tighten central controls over education at all levels, its introduction of cost controls into the popular National Health Service, its privatization of electricity and water industries, as well as its inroads upon what had long been considered established rights in such areas as local government and civil liberties. Moreover, Thatcher was a staunch defender of national sovereignty who distrusted the drive toward monetary and eventual political union in the European Community. She became known throughout the Continent for her unusually sharp attacks on what she regarded as tendencies toward undemocratic statism or technocratic socialism in Brussels.

For the mass electorate, however, nothing seems to have been so upsetting as the introduction of the community charge—a tax on each adult resident that would replace the local property tax or rates as a means of financing local public services. Although the poll tax, as the new charge became known, was very unpopular in Scotland, where it had been introduced a year earlier, Thatcher resisted all pressure to reconsider the measure and followed the plan of extending it to England and Wales in April 1990. Not only did the poll tax appear inequitable or regressive, as compared to one based on property values, it also turned out to be set much higher by local governments than the national government originally had estimated. The politically disastrous result was that the revenue measure appeared to be anything but neutral in its impact. It created an unexpectedly large proportion of losers, that is, people who had to pay considerably more in local taxes than they previously paid, while the far fewer winners tended to be rich people who had previously paid higher property taxes. Not surprisingly, the national and local governments disagreed about who was responsible for the unpopular tax bills, but the voters seemed to have little difficulty in assigning blame to Margaret Thatcher and the Conservative party as originators of the unpopular reform. By the spring of 1990, some observers correctly anticipated that the tax rebellion would undermine Thatcher's position in her own party and become her political Waterloo.

The feisty prime minister had weathered many political challenges, but there was increasing speculation that the Tories might try to replace her with a more attractive leader before the next general election. The issue that finally triggered such a development was Thatcher's stepped-up attacks on closer European union during 1990. It led her deputy prime minister, Sir Geoffrey Howe, to resign on November 1, 1990, with a sharp public rebuke of her attitude to Europe. There followed a leadership challenge in the Conservative party that ended with Thatcher's own resignation toward the end of the same month.

John Major, who was chosen by his fellow conservative members of Parliament to be Thatcher's successor as prime minister and leader of the governing party, had long been regarded as one of her most loyal cabinet supporters. But, although he continued her tough economic policy, which Thatcher herself had described as dry, he appeared to prefer a more compassionate or wet social policy. His governing style turned out to be far less confrontational, and he made early plans for abandoning the hated poll tax. In the Persian Gulf War of 1991, Major continued Thatcher's policy of giving strong British support for firm and ultimate military measures against the government of Iraq, which had invaded and occupied oil-rich Kuwait. Unlike his predecessor after the Falkland Islands conflict, however, he did not follow up on the quick and popular military victory by calling for general elections.

By the time of Thatcher's resignation, Labour appeared to be in a relatively good position to capitalize on the growing electoral disenchantment with the Conservative government. The big political question had become whether Prime Minister Major could recapture some of the lost ground. Under its leader, Neil Kinnock, Labour had moved back toward its traditional center-Left position and now again presented itself as a politically moderate and socially caring reform party. It had moved ahead in some opinion polls, and it won some impressive victories in by-elections to the House of Commons. In the aftermath of the Persian Gulf War, Labour was overtaken by the Conservatives in the polls, but its position improved again a few months later.

As the main opposition party, however, Labour was now troubled by a new version of the social democratic and liberal alternatives that had fragmented the non-Conservative camp in the elections of 1983 and 1987. The two smaller parties, which had operated as an electoral coalition or alliance in those years, had drawn the conclusion that their organizational separation was a hindrance to their own political breakthrough. After the defeat of 1987, they formed a new united party, the Social and Liberal Democrats (SLD), which soon became known simply as Liberal Democrats. Under the leadership of Paddy Ashdown, they promoted themselves as a reasonable centrist alternative to the Conservatives on the right and the Labour party on the left. Their goal was to win the balance of power in a tightly fought election and then, as kingmakers, to enter a government coalition with one of the two big parties. One of their main demands would be that the winner-takes-all electoral system, based on single-member districts, be replaced by one of proportional representation in multimember districts, as used widely in continental Europe. Such a system would almost surely guarantee the Liberal Democrats not only a relatively solid base in the House of Commons, based on their share of the popular vote, but also a pivotal role in a future process of coalition politics in Great Britain. In other words, they would occupy a position as kingmaker or balancer, much like their smaller counterpart, the Free Democratic Party, in Germany.

Writing half a year before the 1992 general election, James E. Cronin provides a good assessment of the changed political landscape in Great Britain. He explains the reasons for the coup against Margaret Thatcher and shows how both Labour and Conservatives had begun to move toward the center, even before the beleaguered prime minister stepped down. This recentering of British politics became evident in the campaign leading to the general election, called by Prime Minister Major for April 9, 1992. The timing of the election seemed highly unattractive for his own governing party, since Great Britain had entered its worst recession in years. On the other hand, there was little time left for delay, for an election had to come before the end of June under Great Britain's five-year limit.

Two articles in this unit analyze the election and its political consequences. It was a very important outcome that confounded many observers who had expected a change in government. Instead of defeat, the result guaranteed the governing party a fourth consecutive term of office, something that had not occurred in British politics for over 150 years. Despite the recession, they were able to garner the same overall percentage of the vote (about 43 percent) as in 1987, while Labour increased its total share only slightly, from 32 to 35 percent. The Liberal Democrats received only 18 percent, almost one-quarter less than the Alliance had won in its two unsuccessful attempts to "break the mold" of the party system in 1983 and 1987. In retrospect, it became clear that there had not been a uniform electoral shift, as the article from the London Sunday Times points out. In the House of Commons, the Conservatives lost 36 seats but ended up with 336 of the 651 members—a clear majority. Labour increased its number of seats from 229 to 271, a net gain of 42, but far short of an opportunity to threaten the majority party. The Liberal Democrats ended up with 20 seats, down from 22, and the rest were occupied by representatives of small regional parties from Northern Ireland, Scotland, and Wales.

One of the most interesting issues in contemporary British politics is the demand for constitutional change. In the late 1980s, an ad hoc liberal coalition launched Charter 88, which called for a written constitution with a bill of rights, proportional representation, and a redefinition and codification of other basic rules of the game in British politics. The chartists chose the tricentennial of Great Britain's Glorious Revolution of 1688 to launch their effort, whose main result until now has been to kindle a broad discussion of citizenship rights in the country. By now, other groups have worked out a number of alternative proposals for a new British constitution. Caroline Ellis summarizes and compares the main features of four of these proposals, two from the socialist Left, one from the Liberal center, and one from the neoconservative Right.

Germany was united in 1990 when the eastern German Democratic Republic (GDR) merged with the western Federal Republic of Germany. The two German states had been established in 1949, four years after the defeat of the German Reich in the World War II. During the next forty years, rival elites and ideologies had set the tone in each of the two successor states. East Germany comprised the territory of the former Soviet Occupation Zone of Germany, and its one-party rule and centrally planned economy had expressed the power monopoly of the Communist party on which the state rested. In contrast, West Germany, which was based on the former American, British, and French zones of postwar occupation, had developed a pluralist democracy and a flourishing market economy.

Mass demonstrations in several East German cities and the westward flight of thousands of citizens brought the GDR government to make numerous concessions in late 1989 and early 1990. The Berlin Wall ceased to be a hermetical seal after November 9, 1989, when this symbol of the cold war and Germany's division was dismantled. Under new leadership, the ruling Communists of East Germany sought to restore stability and gain some legitimacy by introducing a form of power-sharing with non-Communist groups and parties. With the westward flight of East Germans continuing, Prime Minister Hans Modrow, a reform Communist, hurriedly agreed to permit a free election in March 1990.

Popular demonstrations and the willingness of East Germans to "vote with their feet" only had a chance of promoting reform because of two major developments. First, the Soviet leader, Mikhail Gorbachev, had abandoned the so-called Brezhnev Doctrine, according to which the Soviets claimed the right of intervention on behalf of the established Communist regimes in Central and Eastern Europe. And second, the imposed Communist regimes of these countries turned out to have lost their old self-confidence and will to hold on to power at any cost. As Alexis de Tocqueville had observed a century and a half earlier, no popular revolution can succeed until the old regime has developed such symptoms.

The East German Communists slowly gave up their power and positions, and by the time of the March 1990 election it was clear even to them that the pressure for national unification could no longer be stemmed. The issue was no longer whether the two German states would be joined together, but how and when. These questions were settled when an alliance of Christian Democrats, largely identified with and supported by Chancellor Helmut Kohl's party in West Germany, won a surprisingly decisive victory with 48 percent of the vote. It advocated a short, quick route to unification, beginning with an early monetary union in the summer and a political union by the fall of 1990. This also meant that the new non-Communist government in East Germany, headed by Lothar de Maizière of the Christian Democratic Union (CDU), followed the short route to merger with the Federal Republic under Article 23 of the West German Basic

Law. The electoral result for the SPD (Social Democratic Party) was only 22 percent of the vote. That also meant a defeat of its alternative strategy for unification which would have involved the protracted negotiation of a new German constitution, as envisaged by Article 146 of the Basic Law.

During the summer and fall of 1990, the governments of the two German states and the four former occupying powers completed their so-called *two-plus-four negotiations* that resulted in mutual agreement on the German unification process. A monetary union in July was followed by a political merger in October. In advance of unification, Bonn was able to negotiate an agreement with Moscow in which the latter accepted the gradual withdrawal of Soviet troops from eastern Germany and the membership of the larger, united Germany in NATO in return for considerable German economic support for the Soviet Union. The result was a major shift in both the domestic and international balance of power.

The Christian Democrats repeated their electoral success in the contest for the parliaments of the five new (or revived) states of eastern Germany in October 1990. They won again in the first Bundestag election for united Germany in early December, even though their share of the vote dipped somewhat. The only Bundestag party to increase its overall share of the vote (to 11 percent) was the FDP, the small liberal coalition party that has been a majority maker in West German politics for years. It did even better in the eastern part of Germany than in the West. The Greens, on the other hand, failed to get the required minimum of 5 percent of the vote in western Germany and dropped out of the Bundestag.

The composition of the Bundestag was affected by the provision that, for this election only, the two parts of united Germany operated as separate electoral entities as far as the 5 percent threshold was concerned. That made it possible for another Green grouping, an electoral coalition with left-wing reformers calling themselves Alliance 90, to win enough votes (about 6 percent of the total) in eastern Germany to get a small foothold in the Bundestag. The special electoral conditions for 1990 also enabled the former Communist ruling party, in its new identity as the Party of Democratic Socialism or PDS, to gain representation in the Bundestag by winning about 10 percent of the vote in eastern Germany. It appealed to a number of groups that feared social displacement and ideological alienation in a market economy, including not only many former privileged party members but also some rural workers and young people. Ironically, the party was very weak among the wage workers for whom it claimed to speak.

Anyone interested in political development will want to keep a close eye on the difficult transition period in Germany. State and local elections since December 1990 appear to support the view that the Greens are still a small but viable political party, which can expect to return to the Bundestag in 1994. But there is also a possibility that a far Right party, which uses xenophobic slogans against foreign immigrants and asylum-seekers, could gain entry to the Bundestag for the first time since 1949. One such party, the German People's Union (DVU), was elected to the state parliaments in Bremen and Schleswig-Holstein in the fall of 1991 and the spring of 1992 respectively. A similar ultra-Right party, the so-called *Republikaner* or Reps, entered the state parliament of Baden-Wüerttemberg in southwestern Germany by winning over 10 percent of the vote in April 1992. The growth of such parties in Germany and elsewhere in Europe bears careful watching, even if many of these votes seem primarily to be a form of protest against social and economic uncertainties.

In France, the bicentennial of the country's 1789 Revolution was duly celebrated in 1989. It served as an occasion for public ceremonies and a revival of historical-political debates about the costs and benefits of early modern exercise in the radical transformation of a society. Ironically, however, for some years there has been evidence that the ideological cleavages, which marked French politics for so much of the nineteenth and twentieth centuries, are losing much of their significance. Instead, there is now emerging a more pragmatic, pluralist form of accommodation in French public life.

To be sure, this deradicalization and depolarization of political discourse is by no means complete in France. If the Communists have been weakened and become ideologically confused, Le Pen's National Front on the far Right has had some success with a xenophobic rhetoric directed primarily against the many residents of Arab origin found in the country. The apparent electoral appeal of his invective has led some leaders of the establishment parties to voice more carefully formulated reservations about the presence of so many immigrants. An entirely new and different political phenomenon for France is the appearance of two Green parties, one more conservative and the other more socialist in orientation. In the regional elections of March 1992, the environmentalists together received about 15 percent of the vote, slightly more than the share received by the National Front.

Soon after the regional elections, in which the Socialists suffered a calamity by garnering less than 20 percent of the vote, François Mitterrand replaced Prime Minister Edith Cresson. He had appointed her to that position only 10 months earlier, in May 1991, after dismissing Michel Rocard, a possible contender for the leadership of the Socialist party. In contrast to her predecessor, Cresson soon managed to attract a lot of negative press coverage with her blunt manner of speaking. She served as a kind of sacrificial lamb after the electoral debacle in March 1992, and she was replaced by Pierre Bérégovoy, her former finance minister. It was widely reported that Mitterrand's first choice had been Jacques Delors, his finance minister from 1981 to 1984 and current president of the European Commission in Brussels. Delors is highly respected, inside and outside France, and might have given new vigor to the dispirited Socialists. But Delors, who is believed to have his eyes set on the presidency, apparently did not wish to ruin his political future by taking over a weak and unpopular government in France at that time.

Mitterrand's seven-year presidential term does not expire until 1995, but there will be new elections to the National Assembly when its five-year term is up in 1993. Should the Socialists be defeated, Mitterrand would face the question of whether to resign early from the presidency or, as under similar political circumstances in 1986, to enter a period of cohabitation with a conservative prime minister. The latter experiment ended well for the Socialists, with Mitterrand reelected as president in 1988 and the conservatives defeated in the early election of a new National Assembly that followed. But many observers find it doubtful that an aging Mitterrand will wish to repeat the stressful experience of governing with a prime minister who belongs to a rival party.

Mitterrand has indicated an interest in possibly shortening the unusually long presidential term to five years, to coincide with the parliamentary term. Such an institutional reform, were it to be enacted, could have important consequences for the balance of power within the dual executive of the Fifth Republic. It is also possible that Mitterrand will try to change the electoral law to one based on proportional representation, as he did in 1986, in order to fragment the Right and save his own Socialists from a political rout in the 1993 party contest. But such a cynical manipulation of the electoral rules could run into opposition on the grounds of principle.

The articles in this subsection provide a perspective on what some observers call "the new France." In fact, contemporary French politics and society combine some traits that reflect continuity with the past and some that suggest considerable innovation. One recurrent theme among observers of France is the decline of the previously sharp ideological struggle between the Left and the Right. There may well be a sense of loss among some French intellectuals who still prefer the political battle to have apocalyptic implications. They will find it hard to accept that the grand struggle between Left and Right has been replaced by a more moderate and seemingly more mundane party politics of competition among groups that are clustered near the center of the political spectrum. To be sure, they may discover that what they regard as a tedious political competition between those promising a little more or a little less can have considerable practical consequences in terms of who gets what and how. Moreover, such incremental politics need not be without dramatic conflict, since new issues, events, or leaders often emerge to sharpen the differences and increase the apparent stakes of politics.

Still, the loss of the great alternatives may help account for the mood of political malaise that many observers claim to discover in contemporary France. But the French disorientation probably has another major origin as well. The sudden emergence of a larger and potentially more powerful Germany next door cannot but have an unnerving effect on the so-called political class in France, even though opinion polls show a fairly strong public support for the right of the Germans to choose national unification. French elites now face the troubling question of redefining their country's role in a post–cold war world, in which the Soviet Union has lost power and influence while Germany has gained in both.

In this new European setting, some observers have even suggested that we may expect a major new cleavage in French politics between those who favor a reassertion of the traditional French nation-state ideal—a kind of neo-Gaullism found on both the Left and Right—and those who want the country to accept a new European order, in which the sovereignty of both the French and German nation-states would be diluted or contained by a network of international obligations within the larger European framework.

Japan, the fourth country in this study of representative governments of industrial societies, has long been an object of fascination to students of politics and society. After World War II, a representative democracy was installed in Japan under American supervision. This political system has acquired indigenous Japanese characteristics that set it off from other major democracies examined here. James Fallows explores some of these differences, arguing that it is both a mistake and a presumption to believe that Japan is becoming a pluralist Western society.

The Japanese political system has long been dominated by the Liberal Democratic Party (LDP) that, as the saying goes, is neither liberal, nor democratic, nor a party. It is essentially a conservative political force, comprising several delicately balanced factions. These are often personal followerships identified and headed by political bosses who stake out factional claims to benefits of office. In the late 1980s, some observers believed that this system would be replaced when the LDP was shaken by scandals that felled Prime Ministers Noboru Takeshita and Sosuke Uno in quick succession. At the time, the LDP lost its majority in the upper house of the legislature, and for a while the Socialist party seemed to be headed for a political breakthrough.

The political establishment in Japan proved to be more resilient than many foreign journalists had led their readers to expect. In the February 1990 election of the lower house, the LDP won a decisive victory that left it in charge of the government under Toshiki Kaifu, a younger, relatively unknown and, above all, untainted politician. He had become prime minister some months earlier, when he apparently was pushed forward by his party's heavyweights as a seat-warmer until the scandals died down enough for one of the usual factional leaders to take over. After Kaifu's larger-than-expected electoral victory, it seemed that his popularity would make it harder for the old-timers to replace him with one of their own. In the latter half of 1991, however, the LDP promoted one of its old factional leaders, Kiichi Miyazawa, to replace Kaifu as prime minister. Ironically, this power play has been followed by a replay of the LDP's problems, including a setback in the spring 1992 elections for the upper house.

In recent years, the relationship between Japan and the United States has become marred by a number of mutual recriminations. There is a need for greater understanding of the other's culture, both in Japan and the United States, as the two final articles explain.

Looking Ahead: Challenge Questions

Why was Britain once called "the sick man of Europe?" How did Margaret Thatcher differ in her perception of the British problems and her determination to do something about them? How has John Major presided over a recentering of British politics? Why was the outcome of the 1992 general election a surprise to many observers, and how do you explain the result received by the three largest parties? What are some of the problems that constitutional reformers in Great Britain seek to redress?

Would you agree that the democratic order in the western part of Germany has long been sound and stable? What factors may help the eastern part of united Germany to develop a democratic political culture and a prosperous market economy like its western counterpart?

What are the signs that French politics have become more centrist or middle-of-the-road for the main political parties? What are the sources of political support for the National Front? What are the problems that may face President Mitterrand after the parliamentary elections of 1993? What political decisions may he take as a result?

In what significant ways does Japan differ from the socio-cultural pluralism of many Western societies? Why did the LDP replace the relatively popular and untainted Prime Minister Kaifu in 1991?

> "[T]he next election will turn on the state of the economy or issues of the moment. But whatever the election's outcome, the next government will almost certainly eschew the highly controversial and polarizing initiatives that marked the Thatcher era."

The End of an Era in British Politics

JAMES E. CRONIN

JAMES E. CRONIN *teaches modern European history at Boston College. His works include* Industrial Conflict in Modern Britain *(London: Croom Helm, 1979) and* Labour and Society in Britain, 1918–1979 *(New York: Schocken, 1983). His most recent book is* The Politics of State Expansion: War, State and Society in Twentieth-Century Britain *(New York: Routledge, 1991).*

It has been one year since British Prime Minister Margaret Thatcher's fall from power in November 1990—long enough to become accustomed to the relatively innocuous presence of her successor, John Major, but not nearly long enough to become accustomed to Thatcher's absence. Has there been time enough to assess the accomplishments, the legacy, of the 11 years and 7 months of Thatcher's Conservative rule?[1]

Perhaps such assessments should await the outcome of the next election, to be held by June 1992, which might be regarded as rendering a provisional verdict. But it is certain that the Conservative party has conspicuously distanced itself from key tenets of "late Thatcherism." John Major, the new Conservative prime minister, has adopted a "kinder, gentler" personal image than Thatcher's and a more conciliatory stance toward Europe, and in May his government abandoned Thatcher's unpopular poll tax.

It might even be argued that recent changes in the programs and rhetoric of the two major British political parties constitute the best indicators of the fate of Thatcher's vision. Both parties have moved to the center: a Labour party policy review has produced a markedly more moderate program than the ones presented in the elections of 1983 and 1987, while the Conservative party has with equal clarity abandoned the right-wing radicalism that characterized it during much of the Thatcher period.

The movement toward the center suggests that the achievements of Thatcher's first two terms in office—the tax cuts, the attempt to rein in public spending and dampen inflation, the taming of the unions, the selling off of public housing, and the privatization of nationalized industries—were more widely accepted than the initiatives of Thatcher's third and last term. It suggests too that politicians of all sorts recognize that the challenges of the 1990s are likely to require a different mix of policies and a more flexible orientation than Thatcher and her governments exhibited.

The British public's initial response to Thatcher's removal was to reward Major and the Conservatives with their first lead in the opinion polls for some time. That lead persisted throughout the period surrounding the Persian Gulf war of January–February 1991, during which Major took on the role of America's best ally and spokesman in Europe. His performance confirmed his accession to office while muting the debate over Europe. No longer was Britain merely responding to the pressures of its more prosperous economic partners; it was now pushing the reluctant European powers into a "virtuous war." The effect did not last, but the episode ensured that there would be no second thoughts about the decision to drop Thatcher, and that the movement away from her legacy would not be quickly or easily reversed.

WHY THE COUP?

The first and most dramatic of the moves away from Thatcherism had of course been the Conservative party's coup against Thatcher's continued leadership. The coup was an extraordinary event, requiring the courage that is only born of desperation. Many Tories were clearly convinced by the fall of 1990 not only that Thatcher was an electoral liability, but that she was no longer reliable. Thatcher had often been stubborn and strongly ideological, but the persona and the ideas had been kept under control by a keen sense of what was politically possible.

Thatcher may have extended the boundaries within which conservatives could speak and act, but she did so gradually and was careful in her selection of opponents and the timing of her battles. She may have long detested Arthur Scargill, the president of the National

Reprinted with permission from *Current History* magazine, November 1991, pp. 363-367. Copyright © 1991 by Current History, Inc.

Union of Mineworkers, but did not take on the miners until she was quite sure she could win. She may always have been a patriot and fond of military action, but she did little on that score until 1982, when Argentina provided her with a nearly perfect opportunity by invading the Falkland Islands and United States President Ronald Reagan gave his blessing to the British military response.

Between June 1987 and November 1990, Thatcher's behavior changed. No longer guided by her sharp political intelligence, it was instead dominated by a renewed ideological fervor that had not been much on display during the general election. During the 1987 campaign, in fact, the Tories had promised more of the same: a continuation of the government's hard-line policy on defense; a steady hand on the economy to keep inflation down and encourage growth; lower taxes; more legislation aimed at weakening the unions; and further privatization. Thatcher had hoped to wage a positive campaign on behalf of a more radical program, but Labour's unexpected strength forced the Tories to revert to a primarily negative attack. "Britain Is Great Again," Tory party advertisements read, "Don't Let Labour Wreck It."[2]

The election produced unclear results. Labour emerged strengthened but still far short of the votes needed to overtake the Tories. The Alliance party of Social Democrats and Liberals received slightly fewer votes than in 1983, but won a very small number of seats and so was understood to have failed decisively. The Conservatives were not given a mandate to move further to the right, but they scored a victory solid enough to embolden Thatcher. She proceeded to encourage her ministers to develop plans and propose legislation on education, health, and local government that had not been much discussed before the election and that would prove controversial.

In education, for example, the Tories had for some time evinced a hostility to the state sector: they were not happy with comprehensive (non–college preparatory) schools, resented the autonomy and the politics of local education authorities, fought bitterly with teachers unions over pay, and complained endlessly about the decline of standards. A series of more or less radical reforms was promised in the Conservative manifesto, but during the election Education Secretary Kenneth Baker had spoken in moderate tones about reform. The legislation that was passed in 1988 was anything but moderate, however. It allowed parents to vote on whether schools should opt out of local authority control and called for a national curriculum and for testing at ages 7, 11, 14, and 16.

A similar if less drastic approach was adopted toward the National Health Service. Central government funding and universal access were to be maintained, but there would be greater opportunities in the system for internal markets and subcontracting arrangements and for hospitals to become "self-governing." Important constituencies of providers and clients in education and health feared at the time and still fear that behind the Tories' interest in efficiency and choice lies a desire to lower the standards of service.

The most contentious proposal of late Thatcherism was the poll tax, or "community charge." The government's plan, which again received scant publicity during the election campaign, was to eliminate local property taxes based on the rental value of property and to substitute a fixed charge per resident for the cost of local services. The poll tax was to some extent a continuation of earlier efforts to control the spending of local government by means of devices like rate-capping. But it went much further, replacing a flawed but progressive tax with a highly (and visibly) regressive levy.

Thatcher was told repeatedly that the poll tax would not work, but she persisted, and it was adopted in 1988, with implementation scheduled in Scotland for 1989, and in the rest of Britain for April 1, 1990. Collecting the tax proved difficult in Scotland, and the tax's imminent imposition elsewhere prompted large-scale demonstrations throughout England in March 1990, and a violent confrontation in London's Trafalgar Square on the last day of that month. The unpopularity of the tax was a key factor in Conservative defeats in a Mid-Staffordshire by-election on March 22 and in local elections in May.

The government was also hurt by mounting economic troubles. Inflation had fallen in the early and mid-1980s, as unemployment rose and then persisted at extremely high levels. By 1987 inflation seemed to be under control, jobs were being created, and the Conservatives were able to take credit for a modest revival. Growth continued, especially in the south, through the beginning of 1990, but inflation rose from rates as low as 3.3 percent in early 1988 to nearly 11 percent by the fall of 1990. As inflation climbed so did interest rates, especially for home mortgages. The rising mortgage payments were particularly damaging to Conservative fortunes, since they often affected those who had previously benefited the most from Thatcher's policies. Eventually unemployment rose as well and continued to increase through 1990 and into 1991. None of this helped the Tories or Thatcher.

LABOUR'S REVIVAL

Nor was the Conservative party helped out this time by Labour, whose mistakes and disarray had been a boon to Thatcher in the late 1970s and early 1980s. In 1973 Labour activists, disillusioned by the poor prospects for political reform and angry at the duplicity and ineffectiveness of party leaders, had restructured the party to make the leadership more accountable. Labour's program also moved sharply to the left, particularly on defense and the economy. These developments disturbed many voters, and the problem was compounded by the bitter internal arguments that accompanied Labour's transformation. The Conservatives were able to turn Labour's troubles to their advantage in 1979 and in 1983, and in 1987 they could rely on a negative campaign at the end to frighten voters away from Labour.

But Labour's new leader, Neil Kinnock, did much to reassure voters in 1987, and he set out after that to do even better. The fall after the election the party began a policy review that culminated in 1989 in a new, more moderate program that gave the Conservatives far fewer targets for attack. Most important, Labour's gradual move away from a more radical policy on nuclear weapons, combined with the ending of the cold war, removed from the center of political debate the issue of defense, whose prominence usually worked to the benefit of the Tories. Kinnock has also been remarkably successful at managing the party's internal affairs, effectively purging the fringe Trotskyist group, "Militant Tendency"; isolating supporters of Tony Benn, the leader of the party's more moderate left wing; reassuring the right; and keeping the unions behind him.

Kinnock has not, however, impressed the intellectuals and pundits—R. W. Johnson has repeatedly used his column in *The New Statesman* to question Kinnock's intelligence, and Noel Annan recently judged him "spunky but ignorant." The Labour leader has nevertheless presided over a remarkable rebound. Kinnock kept the party together when it seemed to be coming apart, resisted pressures to coalesce with the Liberals and Social Democrats (and went on to see the Alliance expire as a serious threat to Labour), and managed the modernization of the party's appeal and of its machinery for making policy and waging campaigns. Kinnock thereby positioned his party to profit from Conservative losses. By mid-1990, Labour was far ahead of the Tories in all the opinion polls.

THATCHER AGAINST EUROPE

Labour's revival, and its persistent gains throughout 1990, were thus a major factor in convincing Conservatives that Thatcher had to go. But Thatcher showed no sign of leaving, and, more disturbingly, showed few signs of bending before the threat of electoral defeat; on the poll tax, for example, the government made only modest financial concessions. Thatcher also betrayed a troubling lack of realism over Europe.

The prime minister had never been ideologically or emotionally committed to Europe. She spent her first term fighting over Britain's monetary contribution to the European Community (EC) and opposing the EC's Common Agricultural Policy. But the financial arrangement worked out at an EC ministers meeting in Fountainebleau in 1984 temporarily settled these disputes, and for the next three years the Thatcher government played a far more positive role with regard to Europe. The government was especially keen on breaking down barriers to trade and investment, and became a major supporter of the effort to create a single market by 1992. After 1987, however, Thatcher became less enthusiastic

as it became clear to her that integration with Europe would have not just economic, but social, legal, and political dimensions as well.

Thatcher had reasons for resisting a transfer of power to the EC, since Britain was out of line with European practice on several critical issues. The European Court of Justice had forced the British government to strengthen laws relating to sex discrimination and regulating telephone wiretaps and the interception of mail. Britain has also been, and remains, vulnerable to criticism over its treatment of the Irish. British standards on the environment and, more embarrassing, on food inspection, also fall short of European norms; scandals over salmonella in eggs and chicken and over "mad cow" disease have served to underline the potential meaning of closer political integration. British farmers, butchers, and other food processors would not be able to export their products to other EC members unless they raised their standards to EC norms and permitted inspections; while the cost of raising their standards may not be high, the food processors resist such changes as a loss of control over how they do business. Moreover, during the Thatcher decade the level of public services in Britain fell far below that in the rest of the European Community; taxation and public spending now constitute a lower proportion of gross domestic product in Britain than in any other EC country.

Thatcher apparently found the prospect of European institutions imposing European standards on Britain frightening. Particularly upsetting were the efforts of the EC's Commission, headed since 1985 by the French socialist Jacques Delors, to spell out the "social dimensions of the internal market" as the EC nations moved toward integration. In 1987, Michel Hansenne, the Belgian EC president, had raised the issue of the EC's need to specify and guarantee "fundamental social rights" as 1992 approached; by 1989 the Commission had issued a "Social Charter," which was denounced by Thatcher as a "socialist charter" but adopted by the EC's Council of Ministers nonetheless. There was, and remains, no mechanism by which the provisions of the "Social Charter" can be enforced, but its very existence apparently suggested to Thatcher the possibility that socialism, although beaten in Britain, could be reimposed from Brussels.

This was a somewhat extreme vision, but not unreasonable considering the highly ideological worldview held by Thatcher and her closest allies. Unfortunately for the prime minister, it was not shared by the majority of her government or the Conservative party; nor was it the view of most British businessmen. Indeed, business—London's financial establishment especially—was entranced by the prospects of the single market and firmly committed to its implementation. So too were the two ministers who had been primarily responsible for economic policy under Thatcher, Geoffrey Howe (Thatcher's first chancellor of the exchequer and subsequent foreign secretary) and Nigel Lawson (her second chancellor of the exchequer). The result was increasing tension between Thatcher and the most important members of her government.

Thatcher signaled her resistance to Europe in a speech at Bruges, Belgium, on September 20, 1988. Howe and Lawson managed, however, to prevail on her to commit Britain to Delors' plan for European economic and monetary union, which had been worked out at the EC summit in Madrid in June 1989. This meant linking the British pound to other EC currencies and accepting the discipline of the international market.

Thatcher was skeptical, though her arguments concentrated more on sovereignty than economics; she claimed that Delors' plan for economic and monetary union would jeopardize Britain's long tradition of political independence. Her close friend, Trade and Industry Minister Nicholas Ridley, went much further, predicting in July 1990 that the new arrangements would lead to German domination of the entire continent.[3] Ridley was forced to resign over the gaffe, but it seemed to many that he spoke the prime minister's mind.

There may well have been an economic analysis lurking behind Thatcher's patriotic rhetoric. As one commentator has argued, "all Thatcher meant by national sovereignty was her own unfettered discretion to screw up the economy once every four years for electoral purposes."[4] Less cynically, it may be suggested that Thatcher was more aware than her advisers of how precarious the economic recovery of the late 1980s actually was. She certainly knew that wage increases in manufacturing had been consistently high and that industry therefore was less competitive than public pronouncements implied. So long as domestic consumption continued at a high level, the problem did not have to be faced. But if demand fell off, it would have to be confronted.

THE OUSTER

Thatcher persisted in her essentially negative stance through the fall of 1990. Out of step with respectable opinion on Europe, unwilling to back down over the poll tax, and increasingly isolated in her own party, which trailed Labour by roughly 20 points in the polls, she was removed from the Conservative party leadership in November 1990.

The first blow was dealt by Geoffrey Howe. After he and Lawson had pushed the prime minister into the concessions made at the Madrid summit, relations between them and Thatcher deteriorated. Howe had been removed as foreign secretary in July 1989 and replaced by a relative newcomer, John Major. Although Howe was made leader of the House of Commons and deputy prime minister (a largely honorific title), he deeply resented his demotion. Three months later, Lawson, who had been serving as chancellor of the exchequer, was provoked into resigning when Thatcher

refused to repudiate statements by Sir Alan Walters, her personal economic adviser, that implicitly criticized Lawson's position on Europe. Lawson too was replaced by Major, who was obviously seen by Thatcher as quintessentially reliable.

Howe continued in the Cabinet and remained loyal throughout the difficulties over the poll tax, but by the fall he was unable to contain himself. He resigned his two positions on November 1 and two weeks later delivered a scathing attack on Thatcher in the House of Commons. This signaled that Thatcher had lost the confidence of Tory insiders, and it prompted former Minister of Defense Michael Heseltine to declare himself a candidate for leader of the party. In the ensuing vote among Conservatives in the House of Commons, Thatcher failed to gain a sufficient majority, and was pressured to resign. Her supporters threw their votes to Major, who became prime minister on November 29.

THE RIGHTS OF CITIZENS

The circumstances of Thatcher's political demise suggest the distance that politicians and the public had moved away from Thatcherism, if indeed they had ever embraced it. Thatcher had not won her cultural revolution, her crusade to foster "Victorian values" among ordinary citizens, and so could carry neither the public nor the party with her on the initiatives of her third term. It seems that as Thatcher moved further to the right, the Conservative party moved to the center.

Perhaps the most visible manifestation of these movements was the rather curious discussion about citizenship that emerged in the late 1980s. Neither the term nor the concept of citizenship has a rich history in the United Kingdom; British citizens have always been subjects first and only secondarily citizens with rights. Britain has never had a bill of rights, and there is no constitution setting out the rights of citizens and those of the state. Citizens were granted rights through legislation passed by Parliament, whose decisions were supreme but could be withdrawn or redefined.

Over the course of the nineteenth and twentieth centuries the practical meaning of British citizenship was expanded to include a broad range of civil, political, social, and economic rights; indeed, the welfare state put in place after 1945 can to some extent be defined in terms of the extensive set of rights it sought to guarantee. But in fact nothing was guaranteed, for rights could always be taken away. The thrust of public policy under Thatcher was to do precisely that.

Thatcher's opponents responded by arguing for a broadened definition of citizenship. This served both tactical and substantive purposes. Tactically, it was easier to defend citizenship than socialism, which was how Thatcher preferred to frame the debate; it was also easier to defend social programs if they could be described as rights rather than benefits or, worse still, privileges. More substantively, the discourse on citizenship gave her critics a way to point up certain peculiarities of "Thatcherism."

Thatcher was no ordinary conservative, eager merely to wave the flag and reduce taxes for the rich. She had unique insight into the institutional and cultural underpinnings of politics, and deliberately set out to change them. Thatcher sought to shift the boundaries between state and society, shrinking the responsibilities of government and enlarging the role of the private sector. She aimed to restructure and restrict the public sphere, undercutting the very purpose of government participation in society and hence quite consciously redefining the political rights of citizenship. The Thatcher governments also posed a threat to civil rights, for they exhibited a contempt for local government, demonstrated a strong predisposition toward secrecy, and were cavalier in suppressing dissent. Talking about the meanings of citizenship was therefore a way of understanding Thatcher's significance.

It was also a means of mobilizing opposition. One of the most notable anti-Thatcher initiatives of the 1980s was the launching of Charter 88 by an ad hoc liberal coalition. The charter called for a written constitution containing a bill of rights, restrictions on the executive, freedom of information, proportional representation, a reformed and independent judiciary, abolition of the House of Lords and its replacement with a democratically elected upper chamber, protections against the arbitrary exercise of state power, and a more equitable distribution of power between local, regional, and national government. Launched during the 300th anniversary of the Glorious Revolution of 1688, Charter 88 was testimony not only to the broad dissatisfaction with Thatcher shared by the left and center, but also to the new appreciation among her opponents of the value of citizenship.

The argument over citizenship constituted the opposition's most penetrating and effective critique of Thatcher, and it prompted Conservatives to offer their own vision of citizenship. In his speech to the Peel Society in February 1988, Home Secretary Douglas Hurd sought to appropriate and recast the language of citizenship used by the government's critics. He explained the rise in crime rates by the loss of social cohesion. The way to increase cohesion was to encourage active citizenship—his key example was the Neighbourhood Watch scheme—but Hurd also advocated greater participation by parents in the running of schools and an increase in volunteerism. Hurd's theme was echoed by Education Secretary Kenneth Baker, and was deemed sufficiently useful for the government to set up in December 1988 a Commission on Citizenship.

A MOVE TOWARD THE CENTER

The Conservative government's recognition of the need to enter the debate on citizenship was at least an oblique acknowledgment, well before Thatcher herself was removed, of the movement of public opinion away from Thatcherism and toward the center. So too was the revival of Labour's fortunes, for Labour steadily advanced its standing as its policies came to be accepted as centrist. The eclipse of the Alliance (now the Liberal Democratic party) might also be seen in the same terms, for as the two major parties moved to the center, a specifically center party became superfluous.

Perhaps even more indicative of the strong movement toward the political center is the fact that Thatcher's successor, John Major, has chosen to make advocacy of citizenship the "big idea" of his government. Major has broken with Thatcher's legacy in several respects, but nowhere is the difference more noticeable than in his embrace of the concept of citizenship. Major's personal contribution was to issue a White Paper in July 1991 proposing a "Citizen's Charter" that would embody consumers' rights and set up procedures for the redress of grievances against unresponsive bureaucracies.

What will this "recentering" of British politics mean for the major parties? Will it allow Labour to continue its advance back into power, or allow the Conservatives to recapture voters scared away by the extremism of Thatcher's last years? Or will the Liberal Democrats surprise everyone and stage a comeback? The polls suggest almost equal support for Labour and the Conservatives, with little hope for the Liberal Democrats. If such is the underlying balance, then the next election will turn on the state of the economy or issues of the moment. But whatever the election's outcome, the next government will almost certainly eschew the highly controversial and polarizing initiatives that marked the Thatcher era. British politics may become somewhat less exciting, but that is probably a good thing for British citizens.

---

[1]Several writers were tempted by the completion of a decade of "Thatcherism" to publish books that attempted to evaluate it, but these efforts have been overtaken by Thatcher's sudden departure from office, and all would need to be qualified; the experience argues for caution. Among the best of the genre are Hugo Young, *The Iron Lady: A Biography of Mrs. Thatcher* (New York: Farrar, Straus & Giroux, 1989); Peter Riddell, *The Thatcher Decade: How Britain Has Changed during the 1980s* (Oxford: Basil Blackwell, 1989); and Dennis Kavanagh and Anthony Seldon, eds., *The Thatcher Effect* (Oxford: Clarendon Press, 1989).

[2]David Butler and Dennis Kavanagh, *The British General Election of 1987* (New York: St. Martin's Press, 1988), pp. 109–110. See also A. Heath, et al., *Understanding Political Change: Voting in Britain, 1964–1987* (Oxford: Pergamon, 1990); and W. Miller, et al., *How Voters Change: The 1987 British Election Campaign in Perspective* (Oxford: Clarendon Press, 1990).

[3]Dominic Lawson, "Saying the Unsayable about the Germans," *The Spectator*, July 14, 1990, pp. 8–10.

[4]Auberon Waugh, "Why Were All the Tory Wiseacres So Extraordinarily Stupid?" *The Spectator*, December 1, 1990, p. 8.

Having Outwitted the Seers, Tories Wax Conciliatory

William E. Schmidt

Special to The New York Times

LONDON, April 10—Emboldened by the Conservative Party's unexpected triumph in the national election on Thursday, Prime Minister John Major vowed today to lead Britain out of recession and toward the "classless society" he envisioned when he took over the Government from Margaret Thatcher 16 months ago.

Appearing outside 10 Downing Street only hours after voters defied pundits, bookmakers and poll takers who argued the Conservatives were likely to fall to the Labor Party, the Prime Minister chose to strike a deliberately conciliatory tone after one of the most closely fought British election campaigns in recent memory.

He promised he would expand opportunities for education, job training and home ownership, and assured voters he had no intention of ever privatizing Britain's National Health Service, as Labor had asserted during the campaign.

Labor's Despair

"Every government that has ever been elected in this country has had people who didn't vote for it," said Mr. Major, 49 years old, whose personal popularity among voters helped extend the Tories' winning streak to four elections, beginning in 1979. "And my job as Prime Minister is to make sure I never overlook their interests when I frame legislation, and when I decide what the Government does." Not since the Napoleonic wars has a British party been able to form four consecutive governments.

As Mr. Major beamed and Conservatives took solace in their narrow escape—they watched their majority of 86 seats in the House of Commons shrink to just 21—the rival Labor Party was plunged into despair and recrimination over its failure yet again to topple the Tories, in spite of Britain's worst recession since the 1930's.

Neil Kinnock, 50, who as head of the Labor Party has now lost two successive elections to the Conservatives, went into seclusion today, amid speculation that he might resign as the party's leader.

Kinnock's Future

Aides to Mr. Kinnock released a brief public statement that said, "I am consulting with colleagues to inform them of the action which I propose to take in the wake of the election defeat."

Close aides to Mr. Kinnock said the Welsh coal miner's son had been devastated by the defeat, since he believed, on the basis of public opinion polls and the Labor Party's own analysis, that he was headed for victory on Thursday.

With the final results in from balloting in all 651 seats in the House of Commons, the Conservatives won 336 seats; Labor, 271, and the centrist Liberal Democrats, 20. Regional parties won 24 seats.

Experts on parliamentary government said a majority of 21 seats would give the Conservatives just enough of a cushion to insure passage of their legislative program, although party whips would have to exact a stricter discipline among members to assure attendance for critical votes.

For Mr. Major, the election marked a personal triumph, and gave him his first popular mandate to govern. He had assumed the premiership by default in November 1990, when Mrs. Thatcher was ousted in a Conservative Party revolt.

Mr. Major wasted little time today in working to put his own stamp on his new Government, and aides to the Prime Minister said he was likely to announce a reshuffled Cabinet on Saturday.

News of the unexpected Conservative victory sent London stocks and bonds soaring, after weeks of uncertainty among businessmen and traders, who said they feared that plans by Labor to increase taxes and public welfare spending would set back any hope of economic recovery.

Prognosticators Perplexed

Mr. Kinnock was not the only big loser in the election Thursday. Britain's pollsters were also handed one of their worst embarrassments ever.

In the weeks before the ballot, British editorialists and columnists had sharply attacked the Conservatives and Mr. Major for a lackluster and uninspiring campaign, and not a single public opinion poll prior to the election was even close to predicting the final outcome.

Most had shown Labor with a slight lead, but suggested the race was so close that neither Labor nor the Conservatives would win a majority, resulting in a deadlocked Parliament in which Labor would probably have the upper hand.

For example, on the eve of the election, Market & Opinion Research International, which in the last two elections came within one percentage point of accurately predicting the outcome, showed Labor at 39 percent, the Conservatives at 38 percent and the Liberal Democrats at 20. The sample involved 1,731 registered voters, and had a margin of error of 3 percentage points.

Wiping Off the Egg

But the final national returns tabulated today showed most of the actual

From *The New York Times*, April 11, 1992, p. 5. Copyright © 1992 by The New York Times Company. Reprinted by permission.

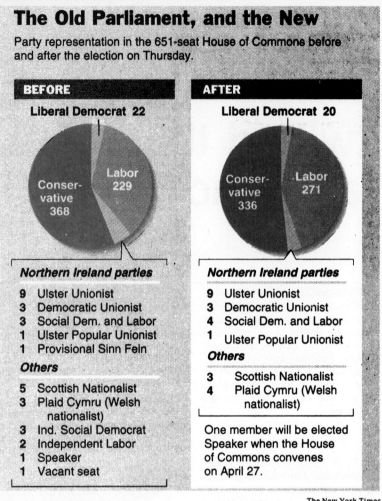

The Old Parliament, and the New

Party representation in the 651-seat House of Commons before and after the election on Thursday.

BEFORE

Liberal Democrat 22

Conservative 368 | Labor 229

Northern Ireland parties

9 Ulster Unionist
3 Democratic Unionist
3 Social Dem. and Labor
1 Ulster Popular Unionist
1 Provisional Sinn Fein

Others

5 Scottish Nationalist
3 Plaid Cymru (Welsh nationalist)
3 Ind. Social Democrat
2 Independent Labor
1 Speaker
1 Vacant seat

AFTER

Liberal Democrat 20

Conservative 336 | Labor 271

Northern Ireland parties

9 Ulster Unionist
3 Democratic Unionist
4 Social Dem. and Labor
1 Ulster Popular Unionist

Others

3 Scottish Nationalist
4 Plaid Cymru (Welsh nationalist)

One member will be elected Speaker when the House of Commons convenes on April 27.

The New York Times

results fell beyond the range of error. Of all ballots cast, the Conservatives won 41.9 percent of the votes; Labor won 34.2 percent, and the Liberal Democrats 17.9 percent. Other parties won 6.1 percent.

Robert Worcester, the chairman of the research and polling group, said it was conducting additional samples today to determine what, if anything, had gone wrong.

"We've got egg on our face," he said. He said a large and unexpected turnout among Conservative voters might have thrown off his findings. Many of these may have decided to vote at the last minute, fearful that Labor's tax plans would cost them money.

British election officials said the turnout of more than 77 percent was the highest since 1974, when Labor and the Conservatives fought to a near draw.

The Tax Factor

Politicians trying to make sense of what happened on Thursday offered a number of alternative explanations. In addition to a late surge as a result of worries about Labor tax policy, others argued that Mr. Kinnock and other La-

For Britain's Labor Party, the crystal ball has become murkey.

bor officials may have hurt themselves in the closing week of the campaign by acting as if they had won the election, when public opinion polls showed them with a four to seven point lead.

Shirley Williams, a former member of Parliament for the Social Democrats, an old centrist party, referred to the chilling effect on voters of a highly orchestrated rally last week in Sheffield, in which Mr. Kinnock appeared, in television news reports, to be in what she described as "a triumphant mode."

"At the last analysis, people stubbornly resisted a Labor government," she said.

The bookmakers also misjudged the election. On election day, some betting shops were giving odds of 14-1 on the Conservatives' winning with a margin of 15 to 20 seats.

The Scottish National Party, which had been banking on polls showing a growing support for Scottish independence from Britain, also ended up losing two of the five seats they held in Scotland, and Sinn Fein, the political arm of the Irish Republican Army, went down to defeat in the one seat it has held for the last nine years in Northern Ireland.

Gerry Adams, the leader of Sinn Fein, was defeated by Joe Hendron, a doctor and a moderate Irish nationalist.

Celebrity Victors

Christ Patton, who ran the Conservatives' national campaign, also was a loser; he was defeated in his Bath constituency, at the same time he was given credit for orchestrating the Conservatives' stunning upset.

Paddy Ashdown, the leader of the Liberal Democrats, Britain's third-largest party, also was a loser. Mr. Ashdown had been banking on holding the balance in a deadlocked Parliament, in the case that neither Labor nor Conservatives held the advantage.

Instead, Mr. Ashdown not only found himself once more dealing with a Conservative majority, but his party actually lost two seats in the election.

Amid the carnage, there were also two well-known winners. Glenda Jackson, the actress, won a Labor seat in the fashionable north London district of Hampstead and Highgate, and Sebastian Coe, a Conservative who won two Olympic gold medals as a runner, crossed the finishing line first in Falmouth-Camborne, a district in southwest England.

British Election of 1992:
How and Why the Votes Were Cast

HOW: Essex Man stays loyal and the older woman is won over

The turnout was high and the Conservatives won a record number of votes. But did the people who created the 1987 landslide support the Tories this time? **Colin Rallings** and **Michael Thrasher** analyse the maths and the geography of John Major's victory

For the fourth election in succession the Conservatives have been returned with an overall majority based on just over 40% of the popular vote. On a high turnout of 77.9%, their share of the vote was close to its 1987 level almost everywhere, with only the southwest showing a drop in Conservative support of more than 2%.

In some regions, most notably in Scotland, their share was actually higher than at Margaret Thatcher's final landslide. The overall swing to Labour was scarcely more than 2% and was almost entirely a consequence of a movement away from the Liberal Democrats to Labour. John Major, no less than Thatcher, owes something of his triumph to a still divided opposition.

In the event the Tories emerged from the election with more votes than any party has ever polled and with a lead of nearly 7% over Labour. However, even with this sort of margin, the political scene this weekend could so nearly have been very different.

With just a dozen fewer MPs, the Conservatives would have been in the much less powerful position of being the largest party in a hung parliament and Major would have been denied his personal mandate. Labour could have achieved its first target of denting the Conservative hegemony if just 3,899 people in these particular constituencies had voted differently.

There are now 17 seats where the Conservative majority over Labour is less than 1,000 and which Labour will naturally believe it can win next time, given the slightest slip in government popularity. However, such a result will also encourage the critics of our capricious electoral system.

That Labour came so close to denying the government its majority on such a small overall swing implies that different types of constituency, even if not different regions, did not behave uniformly.

In the first place, Labour did do a little better in those seats it had targeted. The average swing in its favour in Conservative-held marginals was about 3.5%

and there is little evidence to support the pre-election view that the party was in danger of uselessly piling up votes in its own strongholds.

On the other hand, the Conservatives may have been saved by the personal vote of incumbent MPs. Among Labour's target marginals, the swing in those with a sitting Tory MP was about 1% less than in seats where the Conservatives had a new candidate. Of the 17 Conservatives who now sit on three-figure majorities, no fewer than 15 were incumbents and almost certainly owe their, and the prime minister's, survival to that fact.

In socio-economic terms, Major's supporters look to be much the same people as Thatcher's supporters. "Essex man" did not desert the party and in fact the Conservative share in Thurrock rose, even though Tim Janman lost his seat.

Looking back over the last four elections, it is quite extraordinary how stable the Conservative vote has been. Of course individuals have changed their allegiances and the electorate itself is very different now to 1979. But, in aggregate, the voters who came to the Conservatives in 1979 seeking a fundamental political change have remained with the party through the poll tax, a change of leader and the longest recession since the 1930s.

Although the Conservative vote was solid across most social groups, Major seems to have had an especial appeal for female voters. Among women over the age of 55, Labour did no better than it had in 1987 whereas Conservative support was up by as much as 5%. Strangely, among the youngest voters, the gender gap works in the opposite direction with a majority of women supporting Labour.

Labour does appear to have reaped some reward from its attention to the interests of this group and will hope that they do not desert the party as they get older.

The rise in Conservative support among the unemployed is likely to be a function of the type of people

PORTRAIT OF THE ELECTORATE

% of 1992 voters		1983 vote			1987 vote			1992 vote		
		Con	Lab	L/D	Con	Lab	L/D	Con	Lab	L/D
100	TOTAL	44	28	26	43	32	23	43	35	18
49	Men	42	30	25	43	32	23	41	37	18
51	Women	46	26	27	43	32	23	44	34	18
14	18-24	42	33	32	33	40	21	35	39	19
19	25-34	40	29	29	39	33	25	40	38	18
33	35-54	44	27	27	45	29	24	43	34	19
34	55+	47	27	24	46	31	21	46	34	17
23	Pensioner	51	25	23	47	31	21	48	34	16
19	AB-prof	60	10	28	57	14	26	56	20	22
24	C1-white collar	51	20	27	51	21	26	52	25	19
27	C2-skilled	40	32	26	40	36	22	38	41	17
30	DE-skilled	33	41	24	30	48	20	30	50	15
67	Owner occupier	52	19	28	50	23	25	49	30	19
23	Council tenant	26	47	24	22	56	19	24	55	15
7	Private tenant	41	33	23	39	37	21	33	40	21
7	Men 18-24	41	35	21	42	37	19	39	35	18
7	Women 18-24	42	31	25	31	42	24	30	43	19
9	Men 25-34	37	34	28	41	33	24	40	37	17
10	Women 25-34	42	25	30	37	33	27	40	38	18
16	Men 35-54	42	29	27	42	32	24	40	37	19
17	Women 35-54	46	24	28	47	27	25	46	32	19
17	Men 55+	45	28	25	45	31	23	43	38	17
17	Women 55+	49	26	24	46	32	20	49	32	17
9	Men 65+	50	25	23	47	30	22	44	38	16
9	Women 65+	51	25	23	46	33	20	51	31	17
4	Unemployed (m)	25	49	24	21	56	20	24	52	17
3	Unemployed (f)	32	41	24	23	54	19	26	51	16
17	North (m)	35	39	24	34	42	20	33	46	14
19	North (f)	40	33	25	33	41	22	36	43	15
13	Midland (m)	43	31	23	46	34	19	44	38	16
13	Midland (f)	46	27	24	45	29	24	46	36	16
19	South (m)	48	23	28	49	22	28	46	29	22
20	South (f)	51	19	30	51	24	24	50	27	22
	HOMEOWNERS									
36	Middle-class	58	12	29	57	15	26	56	21	20
31	Working-class	46	25	27	43	32	23	41	39	17
	COUNCIL TENANTS									
2	Middle-class	32	39	25	28	41	24	34	40	18
21	Working-class	25	49	24	21	58	18	22	58	15
	TRADE UNIONS									
23	Members	31	39	29	30	42	26	30	47	19
15	Men	29	41	28	31	42	25	30	48	18
8	Women	34	34	31	29	41	27	31	44	21
3	18-24	31	34	23	29	46	23	30	42	20
5	25-34	29	37	32	28	47	23	28	49	19
10	35-54	30	40	29	29	40	29	31	45	20
5	55+	32	40	26	36	37	24	33	49	16
10	ABC1	38	27	33	37	30	30	36	36	24
8	C2	27	44	27	28	47	24	27	52	17
5	DE	25	50	24	22	56	19	24	59	13
9	North	26	44	28	25	50	21	25	53	14
6	Midlands	32	40	25	35	39	24	32	49	18
8	South	35	32	32	33	34	32	35	38	26

Taken from an aggregate analysis of 23,396 voters in Great Britain interviewed by Mori during the election, weighted to the actual outcome. Key: L/D, Liberal Democrat; m, Men; f, Women

HOW BRITAIN VOTED: REGION BY REGION

HOW THE PARTIES SHARES CHANGED FROM 1987

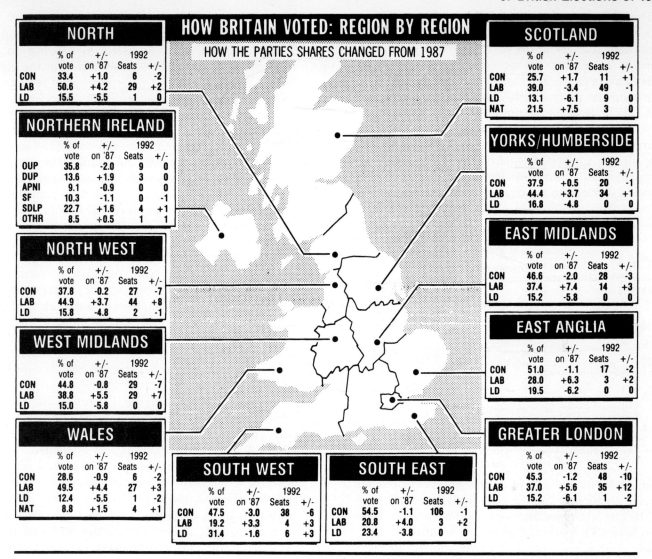

NORTH

	% of vote	+/- on '87	1992 Seats	+/-
CON	33.4	+1.0	6	-2
LAB	50.6	+4.2	29	+2
LD	15.5	-5.5	1	0

NORTHERN IRELAND

	% of vote	+/- on '87	1992 Seats	+/-
OUP	35.8	-2.0	9	0
DUP	13.6	+1.9	3	0
APNI	9.1	-0.9	0	0
SF	10.3	-1.1	0	-1
SDLP	22.7	+1.6	4	+1
OTHR	8.5	+0.5	1	1

NORTH WEST

	% of vote	+/- on '87	1992 Seats	+/-
CON	37.8	-0.2	27	-7
LAB	44.9	+3.7	44	+8
LD	15.8	-4.8	2	-1

WEST MIDLANDS

	% of vote	+/- on '87	1992 Seats	+/-
CON	44.8	-0.8	29	-7
LAB	38.8	+5.5	29	+7
LD	15.0	-5.8	0	0

WALES

	% of vote	+/- on '87	1992 Seats	+/-
CON	28.6	-0.9	6	-2
LAB	49.5	+4.4	27	+3
LD	12.4	-5.5	1	-2
NAT	8.8	+1.5	4	+1

SOUTH WEST

	% of vote	+/- on '87	1992 Seats	+/-
CON	47.5	-3.0	38	-6
LAB	19.2	+3.3	4	+3
LD	31.4	-1.6	6	+3

SOUTH EAST

	% of vote	+/- on '87	1992 Seats	+/-
CON	54.5	-1.1	106	-1
LAB	20.8	+4.0	3	+2
LD	23.4	-3.8	0	0

SCOTLAND

	% of vote	+/- on '87	1992 Seats	+/-
CON	25.7	+1.7	11	+1
LAB	39.0	-3.4	49	-1
LD	13.1	-6.1	9	0
NAT	21.5	+7.5	3	0

YORKS/HUMBERSIDE

	% of vote	+/- on '87	1992 Seats	+/-
CON	37.9	+0.5	20	-1
LAB	44.4	+3.7	34	+1
LD	16.8	-4.8	0	0

EAST MIDLANDS

	% of vote	+/- on '87	1992 Seats	+/-
CON	46.6	-2.0	28	-3
LAB	37.4	+7.4	14	+3
LD	15.2	-5.8	0	0

EAST ANGLIA

	% of vote	+/- on '87	1992 Seats	+/-
CON	51.0	-1.1	17	-2
LAB	28.0	+6.3	3	+2
LD	19.5	-6.2	0	0

GREATER LONDON

	% of vote	+/- on '87	1992 Seats	+/-
CON	45.3	-1.2	48	-10
LAB	37.0	+5.6	35	+12
LD	15.2	-6.1	1	-2

who have lost their jobs in the recession rather than evidence of a new electoral alignment.

What is more significant is that many others who have suffered economic disappointment in recent years continue to find no acceptable alternative to the Tories.

The much-discussed skilled manual workers—the C2s—did show an above-average swing to Labour of 3.5%, but even here Labour's improvement owed as much to desertions from the Liberal Democrats as straight conversions from former adherents of Thatcher.

The same applies to the group of working-class owner-occupiers, whose recent experience that a house is not always an inflation-proof investment has not prevented more of them continuing to support the Tories more than any other political party.

Labour were also hoping to do well among the elderly, who were wooed with a promise of an immediate pensions increase and that future rises would once again be pegged to average wage, rather than price, rises. In fact the Conservative vote among pensioners hardened and there is little sign that a growing and more affluent elderly population will identify with Labour.

Labour's frustration can be seen from a comparison of its local and national electoral performance in the fast-growing centres of the south. In places such as Basildon, Slough, Harlow and Swindon, Labour habitually polls well in local government contests and was convinced that this time that support would translate to the general election.

However, since the May 1991 local elections, when the national swing back to the Conservatives from Labour has been 5%, in those towns it has been of the order of 10%. These are the very voters whose private ballot box decisions are likely to have contradicted the support for extra public services which they pledged to the pollsters. In so doing they saved the career of men such as Slough's John Watts, who hung on with a majority of just 514.

Labour's wider concern must be that it is in danger of being relegated to a party of local and not national government, trusted to provide community public services but not to run the economy.

1. COUNTRY OVERVIEWS: Great Britain

The electoral geography of Britain has not been much altered by this election. Only four regions saw significant changes in the party profile of seats, with London accounting for more than a quarter of all Labour's net gains. The "loony left" image, which so damaged the party in 1987, has almost disappeared but Labour faces another problem in the capital.

Social change means that many inner-city areas such as Battersea and Westminster North are becoming almost Conservative strongholds, whereas depopulation in parts of traditional working-class London will lead to the disappearance of safe Labour

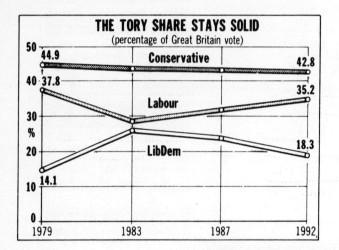

THE TORY SHARE STAYS SOLID
(percentage of Great Britain vote)

seats under the Boundary Commission review, due for implementation before the next general election.

The Liberal Democrats' one cause for muted celebration was their performance in the southwest. They made four gains from the Conservatives, all with similar swings to the 5.2% which led to John Taylor's defeat in Cheltenham. The Conservative vote dropped more here than in any other region.

Elsewhere Ashdown's party failed to live up to its pre-election claims, and it is still dogged by its failure to carve out a distinctive niche of support outside the Celtic fringe. Its level of support dropped among every social group and it is now the second most popular party only among the AB group of professional and managerial workers.

Moreover, the Liberal Democrats will not be able to claim at the next election that they hold more second places than Labour. They are now indisputably the third party and that will inevitably weaken their bargaining position should discussions on an electoral pact ever come about.

The election also marked the final removal from the centre of British politics of the remnant of both the personalities and support of the SDP.

The Liberal Democrats dropped 20% of their 1987 vote in former SDP strongholds such as Norfolk North

West, Plymouth Devonport and Stockton South. In England, at least, only Mike Hancock in Portsmouth South has really been successful in hanging on to votes the SDP garnered with such ease in the early 1980s. Once again he had the frustration of seeing the Tories hold on with a majority of less than 250.

In general, tactical voting was either not widespread or was counter-productive. The collapse of the Liberal Democrat vote to Labour was common to most constituencies and not especially pronounced in Labour's targets. The Liberal Democrats themselves gained little benefit from tactical voting, with all their gains in the southwest coming in seats where the Labour vote had already been squeezed to 10% or less in previous elections.

They gained North Cornwall despite a small increase in the Labour vote. In Oxford West and Abingdon, which had shown signs of tactical voting in 1987, there was almost no further realignment of the anti-Conservative vote. On the other hand, tactical voters will claim a victory in Southampton Itchen where the Green party candidate stood down and advised supporters to vote Labour to help defeat roads minister Christopher Chope.

There were solid gains for Labour in the crucial regions of the West Midlands and the northwest, but nowhere did the party reach the level of support at which all its target marginals could be gained.

In Scotland, Labour's share of the vote slipped below 40% as both the Conservatives and SNP gained support. The Conservatives' performance enabled them to hold on to all their seats and gave them the additional satisfaction of beating the SNP into third place in the popular vote. They won back Kincardine & Deeside, only recently lost to the Liberal Democrats in a by-election, and gained adjacent Aberdeen South.

The SNP lost its by-election gain of Glasgow Govan and will be embarrassed that it now has fewer seats than Plaid Cymru. None the less it is now second in half the Scottish constituencies. Three-quarters of the Scottish population voted for parties advocating constitutional change and the issue of a Scottish parliament will not go away.

For the Liberal Democrats, as much as Labour, the logic of inter-city co-operation may soon become too strong to ignore. Without it, both parties face the prospect of many more years in opposition. Although the electorate has a habit of punishing parties which have the hubris to believe they are the "natural party of government", four election victories will encourage the Conservatives to argue that we now have a one-party dominant political system.

As they do so, they should at least pause to consider that it is the votes of only 3,899 people which allow them that luxury.

Britain's Constitutional Question

Politicians and others urge adoption of a written charter and a bill of rights

By Alexander MacLeod

Special to The Christian Science Monitor

LONDON

BRITAIN has long taken pride in the fact that its constitution, unlike those of most other democracies, is unwritten. But pride is giving way to doubt, and pressure is building for a fresh look at ways of securing the rights of British citizens.

Anthony Barnett, an advocate of a written constitution and a bill of rights, says he thinks that relying on Magna Carta, signed by England's King John at Runnymede in 1215, is an insufficient basis for ensuring that the rule of law prevails.

Mr. Barnett is coordinator of Charter 88, a nonpartisan group of lawyers and intellectuals modeled on Charter 77, the human-rights group that played a major part in destroying communism in Czechoslovakia.

He notes that Britain is the only member of the 12-nation European Community and its 25-nation sister body, the Council of Europe, without a written constitution.

"The result is that Britain is now regularly facing constitutional issues it is ill-equipped to handle," Barnett says.

King John's "great charter" was imposed on him by rebel barons who saw it as a barrier against the monarch's arbitrary actions. It remains the basis of Britain's common-law system and such institutions as the right of trial by jury and habeas corpus.

But growing numbers of British political observers and groups say its rambling provisions do not fit with modern times. The Liberal Democrat party will enter the coming general election with calls for a written constitution guaranteeing civil liberties at the center of its policies.

The opposition Labour Party also is proposing constitutional reforms, including a separate parliament for Scotland, a British bill of rights, and the abolition of the House of Lords.

The ruling Conservatives will fight the election on the "Magna Carta principle" – a defense of the status quo – but Douglas Hurd,

---

'Britain is ... facing constitutional issues it is ill-equipped to handle.'

– Anthony Barnett, constitutional advocate

---

the foreign secretary, whose work brings him into regular contact with European governments, is on record as saying that his party should give "serious thought" to constitutional change.

Prominent members of Britain's political and legal establishment are now counted among those who demand that the country should have a bill of rights.

Lord Scarman, a former judge of the Court of Appeal, has been campaigning for a written constitution for decades, arguing that allowing Parliament to pass laws without regard to a framework of citizens' rights is a recipe for unfairness.

Since Britain entered the European Community (EC) 19 years ago and began rubbing shoulders with countries where human rights are enshrined in written constitutions, Mr. Scarman's campaign has been taken up by a younger generation.

Last November, Charter 88 organized its own convention in Manchester at which four draft constitutions were considered. All the drafts indicated that across the political spectrum there is a demand for fundamental change.

Tony Benn, the left-wing Labour Member of Parliament (MP), proposed an elected upper chamber to replace the House of Lords. He also argued that women should have 50 percent of the seats in the lower and upper houses, and that the government should appoint a human-rights commissioner with the power to refer to Parliament abuses of human rights by the courts.

Frank Vibert, deputy director of the Institute for Economic Affairs, a right-wing think tank that former prime minister Margaret Thatcher favors, presented a draft that called for taking away the queen's right to give final approval to new laws.

Mr. Vibert also proposed that a Parliament-elected official should give formal assent to legislation and that the European Convention on Human Rights should be made part of British law. An elected upper house, he argued, should act as a constitutional

Reprinted by permission from *The Christian Science Monitor,* March 3, 1992, p. 12. Copyright © 1992 by The Christian Science Publishing Society. All rights reserved.

court to monitor observance of a written constitution.

Barnett is convinced that the Charter 88 constitutional convention has already had a major impact on the thinking of the main political parties.

"The European Court of Human Rights in Strasbourg continues to have cases referred to it by British citizens unhappy with the way the law of their own country is administered," he says. "More often than not the court finds in favor of the citizen. The reason is that it is applying a code of human rights that is absent in the British system."

Britain and the European Court are deadlocked on the question of lengthy detention before trial. The Strasbourg court has ruled that such detention is wrong. Britain argues that it is lawful under the Prevention of Terrorism Act used to cope with sectarian violence in Northern Ireland.

Roy Hattersley, Labour's deputy leader who will probably become home secretary if his party comes to power at the general election, is a dedicated supporter of constitutional reform. "For socialists," he says, "reform of the constitution is one of the ways by which a more equal, and therefore more free, society can be created."

The Labour Party has adopted a determined approach to the way members of Parliament are elected. Last year Neil Kinnock, the party leader, appointed a 20-member task force of political and constitutional experts, headed by Raymond Plant, a professor of politics at the University of Southampton, to examine this aspect of Britain's political system.

MPs are elected under the "first past the post" system, whereby a person who gains only one more vote than an opponent receives is automatically elected.

Mr. Plant and his committee are examining several forms of proportional representation (PR), in which voters are asked to rank candidates in order of preference.

Second preferences are distributed to reflect the numerical support gained by candidates of smaller parties. Supporters say that distributing the votes of individual electors among candidates ensures a more representative Parliament and gives smaller parties stronger representation. Most EC parliaments operate under a PR system.

Significantly, Labour says that if it wins the next general election, members of its promised Scottish Parliament will be chosen by a PR system.

Official Conservative policy, however, remains unchanged on either a bill of rights or a new electoral system. John Patten, a Home Office minister, dismisses the former as unwise and the latter as unnecessary. "The reformers want to sweep away the existing constitutional edifice and replace it with grandiose, ill-thought-out schemes," he says. "I think we should call the repairman only when it is necessary."

The myths are dead—so let's get down to business

As the advocates of fundamental change to Britain's system of government gather to discuss their strategies, Caroline Ellis takes a hard look at what is on offer

The enduring myth that a written constitution would be a deeply un-English phenomenon has, at last, been debunked. It may be some time before our culture of cap-doffing is definitively replaced by a continental system of citizenship rights and popular sovereignty, but the idea that the UK might one day adopt such an alien document has firmly taken root.

Just three years after the appearance of Charter 88, which delivered a kick in the pants to the constitutional reform movement, not one but four blueprints for change are on the table, from four corners of the political spectrum. Their existence changes the terms of the debate from why change is necessary to what form it might take and how it would come about.

First off the mark were the Liberal Democrats. The barrister John Macdonald wrote a draft constitution to go with the party's green paper, *"We, the People . . ."*, *Towards a Written Constitution*, published in June 1990. Accessible and concise, it illustrates what might be involved in a major constitutional reform programme. Next was Frank Vibert, deputy director of the free-market think tank, the Institute of Economic Affairs, with proposals for a constitution in the Conservative tradition. Tony Benn's *Commonwealth of Britain Bill*, five years in the making, was delivered in May this year.

The left-of-centre think tank, the Institute for Public Policy Research, had its proposals ready by July. At this weekend's Constitutional Convention in Manchester, hosted by Charter 88 and the *Independent*, all four drafts will be discussed, and defended by their authors. Here, to set the scene, are the main points of each approach.

"We, The People . . .", *Towards a Written Constitution*, Liberal Democrats
As a first step towards a full UK bill of rights, the document argues for incorporation into domestic British law of the European Convention on Human Rights. There would be devolution of power from the centre to a Scottish parliament, a Welsh Senedd, English regional governments, and multipurpose local authori-

ties. The competence of each tier would be defined by the "subsidiarity principle": no executive decision to be taken by the higher authority that could effectively be taken by the lower.

The Commons, under these proposals, would be reduced to 450 MPs. Other changes would include stronger select committees, sensible working hours, improved facilities for members and their staff and state funding of political parties.

In place of the House of Lords, a "Senate" of 100 members would be elected from the nations and regions, with powers to delay legislation other than money bills for up to two years. Other basic changes include:
- elections to all assemblies by single transferable vote;
- a Freedom of Information Act with a general right of access to all but a few narrowly defined areas;
- a Supreme Court nominated by a Judicial Services Commission established by parliament. This would have powers to veto unconstitutional legislation and act as final arbiter in disputes.

A reform timetable would be set up, detailing these changes. MPs would vote, initially, for the temporary disbandment of the Commons by passing legislation for an election under proportional representation. The newly elected Commons would sit as a Constituent Assembly and draw up the constitution, to be amendable only by a two-thirds majority of both houses of parliament.

(Available from Hebden Royd Publications, the Birchcliffe Centre, Hebden Bridge, West Yorkshire HX7 8DG, £4.50 plus 20p p&p)

The Constitution of the United Kingdom, Institute for Public Policy Research
The IPPR document shares the basic structure and features of the Liberal Democrats' draft—the codification and entrenchment of the rights of individuals against the state, and large-scale decentralisation of power. However, several factors make it distinctive.

The think-tank's proposals include wide-ranging ju-

Reprinted from *New Statesman and Society*, November 1, 1991, pp. 24-25.

21

dicial and legal reforms, and would put the police and security services on a constitutional footing. There are more explicit parliamentary checks placed on the exercise of the "crown prerogatives" by the executive (to declare war and peace, and so on), while the residual powers of the monarch are removed. The prime minister, for example, would be elected by the Commons.

The bill of rights would encompass the European Convention and aspects of the International Covenant on Civil and Political Rights, but goes beyond both in strengthening the right to privacy, the right to participate in public life and in guaranteeing a right to asylum.

A stronger commitment to equal opportunities is evident. The article on equality is broadened to cover discrimination on grounds of age, homosexuality or disability, and a duty placed on those appointing judges, police and other public officials to ensure that adequate candidates of both sexes, from diverse racial, religious and social backgrounds are considered.

Social and economic rights appear in a special declaration. The right to work, to an adequate standard of living, to social security and the right to strike would not be legally enforceable, but the state should attempt to facilitate these rights.

Unlike the Liberal Democrats, the IPPR argues that a constitutional convention, followed by a referendum, would be preferable to an act of parliament in the setting up of a constitution.

(Available from IPPR, 30-32 Southampton Street, London WC2E 7RA £20)

Constitutional Reform in the United Kingdom—An Incremental Agenda, by Frank Vibert of the Institute for Economic Affairs

Not so much a blueprint as an inquiry, this contribution from the right highlights key themes for conservative reformers.

Like the Lib Dems and the IPPR, Vibert advocates fixed-term parliaments to reduce a government's ability to manipulate the electoral timetable. He would remove the remaining constitutional functions of the crown, but the monarch would be preserved. An officer elected by one or both chambers could give formal assent to legislation and invite a party leader to form a government. The second chamber should be used as a test-bed before any commitment to electoral reform for the Commons.

Vibert's draft stresses transparency and accountability: an elected second chamber would scrutinise and debate European affairs, and act as a Constitutional Court if the UK adopted a written constitution. Other proposals include:
• switching control of interest and exchange rates to an autonomous Bank of England;
• a national police force, accountable to a parliamentary committee, to operate against serious crime, financial fraud and terrorism;
• incorporation of the European Convention into UK law;
• a comprehensive review of local and regional government, building on Thatcherite reforms.

Finally, a written constitution would put contract and law in place of consensus and convention where these have been eroded. First should come the reforms, then a document reflecting the changes.

(Available free from the IEA, 2 Lord North Street, London SW1P 3LB)

The Commonwealth of Britain Bill, presented to the House of Commons by Tony Benn, MP.

This would establish a democratic, secular, federal "commonwealth". The crown would lose its constitutional status, land, property and tax exemption, and the Queen would be pensioned off in the first parliamentary attempt to abolish the monarchy since 1649. A president elected by both houses on a two-thirds majority would exercise most of the powers of the crown prerogative, subject to the assent of the Commons.

Under the bill, the Church of England would be disestablished, with any state powers over it transferred to the General Synod. The blasphemy law would be abolished.

England, Scotland and Wales (though not Northern Ireland where British jurisdiction would end) would have national parliaments, subject to the authority of a Commonwealth parliament. This would comprise two houses: the Commons, with supreme legislative authority and the House of the People (elected by the nations), a toothless second chamber. In addition:
• women would have 50 per cent of seats in both houses;
• the voting age would be lowered to 16 and anyone resident in Britain for more than five years would have the right to vote in local and parliamentary elections.

Citizens would be entitled to enjoy and campaign for basic political, legal, social and economic rights, including the right to a healthy and sustainable environment. Women would have control over their fertility and reproduction.

A human rights commissioner would monitor observance of these rights, but the balance of power between parliament and courts is the opposite of what the other constitution-mongers envisage. The commissioner could refer abuses by the courts to parliament, which could require the high court to re-examine the matter, but would have no powers to challenge the validity of acts of parliament viewed as contravening the Charter of Rights.

Benn wants magistrates and crown court judges to be elected. And laws passed by the Commonwealth parliament would take precedence over European Community law where the two conflict.

These proposals would be decided by referendum, where voters would also pass their verdict on the need for a new electoral system.

(Available from HMSO Books, 52 Nine Elms Lane, London SW8 5DR, £4 inc p&p)

Very little separates the analysis of the Liberal Democrats from that of the IPPR. They share the same perspective on European integration and pooling of sovereignty and the same comprehensive approach to reform. Charter 88 promoted and popularised general principles for democratic change. The Lib Dems' green paper started to put flesh on the bones and the IPPR filled in the gaps and addressed practical details.

Some might think it foolhardy to consider minutiae at this stage, but James Cornford of the IPPR says someone has to do it. And key questions remain: on regional government in England—do people really want it and would local authorities be better off under regional ruling bodies than under Whitehall? And on rights, how can the definition of fundamental freedoms be extended? Can social and economic rights be entrenched?

Significantly, the IPPR's examination of the British constitution coincides with a major welfare rights project, presided over by Anna Coote. As Ruth Lister wrote in a letter to the *Independent* (12 October 1991): "The effective exercise of political and civil rights requires the firm foundation provided by a comprehensive web of social and economic rights. The three are interdependent." Benn is scoffed at for including social and economic rights in his bill: they are deemed to belong to the sphere of politics, not to the basis of government. But this assumption is likely to come under ever closer scrutiny as work on reform progresses.

The Liberal Democrats' focus is also shifting to deal with these relationships, with the aim of broadening the electoral appeal of constitutional change—not by focusing on specifics, but by enlarging the general picture. Important though it is, *"We, the People"* was not, it seems, considered widely accessible, so the party came up with the Five Es strategy, elucidated in the recent policy document *Changing Britain for Good*. Constitutional reform, the Liberal Democrats argued, would improve the overall quality of decision making.

The IEA, meanwhile, is also taking a step back from the minutiae, if only because there is no consensus on the right that constitutional change is desirable. Vibert and others aim to win the argument by stealth, what they call "an incremental approach", taking a pragmatic look at specific institutions and focusing on themes that strike a chord with Tories. The time is ripe: government-induced recession has led the Institute of Directors, among others, to look again at the kind of institutional arrangements that facilitate such mismanagement (hence the interest in an independent central bank).

Fears over loss of sovereignty to the European Community can be allayed somewhat by arguing that we can, at least, make the mechanisms by which we are gradually surrendering it more transparent. Increasing the legitimacy and efficacy of our governing institutions is thus being touted as a way of staving off the centralising processes of European integration. Intellectually the argument is gaining ground fast. The free market sits easily with more of an emphasis on law and contract, with political pluralism.

Ironically it is not the right-wing proposal that stands apart from the others: it shares much common ground by limiting government powers and modernising state structures, and at least an awareness that all European states are having to rethink their constitutional relationship to each other and the community as a whole.

This passes over Tony Benn's head. While he raises issues of great import—the privileging of Christianity as the state religion and how much of an anachronism this is in a multi-faith society, or the goal of equal representation for the sexes at all levels of government, issues barely addressed in the other proposals—his refusal to budge from the doctrine of parliamentary sovereignty, and inability to come to terms with our place in Europe, guarantee that this is one draft constitution that will not be changing the course of British history.

Despite Integration, Britain Remains an Island Unto Itself

Distrust of their continental neighbors has caused the English to adopt a cautious approach toward implementation of Common Market ideas.

William Tuohy

Times Staff Writer

LONDON—While probably apocryphal, the anecdote about the headline on a long-ago British weather story is famous. "Fog Closes Channel," it supposedly read. "Continent Isolated."

Apocryphal or not, says Sidney Bearman, an editor at the prestigious International Institute of Strategic Studies here, the story reflects a common attitude in this proud island nation, separated by the English Channel from its continental neighbors since the Ice Age. "It's not the island that's cut off—it's everyone else."

And perhaps nowhere has the evidence of that attitude been more apparent than in the history of Britain's stormy relationship with the European Community.

Britain became the "Odd Man Out" from the birth of what is today the EC, rejecting terms of the 1957 Treaty of Rome. When, impressed by the EC's initial success, it finally applied for membership four years later, it ran afoul of France and the late President Charles de Gaulle. It wasn't until Jan. 1, 1973 that Britain was finally admitted into the Community— along with Denmark and Ireland.

Membership didn't end British reservations about the EC, however. Fully one-third of the voters refused in a 1975 referendum to endorse EC ties, for example, and former Prime Minister Margaret Thatcher delighted in denigrating favorite initiatives of the Brussels-based Community as "socialism through the back door."

Just weeks before she resigned in November, 1990, Thatcher said her fellow European leaders, who endorsed the principle of a single European currency, must be living in "cloud cuckoo land."

While Thatcher's successor, John Major, is friendlier to the idea of greater European integration, Britain still acts as a brake on those continental leaders who would accelerate the process.

As a German diplomat based in London put it: "British public opinion can be confusing about the EC—and Europeans in general. Young people in my country look upon a united Europe as a desirable dream. Here it's often regarded as a disease."

If Britain is puzzling to continental Europeans, they are equally mystifying to many Britons.

"I think there are some definite cultural problems that go quite deep," said Robert Elphick, a Briton who works for the European Community in London. "On a basic level, the British are aware that they feel immediately at home in the United States, Canada and Australia—many thousands of miles away. But they travel only 20 miles away, to Calais in France, and they find themselves among people with a different language, different customs and different almost everything else."

At its worst, the British attitude toward outsiders has a racist tinge. "Wogs begin at Calais," according to one old British adage based on a contemptuous slang term for foreigners.

Britain's popular tabloid press—which enjoys far higher circulation than the so-called "quality" press— often seems to pander to the most xenophobic of readers. What other paper anywhere, one wonders, would headline a story about a new proposal by the

Caught in Traffic

Traffic flow in miles per hour during rush hour:

Warsaw	23.0
Rome	22.4
Berlin	18.3
Budapest, Hungary	16.5
Madrid	14.9
Athens	12.4
London	10.4
Paris	8.5
Lisbon	5.8
Los Angeles	19.0

Frantic rush hour in Rome.

SOURCE: Cities, Life in the World's 100 Largest Metropolitan Areas, November 1990

From *Los Angeles Times*, February 4, 1992, p. H6. Copyright © 1992 by Los Angeles Times.

EC's French president, Jacques Delors: "Up Yours, Delors." Britain's Sun newspaper did.

The Sun sells nearly four million copies a day, and as Bernard Ingham, Thatcher's former press secretary, points out: "A quarter of the adult population in this country get their political news from the Sun, if you count how many people read it each day. That's something to think about."

The tabloids like nothing better than Europe bashing—whether in reaction to an EC proposal to change regulations that might affect Britons, or when charging Germans at mass-market Spanish resorts with grabbing all the pool loungers before the sleepy Brits get out of bed.

How Popular Is Unity?

Are you for or against efforts being made to unify Western Europe?

	Very much for	To some extent for	Against	Don't know
Portugal	54	30	4	13
Greece	47	35	8	11
Ireland	44	35	8	12
Italy	43	46	5	7
Spain	42	41	6	11
Germany	32	48	14	7
Britain	27	41	22	11
Luxembourg	26	48	18	8
Belgium	25	55	9	9
France	24	55	12	9
Netherlands	23	53	18	6
Denmark	22	44	33	4

SOURCE: Eurobarometer 36 (Autumn 1991)   NOTE: Figures may not add up to 100% due to rounding.

Suspicion of their continental neighbors is not restricted to Britain's tabloid class, however. Britons of virtually any station are likely to contrast themselves with "Europeans"—as if the French, Spanish, Germans and others were part of a different landmass.

Says one London woman: "These really are crummy first-generation democracies in Europe—while we have been a stable democracy for how many hundred years? Why, really, are we supposed to take our lead from the likes of them?"

"I don't really think we trust the French and Italians," adds another British woman who has lived on the Continent. "The war experience remains very strong among us. We think the French and Italians let us down in World War II. And, of course, we fought the wretched Germans twice. I think if it were not for the obvious benefits of European Community trade, we would prefer to stay here on our own little island."

As for relations with the EC itself, political experts note Britain's late entry into the Community. "It's the only major group they are a member of where they didn't help write the rules," said an EC official, recalling London's role as leader of the British Commonwealth and pivotal member of the North Atlantic Treaty Organization. "Some countries feel Britain is still trying to rewrite the EC rules."

Late to the game or not, enthusiastic about the prospect or not—the sense here now is that Britain is firmly on the road toward closer links with the EC.

6. Despite Integration, Britain Remains an Island

While Major dug in his heels against federalism and retained Britain's right to stay out of a planned currency union at last month's EC summit in Maastricht, the Netherlands, he avoided the confrontational style of his predecessor. What he sought, he said, was compromise; not what is "best for Britain," but what is "best for Europe."

"The EC is now a vibrant organization," Elphick says, "which it wasn't five or six years ago. The revolution in Eastern Europe has concentrated British attention on how to fit in with Eastern Europe, the U.S., Japan, and the EC itself."

An American banker, who has lived in London for three decades, declares: "I don't think there's a great deal of enthusiasm for the EC in the political structure—all those Europeans in Brussels—but out of London, in places like Newcastle, businessmen and industrial managers want to take advantage of the EC.

"I think people like that in responsible positions realize how Britain is falling behind its main trading partners in the country's infrastructure: roads, communications, rail, transport."

And Hugh Dykes, a Conservative member of Parliament who is chairman of the European Movement, says: "A growing number of British people—and not just the younger generation—want to see Europe as one entity for the welfare of its citizens, as well as the peace and well-being of other parts of the Continent."

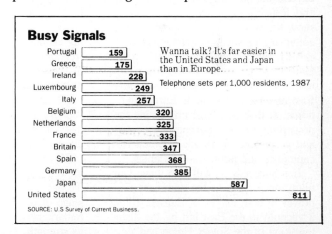

Busy Signals

	Telephone sets per 1,000 residents, 1987
Portugal	159
Greece	175
Ireland	228
Luxembourg	249
Italy	257
Belgium	320
Netherlands	325
France	333
Britain	347
Spain	368
Germany	385
Japan	587
United States	811

Wanna talk? It's far easier in the United States and Japan than in Europe.

SOURCE: U.S Survey of Current Business.

The summit undoubtedly strengthened Major's hand against the so-called Euro-skeptics in Britain, political analysts suggest, enabling him to move closer to that strange continent across the English Channel.

As political analyst Colin Welch puts it: "Mr. Major's ideal Europe is not self-regarding or inward-looking or over-regulatory. It regards Scandinavia, Central and Eastern Europe hospitably, eager to welcome all in."

And columnist Hugo Young, author of a Thatcher biography, concludes about Major's real views on Europe: "Margaret Thatcher was a prewar child with a tribal mistrust of all Continentals. John Major is a postwar child who has no doubt that he is a European, nor that this identity is congruent with winning a British election in 1992."

First year hangover

Integrating the two German states of the post-war period is proving far more difficult than anticipated a year ago when the historic merger took place. Despite the hopes it raised, it is too soon to assume unification will definitely succeed, writes **Quentin Peel**

The worthy analysts of Germany's five leading economic institutes see it as an "historic challenge". Chancellor Helmut Kohl says his country is at a "turning point in history".

There is no doubt about the import of the moment. One year on from German unification, and the success or failure of the process is very much in the balance.

It is a process of importance well beyond the borders of the united Federal Republic. If it succeeds, it can show the way to transformation of the collapsing ex-socialist economies of eastern Europe and the former Soviet Union. It can lay the basis for a re-united Europe, bringing together the East and West in a single European home. If it fails, it will undermine the powerhouse of the European economy and perpetuate the divide between rich capitalists and poor (ex-) socialists.

If it succeeds, it will also leave Germany once again as the dominant power in both halves of Europe, filling a vacuum in the East left by the disintegration of the Soviet Union and increasingly flexing its political as well as economic muscles in the West.

The historic challenge cited by the analysts of the German economic institutes is the challenge of financing the cost of unification: to create self-sustaining growth in the east of the country, without tipping the entire economy into inflation and recession.

All this has to be done against the twin social pressures of widespread unemployment and a drive for almost instant equalisation of living standards with the west.

When the German people celebrated their first anniversary of unification on October 3, it was a half-hearted event. It was overshadowed by the fear of unemployment in the east, by the resentment at the cost of unification in the west, and by the immediate shock of a sudden upsurge in racist attacks against immigrants, underlining the new tension in the nation.

Chancellor Helmut Kohl, the man who knows he has written his name into the history books for seizing the opportunity of reunification, did his best to put a good face on it.

"We are experiencing an epoch-making change under the banners of freedom, democracy and the social market economy," he declared in the historic Hamburg stock exchange.

He urged his electors to recognise, "for all their grumbling and whining," that for the great majority, living conditions had improved.

The truth is that the performance of the old West German economy over the past year, faced by the huge challenge of unification, has been quite remarkable, showing the real depth of its strength. Gigantic transfers from west to east have been made already without the western economy overheating. Soaring demand for western goods has been met by German industry, with costs kept down by a surge in imports from the rest of the recession-struck world economy.

An extraordinary wave of immigration from the east—some 2.5m since 1989, most of them eastern Europeans of German origin, and east Germans before unification—has been absorbed without any serious rise in unemployment.

Since the summer, however, that first boom time for the west has been over and a prolonged period of painful adjustment has begun.

The gloomy scenario was graphically spelt out by the five economic institutes in their autumn economy survey. They warned of the growing conflict between rising wage pressures in both east and west, a failure to restrain public spending outside the east, and the rigid insistence on tight monetary policy imposed by the German Bundesbank.

More precisely, they warned that the pressure for wage equalisation in the east was undermining all improvements in productivity. The result, they predicted, would be a slowdown in private investment, and an increasing reliance on public spending.

In spite of the growth of small business in the east, from a very low base, there has been little progress in privatising the big old heavy industries, the major employers. The Treuhand privatisation agency has transferred 720,000 jobs to the private sector, but another 2m are still in its care, and they are in the industries most difficult to dispose of, such as heavy engineering, chemicals and textiles.

The danger then would be of an east Germany locked in a vicious circle of reliance on state hand-outs from the west, creating increasing resentment in that part of the country, the analysts say. The tax and social security on western workers would fuel new wage demands there, pushing up inflation and encouraging the Bundesbank to raise interest rates and clamp down on money supply.

Meanwhile, the federal government would prove unable to cut any major spending programmes affecting individ-

Reprinted from *Financial Times*, October 28, 1991, p. 1.

ual interest groups—like the still swollen state subsidies to agriculture, steel, coal-mining and shipbuilding. With the need for public subsidies in the east still rising, the prospects for a significant reduction in the DM130bn public sector deficit are slim. The temptation would be for across-the-board, and therefore inflation-stimulating, tax increases.

Thus the institutes argue, grimly and urgently, for the negotiation of a new political consensus, precisely to finance unification.

Against this, the government insists that the upswing is coming in the east. Having promised that the pain would be bearable, Chancellor Kohl is forced to insist that all is for the best, and the worst will soon be past. As the pain continues, and sharpens, the political backlash is palpable.

The whole process means that Germany, the body politic as well as the business community, has become increasingly introverted. And yet the pressures for a more active external policy remain acute. For a united Germany has become once more the swing power of Europe, the intermediary above all others between east and west.

Initial fears in the rest of the European Community that Germany would turn eastwards appear to be unfounded. If anything, the unification process has bound the government to its constant vision of an integrated, federal European Community.

"Our freedom and our well-being are inseparably bound to the European Community and the Atlantic alliance," Mr Kohl declared in his Unity Day address. "Together with our friends and partners, we want to make our contribution to the building of the United States of Europe."

And yet the proximity of an eastern Europe in turmoil is proving profoundly uncomfortable. Germany is concerned, but wishes to share the burden. The reason is not simply financial.

"We are acutely aware that the chance to be the dominant power of eastern Europe is a grave temptation," according to one political analyst. "We don't want to be tempted."

That is why Germany—at least the present ruling generation—remains so profoundly committed to its European vision. That and the fact that Europe has been good for Germany, politically and economically.

"Without the European Community," we might never have been able to get our re-unification," according to a senior diplomat. "Mr Gorbachev might have been the only person prepared to agree."

THE NEW GERMANY

Stephen F. Szabo

Stephen F. Szabo is associate dean for academic affairs at the Paul H. Nitze School of Advanced International Studies of Johns Hopkins University. He is the author of numerous publications on European and specifically German politics, including The Changing Politics of German Security *(1990). His article is based on a chapter in* From Leninism to Freedom, *edited by Margaret Latus Nugent, to be published by Westview Press in 1992, and is reprinted here with permission of the publisher.*

Far from closing the "German question," the unification of Germany has opened it yet again. Especially pertinent is the issue raised over 30 years ago by Ralf Dahrendorf in his classic study of West Germany—namely, why has Germany had such difficulty in establishing liberal democracy?[1] Might not the thread of his inquiry be profitably taken up anew as we ponder the prospects for democratization in Eastern Germany?

Unlike the western two-thirds of Germany, the eastern third has never sustained a successful democracy. Its only experience with democracy came to an end along with the Weimar Republic in 1933. With its incorporation under Article 23 of the Basic Law into the Federal Republic, the territory of the former German Democratic Republic (GDR) is now again part of a democracy. Yet Eastern Germany faces not only many problems common to other postcommunist democracies, but also serious questions about its impact on German democracy.

Eastern Germany's incorporation into the larger and successful democracy of West Germany gives it an advantage not shared by the other new European democracies; few doubt that this will ensure the viability of democracy in the East. But democracy in Eastern Germany could have a decisive impact on the overall balance of German politics. The recent decision to move the German capital from Bonn to Berlin is an example of how the presence of the new legislators

from the East decided an emotional and hard-fought national issue.

In order to assess the prospects for democracy in the former GDR, a look back at the reasons both for the failure and the later success of democracy in Germany should prove instructive. Anyone seeking to explain the demise of Weimar or the democratization of the Federal Republic must examine Germany's political culture, the history of its party system, and the various constitutional and electoral arrangements that it has adopted, as well as the broader international context.

Political Culture and Economic Performance

Most examinations of the fall and rise of democracy in Germany turn sooner or later to political culture. It is often noted that Weimar was, in the words of Peter Gay, a republic without republicans.[2] Its doom was sealed by a deadly combination of economic depression and nationalist resentment against the Versailles settlement. While Britain, the United States, and France were all weathering the social and economic crises of the 1930s without sacrificing democracy, Weimar was forced to navigate the decade's rough waters without the necessary cultural ballast of solid support for constitutionalism among the general citizenry and the intellectual classes. The turn toward authoritarian alternatives was not seen as unnatural or un-German.

Studies of the political culture of the early years of the Federal Republic, including those of Gabriel Almond and Sidney Verba and of the Allensbach Institute, found thin support for such key institutions and practices of democracy as multiparty politics and free speech.[3] On the contrary, support for a single-party state remained high in the early 1950s, and there were positive attitudes toward some aspects of National Socialism. Later studies of the political attitudes and values of the citizens of West Germany concluded that prior to the 1970s, the legitimacy of democracy was "performance based," resting on the continuing vitality of the West German economy, and that the Federal Republic was thus a "fair-weather" democracy. It was only during the 1970s that evidence of a more deeply rooted democratic political culture began to emerge.

Observers cited a number of reasons for this transformation, including especially the long period of postwar economic growth and societal stability that bolstered performance-based legitimacy as Germans came to realize that democracies too can make the trains run on time. A second reason was the successful transfer of power from the ruling Christian Democratic Union (CDU) to the Social Democratic Party (SPD) in 1969, which convinced the SPD and its supporters that the Federal Republic was not merely a *CDU Staat*. Finally, there was the gradual socialization of two generations in the ways of democracy, a process that laid a more lasting basis for legitimacy than mere short-term performance and helped significantly to broaden political participation.

Although it will probably take at least a generation to develop a mature democratic political culture in the former GDR, the East Germans have several advantages over their Western counterparts of 45 years ago. If the West Germans could profit so greatly from the assistance of foreign occupiers, especially the United States, how much more do the Eastern Germans stand to gain from becoming part of a functioning *German* democracy with proven institutions and patterns of political behavior? The Easterners will benefit from the West's half-century of experience with democracy; they will not have to learn how to reinvent the wheel.

Economic growth will play an important role in stabilizing democracy in the East. Recent public-opinion surveys in Eastern Germany have found that two-thirds of those asked believed that democracy can only function in a growing economy, while only 17 percent believed that democracy could work in a poor economy.[4] This association of support for a political system with economic performance is a traditional German characteristic; the state of the economy in the East will be crucial in the early stages of democratic development there.

While the prospects for economic reconstruction seem good, no sudden leap to prosperity is in the cards. An October 1991 report by Germany's five leading economic institutes has concluded that while the East's falling industrial output has bottomed out, leading to a forecast of substantial growth in 1992, inflation there will most likely rise to an annual rate of 12 percent. Most importantly, the report added, the numbers of unemployed will probably continue to grow, going from 950,000 in 1991 to over 1.4 million in 1992. The number of workers on shortened hours will decline from the 1991 figure of 1.6 million, but will not go lower than 750,000 in 1992. Thus about 30 percent of the workforce in Eastern Germany will be either unemployed or underemployed by early 1992. Further-

more, the institutes warned, the growth increases in the East will result from West German assistance rather than increased private investment or improvements in the competitiveness of Eastern industry. Privatization, though substantial in the small-business sector, has lagged in both the industrial and agricultural sectors.[5]

Prospects over the longer term are much better. Their inclusion in the Federal Republic has given Eastern Germans an economic as well as a political edge over their Central European neighbors. The West Germans have begun a program of investment and economic assistance that will top even the Marshall Plan in size and scope. Estimates of the eventual extent of this aid begin at a figure of 100 billion D Marks (about $60 billion) annually for the next ten years, and go up from there. In 1992 alone, public transfers from west to east will add up to 10,800 D Marks (about $6,000) per Eastern resident.[6] While this assistance will strain the German economy and push up public-sector deficits and possibly taxes, it promises to transform Eastern Germany. Within five years, the East's infrastructure will be modernized, its state-run economy privatized, and its new plant equipment installed. These improvements should boost labor productivity and ease unemployment. Even before the end of 1991, signs of construction and renewal were visible throughout the new eastern *Länder* (states).

What is crucial is how Eastern Germans view the situation and their own prospects. It still seems safe to conclude that by the time of the next federal elections in December 1994 the economy in the East will clearly be on the upswing, and most people will believe that they are better off than they were four years earlier.

Assessing Public Opinion

A recent survey of public opinion throughout Europe and the Soviet Union commissioned by the Times-Mirror Foundation provides some interesting insights into the emerging Eastern German political culture.[7] First, the survey found Eastern Germans to be the most optimistic about the future of all the East Europeans polled. Almost half (48 percent) believed that they were better off as a result of unification, while only 5 percent expected unification to make things worse.

Second, the survey provides little evidence to support fears of a Weimar syndrome. Ninety-one percent of Eastern Germans approved of the change to a multiparty system; only 4 percent disapproved. This figure of approval is the highest among the other former "people's democracies," which tend to produce approval ratings of around 70 percent for multiparty democracy. It is also higher than figures from similar questions posed to West Germans in the early 1950s. In April 1991, 70 percent of Eastern Germans believed that democracy was the best form of government—about the same percentage of respondents who believed this to be the case in West Germany during the 1970s.[8] This broad support for political pluralism is mirrored by strong approval of free-market reforms. Despite massive unemployment in the former GDR, 86 percent of Eastern Germans in the survey supported efforts to establish a free market.

Resentment exists, to be sure, against the *Wessies* and their domination of the unification process. The Times-Mirror Foundation survey found that about three-fourths of Eastern Germans feel that East Germany has been "overwhelmed and taken over" by West Germany, and about half feel a great deal of resentment over this. Only a third believed that West German leaders care about East Germany, and 58 percent thought of themselves as East German while only 38 percent viewed themselves as simply German. None of this, however, changes the overall support for unification. Questions about whether unification was worth the cost are raised much more often in Western Germany than in the eastern *Länder*.

In general, then, early indications concerning the state of political culture in the former GDR are surprisingly good, far better than one might have expected in light of the earlier West German experience. It is worth noting in this connection that for the past two decades, close to 90 percent of East Germans have followed West German and Western politics on their living-room TV sets—a circumstances that may have helped compensate for the lack of a democratic political culture at home.

Above all there is the exhaustion of authoritarian alternatives to democracy. For almost all Easterners, authoritarian and totalitarian models of social and political organization are completely discredited. The East German Revolution was not simply about the D Mark and the desire for a Western-style consumer society; it was also about ridding East Germans of the leaden hand of the paternalistic state. Protests focused on a failed and corrupt leadership, and on a state that aspired to superintend every aspect of private life. Few Germans who lived under it are likely to wax nostalgic about it or develop a fresh hankering for an escape from freedom. This stands in marked contrast to the Weimar era, when extremisms of the left and right and their respective brands of totalitarianism held considerable appeal for large segments of the German public.

This is not to imply that democracy will face no serious tests in the years ahead. Resentment toward foreign minority groups has emerged as a serious problem. The Times-Mirror survey shows that unfavorable attitudes are strongest with regard to Gypsies, Vietnamese, Poles, Soviet emigres, Turks, and Romanians. Anywhere from 50 to 60 percent of Germans have unfavorable views of Gypsies, Poles, and Romanians; and 30 to 40 percent have negative images of

Soviet emigres and Turks. Jews are less disliked (with 52 percent of Germans having favorable attitudes toward them as against 24 percent with unfavorable ones). These are disturbingly high levels of what the Germans call *Ausländerfeindlichkeit* (animosity toward foreigners), although lower than those found in the Times-Mirror surveys of other newly liberated Central European countries. The influx of 2.5 million immigrants into Germany between 1989 and the end of 1991 has reinforced the feeling of many Germans that the boat is full. The increasing numbers of people, mostly from Third World countries, seeking entry for political asylum (estimated at 250,000 for 1991) has also fueled a new kind of racism.

This xenophobia is not a larger problem in Eastern Germany than in Western Germany; nor, for that matter, is it more or less a cause for concern in Germany than in other parts of Europe. Despite the palpably higher level of anti-Polish feelings and the more visible presence of skinheads and neo-Nazis in the former GDR, the surveys offer no evidence that the *Ossies* are more xenophobic that the *Wessies*.

Yet the fascist temptation will surely be stronger in the East than in the West both in Germany and in Europe as a whole. Ralf Dahrendorf warns that the greatest risk to democracies in postcommunist Europe is fascism, by which he means "the combination of a nostalgic ideology of community which draws harsh boundaries between those who belong and those who do not, with a new monopoly of a man or a 'movement' and a strong emphasis on organization and mobilization rather than freedom of choice."[9]

The rise of skinhead and neo-Nazi groups in Eastern Germany, while not surprising, is nonetheless a troubling example of what concerns Dahrendorf. There was a dramatic surge in reported incidents of violence against foreigners in the fall of 1991. Federal authorities, who reported 26 such incidents during the first quarter of the year, listed the number at 220 by mid-September. The attacks in the fall tended to be concentrated in the new Eastern states.[10] German authorities estimate that there is a hard core of about 2,000 neo-Nazis in the former GDR, and a broader group of sympathizers numbering about 15,000. Social scientists estimate that about 50,000 young Eastern Germans are open to the appeals of this deviant behavior.[11] Citizens of the eastern *Länder* are more vulnerable to these types of appeals than those in the West for a number of reasons. The higher unemployment in the East creates a larger clientele for radicalization. The collapse of a society, even one as corrupt and debilitating as that of GDR, creates feelings of dislocation and anomie. The decollectivization of the "niche society" of the GDR and what the political scientist Christoph Butterwegge calls "the reprivatization of social risk" are especially disorienting to many.[12] Police forces in the East have not yet been rebuilt, so law enforcement is consequently much weaker there than in the western states.

In addition, the different approach taken to the question of German responsibility for Hitler and the Holocaust in East as compared to West Germany has had consequences for the appeal of extreme right-wing groups. While the Federal Republic accepted responsibility for the crimes of the Nazi regime, making restitution payments to both individual Jews and the state of Israel and undertaking serious efforts to educate the public about what really happened in the Third Reich, the communist rulers of the GDR did nothing of the sort. They took the position that fascism was a legacy of capitalism, for which communism was the cure; the history of the Nazi period was largely ignored by the East German regime. This has left a vacuum on the right which is larger than that in the West. Four decades of suppressing nationalism and patriotism in the name of proletarian internationalism has only increased the potential for right-wing extremism.

Yet despite the disturbing surge in violence against foreigners that began in the fall of 1991, and notwithstanding all these warning signals, it is still true that *Ossies* have so far shown no greater inclination than *Wessies* to vote for right-wing extremist parties. *Die Republikaner* (the Republicans) and other new rightist groups have had even less electoral impact in the East than in the West, while voter turnout in state and national elections remains high. All in all—and especially given their starting point—the political culture of Eastern Germans seems favorable to democratization.

Political Institutions

The democratization of political culture in the former GDR is likely to receive powerful support from stable political institutions transplanted from the West. Here again the Eastern Germans have a great advantage over the new democracies of Eastern and Central Europe, which are struggling to create viable democratic institutions quickly under difficult conditions. In contrast, the East Germans can directly avail themselves of a system that has proven itself to be among the most stable and democratic in Europe.

The new constitution (the Basic Law of the Federal Republic) should fit the requirements of integration comfortably. The decentralized federal system—in which states play large independent roles in administration, cultural policies, and law enforcement—should allow the "new states" the flexibility they need in order to adjust to varying demands. A system that can accommodate the diverse interests and cultural traditions of Hamburg and Bavaria should be able to deal with those of Brandenburg and Saxony. This is not to deny that such searing national issues as abortion will

test the system, but some sort of state-level solution could help to defuse even these divisions.

Similarly, the adoption of the West German party and electoral systems will also ease the transition to democracy. Among the lessons of the Weimar era is the danger posed by a fragmented and ideologically polarized party system, and the consequent weakness of the executive when facing a legislature filled with fractious parties.

While the Weimar party system featured a multiplicity of parties, each with narrow constituencies, and an array of extremist antidemocratic parties, the Federal Republic's party system has long been dominated by centrist, democratic parties. The long-term trend has been toward a stable three-party system in which the centrist Free Democrats hold the balance of power between the center-right Christian Democrats and the center-left Social Democrats. The addition of the Greens as a fourth party has not essentially altered the system, which continues to produce stable coalition governments of the center.

In contrast to Weimar and the early Federal Republic, Eastern Germany begins its move into democracy with stable and moderate parties, reinforced not only by the predominance of Western German politicians and party organizations, but also by the Federal Republic's electoral system and its 5-percent clause. This provision, which requires a party to gain at least 5 percent of the national vote to enter the parliament (Bundestag), has proven as effective a barrier to splinter parties in the East as in the West.[13]

A difficult problem for all the new democracies in Central and Eastern Europe is the shortage of experienced political leaders untainted by collaboration with the old regimes. The leadership vacuum is especially serious in the former GDR, for several reasons. Unlike Poland, where experienced noncommunist leaders grew up within Solidarity, the GDR had no established opposition movement; East German dissidents were quickly jailed and then sent west in exchange for hard currency. Almost to the very end, the GDR police state remained highly efficient at controlling dissent and identifying and isolating potential opposition leaders. The revolution came and went quickly, producing neither a Walesa nor a Havel, let alone a Solidarity. Moreover, the East German police and party state was much more extensive than its Hungarian, Polish, or Czechoslovak counterparts. The GDR's secret-police service, the Stasi, is thought to have employed over 500,000 people. It is estimated that about two million more East Germans (out of a total population of less than 17 million) collaborated with the Stasi, while East Germany's communist party (the Socialist Unity Party or SED) had quite a large membership.

The relative weakness of East German civil society and the lack of effective leaders quickly became manifest in the inability of East Germans to fill the gap left by the communist collapse. Not only were Erich Honecker and his would-be successors swept away, but so also was the most prominent group from the revolution of 1989, New Forum. The incompetence of the GDR's only democratic government, a short-lived coalition led by Christian Democrat Lothar de Mazière, further underlined this problem and opened up East Germany to a friendly takeover. Many key officials in the eastern *Länder* are West Germans who have been appointed or elected by Easterners. The predominance of Western personnel is temporary, of course, and will end in due time as Eastern Germans receive a speedy and practical education in the ways of democratic politics.

As for the problem of collaborators, the relevant examples will most likely be the one set by West Germany in the second half of the 1940s, when it attempted to identify and punish the worst offenders from the Nazi regime while also keeping on many former Nazis and their collaborators for the duration of the democratic transition. Too many are guilty to sweep with too broad a broom. Trials of former East German border guards charged with shooting their fleeing countrymen will serve as a painful reminder of how difficult it is to punish subordinates for carrying out government policies. A series of trials of prominent GDR officials, including former spymaster Markus Wolf and possibly Honecker himself (if the Russians turn him over) can also be expected. Unlike their Nazi counterparts, however, the ex-GDR collaborators have few administrative or economic skills that can be put to use in the new period.

The Bundestag has given Stasi victims the right of access to the files that were kept on them, and to information about who reported them to the police, although media access to these records will remain restricted. The German government will also establish a special office to administer the six million files that the secret police compiled on East and West Germans as well as some foreigners. The office will be administered largely by Eastern Germans and will have a staff of 2,500 and an annual budget of 98 million D Marks (about $60 million).[14]

In addition to these promising domestic indicators, the global and Continental milieux in which the new democracies of the East are taking root also give grounds for hope. The Weimar Republic failed in part because it could not escape the taint of its association with the Treaty of Versailles, which many Germans reviled as an unjust peace imposed upon their country by her foes. Weimar floundered during a period of general crisis in Europe, when fascism, communism, and other aggressive, antidemocratic ideologies were on the rise. Today, while Europe may not have reached the End of History, the clear trend is toward democracy. Attempts to restore undemocratic forms of government would go against the current of trends in

Europe and lead to isolation and exclusion from the promise of the European Community.

Similarly, the openness of modern societies pervaded by mass media and the limits thus placed on political regression—most recently made apparent during the failed Soviet coup—serve as yet another check on authoritarian tendencies.

A New Identity

After the recent experience of unification, one thing is clear: while the impetus for unification may have come from the *Ossies*, its management and the reconstruction of Eastern Germany was and is "made in West Germany." Yet the Eastern Germans will have an impact on the new German democracy. The addition of about 12 million new voters, 140 Bundestag representatives, and five new state governments will have important consequences for the national political balance. Eastern Germans now comprise about 20 percent of the German electorate; the political leadership in Bonn cannot afford to ignore them. More than half the members of the FDP, which holds the balance of power in the current federal government, are Easterners. What impact are they likely to have?

First, the citizens of the five new *Länder* are likely to put their weight on the "social" side of the social market economy by favoring greater government intervention and defending a broad array of social services. This means that both the SPD and the left wing of the CDU will have at least the prospect of more influence than they did in the old Federal Republic.

Second, antiforeign sentiments in the East will probably strengthen parallel tendencies in the West, pushing Germany toward the adoption of a more restrictive immigration policy. The strong pacifist feelings that are common in the East will probably also have a broader impact on German foreign policy.

Third, the distinctiveness of the East will probably strengthen the already strong federalist and decentralist tendencies of the Federal Republic, at least in educational and cultural policies. There is some conflict between the social agenda of the eastern *Länder* and their desire to have flexibility in taking account of special regional problems and traditions, but decentralized approaches are likely to be more prominent in the future.

Finally, the inclusion of the East has, as the debate over moving the capital from Bonn to Berlin showed, reopened yet another discussion of the German identity. In this sense, the changes in Europe as well as those in Germany will force a major reexamination of fundamental assumptions about security policy, foreign policy, and Germany's role in the new Europe. Here too the Eastern Germans will have a voice.

As the new Federal Republic defines itself once again, the question about the balance between continuity and change remains open. Will the new Germany simply be a continuation of the old Federal Republic with five new states? To a large extent, the answer will be yes, especially in terms of institutional structures and political practices. Yet the changing European milieu will not allow Germany to maintain continuity in foreign and defense policy. With the implosion of the former Soviet Union, widespread instability in Eastern and Central Europe, the movement toward integration in the European community, and the prospect of a diminished American role in Europe (especially in the crucial area of military security), many of the fundamental assumptions of postwar German foreign and defense policies are being challenged.

Postwar German Atlanticism is likely to be tested and reshaped by these transformations, and a more "European" Germany will emerge. Germany is once again the Land of the Middle, facing both east and west and probably south as well. It is fully sovereign and will eventually be unified in fact as well as in law. Thus change will come, and will once again reshape what has always been a malleable German identity. Yet whatever the contours of the new Germany in the new Europe may be, it seems virtually certain that the country will mold its new role and identity on the basis of a stable democratic foundation.

NOTES

1. Ralf Dahrendorf, *Society and Democracy in Germany* (New York: Doubleday, 1967).

2. Peter Gay, *Weimar Culture: The Outsider as Insider* (New York: Harper and Row, 1968), see chs. 1, 2, and 4.

3. Gabriel Almond and Sidney Verba, *The Civic Culture* (Princeton: Princeton University Press, 1963); see also David Conradt, "Changing German Political Culture," in Gabriel Almond and Sidney Verba, eds., *The Civic Culture Revisited* (Boston: Little, Brown, 1980), 212–72. The Allensbach surveys can be found in a series edited by Erich Peter and Elisabeth Noelle-Neumann, *The Germans 1947–1966* (Allensbach: Verlag für Demoskopie, 1967).

4. Elisabeth Noelle-Neumann, "Die Vözuege der Freiheit stehen noch nicht im Mittelpunkt," *Frankfurter Allgemeine Zeitung*, 30 September 1991, 13.

5. See "Im kommenden Jahr in den neuen Ländern Wirtschatswachstum von zwoelf Prozent," *Frankfurter Allgemeine Zeitung*, 27 October 1991, 1; Stephen Kinzer, "Facing Down Protest, Eastern Germany Goes Private," *New York Times*, 3 November 1991, A16; Quentin Peel, "Germany is Given Grim Warning on Economy," *Financial Times*, 22 October 1991, 1.

6. Quentin Peel, "Autumn of Discontent," *Financial Times*, 24 October 1991.

7. *The Pulse of Europe: A Survey of Political and Social Values and Attitudes* (Washington: Times-Mirror Center for the People and the Press, 1991).

8. Elisabeth Noelle-Neumann, "Die Vörzuege der Freiheit stehen noch nicht im Mittlepunkt," *Frankfurter Allgemeine Zeitung*, 30 September 1991, 13.

9. Ralf Dahrendorf, *Reflections on the Revolution in Euroep: In a Letter Intended to Have Been Sent to a Gentleman in Warsaw* (New York: Random House, 1990), 111.

10. "Lieber sterben als nach Sachsen," *Der Spiegel*, 30 September 1991, 36; and "Dann macht er dich kalt," *Der Spiegel*, 14 October 1991, 37; Stephen Kinzer, "Klan Seizes on Germany's Wave of Racist Violence," *New York Times*, 3 November 1991, 16.

11. Bartholomaeus Grill, "Auferstanden aus Ruinen," *Die Zeit* (North American edition), 21 June 1991, 3.

12. Quoted in Grill, "Auferstanden aus Ruinen," 3.

13. In the first all-German elections in the Bundestag in December 1990, Easterns voted largely for the three major parties, though in somewhat different proportions than their fellow citizens in the West. The CDU recieved 35.0 percent of the party-list vote in the West and 42.7 percent in the East; the SPD 35.9 percent in the West and only 20.8 percent in the East; and the FDP 10.6 percent in the West and 15.2 percent in the East. It is significant that the extreme-rightist Republicans received even less support in the East (1.3 percent) than in the West (2.3 percent). The former Communists (PDS) did gain 9.9 percent of the vote in the East (as compared with 0.3 percent in the West), and thus were able to gain representation in the Bundestag under a special one-time provision applying the 5-percent threshold separately to the East; they are unlikely, however, to retain representation in future election. For more detailed election results, see *The Week in Germany* (New York: German Information Center, 7 December 1990).

14. "Der Bundestag billigt das Stasi-Unterlagengesetz," *Frankfurter Allgemeine Zeitung*, 15 November 1991, 1.

GERMANY: POWER AND THE LEFT

A New Political Configuration

Andrei S. Markovits

The momentous events of 1989 and the unification of Germany recast the long-standing debate about Germany's role in a changing Europe. Virtually all the English-language newsweeklies ran cover stories on the new "German question," and academic experts weighed in on the op-ed pages. At the risk of simplification, one can divide these commentaries into two categories: optimists, who viewed unification as a boon to Germany, Europe, and global peace, and pessimists, who were concerned that a strong Germany might repeat past mistakes. The optimists are the majority; but, for understandable reasons, both voices are preoccupied by the legacy of Auschwitz. The optimists have made it their mission to convince their audiences (perhaps even themselves?) that the ingredients that produced Auschwitz have been extirpated by "Modell Deutschland"—West Germany's exemplary democracy. Pessimists on the left worry that the Federal Republic's democratic foundations are not really democratic. Liberals fret that its institutions have never been truly tested in a crisis comparable to the depression of the early 1930s and are thus "fair weather" institutions at best. Conservatives, in turn, judge these structures irrelevant in a world ruled by renewed nationalism. Always cynical about the tenuous nature of the Federal Republic's "constitutional patriotism" (Jürgen Habermas's term), conservatives hope that nationalism will make a credible return as a new political force in a strong Germany, thereby challenging the anemic arrangements of the *Bundesrepublik*.

There is truth in both optimistic and pessimistic claims. Among the Federal Repub-

lic's greatest achievements is its eradication of most factors that might engender another Auschwitz. However, the optimists—and the vast majority of Germans—tend to see the future of Germany in Europe through rose-colored glasses, convinced that history—the Auschwitz trauma—now renders them essentially benevolent. Such assertions completely disregard the hegemonic power—resting on economics—already exercised by Germany in Europe. Its future extension is certain. Optimistic liberals and pessimistic conservatives, though from opposite vantage points, all see democratic institutions as mitigating power. But successful democracies, such as Germany's, are powerful because of the consensual nature of their politics and the high productive and distributive efficiency of their markets. Indeed, the adage that Deutsche marks will go much farther than Panzers seems compelling. It is encouraging that a substantial majority of Germans favor a low profile for their country in world affairs, and are, in the *Financial Times*'s words, "peaceable, fearful—and Green." Yet, the power already exercised by a united Germany in Europe and beyond cannot be underestimated.

In virtually every aspect of economic life, the Federal Republic has a formidable lead over its nearest Western European competitors. The existence of the European Community (EC) seems to have benefited Germany more than any other country. West Germany's market share in terms of intra-EC exports has consistently grown since the 1970s, rising to nearly 28 percent by 1989. France, the runner-up, has 15.6 percent, and the United Kingdom 11.4 percent. Germany's share is nearly three times

From *Dissent*, Summer 1991, pp. 354-359. *Dissent*, 521 Fifth Avenue, New York, NY 10017. Reprinted by permission.

that of Italy. Using export prowess as an indicator, there can be little doubt that the Federal Republic in Europe and Japan in expanding parts of Asia have reached hegemonic status. Throughout the 1980s only West Germany had a positive balance of trade among Europe's "big four." Its $208.5 billion surplus for the decade contrasts sharply with the huge deficits incurred by Italy, France, and the United Kingdom. Data corroborate the view that the European Community—at least thus far—has constituted a zero-sum game between Germany and its major rivals. Germany wins what the other three lose.

As a consequence of its singularly advantageous position within the EC, Bonn has been the largest contributor to the community's budget. This makes Germany the major political player inside the EC. The Germans dominate the corridors of the EC headquarters in Brussels. German political prowess was attained quietly and "by doing"—hard committee work—rather than through constant posturing, which has been the French style, or the spoil-sport negativism perfected by the British under Thatcher. Moves now under way to make German into the third official working language of the community (along with English and French) symbolize the political reality.

German influence in Eastern Europe is even more pronounced than in the West. In 1989 West Germany led all Western countries in export sales to Eastern Europe, and the figures are dramatic: $21.2 billion for West Germany, followed by Italy with $6.7 billion and $5.8 billion for the United States. In every category listed by the OECD (Organization for Economic Cooperation and Development), West Germany was the leading Western trading partner with Hungary, Poland, Czechoslovakia, Bulgaria, Romania, Yugoslavia, and the Soviet Union. And in each case Germany's trade was, at a minimum, double that of its nearest Western competitor. German firms have also taken the lead in forming joint ventures in Eastern Europe and the Soviet Union.

Culture and language are among the most decisive transmitters of economic and political influence. In East-Central Europe, German provided a common cultural bond and a *lingua franca* within the political and cultural elites at least until 1945. Despite its repression under communism, German has been reborn in postcommunist *Mitteleuropa*. This region wants to become European again—that is, Western, but in a commercial rather than cultural sense. East-Central Europeans are now learning German in order to converse with

Siemens and Volkswagen, not to read Goethe and Schiller.

Precisely at this moment of national ascendance, the German left finds itself in one of its most serious crises since 1945. Although this malaise is in good part due to Germany's new power, it also stems from internecine battles that contributed to a certain loss of purpose and vision. The unique burden of Germany's past further exacerbates the left's malaise by complicating its relationship to such contemporary issues as nationalism.

December 2, 1990, witnessed the nadir of the German left. Its most important institutional representative, the Social Democratic party (SPD), lost the third national election in a row (1983, 1987, 1990). Its support in the western part of the country declined perilously close to 30 percent. True, the SPD won 23.6 percent in what was East Germany, a 3 percent gain over its March 1990 showing there (in the only democratic election ever held in the GDR—the German "Democratic" Republic). But East Germany was the SPD's cradle, and in such pre-1933 strongholds as Saxony and Thuringia voters gave the party only 15.1 percent and 17.5 percent, respectively. For the Greens, the left's other parliamentary representatives, December 2 ignominiously ended a decade of gains. Founded in 1980 as an "ecological, social, grass-roots democratic, nonviolent" movement, the Greens were arguably the New Left's most important political legacy in the advanced capitalist world. On December 2 they collapsed at the polls.

These setbacks reveal a deep identity crisis. The left is haunted by its memory of the 1950s, when the Christian Democrats were dominant and the SPD was politically "ghettoized" and excluded from power. In 1959 it responded with a dramatic change in direction; the SPD's Bad Godesberg Congress shed Marxism in favor of Keynesianism. Today, a new Bad Godesberg may be required, although perhaps not quite as dramatic.

Identity crises result, in part, from success. Social democracy's difficulties in Germany, indeed across Europe, come from its acceptance by much of the continent's political class. The fact that Helmut Kohl never attempted to pursue anything vaguely resembling Thatcherism or Reaganism has much to do with the successful integration of social democratic values into the mainstream of West German politics.

The SPD was caught between an Old Left

insistence on growth and productivism and a New Left assertion of grass-roots democracy and anti-authoritarianism. In power in the 1970s, social democracy successfully expanded the state sector, introduced educational reforms, and spawned a general liberalization of West German public life. Ironically, this atmosphere helped to create the Greens just as much as did the SPD's failure to respond to the country's energy problems and demands for "new" politics.

The Greens also have a crisis of identity as a result of success. Polls convincingly demonstrate that in the course of the 1980s a majority of West Germans became "green" in attitude, though not "Green" at the ballot box. All three establishment parties (Christian, Free, and Social Democrats) developed strong pro-ecology positions, became advocates of women's rights, and were defenders of disarmament and detente during the last few years. One of the Federal Republic's leading commentators aptly characterized the Greens as "soluble fertilizers on the fields of the classical parties."

One component of the left's identity crisis may be called the postnational consciousness of virtually all the Greens and much of the SPD. One by-product of the Federal Republic's westernization and bourgeoisification was the emergence of a broad milieu of intellectuals devoid of nationalist sentiments—people who are first and foremost "federal republican." Being a German nationalist—in any shape or form—simply became unacceptable for West German leftists, especially after the belated discovery of the Holocaust in the 1960s and the immense impact of the student revolt of the late 1960s, known in Germany as "1968." Indeed, it was at this time—and not immediately after World War II—that much of the West German left developed the notion that the country's permanent division was a just penalty for Auschwitz.

Oscar Lafontaine, the SPD candidate for chancellor last year, is a product of this milieu. Hence, he was simply no match for Helmut Kohl and Hans-Dietrich Genscher in an election that was dominated by the national question (even though it was surprisingly muted in nationalist fervor). It was obvious to all that the Social Democrats and the Greens were uncomfortable addressing the national dimension of German unity. Instead, they harped on its costs, which did not endear them to East Germans and provided insufficient appeal in the West. In short, the left's history rendered it unprepared to address unification on an equal footing with the right. To most West German leftists, the GDR—while certainly no model—had become at least acceptable, if not commendable.

It should come as no surprise that many West German leftists, including a substantial segment of the SPD's left wing, remain profoundly unsettled about the disappearance of the GDR. Their discomfort mixes anger, embarrassment, and nostalgia and seems explainable only through a larger, unhappy context. In the eyes of some in the West German left, the GDR was unequivocally the morally superior of the two German states: it was the first "socialist" experiment on German soil and embodied the only genuine break with the Nazi past. This lent a particular legitimacy to the GDR, a legitimacy bestowed by the left on few other countries, save in the Third World. The GDR's dictatorial ways and bureaucratic repression were criticized, but they paled beside the achievement of a truly antifascist society via the abolition of capitalism. Though poorer than the West and more repressive, the East was perceived to be an experiment worthy in principle if flawed in practice. After all, the GDR claimed the legacy of Marx, Engels, Liebknecht, Luxemburg, Thaelmann, and Brecht in a land where Hitler had ruled not long ago.

This perception of the GDR is linked to the political fate of the left inside the Federal Republic. Until the late 1960s, virtually all West German discourse was engulfed by an anticommunism that often bordered on outright hysteria. In no other European country did anticommunism serve to affirm the existing order as forcefully as in the Federal Republic of Germany. Much of the West German left—led by the Social Democratic party—shared this antipathy for everything communist throughout the 1950s and much of the 1960s.

The year 1968 changed this both "from above" and "from below." It marked the intellectual origins of social democracy's *Ostpolitik*—a policy that, in the long term, contributed decisively to Leninism's eventual collapse. One of *Ostpolitik*'s contradictions was best described by its political architect, Willy Brandt: "In order to shake up the status quo politically, we had to accept the status quo territorially." As for the changes "from below"—little in West German public and private life remained untouched by the challenges posed by the New Left. Concentrated in Berlin, Frankfurt, and a number of university towns, the '68ers created an extraparliamentary movement that confronted all German institutions, including social democracy. Initially operating against social democracy, the New Left was in good part transformed by social democracy's reforms during the 1970s, which led to an uneasy symbiosis between the New Left's successors—the new social movements—and an SPD that, in turn, had become radicalized by its contacts with these movements. The interaction between social democracy, the New Left, and its successors also changed the earlier adherence by the left—and by the general public—to traditional anticommunism. In the course of the 1970s the SPD and much of the West German left tempered its anticommunism and came to accept the GDR. The '68ers were much more critical of the GDR's communism than some of the Greens and a good portion of the SPD would be later. At the same time, they were equally opposed to the repressive aspects of Bonn's anticommunism. Whatever the rivalry between Social Democratic "reformism from above"—the SPD led the government from 1969 to 1982—and its extraparliamentary challengers "from below," both contributed to a broad leftist milieu in which public criticism of the GDR became taboo. This "anti–anticommunism" was challenged only periodically by some daring Greens, but virtually never within the SPD, excepting some pockets of the party's right wing.

Unification upset the left's equilibrium. For a decade, the values of "old" and "new" politics had contended with each other. Just when the "new" priorities triumphed, enter the old GDR. Questions of feminism and ecology were again overwhelmed by bread-and-butter issues. Jobs, growth, energy, and investment all had to be debated again. In the united Germany of the 1990s, East Germany's 1950s-style materialism will undoubtedly challenge West Germany's 1980s-type postmaterialism as the left seeks a new identity.

Finally, a generational factor also helps explain the West German left's discomfort with unification. Surveys show that many young West Germans perceived the GDR as considerably more foreign than Holland, Austria, Switzerland, or even Italy. In other words, the division of Germany and Bonn's successful integration into Western Europe diluted identification with the GDR in favor of cultural empathy with other Western countries. In fact, the contemporary West German left is very much a creature of West Germany's successful integration into Europe. This has led, among other things, to an intellectual and experiential distancing of the left from Eastern Europe on a number of levels.

In recent decades the German left has been, by and large, uninterested in Eastern Europe's dissidents. The contrast with the French and Italian left could not have been more stark—at least in this area. The SPD and the trade unions have an especially ignominious record. Mention of the Soviet invasion of Afghanistan—even in a "politically correct" combination with the U.S. involvement in Central America—was repeatedly shunned by one of the trade unions' main youth organizations. A leading activist (who was prominent in the leftist Media, Printers' and Writers' Union) condemned any union member who protested the dissolution of the Polish writers' union. The Polish union, he declared, was a "fifth column," which undermined "socialism." Some of his colleagues called KOR, the organization of Polish intellectuals associated with Solidarity, "a questionable organization which transforms Solidarity into a political resistance movement." Many unionists and Social Democrats railed against the "Catholic-reactionary" nature of Solidarity (in 1981, *not* 1991). One member of the media union went so far as to compare Polish unionists to Hitler's storm troopers.

Tacit approval of the communist status quo in Eastern Europe reached the highest echelons of the West German Social Democratic hierarchy in a bizarre—though telling—incident in December 1981. SPD Chancellor Helmut Schmidt spent a sequestered weekend consulting with GDR chief Erich Honecker—in the latter's country house—while General Jaruzelski's troops were imposing martial law in neighboring Poland. Schmidt was not sufficiently disturbed by the events to break off the meeting.* The neglect of Eastern Europe by the German left led to an understandable mistrust by East Europeans of the German left. At the celebrations of Willy Brandt's seventy-sixth birthday in December 1989 in Berlin, Pavel Kohut declared that "you [Social Democrats] will yourselves have to analyze why you dropped us in the 1970s, and why you allied

---

* Friends of mine who attended an anti-Jaruzelski demonstration that Sunday in Frankfurt were not surprised by the low turnout in a town known for the political activism of its sizable leftist subculture. Except for some anarchists and Trotskyists, most of the left stayed home. This would not have been the case had it involved comparable developments in Central America or other parts of the Third World, including Iraq, of course.

not with the beaten but with the beaters, or at best stayed neutral." The German left carries a heavy burden concerning Eastern Europe.

Looking West, we find problems of a somewhat different nature. One legacy of the "new" left is a tendency to frown on large-scale projects. Consequently, the German left has been rather uninterested in Europe '92. The Greens, in particular, exhibit substantial hostility toward the project. They have articulated the conventional (and largely correct) criticisms of the plans for a unified internal European market as a distant, overly bureaucratized, dehumanizing, and capitalist megamachine that will trample everything in its way. However, I have yet to see any comprehensive proposal from the German left that could even vaguely serve as a useful political strategy for these fundamentally new conditions. The unions seem completely preoccupied with defending the economic interests of their members and are fearful of a challenge to their position from the working classes of Europe's southern rim. Moreover, they have also been confronted with the onerous task of integrating the increasingly worried workers of the former GDR into a new union structure. This unexpected development demanded the unions' full attention and further diluted their lukewarm commitment to Europe '92. The extreme negativity of the Greens may render them peripheral to the entire debate on Europe's future. And the Social Democrats are once again caught between residues of their "old" left fixation on growth and their "new" left negation of growth and everything related to it. For too much of the German left, endless hearings in the committees of the Brussels-based Eurocracy—concerning issues like the standardization of measurements across the continent—seem boring and irrelevant to the "big picture." The German left is consequently largely absent from the trenches while European capitalism is dramatically reorganized. Its warnings that Europe '92 means a "Europe of capital" may become a self-fulfilling prophecy.

Finally, the German left harbors a fundamental mistrust of power and leadership as a consequence of the Nazi past. Although commendable in many ways, it can also lead to irresponsibility. This became evident in the process of unification, when many Social Democrats, and especially Greens, simply refused to accept a reality that contradicted their image of what should have been—and because this reality demanded forthright leadership from them. Had the Social Democrats recognized that unification—not a two-state solution—was the name of the game as of January 1990 and had they assumed a posture of leadership, German unity might not have become the exclusive preserve of the conservatives. The SPD and the Greens were reactive when they could and should have been active in shaping unity from the very beginning. A similar predicament pertains to Europe. Again the left seems resigned to accept the role of post hoc critic instead of vigorous creator. In fact, the German left has much to contribute in the formation of this new Europe. By virtue of Germany's hegemonic position its left has—despite itself—become Europe's most influential left. Its Social Democratic party, now led by the quiet but very capable Bjoern Engholm—a centrist—remains the dominant force in the Socialist International and on the European scene. Engholm is the SPD's fifth postwar leader (following Schumacher, Ollenhauer, Brandt, and Vogel) and gained national attention by leading the party to impressive successes in the state of Schleswig-Holstein. Although he belongs to the same "restless" generation inside the party as Oskar Lafontaine and Gerhard Schroeder, Engholm seems to be both temperamentally and strategically a conciliator. This is exactly what the party needs. Lafontaine's confrontational style and imperious personality were too divisive for a movement encumbered by serious identity problems. Engholm's quiet confidence will provide the party with fine leadership while at the same time offering it some respite from the frenzied conflicts of the recent past. Once the party is able to adjust to the fact that it operates in an enlarged Federal Republic in a completely new Europe, it will experience an electoral revival similar to the one that boosted it into power in the late 1960s. The absence of the West German Greens from the Bundestag during the following term should give the Social Democrats a much-needed breathing space. They can safely claim to be the sole parliamentary representatives of the left. Unlike in the 1980s, the Greens won't be able to upstage them. If the SPD's elites shed their unification phobia and develop a viable strategy for the new Europe (and, of course, the new Germany), Social Democrats could recapture power before the end of the century.

The Greens, too, can put their identity crisis to good use. Local and state contests after December's Bundestag election have demonstrated that the Greens will remain a permanent political force in Germany. Their disappearance from the federal level is a temporary phenomenon due mainly, though not solely, to the specific circumstances of unification. If the Greens can curtail the internecine battles that have disrupted them so often, they can re-enter the Bundestag in 1994. But both parties must recognize that German—and European—politics in the 1990s will differ dramatically from the previous four decades. Germany is no longer "merely" an economic giant and a political dwarf. It is a new and very powerful country in a new Europe no longer divided into East and West. True, many of the past markings that defined the identity of the German left still remain—relations vis-à-vis the Soviet Union, and the United States, the problems of capitalism and socialism. The surroundings, however, have changed significantly. It was one thing to be the progressive force in a smaller Federal Republic of Germany tied to the United States. It is entirely different to play this role in a united Germany within a transformed, and still changing, Europe. A new self-perception and a new strategic presence are required. *Ostpolitik*, to take one example, will no longer mean accommodation with a formidable communist foe for largely instrumental reasons and purposes of temporary detente. Instead, it will denote the projection of German power in an economically fragile and politically volatile part of an otherwise wealthy and stable continent. A new era in German politics has begun; the future of the German left will depend on its ability to adjust and innovate.

Germany
Such long sorrow

FROM OUR BONN CORRESPONDENT

LIKE Wagner's tragic heroes, coalition governments in Germany tend to take their time to die. Helmut Schmidt's government, an alliance of Social Democrats and Free Democrats (liberals), suffered agonies for years before it expired in 1982. A growing number of people now reckon that its successor, the centre-right coalition under Helmut Kohl, may already have started its last act, though with plenty of pain to come before the final break.

After nearly a decade together, personal strains between Free Democrats and Christian Democrats are beginning to tell. Count Otto Lambsdorff, the Free Democrats' chairman, observed recently that the same people had long been sitting at the same table and boring each other to death with the same arguments. Small wonder that sniping among coalition partners is on the rise, just as it was in the early 1980s among members of the Schmidt government. Might the liberals be preparing to return to the Social Democrats they abandoned before?

At the moment, Free Democrats and Social Democrats together would have no majority in the present parliament. That alone seems to rule out a new coalition for the time being. But there are growing signs that these former partners might get together again after the next general election, due in 1994. The liberals are closer to the Social Democrats than they are to their Christian Democratic partners on abortion, law reform, immigration and even finance policy (about which the Free Democrats hold stern views). German unification may have nudged the Free Democrats to the left. Almost three-fifths of the party's 162,000 members come from the east.

Younger liberal and Social Democratic leaders are starting to replace those who lived through the bitter coalition split nine years ago. Count Lambsdorff was re-elected chairman on November 1st but does not plan to stand again in 1993, when he will be 66. Hans-Dietrich Genscher, who is 64, seems to want to go on for ever with the job of foreign minister he has already held for 17 years. But there is talk that he could be persuaded to stand for election as federal president, a job that would lift him out of party politics in 1994. A switch back to the Social Democrats would be quite conceivable under any of three youngish and middle-of-the-road liberals wanting Count Lambsdorff's job—Jürgen Möllemann, the economics minister, Irmgard Schwätzer, the minister for building, and Klaus Kinkel, the justice minister.

The Social Democratic Party is meanwhile about to choose a new parliamentary leader to succeed Hans-Jochen Vogel who, at 65, is stepping down after eight years in the job. Earlier this year the party picked as new chairman Björn Engholm, the practical-minded 51-year-old premier of Schleswig-Holstein. If he can further insure himself against a bevy of dormant but ambitious party rivals by achieving a strong election result in his home state next April, Mr Engholm looks set to become the Social Democratic candidate for the chancellorship in 1994. Count Lambsdorff admits to having the occasional useful chat with Mr Engholm these days.

Mr Kohl's Christian Democrats believe they are going through a bad patch mainly because of the awful strains of making German unity work. But they argue that the economic recovery in eastern Germany will be obvious to all by 1994 at the latest, that the coalition climate will have improved and that the liberals will decide to stick to a winning team.

That is the party line. But self-doubt is growing. The Christian Democrats have little fresh, young talent to offer at the top and their results in regional elections have been abysmal for several years. Coalition-watchers also reckon that, although Mr Kohl's men are probably right about recovery in the east, they are still, as the Social Democrats have repeated for more than a year, greatly underestimating the costs of unity. The government has already raised taxes this year after pre-election promises in 1990 not to. It may well have to do so again unless, as the Free Democrats demand, it can curb spending and cut federal, state and municipal subsidies officially running at nearly DM100 billion a year. The government looks like being able to do neither.

Deficits soaring; liberals demanding savings which they are too weak to prise out of their government partner; an opposition shouting that state finances will be put in order only when it comes to power. All of that eerily recalls Germany at the start of the 1980s. The difference is that the Social Democrats were then the big spenders; now, safely out of government, they are the preachers of thrift—in unexpected harmony with their former allies. Public finance, which split the Schmidt coalition apart, may yet bring liberals and Social Democrats together again.

From *The Economist*, November 9, 1991, pp. 53, 56. Copyright © 1991 by The Economist. Distributed by The New York Times Special Features.

Germany

Too right

FROM OUR BONN CORRESPONDENT

APART from the jubilant far right, most German politicians would love to forget the regional-election results of April 5th. Buoyed by voter xenophobia and frustration with the political hick-hack in Bonn, extreme right-wingers sailed easily into the parliaments both of the rich southern state of Baden-Württemberg and of poorish Schleswig-Holstein in the far north.

Optimists recall that the far right scored similar regional successes in the late 1960s, but failed to win seats in the federal parliament in the 1969 general election and faded quickly afterwards. But the main causes of the rightist upsurge then were a rare recession and a "grand coalition" between Christian Democrats and Social Democrats in Bonn that brought an extremist backlash. This time the problems behind the swing to the right may prove more durable.

Easily top of the list is resentment over the inflow of asylum-seekers to Germany and rising anger that politicians in Bonn seem incapable of stemming the tide. The Christian Democrats under Helmut Kohl, the chancellor, want to change the constitution so that refugees from states where there is clearly no political persecution (how many would that be?) can be turned back at the border. But they cannot muster the support of the Free Democrats (liberals) and the opposition Social Democrats for the two-thirds parliamentary majority needed. Instead all parties have got together to urge that the processing of asylum applicants be completed in only six weeks, instead of the many months it usually takes, and that those rejected be booted out promptly. It sounds sensible in theory, but many officials landed with the job reckon that it will prove impracticable.

None of this, in any case, will affect the inflow of ethnic Germans from the ex-Soviet Union and Eastern Europe (222,000 last year) who have automatic right of entry. These newcomers are not officially classed as foreigners, but many Germans tend to see them that way and fear the extra competition for housing and jobs.

On top of that come economic worries: inflation close to 5% and record interest rates; the belief (justified) that the government has not come clean about the soaring costs of German unity; a reluctance to sacrifice the reliable D-mark to an obscure European substitute; in general, *Angst* that Germany is being squeezed by developments in East and West over which its leaders seem to have little control. Small wonder the tub-thumpers of the far right have found a truly thumpable tub.

They were already doing unexpectedly well in some elections in 1989, then dropped out of sight in the rush to unity,

but are now back in strength. Campaigning for a "Germany for the Germans", the German People's Union came from nowhere (much as it did in Bremen last October) to take 6.3% of the vote in Schleswig-Holstein. In Baden-Württemberg the Republicans, with a similar message but somewhat softer rhetoric, soared to 10.9% overall and close to 20% in some constituencies. Worse, the results in both states show the far right is pulling in young people as it mostly failed to do at the end of the 1960s. In Baden-Württemberg it attracted support from more than 20% (and in Schleswig-Holstein nearly 15%) of voters under 25.

Despite the onslaught of the right, the ruling Social Democrats in Schleswig-Holstein clung on. They had the narrowest of escapes, seeing their support dwindle by nearly 10%, but they were still able to retain an absolute majority of just one vote in the Kiel parliament. That means the local premier, Björn Engholm, has done well enough to keep himself (albeit ingloriously) in the running to become the party's candidate for chancellor in 1994.

The Christian Democrats never thought they would do well in Schleswig-Holstein. But even the most pessimistic among them hardly expected the fiasco that emerged in Baden-Württemberg—a Christian Democratic stronghold for 20 years and the last western state where the party still rules. By mustering less than 40% of the vote this time, the Christian Democrats are unable to form a government with their preferred partner, the liberals. They would have a parliamentary majority in alliance with the Republicans but refuse to entertain the idea. That leaves them with two unlikely and distasteful alternatives: a grand coalition with the Social Democrats, which might cause more support to rally to the extremists, or an alliance with the Greens that would probably not last long.

Post-war German history shows that voters use regional polls to wrap their rulers' knuckles but then go for middle-of-the-road government at general elections. But the challenge from the right looks trickier this time. Nothing the leaders of the big parties have said or done since the April 5th shock shows they know how to deal with it.

Deutschland, Deutschland, Land für Alle
Number of people seeking asylum in Germany
Excludes ethnic Germans

Inflow of ethnic Germans into Germany, 1991
Total: 222,000, from:
Romania 32,200 — Other 2,400
Poland 40,100 — Ex-Soviet Union 147,300

1981 82 83 84 85 86 87 88 89 90 91   91 breakdown

Other; Vietnamese; Nigerians; Iranians; Bulgarians; Turks; Romanians; Yugoslavs

Source: Government statistics

Germany's state elections				
Baden-Württemberg	**Share of vote (%)**		**Seats**	
	1992	1988	1992	1988
Christian Democrats	39.6	49.0	64	66
Social Democrats	29.4	32.0	46	42
Republicans	10.9	1.0	15	–
Greens	9.5	7.9	13	10
Free Democrats	5.9	5.9	8	7
Other	4.7	4.2	–	–
Total	**100.0**	**100.0**	**146**	**125**

Schleswig-Holstein	**Share of vote (%)**		**Seats**	
	1992	1988	1992	1988
Social Democrats	46.2	54.8	45	46
Christian Democrats	33.8	33.3	32	27
German People's Union	6.3	0.6	6	–
Free Democrats	5.6	4.4	5	–
Danish minority party*	1.9	1.7	1	1
Greens	4.9	2.9	–	–
Other	1.3	2.3	–	–
Total	**100.0**	**100.0**	**89**	**74**

*Excluded from requirement to have at least 5% of the vote to get seats

From *The Economist*, April 11, 1992, p. 51. Copyright © 1992 by The Economist. Distributed by The New York Times Special Features.

The New France

In a transformed Europe, the French contemplate their place, their problems and their purpose

JAMES WALSH

If geography is destiny, the fate of France would assuredly seem blessed. A temperate climate and gentle, well-watered terrain have contrived down the ages to produce a civilization *sans pareil.* It is a culture abrim with connoisseurs of the good life and nature's bounty. Charles de Gaulle, father of the Fifth Republic, used to cite France's prodigious number of cheeses—265 by his reckoning—as an example of the land's lavish variety. Some benighted souls across the Channel may still believe God is an Englishman, but the French have never doubted that heaven is their home.

So why all the buzz today about discontent, about social gloom and political drift, a crisis of faith in the future and a fading sense of national identity? An identity crisis—in France? It sounds as unlikely as the notion of Cyrano de Bergerac fumbling his sword or groping for the mot juste. In his 1983 book *The Europeans,* the Italian journalist Luigi Barzini, a seasoned and mordant observer of the Continental scene, cites Edmond Rostand's fictional Cyrano as the quintessence of French character, at least as outsiders exaggerate it: the boastful, cocksure Gascon whose fellow provincials are defined in Rostand's play as "free fighters, free lovers, free spenders, defenders of old homes, old names and old splendors . . . bragging of crests and pedigrees." Yet now it seems that the rooster, the national symbol, is crestfallen.

How can a people so certain of their birthright be disoriented? More to the point, how can the French feel lost when France has emerged as the master builder of modern Europe? Not since the mid–19th century, when Baron Haussmann thrust his boulevards through rancid slums, has Paris experienced such a fever of construction and renewal. With a Métro that works, streets kept remarkably clean by 5,000 green-uniformed sweepers, parks planted like Impressionist paintings and bakeries galore, Paris may well represent the apogee of civilized city living—for those who can afford the rent. Yet not since Parisians finally ousted Haussmann for his arrogant, free-spending ways has there been such a struggle over progress versus preservation.

The French can look with pride at high-speed trains and modern aircraft, fashion and luxury goods better than most of the world's; yet the country is, more than ever before, obsessed with its ability to compete in a global marketplace. It sees the powerhouse of a united Germany bulking over a Europe destined to become the world's biggest single market in 1993. According to the authoritative *World Competitiveness Report* for 1991, France has dropped to its lowest ranking since 1986 and is listed 15th, behind most other members of the European Community. Industrial growth has lagged, and the trade gap with behemoths like Germany and Japan has grown severalfold. But the world's fourth largest economy, with a gross national product of $956 billion, is far from an also-ran. Under the steady hand of President François Mitterrand, France now stands to become a keystone of 21st century power—so long as the French people manage to keep their cool.

At the moment, their aplomb seems to be deserting them. Judging by opinion surveys and diagnoses in the press, a country that long prided itself on being the *lumière du monde* is awash in dark soul searching. The French are said to be fed up with politics and politicians. There is the hangover from the gulf war, an episode that deflated the vaunted image of French power and influence. Paris waffled about what to do almost to the last minute and ended up sheltering behind U.S. policy. In the harsh judgment of Jacques Julliard, a columnist for the progovernment weekly *Le Nouvel Observateur,* "The gulf crisis revealed the weak influence of our diplomacy, the modest competitiveness of our industrialists and above all the archaic state of our military equipment."

And there is a nagging anxiety over the nation's soul. French culture, so some worry, is in danger of turning into pasteurized processed cheese: wholesome, possibly edible, but lacking distinctive tang and texture. What the country managed to preserve despite humiliations over the centuries—pride in a singular civilization—it now risks losing under the impact of American pop culture and in the homogenizing vat of that mysterious entity called Europe. Chauvinists like the immigrant baiter Jean-Marie Le Pen say the greater threat comes from African Arabs and blacks who have had the inestimable privilege of settling in France but refuse to accept its folkways. Meanwhile, with Marx in the dustbin of history, leftists have no prophet, right-wingers no archfoe.

The French, in short, seem to be losing their bearings, their ideals and dreams. It is a bitter vintage, all the more so considering how high expectations were running. Just last year France looked well placed to become more than the center of gravity of a newly ascendant Europe. By some lights, it was emerging as the best of all possible worlds. Three centuries after the reign of the Sun King, Louis XIV, and nearly two after Napoleon bestrode the Continent, Paris was confidently pulling the strings of Europe, positioning itself to be the capital of a new political-economic imperium.

It may be yet, for France still enjoys copious advantages. Its standard of living is among the best in the world, and the quality of life, as many a visitor will attest, remains as invigorating as it is gracious. Modern arts and sciences flourish in a landscape adorned with Gothic cathedrals, tree-lined avenues and *grand siècle* châteaus. Philosophy is still as much in fashion as fashion is the ultimate philosophy. To-

From *Time,* July 22, 1991 pp. 30-32, 37-38. Copyright © 1991 by The Time Magazine Company. Reprinted by permission.

gether with modern farms, a medieval patchwork of agriculture still yields its plenty to cordon bleu tables in a country better prepared for the 21st century than most—a land crisscrossed by bullet trains, a nuclear-electric power grid, Airbus jetliners and satellites borne aloft in Ariane rockets.

The jewel of French assets in recent years has been stability: a sureness about the nation's place and purpose in the world as well as its material prospects. Inflation was reined in, exports rose comfortably, and a Socialist President managed to guide France's fortunes, at home and abroad, with the confident generalship of a De Gaulle. A people famous for crossing swords over the slightest trespass or ideological difference settled into a harmonious political dispensation.

Now the country seems to be suffering an outbreak of that endemic French affliction called malaise. The symptoms: widespread public unease; a volatile mixture of boredom, anxiety and irritation, carrying the potential for triggering sudden acts of collective furor. Change is beginning to look overwhelming to many of the French, eroding the old certainties that once defined Frenchness for everyone. Traditional institutions are in decline, including the church, marriage, labor unions and even the leisurely lunch. In foreign affairs, defense, economic policy, even eating habits and consumer tastes, the French are becoming more like their neighbors—and they're not sure they like it.

They are no longer strikingly different in the way they dispute power, practicing instead a pragmatism and consensus building that is unfamiliar, perhaps even unwanted. The disturbance involves what the French call the banalization of politics—the end of ideology as the center of political life. Mitterrand's great achievement has been bringing the left into the political mainstream, giving it the respectability that was once a conservative preserve. But with the old partisan banners faded today, people sense a lack of choice in politics and are vaguely spoiling for a fight.

The President's May 15 selection of Edith Cresson as Prime Minister, to shake the nation out of its sullen mood, soured after little more than a month. With only a 38% public-approval rating, the bride of high office may be headed for divorce at a point when she has barely assembled her trousseau. French unemployment has reached 9.5%, and the record number of jobless looks as if it will go higher still. Meanwhile immigrant riots broke out in June, even as municipal policemen went on strike—along with air-traffic controllers, railway workers and doctors.

Cresson's idea was to rally the nation behind a centralized industrial policy, marshaling economic forces in a war footing against competitors—notably her des-

ignated No. 1 enemy, Japan. But her summons to arms has fallen flat at a time when the treasury is tight and Paris is striving to meet the conflicting imperative of a less subsidized, state-driven economy in advance of Europe's experiment with open market frontiers.

The undercurrent of these quarrels is a yearning for a new national myth, a sense of grandeur and destiny. As author Barzini points out, it was François René de Chateaubriand, the great Romantic writer, who said of his compatriots, "They must be led by dreams." De Gaulle, after founding the Fifth Republic in 1958 and establishing a presidential form of government verging on monarchy, set France apart from NATO, apart from "the Anglo-Saxons"—conveniently lumping in superpower America with France's ancient enemy, England—and even, in important ways, apart from Europe.

Though the general often talked up the idea of a like-minded, cooperative Europe, he viewed the infant Common Market circa 1960 largely as a device to control West Germany. From De Gaulle's day on, the E.C.'s chief purpose, as successive Elysée Palace incumbents saw it, was to bind French and Germans so tightly together economically that another war would become unthinkable. In exchange, Paris would champion West German interests in international councils where measures proposed by Bonn might sound Teutonically threatening.

That relationship remains as useful and vital as it was 30 years ago. The trouble is, the French today are no longer in league with *West* Germany. Their chief partner is now a larger, unified country, raising some worst-case nightmares of an old nemesis reborn. The two times in modern history when Germans ventured to consolidate— under Bismarck and under Hitler—France was eclipsed and conquered. Apprehensions today do not envisage anything so dire as a panzer plunge through the Ardennes, but many French wince at the prospect of an expanded Federal Republic overmastering them with its money, industry and technology.

Even France's famous "civilizing mission" to the rest of the world has come under question. French policy toward the Arab countries, supposedly an example of Paris' understanding approach to Third World aspirations, sank practically without a trace in the quicksand of the gulf crisis. Says Gilles Martinet, an ex-ambassador with close links to the Socialists: "For most of our statesmen, whether they belonged to the left or the right, France was always strong, feared, respected, admired and envied—until the gulf war taught us otherwise."

Yet France's seat as one of the five permanent members of the U.N. Security Council still gives the country a leverage in

world affairs far beyond that of Germany, Japan or Italy. The seat explains why Mitterrand insists that any new security arrangements for the Middle East must gain the U.N.'s imprimatur. Moreover, France's nuclear arsenal continues to assure it a place at high table with the superpowers, while its economic clout provides membership in the exclusive Group of Seven. Political punch aside, French humanitarian efforts overseas, such as the war-defying missions of the volunteer doctors known as Médecins sans Frontières, remain leading lights of compassion.

Even in the image department, the hand wringing in Paris before the gulf war measured up favorably, in the end, against Germany's self-paralyzing angst. Bonn's inability to weigh in for battle against Iraq except as a financier was greeted across the Rhine with relief. France's strengthened transatlantic relations have also reinforced the case for keeping U.S. troops in Europe, which Paris endorses as protection against any resurgent Soviet threat and a means of ensuring that Germany remains anchored in the West.

Though Mitterrand continues to exploit the French position in the middle, signaling his country's potential for mischief in dealings with difficult regimes, he can now justify his approaches to China or Iran as those of an *éclaireur,* or scout, for American diplomacy. France's ace in the hole remains its latitude for independence, especially in framing an autonomous "defense identity" and common foreign policy for Europe. Says a senior French military officer: "We will always stand with the U.S. in the great battles of the West. After that, we again become a difficult ally."

Though the fiction of a singularly influential and enlightened French "Arab policy" was exploded in the gulf, the result has been a more realistic, selective outreach across the Mediterranean. Mitterrand and Foreign Minister Roland Dumas are now concentrating attention on their Maghreb neighbors. In many French eyes, the North African lands that were once colonial possessions are a time bomb. Arab immigrants have for the most part rejected assimilation, and in future years may become a heavier challenge to the concept of what it means to be French. Surprisingly, residents of foreign origin constitute no greater a share of the population today—6.3%— than they did in 1931. The novelty is the highly visible intrusion of non-Europeans, largely Muslims, and their practices: schoolgirls wearing the chador, the electronically amplified wails of muezzins from mosques, suburban concrete ghettos where the culture smacks of Algiers or Tunis more than Paris or Lyons.

Mitterrand himself has warned about a "threshold of tolerance" for immigrants, and Jacques Chirac, the conservative mayor of Paris and former Prime Minister, has weighed in to the debate with a vengeance. He voiced sympathy for French families who have to live with the "noise and smells" of tenements inhabited by the newcomers. Cresson proposed last week to charter aircraft to send unlawful immigrants home, but an outburst of protests from fellow Socialists in Parliament caused her to withdraw the idea.

Now the more pessimistic oracles are casting doubt on the nation's ability to absorb the shock of the new, of a more rough-and-ready economic atmosphere, as well as the unfamiliar idea of multiculturalism. While the mainstream political parties cast about for fresh directions, Le Pen's racist National Front can count on a basic 15% of the popular vote in any election.

A recipe for trouble? For a civilization that may be the fastest changing in Europe, France has shown remarkable resilience and political staying power. The existential debate has not deflected Mitterrand from his nouveau Gaullism, a policy of working with and through Germany to secure a decisive say over the Continent's future. In the E.C.'s halls of power France remains paramount, and relations with Washington, prickly at the best of times, are on a surer footing.

If in the past Americans and others in the West often saw Paris as a withered peacock, strutting grandiosely when it was not perversely kicking up dust, the firmness with which Mitterrand steered his nation after the gulf war's outbreak gave their old ally a taller stature. France is still a tough customer on many issues—agricultural subsidies, for example, the big snag in the current troubled round of world-trade talks. Stubbornness is the Gallic style: a demonstrated readiness to scuttle agreements is Paris' way of showing that it means business.

Yet the country views its new challenges as especially dicey. Its postwar identity depended on the postwar system, which has come unglued. Mitterrand's ambitions for E.C. political union and a joint defense policy are central to his design of preserving France's status as the Continent's anchor. Washington-based analyst Jenonne Walker notes, "De Gaulle was never willing to meld France into a Europe able to act as a unit. Mitterrand is willing to do that." Trickier is the question of whether the French people, fearing for their national soul, will go along.

Mitterrand himself has adjusted to the idea of France as a middling power. Under him, says economist Peter Ludlow, director of the Brussels-based Center for European Policy Studies, "France came to terms with the fact that it was the end of the era of medium-size states with protectionist policies." Germany continues to rely on its partner in a relationship that is more a symbiosis than an axis. "Paris and Bonn," says German policy analyst Ingo Kolboom, "are condemned to act in concert." Jean-Pierre Cot, the French chairman of the European Parliament's Socialist bloc, sees a bright future for his homeland. He says, "I am struck by the fact that France seen from the E.C. today looks a lot better than France seen from within France. We are now in the best position to do the job of European integration."

So has the *lumière du monde* lost its way? Not yet, certainly. If the home of the Rights of Man could absorb one-third of its population growth by way of immigration between 1946 and 1982, its cherished identity seems rather safe. After all, 30 years ago, at the Fifth Republic's outset, the living embodiments of sophisticated Frenchness to much of the world were the film stars Yves Montand and Simone Signoret—the former a native Italian from a town near Florence, the latter born in Germany to an Austrian-Polish-Jewish father. As Cyrano himself might have crowed, in a slightly different context, *Vive la différence!*

—*Reported by J.F.O. McAllister/Washington and Frederick Ungeheuer/Paris, with other bureaus*

FRANCE

The state gives way

MARCEL PROUST wrote of the "immense human being called France" and compared it with the "conglomerate of individuals" that is Germany. This idea of France as a person with a will, character and pride of her own has been cultivated by the French for centuries. It makes natural for them statements such as "France wishes it" as a justification for foreign policy. And the recent claim of a leader of the French Socialist Party that "France has acted as midwife to history" in building the European Community sounded no more strange than Marshal Joffre's "I bring you the kiss of France" upon marching into Alsace in 1914.

Odd, therefore, to report that this wilful human being is transforming herself without much debate into a Germanic conglomerate of individuals. That is the legacy of the ten-year reign of President Mitterrand. Over the past 30 years France has become ever more committed to shaping the European Community; and during Mr Mitterrand's decade, it has allowed that Community to turn round and reshape its shaper. The Frenchness is going out of a France that has pledged itself to Europeanness.

This flies in the face of what most outsiders expect of the country. It looks odd, too, set against the forces of national self-determination recently unleashed in Europe. Yet it is only recently that great events in Germany and Eastern Europe have raised doubts about the European course that France has taken. And it is still only a small, though growing, minority of the French on left and right who openly challenge the wisdom of it. Like the *Grande Arche*, and Mr Mitterrand's other dazzling monuments in Paris, the European Community is ordained from above: it is simply there.

"Europe does not cause us an identity crisis, but is an affirmation of our identity," says Valéry Giscard d'Estaing, a former centre-right president of France and would-be contender in the election due in 1995. "We know what we are, but the way in which we choose to express what we are has had to be redefined."

Britain's identity is as an island with well-tried traditions, Germany's as a people, America's in loyalty to a set of principles; for France, the identity of a large and open-frontiered country has always been based on the instruments of state control. Already in the 15th century France was a vast and populous country by European standards—a China-in-Europe that demanded a powerful mandarinate to hold it together.

The Frenchness is being squeezed out of France by the Europe that France itself championed. Nico Colchester, deputy editor, wonders whether Frenchmen will continue to accept this

Exchange rates per dollar		
	1990 average	1991 end-Oct
FFr	5.45	5.70
D-mark	1.62	1.67
£	0.56	0.57
Ecu	0.79	0.82
Yen	145	131

During the past ten years that mandarin-based identity has proved hard to preserve in the modern world. Centralised state planning tends to be overwhelmed by the complexities of rich economies. State control of finance is brushed aside by international flows of money, and state protectionism by Europe's common market. The result has been little short of a silent revolution. Pinch yourself today to remember that in late 1981 the same Socialist government now in power in France controlled the price and allocation of credit, controlled wage rises and many prices, applied exchange controls, controlled the electronic media and had a *dirigiste* industrial strategy.

Remember, too, that this same government was then bent upon nationalising much of French business—a project orchestrated by Jacques Attali, a Frenchman now charged, through the European Bank for Reconstruction and Development, with the privatisation of Eastern Europe. And that those two old handmaidens of centralised power—inflation and exchange-rate devaluation—were deployed to leach away the savings that the French were not allowed to move abroad.

Although vestiges remain, that entire list can now be considered obsolete. In particular, by surrendering control over its monetary policy and fixing its franc to the D-mark, France has won itself an inflation rate of 2.6%, the lowest in the industrialised world. Its unmanipulated, non-inflationary money has become a source of national pride to ordinary Frenchmen and is reflected in their wage demands (whereas in Britain disinflation retains the image of a hair-shirt, the better to be discarded).

French industrialists, too, who were once inclined to see inflation as something that brought them growth, and devaluation as what gave them competitiveness, are now strong-currency converts, despite the painful rates of interest involved. They have progressively been weaned off the state as the centrepiece of their lives. Deprived of *étatisme*, they now find themselves torn between the Anglo-American model of capitalism and Germany's social-market version.

An ancient regime

Yet it is not only market truths that have eroded the old France. The French idea of the state as the embodiment of liberty is another recent casualty—this time of the collapse of communism. The notion of a liberating state was long basic to France's belief that

From *The Economist*, November 23, 1991, pp. 3-8. Copyright © 1991 by The Economist. Distributed by The New York Times Special Features.

its civilisation was a model for the world. An essay on the future of the French identity, published recently by the French planning commissariat, points out that the state's power was considered legitimate in France because the state was believed to be "culturally and morally superior to a hidebound society."

That sense of state-righteousness shaped France's peculiarly Roman approach to colonialism. Across the world, it helped various dictatorships of the proletariat feel virtuous, and numerous post-colonial supremos pass themselves off as l'état émancipateur. It had a good run until recently, when the idea of individual freedom reasserted itself across the third world and exploded in Eastern Europe. So now this aspect, too, of the French model looks dated.

Within France, a reaction against central power became visible in a phase of decentralisation of government. Since 1982 all of France's 22 regions were given new powers above its 96 departments, bringing the number of layers of local government to an unmanageable and extravagant three. Europe—the "Europe of regions"—provided newly empowered local administrators and mayors with their rallying cry. The 12-starred flag flies outside their headquarters. Some of them have representative offices in Brussels and have forged co-operation agreements with the city-states of Italy, the provinces of Spain or the *Länder* of Germany. The regions are, indeed, would-be French *Länder* in the making.

Next in the catalogue of challenges to France's identity is the one to France's defence policy. This remains the great Gaullist symbol of French individualism, with its expensive nuclear *force de frappe*, and its aloofness from NATO but tacit dependence upon America's presence in Europe and nuclear shield. This symbol has been reinforced by France's substantial and politically weighty arms industry, and by its posture as purveyor of arms to the non-aligned world.

The end of the superpower confrontation has left France with no fence to sit on, no non-alignment to exploit, no obvious need for expensive parts of its nuclear arsenal. If it is going to benefit from the defence "dividend" that the rest of the West is cashing, it will have to rethink its defence needs and cut back its arms industry brutally. It will have to reconcile a foreign-policy based upon enthusiasm for Europe with a defence policy inherited without much change from General de Gaulle.

Mounting tensions over immigration; angrily marching farmers; continuing pressure from Brussels against French state subsidy of industry and the protection of its car manufacturers—the list of challenges to French habits can go on and on. Europe runs as a thread through them all—Europe as part of a possible answer to France's immigration flows; Europe, the reshaper of French business; the reformer of French economic policy; the wobbling supporter of its vocal farmers; the supposed surrogate for French state power; the guarantor of continuing peace with unified Germany. Europe as the new expression of France's identity.

France has staked a huge amount on Europe, and this prompts two linked questions that this survey will explore. Will the French electorate go on accepting the changes to their society, expectations,

habits—Frenchness—that loyalty to Europe is imposing? And won't this sacrifice become ever harder to accept if the Community fades away, hijacked by Anglo-American values and diluted into what Mr Mitterrand calls "a vague free-trade area", or dominated increasingly by Germanic values and ambitions, or simply enlarged into an incoherent league of European nations?

There is little debate within France on such points—indeed, at the moment, not much discussion of policy at all, despite a mounting outpouring of grievances. Though big changes to the Treaty of Rome loom closer, Europe and what it imposes on France are not live issues there. That could mean that Europe simply isn't an issue in France, and that no amount of British incredulity will make it so. Or it could mean that it lurks, repressed, within the oddities of the French constitution, fuelling the street-protests of the aggrieved that have broken out this autumn.

■

Vote, don't think

What is called a "consensus" could really be apathy towards a stifling political constitution

WHEN Philippe Séguin, a former neo-Gaullist minister, said recently that "parliament is not just a theatre of shadows, it is a theatre without a script or audience", he was himself playing to the gallery. But not much. The theatre—France's constitution—badly needs a radical overhaul. As for the current script of French politics, still conditioned by decades of ideological fear and strife, it is being changed even as you read this.

The atmosphere and institutions of the country's politics remain strikingly at odds with the wealth and education of the French people. They are permeated with the old-fashioned whiff of political favour. They do not encourage debate. They promote what they are presumably designed to contain: politics played out as a series of physical eruptions, between which Frenchmen shrug their shoulders and follow an old pantomime, livened up, to be sure, with attractive *vedettes* from the *grandes écoles*.

The National Assembly and Senate have long had a poor image in France. From the revolution onwards, the mainly Catholic right perceived parliament as a menace to the structure of centralised authority that it felt happiest with. The left saw it as a bourgeois cabal. The periods of parliamentary government after the first world war were famous for their instability. So the Fifth Republic of today, launched in 1958, neutered the parliament and gave immense power to a president elected democratically only once every seven years.

Here is what Edouard Balladur, a neo-Gaullist and former finance minister, says of the extent of that power.

"In which other democracy is the president in charge of the executive and the legislature and the judiciary; in charge of the order of business in parliament, where by intimidation, force or a reverential majority he gets the votes he wants; in charge of the promotion of magistrats and of the public prosecution that sends them cases; in charge of a government that moves only at his whim?"

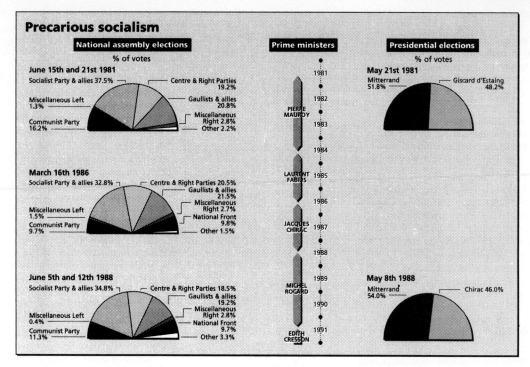

Precarious socialism

National assembly elections
% of votes

June 15th and 21st 1981
Socialist Party & allies 37.5%
Centre & Right Parties 19.2%
Miscellaneous Left 1.3%
Gaullists & allies 20.8%
Miscellaneous Right 2.8%
Communist Party 16.2%
Other 2.2%

March 16th 1986
Socialist Party & allies 32.8%
Centre & Right Parties 20.5%
Gaullists & allies 21.5%
Miscellaneous Left 1.5%
Miscellaneous Right 2.7%
Communist Party 9.7%
National Front 9.8%
Other 1.5%

June 5th and 12th 1988
Socialist Party & allies 34.8%
Centre & Right Parties 18.5%
Gaullists & allies 19.2%
Miscellaneous Left 0.4%
Miscellaneous Right 2.8%
Communist Party 11.3%
National Front 9.7%
Other 3.3%

Prime ministers
1981
1982
PIERRE MAUROY
1983
1984
LAURENT FABIUS 1985
1986
JACQUES CHIRAC 1987
1988
1989
MICHEL ROCARD
1990
EDITH CRESSON 1991

Presidential elections
% of votes

May 21st 1981
Mitterrand 51.8%
Giscard d'Estaing 48.2%

May 8th 1988
Mitterrand 54.0%
Chirac 46.0%

Certainly, set against that arsenal, even the British prime minister looks under-equipped. The parliament, which rises reverentially to its feet whenever a message from the president is read out to it, is further muzzled because it is virtually impossible for a deputy or deputies to bring a private bill to the floor without government approval. And if the president cannot drum up sufficient support for a government bill, he can use article 49-3 of the constitution to push it through unvoted, unless the opposition cares to call for an all-out vote of no confidence.

Small wonder that the parliament has been described as "a device to provide majorities", and that there is little public interest in parliamentary debate. Few people turn to their local deputy to pursue a cause. The person who embodies democracy at the local level is the mayor—especially since central government has granted him new powers. The French like their mayors: they mingle with the locals, play *boules* and fix things across the board. The president might almost be considered the mayor of France—with the Parisian monuments of François Mitterrand showing to what heights the power of the building-permit can be raised.

Whether France's sporadic outbreaks of political violence are the result of this constitution, or what make it necessary, is hard to say. But the improved working of French democracy is a live issue. The way the president and the deputies are elected; the length of the president's term of office; ways of giving the parliament and its deputies more scope to counter the president's powers—all these are now suggested as the possible stuff of referendum.

The length of the president's term is particularly topical at the moment, for a tide is sweeping through French politics that will probably give the right a majority in the legislative elections due in 1993. This would produce another period of "cohabitation" similar to the one the political parties endured in 1986-88, when the Socialist President

Mitterrand controlled foreign and defence policy while the country was run by the neo-Gaullist Jacques Chirac of the RPR as prime minister. Unless, that is, the president considers this a miserable prospect, introduces a shortened term by referendum, departs early, and is succeeded by a candidate of the right.

The nature of the rightward move in French politics will depend importantly upon the voting system used to elect the national assembly. Proportional representation, which the president is again advocating, would help the beleaguered Socialists, but it would also give the nationalist National Front a significant presence in the parliament. The last time PR was applied, in 1986, the National Front won 35 seats out of 577. In 1993, depending upon the system used, that tally could rise towards 70. Small wonder that this aspect of the French constitution is being hotly debated.

The rightward tide has various components. The most important is the demise of the Communist Party, an historic change in French politics. The Communist Party was the party of the French working class—as distinct from the Socialist Party of teachers and the intelligentsia. As late as 1980 it polled 20% of French voters. Now it would be lucky to get 7%.

Mr Mitterrand's original coup was to harness the Communists to his cause in 1981 and then to subdue them. Now they are barely there to harness. His decision in May of this year to replace the centre-left prime minister, Michel Rocard, with the more robustly socialist Edith Cresson was a total miscalculation, designed to bolster an alliance that really needed to be written off. Mr Rocard was appealing to exactly the sort of voter that the Socialist Party must now cultivate; but he and the president do not get on. In this slip-up, quite as much as in his reluctance to concede the passing of the old order in Eastern Europe, Mr

Mitterrand showed himself to be yesterday's fixer.

In terms of policies, too, Mrs Cresson's early whims as prime minister served only to underline what even a left-wing French government no longer has stomach for. A super-ministry to act as a MITI for French industry? The idea was quashed. A robust stance against inward investment by those Japanese "ants"? A minister was sent off to mollify Tokyo. Hold fast to the big chunks of French industry that remain government property? The way for the further sales was promptly prepared.

Until recently the menace of a sizeable Communist Party preserved the polarisation of French politics. In the mid-1970s the then president, Mr Giscard d'Estaing, complained in his book "French Democracy" that, alone among comparable nations, France's political debate was not between two inclinations but was a "clash between two mutually exclusive truths." This was, he surmised, because of France's "Mediterranean passion and Latin absolutism."

Two currents flowing

Today the only passion is on the nationalist right. Across the rest of the political spectrum the parties are shuffling rightwards to adjust to this fact and to the prevailing economic orthodoxy. The Socialists are moving towards social democracy and a German "capitalism with a social conscience". But at the same time they note coyly, in a discussion paper on the Socialists in the year 2000, that they should take more note of nationalism and "not always confuse it with racism."

The centre-right Union pour la Démocracie Française (UDF) has joined the chorus for toughness against immigration and is even starting to redefine its European enthusiasms as the old goal of a federal European Community appears more and more impractical. The RPR, under another would-be president, Jacques Chirac, is turning increasingly against European union and re-emphasising the value of government of all France from the centre.

So there are two axes of opinion superimposed in French politics that make the outlook for the presidential election in 1995 hard to read. The old ideological axis is being reduced to a German-style debate over the size of the social element in a social-market economy. But, according to Mr Giscard d'Estaing, "where the Germans know the difference between an SPD and a CDU, the French don't yet. Because of our arguments within the right we have not yet been able to work up a classic CDU-like platform, or one like the British Conservatives under John Major." This blurring of choice reinforces the electorate's cynicism about politics. The polls show that a majority of Frenchmen do not perceive much difference between left and right.

On top of this lies a reviving debate about national identity, which—quite apart from the personality clashes involved—is going to make that classic CDU platform, and France's answer to Helmut Kohl, hard for the right to agree upon. Is the spreading of power to the regions a good thing? What sort of European Community does France really want to submit itself to? Most powerfully, how should France deal with its immigrants? Such questions lead straight to the phenomenon of Jean-Marie Le Pen.

If Jean-Marie Le Pen's tirades about immigrants appeal in France, what he says about Europe could become important too

Le Pen is mightier

THE mounting clamour over immigration is the most obvious sign that national identity and culture are still neuralgic points for French voters. Jean-Marie Le Pen, the leader of the National Front, has been playing on this theme for decades, gradually shedding the image of leader of a crazed minority. He has recently been flattered by too many imitators for him not to be taken seriously.

Politicians of every major party have this year echoed his refrain. Mrs Cresson talked of the need to fly planeloads of illegal immigrants home. Mr Chirac sympathised with those "driven crazy" by the "noise and smells" of immigrant neighbours. Michel Poniatowski, a senator of the UDF, compared immigrants in France to the German occupation. Mr Giscard d'Estaing has talked of an "invasion."

The facts of the immigrant issue are hard to unravel, partly because the definitions are so confusing, partly because the census for 1990 has not yet been processed—the previous one was in 1982—and partly because France has a relatively generous code of nationality. You can become a French citizen by being born in France, provided you live there, and whether your parents were French citizens or not (*droit du sol*); by being born anywhere in the world of one or two French parents (*droit du sang*); or, while a minor, by being the child of someone who acquires French nationality.

On these definitions, there are about 4m immigrants (foreign-born residents) currently living in France, and about 1.3m of them already have French citizenship. And there are 5m children of immigrants living in France, 4.2m of them with French citizenship. The rate at which immigrant families leave the ranks of "foreigners" (people living in France without French citizenship) and become French may be one reason why many French people are convinced that the unchanging number of foreigners is wrong. (See chart on next page.)

The main problem, however, is that the mix of those foreigners has changed markedly. In 1968 some 72% of foreigners in France were Europeans. By the last census in 1982, this proportion had dropped to 48%, whereas the number from Africa, mainly the Maghreb, had risen to 43%. In short, the visibility and distinctiveness of the foreign-born population and their naturalised descendants have been increasing fast.

Mr Chirac's complaints and much anecdote suggest that it is not so much the race of these people that agitates the French as their habits, religion and culture. There was in 1989 a celebrated row over Muslim schoolgirls veiling their faces; it was considered an affront to the uniformity of the French school system. Equally, Georges Frêche, the mayor of Montpellier, considers it normal that Muslims should have a mosque, but not one with "gold domes that are provocative because they do not correspond to our civilisation." Frenchness, whatever the race or creed, is what counts. Clearly, the dismay at non-Frenchness bites deep, and is likely to lead to a tightening of identity checks and tougher rules for acquiring French nationality.

But if Mr Le Pen strikes a chord with his anti-immigrant tirades, what else does he think might strike a chord with the Frenchman in the street? Your correspondent visited this scourge of the *gauche caviare*—the gilded left—at his fantastic house in the aptly named Parc Montretout on the bluff of St Cloud that overlooks Paris. The mansion was that of the *chef de cabinet* of Napoleon III and was bequeathed to Mr Le Pen by an admirer.

The ex-paratrooper, who entered parliament as a Poujadiste deputy in 1956, has mellowed into a big, beaming uncle of a man, hard to reconcile with his inflammatory creed. His answer to every question is oratory in which he gradually works himself up into a passion. But always he keeps a showman's twinkle in his eye as he selects and savours ever more extravagant words to make his points. Here are some examples on themes other than immigration, both for their form and their content.

On the European Community. "Brussels-style Europeanism is a *fuite-en-avant*. It's the hope offered to voters that problems that can't be solved at home will be solved in Brussels. It's Father Christmas Europe. It's the belief that in 1992 the French tiger will eat the Japanese doe and the German turkey. I reckon that it will be the other way round."

On the open frontiers provided by the Schengen agreement. "It's a paradox to see the spiritual successors of General de Gaulle, like Mr Chirac, dropping the frontiers and joining the Euro-cabal. It's a betrayal. The same people who say that Israel should have secure borders would destroy our own."

On European Monetary Union. "I like the idea of a common unit of exchange, the ECU, but I am against a single currency. As for the idea of one central bank, it would mean the end of national independence, and it would be against the will of the people."

On the lack of open criticism of Europe in French politics. "It's tragic. Europe is a panacea. Touch it with Europe and it's healed. I'm in the European Parliament and make these points every month, but because I'm a nationalist, my ideas are immediately attacked in that assembly of frenetic federasts as racist or fascist."

On free trade. "I don't believe in world liberalism. I don't believe in liberalism that does not take into account the national or European dimension. The hyper-progressive concept of economies just leads to an inhuman quest."

On Brussels banning government aid to Renault, a French car maker. "Good, if that makes Renault adapt to reality. Bad, if it ruins the French car industry, which it will. For 45 years such policies have had Renault walking on crutches. If you add up what Renault has cost the nation, you will be flabbergasted. So I'm for stopping it, because Renault would then have to liquidate the communist *nomenklatura* for which it has been a milch-cow."

On Japanese investment in France. "Japan is liberal in conquering our markets and nationalist in keeping us out of its own. Let's not be naive and forget that to live you must fight."

On the fading of the Communist Party. "Its influence is not through parliament, it is through the key positions that the party holds in France's institutional sclerosis. The most important ministry in France—education—is under Communist influence. Communist union-power has much influence on social security, on our ports, printing and media. I look at the reality of things, not appearances."

On the electoral chances of the right. "The RPR and UDF have a suicidal attitude. They say we have different moral values, but they never say what they are. We say our moral values are Christian-humanism, which is incompatible with socialism, communism, fascism and racism."

On state intervention. "The state plays much too big a role in the economy. There should be a complete denationalisation. The government should give 65% of the shares in all nationalised companies to the fathers of French families."

On unemployment. "The figures say 3m, but actually it's 4m, because there are 1m in training from which they will probably never emerge. We call it a siding for the unemployed. We've let 10m foreigners into our country in 30 years, so we have not respected the basic law of life: preference for family, profession, nation, even Europe."

Mr Le Pen's prescription, in brief, is for government that does not intervene much except to keep France French—fending off foreign immigrants, Japanese predators and the influence of Brussels. The interesting thing is that his anti-European strictures are not loudly trumpeted, perhaps because they do not yet strike much of a chord with the electorate. He has only recently begun to use the word "federast" a lot.

Although France will doubtless tighten its immigration policies, there can be no rapid cure to the cultural suspicions that power Mr Le Pen's beguiling intolerance. But France's currently high rate of unemployment certainly aggravates the xenophobia on which it feeds. Joblessness hits the immigrant workforce particularly hard, leaving almost 30% of immigrant youths footloose amid the rows of high-rise flats that French urban planners have such an odd fondness for, given the space at their disposal. Foreigners make up 6% of the French workforce, and almost a fifth of them are unemployed, as against one-tenth of the workforce as a whole.

France's economic revolution has run but half its course. The jobless need the rest of it

Rapidly French

Immigrants and their children in France on January 1st 1986

	Immigrants' total: 4m	Immigrants' children's total: 5m
French nationality	1.3m	4.2m
Foreigners	2.7m	0.8m

Source: Michèle Tribalat of INED

That unemployment has causes that can be tackled. Almost every analysis of the French economy concludes that while its recent macro-economic policy has been a success, there are habits and expectations built into the French system of government that keep millions out of work.

• • •

Fiefs galore

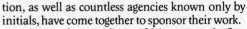

THE idea of spreading the government of France away from Paris was sown under De Gaulle but first blossomed under the Mitterrand administration. The president, who had long criticised the constitution he was later to revel in, needed to offer a counterweight to his socialist prescription. So he nationalised—fleetingly—with one hand, and decentralised more durably with the other.

France's 22 regions were given their first real powers in 1982, and their identity was further boosted in 1986 when they started to choose their regional councils in direct elections. These changes created four levels of government in France: the state, 22 regions, 96 departments, and no fewer than 36,000 communes, some of which are agglomerated into cities.

During the 1980s all these levels of local government were granted more autonomy in spending on regional and local development, in deciding the level of their taxes, in (recipe for graft) granting planning permits, and (recipe for nemesis) in borrowing and guaranteeing the borrowing of others. The prefect, hitherto the Napoleonic ruler of his department, was weakened.

Much local exhilaration was thus unleashed. Any visitor today cannot miss the physical evidence of it. Large towns compete in the splendour of their new pedestrian zones, stadiums, museums and concert halls. No city is complete without its "technopole"—a supposedly critical mass of high-tech skills drawing inward investors into its chain reaction. All airports are now signposted as "international". Bulldozers are everywhere, widening even the most tranquil roads, and billboards proclaim that commune, department, region and na-

tion, as well as countless agencies known only by initials, have come together to sponsor their work.

What are the ingredients of this energy? The first is an undeniable need. France's late development as an industrial country, and its style of government, left it with a curious lack of big cities (see map). Paris not only ruled; it divided to rule. Departments were drawn up on a scale to be governed on horse within a day. And towns, with a few obvious exceptions such as Lyons in its natural corridor, or ports on their natural harbours, remained department-sized. The result was a big country of little towns; surrounded by smaller countries—or German *Länder*, or Italian city-states—armed with region-sized cities. In farming days that did not matter; and perhaps in some cybernetic future it may not matter again. But today it does. Cities alone provide the variety of services and skills needed to support rich, thought-based economies.

France's newly-assertive regional governments are obsessed by city-size. Montpellier, a city of 212,000, sells itself to would-be investors as Montpellier-Nîmes-Ales "pole"—a would-be conurbation of over 700,000, including the city of Nimes, which was once an arch-rival in a different department. Alternatively it might lure you to the Montpellier-Languedoc-Roussillon technopole with its population of 2m. The towns of Saint-Etienne and Lyons, once rivals, today tell investors they can be considered as one great urban resource within the Rhône-Alpes region of France. They are creating a joint industrial zone at Saint Chamond to prove it.

The second ingredient is Europe. It so happened that the freeing of local government coincided with the gestation of the EC's Project 1992. Here was a cartesian justification for new local powers. Open Europe would be more of a "Europe of Regions" or a "Europe of Cities", and less of a Europe of nation-states dominated by self-centred capitals. No French regional-development office is complete, today, without a thematic map of Europe showing how industrial axes, emerging urban corridors, the pull of technopoles and tides of high-tech trade are going to sweep its region into the 21st century—and others off the map.

The regional government of Rhône-Alpes revels in this argument. Rhône-Alpes, say its officials, is a region the size of Switzerland with one-tenth of France's GDP, whose businesses look out at neighbouring Italy, Switzerland and Germany with the same eyes as they do at the rest of France. It has taken the lead in opening representative offices in Brussels and elsewhere. It has forged a co-operation pact with Lombardy, Catalonia and Baden-Württemberg—known as "four motors for Europe", no less. It even wants special ties with Shanghai, Ontario and the Maghreb.

Cynics may smile at such hype—but with an uncertain grin. For it is a fact that the TGV, the French high-speed train, has changed the economic geography of France. It is also a fact that the city of Lyons and the regional government of Rhône-Alpes are paying to alter the southern route of the TGV and bring it, and France's main north-south motorway, past an expanded airport to the east of Lyons.

Officials point to this as a solid example of how a region had to persuade central government that France could have transport nodes other than Paris; and then pay to get the plans changed. In

The regions of France
Showing major conurbations

Napoleon would wince if he saw what French local government was getting up to

Britain, meanwhile, not even the central government can make such a plan for London, let alone the regions challenge it.

The third ingredient in the phenomenon of French regional development is faith that investment in infrastructure, above all in education, will pay for itself. François Dubanchet, the jolly mayor of Saint-Etienne, is bent upon reviving what was till recently a grimy industrial town with failing coal-mines. "My old friend Raymond Barre told me, 'you will not succeed in turning round the economy of Saint-Etienne unless you have culture of high quality, plus higher education of high-quality, particularly in high-tech.'"

So he set to with a will. He spent FFr40m ($7m) creating a splendid museum of modern art. He spent another FFr50m on a 100-hectare golf course, and has 800 children learning golf. He also persuaded region and state to set up a high-tech university in his town to serve all Rhône-Alpes. With help from central government—private investment in Saint-Etienne qualifies for particular help via the DATAR regional development system—Saint-Etienne has been given an upbeat feel. The trouble is that, according to research by *Les Echos*, a French business newspaper, the town is one of the most highly indebted cities in France, owing FFr12,500 per inhabitant.

For mayoral positivism, however, no one touches Georges Frêche, the Socialist mayor of the sunbelt city of Montpellier. With this maestro at the keyboard, a quiet and graceful town has popped up out of the past like a cinema organ. Every stop is out: football team, arts festival, grandiose public housing in hyper-classical style, a stunning opera house, a subterranean maze of roads and carparks, and an echoing international airport.

Montpellier is marketed as a "Eurocity" and a fibre-optic-wired "technopole" as well. Tourism? Heliopolis, if you please. France's oldest faculty of medicine? The "Euromedicine pole". Mayor Frêche, a big, casually-dressed man with all the extroversion and something of the look of Gianni De Michelis, the Italian foreign minister, is everywhere at once. He is on plaques, on bookstands, on front pages, on podiums, fizzing with confidence and hustling his town into the next millennium.

He cannot understand why his predecessor did not *borrow* more. He believes in the virtuous circle of infrastructure investment, growth and tax receipts. His faith is deep. The Corum, a 2,000-seat opera house and conference centre that would make Londoners drool, cost FFr800m. Montpellier is a city with a workforce of 80,000, which has risen by an undramatic 4,000 over the past three years. That one project amounts to FFr10,000 per worker, invested for opera and other staged events. Montpellier's total debt runs to FFr10,000 per inhabitant, according to the *Les Echos* study, which is high, though not strikingly so.

All this points to a sweeping prediction. Local finance will be a source of political drama in France over the next few years. The different levels of local government overlap in their responsibilities. They either compete or egg each other on to spend. The example from the centre does not help: Mr Mitterrand is not modest in his monuments, and even the new finance ministry at Bercy went grossly over-budget. Local sources of tax revenue are intertwined, from one level to the next. The result is that no level of government faces clearly the consequences of its own actions.

The shift of power from civil servants to local politicians has led to an undeniable increase in corruption and projects-for-the-boys. There is no systematic control of indebtedness from the centre, although Crédit Local de France, a state-controlled bank with 40% of French local-government debt on its books, does act as lead-banker. There is not much local experience of debt management. Many towns have agreed to guarantee debts equal in volume to what they owe themselves. The notion of local-government credit not being rock-solid has only recently registered with the financial markets.

Add all those factors together and you can understand the discreet fears of the deputy-mayor of one heavily indebted city. "Our region has gone from building two *lycées* a year to eight. Its revenues cannot cope with the current rate of investment without raising the taxes a lot in a few years' time. Other regions have indulged in Pharaonic investments. If a slump were to force them to honour their off-balance-sheet liabilities, the result could be cataclysmic."

The first rumblings are already audible. The town of Angoulême, in western France, worked up a debt of FFr1.1 billion, or about FFr20,000 per inhabitant, and then defaulted last year and demanded a moratorium from its bankers. The finances of Marseilles, France's second city, are teetering. Pierre Richard, the head of Crédit Local de France, one of the world's largest borrowers on the international bond market, told *Les Echos*, "if the debt-per-head of a commune rises above FFr7,000-8,000, one says "watch out." Yet that newspaper's impressive study found debts of that order to be the average outside Paris and its region.

Unaccustomed deregulation and "moral hazard", all spiced with kickbacks: there is the familiar whiff of the ingredients of the American savings-and-loan mess here. Yet in France there is not, as in America, an entire slice of the banking system at stake. The more modest effect of the showdown will be to help reverse the trend towards the decentralisation of France.

That reversal is becoming ever clearer. The word *deconcentration* is now challenging decentralisation. The latter is political autonomy; the former is greater freedom for local prefects to think for themselves and for their regions—not forgetting, of course, that pay and promotion still come from Paris. National politicians of all hues talk about the danger of *féodalisme*—the creating of fiefs. Socialists flinch when they remember that their decentralisation has led to 18 out of 22 regions with opposition governments.

The outbreaks of urban violence that have shaken France's political calm over the past year have pushed things in the same direction. A new minister of cities has been created. Two laws were passed this spring, one of which forced rich communes and departments to support poor ones, while the other—a so-called "anti-ghetto law"—insists that big towns make more of their housing available for poor people.

In short, local government may once again have to defer to Napoleon's prefects, along with the young elite of the ENA, who serve their apprenticeships under them. It is to those mythical figures of France, and to French education in general, that this survey now turns.

School reform

A RECENT American film, "The Dead Poets Society", became something of a cult in Paris. It is about a teacher who rebels against hidebound practices in an American school. This improbable export struck a chord with the French. Their education system has long had a way of sailing along aloof from the desire of pupils, or the needs of the country, until disaster or revolution strikes it.

Thus French universities had acquired such an image of other-worldliness by the time of the French revolution—the Sorbonne long refused to teach science, seeing it as incompatible with theology—that they found themselves shut down as independent bodies for the whole of the 19th century. The revolutionary government chose instead to develop technocratic *grandes écoles* set up by the *ancien régime* to train the public officials of the state; in 1894 it created a new elite among them, the Ecole Polytechnique, and with it the selection by competitive examination that was to become such a feature of French higher education.

Thus, too, it was the military debacle of 1870 that galvanised France into creating the Ecole des Sciences Politiques (*Sciences-po*) to improve the quality of the senior civil servants who directed those well-trained technocrats. And it was the defeat of 1940, coupled with the shame of Vichy, that led to the founding of the Ecole Nationale d'Administration (ENA) to select and train top administrators with more rigour and protection against the self-interest of the bourgeoisie.

Today, despite many improvements, the impression still lingers that people "drop out" of French education into industry—rejects of a system inherently dedicated to higher things, whether it be

Germany sets the pace for French education. ENA and the grandes écoles are adapting to the new France

administration, the liberal professions or academia. And academia, in its turn, still feels that it is the poor relation of the *grandes écoles*.

There is barely a country in the industrial world that does not worry about its education. The French do so with particular fervour because of the example set by Germany, and because of their youth unemployment. Despite the constraints on the budget, spending on education will be increased by 5.7% in 1992, taking it well ahead of the defence budget. Over the past three years France's spending on education has risen by one-quarter in real terms, involving the creation of 30,000 new jobs.

Good progress is being made towards President Mitterrand's grand goal of preparing four-fifths of the stream of school-leavers for Baccalauréat and thus giving them the chance of going to university; the proportion taking the exam is now up to 64%. French education's next challenges are:
• To provide more university places for that broadened stream.
• To develop the scope and status of the technical and professional education offered after Baccalauréat.
• To develop a French answer to the German apprentice system, particularly with the non-Baccalauréat rump in mind.
• To get more local variety and responsiveness into higher education and further education, as well as more guidance from industry.

The problem is that the teaching establishment—whose million-strong workforce is the bedrock of the Socialist Party—will take some turning. It remains suspicious that Mr Mitterrand's reforms will pervert education for the less well off, leaving the bourgeoisie free to develop their intellects or their influence.

Yet the *grandes écoles* are themselves having to adapt to the silent revolution in French economic management. Despite their roots in state-dominance, they still have enviable effects in France. They have made sure that numeracy and scientific knowledge remain chic credentials. They have, through the skills they give the French elite, helped commerce remain on the same social plane as in-

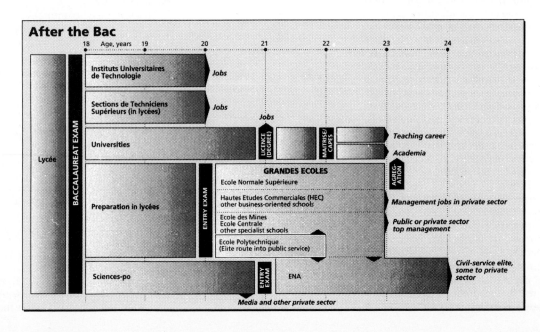

vestment banking and finance—as is also the case in Germany, but not in Britain. They have helped France resist cuts in infrastructure spending as an easy way of budget-trimming. The ex-Polytechnique planners and fast-train builders are not grey engineers struggling against supercilious Treasury men, they are part of a ruling club. At the Treasury the ENA graduates—the énarques—spent part of their apprenticeship building infrastructure themselves.

Nonetheless, ENA finds itself somewhat threatened by the recent changes in France. There is something strongly symbolic about Mrs Cresson's plans to move it gradually to Strasbourg. Unless he or she is set upon a career as a high-flying civil servant, ENA no longer promises a young person that much more than a climb through Polytechnique and a specialist grande école, or through the business-geared grandes écoles, such as HEC (Hautes Etudes Commerciales), where competition for places is now intense. In its heyday in the 1960s and 1970s, ENA was unbeatable as a credential. The state's role in the economy was unchallenged. The school's cumulative output was still small. Its young alumni were assured of powerful government jobs, and after they had served their term as civil servants, they pulled on the pantouffles and shuffled into industry and finance.

Today the choice for the young achiever is getting tougher. As industry becomes less dependent upon government—whether for ownership, loans or orders—its bosses become less inclined to hire énarque fixers. And as the supply of pantouffles dries up, a log-jam mounts in the civil service of 45-year-olds reluctant to abandon their gilded desks to younger men.

Certainly, ENA still provides proof of exceptional brightness, and there has recently been a wave of people passing through it and then buying their way out of their civil-service contracts. But that, too, depends upon the enduring eagerness of employers for people who, in the words of one énarque "have essentially done Sciences-po twice."

That champion of the regional city against the Paris mandarins, the mayor of Montpellier, has no illusions. "France is still run by civil servants. There is no difference between a socialist énarque and a neo-Gaullist énarque. They are intelligent, uncorrupt and absolutely convinced they are right. The country is run by thousands of little Robespierres."

That view remains widespread within France. Yet, beneath the surface, the fraternity of the top grandes écoles is gradually changing the medium through which it exercises its influence—away from the Grand Corps and state control and towards the German-style network of bureaucrats, bankers and businessmen that France is bent upon emulating. ∎

• • •

The last bastion

DURING the 1980s, moral debate about nuclear defence was a powerful fact of political life in Germany and Britain. There was much argument about the deployment of new missiles on German

Defence policy has long been the enduring symbol of France's discomfort with its own European rhetoric. Now that symbol, too, is cracking

soil, and Britain's opposition parties wrestled themselves almost to pieces over the question of unilateral disarmament. In France, a president who held power thanks to a Communist-Socialist coalition was subjected to barely a moral squeak.

The three pillars of French defence—its nuclear forces, its conscript army and its independence of operation from any permanent alliance—are also pillars of national identity. Conscription dates back to the revolutionary ideal of the "citizen in uniform" and is seen as living proof of France's resolve to defend itself. The other two are products of the second world war and de Gaulle's determination to restore France's pride in itself, and to make France unbudgeable from the top table of the United Nations.

All three pillars are now wobbling, rocked from without. The scale of France's nuclear forces is challenged by the same great changes that are affecting the other nuclear powers, as well as by the problem of their cost. Conscription is vulnerable, because the Gulf war showed how France's conventional forces are not structured or equipped to cope with jobs across the world that they could well be called on to do. And while France's proud independence was a viable conceit during the cold war, it flies today in the face of observable realities. The West will often choose to act collectively, and France is having to face up to emerging collective arrangements in Europe.

The nuclear pillar is the least threatened. France will keep its ultimate deterrent. But the present scale of its triad of nuclear forces will be hard to sustain. They currently consume one-third of the defence ministry's spending on equipment, and one-fifth of its total budget. As the threat of a full-scale Soviet assault dwindles, the more probable menace switches to proliferation of nuclear weapons and their use by smaller nations. That means that France will have to be seen to join in the overall reductions in nuclear weapons, now being accelerated by George Bush. It also calls into question France's need for land-based nuclear missiles of any sort, including the short-range Hadès missile now under construction.

The case for being able to threaten a "pre-strategic" strike against massive invasion from the East is no longer credible. France's submarine-launched strategic missiles should suffice to deter a Kazakhstan-gone-wild, and its air-launched missiles will give any nuclear Saddam pause for thought. Apart from budgetary constraints that affect every country, the reason why France must look for nuclear savings is that its conventional forces were shown to have been poorly equipped when they faced their last real military challenge—the Gulf war.

A recent analysis of "French stategic options", published by the International Institute for Strategic Studies (IISS) noted tartly that "With an army less than two-thirds the size of France's, Britain deployed to the Arabian peninsula a two-brigade-strong armoured division, reinforced with corps-level assets, while France was able to deploy only a single brigade-sized division which had to be strengthened with the addition of an American airborne infantry brigade and field artillery brigade."

France's conscript army was another reason for its difficulty in sending troops to the Gulf. There are legal and obvious political problems involved in using them abroad. The Gulf war reinforced the case for a more professional army. Again, that would mean money. France's army cannot be lightly cut without hard choices. France has long land frontiers and much land area to defend at home, and it keeps 30,000 troops expensively abroad in France's overseas departments and territories. In the view of François Heisbourg, the director of the IISS, France faces a decision equivalent to Britain's pull-back from east of Suez in the 1960s.

In the late 1980s the French government indulged in some heavy military spending that will be hard to reverse. The biggest projects include spending FFr24 billion on two full-scale nuclear-powered aircraft carriers. The first, now under development, was initially to be called the *Richelieu*, but was then renamed by canny admirals the *Charles de Gaulle* to make it uncancellable. Based on land and sea will be Rafales, Dassault's go-it-alone bid to build a new fighter, at an estimated cost of FFr120 billion. Then there are 800 Leclerc tanks, for use against Russian invasion; six new missile-launching submarines, plus their new missiles; the Hadès missiles; and, with Germany, the Tiger anti-tank helicopter.

Helping to make these orders hard to cancel is a French defence industry that satisfies almost all France's defence-equipment needs. This industry is facing a trauma. Alain Gomez, the head of Thomson-CSF, is expecting to lose one-quarter of his workforce by the middle of the decade. It is this sort of prospect, at a time of high unemployment, that has made the government abandon any idea of a "peace dividend" in its budget for 1992. Spending will be held steady at 3.3% of GDP.

The determined independence upon which these grandiose purchases are based is getting harder to justify. French defence policy has long indulged in two different sorts of ambivalence. During the cold war it could rely upon the American presence in Europe, and the American nuclear umbrella, without having to participate militarily in NATO. And it could promote the ideal of a political union in Europe that would ultimately involve common defence, without much risk that its defence policy would be compromised by anything really happening.

Now both ruses have been rumbled. First, with the winding down of the cold war and the reunifying of Germany, America's presence in Europe can no longer be taken for granted. The design of a European pillar to the Atlantic alliance is under way, with American encouragement, forcing France to choose whether or not it will become associated with something that will involve America. The dilemma was sharpened this year when NATO revealed plans for a British-led rapid-reaction force in Europe, which pre-empted France's own longer-term plans for a strictly European force.

Second, the fading of the world's ideological strife has suddenly made it possible for multinational forces to be assembled under the United Nations to right international wrongs. Thus France found itself fighting in the Gulf, in an American-led alliance. De Gaulle would not have been amused.

Third, the reunification of Germany forced France to decide what to do with its troops there. They had been in western Germany since the second world war, as one of the guardians of West Ger-

many's liberty. One might have expected the Bonn-Paris axis, working vigorously for political union, to have strengthened its defence dimension at that point. But no, it is only very recently that Mr Mitterrand has moved to set up a Franco-German corps as the kernel of an EC defence policy.

Fourth, the drama in Yugoslavia revealed a rift between France's Europeanist foreign policy and its Gaullist defence policy. The foreign minister, Roland Dumas, urged the Western European Union to send a military force to Yugoslavia. It did not happen, but there was little evidence that the defence ministry was remotely geared up for this.

Most western countries are now having to re-think their defence policies. But France faces a particular predicament—one that touches its sense of identity. To remain a defence loner, it will have to admit that there are limits to Europe's "ever closer" union. To join forces it will have to abandon this last bastion of its America-aloofness and work within a Western European Union that somehow dovetails its activities with NATO's and America's. ∎

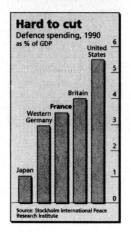

Hard to cut
Defence spending, 1990
as % of GDP

United States

Britain

France

Western Germany

Japan

Source: Stockholm International Peace Research Institute

France becomes Europa

READING of the French ambivalence over defence, some may nod knowingly. It confirms what they had long suspected—that the French are dichard nationalists who are committed not to the reality of European union, only to the rhetoric of it.

That suspicion has to face some awkward truths. The last great step down the road towards European union, the Single European Act of 1987, was negotiated under the Socialists but ratified by a right-wing parliament during the period of "co-habitation"; so, like France's economic reform, it carries the imprimatur of both right and left.

France remains consistently near the top of the "Eurobarometer" polls that the European Commission publishes to check on the enthusiasm of the faithful. Alain Duhamel, a political commentator on French television, reckons that though the term "federalism" remains alien in France, three-quarters of the French population are "federalist without knowing it"—that is to say, they favour a common defence policy, foreign policy and currency, and a sharing of sovereignty.

Take the immigration issue, currently the most visceral topic in French politics. One might have expected anti-European French politicians to have used this to torpedo the Schengen agreement, under which France and initially four—now seven—other EC members agreed to trust each other's border-controls and so allow free flows of people across their mutual frontiers.

Schengen touches sovereignty deeply, requiring much agreement on sensitive matters such as visas, guns and drugs, and mutual trust between police forces. Mr Le Pen hates the idea. Yet in June the agreement sailed through the French national assembly by 495 votes to 61. Several neo-Gaullist deputies complained about it, and there was some intense argument on the right; but the opposition parties still felt they had to back the Socialists.

Or take the more arcane issue of "democratic accountability"—the idea that too much European law is now being imposed upon the EC's members, without proper democratic control. The term means nothing to most Frenchmen. A French parliamentarian, quizzed about it, looked puzzled. European policies are foreign policy, he explained, and are thus a matter for the president. Even if they lead to French law? He smiled at the paradox.

It appears that a people used to being governed by an elected monarch and his civil service do not balk at a Community run by a commission and a council of governments. They can justifiably assume that the machinery of the commission, which France did so much to shape in the late 1950s, will respond well to French interests through the network of bright Frenchmen within it. And they know that its president, Mr Delors, is a French Socialist who has a fair chance of becoming the next president of France.

This fund of European enthusiasm has so far survived recent changes in Europe that have been sour for the French. The apogee of their satisfaction with the EC was probably reached in 1989. The Delors-led single-market programme was then all the rage, without having yet revealed its disciplinary side-effects. Economic growth in France was brisk. And Mr Delors was pushing ahead with France's long-cherished aim of gaining direct influence over German monetary policy through European monetary union.

Then came the prospect of German reunification. Understandably, it threw Mr Mitterrand into a tizzy. It marked the beginning of the end of the Community in which the two dominant members balanced each other: France, economically vulnerable, culturally strong; linked to half-Germany, economically strong, culturally an orphan. Suddenly Germany could forge itself its own fresh identity.

In April 1990, the German chancellor, needing French approval for his reunification, and the French president, anxious to pin Germany down before it became wayward, rushed out their plan for a treaty on political union. In this way the troubled political part of this winter's EC summit in Maastricht was launched.

But the train of unsettling events continued. The Warsaw Pact broke up, and then the Soviet Union. Nordic and neutral countries moved to join the EC. Mr Mitterrand tried to slow the dilution of the Community by proposing that it sit within a broad confederation of Eastern and Western Europe. He was promptly accused of being another Metternich—that arch empire-preserver who insisted that: "The East starts at the bottom of my garden."

The forces remodelling France's European garden now form quite a list. There are pressures to:

• Strengthen European defence co-operation, which France long favoured, as long as it never meant now, and which it has only very recently begun to move towards in practice.
• Organise a common foreign policy, which France thinks should involve a degree of majority voting between foreign ministers, provided the areas of decision are first decided unanimously.

The European Community is changing out of France's control. Despite all the strains involved, France will change prosperously with it.

• Give more power to the European Parliament, which France will concede only to the lowest degree that keeps the Germans smiling.
• Create a monetary union, which has been France's driving ambition all along, to make its surrender of monetary sovereignty less of one to Germany and more of one to Europe.
• Reform the common agricultural policy, a prospect that France fears because its farmers are again on the march, and where the Germans now seem to be less reliable allies.
• Open the European market to Japanese cars and car production. A pan-EC deal negotiated recently with Japan to restrict its imports will almost certainly not prevent much French grief about Japanese car plants in Europe.
• Stop subsidies to industry, which France has grudgingly accepted but which makes it pointless for its government to own many big firms.
• Enlarge the Community more quickly, which France now sees will be hard to prevent, and which must reshape the EC's ultimate dream.

That list contains some good things for France, but it fails two key tests. First, little remains of *Europe à la Française*—the new expression of France's state-based identity. The late-1950s vision of an ever-closer union of six, which was later expanded with strain to accommodate 12, is destined to be redefined in ways that make a Euro-identity less comfortable for the French.

Second, it does not bring the German mastiff to heel. The Community threatens to become, rather, an arena for German habits and techniques, as united Germany and Austria and probably the Nordic countries and—who knows—even Switzerland bring tidy Alpine values to bear on the Community's parliament, commission and council.

So, will those stirrings of resistance in the neo-Gaullist RPR, and the Euro-scorn of the National Front, develop into full-throated revolt? It is not impossible. The long period of unquestioning consensus and dismissive indifference in French politics is worrying. This survey has been a catalogue of pressures on the French and Frenchness. The farmers, or the unemployed young, or unloved civil servants, or redundant defence workers could well take to the streets and pressure the government to wriggle out of the international constraints France has accepted. Indeed, as this is written, they have already started to do so.

Yet France has changed too durably for such *événements* to cause it to revert to type. A gloomy view of that change, put by one quintessential *énarque*, is that "we are in the process of becoming a soft democracy with soft opinions and soft convictions". Mr Gomez, of Thomson-CSF, fears a phase of a "soft, social-democratic establishment" equivalent to the phases of weak conservatism that lulled post-war Britain.

Certainly, it will take political courage to face down the vested interests and tackle problems such as France's bloated bureaucracy, its social-security system, its tax system, its minimum wage. Those, and all the other challenges touched upon, will provide plenty of political tinder as the phase of Mitterrand socialism draws to a close. But what both those comments about "softness" imply is that the argument will rage along classic continental social-democrat versus liberal-democrat lines,

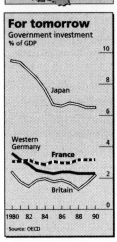

For tomorrow
Government investment
% of GDP

Japan

Western Germany

France

Britain

1980 82 84 86 88 90
Source: OECD

rather than as a nationalist showdown against France's external influences.

An outright relapse into old-style protectionism, planification and introversion is most improbable. Despite this autumn's protests, and sense of political *malaise*, there remains too much confidence in the new France for that. True, many French businessmen still find it hard to shake themselves out of the old state-dependent habit. But the best among them, in big companies and in small, feel that they have much going for them: a competitive workforce, a sound currency, a well-educated elite, a formidable infrastructure. The time for hobbling industrious Germans with Euro-obligations so that France could continue to live a life of cultured rusticism has past. France's game now is to emulate Germany and to compete abroad, rather than repose foppishly, like Shakespeare's *dauphin*, in the courts of a fortress Europe.

Despite de Gaulle's enduring legacy in France's diplomatic posturings, a visitor to France today may notice that the French have become more open-minded, less prickly, much readier—revealingly—to speak other languages (*On s'anglo-saxonise de plus en plus*, as one remarked). Perhaps that is because their enviably equipped nation works so smoothly. Perhaps they see that they have achieved an almost Germano-Nordic level of wealth—with twice the native ability to turn it into the good life. Such strengths explain why the recent paradox of France—that France made Europe, but then Europe remade France—will survive the coming troubles.

Deep Changes in French Society Unsettle Socialist Leadership

Howard LaFranchi

Staff writer of The Christian Science Monitor

PARIS

When François Mitterrand successfully ran for the French presidency in 1981, one of his campaign posters showed the somber Socialist candidate against the backdrop of a rural church. The message was clear: For a better, more "moral" France, put your confidence in me.

Eleven years later, as France prepares to vote in regional elections next month, Mr. Mitterrand's Socialist Party has enlisted Bernard Tapie, a flamboyant entrepreneur and owner of the Addidas sports-equipment multinational and the Marseille soccer team, to head its candidate list in the Bôuches-du-Rhone region of southern France.

The juxtaposition highlights one of the changes that France and its politics have experienced in the decade since Mitterrand took office. They are changes that a worn and unpopular Mitterrand, elected until 1995, may not survive.

• The great left-right divide that has defined French domestic politics since the French Revolution more than two centuries ago has disappeared, erased by generalized middle-class living standards and economic policies dictated increasingly at the European level.

• The left's decade in power has eradicated its image as a "moral force" capable of building a better country. The resulting disillusionment has sent a growing number of the more-motivated French voters in search of "new" alternatives—including the Green movement and the extreme right—and created legions of abstainers.

• In a twist of irony, France in the Mitterrand years has experienced a sea change in its perception of money. Long considered something to be hidden, money in the 1980s lost its shameful connotation for most French and became increasingly associated with such positive concepts as growth and better living.

"A decade ago we elected as president a man who made no secret of his disdain for money, for the conjunction of private money and power, and today Mr. Tapie is a baron of the Socialist Party," says Pascal Perrineau, director of Paris's Center for Studies of French Political Life.

This rehabilitation of money and related concepts of profit and entrepreneurship make possible a political career for Tapie—something unimaginable 10 years ago. Even more striking, it marks a rupture with the country's deep Roman Catholic roots in favor of the Protestant influences of northern Europe.

Politically these changes have devastated the French left.

A "profound transformation" has swept the French political map, replacing the "coherent" left and right with a collection of at least six forces—the Socialists, Communists, and ecologists generally on the left and Centrists, Guallists, and Jean Marie Le Pen's National Front (FN) to the right, says Philippe Moreau-Defarges, a political scientist with the French Institute for Foreign Relations. But none, he adds, can claim to represent a majority, even with traditional alliances.

One reason observers here are awaiting the March regional elections with great anticipation is that they will be the first national test of French voters' thinking since June 1989. They should give some clue to likely results in national parliamentary elections scheduled for spring 1993.

After a series of special partial elections across the country recently, the March regionals seem certain to reveal a greatly weakened Socialist Party, and probably stagnant traditional right-wing parties. Impressive gains are expected for the country's two principal ecology parties and for the FN.

Some analysts suggest that, depending on how many people stay away from the polls, the Socialists could find themselves only slightly ahead of the FN.

Yet analysts say the left's problems will not benefit France's traditional right until it is able to develop a coherent and distinctive message, something it so far has been unable to do. As abhorrent as his racist, nationalistic, and anti-Semitic message is to most, Mr. Le Pen is providing a lesson in this regard.

No one will be watching the March results closer than Mitterrand. Depending on the outcome, he could decide to drop his unpopular prime minister, Edith Cresson, for someone he believes could improve the Socialists' prospects before parliamentary elections. With an ineffective Socialist majority in the National Assembly, he could call early parliamentary elections. He could even step down from office early, some observers say.

The Socialists' slide is irreversible, according to most analysts. They remain saddled with a 1981 image that they have betrayed. "They came to office championing the virtues of the state, but they have embraced private enterprise," says Mr. Moreau-Defarges. "They touted French difference and independence, but pushed European integration and international cooperation to new heights."

Other factors are the multiplying financial and management scandals tarnishing the Socialist Party's image. "It's not that other parties don't have their scandals, but the Socialists presented themselves as different," says Perrineau. "As their claims of virtue began to ring hollow, the electorate judged them more severely."

The dangers for France in this period of political recomposition cannot be ignored, analysts say. With neither the traditional right nor left able to command a legislative majority, France risks becoming increasingly lost in internal affairs as important changes continue across Europe.

"We could end up with a dragging, flaccid political direction, with complaints about an increasingly aggressive Germany, for example," says Moreau-Defarges, "but no viable response for managing the domination."

Others warn that without clearly defined political imperatives and an opposition to battle against, the French could sink deeper into what writer Pascal Bruckner calls "democratic melancholy" typified by growing estrangement from their country's democratic process—even as countries in Eastern Europe and beyond strive to develop their own democratic institutions.

Reprinted by permission from *The Christian Science Monitor,* February 24, 1992, pp. 1, 2. Copyright © 1992 by The Christian Science Publishing Society. All rights reserved.

The lame duck with a long, long way to waddle

FROM OUR PARIS CORRESPONDENT

With his own popularity and his Socialist Party's vote at all-time lows, can President François Mitterrand restore confidence in his regime?

IN ALL its 21 years of existence, France's Socialist Party has never had a worse result at the polls. It won a pitiful 16.4% of the vote in the elections on March 22nd for France's 22 regional councils. It was overtaken by the far-right National Front in five regions, including greater Paris, and by the greens in nine regions. The Socialist government's credibility could hardly sink lower. A general election is not due for another year. But the pressure to reshuffle the government, perhaps even dump the intensely unpopular Edith Cresson as prime minister, is becoming almost irresistible.

Everyone is now waiting to see what President Mitterrand will do. As usual at critical moments, he is biding his time. Before the elections he was reported to be angry at suggestions that a collapse of the Socialist vote might somehow affect his own legitimacy, calling the idea "absurd". Now even his own aides are admitting he can hardly pretend that nothing happened on March 22nd beyond a normal expression of mid-term blues.

The message from the voters was nevertheless confused. Although the Socialists were the evident losers, it is hard to find a clear winner. Far from benefiting from the Socialists' decline, the alliance of the two main conservative parties also lost support: their 33% of the vote was their lowest score in over a decade (see table). Usually, three out of four votes go to the mainstream parties. This time, barely one in two did so. In a high turnout (69%), voters migrated to fringe parties.

The National Front did well, winning 13.9% of the vote, up four points on its score in the previous regional elections six years ago. In some cities, such as Nice, it won at least 30% of the vote. But its overall score was less than the 14.4% won by its leader, Jean-Marie Le Pen, in the 1988 presidential election, and way below the 20% the party had been predicting. Mr Le Pen failed to capture the Provence-Alpes-Côte d'Azur region, as he had hoped to do.

The two green parties combined did better than the National Front: 14.4% of the vote. But they remain fratricidally divided. The older-established Verts blame the new

Le rouge et le noir, et le vert					
% of vote in recent elections in France					
	Regionals 1992	Europe 1989	General June 1988	Presidential April 1988	Regionals 1986
Conservatives*	33.2	37.3	37.7	36.5	39.6
Socialists	16.4	23.6	37.5	34.1	29.9
Communists	8.7	7.7	11.3	6.7	10.4
National Front	13.9	11.7	9.6	14.4	9.6
Greens**	14.4	10.6	0.4	3.8	2.4

* Union pour la Démocratie Française and Rassemblement pour la République; in 1988 presidential election, combined first-round scores of Raymond Barre and Jacques Chirac. ** The Verts and (in 1992 regional elections only) Génération Ecologie

fall in their own party's score. Even the Communists appear to have benefited from the general rejection of the mainstream parties. They managed 8.7% of the vote, a slight improvement on their dismal 6.7% in 1988 presidential election but a far cry from the 20% and more they used to poll before the 1980s.

Why the disenchantment with the political establishment? France is not in such bad shape. The economy is reasonably healthy, though the promised upturn is a little slow in arriving. The franc is strong, inflation is low and the French on the whole live enviably well. Exit polls last Sunday suggested that unemployment, now almost 10% of the workforce, was the main influence on people's choice. Neither the right nor the left seems capable of offering any satisfactory solution for that perennial ill. The voters also said they were bothered about the environment. Immigration and crime, the National Front's two favourite themes, were not considered of prime importance other than by the Front's own supporters.

More than any specific grouses, however, the regional elections seem to have expressed a general discomfort, a bad case of Baudelaire's complaint: *ennui*. The mood in France is one of boredom and frustration, more than of anger. After 12 years of Mr Mitterrand as president, people are fed up. Many would like him to go now (though he is only just over half-way through his seven-year term). Yet they cannot see anything much brighter on the right. Jacques Chirac and Valéry Giscard d'Estaing, the two leading conservative presidential hopefuls, are also regarded as yesterday's men.

Mr Mitterrand does not like acting under pressure. But this time he may have to. There is talk of bringing in a new prime minister before the next parliamentary session begins on April 2nd. Jack Lang, the laid-back culture minister and government spokesman, is the latest person to be mooted as a possible choice. He was one of the few ministers to have done reasonably well in the regional elections. He is also a Mitterrand loyalist, popular with the young and unfussy about socialist dogma. He might therefore be acceptable to the ill-defined new coalition of "progressive forces" that Mr Mitterrand is said to be seeking to cobble together. Some centrists are already in the government. The greens are also being ardently wooed.

Under the present first-past-the-post voting system, the conservatives could expect to win a landslide victory in next year's general election if this month's voting patterns were repeated. Virtually the only way of preventing them from doing so, and thereby of avoiding a new period of left-right cohabitation, would be to introduce proportional representation.

Mr Mitterrand is said to be considering this. It would certainly help to attract the greens, who at present have no representatives in parliament. But it is strongly opposed by many Socialist leaders, who fear that it would kill their party and stimulate the National Front by bringing 60–80 of its representatives into parliament. It is also opposed by the conservatives, who say that it would lead to the same kind of confusion that has been produced by last Sunday's regional elections.

From *The Economist*, March 28, 1992, pp. 45-46. Copyright © 1992 by The Economist. Distributed by The New York Times Special Features.

The Real Japan

James Fallows

**The Enigma of Japanese Power:
People and Politics in.a Stateless Nation**
by Karel van Wolferen.
Knopf, 496 pp., $24.95

**Trading Places: How We
Allowed Japan to Take the Lead**
by Clyde V. Prestowitz, Jr.
Basic Books, 365 pp., $19.95

Karel van Wolferen's *The Enigma of Japanese Power* is the subject of much controversy and has been generally vilified in Japan, even though it has not been officially published there, is written in a language most Japanese cannot read, and does much to explain the roots of the political crisis that has preoccupied Japan for most of the last year. The book would be important for non-Japanese readers even if it had evoked no reaction whatever from the Japanese. *The Enigma of Japanese Power* will, I think, stand with other classic attempts by foreigners to interpret Japanese society and institutions, including Ruth Benedict's *The Chrysanthemum and the Sword* and Chalmers Johnson's *MITI and the Japanese Miracle*. Like those books, this one will change the course of subsequent debate about Japan; it will be very hard for anyone to discuss the Japanese political system without responding to Van Wolferen's argument. The intensity of the Japanese reaction against the book underscores the significance of the messages Van Wolferen is trying to convey.

The furor began three years ago, when "The Japan Problem," a précis of some of the arguments Van Wolferen has developed in his book, was published in *Foreign Affairs*. The article advanced a view that the subsequent twists of Japanese politics would seem to have borne out: that there is not a clear center of power in the Japanese government, but that the "buck" is circulating constantly and does not stop on anyone's desk. The Japanese government is extremely influential, Van Wolferen said, if one considers the cumulative effects of its various parts, but it is not centrally directed or controlled. A variety of Balkanized ministries exercise very strong supervision of trade policy, the schools, public works, prisons, banks, the medical and legal systems, et cetera, but no one stands above the separate organizations, with the authority or power to steer the entire system in a new direction. The best parallel in the American government would be the Pentagon, with its strong but very independent bureaucracies (the ship-building faction of the navy, the long-range bombing faction of the air force, the research-and-development faction, and so on) that fiercely resist the attempts of any president or defense secretary to coordinate them.

Van Wolferen was saying, in short, that Japan may seem structurally and legally a typical liberal democracy, but in practice its politics work differently from those of most other democratic states. One basic difference is that Japan's is effectively a one-party system. Since 1955, when the ruling LDP was formed, the party has constantly dominated the Diet and therefore the prime minister's office and the bureaucracy. (In English it is more appropriate to use the neutral acronym LDP than the full name "Liberal Democratic Party," which is the direct translation of the Japanese name, *Jiyuminshuto*. The *Jiminto*, as it is colloquially known, was created from the merger of Japan's main conservative parties, and the role it plays is exactly the opposite of what Americans think when they hear the words "Liberal Democratic.")

The peculiarities of Japan's electoral system strengthen the LDP's hold and illustrate Van Wolferen's point about the differences between Japan's political behavior and that of other advanced democracies. Japan's version of "one man, one vote" is "one man, three votes"—Supreme Court decisions permit a three-to-one disparity between the most and least populated Diet districts and in reality the disparity is now almost five to one. This gives farmers a hugely disproportionate role in Japanese politics and is much of the reason why Japan's urban consumers and industrial workers have had so little voice in the nation's policy.

The farmers and the LDP are locked together in a kind of "agricultural-electoral complex" that is at least as strong as the "military-industrial complex" is in the United States and is probably more destructive to the nation's overall welfare. For example, the Diet, under the control of the LDP, refuses to let imported rice into the country, even though Japanese rice, grown on tiny plots, costs 600 to 800 percent as much as rice from the vast flatlands of Thailand, Australia, California, or Arkansas. The rice-import ban and other farm quotas force Japanese consumers to pay 30 percent of their income for food, while Americans pay about 15 percent, and the policy indirectly compels them to live in tiny, expensive quarters, since about half of Japan's scarce nonmountainous land is used for these grossly inefficient farms. The farmers, nonetheless, are pleased and grateful, and they recirculate some of their profits into substantial contributions to the LDP.

According to an opinion poll conducted last December by the prime minister's office, only one quarter of the Japanese public feels that government policy reflects the best interests of the public; two thirds feel that, on the contrary, the Japanese government acts against the "popular will." Since "government policy" really means LDP policy, this would seem to be a devastating indictment of the ruling party, and because of year-long bribery scandals, the LDP will probably suffer significant losses in

Reprinted with permission from *The New York Review of Books*, July 20, 1989, pp. 23-28. Copyright © 1989, Nyrev, Inc.

the elections from the Upper House of the Diet in July. But almost no one expects the LDP to lose its control of the government.

A further peculiarity, amplifying Van Wolferen's themes, is that even though the LDP dominates Japanese policy, policy and issues play almost no part in the workings of the LDP. Under the Japanese "multimember district" system, individual LDP members have to run against each other in the same district, a problem that US congressmen face only when redistricting pits two incumbents against each other. Most election campaigns turn into sheer name-recognition contests—more than half the members of the Diet are the sons of former Diet members, riding in on their fathers' established names. Within the Diet, LDP politicians ally themselves with *habatsu*, or "factions" that compete for power the way Republicans and Democrats do in the United States. But while the difference between Democratic and Republican policies sometimes seems slim, there are no differences over policy whatever between the LDP factions. The factions are known by the name of the strong-man who leads them (the Takeshita faction, the Nakasone faction, and so on) and they compete only for political "market share," much as Toshiba does against the electronics conglomerate NEC. In fact, the real opposition party in Japanese politics is the United States. The LDP prides itself on maintaining a smooth relationship with the Americans, but constant pressure from American politicians and trade negotiators serves the function that an opposition party does in other countries, that of pushing policy in a different direction. There is very little push from within.

At about the time Van Wolferen's *Foreign Affairs* article was published, Yasuhiro Nakasone was going into eclipse, in a way that conformed to Van Wolferen's thesis. Nakasone seemed the exception to the general rule of Japanese politics that no one leader becomes dominant: he was a prime minister who tried to behave like a president rather than a committee chairman, and to impose his views on the government. One of Nakasone's goals was to increase Japan's military spending and generally have Japan viewed as a mature world power. Another was to reduce the trade surplus that is America's chronic grievance

against Japan. His military plan succeeded: he pushed military spending above the informal limit of 1 percent of Japan's GNP without making China, Korea, and the Philippines worry about being invaded again. But he failed in his attempt to redefine the prime minister's job. Nakasone's attempts to change Japan's policy seemed too pushy to the Japanese bureaucracy—and too feeble to other world leaders, who doubted Japan's ability to carry out commitments Nakasone had made.

The most powerful illustration was the Maekawa Commission Report, a major study by a panel appointed by Nakasone. This report, which was issued just before the Tokyo Economic Summit meeting in 1986, said that the time had come to transform Japan from an export machine, with long working hours and high prices, into a more relaxed, balanced state with more emphasis on imports. Nakasone put his authority behind the report and offered it to other leaders at the summit as an indication that Japan's trade policy was about to change. But all the entrenched power of the Japanese bureaucracy was against him, and by the time he left office the Maekawa recommendations were moribund. The episode fit the pattern Van Wolferen described:

> If Japan seems to be in the world but not of it, this is because its prime minister and other power-holders are incapable of delivering on political promises they may make concerning commercial or other matters requiring important adjustments [in domestic power arrangements]. The field of domestic power normally leaves no room for an accommodation to foreign wishes or demands.

What has happened since Nakasone left office even more vividly illustrates Van Wolferen's themes. Nakasone's successor, the luckless Noboru Takeshita, came to office through a whimsical, non-democratic process whose closest US counterpart is the way an American presidential candidate chooses his vice-presidential running mate. Through the summer of 1987, Nakasone showily deliberated about the personal merits of the "new leaders," three veteran politicians in their sixties who had waited for their turn in line. He settled on Takeshita as the country's next prime minister, largely because of Takeshita's reputation as a backstage deal-maker and a proven money-raiser.

In office, Takeshita used his skills to push through two highly unpopular measures, a new consumption tax and an increase in beef and citrus imports from the United States. But he spent the last year watching his cabinet fall apart because of the complex "Recruit Cosmos" scandal. One ambitious parvenu businessman, Hiromasa Ezoe, was shown to have illegally given money and shares in his Recruit company to virtually every prominent figure in the LDP, and leaders of most of the non-Communist opposition parties as well. In some cases the donations were bribes for specific favors from the government; in other cases, Ezoe seemed mainly to be investing in future good will. Ezoe was arrested early this year, and by this spring forty-two politicians or bureaucrats had resigned, fourteen had been arrested, and Takeshita himself had had to admit that Recruit had secretly contributed hundreds of thousands of dollars to his political campaigns.

Early in April, opinion polls showed that approval of Takeshita's government had sunk to a ludicrously low 3.9 percent, or one eighth as much support as Richard Nixon had on the day that he resigned. A week after this poll was published, Takeshita announced that he too would resign—but two months later, he was still in office, mainly because the LDP could not find any plausible replacement who was not also tainted by Recruit. The most prominent politician of the LDP who was not implicated in the scandal, the seventy-five-year-old Masayoshi Itoh, refused to take the job unless there were also sweeping reforms in the political fund-raising system typified by the secret payoffs of the Recruit company. "He didn't hear a word I said," Itoh was quoted as saying after a meeting with Takeshita in which he discussed political reforms. "I could just as well have been a clown."

Early in June, Takeshita and a handful of party elders startled the nation by presenting Sosuke Uno as the LDP's savior. Uno is reputedly an intelligent if prickly man, who was serving at the time of his elevation as Takeshita's foreign minister—but the widespread joke was that the only reason he'd escaped the Recruit scandal is that no one considered him important enough to bribe. (Joking became even more widespread a few days later, when a semirespectable weekly magazine carried a geisha's claims that Uno had paid her $25,000 for sexual favors over a several-month period three and a half years ago. As with Nakasone's "minority groups have low IQs" comment three years ago, the Japanese newspapers did not mention the story until an American newspaper, in this case *The Washington Post*, publicized it in the US. Uno now says it is a "private matter" not fit for public comment.) About the time Uno was selected, Nakasone announced that he would "resign" his connection with the LDP (though he would keep his seat in the Diet), Uno's approval rating "soared" to 32 percent, and the public prosecutor's office conveniently declared the Recruit case closed.

This brings us back to Karel van Wolferen, who might have predicted that the scandal would have ended with something less than a full, cleansing investigation of the Recruit case or the "money-politics" system it exemplified. No one part of Japan's recent political saga is unique to Japan. Uno will probably be a mere caretaker leader, but the US has had caretakers too, Gerald Ford, for example. Some American presidents have had trouble carrying out their international commitments, as Jimmy Carter demonstrated with the SALT treaty and Woodrow Wilson long before him with the League of Nations. But the combination of recent traits in Japanese politics is unusual: the near-total unimportance of public opinion, the sequence of prime ministers personally choosing their successors, the disgrace of virtually all prominent politicians in one big scandal, the intervention of one of the ministries to stop the scandal from going further. The combination is also consistent with what Van Wolferen called the "Japan problem."

But when his original article was read in Japan, Van Wolferen became the object of bitter attack—one prominent magazine ran an issue containing half a dozen articles taking him to task. With the publication of Van Wolferen's book, the criticism has become even more personal. In Japanese newspapers, his book is routinely cited as a harbinger of a new, inexplicably hostile attitude to Japan in the US. In my own talks with Japanese journalists, government officials, and businessmen, I've never heard a kind word for Van Wolferen and rarely heard any serious discussion of his argument. Instead I've heard countless times that Van Wolferen, a Dutchman who has lived in Japan for twenty-five years, must simply detest the country and its culture, that his animus against Japan must be racially biased. (Many Japanese intellectuals and officials instinctively see criticism of the Japanese political/economic system as a challenge to the achievements, dignity, and equality of the Japanese "race." Such sensitivity may be understandable, in view of the history of anti-Asian prejudice in the US and Europe, but it is a real barrier to serious discussion of Japan's economic policies.)

Why has one relatively complicated book made so many people so mad? Part of the explanation is no doubt a spillover from other frustrations Japan is encountering just now. In the good old days of the postwar economic miracle, Japan could concentrate on smooth relations with the US and otherwise forget about foreign policy. Now it is besieged by countries that want more Japanese aid, want more—or less—Japanese investment, and in general are unhappy about how Japan is using its wealth. Also, Van Wolferen's rhetorical style is exactly the opposite from the one most Japanese intellectuals prefer. Van Wolferen likes to push every argument to its logical extreme and state everything as bluntly as possible. This makes his book lively to read but violates the Japanese tradition of half-specific, half-vague discourse. "Japanese are treated by their school system and their superiors in the way a landscape gardener treats a hedge; protruding parts of the personality are regularly snipped off," Van Wolferen says. Many Japanese have used this line to illustrate what they see as a contemptuous tone. But it also demonstrates the power, the directness and clarity of the book—and no one who has seen the Japanese schools or corporate-training programs can argue that what he says is wrong.

Because Van Wolferen pushes every point to its limit, inevitably in a few cases he overstates. For instance, I think Japan is not as helplessly dependent on American good will for its security as Van Wolferen says it is. (The US military is more visibly fearful about losing its bases in Japan than most Japanese are about losing US military protection.) Also, Van Wolferen typically contrasts troublesome Japanese practices with an idealized description of how things are done in "the West," where Van Wolferen, after all, has not actually lived for many years. But the book's excesses are only occasional, and the heart of Van Wolferen's argument is strongly argued, original, and important.

The power and originality of his argument are, finally, the real reasons for Japanese outrage at Van Wolferen's book. *The Enigma of Japanese Power* presents a theory of the "differentness" of Japan that is completely at odds with the version that most Japanese believe in, and that Japanese spokesmen have propagated to outsiders. The notion that Japan is different is the starting point for almost every discussion of Japan's place in the world. The explanations of its differentness, even uniqueness, take many forms. Japan is different because it is better run than other societies (universal literacy, scant crime); because it is so fragile and vulnerable (no natural resources, constant threat of earthquakes); because of its tradition of harmony and consensus; because it has uniquely suffered the atomic bomb. The cartoon version of this concept shows up in *nihonjinron*, the "study of Japaneseness," which includes the familiar assertions by Japanese writers that Japanese intestines, brains, snow, and soil are different from those found elsewhere in the world.

Some theories work along the margins between science and crackpottery. For instance, a Japanese government researcher recently wrote that Japanese/Shinto traditions of purity gave Japan a crucial edge in the semiconductor business. (The explanation was that Japan's instinct for purity allowed factories to reduce ambient dust to levels unattainable in the West; in a cleaner environment the percentage of perfect chips was higher.)

Van Wolferen says that Japan is, indeed, different from other advanced societies, but not for biological or mystical or hazily traditional reasons. The crucial difference, he says, lies in the intellectual and practical foundation of Japan's political system, which produces behavior and values unlike those in most of the West. The political phenomenon Van Wolferen is discussing is comparable to the differentness in Japan's economic goals that Clyde Prestowitz analyzed in his carefully reasoned book *Trading Places*, which was published last year.

Americans often complain that Japan's trading practices are "unfair," Prestowitz said, but such objections completely miss the point. To call Japanese practices "unfair," as the US government did last month under the "Super 301" trade law, assumes that Japan's goals are the same as America's and that Japan is taking shortcuts to reach them. In fact, Prestowitz said, Japan's trade and economic policies represent consistent and impeccably "fair" efforts to reach an entirely different set of goals. The United States mainly wanted to improve the individual consumer's standard of living, and therefore it usually permitted imports unless some powerful lobby, such as the beet-sugar growers, stood in the way. Japan mainly wanted to develop industries within its own territory, and therefore it usually resisted imports of high-value products it could make on its own.

The significant fact about Japan's trade patterns is not that it exports so much—West Germany and many other countries export proportionately more—but that it imports so few manufactured goods. In 1986 Germany imported 37 percent of all the manufactured goods it consumed; Japan, 4.4 percent. As Chalmers Johnson of the University of California has recently pointed out, "Japan's imports, particularly of manufactured goods, are between 25 and 45 percent below what would be expected of a country with Japan's economic attributes."[1] The "Four Tigers"—South Korea, Taiwan, Hong Kong, and Singapore—have a combined gross national product only one eighth as large as Japan's, but their combined imports are greater.

Most developed economies have a very high "specialization ratio"—an economic term of art which means that countries both import and export within the same product category. Automobiles, for instance, are a leading export and a leading import for Germany. The United States exports a tremendous amount of food but imports even more. Japan is the only developed country with a very low "specialization ratio."[2] If it can make a certain item for itself, it generally does not buy from abroad.

Americans are often frustrated in their trade negotiations with Japan, Prestowitz writes, because they fail to imagine how different Japan's goals might be from their own. American politicians and negotiators continually say that Japan must "open" its markets, "but the

Japanese had no conception of what the Americans meant by *open*." In the American economic and political system, "openness" meant that anything not specifically forbidden should be permitted; in the Japanese regulatory scheme, "opening" the market meant allowing foreign competitors in one by one. Rather than whine about Japan's failure to pursue the same goals in the same way that America does, Prestowitz argues, Americans should accept Japan for what it is and adjust their policies so as to coexist with it.

In the case of Japan's political system, Van Wolferen says that the difference lies in the essential source of political legitimacy. Western politics, in the slightly idealized version that Van Wolferen outlines, turns on a constant tension between the power of the state and the loyalties that reach beyond the state—to religious values, to ideas of the universal rights of man. In Japan, he says, the forces that offset the power of the state are extremely weak. This, he says, is

> the characteristic that, in the final analysis, is the most crucial factor determining Japan's socio-political reality, a factor bred into Japanese intellectual life over centuries of political suppression. It is the near absence of any idea that there can be truths, rules, principles or morals that always apply, no matter what the circumstances.

Japanese Shinto religion, Van Wolferen says, lacks a strong ideology or even a set of scriptures. LDP-dominated politics rarely turn on issues, which is why the change from one prime minister to another makes so little difference to the outside world. Even the codes of behavior and personal morality that are taught to Japanese youth stress needs springing from different situations, such as duty to friends and family or loyalty to superiors, rather than abstract principles. "Japanese are not expected to take their cues from an inner voice that reminds them of moral absolutes they came to embrace while growing up," he says.

> They cannot appeal to any principle or ideal with which to justify their behaviour in the eyes of their neighbors, fellow workers or superiors. To understand this moral world one must imagine a situation in which good behaviour is constantly deter-

mined by individuals' views of how others expect them to behave.

Van Wolferen's argument that the Japanese have "no absolute truths" has been infuriating to many people in Japan, but not for the reason most outsiders might suspect. The concept itself has not been the main concern of Van Wolferen's critics, partly because so many Japanese theorists have claimed that Japan's ethics are more flexible and "situational" than those of the rule-bound West. It is, instead, Van Wolferen's tone that has stung many Japanese, who see in it raw contempt for Japan and a continuation of the age-old struggle to show the white man's superiority over the devious yellow man. ("How could he have stayed here so long if he hates us so much?" an official of the Japanese foreign ministry asked me after he'd read Van Wolferen's book.)

This reaction, I think, misreads Van Wolferen's intentions, and in a serious way. Van Wolferen clearly prefers the legal and intellectual world of the West to that of Japan, but he is not condemning the Japanese system so much as he is trying to explain it clearly. Similarly, Clyde Prestowitz is renowned in Japan as a "Japan-basher"; yet his book, far from demanding that Japan change its trading practices, merely asked foreigners to understand the practices for what they are. The phrase *wakatte kudasai*—"please understand"—is used frequently by Japanese negotiators. It represents a request to recognize the peculiarities of Japanese politics or society and accept them without criticism. This is the rule that Van Wolferen has violated. His argument about the absence of consistently applicable values could be wrong, but his book leaves the burden of proof on the other side.

Van Wolferen explains one other political difference, which is of much greater practical significance to outsiders dealing with Japan. Japanese spokesmen like to say, and Americans and Europeans seem willing to believe, that Japan's distinctive social traits somehow come naturally to its people. After all the millennia of living in close quarters, the Japanese, it is said, have learned to work well in groups. Because of some instinctive sense of the collective good, Japanese employees are loyal to their companies, and the companies are said to be willing to look past short-term profitability and invest for the long haul. Japanese students concentrate harder on their work; Japanese factory

---

[1] From "The Problem of Japan in an Era of Structural Change," a speech at the International House of Japan (June 2, 1989).

[2] "Analysis of the US-Japan Trade Problem," Report of the Advisory Committee for Trade Policy and Negotiations, report to Carla Hills, US Trade Representative (February 1989).

hands devote themselves to making the best possible product.

No doubt there are some basic behavioral differences between the average Japanese citizen and the average American or Frenchman. Japan's idea that it is monoracial makes it easier to generate a feeling of national unity. (The idea of racial unity, which was propagated during the Meiji era and again in the buildup to World War II, is the important trait, since the Japanese population itself is less homogeneous than, say, Korea's.) For a variety of reasons, Japanese blue-collar workers seem on the whole more diligent than their counterparts in the US or Europe. But for American readers, the most startling part of Van Wolferen's book will be his extensive demonstration that most of these "innate" traits are actually the results of the deliberate use of political and economic power.

The "loyalty" of white-collar workers to their company, in contrast to the constant movement of employees in other countries, is one clear example. Van Wolferen points out that the major corporations tacitly agree never to hire someone who has left another firm. Japanese children are studious in large part because admission to the University of Tokyo, which is based on examination scores, is essentially their only hope for having an influential place in society. In the higher reaches of the US civil service, 11 percent of appointees have some connection to Harvard. In Japan's extremely powerful Ministry of Finance, 88 percent of the senior officials are from the University of Tokyo, as are most of the officials in other agencies.

Japanese are "nonlitigious," not just because of their alleged love of consensus but also because of the acute shortage of lawyers. The Ministry of Justice controls the Legal Training and Research Institute, where future lawyers and judges must train, and it admits only 2 percent of those who apply. (Of the 23,855 who took the entrance examination in 1985, 486 were admitted.) "The widespread idea that the Japanese are reluctant to enter the legal profession is pure myth," Van Wolferen says.

As one specialist has pointed out, the number of Japanese, relative to the total population, who took the judicial examination in 1975 was slightly higher than the figure for Americans taking a bar examination.

Most criminals arrested by the police confess partly out of a sense of remorse but also because they know what a trial would mean: in 99 percent of criminal trials, the verdict is guilty.

Japanese salarymen devote eighteen hours a day to the company partly out of dedication but also because they feel they have no choice. "The phenomenon of a middle class deprived to a large extent of men functioning as husbands and fathers is of relatively recent origin," Van Wolferen says. He quotes an academic study: "If Japanese 'naturally'—because of cultural preconditioning—were prepared to give up their egos to a large organisation, the organisation would not have to work so hard to instill loyalty and identification." That is, the quasi-compulsory morning exercises and company songs that are common in Japanese companies may not indicate how "naturally" the Japanese conform but rather how unnatural the overwhelming emphasis on teamwork is.

A less benign effort to instill the team spirit is now being contemplated. The *monbusho*, or Ministry of Education, has long been one of the most conservative and pig-headedly nationalistic of all Japanese bureaucracies. Every year or two, the *monbusho* provokes outrage throughout Asia when it considers new history texts that gloss over Japan's role in China before and during World War II. Predictably, the Chinese and Korean governments lodge bitter protests, and predictably the *monbusho* is forced to back off. It also typically meets resistance from the *Nikkyoso*, or national teacher's union, which is the main source of organized left-wing sentiment in the country. Early this year, the *monbusho* announced plans for a new emphasis on national pride in Japan's public school curriculum, which is centrally controlled from Tokyo. (In every corner of the country, students cover the same subjects with the same books in the same weeks of the year, as directed by the *monbusho*.)

Japan's schools are already heavily directed toward developing the character traits that have made the Japanese productive system strong. Children go to school six days a week, for instance, even though the academic courses they take could easily be fitted into five days, because the six-day schedule teaches them the value of perseverance and hard work. Onto this existing pattern the *monbusho* proposes to add a stronger emphasis on the narrowly nationalistic glories of Japan: children will learn more about Japan's military heroes and spend more time hearing the national anthem and seeing the flag. It's to be expected that schools will cultivate national pride but there's hardly a shortage of it in Japan. For several years, Japanese diplomats, government spokesmen, and conference-goers have been assuring foreigners that Japan's new motto is *kokusaika*—"internationalization," to reduce the spiritual and psychological barriers between Japan and the rest of the world. Apparently the Japanese school system has not gotten the news.

To point out the remaining factors that make Japan unusual, as Prestowitz and now Van Wolferen have done, is not to foment hostility toward Japan. If anything, it is the best way to ensure smoother relations in the future. In the long run, the greatest source of hostility toward Japan is the myth of *kokusaika*—the idea that, any minute now, Japan's economy and its political system will be just like those in the United States or Western Europe, and that trade imbalances and other misunderstandings will therefore naturally melt away. The Japanese system is not about to transform itself, and it is presumptuous for outsiders to say that it should. Japan has been very successful doing things its own way. It has virtually no street crime, drugs, homeless families, or single parents. Its savings rate is high, and the literacy rate is nearly 100 percent. Every hour of every day, its foreign assets increase by $10 million.

This society does not seem to its leaders such a total failure. And if foreigners like Van Wolferen do not like the social contract on which the success is built, well, no one is asking them to become Japanese. The rest of the world will have no trouble getting along with this society, including its trading practices, if outsiders take Japan's system for what it is, not as some midway point en route to becoming just like the United States. Prestowitz's description of Japan's economy and Van Wolferen's analysis of its political system do more than any other books in many years to encourage a healthy realism about Japan.

POOR, HONEST AND OUT OF A JOB

Japan's Liberal Democratic Party is choosing a new prime minister. Murray Sayle marks the scandal-stained card

Tokyo

The ancient Japanese, imitating, as ever, their wiser Chinese neighbours, once elevated a 17th-century finance minister to the status of a god because he left office poorer than he came in. Since then, politicians qualifying for divinity have been scarce. One may be doing so right now, however, as clouds of numen gather round the boyish head of Toshiki Kaifu, Japan's ever-smiling, honest-as-the-day-is-long, stoically outgoing prime minister.

Readers with memories like hard discs will recall that Kaifu, then 58, was hastily jobbed into the premiership two years ago when the entire leadership of the governing Liberal Democratic Party and a lot of the opposition were engulfed in Recruit, the gigantic, high-tech, only-possible-in-Japan scandal. Briefly, a real estate, information and job-placement firm of that name had boldly set out to buy influence in bulk by bribing every politician of importance on the Japanese national scene, using the ingenious dodge of lending them money to buy parcels of its own shares which, in the bubble market of the 1980s, were certain to go up.

Among many breakthroughs, Recruit was the world's first scandal in which a businessman was shown passing a bribe to a politician on national television, and the first in which a list of those bribed, how much, and their relative importance was stored by the bribers in high-speed computers, greatly aiding the work of investigation. Japan's marriage of modern technology and ancient folkways, so potent in the marketplace, has never better been illustrated.

Spare a thought, however, for the plight of the Liberal Democratic Party, then 36 years in power. With elections in the offing and the shareless back benches envious, the LDP found itself well up a notorious creek. Not only had it just imposed an unpopular consumption tax (was there ever a popular one?) but the opposition Socialist Party was making a great splash with its new leader. Ms Takako Doi, a former law professor with enormous appeal to voters, particularly much-put-upon, seldom-heard Japanese women. The LDP needed a new, clean frontperson, and fast.

An urgent appeal for untainted good men turned up boozy *bon vivant* Sosuke Uno, an elderly backbench fixture Recruit had overlooked in its choice of 172 top people to bribe. Six weeks later—after an angry geisha had accused Uno of hiring her as his mistress, haggling over her fee, trying to get her to floor in an exclusive restaurant and then ditching her when the limelight unexpectedly turned his way—Uno led his party to an electoral disaster, scoring less than a third of the popular vote and losing control of the Upper House for the first time in the party's history. Uno slank back to the back bench and LDP politicians discovered a nasty new phenomenon, the 'Madonna vote', 35 million Japanese women at last discovering the deadly power of the ballot box.

The second hasty search for Mr Conspicuously Clean produced an even less likely candidate, Toshiki Kaifu. A schoolboy debating champion, Kaifu was a mere spear-carrier, not even the leader of the smallest faction among LDP politicians. Apart from a long-ago, unremarkable spell as Education Minister, he had no experience of office, no connections with big business, no secret sources of cash. Recruit had given him only a million yen (£4,250) and no shares, well within the legal limit and the kind of money influence-hungry Japanese firms send out instead of Christmas hams. Kaifu did not frequent geisha houses, drank little, and listed his hobbies as reading and stamp collecting. His only peculiarity was, and still is, a collection of blue polka-dotted neckties—not, as desperate journalists hoped, the symptom of an intriguing fetish, but to help his supporters pick him out from a crowd ('the Prime Minister', mothers tell their children, 'is the nice little man with the funny thing round his neck.') Accused by a scandal-sheet of mothering Kaifu's love-child, the baffled lady named asked reporters to remind her who Mr Kaifu was.

 From *The Spectator*, October 19, 1991, pp. 10-13. Copyright © 1991 by Murray Sayle. Reprinted by permission.

Just the same, forgettable, eager-to-please Kaifu saved his party. He said the right things on television. His wife, a level-headed, intelligent woman gave out cooking recipes. With their lively young children, the family looked good on advertising (actually the Kaifu children are grown up and they were child models, but that's politics). Ms Doi, who favours polka-dotted dresses, was a formidable opponent, but her party has never been able to break out of its base in the big industrial cities, heavily bombed during the war, into the newly affluent, look-ahead suburbs. In the general elections of February 1990, the LDP led by Kaifu, dropped 25 seats but held a comfortable majority in the Lower House, the one that counts.

As Prime Minister Kaifu has done surprisingly well. In the big crisis of his time, the Gulf war, Kaifu dithered and in the end did nothing—but his inactivity turned out to mesh both with unexpectedly robust Japanese pacifism (recalling their own bombed cities) and the doubts of business and bureaucratic circles about American long-term management of the world oil market, combined with Japan's intense short-term interest in keeping the oil flowing now (140 days' supply in hand, and then Japan starves and freezes.) The $9 billion Japan eventually sent to help pay the Gulf bill (Uncle beaten down from $15 billion) now looks to most Japanese like money well spent, while those in Tokyo who claimed that despatching a couple of battalions and a squadron of aircraft with red dots on their wings would have saved Japan both honour and $9 billion are still not taken seriously.

In his two years of office Kaifu's popularity has remained consistently high, the best of any prime minister's in almost 20 years. Although the next general election need not be held until 1995, all the polls indicate that the LDP would do better under Kaifu than under any of his current rivals for the premiership. His health is excellent, and so is the Japanese economy's, with booming exports, infinitesimal unemployment and finally falling interest rates and house prices. No breath of scandal has touched Kaifu in office, despite the tireless burrowing of the Japanese media, far less deferential these days than they used to be. His disclosed personal assets of 110 million yen (£450,000) put him 27th in wealth in his own cabinet. Kaifu's declared political contributions for last year, 28 million yen (£110,000) about average for a politician of his standing, came from blameless business sources in his electorate. He draws no entertainment allowance. Hopeful bribe-givers have, by general consent, left this premier's office sad and full-handed.

The Kaifus have refused to live in the leaky, cockroach-infested Prime Minister's official residence, so his wife has kept house for him in Tokyo on weekdays. On weekends she drove herself to his rural electorate to attend impartially to voters' requests, while Kaifu moved to a Tokyo hotel and got on with his job. The Kaifus' modest Tokyo flat, once valued at 45 million yen has probably fallen with other urban real estate, so that he should be leaving office a wiser, sadder and marginally poorer man—the very stuff that Japanese political gods are made of.

Even cynical, worldly-wise *Spectator* readers may be puzzled at this point. Why does this poll-pleasing paragon, the people's choice and everybody's friend, have to leave office at all? Has the LDP gone mad, ditching a sure election-winner, which is what has happened? Naïve, sentimental (in Japanese matters) Mrs Margaret Thatcher asked exactly the same question, even a trifle wistfully, when visiting in Tokyo in the summer. She was told that Japanese politics are difficult for foreigners to follow. Perhaps they are, but let us at least try.

Things have definitely looked up for the LDP since Toshiki Kaifu was elected president of the LDP, and therefore Prime Minister, in the party's darkest hour two years ago. This spring the LDP did unexpectedly well in nation wide local elections. Then, in June, the dangerous Ms Doi stepped down from the leadership of the socialists, now calling themselves the Social Democratic Party. Her successor, one Makoto Tanabe, is a well-meaning, impractical ideologue who is currently busying himself drafting a Repentance for Japan's Wars and a Pledge to Peace, which he hopes parliament will pass before the forthcoming anniversary of Pearl Harbour. The voter appeal— or point—of this initiative remains to be seen.

Why did Ms Doi give up? The short answer seems to be weariness, not with politics, much less with life (she, too, is in sound health) but with self-righteous, lefter-than-thou intellectuals of her own party, mostly former schoolteachers who prefer to be correct on such cosmic irrelevancies as the constitutional legitimacy of the Japanese military forces or the recognition of North Korea than descend to the everyday questions of homes, food and family that actually win elections, even in mysterious Japan. Responsive government anywhere needs responsible opposition, as Japanese, and many others, still have to learn.

But Ms Doi's departure dispelled the dread of the Madonna vote, the spectre that has haunted the LDP so long. With things apparently back to normal, many restless old pros argued that it was time to cut out all this crowd-pleasing nonsense and pay off some political debts, long over-due. In short, business as usual in the smoke-filled rooms of Tokyo. Now where were we, when those nosey detectives came in and seized all our bank books?

The real power in Japanese politics, both pre-and post-Recruit, is what was formerly known as the Tanaka faction when that wily politician (a victim of the Lockheed scandal) organised it, and since a treacherous disciple wrestled it away from the ailing boss is now called the Takeshita faction. But ungrateful usurper Noboru Takeshita banked £700,000 from Recruit shares in circumstances, never fully disclosed, that led his fund-raising secretary to kill himself. For shame, Takeshita had to step down as Prime Minister, to be followed in quick order by the lecherous Uno and then the vote-pulling Kaifu. Solidly based on a nation-wide network of building contractors, than which a booming economy knows no steadier source of funds or votes, the Takeshita faction commands 108 members of the Japanese parliament. Nothing moves in Tokyo politics except by its orders.

Back in the dear and not-so-dead days before Recruit, boss Takeshita did a private deal, the very essence of Japanese politics. If the second largest faction of Shintaro Abe voted for him as Prime Minister, then Takeshita's boys would vote for Abe on the next turn of the merry-go-round. Abe had clearly inherited a term as premier, being the son-in-law of former Prime Minister Nobosuke Kishi, who . . . well, it's a long story, but a deal is a deal, and once given, a Japanese politician's word is, as we know, his bond.

Last May, Abe died. Are Japanese political debts hereditary? As of last week, it seems not. But, as Damon Runyon used to say, more markers are out. It was distinctly understood that when Abe had served his term, former premier Yasuhiro Nakasone (Recruit's first, and best friend in high places) might have another try at the greasy pole. Then there was gentlemanly, ineffectual Kiichi Miyazawa (72) who had, it was true, also been handsomely Recruited, but who still commanded a useful faction of 81 votes, and had waited so long, and begged so hard for his chance.

To give everyone a turn at the trough of office, LDP Prime Ministers are supposed to be re-elected by the party every two years. Kaifu's term is up on 29 October. Only ten days ago, it was generally assumed that, it being still too early for Takeshita himself to step out of the shadows, the party elders would stick with the proved election-winner, eminently biddable Toshiki Kaifu.

But the lad, it seems, had been nursing ideas above his station. Many people have argued that the factions owe their existence to Japan's system of multi-seat electorates, returning anything from two to five members each. This means that an LDP candidate has first to win LDP votes away from a rival of the same party, which costs loadsamoney, leading to competitive financing by the different factions, which are essentially fund-raising enterprises run by bosses ambitious to be prime minister. Then, controlling government patronage, the boss can hope to keep the cash flowing to his faction.

Kaifu therefore aspired to make his modest mark on history by abolishing the multi-seat electorates. This should make it possible for honest men to run on policy instead of having to buy votes away from party colleagues, thus at a stroke eliminating the cash basis of the factions. 'Political reform', meaning the hobbling of the omnipotence of money in Japanese politics was one of the party's planks when it was founded in 1955. Like a smoker's determination to quit tomorrow, it has been advanced by the LDP at every election since. To a schoolboy debater, Kaifu's idea must have sounded good.

The party elders tried, it seems, to tell him the facts of life. Most of them owe their careers to mastery of factional, that is, money politics. Some of the younger backbenchers, both LDP and Social Democrat, would also like to see the multi-seat constituencies go, but the other opposition parties—scandal-ridden Clean Government, the Democratic (right-wing) Socialists, even the Communists—would be wiped out

in single-seat elections, and the LDP needs them to get money bills through the Upper House. Reform, yes. Of course. Next year, perhaps. Or maybe the one after. One day, certainly. But not this week. Okay, sonny?

Kaifu, it seems, turned uncharacteristically stubborn. He was planning political reform, he told a meeting of faction chiefs, with 'grave determination.' It may simply have been something he ate, but the party strong men decided to take no chances. The constitution gives the Prime Minister the theoretical right to sack all his cabinet (manned by representatives of the factions, in proportion to their strengths) or worse, even to call a costly general election. To past masters of circumlocution 'grave determination' sounds like fighting talk, a mouse roaring his little head off.

Next morning Shin Kanemaru, 77, the veteran string-puller who heads the faction while Takeshita himself, the real boss, lies low, announced that enough was enough. Kaifu was out. Kanemaru accused Kaifu of 'cowardice', presumably in trying to curry favour with the voters instead of obeying his party chiefs. The 1.7 million non-parliamentary members of the party-at-large are supposed to have some say in this, but the party rules give them only 101 votes, so the Takeshita faction alone outnumbers them. Japanese commentators speak of Kaifu's flagrant insubordination as 'temporary insanity.'

With the mouse off the scene the cats are playing, under close supervision. As this is written three candidates have announced for the party presidency, and thus the prime ministership. Hiroshi Mitsuzuka, 64, the current foreign minister, is trying to claim the turn at the premiership promised to the deceased Abe, whose faction he now heads for want of someone more forceful. The claim of Abe himself was based on inheritance, a principle once applied to Shoguns and still of course, governing the Japanese monarchy, but not yet accepted by the LDP. Matsuzuka is considered a hopeless outsider. Recruit thought so too, and gave him nothing.

Michio Watanabe, 69, is a former sergeant in the Imperial Army, twice passed over for a commission. Like Nakasone whose faction he now technically heads (Nakasone, too is lying low) the garrulous Watanabe is proud of his war record, and affects an old soldier's bluntness in calling for a revision of the Japanese Constitution to give the Japanese armed forces freedom of action outside Japan.

Discharged from the defeated Army, ex-sergeant Watanabe, like many of his former comrades became what his campaign biography delicately calls a 'street vendor' or, in more homely Japanese, a barrow boy, hawking whatever he could find to sell on the murky black market of Japan's desperate years after the overwhelming defeat of 1945. This hard apprenticeship has given Watanabe a colorful vocabulary and a reputation for street savviness, no bad thing among Japanese of his generation, but fast losing its appeal as the good times roll on.

In 1984, just as Recruit was drawing up its list, Watanabe was chairman of an LDP 'Special Committee for the Introduction of Private Sector Vitality into Public Works.' Recruit had vitality to burn, in thousandshare blocks, and Watanabe took 5,000 in the name of his eldest son, reselling them at a handsome profit. Unique among Recruit's beneficiaries, Watanabe has made no bones about his windfall. 'Ten or 20 million yen (£42,500 to £85,000) isn't that much money' he has explained. 'Politics is an expensive game to be in. Others did much better than I did, and we have to recognise different shades of grey in this business.' Honesty, at least about his dishonesty, seems to have worked in Watanabe's favour, but the homespun political style of this veteran is fast going out of fashion. Rated a long shot.

Kiichi Miyazawa, 72, comes from the Japanese bureaucratic élite. A graduate of the law faculty of Tokyo University, sure guarantee of a brilliant career of some sort, Miyazawa first went to the Finance Ministry and then into politics. He has held every important post except the premiership in the Japanese government, runs a modest-sized faction of his own, and speaks excellent English, which he has shown off (much to the disgust of barely monolingual rivals like Watanabe) by exchanging wordy platitudes with Henry Kissinger on national television (Miyazawa has the better accent). Even in Japan's years of poverty this brilliant man was spared the same—and also the educational benefits—of a spell behind a barrow.

Recruit naturally marked Miyazawa down for special munificence, a parcel of 10,000 shares. When the scandal broke Miyazawa claimed that his secretary had bought them without his permission. The secretary said that someone must have used his name. On closer investigation, the someone turned out to be Miyazawa himself. The Minister of Finance had signed for the money-for-old-rope shares in his own name, or as Watanabe would put it, was caught like a plain, ordinary or garden mug—not the best of omens for his judgment in a future crisis.

What a former sergeant may be able to brazen out—and even get some wry respect for—a Tokyo University Law Faculty graduate cannot. 'I shall regret it all my life,' Miyazawa lamely tells persistent interviewers, adding the questionable claim that his constituents have absolved him by re-electing him. Just the same, over the weekend Kanemaru announced that the Takeshita faction's block vote was going to Miyazawa, making him a racing certainty for the premiership. Miyazawa's first move was to call, not on boss Takeshita who is still skulking off-stage, but on underboss Kanemaru to discuss (some say to discover) the line-up for the Miyazawa cabinet. Kaifu has until the end of the month to clean out his desk and go back to well-earned obscurity.

Does any of this matter? In the great scheme of things, probably not. The factions are mostly about money, somewhat about style and seniority, and scarcely at all about policies. Speckled frontman Miyazawa will no doubt replace spotless façade Kaifu for his regulation two years, and then it will be some other Buggins' turn. Ever since 1974 the real power in Japan has been in the hands of two men, bosses Tanaka and Takeshita, and for almost all of those years the potent pair have been obliged by scandals to stay behind the scenes, and in Tanaka's case to work hard to stay out of prison (a broken man, he is still theoretically appealing against a five-year sentence.) Yet, in their time, Japan has successfully weathered three oil crises, the stockmarket crash, the Nixon soybean shock and the backwash of two Middle Eastern wars. Someone, the record suggests, must be doing something right.

Government by scandal has many obvious drawbacks. It is, for one thing, hardly the Athenian, or even the Westminster or Washington forms of democracy, although it is not dictatorship either—Japanese voters could get rid of all this dubious crew if they really wanted to. However, the fact that lawful sources of political funds come nowhere near the needs of the system imposes perpetual instability, the statistical certainty that sooner or later someone (as often as not the prime minister, who needs the money more than anybody else) will be caught with his hand in the till.

This is especially frustrating on the international scene in these days of non-stop summit conferences, with politicians from abroad getting steadily more frustrated as they apply in vain to meet the Japanese men of power, or even, from day to day, to learn who they are. This has led some thinkers to the Headless Monster hypothesis, that no one at all is actually in charge in Japan—in which case the islands must have had really extraordinary sleepwalker's luck.

The baroque Japanese political system, however, also has certain advantages, well worthy of study. The tradition of shuffling men (and, once in a blue moon, women) from the different factions though all the cabinet posts mean that everyone has a rough idea of how the government works, although none of them would presume to give orders to the bureaucrats who actually run the economy. The fragility of the parliamentary side has also weakened the influence of professional politicians in the 'iron triangle' of power that dominates Japanese affairs, leaving the other two sides, the bureaucracy and big business, to consumate the cosy relationship generally known as 'Japan Inc.'

Most importantly, the money siphoned into Japanese politics, while essential to the recipients, is trivial compared with the resources wasted in conspicuous consumption and lavish welfare schemes by better-organised élites in rival countries. The result has been that Japan's surplus has gone back into the business (the highest reinvestment rate in the world) the economy has bloomed and, well-financed, the technological mastery on which it all rests has gone from strength to strength. Here, clearly, is the something that someone is doing right.

A friend with a red nose explains: 'Every successful circus is actually run the same way, by an efficient management in a small back room, not by the clowns out in the ring.' Japanese politics may not yet be the biggest, but they are still one of the more entertaining shows on earth.

Trading in Mistrust

The U.S. and Japan: A romance turning to ashes

Don Oberdorfer

Washington Post Staff Writer

In the two months since President Bush's troubled trip to Tokyo, U.S.-Japanese relations have suffered their most serious downturn in decades, according to American officials and other observers.

To a greater degree than in earlier crises, the current disputes have spread beyond specific differences over economic and security policies to a broader collision of two dissimilar societies, their leaders and peoples. Since World War II, the United States and Japan have cooperated extensively in the Pacific and elsewhere, holding in check economic rivalries and cultural differences. Now, however, some of the restraining influences have been shattered by a confluence of developments, including the end of Cold War threats that had cemented the U.S.-Japan alliance, a serious U.S. recession that has deepened American ire about trade frictions and inflammatory politics that have been fanned by the important elections both nations face later this year.

The complicity of U.S. and Japanese leaders in the current trouble is one of its most unusual and serious aspects. Former assistant secretary of State Richard Holbrooke, who calls the downturn "a crisis of leadership," says that in the past "the leaders of the two countries had always been committed to keeping the lid on" disputes and differences. This time, he says, Bush and Japanese Prime Minister Kiichi Miyazawa, who are both internationalists and friends, have not asserted control but rather added fuel to the fire with statements addressed to their home audiences.

Following the Bush trip to Japan, the speaker of the Japanese Diet, Yoshio Sakurauchi, touched off a furor here by calling the United States "Japan's subcontractor" and describing American workers as lazy and illiterate. Americans responded with insults in their "get tough with Japan" campaign slogans and a mushrooming "Buy America" campaign largely directed at Japanese imports.

Late in January, the Los Angeles County Transportation Commission canceled a contract with Sumitomo Corp. for subway cars because of their origin, and Major League Baseball Commissioner Fay Vincent moved to stop a Japanese-led investor group, which had local support, from buying a majority interest in the Seattle Mariners. In Greece, N.Y., a Rochester suburb, the Town Board voted against buying a Komatsu dirt excavator because of Buy American fervor—only to learn that it had been made in the United States, while the John Deere model under consideration had been made in Japan under a joint venture.

In recent weeks, Japanese companies and Japanese Americans have been subjected to vandalism, abusive telephone calls and threatening remarks. Anti-Japan literature, too, has taken a leap to the top of the national bestseller lists with the publication last month of popular novelist Michael Crichton's new book, "Rising Sun."

Surveying recent developments, the U.S. Civil Rights Commission Feb. 28 called for a halt to "Japan-bashing," saying it contributes to bigotry and even violence against Asian Americans. A Washington Post-ABC News survey early last month showed 65 percent of Americans polled saying anti-Japanese feelings in the United States were on the rise, and 63 percent said they were trying to avoid buying Japanese products. Both cases represented sharp jumps in such sentiments over earlier poll results.

The United States and Japan, which together account for 40 percent of global production of goods and services, are today so intertwined economically and politically that a rupture would be so disastrous as to be almost unthinkable. At the official level, U.S. and Japanese diplomats say their governments continue to work harmoniously on a broad array of issues. Yet, they add, if the plunge in political and public tolerance continues, the prospect is for more troubled times ahead.

From *The Washington Post National Weekly Edition*, March 9-15, 1992, pp. 6-7. Copyright © 1992, The Washington Post. Reprinted by permission.

"We could both hurt ourselves pretty bad; for example, Japan holds a lot of our debt, and we are their most important market," says former senator and Reagan White House chief of staff Howard H. Baker Jr., who recently led an extensive Council on Foreign Relations study of the relationship. Although he hopes increased candor will lead to a more mature relationship, Baker says, "we have it within our power to pull a Samson act" to the great disadvantage of both nations.

A veteran U.S. diplomat who has been watching recent events with dismay says, "It is going to take people in both countries to say, 'Cool it.'" He adds that he sees little such leadership emerging, especially in the United States.

Bush's trip Jan. 7–10 was originally planned for late November to affirm the extraordinary postwar alliance between the two nations in the face of the 50th anniversary of the Japanese attack on Pearl Harbor Dec. 7. The presidential journey was suddenly postponed by a panicky White House Nov. 5, the day the Republicans lost a Senate race in Pennsylvania, and later recast as a high-profile effort to obtain trade concessions from Japan to produce jobs in the United States.

The shift by Bush conveyed the "implicit message" that Japan was responsible for U.S. economic problems, says Holbrooke, validating and inadvertently encouraging anti-Japan sentiment. The message was amplified by the presidents of the Big Three automakers, who had been invited to accompany Bush to Japan in an unprecedented display of official solidarity with their cause.

Robert A. Mosbacher, secretary of Commerce at the time, says he helped persuade Bush last fall to include U.S. business leaders in his delegation following an Aug. 14 recommendation from the President's Export Council, a business-government group headed by Michigan industrialist Heinz C. Prechter. Mosbacher says the Big Three auto presidents were invited after he argued that automobiles and auto parts represent about three-fourths of the U.S. merchandise trade deficit with Japan. The automakers dominated the trip in ways he did not anticipate, says Mosbacher, now general chairman of the Bush reelection drive, and the journey became "more political" because of the political and economic climate in the United States.

A source involved in planning the trip says Mosbacher had been told that the only way Bush could win Michigan in the November election was to "demonstrate the president was doing something about the auto problems and this [invitation to the Big Three presidents] would be a good way to do something about it." The source adds, "Who was to know that the Big Three would turn around and be a bunch of crybabies?" Mosbacher denies that domestic political considerations were involved in the invitation.

Views about the Japanese threat to the United States that were previously heard mostly on the fringes of American intellectual and political life have spread to the mainstream in recent months. Starting around 1988, a tide of books analyzing Japan in critical fashion began to be published here, some of which gained a bigger audience in Japan than in the United States.

Alfred A. Knopf, publisher of Crichton's "Rising Sun," moved up the publication date of the book a month to take advantage of the wave of emotion following the Bush trip, and Knopf spokesman says 375,000 copies are in print, an extraordinary number for a new novel. Crichton seeks to surmount detective fiction by including a three-page list of nonfiction books about Japan as a bibliography and writing an afterword charging that Japan has surpassed the United States by inventing "adversarial trade, trade like war, trade intended to wipe out the competition."

Also riding the new wave is "The Coming War with Japan," which was published to minimal attention in this country last spring but received massive publicity and sold 150,000 copies in Japan. Coauthor Prof. George Friedman of Dickinson College says he was "absolutely baffled" to discover it was excerpted last month by the Los Angeles Times and carried as a series two weeks ago by several other U.S. newspapers. Friedman's premise is that, just as the United States and Soviet Union ended World War II as allies but soon discovered deep conflicts, the same thing is happening to the United States and Japan after the Cold War.

William T. Archey, senior vice president of the U.S. Chamber of Commerce, says part of the rise in anti-Japanese sentiment in recent months is due to a search for scapegoats because of the current recession. At the same time, Archey says trade data demonstrate that "increasingly America's trade problem is a Japanese problem." Although it is true that the U.S. merchandise trade deficit with Japan decreased from $60 billion in 1987 to $43 billion last year, the U.S. trade balance with the European Community shifted in the same period from a $27 billion deficit to a $16 billion surplus, Archey says. "In 1991, when U.S. domestic business was terrible, U.S. exports were dynamite everywhere but Japan," he says. Trade frictions, of course, have been a constant feature of the U.S.-Japan relationship given the worldwide competition between American and Japanese firms, enormous flows of trade in both directions across the Pacific and a persistent merchandise trade deficit in Japan's favor for more than two decades. What is new, however, is a growing influence of a minority of U.S. experts on Japan, known as "revisionists," who argue that Japan's society and economy are so fundamentally different that normal remedies for closed markets and commercial advantage are almost useless. The increasing acceptance of this view both reflects and deepens American frustration with Japan.

1. COUNTRY OVERVIEWS: Japan

While expressing concern about Japanese trade practices, Archey and other business leaders also say the U.S. and Japanese economies are so intertwined with joint ventures, sole supply arrangements and other interlocking relationships that a separation is almost impossible. For example, Ford owns a major stake in Mazda autos, General Motors has stakes in Isuzu and Suzuki, and Chrysler holds a part of Mitsubishi autos. Many "American" cars rely heavily on foreign parts and vice versa.

When the Reagan administration considered strong action against Toshiba several years ago, according to a business source, this move was resisted by such U.S. firms as IBM, which was dependent on Toshiba circuit boards for its personal computers, and Motorola, which was dependent on Toshiba computer chips.

"We're intertwined and intermingled, economically speaking, and a great deal of the prosperity of the world will depend on what the two economic superpowers do with one another," says Mike Mansfield, a former Senate Democratic leader and former U.S. ambassador to Japan. The coincidence of a major U.S. recession with a U.S. presidential campaign has produced "a dangerous impasse in U.S.-Japan relations," Mansfield says, adding, "We had better face up to realities, and become less emotional, but more practical and realistic" to get through 1992 without major damage.

Washington Post staff writers Ann Devroy and Stuart Auerbach contributed to this report.

For the Japanese, A Growing Sense of Disillusionment

T. R. Reid and Paul Blustein

Washington Post Foreign Service

Kichijoji, Japan—"When I was a kid, it was such a marvelous place," Junji Izumi says, poking disconsolately with his chopsticks at a dark red slice of raw tuna steak. "We would see it on TV, and it was like the shining light of the world. So rich, so free—it used to be a place where dreams came true."

The "marvelous place" that Izumi, a 39-year-old retailer, was lamenting in nostalgic tones at a teeming bar in this busy Tokyo suburb on a recent night is none other than the United States of America, a country that was once the stuff of dreams for nearly everyone in Japan—but evidently is no more.

"Yeah, it's sad now," chimes in 42-year-old Shogo Miyake, leaning over to pour a cup of hot sake for his friend Izumi. "To think that America would have to send its president over there to beg! To think that all those wonderful department stores in New York—even Bloomingdale's—have gone bankrupt! What is it—a lack of effort?"

That casual conversation between two salarymen and the disparaging blasts of America-bashing from Japanese politicians in recent weeks reflect a new strain in Japan's attitude toward its chief ally: a sense of disillusionment, even contempt, with the economically ailing country across the Pacific.

"The feeling that things have gone badly wrong in the U.S. is strong—much stronger since President Bush's visit in January," says Keio University professor Atsushi Kusano, who has been conducting opinion polls with small samples.

The mixed emotions of sympathy and superiority that color Japan's view of the United States today have

In Japanese, these characters mean bubei, or "contempt for America."

clearly made people more willing to criticize it out loud. Some worry that the seeds of dangerous nationalism are being sown; political scientist Nagayo Honma wrote last month that if Japanese come to see their country as superior in all respects, "then Japanese-U.S. relations will face catastrophe again."

But whether such a disastrous scenario is really in the making remains to be seen.

The Japanese are strongly conditioned to avoid confrontations; the elaborate ritual and stylized politeness of Japan's language and culture evolved to serve that objective.

As a result, the immediate Japanese reaction to the current volley of trans-Pacific name-calling has been to try to find some quick resolution, some way to quiet the immediate uproar. Meanwhile, resentment may be building, just waiting for the next bilateral blowup.

From *The Washington Post National Weekly Edition*, March 9-15, 1992, pp. 7-8. Copyright © 1992, The Washington Post. Reprinted by permission.

"The Japanese tend to suppress anger or resentment," says Tokyo University professor Takashi Inoguchi. "If the Japanese public keeps accumulating this feeling of resentment [toward America], it is bound to come out in some form."

In geopolitical terms, there is no sign that the Japanese government or public wants to break away from its long alliance with, and dependence on, U.S. leadership. The fear of divorce from the United States, of becoming "an isolated child in the world," as analyst Yukio Okamoto puts it, is still the ultimate nightmare for policy planners and ordinary people alike.

In the business community, though, the changed mood has sparked a sharp debate about the goals of Japanese industry. The dispute centers on this question: Is Japanese industry so strong that it must change its ways to avoid wiping out foreign competition?

The Japanese are still edgy about doing or saying anything that might alienate the United States, their biggest market, chief ally and military defender. Although recent criticisms by politicians reflected widely held views here, the critics felt the need to express groveling apologies to the Americans in each case.

The America-bashing is widely regarded as a clumsy mistake, and Japanese officials heave sighs of relief that "buy-American" sentiment appears to be sputtering in the United States. Newspaper and TV analysts blasted the America-bashers for exacerbating U.S.-Japanese friction.

"There might be some truth to these [criticisms of American workers]," said an editorial in the Nihon Keizai Shimbun, a middle-of-the-road newspaper serving the business community. "But speaking in such derogatory terms does not serve U.S.-Japanese relations, especially when the strong language comes from someone . . . who holds high public office."

Japan's ambassador to the United States, Ryohei Murata, has just received an abrupt order from Tokyo to leave Washington midway through his tour. His crime, diplomatic officials say, was acting too aloof and insufficiently chummy with the Americans.

Even in time of recession, Japan maintains an enormous financial stake in the United States, with loans and investments worth hundreds of billions of dollars. The flow of yen toward the United States has slowed, but not ended. When a Japanese company sold the Pebble Beach golf course last month at a staggering loss of $340 million, the buyer was—what else?—another Japanese company.

Still, there clearly seems to be a new attitude toward the United States in Japan, a sadder-but-wiser sense that the former dreamland is snarled in various social and economic nightmares.

In a highly homogeneous, media-saturated nation where the latest fads and fashions seem to spread the length of the land in the blink of an eye, that attitude has quickly become the conventional view of the United States.

"People are surprised and disturbed at all the bad news coming from America, and they're mad that people like Lee Iacocca—with his salary!—blame Japan for their problems," says political scientist Kusano.

"We ask the question, 'What's your favorite foreign country?' Of course it's still America, by far. But among the same people who say that, criticism of America is increasing very much."

There has for years been a political fringe quite willing to bash the United States. The major change is that contemptuous descriptions of America and American products are now mainstream. That trend was clearly accelerated by Bush's trip here in January, when he pushed for more auto and auto parts imports and cut the ribbon to open a new Toys R Us store.

"President Bush . . . erased the mystical image that the Japanese people still had toward the U.S. by making a speech in front of a toy shop," observed a front-page analysis in the Keizai Shimbun newspaper.

But the disillusionment with the United States—a feeling many Japanese also hold toward Western Europe—is tempered by a sense of concern that Japan itself must adjust to avoid becoming an international pariah. Within the business world, these ambivalent sentiments have fueled a new debate about the basic thrust of Japanese commerce.

Akio Morita, the founder of Sony Corp.—himself a fairly tough America-basher in the past—published an article in the influential magazine Bungei Shunju arguing that "the Japanese style of management is dangerous." Morita's article has become a hot topic on TV talk shows and in policy-making circles here because it says the impulse behind Japan's postwar economic miracle may have been too narrow.

Morita argued that Japanese firms are too focused on "producing good products at low prices" in an effort to attain market dominance. More emphasis, he said, should be placed on rewarding workers with higher wages and shareholders with higher dividends. This change would make Japan less competitive in world markets, but the quality of Japanese life would improve, and the world might stop regarding Japan Inc. as an economic juggernaut.

Heretical as it seemed, this view was quickly endorsed by Gaishi Hiraiwa, chairman of Japan's premier big-business group.

Like Morita, Hiraiwa suggests that Japanese industry is simply too excellent for its own good. He says he was "astonished" recently when European business executives told him "that European companies did not have the capacity to compete on an equal basis with Japanese companies, [and] that their companies would perish if the present gap in competitiveness continued."

"In the eyes of Western business executives,"

Hiraiwa continues, "Japanese businessmen and companies appear willing to sacrifice everything and think only of how to win when they compete. . . . Shouldn't we relax somewhat and seek symbiosis with other countries?"

There are, of course, defenders of the Japanese way of business. Takeshi Nagano, chairman of a big business group, has been Morita's most prominent critic, asserting that Japanese workers are already highly paid and that raising wages further could prove disastrous.

"Japan has to export," Nagano says. "We manufacture products from the raw materials that we import, and most of the difference goes into labor cost. So we have to keep the ratio of labor costs at a proper level."

There is evidence—slim but unmistakable—that Japanese companies are adopting some of Morita's new way of thinking.

Toyota, Nissan and Honda have announced they will raise the prices of their cars in the United States by 1.7 to 5 percent, a change that could reduce their share of the U.S. auto market. Publicly, the companies attributed the decision to the strong yen, but industry insiders say a key goal is to help keep the Japanese share of the U.S. market from rising above today's 30 percent to some politically unacceptable level.

Is all this real, or is it just a smoke screen to fool Americans? "I don't just dismiss it," says Clyde Prestowitz, a Washington analyst who has been a strong critic of Japanese trade practices. He says statements such as Morita's "are interesting harbingers of potential, worth following."

But before the attitudes of the Japanese public change, something is going to have to happen in America to make Japan believe that the United States has its economic house in order.

"Of course America is still a country I respect," says Junji Izumi, still talking about this perennial topic at the suburban bar here. "At the time of the [Persian] Gulf War, America was the world's leader, the world's policeman. This is something Japan could never do.

"What Japan can do," Izumi continues, "is make cars as good as the old Ford Mustang. That used to be the state-of-the-art car of the world. Why can't America make cars like that any more?"

Washington Post special correspondent Shigehiko Togo contributed to this report.

Pluralist Democracies: Factors in the Political Process

- Political Ideas, Movements, and Parties (Articles 20–22)
- Women and Politics (Articles 23–24)
- The Institutional Framework of Representative Government (Articles 25–27)
- Nation and State, Unitary and Federal Frameworks (Articles 28–30)

Observers of Western industrial societies frequently refer to the emergence of a new politics in these countries. They are not always very clear or in agreement about what is supposedly novel within the political process or why it is of significance. Although few would doubt that some major changes have taken place in political attitudes and behavior in recent years, it is very difficult to establish clear and comparable patterns of transformation or to gauge their endurance and impact. Yet making sense of continuities and changes in political values and behavior must be one of the central tasks of a comparative study of government.

More than anything else, the end of the cold war and the collapse of communism in Europe have created a situation that seems to demand a reformulation of political and ideological alternatives. Democratic socialists and ecologists stress that the sorry political, economic, and environmental record of Communist-ruled states in no way diminishes the validity of their own concerns for using political tools to advance social justice and environmental protection in modern industrial society. However, many of them appear to be moving toward a greater pragmatic acceptance of the modified market economy as an arena within which to promote their goals.

The first three articles in this unit deal with some of these political ideas, movements, and parties that have in common the attempt to establish a more clearly defined political identity and a more solid political base for themselves. The essay from *The Economist,* "A Tale of Two Families," also includes some useful institutional comparisons among the West European democracies. Its main theme, however, concerns the flattening of the differences between mainstream politics of the Left and Right. To be sure, there are still noticeable ideological and rhetorical differences. The Right accepts more readily the existence of social or economic inequalities as inevitable, and it usually favors lower taxes and the promotion of market forces, with some very important exceptions, intended to protect certain favorite groups and values. The Left, by contrast, emphasizes that government has an important task in promoting opportunities and reducing social inequities, whether they result from differences in inherited or acquired advantages or disadvantages. In a controversial policy area, such as that of higher and more progressive income and property taxation, there can still be considerable differences even between moderates of the Left and Right. In general, however, they seem to have moved closer by adopting what has been called center-Left and center-Right positions respectively. At the same time, there are some signs of a growing distinction in the nonsocialist camp between the economic neoliberals (who speak for business and industry) and the social conservatives (who advocate traditional values and authorities). The former will accept disruptive change far more readily than the latter, who emphasize the importance of continuity and stability in the social order.

On the center-Right, we should not overlook the Christian Democrats as one of the most successful political movements in Europe since 1945, at least until their recent electoral setbacks in Germany and Italy. Here too we can discover something of a political identity crisis, as idealists who subscribe to the social teachings of the Church find themselves with decreasing influence in parties that are now dominated by nonvisionary technocrats and political managers, like Giulio Andreotti in Italy and Helmut Kohl in Germany. The latter kind of politician seems to reflect little of the original ideals of personalism, solidarity, and subsidiarity that originally set the Christian Democrats off from liberals and conservatives in postwar Europe. The article "Europe's Christian Democrats: Hello, Caesar, This Is God" outlines some further differences between the idealists and pragmatists in the Christian Democratic parties, and it suggests that their argument will determine the future of the movement. A major issue is whether the Christian Democrats should line up in Europe with other nonsocialist but secular parties, such as the British Conservatives and French Gaullists.

In another article on political parties, Rone Tempest examines the ultra-Right parties in Western Europe. While the far Left, as represented by the Communists, has seen its support dwindle for over a decade, the extreme Right has found growing support among some socially alienated and economically insecure voters in Italy, France, Belgium, and Germany. There are counterparts to these parties in the Scandinavian countries as well, even if these still appear to be more moderate in style and agenda. They operate under the somewhat incongruous names of Progress Party (Denmark and Norway) and New Democracy (Sweden), and much of their appeal seems to lie in attacks on public bureaucracy and high taxes.

In united Germany, the far-Right Republikaner (or Reps, as they are colloquially known) received just over 2 percent of the popular vote in the Bundestag election of 1990, a considerable reversal of fortunes after an initial success (7.1 percent of the vote) in the European elections of the previous year. Since then, they have done better again at the state level, winning almost 11 percent of the vote in the southwestern state of Baden-Wüerttemberg in April of 1992. Another ultra-Right party, the German People's Union (DVU), was able to enter two other state parliaments after elections in the city-state of Bremen in 1991 and Schleswig-Holstein (6.3 percent) in 1992. Moreover, there are indications that the extreme right-wing potential in Germany is somewhat higher than these electoral results alone suggest. Some poll findings indicate that there is a potential of about 15 percent of alienated voters who would qualify as belonging, but until now they have never united behind one party. Instead, the German far Right has been kept relatively weak not only by the unusual degree of rivalry and divisiveness among the extremist parties and their leaders, but also by the continuing ability of the more moderate parties, such as the conservative Christian Democrats, to absorb some of this potential protest vote.

In France, Jean-Marie Le Pen's National Front for a long time has gotten away with being more explicitly xenophobic, racist, and anti-Semitic than appears to be either legally or socially acceptable in today's Germany. His supporters can be found across the sociological spectrum and include some working-class protest voters looking for simple authoritarian answers to their social and economic problems. In the regional elections of March 1992, the National Front received close to 15 percent of the total vote. In some of its southern strongholds, around the city of Nice, about one-third of the voters supported this party that fulminates against immigrants, especially Arabs from northern Africa. In a proportional system of representation, the party could end up doing quite well. In the process, it would weaken the two moderately conservative parties, the neoliberal Union for French Democracy and the Rally for the French Republic (the Gaullists), but it could also draw some protest voters from the Left.

Women in politics is the subject of the second subsection in this unit. There continues to be a strong pattern of underrepresentation of women in positions of political and economic leadership practically everywhere. Yet there are some notable differences from country to country, as well as from party to party. Generally speaking, the parties of the Left have been readier to place women in positions of authority, although there are some remarkable exceptions, as the center-Right cases of Margaret Thatcher in Britain and Simone Weil in France illustrate.

This is where a policy of affirmative action may be chosen as a strategy. The Scandinavian countries illustrate better than any other example how the breakthrough may occur. There is a markedly higher representation of women in the parliaments of Denmark, Finland, Iceland, Norway, and Sweden, where the political center of gravity is somewhat to the left and proportional representation makes it possible to set up party lists that are more representative of the population as a whole. It is of some interest that Iceland now has a special women's party with parliamentary representation, but it is more important that women are found in leading positions within most of the parties of this and the other Scandinavian countries. It usually does not take long for the more centrist or moderately conservative parties to adopt the new concern of gender equality, and they may even move to the forefront. Thus, women now lead three of the main parties in Norway (the Social Democrats, the Center party, and the Conservatives), which together normally receive more than two-thirds of the total popular vote.

Altogether, there is undoubtedly a growing awareness of the pattern of gender discrimination in most Western countries. It seems likely that there will be a significant improvement in this situation over the course of the next decade if the pressure for change is maintained. Such changes have already occurred in other areas, where there used to be significant political differences between men and women. At one time, for example, there used to be a considerably lower voter turnout among women, but this gender gap has been practically eliminated in recent decades. Similarly, the tendency for women to be somewhat more conservative in party and candidate preferences has given way to a more liberal disposition among younger women in foreign and social policy choices than among men.

In any case, there are some very important policy questions that affect women more directly than men. The survey article on women in the paid labor force of Europe offers statistical evidence to support three widely shared impressions: (1) there has been a considerable increase in the number and relative proportion of women who take paid jobs, (2) these jobs are more often unskilled and/or part-time than in the case of men's employment, and (3) women generally receive less pay and less social protection than men in similar positions. By showing that there are considerable differences among Western European countries in the relative position of their female workers, the article also supports the argument that political intervention in the form of appropriate legislation can do something to improve the employment status of women—not only by training them better for advancement in the labor market but also, and importantly, by changing the conditions of the workplace to eliminate some obvious or hidden disadvantages for women.

In the third subsection of this unit, a number of institutional arrangements are compared: (1) different forms of democratic constitutions, (2) major systems of electoral representation, and (3) the parliamentary and presidential systems of government. Robert Goldwin reminds us that most of the world's constitutions have been very short-lived. There has been a flurry of constitution-writing after the collapse of dictatorships in several parts of the world, and he suggests that the products may turn out to be more lasting if the drafters would consider carefully some basic questions. Above all, the constitution writers should remember to take into account the peculiarities of their own society.

Gregory Mahler focuses on the legislative-executive relationship of parliamentary and congressional systems, drawing mainly upon the British, Canadian, and American examples. He avoids the trap of idealizing one or the other way of organizing the functions of representative government. That is also true for Richard Rose, who compares the governmental leadership and systems of checks and balances found in the United States, Great Britain, and France. He finds that each system has its own constraints upon arbitrary rule, which can easily become obstacles to prompt and decisive action. One could add that the authors of *The Federalist* would not have been surprised by such conclusions.

In the final subsection of this unit, three articles address the old problem of the optimal size and form of a governmental unit. David Lawday develops the argument that the nation-state has become too small to deal effectively with the tasks of economic and monetary policy, let alone the provision of international security or the protection of the environment. At the same time, it is too large and centralized for dealing with matters better left to regional and local governmental units. In another article, Andrew Adonis points out that Great Britain is unusual among larger European countries in not having developed a regional tier of government or anything resembling a regional policy. Norman Ornstein and Kimberly Coursen go beyond this halfway house to consider full-blown examples of federalism.

Looking Ahead: Challenge Questions

How do you explain the apparent centrist movement of parties of the moderate Left and moderate Right in recent years? How do regionalist, environmentalist, and ultra-Right parties represent different challenges to the present status quo?

The Christian Democrats seem to be torn between an idealist and a pragmatic wing. Explain. Where do idealist Christian Democrats differ from more secular conservatives or classical liberals?

Why are women so poorly represented in Parliament and other positions of political leadership? How do institutional arrangements, such as elections systems, sometimes help or hinder an improvement in this situation?

Is there a universal formula for a good constitution? Explain. What are some of the major arguments made in favor of the parliamentary system of government? How does it differ from the U.S. system of congressional-presidential government?

If the nation-state is such a recent phenomenon, how can it be argued that it may already be out of date? Do you think it will be easily supplanted by other arrangements? Why? How do you explain that regionalism and federalism have gained new attention and respect in recent years?

A tale of two families

Across Europe, governments are stabler than at any recent time. Left and right sound more and more alike. Will this calm last?

GIVEN the events—communism's collapse, Germany's unification, the drive towards European union—Europe's voters could find politics gripping. In fact, more and more of them find it a turn-off. About 55% of people in the European Community are "not much" or "not at all" interested in politics, according to the Eurobarometer opinion poll.

A growing proportion of Europeans are not bothering to vote. In Portugal abstentions leapt from 22% in the 1987 general election to 32% in 1991. Abstentions are also breaking records in Germany. Turnout in West Germany was 89% in 1983, 84% in 1987 and only 78% (the lowest since 1949) in the first all-German vote in 1990.

Not only are voters getting blasé. Politicians are staying in power longer. By the end of the 1980s, the average length of time Europe's leaders had held office was a record seven years. Are these two things linked? Perhaps familiarity breeds indifference.

There are other ways to explain those long tenures in office in the 1980s. One lies in rising incomes. Europe's voters rewarded governments for booming economies. Another lies in the widening agreement about how governments should tax, spend and borrow. Opposition parties no longer tout radically different ways to run an economy. As a result, voters may well feel that, the candidates' competence aside, less hangs on their choice than in the past.

Throughout Europe, all the same, most politicians belong to one or other of two ancient tribes, the left and the right. The pattern of support for these two has until recently been astonishingly stable (see box).

Differences of philosophy, style and emphasis distinguish right from left. The right stresses freedom (notably from government interference), low taxes and market forces. The left emphasises equality, social welfare and the guiding hand of the state. (If not misled by the label "socialist" or "social-democrat", Americans will spy in these two tribes close cousins of Republicans and Democrats.)

When it comes to governing, differences between right and left in Europe blur. The left has made its peace with the market and accepted that the state's weight in the economy must be limited. The right recognises that voters want the welfare state improved, not abolished, and that even a slimmed-down state is still a large and inevitable presence in any modern economy. The left talks of "market socialism", the right of the "social market". Who can blame voters for finding it hard, especially on economic policy, to tell the two apart?

A question of identity

Political change reflects shifts in European society. Over the past 30 or 40 years, Europeans became better educated, more middle-class and more middle-of-the-road. Extremism's appeal faded. Class conflict, the storyline of much earlier European history, did not disappear. But it

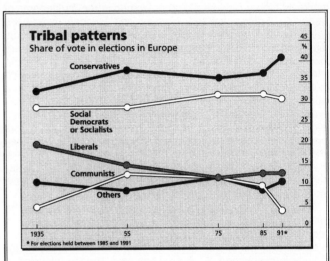

Tribal patterns
Share of vote in elections in Europe

Conservatives

Social Democrats or Socialists

Liberals

Communists

Others

1935   55   75   85   91*

* For elections held between 1985 and 1991

THE pattern of voting for Europe's main political tribes has been broadly steady for 50 years. The chart above shows the share of the total vote each of the big party groupings won in general elections held in Europe in or just before the year given. (In most countries, the election chosen was not more than four years before the date given; in order to include Italy in 1935, the 1921 election had to be used.)

For 1935, 1955 and 1975, a putative European result was calculated by adding up the general-election result (lower house in two-chamber systems) in 15 countries: Austria, Belgium, Britain, Denmark, Finland, France, Germany or West Germany, Holland, Iceland, Ireland, Italy, Luxembourg, Norway, Sweden and Switzerland. For 1985 and 1991, Greece, Portugal and Spain were included.

The four party groups separately identified are those which clearly exist in all or nearly all the countries mentioned. Obviously there are tricky choices, particularly when parties change flavour (Italy's Social Democrats, for example, who are now close to liberals).

In the "other" category are agrarian, nationalist, extreme-right or extreme left, or Green parties. The biggest component of the "other" category for 1935 was the 1932 vote for the Nazis in Germany.

Our sources were "The International Almanac of Electoral History", *The Economist*'s "World Atlas of Elections" and Keesing's Contemporary Archives.

From *The Economist*, November 23, 1991, pp. 59-60. Copyright © 1992 by The Economist. Distributed by The New York Times Special Features.

was muted. The left grew less starry-eyed, the right more tolerant. That created for both political tribes an identity problem.

The collapse of communism leaves the democratic brand of socialism unchallenged on the left. In Western Europe, communism's last bastions were in France and Italy. From 1945 to 1978 France's pro-Soviet Communists routinely won 20-25% of the vote, often more than the Socialists. They will be lucky to get 10% at the next general election.

Italy's mild-mannered Communists won 34.4% of the vote in the 1976 general election. In 1987 their share fell to 26.6% and is likely to drop more, even though the party has changed its name. In the next general election, Italy's Socialists are likely to overtake the former Communists.

Now that the dominant parties on Europe's left can no longer usefully define themselves as non-communist, what does being a democratic socialist or social democrat mean? Socialists have given up revolution, the planned economy, state ownership. Other things they fought for—trade-union rights and the welfare state—are achieved (though under pressure in many countries). The socialists' old base in the industrial working class is dwindling. Budget cuts are eating into its new one: public-service workers. Not surprisingly, Europe's left finds itself foraging for ideas on the right.

During the 1980s, the right's ideas triumphed with Europe's voters. This brought its own problems of success. Now that socialism means little, it is hard for the right to define itself as anti-socialist. The loss of a common enemy also sharpened the old distinction on Europe's right between the advocates of liberty and the defenders of tradition.

The conflict goes back to 19th-century quarrels between economic liberals (speaking for trade and industry) and more authority-minded conservatives (defenders of church, crown and gentry). Its traces remain in the division of Europe's right into two recognisable families.

Germany's Free Democrats, France's centre-right and liberals in Belgium, Holland and Italy stand for personal liberty and the free market. Christian Democrats in Europe (whatever their exact name) and Gaullists in France speak for the "solidarity" of all parts of society, including trade

A rich and varied sameness

Country	A	B	C	D	H	I	Current government	Leader
Austria	P	M(6)	2	PR	Y(4)	N	Left-right	Franz Vranitzky
Belgium	M		2	PR	Y(4)	N	Right-left	Wilfried Martens
Britain	M		2	PL	Y(5)	Y	Conservative	John Major
Cyprus	PE	M(5)	1	PR	N(5)	Y	Conservative	George Vassiliou
Denmark	M		1	PR	Y(4)	N	Centre-right	Poul Schlüter
Finland	PE	(M6)	1	PR	(Y4)	N	Centre-right	Mauno Koivisto
France	PE	M(7)	2	PL	Y(5)	Y	Socialist	François Mitterrand
Germany	p		2	MX	Y(4)	N	Centre-right	Helmut Kohl
Greece	p		1	PR	Y(4)	N	Conservative	Constantine Mitsotakis
Holland	M		2	PR	Y(4)	N	Right-left	Ruud Lubbers
Iceland	P	PL(4)	1	PR	Y(4)	Y	Right-left	David Oddsson
Ireland	P	M(7)	2	PR	Y(5)	Y	Conservative	Charles Haughey
Italy	p		2	PR	Y(5)	N	Right-left	Giulio Andreotti
Luxembourg	M		1	PR	Y(5)	N	Right-left	Jacques Santer
Norway	M		1	PR	N(4)	N	Labour	Gro Harlem Brundtland
Portugal	P	M(5)	1	PR	Y(4)	N	Conservative	Anibal Cavaco Silva
Spain	M		2	PR	Y(4)	N	Socialist	Felipe Gonzalez
Sweden	M		1	PR	Y(3)	N	Right-centre	Carl Bildt
Switzerland	p		2	PR	N(4)	N	Right-left	Flavio Cotti

A Head of state: M = monarch   P = directly elected president   p = indirectly elected president
E = president has executive powers
B How president is elected: M = majoritarian   PL = plurality   (Term of office in years)
C Number of chambers in parliament
D How parliament or lower chamber is elected: PL = plurality   PR = proportional representation
MX= mixed system
H Is dissolution possible? Y = yes   N = no   (Term of office in years)
I Are by-elections possible? Y = yes N = no

unions. They defend "traditional" moral or family values. Britain's Conservatives are hard to place. Their "wets" are most like continental Christian Democrats. Thatcher Conservatives favour both a free market and "traditional" values.

The right now has a share in all but three West European governments (see table). Only in France, Spain and Norway do socialists rule alone—and there precariously. Socialists sharing power are everywhere (except in Austria) junior partners. After holding office for all but six of the past 60 years, Sweden's Social Democrats lost the general election in September 1991.

This reverses the European pattern of the 1960s and 1970s, when social-democratic parties were on top. The right-wing parties need not, though, have the upper hand indefinitely. Parties are not just vehicles for ideas but machines for promoting talent and distributing jobs. Governments get tired. In a healthy democracy, power alternates. The left has a fair chance of winning power at the next elections in Britain, Germany and Italy.

Different democracies

In the past 20 years, Greece, Portugal and Spain have abandoned right-wing dictatorship. In the past two years, one-party rule has all but vanished from Eastern Europe. (A later brief looks at what is taking its place.) Despite the violence surrounding Irish, Basque or Corsican nationalism, there is now only one accepted way of deciding who governs in Europe: the ballot box.

There are, though, important differences in how Europe's democracies work. Consider simply the EC. Among the EC countries there are six constitutional monarchies, five republics with parliamentary government and a largely ceremonial presidency, and one system, France's, where most power lies with the president (except when the president is having to cohabit with a hostile parliament). Eight of the 12 have two houses of parliament, four have a single chamber.

Some countries, such as Britain and France, have strong central government. Others, like Belgium and Spain, have devolved significant power to regional government. Germany is a fully fledged federation.

No two EC countries have quite the same voting systems. The main divide is between those (Britain and, usually, France) with a first-past-the-post system, and those who use proportional representation (PR). In Germany parties need at least 5% of the

vote to win seats, in Holland just 0.66%. Britain votes once. France has two-round elections.

In Italy, Germany, Belgium and Holland, all of which use some form of PR, coalition is a way of life. At best that breeds a habit of compromise. At worst it produces chronic indecision (whence mounting pressure in Italy for constitutional reform). In Britain, France and Spain, single-party rule has been the norm—but may not remain so.

The room for disagreements about economics may have narrowed (and could get smaller still if Europe moves on to economic and monetary union). But disagreement on economics and other issues is not extinct. There is a clash of interest between the poorer nations of the Community (Greece, Ireland, Portugal and Spain) and the others. This divide will matter more if the Community takes in the countries of Eastern Europe. Opinion about the Gulf war and the civil war in Yugoslavia varied or varies from country to country.

Three jokers

The search by left and right in Europe for a new ideology has produced little so far but a loose faith—in Europe. The spectacle of the two political tribes competing to be "good Europeans"

2. FACTORS IN THE POLITICAL PROCESS: Ideas, Movements, and Parties

merely adds to the sense of interchangeability that many voters seem to find.

Partly because gloved conflict between centre-right and centre-left within parliamentary democracies is now the European rule, it is easy to forget that the continent was not always so reasonable. Europeans have fought two world wars and countless civil wars in the past century. Europe is the birthplace of three of the 20th century's more destructive "isms": fascism, communism and nationalism (the malign sort). Balanced competition between socialists and conservatives may well continue. But it ought not to be assumed it will.

There are three political movements that could disturb Europe's calm and tidy pattern: Greens, regionalists and, ominously, the far right. Green parties may already have passed their peak. The best known is Germany's. But German Greens got no seats at all in the general election of 1990. This was partly because they split into zealous "*Fundis*" and more practical-minded "*Realos*", and partly because, as elsewhere, big parties have stolen the Greens' clothes.

Regionalism, on the other hand, is on the rise. The most notable example is in Catalonia, where the Convergence and Union party is doing well at the polls. Regionalism is influenced by the re-appearance of small nations in Eastern Europe. If the Balts can have their independence, so should we, argue, for example, many Basques. It is encouraged also by a sense that the old nation-states are ceding power both upwards, to the Community, and down to lower levels of government.

The far right is a more sinister force. In France the National Front scores 15% in opinion polls. In Italy the Lombard League, which offers a potent mix of regionalism and xenophobia, has sprung from nowhere to be a serious nuisance to the other parties. In recent elections in Germany and Austria, xenophobic parties have made advances.

The far right waves a nationalist flag. But nationalism means many things. Nationalism that reacts to foreign domination, as in Eastern Europe, may be violent at first and then die down as the effects of outside oppression recede. Nationalism meaning pride in language, land and culture is no party's province.

As a reaction, this benign sort of patriotism is liable to strengthen if Europe's countries pool more economic and political sovereignty. But in a more united Europe the far right's foreigner-hating strain of nationalism could survive as well, the foreigners in question being non-Europeans. Pride in Europe—Euro-nationalism—also comes in benign and malign varieties.

EUROPE'S CHRISTIAN DEMOCRATS

Hello, Caesar, this is God

Much of Europe is run by Christian Democratic parties. Will they stay true to their religious roots, or become just another variety of the centre-right?

SINCE 1945 Christian Democracy has been Western Europe's most successful political movement. In Belgium, Holland, Luxembourg, West Germany, Austria, Switzerland and Italy, Christian Democrats have seldom been out of power. Yet many Christian Democratic parties today suffer, just as do Socialist and Communist ones, from doubts about their identity.

The idealists among them want to preserve the movement's original, Christian inspiration, which distinguishes it from liberalism or conservatism. The pragmatists, in contrast, argue that it should line up with European conservatives to confront the left. History seems to be moving the pragmatists' way. For the time being, though, Christian Democrats are a very different breed from conservatives such as Britain's Tories.

The movement springs from the nineteenth-century (and later) quarrels in mainland Europe between clerical parties and lay. What would today be broadly called the right was deeply divided. Clericals thought the church should be integrated into, and privileged within, the state; liberals that the two should be kept firmly apart. The church itself—essentially, the Catholic church—was happy to influence the mighty, but had little zeal for democratic politics of any sort, seeing democracy and the socialist parties that it bred as the road to atheism.

The aim of Luigi Sturzo, the Catholic priest who founded Europe's first Christian Democratic party, in Italy in 1919, was to reconcile Catholicism with democracy. His party was independent of the church and in favour of social reform. Similar parties were founded elsewhere in Europe and in Latin America. When fascism drove Sturzo into exile in 1924, he set up an international grouping in Paris. Among those active in it were an Italian aide, Alcide De Gasperi; a Frenchman, Robert Schuman; and a German, Konrad Adenauer. In the 1920s they talked of a common market and of European integration as a means of preventing

further wars. In the 1950s these men were to achieve their dreams.

After the second world war, the Christian Democratic parties were refounded and immediately won elections. They had an obvious appeal in countries where Christian values had suffered from nazism and were now under threat from communism. Christian Democrats adopted from Jacques Maritain, a French philosopher, the principle of "personalism": the idea that an individual should fulfil his development through responsibility to other people, especially to the family and to the community. Personalists oppose both liberal individualism and socialist collectivism.

Christian Democrats took the rest of their doctrine from the social teaching of the Catholic church. They are thus set apart from conservatives by their principle of "solidarity"—the solidarity, that is, of all parts of society with each other. This means working to improve social conditions and, not least, accepting the role of trade unions. Most Christian Democratic parties (though not the West Germans) have strong trade-union wings. The European People's party (EPP—a get-together of the European Community's Christian Democratic parties) supports the EC's social action programme. Opposing class-consciousness, Christian Democrats claim to represent all social groups. They get votes from all, though relatively fewer among industrial workers.

Another principle, which the Christian Democrats accepted long before the Vatican did, is "subsidiarity": the notion that power should be decentralised as far as possible—but may be exercised at high, if need be even supranational, levels, when that makes sense. Thus Christian Democrats have always been federalists.

Christian Democratic theorists never got round to economics. But it was a Protestant member of West Germany's Christian Democratic Union (CDU), Ludwig Erhard, who dreamed up the "social market econ-

omy"—the free market with a social conscience. His success as West German finance minister during the 1950s helped persuade Christian Democrats elsewhere to rein in their interventionist instincts. This was, by the way, Protestantism's one clear contribution to Christian Democracy. The movement is dominated by Catholics, though 40% of CDU members are Protestant and the Dutch party is a union, formed in 1980, of one Catholic and two Protestant parties.

Decline and revival

The wave of secular liberalism in the 1960s both threatened the Christian Democratic parties and changed their character. The Catholic church, in the past a firm believer in its right to a privileged role in the state, came gradually closer to the liberal concept of their separation. In Italy the Vatican stopped offering direct advice to voters. Voters were listening less to it anyway. Church-going declined, while church views on matters such as contraception were widely disregarded.

The Christian Democratic parties were slow to catch up with such social trends. And though their leaders in the 1940s and 1950s mostly had been men of vision who took their ideals seriously, the new ones tended to be quite simply politicians, some of them pretty cynical politicians at that.

Christian Democracy's hold on power only just survived. As the table shows, in Belgium and Holland the Christian Democratic share of the vote dropped sharply during the 1960s. The fall was less sharp in West Germany. But the Social Democrats there got more votes in the 1972 election, for the first time, and kept the Christian Democrats out of government for the next ten years. France's Christian Democrats had won 28% of the vote in 1946, but later slid, under the weight of

From *The Economist*, March 17, 1990, pp. 17-19. Copyright © 1990 by The Economist. Reprinted by permission of The New York Times Syndicated Sales Service.

2. FACTORS IN THE POLITICAL PROCESS: Ideas, Movements, and Parties

Gaullism, to 10–15%. In the 1970s they traded their independence for a place with Mr Valéry Giscard d'Estaing's centrists.

In Italy, where De Gasperi's party, Democrazia Cristiana, has been in government since 1944, its support held up, close to 40%, until the 1980s. The DC is expert at using its permanent hold on power in local government and in state industries to win votes. But it was on the losing side in the referendums on divorce and abortion, held in 1974 and 1981 respectively, and its vote fell to 33% in the 1983 parliamentary elections. In the 1984 Euro-elections it fell behind the Communists, for the first time ever.

Yet by the late 1980s the rot had stopped. Socialism, as a way of running the economy, has been largely discredited, and left-of-centre parties, little as they may have believed in it, have suffered. The pragmatism of power has helped Christian Democratic politicians to accept, in time, the liberal reforms that they disagree with. And voters care less about, say, abortion, than about jobs, wages and prices.

Party reform too contributed to the revival. The West German CDU, for instance, at one time did little more than run election campaigns. While in opposition, Mr Helmut Kohl supervised its transformation into a mass party, with a machine to rival that of the Social Democrats. Membership rose from 355,000 in 1971 to 734,000 in 1983. The CDU also adopted a popular new programme that combined lower taxation with welfare payments for mothers. In Italy, however, Mr Ciriaco De Mita, the DC party secretary since 1982, had less success. His attempt to shift authority from the competing factions to the party directorate was blocked by the old guard, who last year removed him first from his party post, then from the prime ministership, which he had held since April 1988.

Prose after poetry

For all its success at the polls, many Christian Democrats feel their movement has lost its way. Mr Fernand Herman, one of the most effective EPP members of the European Parliament, and a former Belgian economy minister, speaks for such people: "Christian Democracy has lost its soul and should go into opposition. The leaders now accept anything to stay in power, and they disregard our principles and traditions. They are not helping to renovate our doctrine. We were the first federalists, but now we focus too much on domestic politics, and leave it to socialists like Delors and Mitterrand to push forward European integration."

It is true that the movement has not produced any fresh political thinking since the 1940s, and that the current generation

Holding the voters

Christian Democratic % of vote in lower-house parliamentary elections

Year	Belgium¹	Holland²	W Germany³	Austria⁴	Italy⁵
1945				49.8	
46	42.5	51.5			35.2
47					
48		53.4			48.5
49	43.5		31.0	44.0	
1950	47.5				
51					
52		48.9			
53			45.2	41.3	40.1
54	41.1				
55					
56		50.0		46.0	
57			50.2		
58	46.5				42.4
59		49.1		44.2	
1960					
61	41.5		45.3		
62				45.4	
63		49.2			38.2
64					
65	34.4		47.6		
66				48.3	
67		44.5			
68	31.8				39.0
69			46.1		
1970	30.1			44.7	
71		36.7		43.1	
72		31.3	44.9		38.7
73					
74	32.3				
75				42.9	
76			48.6		38.7
77	36.0	31.9			
78	36.1				
79				41.9	38.3
1980			44.5		
81	26.4	30.8			
82		29.4			
83			48.8	43.0	32.9
84					
85	29.2				
86		34.6		41.3	
87	27.5		44.3		34.3
88					
89		35.3			
1990					

1. Parti Social Chrétien (French) plus Christelijke Volkspartij (Flemish).
2. Christen-Democratisch Appel, formed 1980; till then, Katholieke Volkspartij plus (Protestant) Anti-Revolutionaire Partij and Christelijk Historische Unie, which formed it.
3. Christlich Demokratische Union plus (in Bavaria) Christlich Soziale Union.
4. Österreichische Volkspartei. 5. Partito della Democrazia Cristiana

of leaders—Mr Ruud Lubbers (Holland), Mr Wilfried Martens (Belgium), Mr Alois Mock (Austria), Mr Giulio Andreotti and Mr Kohl—is one of technocrats and party managers rather than intellectuals and visionaries. Rightly, some think. "We are in a period of prose after the heroic age of poetry," says Mr Franco Maria Malfatti, a former president of the EC commission who now heads the

Italian Christian Democrats' political bureau. "It's not a sin to win elections. We have the right and the responsibility to govern."

The argument between the idealists and the pragmatists will determine the future of Christian Democracy. Its more left-wing and/or more religious members think the movement should remain true to its origins, neither conservative, liberal nor socialist. The opposing camp, including most of the Germans, argues for a broader movement, more overtly right-wing and less Christian, that could cover the whole of Europe.

Sparks flew between these two camps in 1978, when a group of ten, mostly conservative, parties, including British Tories and French Gaullists, set up the European Democratic Union. To the horror of Italian and Benelux Christian Democrats, the CDU and the Austrian People's party also took part, while remaining in the European Union of Christian Democrats (first cousin of the EPP, but Europe-wide, not just EC-wide).

In the European Parliament, the need to compete with the left has already spurred the EPP to embrace Ireland's Fine Gael, Greece's New Democracy and, last year, the Spanish People's party, none of which has religious origins. But Christian Democracy's purists still carry some weight. After last year's European elections, British Conservative Euro-MPs applied to link with the EPP. Though the Germans were sympathetic, the Tories were told that their policies on EC integration, monetary union and the social charter made them unacceptable.

Holier than thou

The more Christian of Christian Democrats insist that religious inspiration could once again drive their movement. They rest their hopes on Eastern Europe, where 50 years of persecution have made the new or revived Christian political groups unashamedly forthright.

In the brief gap between liberation in 1945 and the imposition of Stalinism, Christian Democrats flourished in Poland and Hungary. In Poland they are now split between the re-established Labour party, the new National Christian party and Rural Solidarity. After the coming Hungarian elections, there is a chance that three Christian Democratic groupings will work together. Two of them, the Christian Democratic People's party and the Smallholders party, did well in the 1947 elections, while the third group is one of the strongest elements of Democratic Forum. A new Christian party is set to become a leading force in Slovakia. In Romania, the revived Peasants party has merged with a new Christian Democratic group.

Even in Western Europe, for all its secularisation, the Christian Democratic parties retain a firm religious base. Religion determines voting behaviour more than class does. In last year's Dutch elections, for instance, 85% of Christian Democrat voters described themselves as religious; for the Socialists, Liberals and Democrats '66, the figures were 55%, 40% and 25% respectively. In Italy in 1988, 30% of adults claimed to attend church at least once a week, but 50% of DC voters and 75% of delegates to the party's congress did so.

In Italy social and religious movements still play a big part in drumming up support for the DC. The Christian Democratic trade-union confederation claims 3m members. Comunione e Liberazione is a group of (a claimed) 100,000 religious activists who say they want to put Christ at the centre of life and society. It runs radio stations, businesses, publishing houses and "solidarity centres," which offer training for the unemployed; and an annual festival of political debate and entertainment at Rimini, the latest of which drew 700,000 people, most of them young.

For Mr Roberto Formigoni, Comunione e Liberazione's charismatic leader and a Euro-MP, "Faith means action. Other Christian Democrats have relegated faith to an abstract sentiment. While laicising the party, they've forgotten about the poor." This concern for the less fortunate did not stop Mr Formigoni being one of those who played a big part in bringing down the relatively laic but no less concerned Mr De Mita, and in restoring to the prime ministership the wily Mr Andreotti—one of the old guard, and a daily attender at mass.

The West German parties—the CDU and its Bavarian equivalent, the Christian Social Union (CSU)—represent the pragmatic pole of European Christian Democracy. The founders of the CDU included people who before 1933 had been liberals and conservatives, as well as Christian Democrats, and these mixed origins still mark its political complexion. The CDU and CSU do not always see eye to eye, but the differences are over policy—the Bavarians are more nationalist, and less keen on European integration, for instance—not about the place of religion in politics.

The West German parties think it inevitable that, in time, the EPP and the European Democratic Union, complete with its Gaullists and Tories, will merge. Projecting their own essentially bipolar politics on to Europe, they see socialism as the enemy. In Italy, Belgium and Holland, in contrast, Christian Democrats are used to working with socialists. Seeing themselves as centrist, they do not want to sink into the European centre-right.

Which way now?

Which of these tendencies will win? The continuing trend to a more secular society favours the Germans—and it seems unlikely to abate. The triumph of free-market economics makes it hard for Christian Democrats to maintain an economic policy distinct from that of conservatives. And the shift of Europe's left-wing parties towards the centre encourages some Christian Democrats to take a more right-of-centre line: they have to appear different.

Both the Italian and West German parties veered rightwards last year, mainly for their own internal reasons. In Italy the Communists' identity crisis helped to weaken Mr De Mita and his friends on the left of the DC, who would have accepted an alliance with the Communists. The now dominant centre factions prefer close links with the Socialist party. They feared that Mr De Mita's struggle against faction and patronage could endanger the DC's hold on power.

While the DC was purging Mr De Mita's leftish-leaning friends, the CDU in West Germany underwent similar surgery. Mr Kohl got rid of the powerful party secretary, Mr Heiner Geissler, and many of his followers. Mr Geissler's strategy had been to win votes from the centre-left. He had also been a fierce critic of the CSU's leader, Franz Josef Strauss. After Strauss's death in 1988, Mr Kohl feared that the CDU-CSU ticket would not look right-wing enough to get conservatives to bother to vote for it, nor to mask the far-right charms of the new Republican party.

The rightward shift of the German and Italian parties will encourage the EPP to become a broader centre-right grouping. Mr Thomas Jansen, its (German) secretary-general, used to think it should stay a purely Christian Democratic group. But last year he changed his mind: "The success of our link with the Spanish conservatives leaves Britain the only big EC country where we are not represented. In view of the new developments in Europe, it would be worrying if we kept the British out. We must try to persuade them to change their attitudes."

The coming intergovernmental conference on monetary union is likely to boost the powers of the European Parliament. The absence of the British from the EPP, which allows the left to dominate the parliament, will then matter more than it does now. The replacement of Mrs Margaret Thatcher as Tory leader, whenever it comes, will probably tilt the EPP towards opening its door. That would leave many Christian Democrats in Italy and the Benelux countries grumbling; for the founding fathers' vision of the movement would then be blurred beyond recognition.

Europe: Right-Wing Parties Gain

Extremist parties' successes in elections sound alarms on a continent where the rise of fascism before WWII is still a vivid memory.

Rone Tempest

Times Staff Writer

PARIS—Propelled by post–Cold War insecurities, economic recession and building anti-immigrant sentiments, right-wing extremist political parties have made important electoral inroads recently across Western Europe, from Sweden in the north to Italy in the south.

The most recent example in a national election occurred this weekend in Belgium, where the Vlaams Blok—a Flemish nationalist, virulently anti-immigrant party—registered its best showing ever. It gained a plurality in the important northern city of Antwerp and increased its representation from two to 12 seats in the 212-member Parliament.

Flemish Socialist Party leader Willy Claes called the vote "a black day, literally and figuratively, comparable to the elections of 1936"—a reference to the dawn of fascist political strength in Europe.

In Italy, the Lombard League, a right-wing regional party, claimed its first important election victory Monday, winning a plurality of votes in the election for the government of Brescia, a major northern industrial city. The Rome daily newspaper L'Indipendente described the Brescia vote as "a solemn judgment on the failure of the traditional parties, indeed of the whole political class."

Extreme right-wing parties also have had strong showings in Austria, Switzerland, the Netherlands and even in the social-welfare bastion of Sweden, where in September elections the anti-immigrant New Democratic Party won seats in Parliament for the first time.

Far-Right Parties Make Gains

Here is a list of recent European elections in which far-right parties have made significant showings.

■ **ITALY, Nov. 25**
Municipal election in Brescia, Italy. Right-wing, northern Italian regional party Lombard League wins plurality with 25% of the vote. Raises possibility of coalition government led by Lombard League in key northern industrial city.

■ **BELGIUM, Nov. 24**
Extreme right-wing Flemish nationalist party, Vlaams Blok, running on anti-immigrant platform, scores strongly in Dutch-speaking north, increasing its representation from two to 12 seats in the 212-seat Belgian Chamber of Representatives. Vlaams Blok wins plurality in key northern city of Antwerp.

■ **AUSTRIA, Nov. 10**
Far-right Freedom Party under leader Jorg Haider wins 22.5% of the vote in Vienna city elections, surpassing tally of mainstream People's Party. Capitalizing on xenophobic campaign of "Vienna for the Viennese," Freedom Party doubles its score from previous election.

■ **SWITZERLAND, Oct. 20**
Right-wing Parti des Automobilistes (Motorists' Party) wins six seats in national legislature on populist campaign against traffic restrictions. Italian nationalist Ticino League wins 25% of the vote in Italian region of Switzerland.

■ **GERMANY, Sept. 29**
Campaigning on platform of "Germany for the Germans," extreme right-wing Deutsche Volksunion, founded by Munich millionaire Gerhard Frey, doubles its previous high score in state elections in Bremen, winning 6 seats.

■ **SWEDEN, Sept. 15**
Extreme right New Democratic Party wins first seats in Parliament (26) with a campaign against immigrants and political asylum-seekers. Party leaders Count Ian Wachtmeister and Bert Karlsson call for shift in foreign aid from the Third World to neighboring Baltic states. New party captures a surprising 6.6% of the vote.

Although most far-right political parties remain relatively small, seldom surpassing 20% of the vote in local elections and less in national elections, their recent success at the polls has sounded alarms on a continent where the rise of fascism before World War II is still a bitter, vivid memory.

After the Belgian vote, European newspapers rose in a chorus to condemn the rightward trend.

"In election after election," wrote

From *Los Angeles Times*, November 27, 1991, pp. A1, A10. Copyright © 1991 by Los Angeles Times.

Pierre Haski in Tuesday's editions of the Paris daily newspaper Liberation, "from Belgium to Austria, in Sweden and, of course, in France, the extreme right scores its points and installs itself solidly in the European political landscape."

The Guardian, the left-leaning British newspaper, editorialized: "Belgium is the latest European country to wake up to a morning of shame with the news that a far-right party, peddling racism and anti-Semitism and with undeniable connections to the Nazi era, has broken through at the polls."

Although there is no Europe-wide movement linking the emerging right-wing parties, they share a common hatred of immigrants and a feeling of lost national identity in their respective homelands. The prospect of the borderless, united Europe of 1993—proposed by the 12-nation European Community—has added to the insecurities leading to the growth of the extreme right.

"The idea of the common European home, the Great Market," commented French historian Anne-Marie Duranton-Crabol in an interview, "was at first welcomed with open arms. But now it has given rise to an uneasiness, a fear of competition and a concern about the free movement of people across borders, particularly from the East."

Duranton-Crabol, a professor at the Paris Institute of Political Studies, is the author of a recent book on post–World War II extreme-right political movements. In the anti-immigrant, nationalist cause, usually tied to unemployment and other economic concerns, the extremist parties may have found a more potent issue than the old right-wing fight against communism.

"Deprived of its favorite *bete noire,* communism," the French newspaper Le Monde editorialized Monday after the Belgian vote, "the extreme right now exploits unemployment, recession and the fears raised by the construction of a unified Europe."

A Varied Far Right

The nature of the far right varies from country to country and even within countries.

In Switzerland, the populist right-wing Parti des Automobilistes (Motor-

ists' Party) won six out of 200 legislative seats in October national elections after a campaign centered on opposition to increased gasoline taxes, speed limits and speed bumps.

In the same Oct. 20 elections, the Ticino League—a right-wing, ethnic Italian political party, modeled on the Lombard League in Italy won 25% of the vote in the Italian region of Switzerland by campaigning against domination by German and French speakers in Switzerland.

In the Netherlands, the extreme right, represented by two parties, the Centrum Democratum and the Centrum Partij, is essentially an urban phenomenon. In regional council elections last March, the two parties together gained about 7% of the vote in Amsterdam and Rotterdam but almost none in the countryside.

In Belgium and Italy, the right-wing parties began as regional, ethnically oriented movements and have expanded to take on broader national issues. The main issue for the Vlaams Blok political party in Belgium, for example, was Dutch-speaking Flemish resentment of what members felt was political domination by the minority French-speaking Walloon population that controls the Belgian—and European Community—capital in Brussels. Similarly, Italy's Lombard League was mainly a regional protest movement based on perceived inequities between the economically dynamic north, centered in Milan, and the economically depressed south.

Immigration Issue

But when the parties take on the broader issue of immigration—attacking the already existing flow of immigrants from North Africa and the anticipated wave of immigrants from collapsing Eastern Europe—they produce bigger vote counts.

In blatantly racist cartoons distributed during the recent campaign, the Vlaams Blok portrayed black African and Muslim immigrants as responsible for most of the country's problems, ranging from drug addiction to unemployment. The symbol of the party is a pair of boxing gloves. Its motto: "Our Own Folks First."

Similarly, in September, the German ultraright-wing Deutsche Volksunion party used a simple anti-immigrant slo-

gan, "The Boat Is Full," to double its previous best results in the small state of Bremen and to gain six of 100 seats in the state Parliament.

In Germany, right-wing parties have shown only small gains in elections. But resurrected extremist sentiments have surfaced in outbreaks of anti-immigrant violence in several cities. The German anti-immigrant rage is also fueled by the unusually high number of refugees, mainly from Eastern Europe, who have migrated to Germany to take advantage of the country's liberal asylum laws.

In Swedish elections in September, the newly formed New Democratic Party—under a right-wing businessman, Count Ian Wachtmeister, and record promoter Bert Karlsson—won votes by calling for the deportation of immigrants convicted of crimes on Swedish soil. Along the same lines, Wachtmeister and Karlsson said that Swedish foreign aid should be directed to neighboring states with similar cultures, such as the Baltic states, rather than to faraway Third World countries.

Using these issues, the new party shook up the Swedish political establishment, gaining 6.6% of the vote and installing 25 of its members in the 310-member Parliament.

Austrian Rightists

Most European political analysts feel that the most potent extreme right-wing party is in Austria, where earlier this month the anti-immigrant Freedom Party won 22.5% of the vote in municipal elections in Vienna, the capital. The vote doubled the results won by the party in the previous Vienna election and vaulted charismatic Freedom Party leader Jorg Haider into national prominence.

Three years ago, Haider became one of the first extreme right-wing leaders to exercise territorial control when he was elected to the post of governor of the southern province of Carinthia. But he was forced to resign that post this year after creating a scandal by publicly praising Adolf Hitler's Third Reich labor policies.

In national elections last year, Haider's Freedom Party won 20% of the vote by campaigning against crimes attributed to illegal immigrants from Poland, Romania and Czechoslovakia.

2. FACTORS IN THE POLITICAL PROCESS: Ideas, Movements, and Parties

The main campaign theme of the Vienna election earlier this month was "Vienna for the Viennese."

All the extreme-right parties owe an ideological debt to France, where the National Front party, headed by the demagogic Jean-Marie Le Pen, has easily the most broad-based support among far-right parties.

There have been no recent electoral tests to measure the French party's strength. But the National Front lately has recorded some of its highest approval ratings ever in national polls. According to one recent poll, 32% of the French said they were in agreement with many of the fiercely nationalist, anti-immigrant ideas of Le Pen, up from 18% the year before.

The popularity of the National Front's anti-immigrant stand—particularly as directed against Muslim immigrants—has forced establishment parties to take similar positions.

Former French President Valery Giscard d'Estaing, for example, caused a furor last summer when he described the influx of mostly North African Arab immigrants to France as an "invasion"—a clear attempt to woo right-wing votes for his center-right Union for French Democracy.

Former French Prime Minister and current Paris Mayor Jacques Chirac, leader of the Gaullist Rally for the Re-public party, gave a speech in which he complained about the noise and "odors" of immigrant families. Even current Socialist Prime Minister Edith Cresson joined the chorus by threatening to hire charter flights to deport illegal aliens.

Le Pen, a bull-necked, overweight figure whose face turns crimson with rage when he harangues his audiences about Arab immigrants, is widely considered unelectable in France. The same poll, commissioned in October by the newspaper Le Monde, showed that 32% of the French questioned supported his ideas; only 19%, though, felt he was fit to be a minister in the government.

But it is Le Pen, more than any other political figure, who has set the political agenda for France and other parts of Europe with his steady campaign against immigration.

Mainstream political leaders are anxiously awaiting a regional election next March in Nice in which Le Pen, who recently bought a house in the area, is felt to have his first good chance to establish a regional stronghold.

Although the right-wing political movements have mainly stuck to issues of immigration and crises in national identity, some observers feel that other issues lurk not far under the surface.

"One of the other things that links these people together is anti-Semitism," said Antony Lerman, director of the Institute of Jewish Affairs in London. "I think if you scratch any one of these groups, you will find anti-Semitism at the heart of it."

'Sense of Vigilance'

Still, few analysts of the European extreme right feel that the conditions are nearly as threatening as they were in the dangerous years leading up to World War II.

"I think there are too many counterweights now," said Duranton-Crabol. "The fact that so many journalists jumped on the Belgian election proves that there is a sense of vigilance that didn't exist before."

Europeans remember, however, that world-changing political movements can begin in such innocuous locales as a beer hall. As a result, every local election, every hint of a rise of the old European right, is taken seriously.

"Every country has extremists of various hues, fascists, anti-Semites and hooligans," The Independent newspaper of London said in an editorial in its Tuesday editions. "They become seriously worrying only when they get wind in their sails, which is what seems to be happening now."

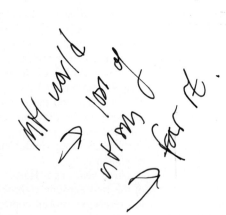

Women, Power and Politics:

The Norwegian Experience

Irene Garland

Irene Garland, a Norwegian social scientist, lives in London.

T hree Scandinavian countries all have more than one third of women representatives in their national assemblies. In Norway the Prime Minister is a woman as are 9 out of 19 cabinet ministers as well as the leaders of 2 of the other political parties.

Commentators trying to explain this phenomenon have looked back through history and pointed to the independence of Norwegian women as far back as the Viking era, when they kept the homefires burning while their menfolk were away plundering. Others have referred to more recent times. Outstanding women, however, are to be found in most countries at some time or another. The reason for Norwegian women being so successful in gaining political power must therefore be found somewhere else. My belief is that the explanation is of a practical nature and is to be found in the post-war era.

Common to the three Scandinavian countries is a structure of progressive social democracy and election systems based on proportional representation. If one compares the number of women in parliaments across the world, one finds that proportional representation is the single most important element for women to gain entry into politics. However, it was the ability to use this system to their advantage, and the fact that a group of women managed to agree on a common course across party lines, that made it possible to break the mold of the male dominated political scene in Norway.

A SPECTACULAR BEGINNING

The year was 1967 and Brigit Wiik—editor, author, mother and leader of the Oslo Feminist Movement—recalls in her book a chance meeting between herself and Einar Gerhardsen on the street in Oslo. Einar Gerhardsen was a leader of the Labor Party and had been Prime Minister almost continuously since the war. He was, at the time, in opposition, having lost the previous election. With the local elections coming up he agreed to a quota for women on the Labor party lists. In doing so he saw an opportunity to activate a new group of voters for his party, and when his agreement was presented to the party in power, they felt compelled to do the same. With the two largest parties both agreeing to give a quota to women, representatives from The National Advisory Council for Women, The Working Women's Association and the Oslo Feminist Movement, formed a group to lead the campaign to get women into politics by harnessing the female vote. They used a professional PR firm to lead the campaign—a first in Norway. The result surprised everyone; there was a national increase in women representatives of 50%, and whereas there had been 179 local communities without women's representation prior to the election, afterwards the number was reduced to 79. Subsequent campaigns further increased the number of women in local government by 50%—except for 1975.

Reprinted from *Scandinavian Review*, Vol. 79, No. 3, Winter 1991, pp. 18-25.

85

2. FACTORS IN THE POLITICAL PROCESS: Women and Politics

WOMEN IN THE NATIONAL ASSEMBLY— THE STORTING

Though there was no campaign to elect women to the national assembly, there seems to have been a spillover effect. Political parties were quick to recognize the advantage in gaining the female vote and soon extended the quota system to parliamentary elections.

Women's representation in parliament increased steadily from the 1969 election in parallel with what happened in the local elections.

WOMEN START WINNING THE ARGUMENTS

After the 1967 election the Central Bureau of Statistics started to separate voters by gender for the first time, and the 1970s saw an upsurge in research into the history of women's lives and living conditions. Young female researchers were for the first time given the opportunity and the funding to look into their own past, a hitherto ignored area of academic research, and much empirical data was collated during this decade. The history of women's lives ran to 18 volumes and a history of women writers to 3 volumes.

Once they gained entry into the corridors of power, women were increasingly taking up issues of importance to themselves and to the family. Such issues gained in importance by producing results at the ballot box. They could, therefore, not be ignored in party politics and as a result, became part of the overall political agenda.

Enabling policies such as the right to maternity leave and the ability to return to work after giving birth were important for women who wanted to have the choice between having a career and becoming a full-time housewife. With the increased number of women investing in higher education, going back to work was not only seen as a means of personal fulfillment, but became an economic necessity for those who needed to pay back their student loans. The availability of choice was also seen as central to the equality debate— why should men be able to have both a family and a career while women were forced to make a choice? The idea that there was such a thing as a "natural" place for a woman in the home despite qualifications or inclinations was rejected. If women were designed for domesticity by nature itself, then how could one explain the fact that women, given a chance, did very well in the outside world? The patriarchs were at a loss for an answer.

LAWS ARE CHANGED

The 1970s saw a number of typical feminist arguments being brought forward and legislation or common practices changed as a result. One such issue was the one over Miss and Mrs. Throughout the 1960s feminists had opposed the use of these titles and the alternative Ms. had not won approval. During the 1960s ardent feminists would reply to anyone asking if

THE INCREASE IN WOMEN'S REPRESENTATION

Local government elections	pre-1967	1967	1971	1975	1979
Women as a % of total	6.3	9.5	15	15	22.8
Parliamentary elections	1945–53	1969	1973	1977	1981
Women as a % of total	4.7	9.3	15	23.9	25.8

Maternity leave	2 weeks prior to confinement 30 weeks after confinement with full pay
Leave from work & the right to return	mothers have the right to a further year off work without pay
Paternity leave	fathers have the right to 2 weeks off work with pay, dependent on trade union agreement (applies to all civil servants)
Breast-feeding	mothers have their hours of work cut to accommodate breast-feeding
Children's illness	both parents have a right to 10 days off work with pay when a child under 12 is ill

	Born	Married	Chil-dren	Education
Gro H. Brundt-land Prime Minister (Labor)	1939	1960	4	Degree in med-icine; MA (Harvard)
Ase Kleveland Minister of Cul-tural Affairs (Labor)	1949	Co-habits	None	Part law degree; Studied music
Anne E. Lahn-stein Leader, Centre Party	1949	1975	3	Social worker
Kaci K. Five Leader, Conser-vative Party	1951	1972	2	Political Sci-ence degree

they were Miss or Mrs. that it was none of their business whether they were married or not. These days no one would ask and such titles are not in general use.

Another issue was that of surnames upon marriage. Women regarded giving up their own names as losing their identities. The law on surnames has now changed so that couples can choose which name to use. Some prefer to keep their maiden name. Some couples take on her name after marriage instead of his, but many women prefer to attach their husbands' name to their own. The latter is the case with the three female party leaders. Children are no longer automatically given their fathers' surname—again it is subject to parental choice.

The debate on surnames formed part of a wider debate about the right to a separate identity for women after marriage. The argument was for women to be able to carry on with their own careers and not to take on the role of supporting player to that of their husbands. Marriage should not become synonymous with taking on the cooking, cleaning and entertaining in addition to their own jobs. Entertaining could equally well be done in a restaurant anyway. Men would have to grow up and stop relying on their wives taking over where their mothers had left off. Cooking and darning became part of every boy's curriculum at school—the emphasis was on enabling men to become self-sufficient.

This also extended to quotas being set for men in certain professions, such as nursing, which until then had been dominated by women.

WOMEN IN POWER TODAY

The quota system helped the Prime Minister, **Gro Harlem Brundtland,** on her way to power. When she became Prime Minister in 1981 for the first time, it was she who introduced the idea of 50/50 gender representation in the cabinet. Having formed her third government at the most recent election, she has taken with her a team of young and capable women. Mrs. Brundtland followed in her father's footsteps—he was a doctor and a cabinet minister—and has been involved in politics from an early age. She is known for her enormous capacity for work, and certainly her record of achievements bears witness to just this. In addition to working full time she has managed to raise a family of four children. Her first job was as a medical officer on the Oslo Board of Public Health. The first ministerial position came in 1974 when she was appointed Minister for the Environment. She was appointed leader of the Labor Party in 1981, the same year that she became Prime Minister at the age of 42, the youngest ever to hold this office.

Internationally she has served on The Palme Commission which published its report on "Common Security" in 1982. This was followed by her chairing the World Commission on Environment and Development whose report, "Our Common Future," was published in 1987. She has published many scientific papers and received numerous prizes in acknowledgement of her work in different fields.

The new leader of the Conservative Party, **Kaci Kullman Five,** also started in politics quite young. Her mother, an elegant looking lady in her 60s, is still active in the local conservative party in Baerum where Mrs. Five first started out. After serving as deputy leader locally, she joined the national party, and was elected to parliament in 1981. Her first major office was as Deputy Secretary of State for commercial affairs in the Foreign Office in 1989. Having a degree in political science, she has served on the standing committees for foreign policy and constitutional affairs and on the finance committee. She has also published a book.

The third female party leader is **Anne Enger Lahnstein** of the rural Centre Party, who comes from a farming background. She headed the national action against free abortion in 1978–79, and was a member of the Nordic Council from 1979 on, but she did not enter parliament until 1985. She was head of the Oslo Centre Party from 1980–83. From 1983 on, she served as the deputy leader of the national party until she took over as its leader this year.

Ase Kleveland, the new Minister of Culture, differs from the others in that she has not gone through the rank and file of a party. She studied classical guitar and music theory for a number of years and during the '60s and '70s was one of Norway's best known popular singers. Ms. Kleveland won the Norwegian finals of the Eurovision Song Contest and later hosted the TV program for this contest the year it was held in Norway. She headed the Norwegian Musician's Union for a period and her most recent job was as a manager of the first amusement park in Norway. She was due to take over as Cultural Director for the Olympics to be held in Lillehammer in 1994 on the very day she was offered her cabinet post.

COMBINING CAREER AND FAMILY

Combining career with family commitments is no easy task, though office hours in Norway are short—9 to 4—giving more time for both parents to spend with their children. The smaller towns and communities constitute less danger to children which also makes it easier on working parents. Often though, it would seem that having a husband with flexible working arrangements such as a researcher or a journalist helps, and there is no doubt that joint efforts are necessary when both parents work. Fathers do take a much greater part in the up-bringing of their children and in the running of homes, than previously. This "new" role for fathers has now become the norm.

The Prime Minister's children are all grown up now and she is in fact a grandmother, but her husband's job as a researcher and writer no doubt being able to work from home when the need arose, must have been a help. Anne Lahnstein's children are in their teens, only Kaci Five has a young child (8 years old), and she said in an interview that she had to work very hard in order to make time for the family—something she viewed as important. Her husband is an editor and doubtless has to take his turn in looking after the children.

SOUR GRAPES?

It is perhaps inevitable that dissenting voices be heard when so many women reach such high positions in society. Recently a study has been published suggesting that men are leaving politics in Norway because, since it has become dominated by women, it is also becoming a low-paid occupation. Men, it is claimed, are opting for the better paid, higher status jobs in the private sector.

With increased internationalization, they argue, there are many constraints on national assemblies, and important decisions are being made elsewhere; Parliament is no longer the power house it used to be.

Research by Ms. Hege Skjeie from the Institute for Social Studies, disagrees with these conclusions. It is quite true that politicians whose wages are part of the civil service wage scale are lower than those received for the top jobs in the private sector and also that many professions dominated by women are badly paid. However, wages in the state sector have always been considered low relative to private industry, and this was the case before women started to take an interest in a career in politics. Ms. Skjeie's studies found that the men leaving politics did so because of age—they had all served for quite some time. Others had in fact lost their seats or been ousted from positions of leadership within their parties—some by women. There was certainly no difficulty in recruiting young men into

politics, and as regards the power and status associated with politics one could point to Ase Kleveland, Minister of Culture, who had the choice between politics and the Olympic Committee, and chose politics in spite of its uncertainties.

"I'M ON QUOTA—AND I LOVE IT!"

There can be no doubt that it was the quota system that made it possible for Norwegian women to enter politics in such a big way. The power that comes from parliament cannot be underestimated—it has given weight to arguments that had been previously ignored and as such has changed social attitudes of both sexes to the roles and rights of men and women alike. This change could not have taken place without political backing and without such backing, it would not have received such broad social acceptance. However, it is clear that when women work together across party lines, as was the case in Norway during the early days, that is when they achieve the most. Campaigning is also necessary as the experience of 1975 showed—no campaign, no increase in women's representation. The clock cannot be turned back, but even in Norway many women feel that there is no ground for complacency.

How the other half works

EUROPE'S WOMEN

The past two decades brought more paid jobs for Europe's women. But often the pay was poor and the job short-lived. The 1990s will need to adapt women better to the labour market—and the market better to them

NO LONGER do Britain's taxmen address their queries about a married woman's earnings to her husband. Spanish noblewomen have won a court decision—subject to appeal—that they, not a younger brother, can inherit a father's titles. The Anglican Church of Ireland has just ordained its first women priests. Italy last year got its first woman airline pilot. Europe's women are moving out of the home, into the workforce and into a semblance of equality.

Women in the European Community now, on average, have one fewer child apiece than 25 years ago. They have more freedom to work—and often more need to. As marriage has become less common, and divorce more so, the single-parent family, once a rarity, has become common. Most such families—more than 90% in Britain, for instance—are headed by women.

Equal-opportunities legislation made it more possible for women to work outside the home during the flush years of the early 1970s. Economic recession later made it more necessary. Women were 37% of the EC's civilian workforce in 1980, but around 40% by 1988. Among them, the Danes, followed by the British, are now, as for decades past, the most likely to have jobs. But the proportion of women who do so has risen markedly in other countries, such as Belgium and Portugal. Though Spanish women are still among the EC's least likely to work outside the home, one-third more of them do so now than in 1980.

Quantity, not quality

Women's share of employment has grown accordingly. Men lost almost 3m jobs in the EC between 1980 and 1987; women gained almost as many. This is not pure gain, however. It stems partly from the inevitable run-down of manufacturing jobs, typically done by men, and the rise in services, which employ almost three-quarters of Europe's working women. But it also reflects a strong growth in part-time and temporary working.

This kind of work suits employers looking for flexibility and lower costs. It suits some women, enabling them to combine paid work with child-care. But such jobs are often unskilled. They generally offer little training and no prospect of career advancement. The pay is usually low, lower than that, pro rata, for a full-time job, let alone a man's full-time job. In Britain, women in part-time manual work earn only half the basic hourly pay of male full-time workers, says that country's Equal Opportunities Commission.

Some 70% of the jobs created in the EC between 1983 and 1987 were part-time, says a report by the Centre for Research on European Women. Women hold most of them. In all, about 30% of the EC's working women (against 4% of men) work part-time: around 60% in Holland, 40-45% in Britain and Denmark, 25-30% in Belgium, France and West Germany, 10-15% elsewhere.

Women also have more than their fair share of other unusual work including temporary contracts, homeworking and helping (often unpaid) in family businesses. They are prominent in the black economy: sweated labour, the trade unions call some of this work, and often—in Italy's back-street shoe-making, for instance, or Britain's clothing sweat-shops—they are right.

So the gap between average women's and men's earnings is large. It has shrunk in all countries since the early 1970s and the EC directive on equal pay for equal work, but not so consistently since the early 1980s. Danish, French and Italian women manual workers are nearest to the hourly wages of their male counterparts; Irish and British women get only about 70% as much as men. Patchier figures on non-manual hourly earnings show a roughly similar pattern. The overall gap remains at least 25%, even without counting men's more frequent overtime.

Low pay is not the only disadvantage. In Ireland, anyone who works fewer than 18 hours a week is ineligible for maternity leave; about half of all EC countries require a minimum number of hours a week to qualify for equal, or any, social benefits. Temporary workers everywhere get no redundancy payments when their jobs end. Women also suffer more than their share of unemployment. Accounting for a bit more than two-fifths of the EC's workforce, they make up more than half of its unemployed. Unemployment among them is running about five percentage points above that of European men.

Slowly to the top

The pace at which women are storming male bastions is not exactly heady. About one-third of doctors in Britain, Denmark and, surprisingly, Portugal are women. But only 10% of Britain's senior corporate managers are, and fewer than 1% of executive directors. A senior Spanish scientist claims to be the only woman in the room as she travels Europe to discuss technological collaboration with her peers.

In two areas women are advancing faster than is generally thought. Between the extremes of Britain's buttoned-up Mrs Margaret Thatcher and Italy's bare-breasted parliamentarian Ms Ilona Staller, better known as the entertainer La Cicciolina, women are becoming visible in politics.

At or near the top, women are still rare. Mrs Thatcher apart, Gro Harlem Brundtland, briefly Norway's prime minister, is the only woman in Europe ever elected to lead her country. Only two of the 17 (appointed) members of the European Commission, Ms Vasso Papandreou and Mrs Christiane Scrivener, are women.

Yet women are working their way in. They won more seats than before in all but one of the national legislative elections in 1989. The gain was most dramatic in Spain, where two of the three leading parties established quotas for female candidates. Women make up 31% of Denmark's parliament and

From *The Economist*, June 30, 1990, pp. 21-22, 24. Copyright © 1990 by The Economist. Reprinted by permission of The New York Times Syndicated Sales Service.

25% of Holland's (taking its two chambers together). In contrast, they account for less than 7% of Britain's House of Commons or the French national assembly. Women won 19% of the seats in the European Parliament last year, a three-point rise.

There seem also to be more women entrepreneurs these days, though figures are uncertain. In Britain the number of self-employed women doubled during the 1980s, and one-third of them now employ other people. In West Germany it is estimated that one in every three new enterprises is set up by a woman; the French estimate is one in four. A fair for female entrepreneurs in Madrid last year was well attended.

Europe needs you

Women's work is attracting increasing attention for two good reasons. First, it is more than ever needed. Europe is running out of new young workers. Only in Ireland are women having enough babies to replace the population. By 2025 there could be about 2% fewer people in the EC than there are now.

The European Commission has calculated, for the first nine countries of the Community, that if labour-force participation kept to the 1985 pattern and demographic trends stayed the same, by 2000 the labour force in these countries would be shrinking by 300,000 a year. If something like this is not to happen, more women will have to work. Britain's labour force is expected to grow in the 1990s; women are likely to account for 90% of the net increase.

Secondly, even while more women workers are needed, their jobs are under threat as the EC moves toward a single market. This may in time bring more employment. But, as Miss Pauline Jackson, the author of an excellent report on what the 1992 programme will mean for women, points out, many women work in the industries

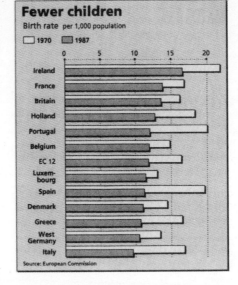

Fewer children
Birth rate per 1,000 population

that face the biggest shake-out from European integration, new technology, and low-wage competition from outside Europe.

Women make up 45% or more of employees in such industries as clothing, textiles and footwear, toys and photographic equipment. They are less numerous in other sensitive industries such as industrial and consumer electronics, but still fill the majority of the manual, assembly-line jobs. And if unemployment strikes, married women are even less free than are their husbands to move house in search of work.

Reshaping the job market

Women's interest groups and employment experts are shifting away from hammering home the message of legal equality to arguing for practical reforms to enable more women to work more productively.

Several governments are moving to ditch income-tax systems that bear relatively hard on a wife's earnings. Harder to solve are the unavoidable conflicts between employment policy and welfare policy. If a household—couple or single-parent—is receiving welfare benefits, these will often be cut if the woman goes out to earn extra money. Given the time and the extra costs, and the low wages that are the best many women can hope for, she may well ask why she should bother. Equally, the greater social protection that the EC's social charter recommends, and that some governments have already provided, for part-time or temporary workers is fine for those who already have such jobs; but it may well discourage employers from hiring more of this kind of worker.

Far the biggest obstacle to women's work, however, is the need for child-care. EC countries vary widely in the extent to which the state looks after children below school age. Mid-1980s figures from a 1988 study done for the European Commission show this, and its effects. In France, Belgium, Italy and Denmark, more than four-fifths of children aged three to five get at least some daytime care at the state's expense. Those are the countries where the most mothers of children under five work full-time: 45% of Danish mothers, 39% of Belgian, 38% of French and 34% of Italian. In Britain only about two-fifths of such children get any of this state care, and under 10% of the mothers concerned have full-time jobs.

Care for pre-school children is not the only need, however. Most schools' working day ends before that of a typical employer. So young children at least need to be looked after somehow in the afternoon, while their mother may still be at work.

Most countries are now taking some steps to improve the quantity and quality of child-care. In Spain, where state-financed nursery schools already look after two-thirds of all three-to-five-year-olds, a new education bill promises total coverage. Some of Holland's main cities have changed school hours, or added extra supervised activities, to bring them more into line with normal work days. The British government has just allowed employers to treat the cost of providing worksite creches as a business expense, while employees will not be taxed on the benefit. Several countries (though not Britain) allow parents a tax deduction for other forms of child-care costs.

The invention of statutory maternity leave (and in some countries paternity leave) has made it easier for women to have children and go back to work. All countries provide for maternity leave, variously defined and paid, though not for everyone. Spain,

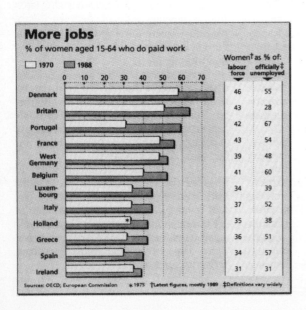

More jobs
% of women aged 15-64 who do paid work

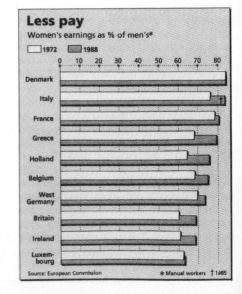

Less pay
Women's earnings as % of men's*

for example, has recently increased its leave to 16 weeks at full pay, and allows the father to take four weeks of it. Most countries, though not Britain or Ireland, also offer some sort of all-purpose parental leave.

Flexible working hours, for either parent, can make a big difference. This practice—"you work 36 hours a week, but, except for core times when you must be present, it is up to you which hours they are"—has increased in most countries, especially in the public sector. It is not a system that many commercial employers fancy. But it could do much to open jobs to women. And as more workers find themselves looking after old parents, flexibility will be of double value.

Even if all these practical difficulties can be overcome, many women still lack the skills to get into (or return to) good jobs. The trouble starts at school. In Greece and, to a lesser extent, Portugal, illiteracy among women is still seriously higher than among men. More widely, the issue is who studies what. The school-leaving age is the same everywhere for girls as for boys. And these days about as many young women as men get higher education too (though not in all countries: even in the mid-1980s women lagged behind in countries as advanced as West Germany, Holland and Britain). But boys are likelier than girls to study subjects that will help toward a skilled job. In Britain, boys were twice as likely as girls in the mid-1980s to sit "A-level" examinations (for 17-year-olds) in mathematics and almost four times as likely in physics.

France, Spain and others are trying to coax girls into school subjects, and then into professions, in which they are under-represented. In Britain and France government and business are working together to increase the number of women technicians and engineers. Greece, Spain and West Germany are among those that subsidise companies to recruit and train women. Dutch and British companies are setting up work-site nurseries. German companies including BASF and Audi have guaranteed re-employment to female workers who leave for domestic reasons, and encourage them to keep up their skills by standing in for absent colleagues meanwhile.

Counting the costs

Helping more women into better jobs at higher pay is all very well, but it will have its costs. These are more than financial. State-subsidised creches and nurseries will have to multiply in most countries, and to improve in all. Yet it is not only reactionaries who suspect that little children lose something by spending eight hours a day away from their mothers, however good the alternative. With divorce, drugs and delinquency on the rise, protecting the family unit must also deserve some priority.

The economic adjustment will not be easy. Women have been a convenient source of cheap labour for European employers. Their wages will have to rise. Few companies will have the nerve to take the opposite road to pay equality, real-wage cuts for men (though Marks & Spencer, a leading British retailer, is trying: while British prices soar, it recently announced a three-year (money) wage freeze for its warehouse jobs, typically held by men). So, in the short term, women may find they have won higher wages but have fewer jobs. Social protection for part-time and temporary workers could have the same effect.

A good deal will depend on attitudes in Brussels. The European Commission is likely to push hard now for practical changes in working conditions, as it did earlier for a legal framework to guarantee equal opportunities and pay. Spurred by an increasingly assertive and increasingly female European Parliament and, from September, by a new Brussels-based pan-European women's lobby, the commission has two instruments to hand.

It is now discussing plans for a new five-year (1991-95) action programme for equal opportunities. The social charter, vigorously pushed by Ms Papandreou and accepted, as a set of voluntary principles, by all heads of government except Mrs Thatcher at the Strasbourg summit last December, also touches on women's issues, and the commission's work programme to implement it makes these goals specific. High on the list are favourites, previously blocked, like a proposed directive on parental leave. A recommendation on child-care is among the suggested new initiatives.

The commission will have to tiptoe more carefully on these issues, though, than it has in the straight job-and-pay crusades of the past. Even among its own officials some question whether the EC has competence under the Treaty of Rome to prescribe in social matters such as child-care. The British government is sure it does not. Recommendations rather than directives may be the outcome.

In the end, it is Europe's governments and the societies they represent—especially the employers—who must make up their minds. How far, how fast and how expensively—for the costs will come before the gains do, and, as with most social advance, they will be enduring costs—are they prepared to act so that men and women can compete in Europe's labour market on equal terms? Or are they content to see that market go on giving most of the best jobs to men, while it increasingly divides women into those with a career and those scrabbling for an occasional piece of work?

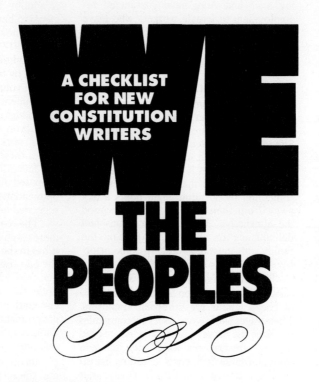

WE

A CHECKLIST
FOR NEW
CONSTITUTION
WRITERS

THE

PEOPLES

ROBERT A. GOLDWIN

*Robert A. Goldwin is a resident scholar at the
American Enterprise Institute. He was director
of AEI's Constitution Project. This article draws
on the introductions of two of his books:*
Constitution Makers on Constitution Making
and Forging Unity Out of Diversity.

AMERICANS ARE ACCUSTOMED to thinking
of constitution writing as something done hundreds of years ago by bewigged gentlemen
wearing frock coats, knee breeches, and white
stockings, but for the rest of the world, constitution writing is very much an activity of the
present day. The Constitution of the United
States is now more than 200 years old, but a
majority of the other constitutions in the world
are less than 15 years old. That is, of the 160
or so written national constitutions, more than
80 have been adopted since 1975. This means
that in the last few decades, on average, more
than five new national constitutions have come
into effect every year.

Some of these new constitutions are, of
course, for new nations, but the surprising fact
is that most were written for very old nations,
such as Spain, Portugal, Turkey, and Greece.
And now, in the old nations of Eastern Europe
and possibly also in the Soviet Union or newly

independent parts of it, new constitutions are
about to be written to replace outdated, one-
party constitutions.

Those who are responsible for writing
these new constitutions know they need assistance. As Professor Albert Blaustein of Rutgers
University Law School recently reported, many
East European legal experts "haven't seen a
constitutional law book for 45 years." They
need not proceed without advice, though, because there are so many still-active, experienced
constitution writers in scores of nations around
the world that have recently adopted new
constitutions. There are also experts in international constitutional law in the United States
and in many other nations who would be only
too glad to offer their services.

Nonetheless, except perhaps for narrow
technical matters, outsiders, however expert,
are limited in the help they can provide. A
successful constitution must be deeply rooted
in the history and traditions of the nation and
its people, and its writers need a clear sense of
what is central to the way the nation is constituted. For millennia, East European nations
have been battlegrounds for innumerable inva-
sions, conquests, and consequent migrations.
As a result, there is a great mixing of peoples
who cannot be sorted out even by computer-
guided drawing of borders. These peoples, who

From *The American Enterprise,* May/June 1990, pp. 70-75. Copyright © 1990, The American Enterprise Institute for Public
Policy Research.

have no choice but to live side by side, are not necessarily able to love their neighbors. It seems as though everyone's grandfather was murdered by someone else's grandfather. As a result, most of these nations have diverse populations characterized by passionate hostilities. The constitutional task to make "one people"—to strengthen a sense of national unity by constitutional provisions—is a much greater concern for these nations.

Destructive Diversity

That all human beings are fundamentally equal is a central tenet of modern constitutionalism that is essential to all systems of political liberty. To assert that we are all equal means, necessarily, that we are all equally human, sharing one and the same human nature. This view is widely held and advanced, sometimes as fact, sometimes as aspiration, and denied or disputed for the most part by those who are thought to be benighted, or bigoted, or both. The universality of human nature, the oneness of humankind, is a vital element of modern democratic thought.

And yet, wherever we look in the world, we see mankind divided into tightly bound groups, set apart by racial, religious, language, or national differences. The bonds of loyalty these differences engender often override all other considerations, including even the obligations of national citizenship. Whether or not we are "all brothers and sisters under the skin," two indisputable, and indisputably linked, facts are evident everywhere: first, there is a natural, powerful fraternal bond among persons who share the same religion, or race, or language, or nationality; second, the same inclusive bond commonly has the effect of excluding those who are different, engendering hostility toward "outsiders."

In almost all countries with diverse populations—and almost all countries around the world do have significant diversity—we see, not the "domestic tranquillity" spoken of in the preamble to the Constitution of the United States, but domestic hostility between fellow citizens of the same nation-states: Protestants and Catholics in Northern Ireland, Muslims and Christians in Lebanon, Jews and Muslims in Israel, blacks and whites in the United States, Flemish and French speakers in Belgium, Armenians and Azerbaijanis in the Soviet Union, Serbs and Albanians in Yugoslavia, Greeks and Turks in Cyprus, Hausas and Ibos in Nigeria—and this list does not come close to being exhaustive. Given historic animosities in many countries of Eastern Europe, diversity presents a problem for their constitution makers.

Citizens who are members of groups significantly different from others of the population can reasonably have grave concerns: fear for their safety, concern that they will not be allowed to participate in the political, social, and economic life of the nation, and fear that they will be restricted in the practices that are characteristic of their special way of life. To address these fears, many constitutions have special provisions, usually addressed directly to groups by name, assuring them of participation in the national life and guaranteeing freedom of religion or use of language, or promising preferences in education or employment on the basis of nationality or race. The dilemma such provisions pose, however, is that they raise the differences within the population to a constitutional status and tend thereby to identify, emphasize, and perpetuate the divisions within society. Our own constitution is silent in this regard, aiming for unity by assimilation.

No Universal Formula

Years of study of constitutions confirm what common sense would suggest: that there is no universal formula for a successful constitution. A sound constitution for any nation has to be something of a reflection, although more than that, of the essence of a particular nation, and this is inescapably influenced by the character of each nation's people, or peoples, and their history.

Constitution writers may wish to make a break with their past, to make a completely fresh start, but they never have the luxury of a clean slate. They start with a population having certain characteristics (for example, homogeneous or diverse), an economy tied to its geographic characteristics (a maritime nation or landlocked), neighboring nations (peaceful or warlike) that cannot be moved or ignored, and a history that has shaped their understanding of themselves and their national aspirations. The constitution must reflect all of these elements of the nation, and the more it is in accord with these national characteristics, the better the constitution will be.

One day in Athens some years ago, while talking to a Greek judge who is also a constitutional scholar, I referred to the newness of the Greek constitution. He asked me what date I put on it, and I, somewhat surprised, said, "1975, of course." "Yes, I understand," he said, "but you could also say 1863." "But," I replied, "Greece has had nearly a dozen constitutions since then." "Yes," he said, "that's right, but they are always the same." He was exaggerating, of course, but not much. When Greece adopted its latest constitution, two

QUESTIONS FOR CONSTITUTION WRITERS

The Preliminaries

• How will delegates to the constitutional committee or constituent assembly be chosen? Will the new constitution be drafted by the legislative body or by a body chosen specifically for the purpose? If there is controversy about the method of selection, how and by whom will it be resolved?

• What will be the rules and procedures of the constitution-making body, once chosen, and how and by whom will controversies on this question be resolved?

Powers and Power Relationships

• What are the different branches of government, and what is their constitutional relationship? Are the executive and legislative branches separated or combined?

• Is there a single chief executive, or an executive cabinet, or some form of executive council? What are the executive powers, and how are they limited? Does the executive have some share in the legislative process: for instance, do laws require his signature; does he have veto power, the right to propose legislation? Does the executive have treaty-making powers, the power to declare war, command of the armed forces, law-enforcement powers, some degree of responsibility to appoint judges, power of executive pardon or clemency? Are police powers national, or is there some form of local authority? How are the executive departments established, and how and by whom are the department heads appointed and fired? How are executive salaries determined? How is the chief executive chosen, and what is the term of office?

• Is the head of state separate from the head of government, and if so, what is the role of the head of state? How is the head of state chosen? What is the term of office? If a monarch, what is the role of the crown? Does the head of state act to dissolve the legislature, call for new elections, name a new prime minister?

• Is the legislature unicameral or bicameral? What is the principle of representation, or is there more than one principle (for example, some legislators chosen on the basis of population, some by states or provinces)? What is the length of term for members? Under what conditions and by whom are new elections called? How are salaries of members determined and varied? Does the legislature have the power of the purse, taxing power, oversight powers, a role in executive and judicial appointments, budget-making powers, power over the monetary system, power to regulate domestic trade, foreign trade, a role in war making and treaty making, power to investigate and compel testimony, power to impeach executive and judicial officers? Do legislators have immunity from arrest? What are the conditions for dissolution of the legislature?

• What is the system of justice and law enforcement? What is the structure of the judicial system, and how and by whom is it established? In what ways, if any, are judges subject to legislative and executive controls? How independent are judges from executive and legislative control? How are judges appointed or elected and for what terms? Are judicial salaries protected? Do the courts of law have powers of judicial review of the constitutionality of legislative and executive actions, or is there a separate constitutional court?

• To whom are the powers assigned for the conduct of foreign policy? To what extent are they shared, and on the basis of what principle? Where is the power assigned to declare war and to make and ratify treaties?

• Are there powers to suspend the constitution in emergencies? If so, by whom and under what conditions? Are there protections against abuse of emergency powers?

• Are all public officials required to take an oath of office to uphold this constitution?

• To what extent are the executive, legislative, and judicial powers separated, and by what provisions are the separations maintained?

• Is the national government unitary or federal, and if the latter, what form of federalism? Whether unitary or federal, is it centralized or decentralized, or some combination?

• What are the limits of the powers of the government and of the various branches and officers, and by what means are the limits sustained?

---

issues were foremost, the roles of the armed forces and of the monarchy. However much Greek constitutions and regimes changed through the decades, these questions remained constant. There was not much leeway, not much discretion on many of the most important points. The same will be true for the nations of Eastern Europe.

Although there can be no universal formula for successful constitution writing—no canned answers that can be applied to any country in search of a new constitutional order—there are standard, universal questions that must be asked. A comprehensive list will include some questions that at first glance seem archaic or unnecessary to consider. Turkey or Portugal, for instance, did not have to dwell on the question of the role of the monarchy as Greece and Spain did, but considering how many modern nations are constitutional monarchies, it is not impossible that one or another East European nation might consider some form of constitutional monarchy before the turmoil is over.

Therefore, in the conviction that it is possible to develop a substantial, if not complete, list of the questions constitution writers must ask themselves in writing the constitution of any country, I offer this enumeration for guidance (see box above):

Elections and Political Parties

• By what methods are the various offices filled: direct popular election by universal suffrage or some indirect method; winner-take-all or some form of proportional representation? Which offices, if any, are not elective, and what is the method of appointment? Are there different methods of election or selection for different offices?

• What is the constitutional status of political parties, or is that left undetermined?

Nonpolitical Institutions

• What is the structure of the education system, and how is it supervised? Is the school system centralized, regional, local, or some combination? Are there provisions for ethnic, religious, or language schools? Are private schools allowed, and if so, what controls are imposed on them? Is the freedom of inquiry in university teaching and research protected?

• What are the provisions for the media? Are there government-owned, political party-owned, or privately owned newspapers, television channels, and radio stations? Are the media regulated or licensed? What protections are there for freedom of the press, and how are abuses prevented?

• What is the constitutional status of the military? Who is the commander in chief of the armed forces? How much and what form of civilian control is there?

• What is the role of religion? Is there an established church, and one or more official religions? Are there church subsidies from public funds, and if so, are they on a basis of equality or are they preferential? Is there separation of church and state? Is freedom of religion protected and by what means?

Rights

• Is there a bill of rights? What protections are there for the rights of individuals: speech, press, religion, peaceable assembly, habeas corpus, public trial, and so on? Is there equality of all persons, or are there constitutional preferences based on race, religion, sex, nationality, or different levels of citizenship? Are the rights primarily political and legal, or are social and economic rights included? Are the rights provisions stated negatively or affirmatively? Is there a list of duties of citizens listed, and if so, are the duties linked to rights? Are there protections of rights of aliens? What are the provisions for immigration and emigration? What is the status under the constitution of international declarations of rights? Are only the rights of individuals acknowledged, or are there also protections for the rights of religious, ethnic, racial, or regional groups?

• Are there different levels or kinds of citizenship; that is, are there qualifications or restrictions of voting rights, property rights, representation, access to education, or eligibility for public office based on race, sex, religion, language, or national origin? Do naturalized citizens have the same rights, privileges, and immunities as natural-born citizens? What are the naturalization provisions?

• Does the constitution specify any national or official languages? Are there provisions for schools, courts, government offices, churches, and other institutions to conduct their activities in languages other than the national or official ones?

The Economic System

• Does the constitution specify what kind of economic system shall prevail (for instance, that this nation is a socialist democracy or that the means of production shall be owned privately)? Are there provisions for managing the economy, or is a market economy of private enterprise assumed? What is the status of private property? What is the status of banks, corporations, farms, other enterprises? What are the regulatory and licensing powers? Are there government monopolies and, if so, what kind? What are the copyright and patent provisions? Is there protection against impairing the obligation of contracts?

• What is the status of international law and international organizations in relation to national laws and institutions? What is the legal status of treaties and other international obligations?

Final Questions

• What is the amendment process? Is it designed to make amending the constitution easy or difficult? Does the amending process include the people as a whole, or is it limited to the legislature and other officials?

• What is the process for ratifying the constitution?

A Rare Activity

The frequency of constitution writing tells us two things. First, constitutions are very important, and great investments of time and effort are needed to write them; and second, it is very difficult, and rare, to write a constitution that lasts—which is why there have been so many of them.

A complete list—and this one surely has omissions—gives no assurance of finding the right answers in writing a constitution. But an enumeration such as this provides reassurance that major issues will not be overlooked.

It also reminds us what an extraordinary accomplishment our own 200-year-old Constitution is.

Making a constitution is a special political activity. It is possible only at certain extraordinary moments in a nation's history, and its success or failure can have profound and lasting consequences for a nation and its people. That is the challenge facing the constitution makers and the peoples of Eastern Europe.

Parliament and Congress:

Is the Grass Greener on the other side?

Gregory S. Mahler

Gregory Mahler is chair of the Political Science Department at the University of Mississippi.

Aristotle long ago observed that man is a "political animal." He could have added that man, by his very nature, notes the political status of his neighbours and, very often, perceives their lot as being superior to his own. The old saying "the grass is greener on the other side of the fence" can be applied to politics and political structures as well as to other, more material, dimensions of the contemporary world.

Legislators are not immune from the very human tendency to see how others of their lot exist in their respective settings, and, sometimes, to look longingly at these other settings. When legislators do look around to see the conditions under which their peers operate in other countries, they occasionally decide they prefer the alternative legislative settings to their own.

Features which legislators admire or envy in the settings of their colleagues include such things as: the characteristics of political parties (their numbers, or degrees of party discipline), legislative committee systems, staff and services available to help legislators in their tasks, office facilities, libraries, and salaries. This essay will develop the "grass is greener" theme in relation to a dimension of the legislative world which is regularly a topic of conversation when legislators from a number of different jurisdictions meet: the ability or inability of legislatures to check and control the executive.

The Decline of Parliament

The theme of the "decline of parliament" has a long and well-studied history.[1] It generally refers to the gradual flow of true legislative power away from the legislative body in the direction of the executive. The executive does the real law-making — by actually drafting most legislation — and the legislature takes a more "passive" role by simply approving executive proposals.

Legislators are very concerned about their duties and powers and over the years have jealously guarded them when they have appeared to be threatened. In Canada (and indeed most parliamentary democracies in the world today), the majority of challenges to legislative power which develop no longer come from the ceremonial executive (the Crown), but from the political executive, the government of the day.

It can be argued that the ability to direct and influence public policy, is a "zero sum game" (i.e. there is only room for a

limited amount of power and influence to be exercised in the political world and a growth in the relative power of the political executive must be at the expense of the power of the legislature). It follows, then, that if the legislature is concerned about maintaining its powers, concerned about protecting its powers from being diminished, it must be concerned about every attempt by the political executive to expand its powers.

Others contend that real "legislative power" cannot, and probably never did reside in the legislature. There was no "Golden Age" of Parliament. The true legislative role of parliament today is not (and in the past was not) to create legislation, but to scrutinize and ratify legislation introduced by the Government of the day. Although an occasional exception to this pattern of behavior may exist (with private members' bills, for example), the general rule is clear: the legislature today does not actively initiate legislation as its primary *raison d'être*.

Although parliamentarians may not be major initiators of legislation, studies have indicated a wide range of other functions.[2] Certainly one major role of the legislature is the "oversight" role, criticizing and checking the powers of the executive. The ultimate extension of this power is the ability of the legislature to terminate the term of office of the executive through a "no confidence" vote. Another role of the legislature involves communication and representation of constituency concerns. Yet another function involves the debating function, articulating the concerns of the public of the day.

Professor James Mallory has indicated the need to "be realistic about the role of Parliament in the Westminster system."[3] He cites Bernard Crick's classic work, *The Reform of Parliament*: "...the phrase 'Parliamentary control, and talk about the 'decline of parliamentary control,' should not mislead anyone into asking for a situation in which governments can have their legislation changed or defeated, or their life terminated... Control means influence, not direct power; advice, not command; criticism, not obstruction; scrutiny, not initiation; and publicity, not secrecy."[4]

The fact that parliament may not be paramount in the creation and processing of legislation is no reason to condemn all aspects of parliamentary institutions. Nor should parliamentarians be convinced that legislative life is perfect in the presidential-congressional system. In fact, some American legislators look to their parliamentary brethren and sigh with envy at the attractiveness of certain aspects of parliamentary institutions.

Reprinted courtesy of *Canadian Parliamentary Review*, Winter 1985–86, pp. 19–21.

Desirability of a Congressional Model for Canada?

Many Canadian parliamentarians and students of parliament look upon presidential-congressional institutions of the United States as possessing the answers to most of their problems. The grass is sometimes seen as being greener on the other side of the border. The concepts of fixed legislative terms, less party discipline, and a greater general emphasis on the role and importance of individual legislators (which implies more office space and staff for individual legislators, among other things) are seen as standards to which Canadian legislators should aspire.

A perceived strength of the American congressional system is that legislators do not automatically "rubber stamp" approve executive proposals. They consider the president's suggestions, but feel free to make substitutions or modifications to the proposal, or even to reject it completely. Party discipline is relatively weak; there are regularly Republican legislators opposing a Republican president (and Democratic legislators supporting him), and vice versa. Against the need for discipline congressmen argue that their first duty is to either (a) their constituency, or (b) what is "right", rather than simply to party leaders telling them how to behave in the legislature. For example, in 1976 Jimmy Carter was elected President with large majorities of Democrats in both houses of Congress. One of Carter's major concerns was energy policy. He introduced legislative proposals (that is, he had congressional supporters introduce legislation, since the American president cannot introduce legislation on his own) dealing with energy policy, calling his proposals "the moral equivalent of war." In his speeches and public appearances he did everything he could to muster support for "his" legislation. Two years later when "his" legislation finally emerged from the legislative process, it could hardly be recognized as the proposals submitted in such emotional terms two years earlier.

The experience of President Carter was certainly not unique. Any number of examples of such incidents of legislative-executive non-cooperation can be cited in recent American political history, ranging from President Wilson's unsuccessful efforts to get the United States to join the League of Nations, through Ronald Reagan's contemporary battles with Congress over the size of the federal budget. The Carter experience was somewhat unusual by virtue of the fact that the same political party controlled both the executive and legislative branches of government, and cooperation still was not forthcoming. There have been many more examples of non-cooperation when one party has controlled the White House and another party has controlled one or both houses of Congress.

This lack of party discipline ostensibly enables the individual legislators to be concerned about the special concerns of their constituencies. This, they say, is more important than simply having to follow the orders of the party whip in the legislature. It is not any more unusual to find a Republican legislator from a farm state voting against a specific agricultural proposal of President Reagan on the grounds that the legislation in question is not good for his/her constituency, than to find Democratic legislators from the southwestern states who voted against President Carter's water policy proposals on the grounds that the proposals were not good for their constituencies.

Congressional legislators know that they have fixed terms in office — the President is simply not able to bring about early

elections — and they know that as long as they can keep their constituencies happy there is no need to be terribly concerned about opposing the President, even if he is the leader of their party. It may be nice to have the President on your side, but if you have a strong base of support "back home" you can survive without his help.

Are there any benefits to the public interest in the absence of party discipline? The major argument is that the legislature will independently consider the executive's proposals, rather than simply accepting the executive's ideas passively. This, it is claimed, allows for a multiplicity of interests, concerns, and perspectives to be represented in the legislature, and ostensibly results in "better" legislation.

In summary, American legislative institutions promote the role of the individual legislator. The fixed term gives legislators the security necessary for the performance of the functions they feel are important. The (relative) lack of party discipline enables legislators to act on the issues about which they are concerned. In terms of the various legislative functions mentioned above, congressmen appear to spend a great deal of their time in what has been termed the legislative aspect of the job: drafting legislation, debating, proposing amendments, and voting (on a more or less independent basis).

While many parliamentarians are impressed by the ability of individual American legislator to act on their own volition it is ironic that many congressional legislators look longingly at the legislative power relationships of their parliamentary brethren. The grass, apparently, is greener on the *other* side of the border, too.

Desirability of a Parliamentary Model

The "decline of congressional power" is as popular a topic of conversation in Washington as "the decline of parliamentary power" in Ottawa or London. Over the last several decades American legislators have sensed that a great deal of legislative power has slipped from their collective grasp.[5] Many have decried this tendency and tried to stop, or reverse this flow of power away from the legislative branch and toward the executive.

One of the major themes in the writings of these congressional activists is an admiration for the parliamentary model's (perceived) power over the executive. Many American legislators see the president's veto power, combined with his fixed term in office, as a real flaw in the "balance of powers" of the system, leading to an inexorable increase in executive power at the expense of the legislature. They look at a number of parliamentary structures which they see as promoting democratic political behavior and increased executive responsibility to the legislature, including the ability to force the resignation of the executive through a non-confidence vote. The regular "question period" format which insures some degree of public executive accountability is also perceived as being very attractive .

Critics of the congressional system do not confine their criticism only to the growth of executive power. There are many who feel there is too much freedom in the congressional arena. To paraphrase the words of Bernard Crick cited earlier, advising has sometimes turned into issuing commands; and criticism has sometimes turned into obstruction. This is not to suggest that congressional legislators would support giving up their ability to initiate legislation, to amend executive proposals, or to vote in a manner which they (individually) deem proper. This does suggest, however, that even congressional legislators see that independence is a two-sided coin: one side involves individual legislative autonomy and input into the legislative process; the other side involves the incompatibility of complete independence with a British style of "Responsible Government".

In 1948 Hubert Humphrey, then mayor of Minneapolis, delivered an address at the nomination convention of the Democratic Party. In his comments he appealed for a "more responsible" two party system in the United States, a system with sufficient party discipline to have *meaningful* party labels, and to allow party platforms to become public policy.[6] Little progress has been made over the last thirty-seven years in this regard. In the abstract the concept of a *meaningful* two party system may be attractive; American legislators have not been as attracted to the necessary corollary of the concept: decreased legislative independence and increased party discipline.

While American Senators and Representatives are very jealous of executive encroachments upon their powers, there is some recognition that on occasion — usually depending upon individual legislators' views about the desirability of specific pieces of legislation — executive leadership, and perhaps party discipline, can serve a valuable function. Congressional legislators are, at times which correspond to their policy preferences, envious of parliamentary governnments' abilities to carry their programs into law because MPs elected under their party labels will act consistent with party whips' directions. They would be loath to give up their perceived high degrees of legislative freedom but many of them realize the cost of this freedom in this era of pressing social problems and complex legislation. Parliamentary style government is simply not possible without party discipline.

A Democratic Congressman supporting President Carter's energy policy proposals might have longed for an effective three-line whip to help to pass the energy policies in question. An opponent of those policy proposals would have argued, to the contrary, that the frustration of the president's proposals was a good illustration of the wisdom of the legislature tempering the error-ridden policy proposals of the president. Similarly, many conservative Republican supporters of President Reagan have condemned the ability of the Democratic House of Representatives to frustrate his economic policies. Opponents of those policies have argued, again, that the House of Representatives is doing an important job of representing public opinion and is exercising a valuable and important check on the misguided policies of the executive.

Some Concluding Observations

The parliamentary model has its strengths as well as its weaknesses. The individual legislator in a parliamentary system does not have as active a role in the actual legislative process as does his American counterparts, but it is not at all hard to imagine instances in which the emphasis on individual autonomy in the congressional system can be counterproductive because it delays much-needed legislative programs.

The problem, ultimately, is one of balance. Is it possible to have a responsible party system in the context of parliamentary democracy which can deliver on its promises to the public, and also to have a high degree of individual legislative autonomy in the legislative arena?

It is hard to imagine how those two concepts could coexist. The congressional and parliamentary models of legislative behavior have placed their respective emphases on two different priorities. The parliamentary model, with its responsible party system and its corresponding party discipline in the legislature, emphasizes efficient policy delivery, and the ability of an elected government to deliver on its promises. The congressional model, with its lack of party discipline and its emphasis on individual legislative autonomy, placed more emphasis on what can be called "consensual politics": it may take much more time for executive proposals to find their way into law, but (the argument goes) there is greater likelihood that what does, ultimately, emerge as law will be acceptable to a greater number of people than if government proposals were "automatically" approved by a pre-existing majority in the legislature acting "under the whip".

We cannot say that one type of legislature is "more effective" than the other. Each maximizes effectiveness in different aspects of the legislative function. Legislators in the congressional system, because of their greater legislative autonomy and weaker party discipline, are more effective at actually legislating than they are at exercising ultimate control over the executive. Legislators in the parliamentary system, although they may play more of a "ratifying" role in regard to legislation, do get legislation passed promptly; they also have an ultimate power over the life of the government of the day.

The appropriateness of both models must also be evaluated in light of the different history, political culture and objectives of the societies in which they operate. Perhaps the grass is just as green on both sides of the fence.

Notes

[1]There is substantial literature devoted to the general topic of "the decline of legislatures." Among the many sources which could be referred to in this area would be included the work of Gerhard Loewenberg. *Modern Parliaments: Change or Decline?* Chicago: Atherton. 1971; Gerhard Loewenberg and Samuel Patterson, *Comparing Legislatures*, Boston: Little, Brown, 1979; or Samuel Patterson and John Wahlke, eds., *Comparative Legislative Behavior: Frontiers of Research*, New York: John Wiley, 1972.

[2]A very common topic in studies of legislative behavior has to do with the various functions legislatures may be said to perform for the societies of which they are a part. For a discussion of the many functions attributed to legislatures in political science literature, see Gregory Mahler, *Comparative Politics: An Institutional and Cross-National Approach* (Cambridge, Ma.: Schenkman, 1983, pp. 56-61.

[3]J. R. Mallory, "Can Parliament Control the Regulatory Process?" *Canadian Parliamentary Review* Vol. 6 (no. 3, 1983) p. 6.

[4]Bernard Crick, *The Reform of Parliament*, London, 1968, p. 80.

[5]One very well written discussion of the decline of American congressional power in relation to the power of the president can be found in Ronald Moe, ed., *Congress and the President*, Pacific Palisades, Calif.: Goodyear Publishing Co., 1971.

[6]Subsequently a special report was published by the Committee on Political Parties of the American Political Science Association dealing with this problem. See "Toward a More Responsible Two-Party System," *American Political Science Review* Vol. 44 (no. 3, 1950), special supplement.

Presidents and Prime Ministers

Richard Rose

Richard Rose is professor of public policy at the University of Strathclyde in Glasgow, Scotland. An American, he has lived in Great Britain for many years and has been studying problems of political leadership in America and Europe for three decades. His books include Presidents and Prime Ministers; Managing Presidential Objectives; Understanding Big Government; *and* The Post-Modern Presidency: The World Closes in on the White House.

The need to give direction to government is universal and persisting. Every country, from Egypt of the pharoahs to contemporary democracies, must maintain political institutions that enable a small group of politicians to make authoritative decisions that are binding on the whole of society. Within every system, one office is of first importance, whether it is called president, prime minister, führer, or dux.

There are diverse ways of organizing the direction of government, not only between democracies and authoritarian regimes, but also among democracies. Switzerland stands at one extreme, with collective direction provided by a federal council whose president rotates from year to year. At the other extreme are countries that claim to centralize authority, under a British-style parliamentary system or in an American or French presidential system, in which one person is directly elected to the supreme office of state.

To what extent are the differences in the formal attributes of office a reflection of substantive differences in how authority is exercised? To what extent do the imperatives of office—the need for electoral support, dependence upon civil servants for advice, and vulnerability to events—impose common responses in practice? Comparing the different methods of giving direction to government in the United States (presidential), Great Britain (prime ministerial and Cabinet), and France (presidential and prime ministerial) can help us understand whether other countries do it—that is, choose a national leader—in a way that is better.

To make comparisons requires concepts that can identify the common elements in different offices. Three concepts organize the comparisons I make: the career that leads to the top; the institutions and powers of government; and the scope for variation within a country, whether arising from events or personalities.

Career Leading to the Top

By definition, a president or prime minister is unrepresentative by being the occupant of a unique office. The diversity of outlooks and skills that can be attributed to white, university-educated males is inadequate to predict how people with the same social characteristics—a Carter or an Eisenhower; a Wilson or a Heath—will perform in office. Nor is it helpful to consider the recruitment of national leaders deductively, as a management consultant or personnel officer would, first identifying the skills required for the job and then evaluating candidates on the basis of a priori requirements. National leaders are not recruited by examination; they are self-selected, individuals whose driving ambitions, personal attributes, and, not least, good fortune, combine to win the highest public office.

To understand what leaders can do in office we need to compare the skills acquired in getting to the top with the skills required once there. The tasks that a president or prime minister must undertake are few but central: sustaining popular support through responsiveness to the electorate, and being effective in government. Success in office encourages electoral popularity, and electoral popularity is an asset in wielding influence within government.

The previous careers of presidents and prime ministers are significant, insofar as experience affects what they do in office—and what they do well. A politician who had spent many years concentrating upon campaigning to win popularity may continue to cultivate popularity in office. By contrast, a politician experienced in dealing with the problems of government from within may be better at dealing effectively with international and domestic problems.

Two relevant criteria for comparing the careers of national leaders are: previous experience of government, and previous experience of party and mass electoral politics. American presidents are outstanding in their experience of campaigning for mass support, whereas French presidents are outstanding for their prior knowledge of government from the inside. British prime ministers usually combine experience in both fields.

Thirteen of the fourteen Americans who have been nominated for president of the United States by the Democratic or Republican parties since 1945 had prior experience in running for major office, whether at the congressional, gubernatorial or presidential level. Campaigning for office makes a politician conscious of his or her need for popular approval. It also cultivates skill in dealing

Published by permission of Transaction Publishers, from *Society,* Vol. 25, No. 3, March/April 1988, pp. 61-67. Copyright © 1988 by Transaction Publishers.

with the mass media. No American will be elected president who has not learned how to campaign across the continent, effectively and incessantly. Since selection as a presidential candidate is dependent upon winning primaries, a president must run twice: first to win the party nomination and then to win the White House. The effort required is shown by the fact that in 1985, three years before the presidential election, one Republican hopeful campaigned in twenty-four states, and a Democratic hopeful in thirty. Immediately after the 1986 congressional elections ended, the media started featuring stories about the 1988 campaign.

Campaigning is different from governing. Forcing ambitious politicians to concentrate upon crossing and recrossing America reduces the time available for learning about problems in Washington and the rest of the world. The typical postwar president has had no experience working within the executive branch. The way in which the federal government deals with foreign policy, or with problems of the economy is known, if at all, from the vantage point of a spectator. A president is likely to have had relatively brief experience in Congress. As John F. Kennedy's career illustrates, Congress is not treated as a

---

Looking presidential is not the same as acting like a president.

---

means of preparing to govern; it is a launching pad for a presidential campaign. The last three presidential elections have been won by individuals who could boast of having no experience in Washington. Jimmy Carter and Ronald Reagan were state governors, experienced at a job that gives no experience in foreign affairs or economic management.

A president who is experienced in campaigning can be expected to continue cultivating the media and seeking a high standing in the opinion polls. Ronald Reagan illustrates this approach. A president may even use campaigning as a substitute for coming to grips with government; Jimmy Carter abandoned Washington for the campaign trail when confronted with mid-term difficulties in 1978. But public relations expertise is only half the job; looking presidential is not the same as acting like a president.

A British prime minister, by contrast, enters office after decades in the House of Commons and years as a Cabinet minister. The average postwar prime minister had spent thirty-two years in Parliament before entering 10 Downing Street. Of that period, thirteen years had been spent as a Cabinet minister. Moreover, the prime minister has normally held the important policy posts of foreign secretary, chancellor of the exchequer or both. The average prime minister has spent eight years in ministerial office, learning to handle foreign and/or economic problems. By contrast with the United States, no prime minister has had postwar experience in state or local government, and by contrast with France, none has been a civil servant since World War II.

The campaign experience of a British prime minister is very much affected by the centrality that politicians give Parliament. A politician seeks to make a mark in debate there. Even in an era of mass media, the elitist doctrine holds that success in the House of Commons produces positive evaluation by journalists and invitations to appear on television, where a politician can establish an image with the national electorate. Whereas an American presidential hopeful has a bottom-up strategy, concentrating upon winning votes in early primaries in Iowa and New Hampshire as a means of securing media attention, a British politician has a top-down approach, starting to campaign in Parliament.

Party is the surrogate for public opinion among British politicians, and with good reason. Success in the Commons is evaluated by a politician's party colleagues. Election to the party leadership is also determined by party colleagues. To become prime minister a politician does not need to win an election; he or she only needs to be elected party leader when the party has a parliamentary majority. Jim Callaghan and Sir Alec Douglas-Home each entered Downing Street this way and lost office in the first general election fought as prime minister.

The lesser importance of the mass electorate to British party leaders is illustrated by the fact that the average popularity rating of a prime minister is usually less than that of an American president. The monthly Gallup poll rating often shows the prime minister approved by less than half the electorate and trailing behind one or more leaders of the opposition.

In the Fifth French Republic, presidents and prime ministers have differed from American presidents, being very experienced in government, and relatively inexperienced in campaigning with the mass electorate. Only one president, François Mitterrand, has followed the British practice of making a political career based on Parliament. Since he was on the opposition side for the first two decades of the Fifth Republic, his experience of the problems of office was like that of a British opposition member of Parliament, and different from that of a minister. Giscard d'Estaing began as a high-flying civil servant and Charles de Gaulle, like Dwight Eisenhower, was schooled in bureaucratic infighting as a career soldier.

When nine different French prime ministers are examined, the significance of a civil service background becomes clear. Every prime minister except for Pierre Mauroy has been a civil servant first. It has been exceptional for a French prime minister to spend decades in Parliament before attaining that office. An Englishman would be surprised that a Raymond Barre or a Couve de Murville had not sat there before becoming prime minister. An American would be even more surprised by the experience that French leaders have had in the ministries as high civil servants, and particularly in dealing with foreign and economic affairs.

The traditional style of French campaigning is plebiscitary. One feature of this is that campaigning need not be incessant. Louis Napoleon is said to have compared elections with baptism: something it is necessary to do—but to do only once. The seven-year fixed term of the French president, about double the statutory life of many national leaders, is in the tradition of infrequent consultation with the electorate.

The French tradition of leadership is also ambivalent; a plebiscite is, after all, a mass mobilization. The weakness of parties, most notably on the Right, which has provided three of the four presidents of the Fifth Republic, encourages a personalistic style of campaigning. The use of the two-ballot method for the popular election of a president further encourages candidates to compete against each other as individuals, just as candidates for the presidential nomination compete against fellow-partisans in a primary. The persistence of divisions between Left and Right ensures any candidate successful in entering the second ballot a substantial bloc of votes, with or without a party endorsement.

On the two central criteria of political leadership, the relationship with the mass electorate, and knowledge of government, there are cross-national contrasts in the typical career. A British or French leader is likely to know far more about government than an American president, but an American politician is likely to be far more experienced in campaigning to win popular approval and elections.

Less for the President to Govern

Journalistic and historical accounts of government often focus on the person and office of the national leader. The American president is deemed to be very powerful because of the immense military force that he can command by comparison to a national leader in Great Britain or France. The power to drop a hydrogen bomb is frequently cited as a measure of the awesome power of an American president; but it is misleading, for no president has ever dropped a hydrogen bomb, and no president has used atomic weapons in more than forty years. Therefore, we must ask: What does an American president (and his European counterparts) do when not dropping a hydrogen bomb?

In an era of big government, a national leader is more a chief than an executive, for no individual can superintend, let alone carry out, the manifold tasks of government. A national leader does not need to make major choices about what government ought to do; he inherits a set of institutions that are committed—by law, by organization, by the professionalism of public employees, and by the expectations of voters—to appropriate a large amount of the country's resources in order to produce the program outputs of big government.

Whereas political leadership is readily personalized, government is intrinsically impersonal. It consists of collective actions by organizations that operate according to impersonal laws. Even when providing benefits to individuals, such as education, health care, or pensions, the scale of a ministry or a large regional or local government is such as to make the institution appear impersonal.

Contemporary Western political systems are first of all governed by the rule of law rather than personal will. When government did few things and actions could be derived from prerogative powers, such as a declaration of war, there was more scope for the initiative of leaders. Today, the characteristic activities of government, accounting for most public expenditure and personnel, are statutory entitlements to benefits of the welfare state. They cannot be overturned by wish or will, as their tacit acceptance by such "antigovernment" politicians as Margaret Thatcher and Ronald Reagan demonstrates. Instead of the leader dominating government, government determines much that is done in the leader's name.

In a very real sense, the so-called power of a national leader depends upon actions that his government takes, whether or not this is desired by the leader. Instead of comparing the constitutional powers of leaders, we should compare the resources that are mobilized by the government for which a national leader is nominally responsible. The conventional measure of the size of government is public expenditure as a proportion of the gross national product. By this criterion, French or British government is more powerful than American government. Organization for Economic Cooperation and Development (OECD) statistics show that in 1984 French public expenditure accounted for 49 percent of the national product, British for 45 percent, and American for 37 percent. When attention is directed at central government, as distinct from all levels of government, the contrast is further emphasized. British and French central government collect almost two-fifths of the national product in tax revenue, whereas the American federal government collects only one-fifth.

When a national leader leads, others are meant to follow. The legitimacy of authority means that public employees should do what elected officials direct. In an era of big government, there are far more public employees at hand than in an era when the glory of the state was symbolized by a small number of people clustering around a royal court. Statistics of public employment again show British and French government as much more powerful than American government. Public employment in France accounts for 33 percent of all persons who work, more than Britain, with 31 percent. In the United States, public employment is much less, 18 percent.

The capacity of a national leader to direct public employees is much affected by whether or not such officials are actually employed by central government. France is most centralized, having three times as many public employees working in ministries as in regional or local government. If public enterprises are also reckoned as part of central government, France is even more centralized. In the United States and Great Britain, by contrast, the actual delivery of public services such as education and health is usually shipped out to lower tiers of a federal government, or to a complex of local and functional authorities. Delivering the everyday services of government is deemed beneath the dignity of national leaders in Great Britain. In the United States, central government is deemed too remote to be trusted with such programs as education or police powers.

When size of government is the measure, an American president appears weaker than a French or British leader. By international standards, the United States has a not so big government, for its claim on the national product and the national labor force is below the OECD average. Ronald Reagan is an extreme example of a president who is "antigovernment," but he is not the only example. In the past two decades, the United States has not lagged behind Europe in developing and expanding welfare state institutions that make government big. It has chosen to follow a different route, diverging from the European model of a mixed economy welfare state. Today, the president has very few large-scale program responsibilities, albeit they remain significant: defense and diplomacy, social security, and funding the federal deficit.

By contrast, even an "antigovernment" prime minister such as Margaret Thatcher finds herself presiding over a government that claims more than two-fifths of the national product in public expenditure. Ministers must answer, collectively and individually in the House of Commons, for all that is done under the authority of an Act of Parliament. In France, the division between president and prime minister makes it easier for the president of the republic to avoid direct entanglement in low status issues of service delivery, but the centralization of government necessarily involves the prime minister and his colleagues.

When attention is turned to the politics of government as distinct from public policies, all leaders have one thing in common, they are engaged in political management, balancing the interplay of forces within government, major economic interests, and public opinion generally. It is no derogation of a national leader's position to say that it has an important symbolic dimension, imposing a unifying and persuasive theme upon what government does. The theme may be relatively clear-cut, as in much of Margaret Thatcher's rhetoric. Or it may be vague and symbolic, as in much of the rhetoric of Charles de Gaulle. The comparative success of Ronald Reagan, an expert in manipulating vague symbols, as against Jimmy Carter, whose technocratic biases were far stronger than his presentational skills, is a reminder of the importance of a national political leader being able to communicate successfully to the nation.

In the United States and France, the president is both head of government and head of state. The latter role makes him president of all the people, just as the former role limits his representative character to governing in the name of a majority (but normally, less than 60 percent) of the voters. A British prime minister does not have the symbolic obligation to represent the country as a whole; the queen does that.

The institutions of government affect how political management is undertaken. The separate election of the president and the legislature in the United States and France create a situation of nominal independence, and bargaining from separate electoral bases. By contrast, the British prime minister is chosen by virtue of being leader of the largest party in the House of Commons. Management of Parliament is thus made much easier by the fact that the British prime minister can normally be assured of a majority of votes there.

An American president has a far more difficult task in managing government than do British and French counterparts. Congress really does determine whether bills become laws, by contrast to the executive domination of law and decree-making in Europe. Congressional powers of appropriation provide a basis for a roving scrutiny of what the executive branch does. There is hardly any bureau that is free from congressional scrutiny, and in many congressional influence may be as strong as presidential influence. By contrast, a French president has significant decree powers and most of the budget can be promulgated. A British prime minister can also invoke the Official Secrets Act and the doctrine of collective responsibility to insulate the effective (that is, the executive) side of government from the representative (that is, Parliament).

Party politics and electoral outcomes, which cannot be prescribed in a democratic constitution, affect the extent to which political management must be invested in persuasion. If management is defined as making an organization serve one's purpose, then Harry Truman gave the classic definition of management as persuasion: "I sit here all day trying to persuade people to do the things they ought to have sense enough to do without my persuading them. That's all the powers of the President amount to." Because both Democratic and Republican parties are loose coalitions, any president will have to invest much effort in persuading fellow partisans, rather than whipping them into line. Given different electoral bases, congressmen may vote their district, rather than their party label. When president and Congress are of opposite parties, then strong party ties weaken the president.

In Great Britain, party competition and election outcomes are expected to produce an absolute majority in the House of Commons for a single party. Given that the prime minister, as party leader, stands and falls with members of Parliament in votes in Parliament and at a general election, a high degree of party discipline is attainable. Given that the Conservative and Labor parties are themselves coalitions of differing factions and tendencies, party management is no easy task. But it is far easier than interparty management, a necessary condition of coalition government, including Continental European governments.

The Fifth Republic demonstrates that important constitutional features are contingent upon election outcomes. Inherent in the constitution of the Fifth Republic is a certain ambiguity about the relationship between president and prime minister. Each president has desired to make his office preeminent. The first three presidents had no difficulty in doing that, for they could rely upon the support of a majority of members of the National Assembly. Cooperation could not be coerced, but it could be relied upon to keep the prime minister subordinate.

Since the election of François Mitterrand in 1981, party has become an independent variable. Because the president's election in 1981 was paralleled by the election of a Left majority in the assembly, Mitterrand could adopt what J.E.S. Hayward describes in *Governing France* as a "Gaulist conception of his office." But after the victory of the Right in the 1986 Assembly election resulted in a non-Socialist being imposed as premier, Jacques Chirac, the president has had to accept a change of position, symbolized by the ambivalent term *cohabitation*.

Whether the criterion is government's size or the authority of the national leader vis-à-vis other politicians, the conclusion is the same: the political leaders of Great Britain and France can exercise more power than the president of the United States. The American presidency is a relatively weak office. America's population, economy, and military are not good measures of the power of the White House. Imagine what one would say if American institutions were transplanted, more or less wholesale, to some small European democracy. We would not think that such a country had a strong leader.

While differing notably in the separate election of a French president as against a parliamentary election of a British prime minister, both offices centralize authority within a state that is itself a major institution of society. As long as a French president has a majority in the National Assembly, then this office can have most influence within government, for ministers are unambiguously subordinate to the president. The linkage of a British prime minister's position with a parliamentary majority means that as long as a single party has a majority, a British politician is protected against the risks of cohabitation à la française or à la americaine.

Variations within Nations

An office sets parameters within which politicians can act, but the more or less formal stipulation of the rules and resources of an office cannot determine exactly what is done. Within these limits, the individual performance of a president or prime minister can be important. Events too are significant; everyday crises tend to frustrate any attempt to plan ahead, and major crises—a war or domestic disaster—can shift the parameters, reducing a politician's scope for action (for example, Watergate) or expanding it (for example, the mass mobilization that Churchill could lead after Dunkirk).

In the abstract language of social science, we can say that the actions of a national leader reflect the interaction of the powers of office, of events, and of personality. But in concrete situations, there is always an inclination to emphasize one or another of these terms. For purposes of exposition, I treat the significance of events and personality separately: each is but one variable in a multivariate outcome.

Social scientists and constitutional lawyers are inherently generalizers, whereas critical events are unique. For example, a study of the British prime ministership that ignored what could be done in wartime would omit an example of powers temporarily stretched to new limits. Similarly, a study of Winston Churchill's capacities must recognize that his personality prevented him from achieving the nation's highest office—until the debacle of 1940 thrust office upon him.

In the postwar era, the American presidency has been especially prone to shock events. Unpredictable and non-recurring events of importance include the outbreak of the Korean War in 1950, the assassination of President Kennedy in 1963, American involvement in the Vietnam War in the late 1960s, and the Watergate scandal, which led to President Nixon's resignation in 1974. One of the reasons for the positive popularity of Ronald Reagan has been that no disastrous event occurred in his presidency—at least until Irangate broke in November 1986.

The creation of the Fifth French Republic followed after events in Vietnam and in Algeria that undermined the authority and legitimacy of the government of the Fourth Republic. The events of May 1968 had a far greater impact in Paris than in any other European country. Whereas in 1958 events helped to create a republic with a president given substantial powers, in 1968 events were intended to reduce the authority of the state.

Great Britain has had relatively uneventful postwar government. Many causes of momentary excitement, such as the 1963 Profumo scandal that embarrassed

---

The French tradition of leadership is ambivalent.

Harold Macmillan, were trivial. The 1956 Suez war, which forced the resignation of Anthony Eden, did not lead to subsequent changes in the practice of the prime ministership, even though it was arguably a gross abuse of power vis-à-vis Cabinet colleagues and Parliament. The 1982 Falklands war called forth a mood of self-congratulation rather than a cry for institutional reform. The electoral boost it gave the prime minister was significant, but not eventful for the office.

The miner's strike, leading to a national three-day working week in the last days of the administration of Edward Heath in 1974, was perceived as a challenge to the authority of government. The prime minister called a general election seeking a popular mandate for his conduct of industrial relations. The mandate was withheld; so too was an endorsement of strikers. Characteristically, the events produced a reaction in favor of conciliation, for which Harold Wilson was particularly well suited at that stage of his career. Since 1979 the Thatcher administration has demonstrated that trade unions are not invincible. Hence, the 1974 crisis now appears as an aberration, rather than a critical conjuncture.

While personal factors are often extraneous to government, each individual incumbent has some scope for choice. Within a set of constraints imposed by office and events, a politician can choose what kind of a leader he or she would like to be. Such choices have political consequences. "Do what you can" is a prudential rule that is often overlooked in discussing what a president or prime minister does. The winnowing process by which one indi-

---

Campaigning for office makes a politician conscious of a need for popular approval.

---

vidual reaches the highest political office not only allows for variety, but sometimes invites it, for a challenger for office may win votes by being different from an incumbent.

A president has a multiplicity of roles and a multiplicity of obligations. Many—as commander in chief of the armed forces, delivering a State of the Union message to Congress, and presenting a budget—are requirements of the office; but the capacity to do well in particular roles varies with the individual. For example, Lyndon Johnson was a superb manager of congressional relations, but had little or no feel for foreign affairs. By contrast, John F. Kennedy was interested in foreign affairs and defense and initially had little interest in domestic problems. Ronald Reagan is good at talking to people, whereas Jimmy Carter and Richard Nixon preferred to deal with problems on paper. Dwight D. Eisenhower brought to the office a national reputation as a hero that he protected by making unclear public statements. By contrast, Gerald Ford's public relations skills, while acceptable in a congressman, were inadequate to the demands of the contemporary presidency.

In Great Britain, Margaret Thatcher is atypical in her desire to govern, as well as preside over government. She applies her energy and intelligence to problems of government—and to telling her colleagues what to do about them. The fact that she wants to be *the* decision-maker for British government excites resentment among civil servants and Cabinet colleagues. This is not only a reaction

to her forceful personality, but also an expression of surprise: other prime ministers did not want to be the chief decision-maker in government. In the case of an aging Winston Churchill from 1951-55, this could be explained on grounds of ill health. In the case of Anthony Eden, it could be explained by an ignorance of domestic politics.

The interesting prime ministers are those who chose not to be interventionists across a range of government activities. Both Harold Macmillan and Clement Attlee brought to Downing Street great experience of British government. But Attlee was ready to be simply a chairman of a Cabinet in which other ministers were capable and decisive. Macmillan chose to intervene very selectively on issues that he thought important and to leave others to get on with most matters. Labor leader Neil Kinnock, if he became prime minister, would adopt a noninterventionist role. This would be welcomed in reaction to Thatcher's dominating approach. It would be necesary because Kinnock knows very little about the problems and practice of British government. Unique among party leaders of the past half-century, he has never held office in government.

In France, the role of a president varies with personality. De Gaulle approached the presidency with a distinctive concept of the state as well as of politics. By contrast, Mitterrand draws upon his experience of many decades of being a parliamentarian and a republican. Pompidou was distinctive in playing two roles, first prime minister under de Gaulle, and subsequently president.

Differences between French prime ministers may in part reflect contrasting relationships with a president. As a member of a party different from the president, Chirac has partisan and personal incentives to be more assertive than does a prime minister of the same party. Premiers who enter office via the Assembly or local politics, like Chaban-Delmas and Mauroy, are likely to have different priorities than a premier who was first a technocrat, such as Raymond Barre.

Fluctuations in Leaders

The fluctuating effect upon leaders of multiple influences is shown by the monthly ratings of the popularity of presidents and prime ministers. If formal powers of office were all, then the popularity rating of each incumbent should be much the same. This is not the case. If the personal characteristics of a politician were all-important, then differences would occur between leaders, but each leader would receive a consistent rating during his or her term of office. In fact, the popularity of a national leader tends to go up and down during a term of office. Since personality is held constant, these fluctuations cannot be explained as a function of personal qualities. Since there is no consistent decline in popularity, the movement cannot be explained as a consequence of impossible expectations causing the public to turn against whoever initially wins its votes.

The most reasonable explanation of these fluctuations in popularity is that they are caused by events. They may be shock events, such as the threat of military action, or scandal in the leader's office. Alternatively, changes may reflect the accumulation of seemingly small events, most notably those that are reflected in the state of the economy, such as growth, unemployment, and inflation rates. A politician may not be responsible for such trends, but he or she expects to lose popularity when things appear to be going badly and to regain popularity when things are going well.

Through the decades, cyclical fluctuations can reflect an underlying long-term secular trend. In Europe a major secular trend is the declining national importance of international affairs. In the United States events in Iran or Central America remain of as much (or more) significance than events within the United States. In a multipolar world a president is involved in and more vulnerable to events in many places. By contrast, leaders of France and Great Britain have an influence limited to a continental scale, in a world in which international relations has become intercontinental. This shift is not necessarily a loss for heads of government in the European Community. In a world summit meeting, only one nation, the United States, has been first. Japan may seek to exercise political influence matching its growing economic power. The smaller scale of the European Community nations with narrower economic interests create conditions for frequent contact and useful meetings in the European arena which may bring them marginal advantages in world summit meetings too.

If the power of a national leader is measured, as Robert A. Dahl suggests in *Who Governs?*, by the capacity that such an individual has to influence events in the desired direction, then all national leaders are subject to seeing their power eroded as each nation becomes more dependent upon the joint product of the open international economy. This is as true of debtor nations such as the United States has become, as of nations with a positive trade balance. It is true of economies with a record of persisting growth, such as Germany, and of slow growth economies such as Great Britain.

A powerful national leader is very desirable only if one believes that the *Führerprinzip* is the most important principle in politics. The constitutions and politics of Western industrial nations reject this assumption. Each political system is full of constraints upon arbitrary rule, and sometimes of checks and balances that are obstacles to prompt, clear-cut decisions.

The balance between effective leadership and responsiveness varies among the United States, Great Britain, and France. A portion of that variation is organic, being prescribed in a national constitution. This is most evident in a comparison of the United States and Great Britain, but constitutions are variables, as the history of postwar France demonstrates. Many of the most important determinants of what a national leader does are a reflection of changing political circumstances, of trends and shock events, and of the aspirations and shortcomings of the individual in office.

NTL IDENTITY

EUROPE

My Country, Right . . . or What?

No DISRESPECT to Kuwait and its right to life, but its temporary disappearance does invite a question that can be crudely summarized thus: What use are countries these days? The United States, comfortable with its nationhood, is surely in no mood to ask itself what purpose it serves. But the countries of old Europe are. The continent that gave us the modern notion of country—or nation-state, as the political scientists would have it—is wondering what future its invention has.

There is nothing sacrosanct about countries as we know them. Most are too young. Half the countries of the world are less than forty years old. To peruse a nineteenth-century map of Europe is to recognize the reckless impermanence of history, with its squandered Prussias, Bohemias, and city-statelets, its departed Hapsburg, czarist, and Ottoman realms. It would be unreasonable to think that a map drawn in the twenty-first century won't hold larger surprises. Rearranging countries by one means or another is among man's favorite activities. Communism has been a great cementer of countries; it bullied them into staying the way they were. Its end is causing territorial havoc, not least by permitting the lid to come off ethnic rivalries that had been contained. At the moment, the Soviet Union and Yugoslavia are prime candidates for redesign.

The modern nation-state is little more than 200 years old, dating from around the time of the French Revolution. Only a few countries with long and coherent histories, like Britain, France, and Spain, had backgrounds perfectly suited for the role. Many European states exist because worried kings and wily statesmen simply hammered bits and pieces of land together.

The objective was not only to maintain a centralized government but also to graft a new popular awareness of national identity onto it. This latter goal grew out of overwhelming pressure to extend to ordinary people the political powers that monarchs, aristocrats, and churchmen had hitherto kept for themselves. As time went by, the goal came to be associated in the West with capitalism and democracy. So it is ironic that one of the crisper definitions of the modern nation (and a perfect explanation, for that matter, for why the Soviet Union is now falling apart) comes from Stalin: "A nation is a historically evolved, stable community of language, territory, economic life, and psychological makeup manifested in a common culture." Put a centralized government on top of that, allow for neutralized monarchs to remain in place where the populace retains a lingering respect for royalty, and you have the kind of modern country with which we are all familiar.

In the West the concept has brought great economic advances, though the nationalism it also encourages has at times had an abominable downside—as Nazi Germany illustrates. From the start much ingenuity and social engineering on the part of new political leaders was required to turn people into nations with a sense of patriotism, territory, and common purpose. "We have made Italy; now we have to make Italians," the Italian patriot Massimo d'Azeglio declared, with perhaps a touch of pessimism, as Garibaldi completed his territorial roundup. Hence national anthems, flags, and symbols were contrived. "They are much less ancient and traditional than everyone supposes," says the London University historian Eric Hobsbawm, the author of *Nations and Nationalism Since 1780*. The most reliable ruse for bonding together stray folk speaking miscellaneous dialects and having no particular sense of motherland, Hobsbawm says, was to unite them against outsiders.

KNOW YOUR ENEMY: this was always Britain's national forte, and it still is. Margaret Thatcher offered her people Europe to dislike, until finally her prejudice appeared counterproductive to her political princes. She was wrenched from her post as guardian of British sovereignty. But disregard for outsiders is in the nation's bones. Though Thatcher's successors are turning pro-European, Britain's diminishing sovereignty retains a vigorous defender in a tabloid press that curses "Argies," "Huns," and "Frogs" with equal relish. Similarly, Canadians seem to pursue their uneasy existence as a nation mainly to keep separate from the United States. In contrast, Americans stick together through an uncommon attachment to their institutions, which may be a healthier way to sustain national pride.

Even the French, so confident of their identity, are having nightmares about it. The Paris government has wanted to pander to the Corsicans by designating them the "Corsican people." Since the autonomy-minded Corsican islanders are, as clearly as the Danes or the Basques, a "people" with their own identity, this would not seem a startling departure. But it sets a most disagreeable precedent, opponents say. Soon the Bretons and the Alsatians will demand to be official peoples too. And when you are designated a people, you get big hitters on your side like the United Nations, which holds

From *The Atlantic*, July 1991, pp. 22, 24, 26. Copyright © 1991 by David Lawday.

that all peoples have the right to self-determination. Where will it all end?

Disillusionment with the nation-state is also strongly felt in Germany. Germans have been running away from nationalism since 1945. Reunification was carried out with not a hint of aggressive nationalist fervor. The accent was instead on the successful federal system that gives Germany's local regions more political responsibility than regions anywhere else in the European Community. East Germany was taken into the new Germany not as a state but in the form of six regions (Berlin included). Chancellor Helmut Kohl means to lock the door against a centralized system like those still operating in France, Britain, and other EC countries: "I believe there can be no return to the nation-state of the nineteenth century," he says. In the hesitancy of politicians to switch the capital from provincial Bonn to Berlin, with its patina of imperial power, one senses the German misgivings about re-emphasizing national identity.

Italians spend much time complaining about the futility of their government. Though the country seems to keep booming, one can see their point. The administration, dominated since Mussolini's fall by a single party, the Christian Democrats, settles for a budget deficit proportionally three times as big as the U.S. monster. Italy's public transport and postal services are awful by regular European standards. Enterprising Milanese firms send Alpine bearers north to Switzerland with the company mail to post it from there. "The Mafia is better organized than the Italian state, and more powerful," a Milan City Hall spokesman confided to me recently. Italians are fond of saying that in America the Mafia runs rackets while in Italy it runs the country. But the habitual complaint of the Milanese, and of most northerners, is that the wealth they create through their hard work is carried off to Rome in taxes and transferred as aid to the backward south, where it ends up in the Mafia treasury. Some $300 billion has taken the southbound route in the past forty years, but personal income in the south has slipped even further behind that in the north, so there must be something to the north's grousing. I asked Indro Montanelli, the editor of the Milan daily *Il Giornale* and the grand old man of Italian journalism,

about this. Sadly he told me, "Our state is completely decomposed."

A new Italian political movement succinctly demonstrates the quandary of the nation-state. The Lega Lombarda (Lombard League) wants to undo Garibaldi's work and split Italy into several autonomous parts. This would allow plump, serious Lombardy to exploit its talents in more suitable company—that is, in the company of the European Community heartland to the north. History has always put Lombards in closer contact with industrious Germans, Austrians, French, and Swiss than with southern Italians. Lombardy extends from the Alps to the River Po and from Piedmont to Lake Garda. Its nine million inhabitants, around 15 percent of Italy's population, are among Europe's high-flyers, hovering near the top of the living-standards lists. The province hums with small and medium-sized industry, accounting for some 25 percent of Italian national output. It retains a solid sense of administration from the disciplined Hapsburgs, who formerly ruled it.

If the Lega ruled Lombardy, it would take full control of taxes raised in the region, guarantee preferential jobs, social security, and housing to Lombards, and protect their culture and dialect. That done, it would slip Lombardy into the EC's direct embrace under cover of participation in some loose kind of new Italian confederation. "Europe has three levels now—the EC, the state, and the region," says Francesco Speroni, a founder of the Lega. "The weakest of these is the state. The state may well disappear. You can't tell me that states really represent the people in the new Europe. Often they were formed for the wrong reasons, by diplomats and generals." With an air of total conviction Speroni adds, "Italy is not a nation." Indro Montanelli, though more moderate politically, would agree with that. He holds that the country was never unified, not by Garibaldi and certainly not by Mussolini, with his bizarre dream of re-establishing the ancient Roman Empire. He sees Lega Lombarda supporters as simple people who feel more at home in Europe than in Italy.

W HAT WENT WRONG with the nation-state? Eric Hobsbawm reckons that the world econo-

my became too big for it. Just ten years ago the new President of France, François Mitterrand, tried a free-spending socialist experiment within French borders to get the national economy moving and make the poor rich, but was forced to abandon the experiment he had been elected to conduct. It was essentially the opposite of what the rest of the industrial world was then doing. "The nation-state has lost control," Hobsbawm concludes. "The world economy became so transnational that the state was bypassed."

Europe's established countries are, then, in an uncommon squeeze. The classic nation-state is too small for big things and too big for small things. The British political scientist David Marquand says that the growth of the EC—which could become a United States of Europe before the 1990s are out—has forced individual countries to recognize that they are too small to carry out their own separate economic, monetary, and environmental policies, let alone manage their own defense. Such matters used to lie at the jealous heart of sovereignty. They will be more effectively handled at the EC level. And yet, Marquand argues, European states remain too centralized or "big" to be effective in developing their own regions; they are simply not sensitive to local needs.

So the European state is squeezed by the EC on one side and by local regions that largely pre-date any sense of nationhood on the other. The economic and cultural identities of some of these ancient regions—Catalonia in Spain, Scotland in Britain, Bavaria in Germany, and so on—are far stronger than those of the countries in which they lie. These days, for self-advancement such regions are increasingly tempted to leapfrog their central governments and look straight to the EC as the mistress of their future.

What bids to replace the nation-state in Europe is a peculiar contraption, one that at first view seems a contradiction. The countries of Europe are simultaneously splintering into local units and consolidating into something bigger than any of them. If this begins to look a little like the United States, perhaps it's with good reason. An American, Hobsbawm says, is someone who wants to be one. Many Europeans have a like aspiration.

—*David Lawday*

AS THE WORLD TURNS DEMOCRATIC, FEDERALISM FINDS FAVOR

*Norman Ornstein and
Kimberly Coursen*

*Norman Ornstein is a resident scholar in
social and political processes at the
American Enterprise Institute. Kimberly
Coursen is a research assistant at the
American Enterprise Institute.*

NO WORD IN POLITICAL THEORY more consistently causes eyes to glaze over than "federalism." Yet no concept is more critical to solving many major political crises in the world right now. The former Soviet Union, Yugoslavia, Eastern and Western Europe, South Africa, Turkey, the Middle East, and Canada are suffering from problems that could be solved, if solutions are possible, by instituting creative forms of federalism.

Federalism is not a sexy concept like "democracy" or "freedom"; it describes a more mundane mechanism that balances the need for a central and coordinating authority at the level of a nation-state with a degree of state and local autonomy, while also protecting minority interests, preserving ethnic and regional identification and sensibilities, and allowing as much self-government as possible. Federalism starts with governing structures put in place by formal, constitutional arrangements, but beyond that it is a partnership that requires trust. Trust can't be forged overnight by formal arrangements, but bad arrangements can exacerbate hostilities and tensions. Good ones can be the basis for building trust.

Why is federalism so important now? There are political reasons: the breakup of the old world order has released resentments and tensions that had been suppressed for decades or even centuries. Ethnic pride and self-identification are surging in many places around the globe. Add to this the easy availability of weapons, and you have a potent mixture for discontent, instability, and violence. There are also economic considerations: simply breaking up existing nation-states into separate entities cannot work when economies are interlinked in complex ways. And there are

Each country has unique problems that require different kinds of federal structures, which can range from a federation that is tightly controlled at the center to a confederation having autonomous units and a loose central authority.

humane factors, too. No provinces or territories are ethnically pure. Creating an independent Quebec, Croatia, or Kazakhstan would be uplifting for French Quebecois, Croats, and Kazakhs but terrifying for the large numbers of minorities who reside in these same territories.

The only way to begin to craft solutions, then, is to create structures that preserve necessary economic links while providing economic independence, to create political autonomy while preserving freedom of movement and individual rights, and to respect ethnic identity while protecting minority rights. Each country has unique problems that require different kinds of federal structures, which can range from a federation that is tightly controlled at the center to a confederation having autonomous units and a loose central authority.

The United States pioneered federalism in its Union and its Constitution. Its invention of a federation that balanced power between a vigorous national government and its numerous states was every bit as significant an innovation as its instituting a separation of powers was in governance—and defining the federal-state relationship was far more difficult to work out at the Constitutional Convention in 1787.

The U.S. federalist structure was, obviously, not sufficient by itself to eliminate the economic and social disparities between the North and the South. Despite the federal guarantees built into the Constitution, the divisive questions of states' rights dominated political conflict from the beginning and resulted ultimately in the Civil War. But the federal system did keep conflict from boiling over into disaster for 75 years, and it has enabled the United States to keep its union together without constitutional crisis or major bloodshed for the 125 years

From *The American Enterprise*, January/February 1992, pp. 20-24. Copyright © 1992, The American Enterprise. Distributed by The New York Times Special Features.

since the conclusion of the War Between the States. It has also enabled us to meliorate problems of regional and ethnic discontent.

The American form of federalism fits the American culture and historical experience—it is not directly transferable to other societies. But if ever there was a time to apply the lessons that can be drawn from the U.S. experience or to create new federal approaches, this is it. What is striking is the present number of countries and regions where deep-scated problems could respond to a new focus on federalism.

A World in Ferment

• **The former Soviet Union.** Its crisis is particularly acute and salient now as Mikhail Gorbachev, Boris Yeltsin, and leaders of the other republics struggle to find a way to keep some remnants of a union together while allowing extensive political and cultural autonomy.

In the wake of the hard-line coup in August, Gorbachev proposed that the all-Soviet Congress of People's Deputies relinquish the bulk of its power to the 12 republics. The plan included the rough outlines of a central governmental system. The system was to consist of a State Council, responsible for foreign affairs, the military, defense, and law enforcement; a bicameral parliament, with voting members from each of the participating republics; and an Interrepublic Economic Committee, which would manage the economy and implement reform. Seven republics indicated that they would sign on.

Taken together, these changes represented a near-180-degree change from a strongly centralized government to one of the most decentralized confederations anywhere. Nevertheless, some of the largest republics persisted in the view that any degree of power held by the center was too much. Ukraine voted overwhelmingly for independence on December 1, and on December 8, Russia, Ukraine, and Byelorussia teamed up to create a "Commonwealth of Independent States." The trio of republics, which together comprise 73 percent of the population and produce 80 percent of the industrial output of what was the Soviet Union, declared that "the U.S.S.R. as a subject of international law and geopolitical reality is ceasing to exist."

Specifically, what the group has pro-

posed is the establishment of "coordinating bodies" to control economic and foreign policy as well as the union's vast nuclear arsenal. In addition, the republics would share a common currency and common transportation and communications systems. The details are still sketchy, and they will undoubtedly meet with resistance, particularly from those who were not included in the negotiations leading up to this historic proposal.

The Gorbachev and the Commonwealth plans have some similarities: both are loose confederations of independent states that would join together for mutual advantage yet maintain a significant degree of autonomy over most issues. The difference between the two plans is one of degree. The greatest obstacle will be to define the precise relationship between the center and the republics.

Even when that is done, the new structure will have to deal with the simmering problem of ethnic distrust. A recent Times Mirror survey of three Soviet republics—Russia, Ukraine, and

> **In the former Soviet Union, the greatest obstacle will be to define the precise relationship between the center and the republics. Even when that is done, the new structure will have to deal with the simmering problem of ethnic distrust.**

Lithuania—showed strikingly high levels of animosity between ethnic groups. For example, four in ten Russians and Ukrainians said they had an unfavorable opinion of Azerbijanis (by comparison, only 13 percent of white Americans hold unfavorable opinions of blacks).

In describing the Commonwealth proposal, Russian Foreign Minister Andrei Kozyrev raised the specter of ethnic fracturing when he said, "This is the only and possibly the last opportunity to avoid what has happened in Yugoslavia." Ethnic animosity creates difficulties between Soviet republics but also within them. The republics, after all, are not ethnically pure. Any federal approach, if there is to be one, will have to include some innova-

tive forms of protection for minority populations.

• **Yugoslavia.** Here the problems start with ethnicity. The ethnic and political differences between Serbs and Croats have precipitated a bloody civil war, which is diverting attention from the deep divisions and suspicions between Bosnians, Macedonians, Slovenians, and Montenegrans.

The six republics that now make up Yugoslavia were created in the wake of World War I from the Ottoman and Austro-Hungarian Empires. After World War II, those six republics and two autonomous regions were forged into a federation under Marshall Josip Broz Tito. For nearly 50 years, his and his successors' harsh dictatorial control from Belgrade kept historic ethnic hatreds suppressed enough to keep the nation-state together.

In the late 1970s, in response to growing ethnic strife, the tightly controlled central government began to decentralize its activities. The individual republics and provinces were granted a great deal of autonomy, and representatives from the regions were given a say—through a de facto veto power—in economic and social policies decided at the federal level. But the new arrangements did not encourage any kind of cross-regional cooperation; ultimately, they resulted in a highly decentralized federation in which ethnic identities and inter-ethnic rivalries became increasingly institutionalized.

Tito's strong hand kept things together until his death in 1980, but his departure left a government unable to manage an integrated economy or to create any level of trust between republics or across ethnic lines. When the Communist Party, the only remaining entity sustaining the Yugoslav state, collapsed in 1990, the country fell apart. Had Tito created a loose confederation of states with economic incentives to cooperate and with legal and other guarantees built in for protection of ethnic minorities—and had he worked to infuse the central government with more of an ethnic mix—the country might have been able to cope with the revolutionary changes of the 1990s. Instead, there emerged a system of freely elected leaders in the various rival republics who are now pursuing their own agendas. Slovenia and Croatia have already declared their independence. While the situation in Slovenia stabilized after an initial period of violence, Croatia is a different story. The large number of ethnic Serbs living in Croatia, fearing to lose their own status, have resisted becoming a part of an independent state. They have been supported by Serbia, which controls the army, and the result has been a Serbo-Croatian civil war.

The situation is made even more complicated by the fact that the drive for a continuing central authority for a Yugoslav federation is coming mainly from Serbia, whose leader, Slobodan Milosevic, an unreconstructed communist and a Serbian nationalist, is not trusted by anybody except the ethnic Serbs.

It may not be possible to keep Yugoslavia from splintering into six or more separate fiefdoms, each eager to suppress the ethnic minorities that reside within its borders. If there is any chance to hold Yugoslavia together—as recent European action is designed to do—it will come through some innovative federal arrangement that guarantees ethnic safety and freedom, safeguards provincial autonomy, and yet retains some form of national economic coordination and sovereignty. Questions of minority rights are the first ones that have to be answered, but they will be followed by other knotty questions of economics, common foreign policy, and what kind of central authority can exist.

Ultimately, formulas for creative federalism may be needed in Czechoslovakia, Romania, Bulgaria, and other countries in Eastern and Central Europe that also have histories of ethnic dominance and conflict.

• **Canada.** The Quebec crisis demands a new balance of power between the central government in Ottawa and the provinces, something that was nearly achieved by the Meech Lake Accord in 1990 but is now in serious jeopardy. Prime Minister Brian Mulroney has created a new plan specifically aimed at preventing the secession of Quebec. It proposes the most comprehensive restructuring of Canada's federal system since the nation's founding in 1867. The plan would grant Quebec constitutional recognition as a "distinct" society, based on its unique language, culture, and civil law, but it also envisions sweeping changes in economic and political power between Ottawa and the provinces. Interprovincial trade barriers would be eliminated, and a new Council of the Federation would be installed to mediate

disputes that might arise between the provinces.

In exchange for this increase in central control, the provinces would be granted more influence over issues of national economic policy as well as greater authority over immigration and cultural matters. In addition, at the insistence of the western provinces, the current appointed Senate would be replaced by an elected, more representative, and more consequential upper house.

Meech Lake II, as Mulroney's new plan is called, has a better chance to succeed than the original accord. But it causes discontent in minority groups, such as Indians and Eskimos, and continues to be viewed with skepticism and even outright hostility by many of the western provinces. Several of these are now governed by the New Democrats, who are less wedded to the plan devised by the Progressive-Conservative prime minister.

Meech Lake II would grant Quebec constitutional recognition as a "distinct" society, but it also envisions sweeping changes in economic and political power between Ottawa and the provinces.

• **South Africa.** The issue here is not only minority rights but also political balance. Any long-term solution to the political crisis in South Africa has to provide some sense of assurance and some real and meaningful political role for the white minority, at the same time providing full political rights and a full political role for the black majority. Both the African National Congress (ANC) and President de Klerk have offered their own plans. There are similarities: both institute universal suffrage; both propose a bicameral parliament, with one house elected by population and the other organized on regional lines; both establish an independent judiciary and a bill of rights.

But there are major differences between the plans. De Klerk's plan calls for a decentralized system for nine regions rather than the four provinces that now exist, with a central government headed by an executive council rather than by a powerful single president. The ANC plan

envisions a much more centralized system than de Klerk's, with a strong executive able to appoint his own prime minister. Negotiations between de Klerk and the ANC will include discussions not only about federal political arrangements and guarantees for blacks and whites but also about the degree of central control over the economy.

• **Hong Kong.** As the result of a 1984 treaty, Britain will turn control of Hong Kong over to the People's Republic of China in 1997. The treaty guarantees that the Chinese government will not interfere in Hong Kong's economic system, that it will be "one country, two systems"; however, the language of the treaty is vague and open to a variety of interpretations. Because of Tiananmen Square, there is widespread fear in Hong Kong and doubt that China will honor the letter or the spirit of the treaty. Thus, there has been increased emigration and substantial capital flight from Hong Kong, and some are predicting political and economic chaos before the turn of the century.

To keep Hong Kong a free-market democracy while bringing it into the orbit of the People's Republic may require more innovative forms of federalism. There are many incentives for China to explore such options—more than just the economic one of keeping alive the goose that lays the golden egg of hard foreign currency. There is also the desire to find a form of governance for Hong Kong that might be a model attractive enough to make a political, federal alliance possible between the People's Republic and the Republic of China on Taiwan.

• **The Middle East.** The peace conference in Madrid in October and the talks in Washington in December were times for posturing, deciding who is represented, who is representing the represented, and how to proceed from there. The underlying issue—resolving the Arab/Israeli conflict—has yet to be addressed. When it is, the resolution of the Palestinian/Israeli component will inevitably turn to how to govern the West Bank and Gaza—how Jews and Arabs can co-exist politically, economically, and socially.

Some form of co-federation, with shared governance, will have to be on the table. The issue would be much easier to resolve if Jordan east of the Jordan River were considered the base of a

Palestinian state, making the West Bank an ancillary, not a central, territory. But Jordan's role aside, creative federalist solutions for these disputed territories is a must. They might include some form of co-citizenship with Israel, Jordan, and the West Bank itself; they might include some innovative economic arrangements. Federalism may also be invoked to resolve the Golan Heights dispute with Syria.

• **Western Europe.** The Soviets and others are carefully watching Europe's attempt at economic and political union known as Europe '92. Their interest is more than geopolitical. In a way, the European Community faces a situation similar to that faced by struggling nations around the world. The EC consists of a group of ethnically and culturally diverse nation-states attempting to establish an integrated and coordinated economic and political system. The compromise reached at the historic meeting in December 1991 may serve as a model of sorts for other countries experimenting with both democracy and new forms of federalism.

The European Community has been predicated primarily on common economic interests. The 12 member-states have already agreed that by January 1, 1993, the EC will be a single economic market, with free movement of capital, goods, and services among its members, making it the most powerful trading bloc in the world. Members have also agreed, more problematically, to establish a common currency and a regional central bank.

Real political union is a less certain proposition. There is a consensus that economic union has to be complemented by some common political structure. But the Europeans divide sharply over whether the community should become a tightly knit federation with central political control over foreign and defense policy and legal matters as well as economic ones, or whether it should be a loose confederation of independent states linked primarily for economic reasons. Germany and France prefer the former, Britain the latter. Eventually, the inherent French suspicion of the Germans may move them into a closer alliance with the British.

> **There is also the desire to find a form of governance for Hong Kong that might be a model attractive enough to make a political, federal alliance possible between the People's Republic and the Republic of China on Taiwan.**

Even after the departure of Margaret Thatcher and her tough anti-Community rhetoric, the British have continued to make clear their deep reluctance to embrace the centralized system of majority rule that the French have proposed. Currently, the European Commission, the executive arm of the EC, operates under a system of unanimous rule in which each member-state retains a veto power. The British are adamant about keeping this system intact. The bigger issues of political power aside, arguments going on now over standards and regulations for transcontinental construction, disputes over how to handle defense and regional security, and questions of whether and when Eastern European nations should be invited to join the Community suggest that it will be a long time before a true European federation takes shape.

Summary

In the final analysis, nations and regions will hold together or come together in the modern world if their economic interests demand it. Even then, the potential for self-destruction, atomization, substantial bloodshed, even all-out war, is very great. A common interest in economic advancement provides the incentive to try to find structural solutions to political and social problems. But it is a delicate matter to find structures that can allay primal fears of genocide, legitimize emerging national identities, and divide up economic and political powers and goodies in a fashion that will be seen as fair to everybody. It is here that creative federalism can play its role.

The United States may be able to at least point the way. Our innovations in decentralized federal arrangements as well as our experience in sorting out powers and rights between Washington and the states could well be adapted to many troubled situations elsewhere today. One especially significant American example may well turn out to be the U.S. Senate. Creating a second legislative chamber with real authority, prestige, and legitimacy, that is divided along state (or regional, or ethnic, or racial) lines, may be an initial way for shaky unions to balance their centrifugal forces and centripetal needs. Creative structures alone will not solve the problems of a prostrate Soviet central economy, keep Serbs and Croats from murdering one another, or bring blacks and whites together in South Africa, much less Palestinians and Israelis in the Middle East. While creative federalism may not be enough, it is surely essential for peaceful transition and successful governance.

Staging post on the path to federalism

Regional policy in the EC is here to stay, writes **Andrew Adonis,** despite the government's qualms

[It] is not just on a single currency and Social Chapter that Mr John Major finds himself isolated in Europe. The prime minister's hostility to the creation of a regional tier of government—even in Scotland—leaves Britain in another minority of one among the Community's larger states. It also leaves the Conservatives as lone defenders of the status quo at home: Labour is committed to Scottish home rule and regional assemblies for England and Wales, while the Liberal Democrats are proposing a virtually federal future for the UK.

It is not just regional *government* that raises Tory hackles: ministers are at odds over anything resembling a regional *policy.* Nevertheless, regional policy is here to stay: at the Maastricht summit Mr Major signed the protocol on "economic and social cohesion", which pledges the Community to spend more on "reducing the disparities between the levels of development of the various regions". The structural funds, to help backward or declining areas, have doubled—to Ecu 14bn (£10bn)—in the past three years: their future funding is to be reviewed next year, and a new "cohesion fund" is planned for 1994.

Britain's self-styled regions are already energetic supplicants in Brussels.

The Assembly of Welsh Counties is, jointly with the Welsh Development Agency, about to set up a permanent office in Brussels, and Scottish councils will follow suit.

Britain has only become the odd man out in the past two decades. When the Community was founded in 1957, only one of its member states had institutionalised regions: by 1987, most of the 12 did. Individual regions came together in 1985 in their own pan-European body. The Assembly of European Regions (AER) has long pressed for a formal Community role, and got it at Maastricht (Britain assenting) in the form of an advisory Committee of the Regions. Within the Community, "Europe of the Regions" is a slogan mouthed as much as "1992" nowadays.

Not content with its gains, the AER's congress last month called on "the governments of those member states which have not initiated the process of regionalisation [read Britain] to make the necessary institutional changes to this end". This implies that there is a regional model Britain ought to follow.

Is there and should it?

Political scientists have laboured hard to define "regionalism", and to relate it to theories of the state and of

the allocation of functions and intergovernmental relations within it. In essence, however, if regionalism means anything other than glorified local government, it is a staging post to federalism, a state in which sovereignty is shared between governmental tiers.

There is, however, no single regional mode going. "There is no such thing as a standard intermediate tier in Europe, just a set of contrasting regional systems," says Mr Michael Hebbert, a regional expert at the London School of Economics.

The move towards regions, and their form, has had as much to do with the culture and political evolution of particular countries as with theory. Perceptions of cultural autonomy on the one hand, and reactions to the authoritarian rule on the other, have been the strongest influences.

The German case needs little explanation—a number of Länder (states) were, in 1949, artificial creations. The two influences combined also lay behind the commitment to regions in Italy (a state only since 1860) and Spain (five languages, no central administration to speak of until the mid-18th century, and two civil wars since).

In Belgium, the bitter cultural divide

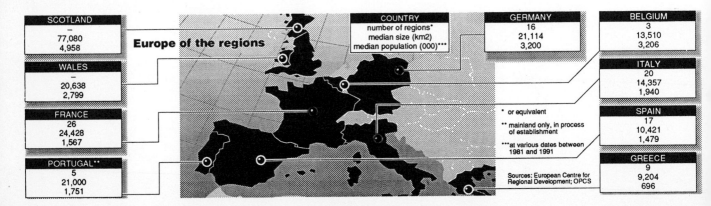

Europe of the regions

SCOTLAND		COUNTRY	GERMANY	BELGIUM
–		number of regions*	16	3
77,080		median size (km2)	21,114	13,510
4,958		median population (000)***	3,200	3,206

WALES				ITALY
–				20
20,638				14,357
2,799				1,940

FRANCE				SPAIN
26				17
24,428				10,421
1,567				1,479

PORTUGAL**				GREECE
5				9
21,000				9,204
1,751				696

* or equivalent
** mainland only, in process of establishment
***at various dates between 1981 and 1991

Sources: European Centre for Regional Development; OPCS

Reprinted from *Financial Times*, December 20, 1991, p. 15.

between Flanders and Wallonia precipitated repeated political crises in the 1960s, and the introduction of regions in 1971 recognised demands for devolution long formulated by the two linguistic communities. Even in France, the creation of elected regions by Mitterrand's socialists in 1982 was a response to their 23 years in the political wilderness.

For the most part, defining regions geographically has not been a problem. Kingdoms, cities, principalities, islands, linguistic communities have formed most of the boundaries. In France, regions are amalgamations of *départements*.

Accordingly, regions come in all sizes. The typical European region is about the size of four English county councils. Yet Germany's Saarland, Italy's Umbria and Spain's Cantabria have smaller populations than Kent and Lancashire, while two German Länder have larger populations than Belgium—and without the likes of Bavaria (11m residents) and North Rhine-Westphalia (16.9m) the Länder would wield far less political clout.

Europe's regions differ in functions almost as much as in size. Constitutionally, the 16 German Länder have the greatest autonomy, with each Land enjoying its own legal system, a share in national law-making, control over most of the country's civil service, and sole or shared powers over education, health, criminal law, local government, economic development, housing, roads and the environment.

Belgium's regions now enjoy legal powers almost as wide, while, at the other extreme, French regions are largely confined to regional economic development, cultural promotion and the submission of plans and opinions for Paris to approve. Spain is exceptional in that each of its 17 "autonomous communities" has its own "statue of autonomy", specifying devolved powers, with Andalucia, Catalonia, the Basque country and Galicia—regions with a strong sense of autonomy—first in the queue.

Nonetheless, concentration on regions' legal powers can be misleading. In the first place, regional tax-raising powers are, without exception, constrained. Even the west German Länder raise only a small proportion of their income, and are dependent upon assigned revenues or grants for the rest.

Conversely, regions wield much of their influence on a co-operative or informal basis. Italian regions, for example, are represented on national parliamentary committees, and their presidents meet the Rome government regularly. In Germany, Mr Helmut Kohl is a former Land prime minister; his Social Democrat opposite number, Mr Bjorn Engholm, is prime minister of Schleswig-Holstein. Imagine Mr Kinnock president of Wales; or Mrs Thatcher mayor of London.

What are the more likely implications for Britain? The European experience is most applicable to Scotland, where elections and opinion surveys show greater Scottish alienation from Westminster than at any time this century. Moreover, the practicalities of devolution from London to a Scottish parliament get simpler by the year, as ever more powers are devolved to the Scottish Secretary.

Wales is similarly placed, though with less devolution and alienation. England, however, is highly problematic.

Much of England does not belong to "self-regarding" regions—though the likes of Cumbria and Cornwall could be made regions if local sentiment necessitated it. Equally important is the absence of any equivalent of the French prefectoral system imposing a settled regional pattern to national administration.

Each UK government department and quango has its own regional boundaries for its activities, and they rarely match. Periodically since the war attempts have been made to align regional boundaries with the government's so-called "standard regions"—but with little success, according to Professor Brian Hogwood of Strathclyde University.

The first step to regional government in England would, therefore, have to be the aligning of *existing* boundaries. Beyond that, rolling devolution, with Scotland and possibly Wales leading the way, appears the only practical course. It looks Spanish in style, but if voters ever decide that Westminster and Whitehall do not always know best, it may be the only way.

Europe—West, Center, and East: The Politics of Integration, Transformation, and Disintegration

- The European Continent (Article 31)
- The Politics of European Integration (Articles 32–35)
- Post-Communist Central and Eastern Europe (Article 36)
- Russia and the Other Post-Soviet Republics (Articles 37–42)

All the articles in this unit are in some way linked to one of two major developments that fundamentally have altered the political map of Europe in recent years. The first of these major changes is the gradual integration of many Western European states within the supranational framework of the European Community (EC). Here the development is primarily one by which sovereign states have piecemeal given up some of their traditional independence, especially in matters dealing with economic and monetary policy. Some important decisions that used to be made by national governments in Paris, Rome, Bonn, and Copenhagen have become the province of the EC representatives in Brussels.

The second major disruption of the established state system goes in the other direction. It consists of the more recent and rapid disintegration brought about by the collapse of Communist rule in Central and Eastern Europe. Here states, nations, and nationalities have broken away from an imposed system of central control, and now assert their political and societal independence from the previous ruling group and its Communist ideology.

A closer look at the countries of Western Europe reveals that they also have their share of problems, even if in a far less acute form than their counterparts to the east. Their relative affluence rests on a base built up during the prolonged postwar economic boom of the 1950s and 1960s. Between the early 1970s and the mid-1980s, Western industrial societies were beset by economic disruptions that brought an end to the long period of rapidly growing prosperity. The last half of the 1980s marked some improvement to the economic situation in most of Western Europe, partly as a result of some favorably timed positive trade balances with the United States.

The economic downturn had come in the wake of sharp rises in the cost of energy, linked to successive hikes in the price of oil imposed by the Organization of Petroleum Exporting Countries (OPEC) after 1973. In the 1980s, OPEC lost its organizational bite, as its members began to compete against each other by raising production and lowering prices rather than abiding by the opposite practices in the manner of a well-functioning cartel agreement. The resulting improvement for the consumers of oil helped the Western European economies recover, but as a whole they did not rebound to their earlier high growth rates. The short Persian Gulf War did not seriously hamper the flow of Middle East oil in 1991, but it once again underscored the continuing vulnerability of Europe to external interruptions in its energy supply.

Because of their dependence on international trade, West European economies are vulnerable to the kind of global recessionary tendencies we have known during the past couple of years. Another important challenge to these affluent countries is found in the stiff competition they face from the new industrial countries (NICs) of East and South Asia, where productivity is high and labor costs remain lower than in Western Europe. The emergent Asian factor has probably contributed to the increased tempo of the European drive for economic integration. Some observers have warned of the possibility that major trading blocs in Europe, North America, and Eastern Asia could replace the relatively free system of international trade established in the post-1945 period.

In the mid-1980s, there was widespread talk of a malaise or "Europessimism" that had beset these countries. Thereafter the mood appeared to become more upbeat, and for a while some observers even detected a swing toward a supposed "Europhoria." It is advisable to add some salt to such generalizations about public moods, but there does seem to be a more sober spirit abroad once again. Some observers plausibly link this change to the economic and social problems associated with an international recession as well as the dislocations that have accompanied the end of the cold war. There can be little doubt that the countries of Western Europe have been affected by the chaotic conditions left behind by the former Communist regimes to the east. There is a competition for scarce capital, as the countries in Eastern Europe seek to attract investments that will build a new and modern economic infrastructure. At the same time, the daily pain and poverty of life in Eastern Europe has encouraged a migration to the relatively affluent societies of the West. Those who attempt the big move resemble in many ways the immigrants who have been attracted to the United States in the past and present. The major point of difference is that many West Europeans are unwilling to accept what they regard as a flood of unwanted strangers.

There can be no doubt that the issues of immigration and multicultural tensions in Western Europe will occupy a central place on the political agenda in the coming years. We have already discussed the symbolic and substantive accommodations that some of the established parties have made to appease protesting voters, who are seen as potential supporters of right-wing extremist movements. But there are also groups that make no such compromises but instead oppose directly the racist and xenophobic elements in their own societies. Some enlightened political leaders and commentators seek to promote the reasonable perspective that the immigrants could turn out to be an important asset rather than a liability. This argument may concede that the influx of immigrants involves some social cost in the short run, at least during a recessionary period, but it emphasizes that the newcomers can be a very important human resource that will contribute to mid- and long-term economic prosperity.

The European Community took another leap forward, even if a

somewhat tentative one, during its Maastricht meeting in December of 1991. Two articles from *The Economist* chart the growth and the open future of the EC, while an article from the *Los Angeles Times* explains the set-up and workings of its main institutional arrangements. There will be a need for further institutional reform, and the European Community will have to deal with the problem of a possible rise of international trade blocs. Some keen observers warn that the celebration of Europe 1992, which really refers to the abolition of restrictions in the flow of goods, capital, services, and labor by January 1, 1993, has served to cover up some remaining or newly emerging obstacles to a full economic integration of the Community.

While much ink has been spilled on the problems of a transition from a market economy to state socialism, we have little theory or practice to guide East Europeans who are moving in the opposite direction. A new and major theoretical argument, which has important policy consequences, thus concerns the best strategy for restructuring the economies of the former Communist countries.

The same debate has been carried out in the former Soviet Union during the past few years. In some ways, it could be argued that Mikhail Gorbachev failed to opt clearly for one or the other approach to economic reform. But he seems not only to have been ambivalent about the means but about the ends of his *perestroika* or restructuring of the centrally planned economy. He remained far too socialist for some born-again marketeers in his own country, while Communist hard-liners never forgave him for dismantling a system in which they had enjoyed a modicum of security and privilege.

But the Achilles' heel of the now defunct Soviet Union turned out to be its multiethnic character. Gorbachev was not alone in underestimating the potential centrifugal tendencies of a country that was based on an ideological and political redefinition of the old Russian Empire. Many of the non-Russian minorities were ethnic majorities within their own territory, and this made it possible for them to long for greater autonomy or even national independence in a way that the scattered ethnic groups of the United States do not.

Most important of all, glasnost and democratization gave those ethnic minorities in the Soviet Union, who had a territorial identity, an opportunity to demand autonomy or independence. The first national assertions came from the Baltic peoples in Estonia, Latvia, and Lithuania, who had been forced back under Russian rule in 1940, after some two decades of national independence. Very soon other nationalities, including the Georgians and Armenians, expressed similar demands through the political channels that had been opened to them. The death knell for the Soviet Union sounded in 1991, when the Ukrainians, who constituted the second largest national group in the Soviet Union after the Russians, made similar demands for independence.

In a very real sense, then, Gorbachev's political reforms ended up as a threat not only to the continued leadership role by the Communist party but also to the continued existence of the Soviet Union itself. Gorbachev seems to have understood neither of these consequences of his reform attempts until quite late, and that would seem to explain why he could set in motion forces that would ultimately destroy what he had hoped to make more attractive and productive. The attempted coup against the reformer and his reforms, in August 1991, came far too late and was too poorly organized to have succeeded. In fact, the would-be coup d'état became instead a coup de grace for the Soviet Communists and, in the end, the Soviet Union as well. Some-what reluctantly, Gorbachev declared the party illegal soon after he had been returned to office by the resistance, led by Russian President Boris Yeltsin, who had broken with communism earlier and more decisively.

After his formal restoration to power, Gorbachev became politically dependent on someone who had once been his protégé and then became his bitter critic before turning out to be his rescuer. It was a remarkable development, which is described and analyzed in some of the articles of the last subsection. But Gorbachev had become a transitional figure, as some observers concluded right after the abortive coup. His own days as Soviet president were numbered when the Soviet Union ceased to exist at the end of December 1991. It was replaced by the Commonwealth of Independent States, a very loose union without any important institutional framework to hold it together. The CIS seemed destined to be a transitional device that could serve as a useful link between the former Soviet republics, as they negotiate what to do with the economic, military, and other institutional leftovers of the old system and try to shape new and useful links to each other for the future.

The article by Serge Scheeman takes the form of an obituary on the Soviet Union, which died in December 1991, soon after entering its seventy-fifth year. In another contribution, Michael Dobbs reviews the strengths and shortcomings of Mikhail Gorbachev, who ended up destroying a system that could have held on longer but, apparently, could not be reformed. Not everyone would agree with such a conclusion, as we learn from the interview with Stephen F. Cohen, long recognized as one of the foremost American experts on Soviet communism. A careful reader will notice that Cohen responds in part to a criticism of his views that is contained in the article by Martin Malia, who appears to be more impressed by Boris Yeltsin's attempt to build a post-Communist order. An internationally-known Russian dissident, Vladimir Bukovsky, draws some distressing historical parallels to Weimar, Germany, in his portrayal of economic chaos and political instability in today's Russia.

Looking Ahead: Challenge Questions

What are the major obstacles to the emergence of a more unified Europe? What differentiates the optimists and the skeptics as they assess the outlook for greater integration?

What was the Maastricht Treaty of December 1991 about? Why do some supporters of European integration see it as yet another leap forward?

What are the main problems facing the newly elected governments in Eastern and Central Europe? How well are they doing in coping with the transition to political pluralism and a market economy?

Was Gorbachev mistaken to believe that the Soviet Union could be reformed without being dissolved? How did he and Yeltsin differ in their views about reform before the abortive coup in August 1991?

How do Stephen F. Cohen and Martin Malia differ in their assessments of both Gorbachev and Yeltsin?

A Divided Continent Sees Shared Destiny

The breeding ground of two world wars is trying to erase old boundaries. Up to 30 nations hope to meld into history's largest voluntary confederation.

Joel Havemann

Times Staff Writer

BRUSSELS—It won't happen in 1992. It won't even happen in the 1990s. But, gradually and painstakingly, the continent whose bloody rivalries bred this century's two cataclysmic world wars is transforming itself into something that might one day resemble a "United States of Europe."

Never in the history of humankind have so many nations voluntarily come together to sacrifice so much of their sovereign power. From mighty Germany to tiny Albania, as many as 20 or 30 nations are in various stages of binding themselves into a confederation that will share a common economic and even political destiny.

This is not the equivalent of 13 new and largely similar American states forming a more perfect union. Europe's nations have existed side by side for centuries, speaking different languages and developing distinct cultures. Their shared history mostly involves centuries of fighting wars against one another.

Many Europeans even object to the label "United States of Europe" as carrying the wrong connotations: a powerful central government and devotion to laissez-faire capitalism, American style.

Although the implied comparison is inevitable, what is actually evolving here is a much looser confederation of democratic nations built around Western Europe's 12-nation European Community. For the EC, this is a landmark year; under the program dubbed "EC '92," its member nations are supposed by the end of 1992 to have torn down most artificial barriers to commerce among themselves.

Europe has just set off down a long road. If it reaches the end, its national economies will be tightly integrated in a system of free markets tempered heavily by social welfare. A central authority will formulate foreign, social and environmental policies. The individual nations will retain authority over actually running things.

"A united Europe will not be based on the American principle of the melting pot," says Peter Ludlow, director of the Center for European Policy Studies in Brussels. "It will be based on the principle of the diversity of nation-states."

This Europe promises to become an increasingly strong economic competitor of the United States. More than that, it could pose a challenge—a healthy one, in many Europeans' eyes—to America's post–Cold War status as the globe's dominant diplomatic power.

Speaking publicly, U.S. leaders welcome the prospect of a united Europe as a strong ally on the world scene. Privately, however, some express concerns about Europe's challenge.

"It is evident that Americans will have much difficulty with Europe if unity succeeds," says Jacques Delors, Europe's leading unifier as president of the EC's Executive Commission. In fact, Delors says, the United States should realize that a united Europe would provide it with a more powerful ally in crises such as last year's Persian Gulf War.

The Skeptics Speak

Europe may never get that far. Especially on the American side of the Atlantic, many skeptics simply do not believe that Europe is ready to set aside centuries of hostility and embrace a common destiny. Britain and Greece sharing a common policy toward Turkey? Forget it. The same monetary policies for Germany and Portugal? Not a chance.

"The interests of national governments remain compelling," says John Yochelson, a vice president of Washington's Center for Strategic and International Studies. "There hasn't been any real change in decision making, just more cumbersome decision-making procedures."

From the U.S. vantage point, Western Europe is swimming against the tide of history. Yugoslavia and the Soviet Union have disintegrated. Canada is shifting power from the national capital to the provinces. In the EC itself, Belgium and Spain are doing the same. In that global environment, how can the nations of Western Europe come together?

What's more, unity seems to depend on prosperity. A European unity campaign in the early 1970s dissolved in intramural squabbling during the Arab oil shocks. Progress since the mid-1980s has depended upon steady economic growth. That can't last forever—and when it stops, Euro-unity may topple with it.

 From Los Angeles Times, February 4, 1992, pp. 1, 4. Copyright © 1992 by Los Angeles Times.

Even in Western Europe, where polls show large majorities in favor of ever-greater powers for the EC, some advocates of Eurounity are beginning to fear that the Continent is not up to the challenge.

"Where is a creative architect for the new Europe?" demands Norbert Walter, chief economist for Deutsche Bank, Germany's biggest. "Where are the untiring men and women who are willing to roll up their sleeves and get on with building a bigger and better Europe?"

Walter laments that EC nations, preoccupied with their own problems, have failed to stop the civil war in Yugoslavia or to help the newly independent Soviet nations to their feet. Jingoism and blinkered thinking," he says, "are in danger of throwing away the chance of the epoch."

The German Factor

The doubters point to two trouble spots—one within the EC, one outside.

On the inside it is not Britain, which has balked at much of the European agenda, that is causing the most serious concern. Continental Europeans expect Britain ultimately to hitch its wagon to unity, kicking and screaming all the way, rather than be left behind. The concern is focused instead on

---

'It is evident that Americans will have much difficulty with Europe if unity succeeds.'

Jacques Delors

President of EC Executive Commission

Germany, which has embraced unity in principle but struck out on its own when its national interests so dictated.

One of the great promises of Eurounity is binding Germany once and for all to the rest of Europe. But that country—since reunification the EC's biggest member as well as its economically dominant one—rang alarm bells all over Europe in December with its unilateral decision to raise interest rates as part of its campaign against inflation.

Many of Germany's neighbors were forced to follow suit, lest their currencies lose value against the Germany mark, even though higher rates could push their less-robust economies into recession. French Finance Minister Pierre Beregovoy, condemning Germany for its "egoism," fumed: "If each country thinks first of itself, Europe will mark time."

Germany remains undaunted. Chancellor Helmut Kohl has stepped up his campaigns to make German the EC's third official language (English and French are the first two) and to make Frankfurt the home of the European Central Bank, which is to replace national central banks when the EC switches to a common currency late in the 1990s.

But even the German problem may prove nothing next to what is happening just to the Community's east. No fewer than nine Eastern European nations, newly freed from the Soviet yoke, are pounding on the EC's door. Nobody knows how many fragments from what used to be the Soviet Union and Yugoslavia will ultimately join the line.

Worries in the East

The EC cannot afford to barricade the gates. Two Europes—a prosperous West next to a desperate East—is a sure formula for strife. At the very least, Western Europe would find itself flooded with unwelcome immigrants seeking a life not available in the East.

But can the EC afford to open up? Already the wealthy countries of the EC are chafing under the strain of propping up the economies of its "poor four"—Ireland, Spain, Portugal and Greece. Only after a year of hard bargaining did the EC last year accept Poland, Czechoslovakia and Hungary as associate members, with greater (but far from full) access to EC agricultural, textile and steel markets.

Delors has no illusions that the road to unity will be smooth. "It will take a great deal of time," he says, "and if history has some bad surprises in store for us, there could be a new period of stagnation in the construction of Europe."

But to Delors, and apparently to the great majority of Europeans, standing still is not an option. The image of a Europe divided, on the brink of two world wars in the first half of the century, remains chillingly vivid. Delors says, simply and compellingly: "I don't want to live in a Europe that is like it was in 1914."

Delors is the first to admit that unity is easier in some areas than others. It is one thing to eliminate internal barriers to trade between EC nations. But it is quite another to ask nations to yield authority to a Pan-European government over monetary policy and foreign policy.

"We are facing 12 sovereign nations that have long traditions, that have geopolitical interests that are sometimes different, sometimes contrary," he reminds. "Little by little, they have to learn to think in common and act in common. . . . Thanks to McDonald's, you can have lunch in 10 minutes, but you can't build a grand political system in a year."

In Delors' seven years at the helm, the EC has already come a long way. Founded in 1957 with only six members (Germany, France, Italy, the Netherlands, Belgium and Luxembourg), the EC was initially known in the United States as the "Common Market."

It was a misnomer. Barriers such as tariffs and differing national product standards still stood in the way of the free movement of goods among the six EC members.

All that is beginning to change. Under the so-called Single European Act, which took effect in 1987 after adoption by the 12 national parliaments, the EC is more or less on course toward bringing down most barriers to the movement of goods, services, money and people across national boundaries by Jan. 1, 1993.

The Three Europes

This year is crucial to the drive for greater unity among the 12 nations of the European Community — "EC '92," as the effort is known. But the dream of a United States of Europe encompasses more — the integration of what are today three Europes. Besides the EC, they include the seven nations of the European Free Trade Assn. (EFTA) and at least 10 newly liberated Central and East European countries.

Amid its incredible diversity, Europe is slowly emerging as a bloc, challenging the United States and Japan as an economic gladiator in the 1990s.

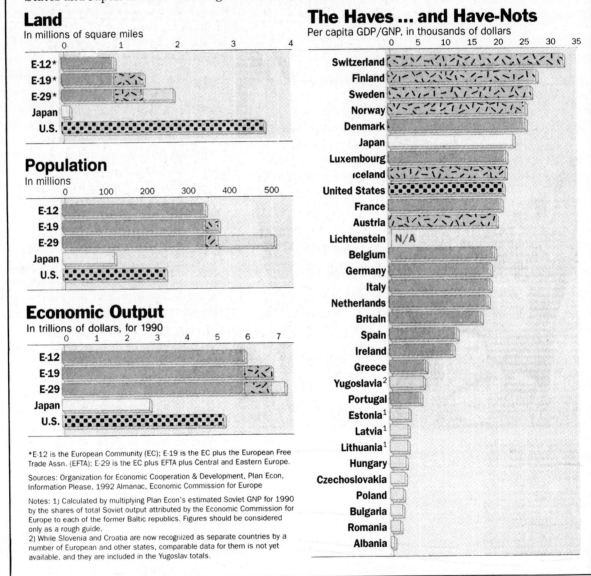

Land
In millions of square miles

E-12*, E-19*, E-29*, Japan, U.S.

Population
In millions

E-12, E-19, E-29, Japan, U.S.

Economic Output
In trillions of dollars, for 1990

E-12, E-19, E-29, Japan, U.S.

The Haves ... and Have-Nots
Per capita GDP/GNP, in thousands of dollars

Switzerland, Finland, Sweden, Norway, Denmark, Japan, Luxembourg, Iceland, United States, France, Austria, Lichtenstein N/A, Belgium, Germany, Italy, Netherlands, Britain, Spain, Ireland, Greece, Yugoslavia[2], Portugal, Estonia[1], Latvia[1], Lithuania[1], Hungary, Czechoslovakia, Poland, Bulgaria, Romania, Albania

*E-12 is the European Community (EC); E-19 is the EC plus the European Free Trade Assn. (EFTA); E-29 is the EC plus EFTA plus Central and Eastern Europe.

Sources: Organization for Economic Cooperation & Development, Plan Econ, Information Please, 1992 Almanac, Economic Commission for Europe

Notes: 1) Calculated by multiplying Plan Econ's estimated Soviet GNP for 1990 by the shares of total Soviet output attributed by the Economic Commission for Europe to each of the former Baltic republics. Figures should be considered only as a rough guide.
2) While Slovenia and Croatia are now recognized as separate countries by a number of European and other states, comparable data for them is not yet available, and they are included in the Yugoslav totals.

Delors coined the phrase "EC '92" to describe the movement toward a single market. That may have misrepresented the date, but it proved to be a public relations masterstroke.

Business had complained for years about costly customs inspections of goods shipped across EC borders, about varying national product standards that prohibited mass production of goods for the entire EC market, about national regulations that impeded the flow of capital from one EC country to another. The tantalizing prospect that all this would soon give way lit a fire under European (and foreign) businesses, some of which are expanding their European operations at a furious pace in anticipation of the single market.

Yet next Jan. 1 will mark only the beginning of Europe's

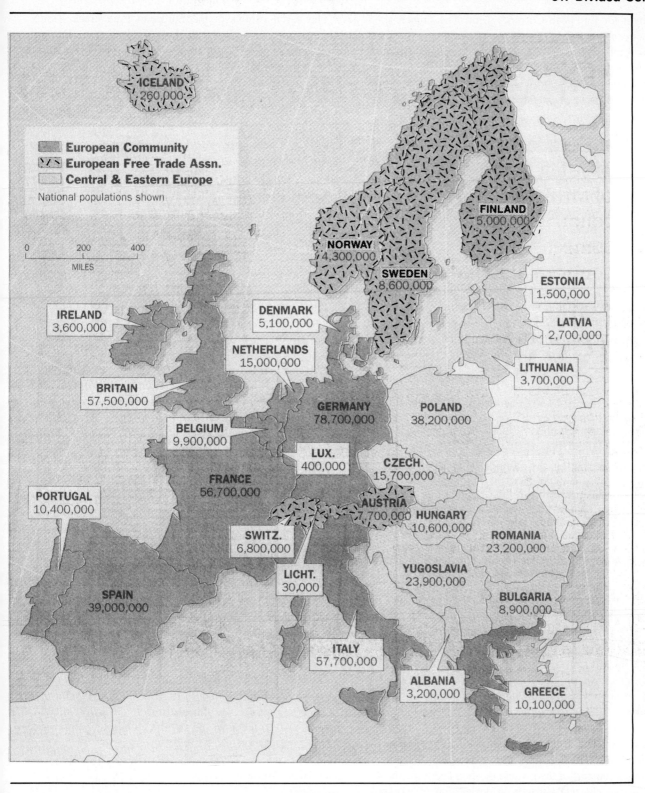

ICELAND
260,000

European Community
European Free Trade Assn.
Central & Eastern Europe
National populations shown

0   200   400
MILES

FINLAND
5,000,000

NORWAY
4,300,000

SWEDEN
8,600,000

ESTONIA
1,500,000

IRELAND
3,600,000

DENMARK
5,100,000

LATVIA
2,700,000

NETHERLANDS
15,000,000

LITHUANIA
3,700,000

BRITAIN
57,500,000

GERMANY
78,700,000

POLAND
38,200,000

BELGIUM
9,900,000

LUX.
400,000

CZECH.
15,700,000

FRANCE
56,700,000

AUSTRIA
7,700,000

HUNGARY
10,600,000

PORTUGAL
10,400,000

ROMANIA
23,200,000

SWITZ.
6,800,000

LICHT.
30,000

YUGOSLAVIA
23,900,000

SPAIN
39,000,000

BULGARIA
8,900,000

ITALY
57,700,000

ALBANIA
3,200,000

GREECE
10,100,000

economic integration, not the end. In most of the cutting-edge industries—computers, electronics telecommunications—European companies will still lag far behind their global rivals.

"The best we can hope for is to be moving toward becoming as competitive as the United States and Japan," says Stanley Crossick, chairman of the Belmont European Policy center, a Brussels think tank.

Money, Money, Money

More help may be just over the horizon. Two months ago, meeting in the Dutch town of Maastricht, the heads of the 12 EC countries agreed that the most prosperous among them—probably Germany, France and several others—will replace their national currencies with a common currency no later than 1999. As of now the common currency is called the *ecu*, an acronym for European Currency Unit. The French approve—an *ecu* was a gold coin in medieval France. But the Germans want to go back to the drawing board because *ecu* resembles German slang for *cow*.

"Surely there's a better name," Kohl says.

Except for Britain, whose Parliament retained the right to stay out of the currency union, European countries judged to have sufficiently sound budget policies and inflation rates will automatically jettison their currencies.

The economic consequences could be enormous. No longer would the Bundesbank set interest rates and govern the amount of money in circulation in Germany. Likewise for the central banks of other countries that switch to the *ecu*.

Instead, a European central bank (already dubbed the "Eurofed" after the U.S. Federal Reserve) would make monetary policy for all countries using the *ecu*. In practice, everyone expects Germany's tight, anti-inflationary monetary policies to become the Eurofed's own, much as many EC central banks already follow the Bundesbank's lead.

Europe wastes $17 billion a year converting one EC currency to another, according to the European Round Table, whose members are the chief executives of 45 major companies.

"Japan has one currency," the Round Table said in a recent report. "The U.S. has one currency. How can the Community live with 12?"

"Money," the Round Table declared, "is the lifeblood of an economic system."

It is more than that. It is also a central element of a nation's ability to control its own destiny.

"Money is sovereignty," says Dominique Moisi, deputy director of the French Institute for International Relations. "Monetary union will drag political union along with it."

The Ultimate Union

That is the not-so-hidden agenda of the Eurounifiers. "Political union" is shorthand for a grab bag of powers—notably foreign policy, defense planning, immigration policy and regulation of working conditions—that proponents of Euro-unity want to shift from the national governments to the EC.

"The agreement on political union [at the Maastricht summit] is slightly disappointing," says Moisi, an avid Eurounionist. "It's extremely vague. There was no substantial progress."

In their most bizarre decision of all, the heads of government agreed that 11 nations (British Prime Minister John Major wanted no part of this) would develop and implement an EC "social charter"—that is, a declaration of worker rights ranging from a maximum 48-hour work week to advance consultations about plant closings. Even though Britain will not be affected by the social charter, its officials at the EC will apparently have a role in shaping it.

The European Community will be at the core of whatever pan-European government evolves. At 12 nations, the EC has become large enough to exert a gravitational pull on everything around it.

The seven nations of the European Free Trade Assn., which constitute virtually all the rest of Western Europe, have agreed to form a free-trade area with the EC as of next Jan. 1, when most of the EC single-market program will take effect.

The EC's court, the European Court of Justice, has ruled the EC-EFTA accord invalid because it would set up overlapping jurisdictions between the EC court and a new court designed to rule on disputes between the EC and EFTA. If negotiators from the two camps can surmount that obstacle, the new "European Economic Area," with about 377 million residents and economic production 30% greater than that of the United States, would be the world's biggest economic bloc.

Already two EFTA nations, Austria and Sweden, have applied for outright EC membership, and most or all of EFTA could be folded into the EC before the end of the decade.

It's one thing for the EC to welcome its Western European neighbors from EFTA, which as a group are even more prosperous than the EC 12. It will be quite another to open its arms to the likes of Poland and Albania and the debris from Yugoslavia and the European part of the Soviet Union.

Even the EC's two poorest members, Portugal and Greece, are about twice as rich as the most prosperous of the new democracies of Eastern Europe.

More than that, Eastern Europe dwarfs the poor EC members in population. Portugal and Greece have about 10 million residents each; Eastern Europe (excluding all former Soviet republics except Lithuania, Latvia and Estonia, which have already begun preliminary discussion with the EC) is home to 132 million.

Many analysts believe Western Europe has been short-sighted and stingy in its dealings with Eastern Europe's new regimes. The EC, says David C. Roche, managing director of the London-based investment house Morgan Stanley International, "is far too slow in opening its markets to manufactured products where Eastern Europe has a competitive advantage (steel, textiles, etc.)." And the agreements that make Poland, Czechoslovakia and Hungary associate EC members leave most EC quotas on farm imports in place.

Delors replies that EC purchases of East European goods have shot upward since the Berlin Wall fell in 1989. (Indeed, EC imports from Eastern Europe grew by 29% from the first half of 1990 to the first half of 1991, while U.S. purchases from Eastern Europe fell by 10%, according to the Organization for Economic Cooperation and Development.) Delors adds that Western Europe's foreign aid far outpaces America's.

"I am outraged when I hear it said that we are not doing our duty," he says. "We are opening our frontiers and we are spending a lot. It is very dishonest to pretend the contrary, as is sometimes done across the Atlantic."

He acknowledges that Western Europe could do more. "But this is a democracy," he says. Western Europe is not about to throw large numbers of its own farmers out of work by importing vast quantities of food from the East.

Daunting though the obstacles to unity may be, Delors warns Americans not to underestimate their neighbors across the Atlantic. "Americans always are like amazed children when they look at what Europeans do," he says.

If Europe can stay the course, it will fulfill the dreams of its post–World War II founders. It has been 30 years since an EC committee headed by French politician Jean Monnet declared:

"New bonds between peoples and the realization of their mutual solidarity are already beginning to take hold. As the Community's impact gradually increases, these bonds will be strengthened. Then it will become possible to find the way towards establishing a political union and reaching the Community's objectives: the United States of Europe."

My, how you've grown

Can the European Community put on both more muscle and new members? Or must it choose? There are clues in how its powers have grown so far

WHAT makes the EC's power and workload grow? They have both expanded hugely over the past 35 years, as members pooled more and more national sovereignty. A lot of Europeans think this process will go on if only because the forces eroding Europe's nation-states are too great to resist and because the Community's success will continue to feed on itself.

Others think the transfer of power to the EC is reaching a double limit. To them, the Community has already grown quite strong enough; and adding new members—the queue is long—will make collective decision-making in Brussels ever harder.

The EC is neither a tadpole nor a mathematical series, so what comes next is hard to guess. The past, though, offers clues. Up to now, power has moved to Brussels because:

• Post-war France and Germany wanted a framework for good-neighbourliness, and post-colonial Britain, for all its doubts, wanted a place in Europe.
• Open markets and closer-knit economies looked the best solution to lagging European competitiveness.
• A steady narrowing of the range of political and economic debate among the Twelve widened the scope for common agreement in Brussels.
• One EC common policy led to another by a mechanism (or deliberate technique) of job expansion known, in English, as "spillover" or, in French, as *engrenage*. Internal free trade, for example, was assumed to require common rules on mergers, state aids, product standards, work conditions, pollution safeguards and so on.
• European federalists, who see the EC as the United States of Europe in embryo, nourished its development however and wherever they could.
• Non-federalists supported federalist-looking schemes (a single market, a common currency) because they saw in them limited pay-offs (greater economic competitiveness, lower currency-transactions costs for business).

The EC's development falls into three periods: 1957-66 (birth and growth); 1966-85 (stagnation and renewal); and 1985-92 (the Great Leap Forward). In each of these, certain patterns repeated themselves: federalist and nationalist impulses competed with each other; the EC did best when Germany and France were close; Britain was always slow to join in; and progress was smoothest on economic matters.

At the creation

The idea of European union is not new. Victor Hugo, one of France's best known writers, and Richard Cobden, an English free-trader, pleaded for it in Paris in 1849. Few listened. After the first world war an Austrian count, Richard Coudenhove-Kalergi, revived the idea in a book, "Paneuropa". It flopped. A second war was needed to get Europe moving.

In 1950 Robert Schuman, France's foreign minister, and Konrad Adenauer, West Germany's chancellor, dreamed up the European Coal and Steel Community as a way to link and reconcile their countries. This got under way in 1952; Italy, Belgium, Holland and Luxembourg joined in, to make it the Six. It had an executive (the High Authority) to make proposals, a council of ministers to decide on them, an assembly to offer advice and a court of justice to settle disputes. Here was the institutional template for the European Economic Community (EEC).

The High Authority's first president was Jean Monnet, a French *haut fonctionnaire*. Like Schuman and, in certain moods, Adenauer, he was a federalist. Only strong European institutions, he believed, could tame national passions. Jacques Delors, the Frenchman who currently heads the European Commission in Brussels, is Monnet's intellectual heir.

One early federal ambition—a European defence community—collapsed before the opposition of France's parliament in 1954. That left European security to the American-led North Atlantic Treaty Organisation (NATO). Europe's federalists concentrated instead on economics.

The Europeans feared they would never catch America's soaring economy if their own ones remained closed to each other. At Messina in 1955, the Six asked Paul-Henri Spaak, Belgium's foreign minister, to report back with a plan for a common market. His committee's work culminated in the Treaty of Rome, signed in March 1957, which created the EEC. Besides commission, council and court, it had a mainly consultative parliament.

Internal tariffs were to be abolished by 1970. There would be one European policy on foreign trade and on farming. European institutions would be strengthened. By 1966 the council was supposed to begin conduct-

Ever more work . . .

COMMISSION'S FULL-TIME EMPLOYEES‡

Year	Number
1970	5,234
1990	12,887

COUNCIL OF MINISTERS‡

Year	Number of meetings
1967	20
1970	41
1975	56
1980	63
1985	69
1987	81
1990	92

EC LEGISLATION‡

Number of:	1970	1983	1987	1991
Regulations	249	395	458	na
Decisions	71	108	125	na
Directives	25	41	40	63

‡ Source: European Commission

. . . and money

EC BUDGET bn ecus‡

	Current prices	1983 prices*	1990 prices*
1983	22.99	22.99	32.21
1987	37.41	30.37	42.55
1990	46.93	33.50	46.93

*Using GNP deflator ‡Source: European Commission

From *The Economist*, January 25, 1992, pp. 49-50. Copyright © 1992 by The Economist. Distributed by The New York Times Special Features.

ing certain business by a form of majority voting (though the blocking minority would still be quite small). Rather than relying on contributions from members, as most international bodies must, it was soon proposed that the EEC should have its own revenues.

France, in the throes of decolonisation and eager to shore up its national self-confidence, resisted. Its president, General de Gaulle, had in 1960 proposed an inter-governmental model for Europe with a weak or non-existent central executive. The Benelux countries rejected this. They wanted a strong commission to counterbalance France, Germany and Italy.

But de Gaulle's counterattack against creeping supranationalism had barely begun. He blackballed Britain's application for membership (1963), threatened to block the Community's work if majority voting were used (1965), and pulled France's troops out of NATO's peacetime command (1966).

Two troubled decades

The "Luxembourg compromise" (January 1966) brought the French back into the council, which they had briefly boycotted. It was agreed that majority voting would not be used when important national interests were at stake. Individual governments, that is, still had a veto. For the next 20 years, in matters great and small, the veto or the threat of the veto hung over the work of the EC.

Despite this, much got done. Regular consultation on foreign policy, known as Political Co-operation, began (1969); import dues and a slice of national VAT collections were allocated to the Community as revenues (1970); Britain, Denmark and Ireland joined (1973); Community leaders began to meet at regular summits called European Councils (from 1975 on); nine of the Ten (minus Britain) linked their currencies in the European Monetary System and the first direct election was held for a now more assertive European Parliament (1979).

Greece joined (1981), followed by Spain and Portugal (1986). There was plenty of spillover as Community legislation dyed the fabric of national law. In the teeth of two recessions (1974-75 and 1979-81) and amid a long wrangle over Britain's budget

---

That democratic deficit

ACCOUNTABILITY in Europe has not kept up with the pooling of national sovereignty. That has left a "democratic deficit". There are broadly two views about how to close it. One looks to national parliaments. Denmark's is the extreme model: its parliament has aimed to vet all the Danish government's EC decisions. The snag is reconciling national scrutiny with majority voting in the council: if a government's objections can be overruled in the council, so by implication may a parliament's.

Others look to the European Parliament. Its powers, in many ways, are limited: it cannot raise revenue and it has no legislative initiative. But its powers are growing. The Maastricht summit was a step forward. The parliament has a fair say over the EC budget, can sack the commission and may veto some EC bills.

As for representativeness, parliament's members tend to reflect Europe-wide rather than national or local interests. On the other hand, it is the one Community body where opposition voices are heard.

---

contribution (1975-85), this was considerable work.

But it was not, for many Europeans, enough. Businessmen complained about Europe's flagging competitiveness. Europe's reedy voice in world affairs was felt to be out of keeping with its economic girth. The EC's workload had indeed grown, but it was inefficiently run and inadequately scrutinised (see box).

The Great Leap Forward

"One must remember the two essentials of progress in Europe: an institutional framework and deadlines." Thus Monnet. Mr

Delors agreed. The very year he took over as commission president (1985), he nudged governments to accept the Single European Act. This set a deadline of December 1992 for completing the Community's single market and, to meet it, widened the scope of majority voting in the council. Dropping its middle initial, the EEC became commonly known as the European Community.

Mr Delors and other federalists argued that the 1992 campaign required a commitment to economic and monetary union (EMU), and that EMU in its turn

entailed political union. This was attempted *engrenage* at its boldest. Not all economists thought a common currency would need close fiscal co-ordination. Nor did all politicians think EMU required another large shift of power to Brussels. Yet non-federalists went along because they favoured a single currency and more limited political reforms.

The 1989 revolution in Eastern Europe added urgency to reforming the Community. The new democracies looked to the EC not just to co-ordinate aid but to admit them before long as members. Federalists, afraid that "widening" would weaken the EC, strove to get their strengthening done first. The unification of Germany also encouraged loud commitments to Europe: from non-Germans worried by its new size, and from Germans keen to allay their neighbours' fears. A series of summits—Dublin (June 1990), Rome (December 1990) and Maastricht (December 1991)—channelled these pressures into a new Community treaty.

What Maastricht meant

On EMU, the treaty agreed upon at Maastricht in Holland has enough deadlines to please the ghost of Monnet: a European Monetary Institute is to be set up in 1994 to co-ordinate monetary policies; by July 1998 this is to become the European central bank; and by January 1999 the ecu is meant to be a common European currency. EC economies whose price and budgetary behaviour are alike enough may join the system. (If most achieve the necessary convergence, the last phase could begin in January 1997.) Britain, true to form, won the right not to adopt the ecu even if its partners do.

Germany got its way on the design of a central bank independent of elected politicians. Fighting inflation will be a duty, and EC finance ministers will be able to fine governments with overlarge budget deficits lest they try to encourage the European bank to lower interest rates.

The Maastricht treaty on political union disappointed federalists. It skilfully deflects attempts to draw power in the Community away from governments. In a mixture of metaphors rich even by the standards of the EC, the European Council is to sit astride three "pillars" known as the European Union. One pillar—that is, a Euro-institution

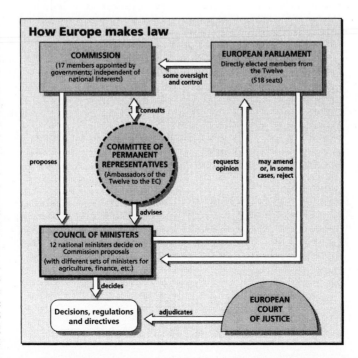

How Europe makes law

COMMISSION
(17 members appointed by governments; independent of national interests)

EUROPEAN PARLIAMENT
Directly elected members from the Twelve
(518 seats)

some oversight and control

consults

COMMITTEE OF PERMANENT REPRESENTATIVES
(Ambassadors of the Twelve to the EC)

proposes

requests opinion

may amend or, in some cases, reject

advises

COUNCIL OF MINISTERS
12 national ministers decide on Commission proposals
(with different sets of ministers for agriculture, finance, etc.)

decides

Decisions, regulations and directives

adjudicates

EUROPEAN COURT OF JUSTICE

with a certain job-description—will be the old Community with its likely new single-currency responsibilities.

The second pillar is for foreign and security policy, the third for co-operation on such topics as immigration, asylum and policing. These will both be inter-governmental bodies of the Twelve in which the commission, parliament and court are to get less say than they have in the EC. Pierre de Boissieu, the French diplomat who thought up this intricate inter-governmental scheme, is de Gaulle's grandson.

The Maastricht treaty, in other words, broadened the Twelve's range more than it strengthened the commission and the parliament. But it did increase their powers a bit. The commission may now make proposals on visas, industrial policy, health, education, culture and consumer protection. It has also won itself a statutory part, if a small one, in Euro-discussions on foreign policy and internal security.

The parliament may veto EC laws on most of these things, as well as on the single market and on environmental and research programmes. (The council may vote about many of these issues by majority.) Of the Twelve, all but Britain wanted a wider common policy on social issues. The Eleven, it was agreed, should do this with the help of the Community's institutions in ways that would not be legally binding on Britain.

One last deadline should not be overlooked. It is for the next big treaty revision, in 1996. As it looms, federalists will argue that the Community proper should take over European co-ordination of foreign policy and internal-security questions. The struggle to define Europe will go on. The European Union may not be a federal government, but it is a long way from being simply a concert of nations.

Neither a State Nor International Organization

The workings of the European Commission may be arcane, but it has power.

Joel Havemann

Times Staff Writer

BRUSSELS—It was Friday, Jan. 10, another variable feast for the 17 members of the European Commission.

Frans Andriessen, the commissioner for external relations, was huddling with the foreign ministers of the 12 European Community nations to discuss crises in the former Soviet Union and Yugoslavia. Meanwhile, Bruce Millan, responsible for developing the Community's poor regions, met with members of a Scottish association demanding development money for their area. And Jean Dondelinger, whose portfolio is cultural affairs, participated in the opening ceremony of the Brussels International Film Festival.

Holland's Andriessen, Britain's Millan and Luxembourg's Dondelinger sit at the top of what is, in the United States, one of Europe's least-understood yet most influential governmental institutions. It was the European Commission, for example, that initiated "EC '92"—the drive to tear down barriers to internal European Community trade—and has now set Europe on a course for political as well as economic union.

The commission, in turn, is just one element of a four-part government system unlike anything found in the United States or anywhere else on the globe.

"The European Community is not a political entity that is easily understood," writes University of Pittsburgh political scientist Alberta M. Sbragia. "Unique in its institutional structure, it is neither a state nor an international organization."

These are the pieces:

• The European Commission (based in Brussels). Although it is commonly described as the European Community's executive branch, the commission generally does not execute policy. (That job is left to the 12 member nations.) Rather, the commission derives most of its power from being the only unit of EC government that can initiate policies.

• The European Parliament (which meets one week a month in Strasbourg, France, but whose administrative offices are in Brussels). This is a 518-member legislative body that, by and large, does not legislate. Although it can veto some proposed EC policies, it acts mostly in an advisory role.

• The Council of Ministers (which meets wherever it chooses). This is the unit of government that makes most EC policy, subject in some cases to veto by the European Parliament and in many to approval by the 12 national parliaments. The heads of the 12 EC governments meet at least twice a year to set Community policy. But most decisions are delegated to a subordinate level: foreign or trade ministers, for example.

• The European Court of Justice (based in Luxembourg). The court actually does what its name implies: It adjudicates disputes between EC institutions and between the EC and its member nations.

In this constellation of peculiar institutions, the commission may be the most bizarre of all.

With one exception, its members are chosen for four-year terms by the leaders of the 12 national governments—and many of them were sent to Brussels to get them out of the way back home. "It's often akin to being put out to grass," admits one commission official.

The one exception is the commission president, who is chosen by a consensus of the heads of the 12 EC countries. In 1985 and again in 1989, the EC heads picked Jacques Delors, who had been France's finance minister.

Delors has, by all accounts, proved easily the most effective president the commission has ever had. As French President Francois Mitterrand's popularity at home has plunged, Delors has become France's most highly regarded politician, and he is considered likely to run for president when Mitterrand's term expires in 1995.

The other 16 commissioners come to Brussels without portfolios. It is the president's unenviable task to divvy up the jobs.

Most commissioners do not rank among Europe's leading political lights. A 1990 EC poll showed that only 45% of EC citizens knew of the commission; of that 45%, slightly more than half had a favorable impression.

The commissioners are not accountable to any voters; their allegiance is to the commission itself—and, if they want to be reappointed, to the prime minister who sent them to Brussels.

The commission generally meets every Wednesday. A majority of nine commissioners is enough to exercise the commission's unique power to send a proposal whirling through the EC's labyrinthine decision-making process.

Unlike a U.S. President's Cabinet, the EC's commissioners range all over the political spectrum. The present commission has room for Leon Brittan, a card-carrying British Conservative who is responsible for antitrust policy, and for Vasso Papandreou, an activist Greek Socialist who is in charge of such volatile issues as workers' rights.

Some of the commissioners manage to use their stints in Brussels to enhance their political standing back home. Delors is not the only commissioner in this category; Ray MacSharry of Ireland, who as the agriculture commissioner has drawn up a far-reaching and imaginative (if controversial) proposal to reform the EC's complex web of farm subsidies, is considered a potential prime minister.

From *Los Angeles Times*, February 4, 1992, p. H9. Copyright © 1992 by Los Angeles Times.

The Machinery of European Decision Making

EC Council of Ministers

The decision-making representatives from the 12 member countries of the European Community. The Council sets Community strategy and makes final decisions on whether proposals become Community law. On some issues, the heads of the 12 countries make decisions themselves; on most they delegate decision-making authority to their relevant ministers—foreign affairs, trade, agriculture, etc. Within the Council, decisions on most issues are made by majority vote, with the votes of the bigger countries (Britain, France, Germany, Italy and Spain) getting extra weight. On the most important issues, unanimity is necessary.

European Commission

The European Community's civil service, composed of Commission President Jacques Delors and 16 other commissioners, each with a different portfolio. These include international relations, competition policy, environment, etc. There are two commissioners from each of the five biggest Community countries and one each from the other seven. The commission initiates proposals for Community regulations and legislation. While its work is subject to the Council of Ministers' final approval, the commission exercises influence by defining issues and controlling the flow of information to the Council.

European Parliament

A largely advisory body of 518 members elected by popular ballot in the member countries. The full Parliament meets one week each month in Strasbourg, while its committees meet in Brussels. European Commission proposals are sent to the relevant parliamentary committee for review and suggested changes. The goal of this back-and-forth process is ultimately to have the council adopt a "common position" on a proposal.

European Court of Justice

The 13-member court (one member per Community country plus one extra), based in Luxembourg, theoretically has the power to rule on the validity of Community laws. That power remains largely untested, although the court recently ruled that an agreement between the Community and the European Free Trade Assn. to create a "European economic area" was invalid because it set up a new court that would conflict with its own prerogatives.

For other commissioners, the political landscape back home is not so appealing. The Greek Socialist government that sent Papandreou to Brussels has since been toppled, leaving her without much of a political future in her native land.

After Delors, the most uniformly well-regarded commissioners include Brittan; MacSharry; Henning Christophersen of Denmark, who helped gain approval by the 12 EC heads in December of a single European currency by 1999; and Martin Bangemann of Germany, who is responsible for proposing the regulations to implement the "EC '92" single-market program.

The hardest job, apart from Delors', belongs to Holland's Andriessen. As commissioner for external relations, he is not only the EC's chief trade negotiator, but he is also responsible for talks with the many Eastern European nations that, freed of Soviet domination, are seeking some sort of association with the EC.

Brittan, who resigned as former Prime Minister Margaret Thatcher's trade and industry secretary in the aftermath of the 1985 Westland helicopter scandal, has proved the most aggressive of the commissioners. It was he, for example, who proposed blocking a French-Italian consortium's takeover last year of De Havilland, a Canadian manufacturer of turbo-prop aircraft for commuter airlines. Over loud objections from France and Italy, Brittan mustered a bare majority of nine commissioners behind his argument that the takeover would have severely reduced competition in the European market.

The commissioners sit atop a bureaucracy of 16,720 civil servants who are divided into 23 directorates, or departments. (Some commissioners are responsible for more than one directorate.) About 15% of the Eurocrats have the job of translating EC documents into the Community's nine languages.

EC pay is good: about $240,000 a year for Delors, $217,000 for each of the six commission vice presidents and $196,000 for the other 10 commissioners. Salaries for the Eurocrats range from an entry-level $22,000 to $150,000 for the most senior officials, and taxes, paid directly to the EC, are low compared with most national tax regimes in Europe.

The EC's 1992 budget is about $84 billion, mostly raised from customs duties and a share of each member nation's value-added tax proceeds. More than half—about $48 billion—is to be spent for agricultural subsidies, the one major governmental program that is financed by the EC itself rather than the 12 individual countries. Regional development, social and related programs will cost another $23 billion. Miscellaneous programs, including direct aid to poorer EC countries, will add another $10 billion; the budget for the EC staff itself is slightly more than $3 billion.

The four-year terms of the present commissioners run out at the end of this year. But the heads of government have already decided to switch commissioners' terms to five years as of 1995, to make them coincide with the term of the European Parliament. That leaves 1993 and 1994 uncovered; a likely solution is simply to hold over the current commissioners for those two years.

That would enable Delors, if he chose, to remain in his high-profile job in Brussels, outside the rough and tumble of French politics, until the eve of France's next presidential election. The leading candidate to succeed Delors, whether in 1993 or 1995, is Dutch Prime Minister Ruud Lubbers, but Spanish Prime Minister Felipe Gonzales is moving up fast.

EC Girds Itself for Inevitable Expansion

By Howard LaFranchi

Staff writer of The Christian Science Monitor

PARIS

AT a recent demonstration in Minsk supporting democracy and closer ties with the West, marchers mixed flags of their native Byelorussia with the flag of the European Community.

Byelorussia is not a likely candidate for EC membership, especially if plans succeed for a "Euro-Asian" commonwealth replacing the Soviet Union. But the sprouting of the EC symbol at a domestic demonstration as far away as Minsk demonstrates just how attractive the EC has become to its neighbors.

With nearly 20 European countries either already applying for membership or making loud noises about joining, the issue of the Community's enlargement from its current membership of 12 is set to dominate the EC's agenda throughout the 1990s.

Deeper vs. wider

The old debate over whether to "deepen" the Community's institutions before "widening" them to include new members has been surpassed by events.

Now as EC leaders debate everything from budgets, immigration, regional development, and

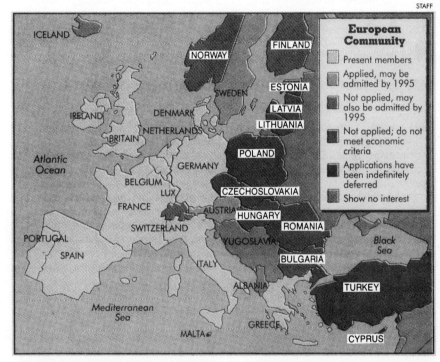

STAFF

European Community

Present members

Applied, may be admitted by 1995

Not applied, may also be admitted by 1995

Not applied; do not meet economic criteria

Applications have been indefinitely deferred

Show no interest

trade, to further reforms of Community institutions, it will be done against a backdrop of an expanding and increasingly diverse union.

Steps taken at the EC's recent landmark summit in Maastricht, Netherlands, "settle the deepening and widening debate, because we will now do both of those things" at the same time, said British Prime Minister John Major at the summit's close.

Community integration in "1992 will begin a long debate on the enlargement – ... the transformation – of the Community,"

says Philippe Moreau-Defarges, a European specialist with the French Institute for International Studies in Paris.

The Maastricht meeting fixed 1999 as the latest date for creating a single European currency, and took some important steps, including laying the foundation of a future EC common defense, reinforcing the Community's political integration. But it also moved up the date for beginning membership negotiations with Austria and Sweden from 1993 to the second half of next year.

Reprinted by permission from *The Christian Science Monitor,* December 24, 1991, p. 5. Copyright © 1991 by The Christian Science Publishing Society. All rights reserved.

More importantly, leaders set 1996 as the date for the next EC treaty revision, which most observers believe will be dominated by the institutional reforms the Community's expansion will require.

Some officials, notably among the Germans, do not think that revision will come soon enough. Issues such as unanimous versus majority voting, already controversial among the EC's 12 members, will become more problematic and central to the organization's effectiveness when new members arrive.

"The whole [enlargement] process is going to have some unpopular effects," says one German official.

Reasons for the push to join the Community vary. For the wealthy countries of the European Free Trade Association (EFTA), whose economies are well integrated into the EC's, membership is a way to gain a say in policies that already affect them profoundly.

The poor, newly democratic countries of Eastern Europe see membership as the best path to prosperity and solid democratic institutions. They look to the astounding progress of countries like Spain and Portugal, EC members for less than six years, as their guide.

A possible calendar might go something like this: Sweden and Austria will be members by 1995, if not before. Finland is to decide during the first six months of next year whether to apply, but some leaders are calling for an acceleration to "catch up" with Sweden and Austria. An ambivalent Norway would probably be pushed to join if Finland does.

Switzerland is leaning toward "eventual" membership, although some Swiss leaders are calling for a referendum next year to speed up the process.

Poland, Czechoslovakia, and Hungary, which just last week signed economic association agreements with the EC, should be members by the end of the decade or early in the next century. Romania, Bulgaria, and the Baltic states are likely to follow closely, as are some or all of the Yugoslav republics and Albania.

In addition, Turkey, Cyprus, and Malta have already applied, but have each hit either political or demographic obstacles – Malta because it is so small, Turkey because it is so large and growing so fast. Although EC officials don't like to say it aloud, Turkey also poses troublesome cultural questions because it is a largely Islamic country. The officials also worry about Turkey's "uneven" human rights record.

Views of expansion

The views of present members will largely determine the pace of Community expansion. It is not an issue that fosters unanimity.

Germany, Italy, and Great Britain are strong supporters of opening the EC to Eastern Europe, though not always for the same reasons. Germany and Italy, the EC countries geographically farthest east, equate enlargement with European stability. Both countries have had recent experiences with East European refugees streaming over their borders. Instability in Eastern Europe means instability for them.

Both countries also already have significant investments in Eastern Europe, and see enlargement as a two-way boon.

Britain also supports admitting Eastern Europe, criticizing any expression of doubt or caution as reflective of a rich man's club too focused on its own affairs. But the Britain that opposes any moves towards a "federal" Community is also suspected by its partners of pushing enlargement as a way of rendering a supranational Europe less likely.

France has been the strongest opponent of enlargement since the fall of the Berlin Wall in 1989. The French feared that expansion to the east would result in a German-dominated Community, replacing the EC's traditional Paris-Bonn axis of power and initiative. The French also preferred first creating a "deeper" union in the image of France's highly centralized political system – thus President François Mitterrand's comment early this year that it would be "dozens and dozens of years" before Eastern Europe joined.

That point of view has begun to evolve over recent months, however. One reason is that the French are beginning to see enlargement as a means of diluting Germany's growing power.

One example is France's very keen desire to see a single European currency by 1997. Last week's hike in German interest rates, almost certain to force another painful increase in French rates, will only increase France's desire for a currency managed by a European central bank and for a Europe out from under the German Bundesbank.

Economic standards

But a single currency in 1997 – the earliest date possible – can only happen if a majority of EC members meet the strict economic criteria set at Maastricht by 1996. Thus France's recent warming to membership of EFTA countries, the most likely candidates to meet those criteria.

Mr. Mitterrand is even said to have told Swedish leaders last week that a fast track might get them in the EC by 1993 or 1994, although the Swedes say that for now they prefer a 1995 entry.

As for the Community's poorer members, Spain, Portugal, Greece, and Ireland figure they have perhaps a decade before other "poor" countries gain entrance. But they will remain cautious over economic moves that would damage their own growth or reduce their own access to Community development funds.

"Certainly we want to encourage Eastern Europe in its economic and democratic development," says a Spanish official in Madrid, "but we can't forget that many of our own people live at levels considerably below the Community average."

The enlargement issue on the horizon is one reason Spanish Prime Minister Felipe González Márquez fought so hard in Maastricht for a commitment to higher funding for the EC's poorer members.

Money is an important reason the EFTA countries are unlikely to confront many objections to their membership – they will be net payers into the system. Beyond the EFTA countries, however, "People will start realizing that enlargement is going to be very expensive, and that's going to upset carts across the EC," says Mr. Moreau-Defarges. "Germany wants to be heard saying 'yes' to the East, but [the Germans] don't say they're ready to pay."

Questions remaining

Yet ultimately more threatening than money issues to the Community's effectiveness, cohesion, and perhaps even its existence, will be the prickly institutional questions that determine how the Community works, how it meets its members' needs, and how it operates in the world.

Leaders must determine how to keep the Community democratic and maintain its effectiveness as it expands. "Cultural and historical differences are going to intensify, not lessen," says Moreau-Defarges. "It's one thing to operate at 12 or 15, but it's another thing to do it as a Europe of 25 to 30."

"The number of small members is going to grow," he says, adding that the Community has traditionally been dominated by its larger members. Leaders will have to address smaller members' concerns over representation.

■ *Staff writer Francine S. Kiefer contributed to this report from Bonn.*

Europe's Open Future

IN THE first half of this century Europe was a disaster. The economy slumped, democracy failed, hatreds started two world wars. The second half, by contrast, has been an astonishing success, at least in the western bit of Europe lucky enough to have been liberated (or defeated) by the Americans.

Since 1945 Europeans have had 47 years of peace with each other—a respite unmatched since the emergence of modern states in the 16th century. The average West European's income (at 1990 prices) has risen more than 300%, from $4,860 a year in 1950 to $20,880 in 1990. Life expectancy for West Europeans went up in that time from 67 to 76 years. Between 1960 and 1990 a West European schoolchild's chance of going on to higher education more than tripled.

In these years West Europeans grew more alike—in how many children they had; in where they worked; in how they voted, saved and invested. Their governments were able to take more and more economic decisions in common. Rising incomes and increasing co-operation reinforced each other in a virtuous circle.

The institutional framework for this was the European Community. It has steadily grown in power and numbers. It already accounts for 69% of Europe's population and 81% of its GNP. Between 1958 and 1986 the Community doubled its membership. Success seems magnetic. To judge by the queue of plausible applicants, it could now double again in half that time.

Given pre-war failure, a natural question is whether Western Europe's post-war success was a temporary freak or something durable in which East Europeans can now expect to share. Though favouring the optimistic view, these briefs have also stressed how much the Soviet-American struggle known as the cold war sheltered Western Europe. Its passing raises three questions that West Europeans, in their modern greenhouse, have not really had to think about.

The eastern question

The first is the unfreezing of their eastern border. If Europe is no longer divided at the Elbe, where to the east does Europe stop? At Poland's eastern frontier? Which of the westernmost states of the ex-Soviet Union—Belorussia, Estonia, Latvia, Lithuania, Moldavia and Ukraine—are in Europe?

This is more than a geographers' puzzle. Poverty and turmoil, with their threat of unwanted migrants, now loom in western politicians' minds as an eastern threat to be feared almost as much as Soviet missiles once were. A common first reaction was to offer advice and some aid, but otherwise to keep the easterners and their problems at arm's length until westerners could think through the upheavals of the past two years and sort out where they wished to go.

Economic aid and advice, though welcome, are not substitutes for market access and, eventually, membership of the EC. In December 1991 Czechoslovakia, Hungary and Poland signed association agreements with the EC, which opened western markets only somewhat. In keeping East European exports out, the EC is being short-sighted. Letting in farm goods (in particular) could do two things. Not only would it be one of the best ways to help East European economies. It might also help wreck the EC's wasteful farm policy.

Westerners have a range of discouraging arguments against easterners asking to join the EC. Their heavy punch is that the difference in wealth is simply too large. This is not the knock-out it sounds. Ireland's GDP per head in 1990 (using purchasing-power parities) was 63% of the EC average, Greece's 58% and Portugal's 53%. Comparable figures for Czechoslovakia were 66% and for Hungary 53%.

Opinion in the West is shifting. The "wideners", who want to enlarge the Community, seem to be winning. Enlargement appeals to anti-federalists who

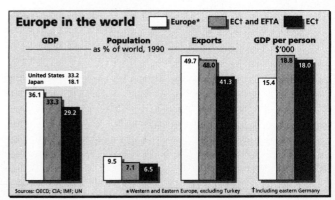

Europe in the world Europe* ECt and EFTA ECt

GDP Population Exports GDP per person
— as % of world, 1990 — $'000

United States 33.2
Japan 18.1

36.1 33.3 29.2 9.5 7.1 6.5 49.7 48.0 41.3 15.4 18.8 18.0

Sources: OECD; CIA; IMF; UN *Western and Eastern Europe, excluding Turkey †Including eastern Germany

From *The Economist*, February 22, 1992, pp. 47-48. Copyright © 1992 by The Economist. Distributed by The New York Times Special Features.

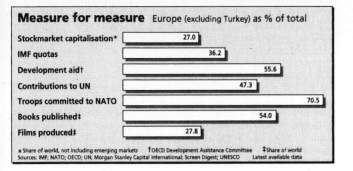

Measure for measure Europe (excluding Turkey) as % of total

Stockmarket capitalisation*	27.0
IMF quotas	36.2
Development aid†	55.6
Contributions to UN	47.3
Troops committed to NATO	70.5
Books published‡	54.0
Films produced‡	27.8

*Share of world, not including emerging markets †OECD Development Assistance Committee ‡Share of world
Sources: IMF; NATO; OECD; UN; Morgan Stanley Capital International; Screen Digest; UNESCO Latest available data

think that widening the EC means weakening its supra-national drive. Enlargement is gaining a more general appeal among those who see it, despite the costs, as the safest and tidiest way to meet the eastern problem.

A boost to the wideners is that it is almost certain that the EC will open its doors soon to countries from the European Free Trade Association (EFTA). Austria and Sweden have applied. Finland intends to soon. Switzerland, chaperoning tiny Liechtenstein, and Norway are likely to apply later this year. (Iceland says it does not want to join.)

Entry talks would be swift. The hard work was done in an EC-EFTA agreement initialled in February 1992. This was to create a common market between the two. EFTA countries would not pay EC taxes or get more than a minor say in EC decisions affecting them—in effect, a B-grade membership. If entry talks started this year or next, up to six EFTA countries could be grade-A members by January 1995.

That date matters. In 1996 the Twelve are to have another go at institutional reform. The EC summit at Maastricht in December 1991 was in a sense the closing of an old agenda. The next set of internal changes must almost certainly make adjustments for an expanded Community.

Not long after that, the EC could be in position to consider poor easterners. Czechoslovakia, Hungary, Poland, the three Baltic states and Slovenia look the most likely. If these are politically stable and press on with economic reform, they could be rich enough to join by, say, the year 2000. Hungary hopes, optimistically, to join by 1996. Exact timing matters less than the final goal. Confidence in eventual EC membership helped steady democracy in Spain and Portugal, even though it took them almost ten years to get it.

Enlargement raises an invidious question: who to leave out. Turkey has already been rebuffed once. Cyprus and Malta, who have applied, may also be asked to come back later. It is not only to the east that Europe's borders grow fuzzy. The Mediterranean helps, but where, to the south, does Europe stop?

The countries that are likely to join pose problems of neutrality, institutional clogging and budgetary overload. None looks insurmountable.

The end of the cold war makes **neutrality** less of an issue than it was. Norway and Iceland belong to NATO and most easterners want to join it. Austria's and Finland's neutrality—non-membership in either cold-war camp—was imposed on them. Sweden's and Switzerland's neutralism—no military alliances in peace, keeping out of others' wars—is a deliberate and long-held policy. Neutralism could still clash with EC membership as it develops common foreign and defence policies. (This is theoretically a problem for Ireland, which is not in NATO.)

To stop an enlarged Community from **clogging up**, it is likely that it would have to:

• Cut the ratio of commissioners to countries, currently 17 to 12.
• Lower the number of official languages (nine) to three or four.
• Make debate in the Council of Ministers more parliamentary: at the moment all 12 ministers speak in turn, however little they have to say.
• Keep the parliament's size (now 518 members) below 700-750.
• Reallocate the votes in the council and, for some issues, lower the majority required.

Adding poorer countries means more revenue-sharing or regional spending. That risks **budgetary overload**. To some extent rich countries would merely be passing through the EC budget money otherwise spent as aid

to the newcomers. The balance of poor and rich countries in the council would, all the same, shift dramatically: from four out of 12 now to 11 out of 25.

Some say that a Community that worked at six and again at 12 will work at 18 or 25. Deals can be made in an expanded council, just as they are now. Others say that 18 or so is a maximum beyond which the Community would lose its character as a tight-knit group of nations with common positions on world trade and foreign policy.

Neither view is right. With 18 or 25 members, the EC will not be able to go on as before. But nor will it seize up or collapse back into a collection of individual sovereignties. As it grows, members will sign up for different things at different times. This is known as a "variable-geometry" or "many-speed" Europe. Though federalists do not always like it, such a Europe is already taking shape.

The German question

German nationalism started or helped start three European wars between 1870 and 1945. Defeat in the last one cost Germany full nationhood. Now it has it back, the rest of Europe wants to know how it will be used. Most Europeans would prefer, as a trio of world powers, America, Japan and the Community to America, Japan and Germany. So probably would most Germans. The question is not "Germany in the EC or out?" but how Germany will it use its weight within.

Germany can be awkward if it chooses. It has the same number of seats in the parliament as Britain, France and Italy. But its population is almost half as big again and it wants more seats. Germany is the largest net contributor to the EC budget, to the tune of 9 billion ecus ($11.3 billion) a year. It is busy absorbing eastern Germany and in no mood to be so generous. Its push for European recognition of the breakaway Yugoslav republics, Croatia and Slovenia, showed a readiness to brush aside British and French pretensions to run Europe's foreign policy.

It is, though, historical fatalism to think that modern, democratic Germany must repeat its non-democratic past. Geography, certainly, gives it a special interest and a privileged position in the east. Yet for the foreseeable future Germany will have a

much bigger trade and investment stake in Western Europe.

Germany's weight in the EC is known. What is not known (most of all, it seems, by the Germans themselves) is how they are to use it. Will Germany nudge Europe towards a more *dirigiste* (French) or more free-market (British) capitalism? Will it push for an open trading block or a closed one which shuns investment from non-European multinationals? Will it continue to favour an Atlantic alliance linked to America or a more continental-minded Europe?

Though Germany will often be the deciding vote, on many of these points German opinion is divided. That leaves its smaller partners room to bargain and argue. As sumo wrestlers know, weight is not everything.

The western question

Western policy during the cold war was to contain the Soviet Union. But cold-war containment worked in a less expected way as well, by keeping economic friction between America, Europe and Japan within reasonable limits. Now that they are no longer united as anti-communists, might these three compete ever more aggressively among themselves as regional power blocks? And in that three-cornered fight, might a European patriotism be born?

Extrapolating the past suggests that, without a common enemy, the western powers could slip from being allies to being antagonists. But extrapolationism is dangerous. Shared interests can override economic conflicts. It is too soon to talk of world economic government. But the GATT, the IMF and the G7 all work so as to lessen economic frictions.

The metaphor of "power blocks" is itself misleading. Only America currently has the combination of wealth, military strength and political cohesion to make it a world power. Japan lacks the military strength, Europe the political cohesion. In terms of social and economic indicators (see charts), the countries of Europe add up to a large and growing presence in the world. As a world power, though, Europe does not yet exist.

The optimum unit of economic government is now larger than the European nation-state. For that reason alone, the European Community is likely to endure and prosper. There are other reasons for confidence in its future. Compared with other options, it still offers Germany and its neighbours the internal balance that Europe needs. Its economic work is far from done. There is almost a decade of change ahead to get Europe a single currency, and perhaps 20 years to complete the single market (1992 was just a beginning).

Despite common interests and shared views, many European states are hesitant about pooling diplomatic and military sovereignty. A benchmark of progress in this direction would be the EC's readiness to take a single seat on the Security Council at the United Nations. That still looks some way off.

The Community of the future will most probably remain a flexible hybrid with federal and in-ter-governmental features. It is a novel creature in world politics that could in time be imitated in Africa, America and Asia.

A leap from this sort of EC to a United States of Europe looks less probable. The pressures on European governments to pool economic sovereignty are different from those that produced modern nation-states. There is no urge for unification (19th-century Germany and Italy), no drive for separation (Muslim India in 1947; the Soviet republics in 1991), no desire for independence (decolonisation).

Two other things can help forge a sense of nationhood. One is democracy. Citizens, after all, have to be citizens of something. European voters do seem to want more control over the EC: they want their voice represented at the European level. But it is not clear they want a European authority to command their chief loyalty as citizens.

Outside pressure is another nation-former. Some Europeans see their continent as a 19th-century nation writ large, with interests to defend against all sorts of external threat, real or imagined: not just economic encroachment by Japan or America, but immigration from the east or the spread of Islam from the south. Yet these dangers do not look real enough to create Europeans. Where believed in, they seem to be fostering bitter nationalism more than Europeanism.

What is Europe? Who is a European? Herodotus thought that, scattered as they were, Greeks were one people because they spoke Greek and had distinctive common values. By that test, Europeans are not a people. No sane European speaks Esperanto or Volapuk. Europe's political values—democracy and human rights—are not Europe's alone. Even if race, religion or colour did define Europeans, they would be tests used by bigots.

An Italian patriot, Massimo d'Azeglio, said, "We have made Italy; now we must make Italians." Treating Europe as whatever Europeans believe it to be seems equally circular. Is Europe, then, a cultural area where musicians use the diatonic scale? Or a geographic one bounded by southern olive groves and northern beech forests?

The fact is that Europe does not need to be defined. It is by its nature open-ended. Whatever 21st-century Europe proves to be, it will not be a 19th-century nation-state built on a continental scale.

"The basis exists for democratic party-building and for economic development in post-Communist Eastern Europe. If the United States does not join the European Community in throwing an economic lifeline to these countries, the long-run cost may be much higher than the cost of taking part in the rescue effort."

Eastern Europe after the Revolutions

ROBIN ALISON REMINGTON

ROBIN ALISON REMINGTON is *professor of political science at the University of Missouri-Columbia. During 1988 and 1989 she was a Fulbright fellow at the Institute for International Politics and Economics in Belgrade, Yugoslavia. An earlier version of this article was presented in April 1991 at the Fulbright Institute of International Relations at the University of Arkansas, Fayetteville, and at a conference on introducing democracy in one-party systems at University of Central Arkansas, Conway, Arkansas.*

When the attempted coup by "the gang of eight" in the Soviet Union backfired in late August, it swept the opponents of perestroika off the political stage and the Soviet Communist party onto the rubbish heap of history. The results were momentous. The Soviet Union that had operated as the "significant other" of United States foreign policy in the post–World War II international system is, like the Warsaw Pact, history, and the North Atlantic Treaty Organization (NATO) an alliance in search of a mission. The cold war that defined and divided Europe is over.

In short, the Europe that set out on the road to economic unity in 1992 has disappeared. The member states of the European Community (EC) must now work through their differing conceptions of European integration in a radically changed political economy. Germany has been reunified. The Baltic states—Latvia, Lithuania, and Estonia—have been recognized as independent countries and accepted as members of the United Nations (UN). The EC can do little more than watch the possible emergence of new and needy states from the Soviet Union or the once federal Yugoslavia.

The success or failure of post-Communist Europe's transition to multiparty democracy and market economics will determine whether the European order taking shape mirrors the vision of 1992 or reflects a quagmire of national fragmentation and ethnic conflict. Politicians must adjust to a Europe in which the threat from the Soviet Union is not communism, but chaos; the danger is not an alien ideology, but a lack of conviction that the democratic model can do the job.

To understand the problems and prospects for building democracy in post-Communist Europe, we must remember that the cold war was not won on the battlefield. With the exception of the short, bloody battle to oust the dictator Nicolae Ceausescu and his "socialism in one family" in Romania, the collapse of Communism in Eastern Europe came without the threat or use of force. This was a victory of ideas, not military hardware.

The ideas at the heart of post-Communist Europe are not new. When Lithuanian President Vytautas Landsbergis spoke to the UN as his country was admitted to that body in September, he said, "our renunciation of fear and falsehood proved stronger than tanks and missiles." He echoed the conviction of the Czechoslovak playright Karel Capek, who wrote that "truth is more than power. . .violence cannot hold out against mankind's need for freedom, peace, and equality among peoples and nations."[1]

The realization that command economies designed to meet the challenges of the nineteenth century could not assimilate the potential of the scientific, technical, and information revolutions dominating the international political economy in the late twentieth century ultimately led Soviet President Mikhail Gorbachev to renounce the Brezhnev doctrine.* With that, the

---

*Editor's note: In 1968, Soviet President Leonid Brezhnev declared that the Soviet Union would regard any "threat to socialism" in its satellites, including internal liberalization, as sufficient justification for invasion. The Prague Spring of 1968 provided such a justification. Gorbachev rejected this doctrine in a speech before the Council of Europe in Strasbourg on July 7, 1989, acknowledging that European states belong to "different social systems. . . . Social and political orders [have] changed in the past and may change in the future. But this change is the exclusive affair of the people of that country and is their choice. Any interference in their domestic affairs and any attempts to restrict the sovereignty of states, both friends, allies, or any others, are inadmissible." See Lawrence Freedman, ed., *Europe Transformed: Documents on the End of the Cold War* (New York: St. Martin's Press, 1990).

[1] Karel Capek, *Lidove noviny*, September 9, 1938.

Reprinted with permission from *Current History* magazine, November 1991, pp. 379-383. Copyright © 1991 by Current History, Inc.

stranglehold the cold war had imposed on Eastern Europe was broken.

Throughout 1989 the power of the "new political thinking" that Gorbachev had unleashed in the Soviet Union found expression in Eastern Europe in demonstrations of "people power." In May 1989 ordinary citizens helped Hungarian soldiers tear down the barbed wire fence between Hungary and Austria. During the summer, East Germans, fed up with their government's refusal to reform, fled into Hungary and across the newly opened border between Hungary and Austria. The Berlin Wall crumbled in November, and Communist parties and governments began to fall throughout Eastern Europe.

EASTERN EUROPE'S REBIRTH

The rebirth of Eastern Europe is best understood as political theater. There is no director or permanent cast of professional political actors. Those who remain must assume new roles. Old rituals, myths, and behaviors are inappropriate. Symbolically, the Goddess of Democracy, whose statue was crushed by Chinese tanks in Tiananmen Square in Beijing in 1989, plays opposite the ghost of the crushed 1968 Prague Spring. The audience is constantly shouting demands; offstage actors (such as the International Monetary Fund [IMF]) give advice from the wings. And the politicians and peoples who will decide her fate have no script.

Scholars of the Soviet Union and Eastern Europe were accustomed to another political theater, one that was a stylized, well-rehearsed play. Like the Communist politicians who lost their jobs, they were caught off balance. Even those who thought change would come in Hungary and Poland did not foresee the political earthquake that shaped the territory of post-Communist Europe. No one knows how this new play will end, or has inside information on the ability of the new political leaders—the writers, dissidents, and born-again Communists—to safeguard the Goddess of Democracy. It is more useful to focus on the political scene, the political actors, and the fundamental passions that determine their relationships.

THE POLITICAL STAGE

The difference between Eastern Europe and post-Communist Europe must be kept in mind. The Eastern Europe we knew after World War II has disappeared. In a geographic sense, it never existed. When scholars and policymakers talked about Eastern Europe, they used an ideological shorthand for political and economic boundaries that divided Europe into two blocs.

Eastern Europe included six members of the Warsaw Pact (Bulgaria, Czechoslovakia, East Germany, Hungary, Poland, Romania), nonaligned Yugoslavia, and isolated Albania. The eight states that made up this region ranged in size from tiny Albania, with a population of 3 million, to Poland, with 38 million people. The coun-

tries of the region had varying levels of economic development, and different histories, nationalities, languages, and religions.

The Communist systems that came to power in Eastern Europe were thus superimposed on very different environments, and indigenous Communist politicians operated under different restraints. For 40 years local political cultures eroded the ideological superstructures coming from Moscow. However, notwithstanding Yugoslavia's socialist self-management and Romania's national Stalinism, the imperatives of the Communist subsystem, central economic planning, and the "leading role" of the party created a collective Eastern European identity from which even Yugoslavia was not immune. The legacy of shared economic problems, high political expectations, and low political institutionalization flowing from that identity is the wellspring of Eastern Europe's multiparty political systems.

THE PLAY AND ITS ACTORS

As Czechoslovak President Vaclav Havel has put it, the poetry is over, and the prose is beginning. Instead of imposed uniformity and ritualized ideological jargon, Eastern European politicians now speak with many voices. Western scholars and policymakers, like Eastern European voters, must sort out signal from noise in these new political systems.

These new governments face the problems of economic reform, ethnic hostility, and territorial conflicts. Establishing democratic governments and market economies involves a tug-of-war between national self-determination and economic viability. This creates political pressures for fragmentation that are countered by economic pressures for the cohesion that will allow post-Communist Europe to join the EC's march toward European integration. Much will depend on how quickly politicians learn or rewrite the rules of the new political game, on which political parties survive, on the ratio of frustration to patience in populations who now know they can throw out politicians who do not deliver, and on armies no longer inhibited from intervening in the political process.

The political actors in post-Communist Eastern Europe are a varied group. In four countries the Communist party is a minority partner in a coalition government (Czechoslovakia, Hungary, Poland, and Romania); in Bulgaria a reform Communist majority government is headed by a non-Communist president; in Yugoslavia the Communist government's ruling party has essentially collapsed from within, and the government itself may become the victim of civil war; and Albania's ruling Communist party is trying desparately to adapt to demands for economic reform and democratization. As of October 3, 1990, post-Communist East Germany had become an internal problem for a united Germany and as such will share—if not equally—German space in the common European home.

THE SEARCH FOR IDENTITY

The political dynamics in the seven countries that make up post-Communist Eastern Europe consist of the search of peoples and politicians for identity and security. On one level the revolutions of 1989 were a popular rejection of ideological, class-defined identity. The "nation" was rehabilitated. Look at any map of new or old Europe and the political implications of a return to historic national and ethnic identities are evident. The search for a new Yugoslavia could not withstand the June 1991 demands for Slovenian and Croatian independence. These two republics' declarations of independence collided with the unwillingness of militant Serbs in Croatia to live in an independent Croat state, and the determination of Serbian politicians to redraw Serbia's borders before the dissident republics divorced themselves from a federal Yugoslavia.

Romanians and Hungarians squared off over the issue of Transylvania. In Czechoslovakia, Slovak has become the official language of Slovakia, while the roughly half-million ethnic Hungarians living in that part of the republic may use Hungarian for official business in communities where they make up at least 20 percent of the population. This spring Slovaks hurled abuse at President Havel in Bratislava, and he has submitted a bill to parliament to hold a referendum on Czech-Slovak unity. Even in Poland, where 98 percent of the population is Polish, there are demographic and legal questions concerning the ethnic Germans who reside in territory that became part of Poland after World War II.

Among the political parties proliferating throughout the region (by October 1990 some 172 were registered in Yugoslavia) are those that are based on historic nations and those who view their mission as protecting the rights of national minorities such as the Macedonians in Bulgaria, Hungarians in Romania, or Gypsies in Czechoslovakia. Regardless of whether these parties make significant electoral inroads, no Hungarian government can afford to ignore the plight of the Hungarian minority in Transylvania, and no Macedonian politician will decline to speak out about what Yugoslav Macedonians consider cultural oppression of Macedonians in Bulgaria. Inevitably, the fate of "our brothers martyred in Kosovo" (a predominantly Albanian region in Yugoslavia) is high among the concerns of the opposition Albanian Democratic party. The search for identity increases the potential for violence both within the countries of Eastern Europe and between them.

THE SEARCH FOR SECURITY

The dissolution of the Warsaw Pact and the search for identity have changed the mission of the region's armies to one of providing internal security or satisfying regional foreign policy objectives. Under these circumstances, it is likely that, despite the acknowledged end of the cold war and a declining East-West threat, there will be no "peace dividend" for post-Communist Europe. Fear of national and ethnic regional conflict may not allow post-Communist leaders to reduce their armed forces and redirect the flow of resources to civil society. But this brings up another dimension of security that is especially important to Eastern Europe's workers: economic security.

The social contract the Eastern European Communist regimes offered their populations was that acceptance of one-party hegemonic systems and limited sovereignty within a family of socialist nations would bring a steady, if slow, improvement in their standard of living as their countries moved forward on the road to socialism. One of the reasons that Communist politicians adopted the "borrow now, pay later" strategy of the 1970s was to postpone cuts in subsidies on basic goods that their citizens had come to take for granted.

However, for soft-currency economies, hard-currency debts are like being addicted to crack. It is clear that, by the 1980s, these export-driven economies were hooked on foreign debt, like much of the third world. Debt servicing absorbed more and more of their hard-currency earnings and depleted investment funds. Borrowing hard currency to service these debts was equivalent to putting a Band-Aid on a problem that required major surgery.

With the dramatic collapse of communism, post-Communist politicians and planners look to the market as a panacea. They are undoubtedly right that a "great leap" into market economics will mobilize whatever external aid is available. However, the problem with using the market to regulate these economies is that the institution of market mechanisms will be followed by unemployment, inflation, and the imposition of IMF austerity programs.

The miners who rioted and called for the resignation of Romanian Prime Minister Petre Roman and President Ion Iliescu in September 1991 were not concerned with Iliescu's lack of democratic credentials. They demanded higher pay, lower prices, and an end to market-oriented reforms that were making their lives even more miserable than they had been under Ceausescu's iron rule.

Whatever the fate of Iliescu's government, it is a sobering reminder that when Eastern European workers, students, and housewives took to the streets against their Communist leaders, they did so in large part because their increasingly paralyzed command economies had failed to deliver. Measures to alleviate the hardships of the transition to a market economy are thus high on popular public policy agendas.

But for market economies to become a reality, post-Communist workers and consumers must learn new ways of thinking and new economic behavior. Workers must become more productive, but accept salaries that buy less. Subsidies must be eliminated. For many Eastern Europeans, the situation will deteriorate further before it improves. Economic security is not in the cards.

OBSTACLES ON THE ROAD TO CAPITALISM?

Poland and Yugoslavia offer two case studies on the adoption of market economics. Poland, which became the first country in Eastern Europe to have a non-Communist coalition government since 1945, has had huge difficulties in its attempt to apply "cold turkey capitalism" to the tottering Polish economy. In December 1990, Solidarity Prime Minister Tadeusz Mazowiecki did not even make the runoff in the country's presidential elections, which speaks volumes about the appeal IMF prescriptions had for Polish voters.

Former Solidarity leader Lech Walesa won the runoff against Stanislaw Tyminski, a Polish-born Canadian millionaire whose rags to riches story captured the Polish people's imagination. Notwithstanding the government's subsequent ability to negotiate a substantial reduction in Poland's $48-billion foreign debt, multiple opposition parties are challenging Prime Minister Jan Bielecki's economic program.

In Yugoslavia, the other experiment with the "Polish road to capitalism" is less well known because the American media has largely abandoned reporting on anything other than ethnic battles between Serbs and Croats, cease-fires, and rumors of army coups. Yet before the collapse into virtual civil war this summer, the Yugoslav economy was a relative success story.

At the end of 1989, Prime Minister Ante Markovic tackled an official annual inflation rate of 2,600 percent (unofficially thought to be much higher) with a six-month anti-inflation package worked out with the advice of Harvard University economist Jeffrey Sachs and under IMF supervision. By April 1990 Yugoslavia had a negative monthly rate of inflation. Notwithstanding the impact of summer wage increases, the annual inflation rate was projected to be about 20 percent (unofficially it was estimated at more than 100 percent).

However, the prime minister could not deliver on his promise that Yugoslavia would continue to function with or without the Communist party. During the spring of 1990, center-right oppositions won elections in Slovenia and Croatia. In May, Markovic announced that he would assemble an Alliance of Reform Forces and hold federal elections by the end of the year. Serbian president Slobodan Milosevic countered by merging the Serbian League of Communists with its own mass organization, the Socialist Alliance, to form the Socialist party of Serbia. Although he reluctantly allowed

opposition parties to take part in the subsequent Serbian elections, Milosevic continued to seek his legitimacy in the whirlwind of Serbian nationalism. His insistence on playing "the Serbian card" and economic mismanagement greatly sabotaged Markovic's economic progress and pushed the negotiations over the confederal or federal future of Yugoslavia into armed conflict.

Milosevic shares the blame for the ongoing "Lebanonization" of Yugoslavia. Croatian politicians who insisted on rewriting the Croatian constitution in a manner that played into his hands by inflaming the fears of the Serbian minority are also to blame; so are those in the Yugoslav federal army who either supported Serbian militants in the self-declared autonomous region of Krajina or would not protect the Croatian and Yugoslav economy by keeping the road through Krajina to the Dalmatian coast open. Slovenian decision makers, who backed out of their agreement to allow the joint presence of federal and Slovenenian customs officials on Slovenia's borders while negotiations about the future Yugoslavia continued, share blame with those in the increasingly paralyzed federal government who decided to use the army to escort federal customs officials back to their posts. The same goes for the Slovenians who gloated over the humiliation of the Yugoslav army when Slovenian defense forces kept firing after the army had agreed to a cease-fire.

The European Community contributed to stabilizing the conflict in Slovenia, but has been largely powerless to cope with escalating violence in Croatia. And Germany's threat to recognize Slovenia and Croatia essentially backfired when the Croatians attempted to speed up the republic's progress toward independence by isolating and cutting off food, water, and electricity to federal army garrisons in Croatia. As it became clear that neither EC recognition nor armed peacekeeping forces were in the offing, a fragile truce emerged between Croatian leaders and the federal forces, themselves challenged by a growing opposition within Serbia itself as well as by open resistance from Bosnia-Herzegovina and Macedonia.[2]

The concept of Yugoslavia as a federal republic is in tatters. If the fighting continues, what will be left of an "independent Croatia?" If "a greater Serbia" is the "winner," Serbs will be prisoners of the war economy that will be required to keep those who consider themselves "captive nations" in line. This is not a zero-sum game; it is a lose-lose scenario.

CONTRIBUTIONS FROM THE AUDIENCE

Ideally, the collapse of the Communist monopoly of power and the rise of multiparty systems in post-Communist Europe would allow Eastern Europeans to become masters of their fate. However, in the political economy of the twenty-first century, that is probably wishful thinking. Unless the West is willing to prime the pump of post-Communist economies to help these

---

[2]*The New York Times*, September 20, 1991. The German preference for a more active peacekeeping role was strongly resisted by British Foreign Secretary Douglas Hurd, who reminded his EC colleagues of the tribulations of British forces in Northern Ireland. Indeed, strains that emerged during the tense days of EC efforts at conflict resolution pointed to the larger danger that Zoran Sekulic referred to as "a Yugoslavization of Europe." See *The International Weekly* (Belgrade), September 14–20, 1991.

fragile democratic coalitions deliver some short-term economic success while they consolidate electoral victories, their governments will not survive.

The most effective strategy would be for the EC and the United States to collaborate on a Marshall Plan for post-Communist Europe. But Western financial resources are undeniably limited. A fallback position that would buy time and credibility would be to grant debt-servicing moratoriums of between three and five years. The United States has suggested that such an option might be available for Latin America debtors under some circumstances. A similar option should be made available to the countries of post-Communist Eastern Europe.

---

[3]Richard A. Gephardt, "America's Role in the New Europe" (Presentation to the Belgian Commission on Security, a Symposium on a New Security Model for Europe, Brussels, Belgium, February 23, 1990).

[4]Richard A. Gephardt, "American Leadership in the New World" (Presentation to the Center for National Policy, Washington, D.C., March 6, 1990).

Legislation in the 1990 United States Congress reportedly provided "more than half a billion dollars as . . .an investment in East European democracy"[3] Considering the cost involved in containing communism, it is not much of an investment in democracy. It is not even a very serious beginning, especially if we take House Majority Leader Richard Gephardt (D-Mo.) at his word that the Marshall Plan would cost $82 billion today.[4]

Post-Communist Europe has evolved into a mixed bag of multiparty systems. In order for stable, democratic polities to develop, there must be a solid foundation of economic development. Without credible economic performance, post-Communist politicians risk being reduced to nationalist rhetoric and anti-Communist witch hunts in their search for legitimacy.

The basis exists for democratic party-building and for economic development in post-Communist Eastern Europe. If the United States does not join the European Community in throwing an economic lifeline to these countries, the long-run cost may be much higher than the cost of taking part in the rescue effort.

The Soviet State, Born of a Dream, Dies

Serge Schmemann

Special to The New York Times

MOSCOW, Dec. 25—The Soviet state, marked throughout its brief but tumultuous history by great achievement and terrible suffering, died today after a long and painful decline. It was 74 years old.

Conceived in utopian promise and born in the violent upheavals of the "Great October Revolution of 1917," the union heaved its last in the dreary darkness of late December 1991, stripped of ideology, dismembered, bankrupt and hungry—but awe-inspiring even in its fall.

The end of the Soviet Union came with the resignation of Mikhail S. Gorbachev to make way for a new "Commonwealth of Independent States." At 7:32 P.M., shortly after the conclusion of his televised address, the red flag with hammer-and-sickle was lowered over the Kremlin and the white-blue-red Russian flag rose in its stead.

No Ceremony, Only Chimes

There was no ceremony, only the tolling of chimes from the Spassky Gate, cheers from a handful of surprised foreigners and an angry tirade from a lone war veteran.

Reactions to the death varied widely, according to Pravda, the former mouthpiece of the empire: "Some joyfully exclaim, 'Finita la comedia!' Others, heaping ash on their heads, raise their hands to the sky in horror and ask, what will be?"

The reaction depended somewhat on whether one listened to the ominous gunfire from Georgia, or watched spellbound the bitter if dignified surrender of power by the last leader of the Union of Soviet Socialist Republics, Mr. Gorbachev.

Most people vacillated. The taboos and chains were gone, but so was the food. The Soviet Union had given them pitifully little, but there was no guarantee that the strange-sounding "Commonwealth of Independent States" would do any better.

As for Mr. Gorbachev, public opinion polls indicated a virtually universal agreement that it was time for him to move on—not because he had failed, but because there was nothing more he could do.

It was perhaps a paradox that the ruler who presided over the collapse of the Soviet Union was the only one of its ill-starred leaders to leave office with a measure of dignity intact. It was possible that history would reach a different verdict, but among many thoughtful Russians, it was to his undying credit that he lifted the chains of totalitarian dictatorship. Whether he could also have saved the economy was another question.

"Gorbachev was unable to change the living standards of the people, but he changed the people," Komsomolskaya Pravda wrote in a sympathetic farewell that seemed to capture the dominant mood. "He didn't know how to make sausage, but he did know how to give freedom. And if someone believes that the former is more important than the latter, he is likely never to have either."

Another man might have done things differently. But it was difficult to conceive that any of those then available— the conservative Yegor K. Ligachev, the rough-hewn Boris N. Yeltsin, the bureaucratic Nikolai I. Ryzhkov or the scholarly Eduard A. Shevardnadze— possessed just that blend of reformer and ideologue, of naïveté and ruthlessness, that enabled Mr. Gorbachev to lead the Communists to the edge of the cliff.

"Gorbachev was a true instrument of fate," declared Viktor Yerofeyev, a writer and literary critic. "He had just enough intelligence to change everything, but not enough to see that everything would be destroyed. He was bold enough to challenge his party, and cautious enough to let the party live until it lost its power. He had enough faith in Communism to be named its head, but enough doubts about it to destroy it. If he had seen everything clearly, he would not have changed Russia."

Mr. Gorbachev struggled to the end, and beyond it, to keep the union alive. But in the end, it was by letting the union die and by stepping aside that he gave a new lease on life to the great Eurasian entity, whatever its name.

The Union
EPIC ACHIEVEMENT AND EPIC FAILURE

Measured against is own ambitions, the U.S.S.R. died a monumental failure.

It had promised no less than the creation of a "Soviet new man," imbued with selfless devotion to the common good, and it ended up all but crushing the initiative and spirit of the people.

From *The New York Times*, December 26, 1991, pp. A1, A14-A15. Copyright © 1991 by The New York Times Company. Reprinted by permission.

making many devoted only to vodka. It had proclaimed a new humanitarian ideology, and in its name butchered 10 million of its own. It envisioned a planned economy in which nothing was left to chance, and it created an elephantine bureaucracy that finally smothered the economy. Promising peace and freedom, it created the world's most militarized and ruthless police state.

Promising a people's culture, it created an anti-culture in which mediocrity was glorified and talent was ruthlessly persecuted. An entire department of the K.G.B. existed to wrestle with art, trying first to co-opt any rising talent "to the service of the state" and if that failed, to muzzle or exile it. The roll-call of repressed or exiled artists is a stunning indictment: Mandelstam, Malevich, Pasternak, Solzhenitsyn, Rostropovich, Brodsky, and so many more.

In the end, promising a new life, it created an unspeakably bleak society—polluted, chronically short of everything, stripped of initiative and spirituality. While the bulk of the nation stood in line or guzzled rot-gut vodka, the Communist elite raised corruption to new heights: The likes of Leonid I. Brezhnev and his cronies pinned endless medals on one another and surrounded themselves with a peasant's notion of luxury—grandiose candelabras, massive cars, vast hunting estates, armies of sycophants, secret hospitals filled with the latest Western technology.

And yet the Soviet Union was also an indisputable superpower, a state and a people that achieved epic feats in science, warfare, even culture.

Perhaps all this was achieved despite Communism, not because of it. Yet by some combination of force and inspiration, the system begun by Lenin and carried out by Stalin unleashed a potent national energy that made possible the rapid industrialization of the 1930's, the defeat of Nazi Germany in the 1940's, the launching of the first Sputnik in the 1950's, the creation of a nuclear arsenal in the 1960's and 1970's. Even now, for all the chaos in the land, two astronauts, Aleksandr A. Volkov and Sergei Krikalev, continue to circle the globe.

In culture too, both the "thaw" of Nikita S. Khrushchev in the 1960's and the "glasnost" of Mr. Gorbachev offered testimony that the enormous creativity of the nation was as tenacious as the people.

And in sport, the tangle of Olympic medals and international victories were a tacit source of national pride even among the staunchest critics of the Communist regime.

The Dream
A UTOPIAN ILLUSION SURVIVED INJUSTICE

It is easy now, gazing over the smoldering ruins of the Soviet empire, to enumerate the fatal illusions of the Marxist system. Yet the irresistible utopian dream fired generations of reformers, revolutionaries and radicals here and abroad, helping spread Soviet influence to the far corners of the globe.

Until recently, rare was the third world leader who did not espouse some modified Marxist doctrine, who did not make a regular pilgrimage to Moscow to join in the ritual denunciations of the "imperialists."

Much of it was opportunism, of course. In the Soviet Union as in the third world, Communism offered a handy justification for stomping on democracy and keeping one party and one dictator in power.

Yet it was also a faith, one strong enough to survive all the injustices done in its name. Lev Kopelev, a prominent intellectual now living in Germany, recalled in his memoirs how prisoners emerged from the gulag after Stalin's death firmly believing that at last they could start redressing the "errors" of Stalinism and truly building Communism.

And only last March, Mr. Gorbachev would still declare in Minsk, "I am not ashamed to say that I am a Communist and adhere to the Communist idea, and with this I will leave for the other world."

The tenacity of the faith testified to the scope of the experiment. It was a monumental failure, but it had been a grand attempt, an experiment on a scale the world had never known before.

Perhaps it was the height of folly and presumption that Russia, a country then only at the dawn of industrialization and without a bourgeoisie or proletariat to speak of, would have been the one to proclaim itself the pioneer of a radically new world order.

Two Worlds
'WESTERNIZERS' vs. 'SLAVOPHILES'

But Russians have always had a weakness for the broad gesture. The greatest czars—Ivan the Terrible, Peter the Great—were those with the grandest schemes. The greatest writers, Dostoyevsky and Tolstoy, explored ultimate themes in immense novels. The Russian Orthodox Church embroidered its churches and its liturgy in the most elaborate gilding and ceremony.

Nothing happened small in the Soviet era, either. Twenty million died in the war, 10 million more in the gulag. And the pride of place was always given to grandiose construction projects—the world's biggest hydroelectric plant at Bratsk, the world's biggest truck factory at Kamaz, the trans-Siberian railroad.

The czarist merchant wrapped in coats of gold and sable racing in his sleigh through wretched muzhiks in birch-bark shoes translated into the ham-fisted party boss tearing through Moscow in his long black limousine.

Many theories have been put forward to explain these traits. There is the sheer expanse of a country that spans 11 time zones. There is the climate, which imposed a rhythm of long, inactive winters punctuated by brief summers of intense labor. Some posited the absence of a Renaissance, which stunted the development of an individual consciousness and sustained a spirit of collectivism.

Above all it was a nation straddling two continents and two cultures, forever torn and forever fired by the creative clash at the faultline of East and West.

Russians have ever split into "Westernizers" and "Slavophiles," and the death of the Soviet Union had everything to do with the struggle between the "Westernizing" democrats and free-marketeers and the anti-Western champions of powerful statehood and strong center.

The West has always been deemed both attractive and dangerous to Russia. Peter the Great campaigned desperately to open his nation to the West, but Westerners remained suspect and isolated. Communism found nourishing soil in the Russian spirit of collectivism, but its Western materialism proved alien.

Western democracy is foundering here on the same ambivalence. The Soviets plunged whole-heartedly into the plethora of new councils and parliaments inaugurated by Mr. Gorbachev. But their endless debate and inability to organize into cohesive interest groups soon diminished public attention, and at the end the parliaments readily transferred most of their powers to Mr. Gorbachev, Mr. Yeltsin and other powerful men.

"What remains after the Soviet Union is this Eurasian essence, this unique interplay of Europe and Asia, which will continue to amaze the world with its culture and totally unexpected actions," Mr. Yerofeyev said.

"What was imported in Western Marxism will vanish," he continued. "But Communism will not disappear, inasmuch as the spirit of collectivism is at the heart of this nation. The nation will always say 'we' rather than the Anglo-Saxon 'I'.

"This was Lenin's deftness, that he realized Russia was ready to accept Communism, but needed only 'class struggle' for everything to fall into place. As soon as it had an enemy, the collective consciousness became dynamic."

Contrasts
IMPRESSIVE FEATS, AWESOME LITTER

That spirit was forever captured in the revolutionary posters, with their capitalists in top hats dripping workers' blood, or the muscular young Communists crushing bourgeois vipers.

Lenin's successors understood this equally well, that it was easier to fire Soviets to enormous feats and extraordinary sacrifice than to organize them for sustained work and steady growth.

The capacity for suffering and sacrifice, whether in the war or in the endless lines today, is something that still awes foreigners. The ability to focus enormous talent and energy on a grand project is equally impressive, and from this came the great achievements in science, weaponry and construction.

Yet the sloppiness and inefficiency of

everyday life make an even stronger impression on visitors. The shoddiness of even the newest apartment block or hotel is shocking. Old houses seem to list precariously in the mud. Wreckage litters every yard. Cars come off the assembly lines half broken.

The planned economy served only to intensify the squalor. It made volume, not quality or inventiveness, the primary measure of production, and it put a premium on huge factories over flexibility or distribution.

The system also gave consumer goods the lowest possible priority, thus institutionalizing shortages and reducing ordinary people to a permanent state of dependence on the state and rude salespeople.

Icons
THE CULTS END IN STATE'S DOTAGE

Whether Lenin would have built the Soviet state this way is not certain. Three years before his death, in 1921, he replaced "War Communism" with what became known as the "New Economic Policy," but was in fact a return to a measure of old laissez-faire. The national income rose to pre-revolutionary levels, but that failed to dissuade Stalin from starting the first Five-Year Plan.

Nonetheless, it was Lenin who became the first deity of the new order. He was a convenient hero: He had died while still enormously popular, and he left behind enough writings on every topic to support whatever position his successors chose to take.

Thus his goateed visage soon became the mandatory icon in every official building or every town square, and his words became scripture. All the powers of science were summoned to preserve his remains forever, and his mausoleum became the spiritual heart of the new empire. His name became an adjective denoting orthodoxy, as in "the Leninist way." Plaques were raised at every building he stayed in, and an enormous temple was built over his childhood home.

The cult seemed only to gain strength with the passing years, as his successors denounced one another and struggled to portray themselves as the one true interpreter of Lenin. Stalin set the trend, killing most of Lenin's

comrades as he perfected the machinery of repression, all the while claiming to act in the name of the great founder.

Next, Khrushchev dismantled the Stalin cult and halted the worst of the terror in the name of restoring "true Leninism," only to be overthrown himself. Before long, Brezhnev was the sole heir, and Khrushchev's "voluntarism" joined Stalin's "personality cult" among the heresies of Leninism.

With Brezhnev, the Soviet state passed visibly into dotage. As he grew bloated and incoherent, so did the state. Production fell while an uncontrolled military machine devoured ever-larger portions of the national product. Foreign policy sank into a pattern of stagnant coexistence and fierce military competition with the West, while at home the political police steadily put down the small but brave dissident movement inspired by the brief Khrushchevian thaw.

After 18 years in power, Brezhnev was succeeded by two other old and sick men, Yuri V. Andropov and Konstantin U. Chernenko, and by the time Mr. Gorbachev took the helm in 1985, it was obvious to all that the state was in radical need of help.

Mr. Gorbachev, at 54 the youngest Soviet leader since Stalin, electrified the land almost immediately with the introduction of "glasnost," or openness. Suddenly the people could talk and think freely, taboos began to crumble, East-West hostilities evaporated, and dissidents emerged from labor camps and exile. The sweet perfume of hope scented the air.

But Mr. Gorbachev's parallel attempts to reform the economy perished on the same shoals as all previous reforms—the thick and privileged Communist party apparat. The more glasnost flourished, the more it became evident that perestroika was foundering, and everything Mr. Gorbachev did seemed to be too little or too late.

Floundering in the end, he lurched first to the left, ordering a radical "500 day" reform plan in the summer of 1989, then to the right, rejecting the plan and encircling himself with party stalwarts and letting them use force, then back to the left last spring, opening negotiations with the republics on a new Union Treaty.

By then it was too late. The rejected right-wingers tried to seize power by force in the August coup, and with their defeat, the republics had no more need for or faith in Mr. Gorbachev or the remnants of his union.

On Dec. 8, the leaders of Russia, Ukraine and Byelorussia pulled the plug, proclaiming a new Commonwealth of Independent States, and after that it was only a question of time before the breathing stopped.

Afterlife
PROBLEMS SURVIVE BUT WILL PRIDE?

The union was dead. But the great Eurasian entity on which it fed remained very much alive—as Russia, as a new Commonwealth of 11 republics, as a culture and a worldview, as a formidable nuclear arsenal, as a broad range of unresolved crises.

The gunfire in Georgia, the long lines across the land, the closed airports and the myriad unanswered questions about the new Commonwealth—would it confer citizenship? would it remain a single military and economic entity? would it manage transport and communications?—made clear that the legacy of the union would long survive.

Mr. Gorbachev had given people a new freedom. But the Soviet Union had also given them something tangible—the pride of superpower. Whatever their problems and shortages, they had been one of the two arbiters of global destinies, a nation that nobody could intimidate or bully.

Now that was being taken away, too, and how the humiliation would play out, especially in conditions of hunger and poverty, was among the troubling questions for the future.

"The parting with the Union of Soviet Socialist Republics will be long and difficult," Izvestia warned. "We must acknowledge that many will not believe or agree to the end of their days with the death warrant written in Minsk and confirmed in Alma-Ata. The idea of superpower has a force equal to nationalism, and in certain conditions it is also capable of uniting millions of fanatic supporters."

Left With a Kingdom of Air

How Gorbachev was swept aside by the tide of history

Michael Dobbs

Washington Post Foreign Service

The people feel no mercy: You do good and no one thanks you.

— Czar Boris Godunov,
in a poem by Alexander Pushkin

MOSCOW—How will history judge Mikhail Sergeyevich Gorbachev? Of all the remarkable leaders to emerge in the 20th century—Lenin, Hitler, Roosevelt, Churchill, Mao—the last general secretary of the Soviet Communist Party and the last president of the Soviet Union is the most enigmatic. He was the Communist who dismantled communism, the reformer who was overtaken by his own reforms, the emperor who permitted the world's last multinational empire to break apart. In the eyes of some, he was the deliverer of freedom. For others, he was the defender of the old, repressive order.

Gorbachev was reduced to presiding over a kingdom of air: ignored by the leaders of the Soviet republics as they formed a new Commonwealth of Independent States; disliked by his own people and blamed by many for the economic chaos sweeping the country; prodded to leave office by nearly all his former colleagues; and seemingly powerless to alter this last, sad chapter of the Soviet saga.

Future generations are likely to associate Gorbachev with something that was the very opposite of his original intention: the destruction of Soviet communism and the fatal weakening of the world's second superpower. When he came to power in 1985, he promised to make the Soviet Union stronger by breathing new life into its socialist system and revitalizing its moribund economy. As he was leaving office in December 1991, the Soviet Union is no more and socialism is totally discredited. The economy is in a bigger shambles than ever.

But the peasant boy from southern Russia who rose through the Communist bureaucracy to become master of the Kremlin will also be remembered as the man who helped end the Cold War and returned free speech to a great nation. Except for the odd historical interval, Russia has always been a land of censors and secret policemen making conformists out of all but the boldest. Gorbachev made it possible for everyone to speak his mind, opening the floodgates to a torrent of complaints and wildly conflicting opinions that eventually swept him aside.

"Many different emotions boil up inside me when I think of Gorbachev," says Anatoly Medvedev, a centrist Russian legislator whose political career would not have been possible without the reforms introduced by the last Communist czar. "He started the process of liberating us from totalitarian rule and created the conditions for the end of communism. But, through his vacillation and indecision, he also undermined our common statehood."

"Gorbachev is a mystery. It is not clear whether he is a reformer or a destroyer, a worthy holder of the Nobel Peace Prize or the man who disrupted a country that covers one-sixth of the Earth's surface," says Yuri Shchekochikin, a leading Soviet commentator and one of the last journalists to interview the Soviet president. "He tried to reconcile the irreconcilable: communism and democracy. He gave the slaves freedom, and they ended up cursing him."

Perhaps the best explanation for the Gorbachev enigma lies in his unique historical mission. He was the agent chosen by history for the subversion of the totalitarian order established by Lenin and Stalin. To destroy this monster, Gorbachev had to proceed by stealth. A master of Kremlin intrigue, he bobbed and weaved between rival factions, hiding his true intentions in a fog of Communist rhetoric. Sometimes, it seemed, he was unable to admit even to himself the revolutionary consequences of his actions.

From *The Washington Post National Weekly Edition*, December 23-29, 1991, pp. 6-7. Copyright © 1991, The Washington Post.

"I knew the system from the inside. After all, I had spent 10 years as a regional party secretary," Gorbachev told Shchekochikin in a revealing interview in Literaturnaya Gazeta. "I knew the strength [of the party and KGB security police]. And what I am able to say now, I was unable to say before. I had to outmaneuver them."

"Gorbachev had no choice but to be duplicitous," says Alexander M. Yakovlev, a prominent constitutional lawyer. "If he had revealed his hand, the hard-liners would have acted much more decisively. They would not have behaved as they did in the coup last August, when they thought that they might be able to persuade him to come over to their side. His duplicity saved us from enormous bloodshed."

Gorbachev's talent for compromise and prevarication was both his strength and his weakness. His tactical maneuvers probably saved the country from a return to hard-line Communist rule on several occasions. But by refusing to make a decisive break with the past, he lost his chance to introduce meaningful economic reforms. He bought time politically but squandered it economically. While the president was playing his games with the party apparatus, both the economy and the state were rapidly disintegrating. It finally cost him not only his job, but also the superpower he had sworn to reconstruct.

To understand Mikhail Gorbachev, it is necessary to understand the age that produced him. He is the child of a generation that experienced terror, hunger and war—along with a primitive Communist idealism. He was born in the rich agricultural region of Stavropol near the Caucasus mountains in 1931, when Stalin's murderous campaign against the independent peasantry was at its height. Millions of peasants were killed or deported to Siberia. The rest were herded onto collective farms.

For many years, Gorbachev never talked about these times or the fate of his own family. Only recently did he reveal that one of his grandfathers was arrested in Stalin's great purge of Communist officials in 1937, while another grandfather was sent to Siberia for failing to fulfill the spring crop-sowing plan. During the terrible famine of 1933, three of Gorbachev's uncles and aunts died of hunger.

In his interview with Literaturnaya Gazeta, Gorbachev traced his decision to launch his *perestroika* reform movement to this terrible period. "All this is in me," he said. "If I hadn't come to the inner conviction that everything had to change, I would have acted like the leaders before me acted. Like Brezhnev. I could have lived like an emperor for 10 years and not given a damn about what happened after me. . . . Is there another case in history when a man, having acquired so much power, has given it up?"

But mixed in with the horror at what Gorbachev later described as the "boundless cruelty and sinister disrespect for human life" was a naive belief in a shining, socialist future. For millions of people, Gorbachev included, the Communist Party became a means of personal advancement. They knew the system had terrible flaws, but they were also impressed by the scale of post-war reconstruction. After Stalin died in 1953, his successor, Nikita Khrushchev, encouraged them to dream of a socialism with a human face.

Gorbachev has identified himself with the generation that came of age during the Khrushchev "thaw," the so-called *shestidesyatniki*, or men of the '60s. (Some of the relatively liberal policies that Khrushchev initiated lasted until the Soviet invasion of Czechoslovakia in 1968, even though Khrushchev was ousted in 1964). It was a generation that was both supportive and critical of the system, perhaps the last generation of Communist believers before the onset of general cynicism under Leonid Brezhnev.

"The shestidesyatniki believed in socialism for a long time, but a different kind of socialism from the socialism of their everyday experience. They wanted a free democratic society in which they could realize their own potential," says Len Karpinsky, a political commentator who worked with Gorbachev in the Communist youth league, Komsomol. "Many became disillusioned after 1968, but Gorbachev remained true to his convictions."

It is difficult to tell whether Gorbachev's repeated assertions of his faith in socialism were a matter of ideological conviction, political opportunism or sheer emotional stubbornness. At a meeting with intellectuals a year ago, he said that betraying socialism would be like betraying his father and grandfather. "I am not ashamed to say that I am a Communist and am devoted to the socialist idea," he told the intellectuals. "My choice was made a long time ago, and it is a final one."

Unlike Russian President Boris Yeltsin, another former regional party boss, Gorbachev was never able to break with the milieu from which he came. His political authority derived from his leadership of the ruling party, rather than a genuine popular mandate. Right up until the August coup, he remained a man of the party, at home with its petty intrigues and its stilted bureaucratic language. Even after the bulk of the party leadership betrayed him during the coup, he still remained rhetorically committed to "the cause of socialism."

In the end, Gorbachev's fatal flaw proved to be his loyalty to a party that had discredited itself in the eyes of most Soviets. It meant that he was unable to forge a bond with the people and acquire the popular legitimacy he needed to make a decisive break with the past. His rationale for remaining party leader was clear: He feared that the most powerful and organized political force in the country could slip out of his control. But, in trying to control the party bureaucracy, he also became its hostage.

"Gorbachev clung for far too long to the illusion that the Communist Party was capable of reforming itself," says Karpinsky, the Soviet leader's former Komsomol colleague. "He was more influenced by the people who surrounded him than the democratic forces he had himself unleashed. He sided with them until the very last moment."

Like many reforming czars, Gorbachev faced the problem of how to break the power of the boyars, the conservative elite. Through his policy of *glasnost*, or openness, he sought to give the hitherto quiescent population a political voice to counteract the influence of the modern-day boyars, the Communist Party *nomenklatura*, or key cadre. But he was still playing court politics. In contrast to Yeltsin, he was never willing to turn his back completely on the boyars and rely on the people. There was always the fear that he might be thrown out of office.

"It was hard to break through the cement of the totalitarian system," says Georgi Shakhnazarov, Gorbachev's longtime political adviser. "This explains his hesitations, his occasional lack of confidence, the fact that he sometimes lagged behind events. Every step of the way, he had to think how to stay in office in order to be able to continue carrying through reforms."

A decisive moment came in 1989 when Gorbachev rejected the idea of a direct presidential election and allowed himself to be nominated to a bloc of uncontested seats specially reserved for the Communist Party in the semi-free Soviet legislature. Up to that point, he could probably have won a popular mandate: The economy had not yet started to unravel, and his prestige as the father of perestroika and glasnost was still high. But he chose to show solidarity with his colleagues in the Communist Party Politburo.

After Russia and the other republics held freely contested

elections in 1990, the Soviet president began to be identified in the public mind with resistance to reform. The struggle for democracy in the Soviet Union became a struggle of the republics against the center, as personified by Gorbachev. The triumph of democracy inevitably meant the collapse of the centralized Soviet state and the emergence of 15 independent republics.

When Gorbachev was elected general secretary of the Soviet Communist Party on March 11, 1985, succeeding Konstantin Chernenko, the Communist superpower was mired in stagnation and self-doubt. Economic growth had dwindled to virtually zero. Technologically, the Soviet Union was falling way behind its Western rivals, even in the military field, which was gobbling up most of its resources. There was a widespread consensus that something drastic had to be done to get the Soviet colossus moving again.

As the youngest and best-educated Soviet leader since Lenin, Gorbachev seemed to be the man for the job. He was energetic and flexible, and he had an attractive wife. Overnight, Kremlin politics was transformed from a deathwatch to a passionate and increasingly open debate. Old dogmas were discarded one by one as Gorbachev and his colleagues looked for innovative solutions to their country's pressing problems.

But the more Gorbachev tinkered with the system, the more it became clear that tinkering alone would not be enough. The slogan of *uskorenie*, or acceleration, gave way to the slogan of perestroika, or restructuring. Eventually, perestroika itself became discredited. The whole rotten edifice had to be rebuilt. What had started off as an attempt to renovate the Communist system led inexorably to an anti-Communist revolution.

"Gorbachev did not know what would become of his experiment when he started out. I am sure that he would have liked to have stopped earlier. But as soon as he made that first fatal step, it was too late," wrote commentator Leonid Guzman in a political obituary of the Soviet leader published by the progressive weekly journal Ogonyok. "No matter how much he may now regret the choice, he made it . . . and even though it is no longer trendy to express gratitude to the president, I consider it my duty to thank him."

Reform communism turned out to be a contradiction in terms, like fried snowballs. The Communist system devised by Lenin and Stalin was a tightly interlocking political and economic structure, based on state ownership of all the means of production, a monolithic ideology and a vast machinery for the repression of dissidents. As soon as anyone began fiddling with one part of the system, the other parts were also undermined. By attempting to reform communism, Gorbachev ultimately hastened its complete demise.

The last Soviet leader also hastened the end of communism through his profligate financial policies—and his inability to make painful economic decisions such as freeing prices or closing money-losing factories. The hole in the state budget rose from just over 3 percent when he took office to a staggering 30 percent to 50 percent by the time he stepped down. The disastrous anti-alcohol campaign of 1986-87 contributed to the deficit by drying up the single most productive source of government revenue. In order to plug the deficit, government printing presses worked overtime, churning out increasingly worthless paper rubles.

In a way, Gorbachev's mistake was a typically Bolshevik one. Ignoring Marxist teaching that politics ultimately boils down to economics, the Bolsheviks behaved as if they could reshape the world through the sheer force of their political will. Preoccupied by the political struggle, Gorbachev made the fatal mistake of assuming that the economy would take care of itself. The result was one of the most disastrous economic slides ever experienced by a major industrial country. This year alone, production is expected to slump by about 14 percent.

The Soviet Union was able to live off its fabulous economic wealth for seven decades. The abundant reserves of oil, gold and other natural resources in Siberia effectively maintained the world's largest standing army and an empire upon which the sun never set. Hard-currency oil revenues of $200 billion between 1970 and 1985 helped fund the Soviet invasion of Afghanistan, a network of sympathetic regimes from Nicaragua to Angola and a succession of grandiose economic projects at home.

By the time Gorbachev came to power, it was clear to everyone that the oil money was running out. The traditional Soviet approach to economic development—which amounted to the rape of the natural environment—would have to be abandoned in favor of intensive development. This was what perestroika was ultimately about. But although the new leadership succeeded in reducing the burden of empire by pulling out of Afghanistan and Eastern Europe, it continued to plunder the national treasure chest.

During the Gorbachev years, the Soviet Union's foreign debt virtually quadrupled to $67 billion. Gold reserves plummeted by around 90 percent to 240 tons. Starved of investment, oil production began falling sharply in 1988, depriving the Kremlin of its most reliable source of Western currency. One recent week, half the airports in the country were forced to close down because of lack of fuel. Russia's economy minister announced recently that the Soviet bank that has a monopoly on foreign trade was, in effect, bankrupt.

It is both symbolic and significant that Gorbachev should be pushed to leave office at this particular moment. As long as Western banks were prepared to continue lending the Soviet Union money, and the gold reserves had not been completely run down, serious economic reforms could be postponed. When the entire country went bankrupt, the master politician was left with no further room for maneuver.

So how should history judge Mikhail Gorbachev—as visionary statesman or shortsighted politician?

There was a historical inevitability about the fall of communism and the collapse of the Soviet empire: Neither could have lasted forever. But the fact remains that the end did not have to come as it did, nor when it did. Gorbachev was probably correct when he argued that the totalitarian system could have remained in place for a few more years. It was he who set events in motion and helped shape the way they unfolded.

"If a hard-liner had succeeded Chernenko in 1985, the results would have been tragic. War might have broken out between the two superpowers," says Ales Adamowich, a Byelorussian writer and filmmaker. "Gorbachev ended the division of the world into two systems—democratic and totalitarian—that were on the point of eliminating each other and the rest of mankind in the bargain. There is no question in my mind that he deserved the Nobel Peace Prize."

Unlike many revolutionaries, Gorbachev sought not to change the course of history, but to swim in its tide. Perhaps this was his greatest virtue. He recognized that Eastern Europe would one day free itself of Soviet domination, that East and West Germany would be united and that the one-party state was doomed. Any attempt to reverse these natural historical processes could have led to enormous human suffering.

"I would set up a golden monument to Gorbachev for not resisting the course of history," says Gleb Yakunin, a dissident priest who was one of hundreds of political prisoners released by the Soviet leader. "Throughout world history, big empires have never disintegrated peacefully, by themselves. It's largely thanks to Gorbachev that we have been able to dismantle the Leninist-Stalinist system without too much bloodshed."

Gorbachev cites the peaceful dismantling of the totalitarian state as his main historical legacy. He points to the defeat of the August coup as proof that democracy is finally taking root in the somewhat inhospitable Russian soil. "My aim was to enable our country, for the first time in its centuries-long history, to pass through a vital turning point without bloodshed," he told Literaturnaya Gazeta.

The jury is still out on whether Gorbachev has achieved his primary goal. So far, the Second Russian Revolution has been relatively bloodless, given the scale and pace of events. The liberation of Eastern Europe and the collapse of the external empire went as smoothly and as peacefully as could reasonably be expected. But events in the former Soviet Union have not yet run their course. The present economic chaos makes virtually any outcome possible, including the violent restoration of some kind of authoritarian or fascist regime.

"I have tried my best," the last president of the Soviet Union said in a recent interview. "If the end result is a happy one, then the attacks against me will have no meaning. But if things do not work out, then even 12 angels swearing that I was right will change nothing."

TUMBLING BACK TO THE FUTURE

Vladimir Bukovsky

Vladimir Bukovsky, who spent 11 years in Soviet prisons before coming to the West in 1976, is the author most recently of "U.S.S.R.; From Utopia to Disaster."

Most of us who challenged soviet Communism some 30 years ago, founding what later became known as the dissident movement, always knew that the regime would one day collapse. The questions were when and how. Only a few of us hoped to live long enough to see its end; Andrei A. Amalrik seemed wildly optimistic in 1969 when he published his famous book, "Will the Soviet Union Survive Till 1984?"

It would have been sheer lunacy to hope for a bloodless revolution against one of the bloodiest political systems in human history. Therefore, we never advocated revolution, bloodless or otherwise, and never tried to create a political organization. Ours was a purely moral opposition, simply a refusal to be a part of that vicious system.

Perhaps our strategy of moral resistance contributed in some way to the "velvet" nature of the anti-Communist revolutions. Yet, if that is so, our refusal to organize an opposition political force must also bear some responsibility for the messy transition the

country now faces—and the peril that presents for democracy.

The Communist regime ended as it started, in a coup, as if history decided to correct itself and to give us a second chance 74 years later. We are going through the events of 1917, only in reverse. This time the Bolshevik coup failed, leaving us with the Provisional Government of Aleksandr F. Kerensky. The party has been outlawed and gone underground, the army has sided with the people, the K.G.B. is doomed and the union has been replaced by a formless commonwealth.

Yet, the problems did not end with the Communists. Boris N. Yeltsin's team, magnificent throughout the crisis in August, disintegrated as a result of the victory and still seems overwhelmed. In trying to replace central structures and positions with his own people, Yeltsin overstretched his human resources.

Yeltsin was unprepared to take power. Lacking either an oppositional political structure, which could have been deployed as a new ruling party, or a comprehensive alternative program, he was left stranded. He lost momentum and got bogged down in the daily routine of government, having no government to

speak about. As usually happens, the vacuum of power was quickly filled by the bureaucracy, a fast-growing and odd mixture of old apparatchiks and new amateurs. And it is a 64,000-ruble question who of them is more corrupt.

AS AN ILLUSTRATION OF the confusion that ensued, consider the overlapping authorities just in the city of Moscow. These consist of a city soviet of a few hundred deputies, complete with its own presidium and chairman; city government; mayor and his staff; prefects of different districts and their staffs; regional soviets with their chairmen and governments. All in all, several thousand people with vaguely defined powers and duties, mostly fighting one another over the former Communist Party's property.

In the aftermath of the coup, the Russian republican "government" was hardly better organized. To the old Council of Ministers, Yeltsin had added a Council of State, and no one could tell whose power was superior. Then there was the Supreme Soviet of the Russian Federation, elected under an old balloting procedure concocted by the former Soviet President, Mikhail S. Gorbachev, and still dominated by former Commu-

nists who, legally, could block any initiative. (In fact, they proceeded to block two enormously important measures: a new Russian constitution and a law on private ownership of land.)

RUSSIA HAS BEEN GIVEN A SECOND CHANCE, A ONE-TIME DISSIDENT SAYS. BUT THIS TIME, IT'S 1917 IN REVERSE.

▼

On top of all this, there was still the Union Government, although its power rapidly faded.

As in 1917, all these "governments" were locked in constant fighting and, needless to say, incapable of

From *The New York Times Magazine*, January 12, 1992, pp. 34, 39-40, 42, 44. Copyright © 1992 by The New York Times Company. Reprinted by permission.

functioning properly. Yeltsin later reorganized the two councils into one administrative body run by his people and securely under his control. But the damage, a three-month delay of the reforms, had been done, and a cold, hungry winter loomed high on the horizon.

This bureaucratic constipation, only somewhat eased by administrative reforms, the demise of the union, the dissolution of the Supreme Soviet and the formation of the commonwealth, is the main source of danger for the young democracies. Although its backbone is definitely broken, the old regime is still very much alive, particularly in the periphery.

This year, as in 1917, revolution triumphed in the center, mostly in the large cities like Moscow, St. Petersburg and Yekaterinburg (formerly Sverdlovsk), while the provinces remained untouched. It happened so quickly that local bosses did not have time to reveal their sympathy for the coup and, therefore, cannot now be easily replaced, although more than 70 percent of them supported the putsch.

Political paralysis in the center is allowing the old guard in the provinces time to regroup and work up a new strategy. I doubt they would ever be so strong as to organize another coup, but they can sabotage and subvert new democracy. A cold, hungry winter will heighten social tensions, which can easily be used to discredit the democratic leadership — particularly as this leadership, with the exception of Yeltsin, is unpopular because of its Communist past and its corrupt present.

The quick defeat of the coup also deprived democratic forces of time to consolidate and to create their own structures. Theoretically, therefore, they bear the responsibility of a party in power; in reality they have no power in the provinces. Very often they do not have even their own local newspapers or printing presses.

Lenin, in similar circumstances in 1917, moved aggressively to undercut the counterrevolution. First, he dispatched groups of activists to the provinces to spread his revolution. Then he issued two decrees: on peace with Germany and on distribution of land to peasants, thus resolving the problems that brought revolution in the first place.

Painful as it must have been for him, he signed what Russians almost universally came to regard as the "shameful" Treaty of Brest-Litovsk with Germany. In the process, he gave up Ukraine, Finland and the Baltic states and split his own party, almost getting himself killed by assassins from opposing factions. But he knew it was his only chance. Even so, he still had to fight a civil war that he nearly lost.

In the end, he won not because his ideas were accepted in Russia but because an exhausted population accepted the Bolsheviks as a lesser evil than chaos, typhoid, hunger and marauding gangs. Any order seemed to be better than no order at all.

By contrast, Yeltsin remained inactive after the coup. No democrats were dispatched, nor did Yeltsin immediately resolve the two main problems of the current revolution, roughly equivalent to Lenin's peace and land issues: dissolution of the union and the introduction of a market economy.

In fact, as far as the first issue is concerned, he did worse than nothing. For months, he tried to hold together a disintegrating empire. Apart from wasting precious time in a futile attempt at making peace between Armenians and Azeris, or with Chechen separatists, he actually almost plunged the country into a war with the Muslim nations of the North Caucasus. His handling of the Chechen crisis, as well as his clumsy effort to pressure Ukraine to hand over the Crimea, were grave political errors. They could not evoke any other response but a backlash of nationalism in the republics.

As a result, Ukraine dragged its feet before agreeing to hand over its nuclear weapons to Russia, and other republics began to view Yeltsin with a new wariness. Needless to say, such elephantine behavior in the most sensitive sphere of international relations is bound to be exploited.

Meanwhile, the implacable logic of the revolution did, quite predictably, force Yeltsin to accept the inevitable anyway, leading to the formation of the new commonwealth and the dissolution of the union. One wonders what took him so long to deliver that coup de grâce.

Yeltsin did at last, in late October, announce a general plan of price reform and ruble convertibility. Only scanty details were revealed, however, and in any case the reforms came too late to help this winter, if not for most of this year, as Yeltsin himself has acknowledged.

One can only hope that Yeltsin's political reorganization, which brought many younger people into the leadership, and his economic reforms will improve the situation before popular discontent sweeps his government away. The chances for their success, however, are very slim, as these changes will have to be implemented through the same bureaucratic machine that has blocked them in the past.

Besides, although words like "free market," "free prices" and "privatization" have become quite fashionable, the question remains whether anyone really understands them.

I remember listening a year ago to Anatoly A. Sobchak, pillar of the new democracy and Mayor of what was then Leningrad, explaining why it would be so difficult to privatize in his city. "Leningraders have no money," he said. "So if we open this process, the city will be bought over by the Central Asians and Caucasians with their illegal capital." When asked how he planned to solve this problem, Sobchak insisted that the authorities would "investigate the origin of money in each case." The prospect of introducing "capitalism" to Russia with the helping hand of the police is sufficiently disheartening to make a skeptic even of Adam Smith.

More important, this episode reveals how little Sobchak and other leading reformers really understand about free markets. Even if the property was divided equitably among Leningraders, not even Sobchak could prevent its subsequent redistribution from those who have no money to those who do.

In the meantime, the delay in announcing a sweeping privatization measure gave the new bureaucracy the chance to "privatize" in its own corrupt ways. Former party functionaries — the most clever of them who were smart enough to jump off the party train before it crashed — turned to "private business," grabbing more than a fair share of desirable state-owned properties in this de facto "privatization." Black-market operators and outright criminals got the rest.

Thus, most profitable enterprises appear to have been "privatized", even before any law was passed, leaving law-abiding citizens only the least profitable leftovers. This, of course, is bound to generate a considerable public resentment and give a bad name to the whole idea of a market economy.

CLEARLY, BUREAUCRATS do not make revolutions, and the former Communist apparatchiks who constitute the bulk of the present leadership are hardly any exception. Even those who, like Yeltsin, seem sincere still carry the blinders of socialism. They lack a vision of a future society in which the central government plays a much smaller role, and bits and pieces of the former empire are glued together by market forces rather than by administrative means.

They lack faith in that future as they lack faith in the people they suppose to govern, and in the principles of the free markets they suppose to introduce. Steeped in Marxist political economy, they still live by the 19th-century notions that the bigger and more centralized the country, the richer and stronger it must be. Otherwise, why were they so reluctant to dissolve the old union? Surely, if the bonds of centuries of common history and economic interdependence are as strong as they claim, then they will survive the collapse of empire without coercion. But if they did not, no amount of coercion will preserve them.

Above all, the current leaders lack the moral authority to lead the country into the future. As former Communists, they will always be mistrusted by the people and, therefore, are reluctant to introduce and stick with unpopular and painful yet unavoidable radical changes. After all, even Solidarity's leaders lost public support and were nearly beaten by former Communists in the recent Polish elections because they adopted shock therapy.

Former Soviet Communists who try to do the same are doomed. But if they do not act, the country will turn into a Weimar Republic, marked by economic chaos and chronic political instability. They are in a no-win situation — the wrong people who just happen to be in the right place at the right moment.

In short, the Yeltsin Government looks more and more like the Provisional Government in 1917, with its inability to solve main problems, lack of political support structures and dwindling popularity. I doubt it will last. Frustrated multitudes already feel themselves robbed of the fruits of their revolution and deceived by former Communists (for whom they have coined the new and very expressive name "commutants"). Before long, they will fill the streets again.

New elections, which may be held as early as this summer, will bring forth new leaders who, in the absence of strong and well-organized democratic structures, will be either dangerous demagogues playing to the lowest sentiments of the crowd or more skillfully camouflaged commutants. Neither is a healthy and a desirable option, but as long as there is no strong, well-organized democratic force in the country, capable of presenting an alternative, one cannot realistically expect anything else.

Such a force, however, is unlikely to appear very soon. On the contrary, "Democratic Russia," the only existing democratic organization is really just a loosely knit coalition of parties. Indeed, it split at its Second Congress this fall because it could not define its position toward the present Russian Government.

While democrats quarrel and split into smaller and smaller groups, however, commutants are busy creating substitutes for the defunct party. Of course, they are all democrats now; no mentioning of Communism or even socialism, please. The former K.G.B. general and Politburo member Eduard A. Shevardnadze, along with Anatoly Sobchak and the Mayor of Moscow, Gavriil K. Popov, create the "Democratic Reforms Movement." The former Central Committee member and present Vice-President of Russia, Aleksandr V. Rutskoi, founds the "People's Party of Free Russia." The former Central Committee member and "dissident-historian," Roy A. Medvedev, creates the "Party of the Socialist Choice."

Each claims to be the legal heir of the Communist Party, at least where its assets and property are concerned. Each expects to unite in its ranks millions of former party functionaries across the country. But, somehow, there are no quarrels among them. Or between them and Gorbachev, with whom they officially cooperate as members of his Presidential Council. I have a strange premonition that, to the utter delight of progressive mankind, they all will form a cozy coalition of commutants by next spring, with Rutskoi emerging as the potential leader.

They will be waiting in the wings, exploiting Yeltsin's every mistake — or even creating them because, like their forefathers at the beginning of this century, they can only hope to be accepted by a desperate population as a lesser evil than chaos, typhoid, hunger and marauding gangs. They need chaos and hunger to succeed in the next elections.

And they might even succeed in their bid for power, like Ion Iliescu in Rumania, but only for a short time. For, unlike their forefathers at the beginning of the century, they have no long-term solutions, even the wrong ones.

The sad reality is that, 74 years later, we still haven't gotten it right. While there were far too many revolutionaries in 1917, this time there are two few.

Yeltsin Mystery:
True Democrat or Tyrant?

Kremlin:

The enigmatic Russian,
facing enormous challenges,
draws open criticism
from former backers.

Michael Parks

Times Staff Writer

MOSCOW—Boris N. Yeltsin has overthrown one of the most powerful states in modern history, forcing the breakup of the Soviet Union and the resignation of Soviet President Mikhail S. Gorbachev. But Yeltsin's next moves as Russian leader are question marks.

Just how will he pull Russia from the ruins of Soviet socialism?

His actual policies remain formulated in vague, sometimes contradictory terms. And further questions arise from the sharpening conflicts among his supporters and advisers, from his staff's penchant for operating in secret and from a character that he himself describes as "impetuous" in some circumstances and "harsh and rigid" at other times.

"The phenomenon of Yeltsin must still be revealed before we can characterize him fully as a politician," Gorbachev said this week before he resigned. "So far, we have studied Yeltsin largely as an opposition figure, and here he has shown he can do a great deal, and he has done a great deal.

"We hope that he is fully aware of the great responsibility now on his shoulders," Gorbachev added. "The euphoria of election campaigns is over, the rights have been achieved, power has been achieved. With this has come a great responsibility, and he still needs to understand that."

Yeltsin came to power with the broadest, noblest of goals: Full democracy for a people who have never been free; economic prosperity through development of a market economy and an international role for Russia that promotes mutual security, disarmament and peace.

As pragmatic and tough a politician as ever emerged from the Soviet system, Yeltsin, 60, a construction engineer and former Communist Party boss from Sverdlovsk, courageously proved his commitment to democracy last August when he rallied the popular opposition to the conservative coup.

He demonstrated it again in recent weeks when, convinced of the impossibility of fundamental reform within even a reconstituted Soviet Union, he forced its dissolution to bring socialism to an end.

And his record over the past three years battling Communist Party conservatives and often Gorbachev in making his political comeback shows a radical but consistent approach to the country's problems—an increasing conviction that only after ending socialism would the crisis ease—and a willingness to act boldly where Gorbachev hesitated.

But open criticism, not just questions, now comes from many of Yeltsin's former supporters.

"There is no democracy in Russia, there is no power, only chaos and anarchy," Maj. Gen. Alexander V. Rutskoi, Yeltsin's own choice for Russian vice president, said this month, complaining to the press that the president has become a captive of his staff. "Everything is falling into an abyss—the economy, finances and, most important, the trust of the people.

Tatyana Koryagina, a radical, free-market economist Yeltsin once considered for his Cabinet, said this week that Yeltsin's "chief characteristic as a politician is his total unpredictability. Wild expectations are generated, but the deeds that follow tend to dishearten the people. This produces a kind of psychological stupor that can, in an instant, turn into a social volcano as people come to. The new sum of his policies leads us inexorably to a non-parliamentary regime."

And Yeltsin himself, sometimes as candid in power as he was in opposition, has acknowledged serious errors as president, including the dispatch of troops, later recalled, to the troubled Chechen-Ingushetia region when he was misled by his personal representative who was feuding with the popularly elected leadership there.

From *Los Angeles Times*, December 27, 1991, p. A1, A16. Copyright © 1991 by Los Angeles Times.

THE END OF THE EMPIRE

NAMES TO WATCH IN THE

Post-Gorbachev Era

As the Commonwealth of Independent States rises on the ruins of the Soviet Union, who will be its most important figures? Here are some of the VIPs taking charge of the new, post-Soviet world:

'It is difficult for all of us now, and it is not going to get easier in the next few months. The main thing is confidence. And faith. Don't give up, don't sink into pessimism, don't lose hope. New times are on the way.'

 BORIS NIKOLAYEVICH YELTSIN
Age: 60
Position: President of Russia
Background: Graduated from Ural Polytechnic Institute in 1955 . . . spent 30 years in hometown of Sverdlovsk, western Siberia, before coming to Moscow in 1985 as chief of Communist Party Central Committee's construction department. That December, he became first secretary of Moscow City Party Committee . . . Mikhail S. Gorbachev, who has assigned Yeltsin to the key Moscow post in his campaign for younger, more energetic leaders, dismissed him less than two years later for criticizing slow pace of *perestroika* reforms . . . In 1989, elected to Congress of People's Deputies in Soviet Union's first multi-candidate

parliamentary elections . . . In 1990, elected chairman of Russian Parliament, and last June he won first election for Russian presidency . . . Since his key role in thwarting August coup, he has gained power and is now boss of largest and strongest remnant of what was once Gorbachev's Soviet Union.

'We will naturally insist that Ukraine become a member of all European organizations, including financial, and I think that our requests will be met.'

 LEONID MAKAROVICH KRAVCHUK
Age: 58
Position: President of Ukraine
Background: Grew up in rural Ukraine, studied at cooperative technical school before graduating from Kiev University with degree in economics . . . For most of his long career as a party apparatchik, he was involved in ideology, becoming chief of Ukrainian Communist Party Central Committee's propaganda department during 1980s. Republic's Parliament elected him chairman in July . . . Opponents, such as members of Rukh, Ukrainian independence movement, accuse him of slyness and note his tendency to change public views according to prevailing political winds . . . But in same referendum that brought Ukraine independence, Kravchuk was elected president.

'There remains one path, the path along which the whole world is moving, the path of . . . the market.'

 NURSULTAN ABISHEVICH NAZARBAYEV
Age: 51
Position: President of Kazakhstan
Background: A wrestler in his youth, Nazarbayev was educated at technical college attached to a metallurgical factory and worked for 10 years at a blast furnace . . . Graduated from Communist Party Central Committee's Higher Party School and

had classic party career, becoming first secretary of Kazakhstan's Communist Party in 1989, a post he quit last summer . . . Ran unopposed for president of Kazakhstan in December . . . Leadership approach has been described as "authoritarian for modernization" . . . A longtime supporter of economic reforms and transition to a free market.

'President Yeltsin enjoys the most powerful credit of trust from the people . . . This is a critical juncture for us, but we know where we want to go.'

 GENNADY EDUARDOVICH BURBULIS
Age: 46
Position: First deputy prime minister of Russia, secretary of state
Background: Born in Pervouralsk, where grandfather had immigrated from Lithuania . . . Graduated from Urals State University with degree in philosophy, then taught that subject himself . . . Came to Moscow as people's deputy in 1989 . . . Referred to by some as "Yeltsin's gray cardinal," he managed Russian president's campaign last June and is now his chief adviser . . . Told Yeltsin before August coup that he should "consolidate the moral and political prestige undoubtedly enjoyed by Russia's leadership" and prepare for "the final disintegration of this totalitarian system."

'The White House [Yeltsin's headquarters] has become a place of intrigues. And no one knows anymore where we're going and what our goal is.'

 **ALEXANDER VLADIMIROVICH RUTSKOI**
Age: 44
Position: Vice president of Russia, air force major general
Background: As a flier, shot down and captured by Afghan rebels twice in the 1980s, named a "Hero of the Soviet Union" after his escape . . . Yeltsin picked him as running mate in 1991 Russian presidential elections to

gain support of military and party rank and file . . . Has recently sparred with Yeltsin over speed of economic reforms—he advocates more gradual transition to free market—and has attacked "anarchy" that he feels present Russian government has wreaked upon nation.

'Behind Yeltsin we can glimpse people even more radical than he is. This is a frightening thought, and this process, so resembling the French Revolution, must be stopped.'

■ ANATOLY ALEXANDROVICH SOBCHAK

Age: 54
Position: Mayor of St. Petersburg
Background: Born in Siberian city of Chita, raised in Uzbekistan, he came to Leningrad as student . . . Graduated from Leningrad State University's law school, later serving there as professor and dean . . . Elected people's deputy of Soviet Union in 1989, mayor of Leningrad (now St. Petersburg) in May, 1990 . . . Before August coup, Sobchak—early supporter of Yeltsin and advocate of radical market reforms—enjoyed one of highest popularity ratings in country . . . Had favored "new union of sovereign states" proposed by ex-Soviet President Gorbachev . . . Lost popularity because of anger over lack of food in St. Petersburg.

'We think that [Russia's role in combating the August coup] is no reason for [Russia] aspiring to the leading role of the union, and to place itself above other republics.'

■ ISLAM ABDUGANIYEVICH KARIMOV

Age: 53
Position: President of Uzbekistan
Background: Born in Samarkand, graduated from Central Asian Polytechnic Institute and Tashkent Institute of National Economics . . . Began political career in 1966 with Uzbek state planning body, becoming finance minister in 1983 . . . Named first secretary of Uzbekistan Communist Party in 1989, chosen president

by republic's legislature in March, 1990 . . . Reelected in republic-wide popular elections this month.

'There can be no putsch with participation of the army. We have learned from the bitter experience of the August events, when they tried to use the military for political ends.'

■ YEVGENY IVANOVICH SHAPOSHNIKOV

Age: 49
Position: Air marshal, interim commander in chief of Commonwealth of Independent States' armed forces
Background: Born in Bolshoi Log, a Cossack village in southern Russia, he later chose flying as career because there was an airfield near his hometown . . . A fighter pilot, he rose quickly through ranks, becoming Soviet air force commander in East Germany in 1987, later commander in chief of Soviet air force . . . Gorbachev named him defense minister on Aug. 23 to replace coup plotter Dmitri Yazov . . . During putsch, he is said to have been instrumental in ordering withdrawal of troops from Moscow streets.

'In the concrete situation of this country, any long-term discussion about very nice things like structural reform or privatization is absolutely out of touch with the financial reality.'

■ YEGOR TIMUROVICH GAIDAR

Age: 35
Position: Russia's deputy prime minister for economic policy
Background: Grandfather Arkady was Red Army regiment commander at 16, later author of popular children's books . . . Before appointment by Yeltsin in November, Gaidar was director of Institute of Economic Policy . . . He has pressed for radical economic reforms while admitting that they will initially be painful for public . . . Recently he announced that Russia's economic reform plan, which includes ending state subsidies and raising prices to compensate, will begin Jan. 2.

'Armenian and Azerbaijani peoples, during all of ancient history, always bore more kindness than evil, which is introduced, I consider, by definite forces during the years of perestroika.'

■ AYAZ N.O. MUTALIBOV

Age: 53
Position: President of Azerbaijan
Background: Born in Baku, educated at Azerbaijan Institute of Petroleum and Chemistry . . . During 1960s, worked at land reclamation institute, and in 1977 began political career in Baku Communist party . . . Elected first secretary of Azerbaijan Communist Party in 1990, has been republic's president since May of that year . . . Earlier this month, he announced he was taking control of Soviet armed forces on his territory.

'Holy Russia is coming back to life.'

■ ALEXEI II

Age: 62
Position: Patriarch of Moscow and all Russia
Background: leader of Russian Orthodox Church was born Alexei Ridiger, into an ethnic German family, in Tallinn, Estonia, where father was an Orthodox priest . . . Studied at Leningrad Theological Seminary and Academy, receiving doctorate in theology in 1953 . . . While advancing in church hierarchy in Estonia, he held important post of administrative head of Moscow Patriarchate . . . He headed church in Estonia, then Leningrad, finally was named patriarch of Moscow in June, 1990 . . . With religious freedom granted that year after decades-long hiatus in Soviet Union, he has become a more prominent figure in Russia, more outspoken on both religious and political matters than previous Russian church leaders . . . Gave his blessing to Yeltsin during Russian presidential elections last summer and urged soldiers "not to allow fraternal blood to be spilled" during *coup d'etat* last August.

—Compiled by Steven Gutterman, a researcher in The Times' Moscow Bureau.

"A sincere man," Gorbachev said of Yeltsin during an interview last weekend with CBS Television. "I wish he could always be consistent, without vacillating. I wish he wouldn't give in to pressure, and I would wish the same thing for myself. . . . And I wish he were more democratic—it wouldn't hurt him."

Whether Yeltsin is a true democrat—or a potential dictator—matters far more today than it did just months ago. The question had less import before, because Gorbachev appeared likely to remain as president of a "confederative state" pulled together from the remnants of the Soviet Union, and Yeltsin would be president of Russia, its largest member. Yeltsin's role was to be the "bulldozer," breaking down opposition to Gorbachev's reforms and marshaling popular support for them. "If Gorbachev did not have Yeltsin, he would have to invent him," the burly Siberian was fond of saying of his often testy relations with the Soviet president.

But Yeltsin broke with Gorbachev late last month in a final, telling dispute. It brought about the collapse of the Soviet Union and the ascendancy of Russia in its place.

Yeltsin believed that he, the other republic presidents and Gorbachev had agreed on a new union treaty that left a minimal central government in a major decentralization of power; when he saw that the draft retained more than that, he refused to sign, arguing that it amounted to preserving the Soviet system.

"Boris Yeltsin is not a man who blinks," a Russian official commented later. "That's what Gorbachev expected—for him to blink, to say, 'Yes, we have come this far, so let's sign and fix it later.' "

But Gorbachev aides accused Yeltsin of negotiating in bad faith, of waiting for a decisive moment, then overturning the agreement on a pretext to maximize power in his own hands.

"In one blow, Yeltsin ended Soviet power and socialism, restructured the state and ousted Gorbachev," one of the former president's political advisers said. "It was a brilliantly plotted strategy, and it was well played, but it was done with total disregard for the country. Yeltsin's partners and his adversaries should learn from this."

Of himself, Yeltsin said the confrontation had brought out the "steel" in him, a result of the 30 years he worked in Sverdlovsk, an industrial center in the Ural Mountains that is now known again as Ekaterinburg. "The people there are tough and exacting," he commented. "They don't like blather, empty talk. I

One of the country's boldest free-market economists sees crucial flaws in Yeltsin's program.

was raised in that atmosphere. That is certainly what makes me tick."

But Yeltsin is seen by his increasingly numerous critics, who range across the political spectrum from ousted Communist bureaucrats to Gorbachev aides to leftist radicals, as gathering for Russia, and for himself, the very powers—and more—that he denied Gorbachev and a continued central government. Under Yeltsin, his critics warn, Russia is plunging into a *demokratura,* a term combining *demokratiya* with *diktatura*.

"I have ventured to take unpopular measures," Yeltsin commented recently. "Therefore, I don't think I can expect ardent affection from the Russians. On the contrary, there is growing criticism of me. So, if portraits of me have sprung up in some places [such as government offices], then no doubt

they will soon start tearing them down. I am even expecting that."

But Yeltsin's supporters, still by far the Russian majority, gave him a mandate for radical change when they elected him in June over five rivals; Yeltsin said he will forge ahead on economic reforms on Jan. 2, ending state subsidies and raising prices up to fivefold to cover production costs.

"Everything depends on economic reforms, which have been hindered in all possible manner until now," Yeltsin told the Russian lawmakers this week. "The situation will deteriorate for a period of six months after the liberalization of prices."

The great fear, as he conceded, is public protests as food prices triple and unemployment then soars as enterprises try to cut their costs: "We shall try to explain to our people that these will be temporary sacrifices, that the situation will stabilize in a year and we will yet see a brighter future. People should be given something to believe in, but six years of *perestroika* did not raise their living standards and the situation even deteriorated. We have to do better if there is to be hope."

New Burst of Fighting Erupts in Georgian Capital

From Reuters

TBILISI, Georgia—Heavy gunfire erupted early today in the most intense fighting in five days of battles between government and opposition forces in this Georgian capital.

Fires raging around the battered Parliament building lit the night sky as rebel national guardsmen poured artillery and rocket fire into President Zviad Gamsakhurdia's stronghold.

There was no immediate word on new casualties in the fighting, which has already taken at least 42 lives since Sunday.

"We don't know what is happening, just that there is heavy firing around Parliament," a Health Ministry spokesman said.

Ambulances could not get through to the barricaded Parliament and other government buildings on Tbilisi's central Rustaveli Avenue.

Electricity was cut off to large parts of the city that lies south of the Caucasus mountains, plunging its population of 1.2 million people into darkness.

The fighting, after a lull on Thursday, was the heaviest since Sunday

when opposition forces launched their latest bid to topple Gamsakhurdia, whom they accuse of trying to stifle the former Soviet republic's fledgling democracy.

Gamsakhurdia, 52, elected by a landslide last May, denies that he is anti-democratic.

"This is a lie. We have all the rights and freedoms, a free press and free political life," he said in an interview with the ABC Television on Thursday.

He refused to surrender. Both sides said they are ready for a cease-fire and peace negotiations, but accused the other of refusing to talk.

Georgia is the only one of the 12 former Soviet republics that has not joined the new Commonwealth of Independent States.

Meanwhile, Georgia's Foreign Minister Murman Omanidze assailed a recent speech by Secretary of State James A. Baker III, saying it only encouraged the violence raging here. In the speech, Baker criticized the Tbilisi government as "undeserving of our acceptance and support."

But Koryagina, one of the country's boldest free-market economists, sees crucial flaws in Yeltsin's program—notably, the failure to privatize the economy first and break the monopolies that state enterprises now have—adding to the social pressures and defeating the reform.

"Yeltsin does not seem to realize how dangerous our economic situation has become," she said. "Worn-out pipelines, the lack of spare parts for nuclear power stations, broken-down sewage systems—everything threatens disaster, and any can cause a volcanic eruption."

The program for a fast-paced push to a market economy that Yeltsin outlined two months ago remains "operative," according to Yegor T. Gaidar, the Russian deputy prime minister for economic policy, and scores of implementing decrees and orders have been prepared.

Yet such is the secrecy now among Yeltsin's top advisers that no one outside that circle—not members of the Russian Parliament, not his allies in the Moscow and St. Petersburg city governments, not the commentators in the pro-Yeltsin press—knows what precisely the program is and how it fits together.

"Let's wait three months," Alexander N. Yakovlev, for almost seven years Gorbachev's closest adviser and the intellectual father of *perestroika,* said in an interview when invited to criticize Yeltsin's program. "I was never afraid to criticize anybody. But times are so tough now that I think if a man takes up this burden let him try. Yeltsin should be given this chance."

Criticism, in fact, is multiplying.

Newspapers on both the radical left and the right complain that new Russian government regulations reducing or eliminating subsidies, increasing delivery costs and raising prices for paper and printing aim to silence those with views different from Yeltsin's.

Moscow Mayor Gavriil Popov and St. Petersburg Mayor Anatoly Sobchak, both one-time Yeltsin allies, are now sharply critical of him—over economic reforms, over the breakup of the Soviet Union, over the closed character of Russian policy-making in recent months, over the way Yeltsin's policies and style of leadership are dividing democratic forces.

But Yeltsin has an electoral mandate unparalleled in Russian, or Soviet, history: He is the nation's first popularly elected leader.

"Boris Yeltsin can say, 'I am the people's choice,' and that is a first that carries a lot of weight," Sergei Plekhanov, a political observer here, remarked. "Yeltsin can then say, 'This is what they want me to do,' and who can argue with him? In fact, people voted for Yeltsin precisely because they wanted change."

And Yeltsin's mandate was validated in August when he led the opposition to the rightist putsch—and saved all the gains of the Gorbachev years.

It was renewed again in the minds of most people when Yeltsin brought to an end, as painful and poignant as it was for many, the Soviet experiment in socialism.

Now, Yeltsin is trying to rally this popular support he has commanded and is preaching confidence in the future.

"It is difficult for us all now, and it is not going to get any easier in the next few months," Yeltsin told the trade union newspaper Trud this month. "The main thing is confidence. And faith. Don't give up, don't sink into pessimism, don't lose hope. That is the important thing now. New times are on the way."

The case for support.

THE YELTSIN REVOLUTION

Martin Malia

Martin Malia is professor of Russian history at the University of California, Berkeley. He has written The Soviet Tragedy *(1992, Free Press).*

Over the last five years, it has become clear that the process of communism's disintegration is as revolutionary as the process that established it in power. And this second revolution, a revolution against the heritage of the first revolution, has just as clearly not yet run its course. So far this new revolution has known three phases. The first was Gorbachev's perestroika, which one of his idea men, Fedor Burlatsky, now characterizes as "a revolution of the dilettantes," an impossible wager to reform the system without abandoning its socialist foundations. The second was the actual demise of communism, when the wager ended in the total collapse of the system: the fall of Eastern Europe in 1989, which demonstrated that the "conquests of socialism" were reversible, and hence the system everywhere was mortal; then the coup de grace in the heart of the system, Russia, last year. At present Boris Yeltsin and the Russian democrats are launching a third phase, that of building a post-Communist order, or as they would put it, of "returning Russia to Europe" by creating a "normal society." The great question now is whether this, too, will turn out to be an impossible wager.

Clearly no one in the West takes Yeltsin for a miracle worker, as some once did Gorbachev, and there is no Western cult of his personality. Quite the contrary, his government is regarded with suspicion, if not hostility. At best he is accorded grudging support in the interests of post-Soviet stability. The lack of a positive Western response to the Yeltsin wager could weigh against its chances of success. This is a government, after all, that aims at integration into the world community.

But the principal factor governing the prospects for Yeltsin's reform is the legacy of Soviet failure, including perestroika. The scope of the Soviet collapse is unprecedented in modern, indeed world, history. This point bears emphasis because mainline American Sovietologists have long misconstrued the Soviet system, making it appear much more of a success than it really was. They argued that the USSR was no longer totalitarian but had developed into an "institutional pluralism," and was thus capable of a "transition" to some sort of social democracy. Their processing of flawed Soviet data through Western models for calculating the GNP produced an economic success story that augured well for an evolution to democracy and that also informed the CIA's absurd belief that the Soviet economy was some 60 percent of the American.

Thus we were presented with a maturing Soviet society quite prepared to make the wager of perestroika a success. And so such authorities as Professors Jerry Hough and Stephen Cohen, for five years, regularly assured us. But the exit from communism, when it came, was not a transition or an evolution. It was a brusque collapse, a total implosion, of a sort unheard of in history: a great state abolished itself utterly—in a matter of weeks—and right from under its president. The reason this happened is that the Soviet Union, *pace* most Western Sovietology, was in fact a total society, with all aspects of life linked in what one scholar called a "mono-organization" whole. At its core was the Party to which all aspects of life were subordinated: the economy, government, culture, private life itself. This total society logically ended in a total collapse of all its interrelated parts at once. Thus we now have in the midst of the resulting rubble a total problem embracing every aspect of life.

What is Yeltsin's program for coping with this universal crisis? Indeed, does Russia's first democratic government have a coherent program at all? And how do its policies relate to Russian nationalism, the matter that seems to worry the West most about post-Sovietism? The bedrock of the Russian democratic program since 1989 is to undo everything that communism has done since 1917, including Gorbachev. As such, the program is truly revolutionary, its notion of "democracy" a post-Communist and revolutionary notion. Yeltsin and the democrats have too often been presented in the West simply as populist rivals of Gorbachev, out for power. But all Yeltsin's statements, from his June presidential campaign through his recent New Year's address, show that he seeks to effect the "rebirth of Russia" by "liberating" her from the "destructive disaster of communism." This aim should be taken quite seriously, and literally.

Thus, Russian democracy means, first, refusal of the Communist monopoly of political power, which translates as the principle of a multiparty order. Democracy means, second, refusal of the Communist monopoly of

Reprinted by permission from *The New Republic*, February 10, 1992, pp. 21-25. Copyright © 1992, The New Republic, Inc.

economic power, which translates as the principle of private property. And the rule of law derives logically from the first two principles. Finally, at the end of the process of challenging the Communist order came the challenge to still another Party monopoly of power—that of state authority—which translates as the dissolution of the pseudo-federation, or Union.

The history of this program's development bears repeating, since it was generated by a series of shocks, of collisions with Party authority. The first came at the Congress of People's Deputies in May-June 1989. Even though Gorbachev had an overwhelming, and in the words of Yuri Afanasiev, "aggressively submissive" majority, a liberal minority of the Congress spoke out, on national TV, against the appalling ills of the system. The result was a "demystification" of communism from which it never recovered. At the same time these liberals, largely from the *Moscow Tribune* group, became convinced that Gorbachev in no way contemplated power-sharing and must be openly opposed. They formed the Interregional Group of Deputies, under Andrei Sakharov and Yeltsin, which brought together all the future stars of Russian democracy, from Gavriil Popov and Sergei Stankevich to Anatoli Sobchak. Russian "civil society," as all groups independent of the state now came to be known, thereby received a political expression; and its program was the end of the Party's "leading role" in all spheres of life.

At first the heretical right to private property was mentioned only sotto voce by the democrats. But with the collapse of Eastern European communism in the fall of 1989 this issue, together with its corollary—the market, now came to the fore. By spring 1990 the example of Poland's "big bang" transition to the market led the Soviet government to draft plans for transition to a "regulated market," another self-defeating half-measure. But they were soon forced to go further when a new front against the Party-state was opened up in June 1990 by the movement for the sovereignty of the Union republics. Launched by Russia, following the Baltic example, this movement by the end of the summer had spread throughout the Union. The very existence of the "center" was now called into question.

Because of this weakening of the center, it became possible for the democrats to force the issue of private property. The result was the "500-Day Plan" associated with Stanislav Shatalin and Grigori Yavlinsky. This plan was not exactly "shock therapy," because the shift to the market was spread over a year and a half, but it had revolutionary implications. A political as much as an economic document, it emanated from a group of younger economists under Yavlinsky who wanted simply to finish with the system. They planned to do this by establishing republic, or local, control in moving to the market, an approach that would automatically undermine the Party-state's "center." Yeltsin quickly espoused this plan, and then prevailed on Gorbachev to accept it also. But in September Gorbachev suddenly drew back, as he and the rest of the establishment realized the political threat this economic program entailed.

From the fall of 1990 to the spring of 1991 Gorbachev moved to the "right," back to the Party, police, army, and military-industrial hierarchies. The Yeltsin democrats, sensing they could soon be eliminated, fought back with demonstrations and strikes. As a result, Gorbachev in April flipped again to the left, giving way to Yeltsin and the republics on most points in a new, more flexible Union treaty. But this capitulation appeared to the old guard as the death sentence of the Party-state. Just before the new treaty's signing on August 19, this group declared their president to be incapacitated and took over, as a prelude to quashing the democrats by force.

Two things about this famous "coup" require emphasis, because both are prudishly ignored in the Western press. First, this "coup" was in fact no coup at all, because the "coup plotters," as they are quaintly called, were none other than the Soviet government: the vice president, the prime minister, the ministers of defense and interior, the head of the KGB, the chairman of the Supreme Soviet, and the chief of staff of Gorbachev's personal Cabinet. They were quite simply the whole Communist establishment; their aim was to depose a chief whose indecision they believed, correctly, was leading the system to catastrophe. If Gorbachev did not know that these close collaborators, all of whom he had appointed, were working toward a state of emergency, then he was incompetent, which is as bad as complicit.

The second notable thing about the August coup is that Yeltsin and the democrats were ready not only to resist it, but also to escalate this resistance into a counter-coup against the Party-state. Once the junta's military thrust had been thwarted, Yeltsin suspended the Communist Party, took over the KGB and army command, appointed an economic committee under Yavlinsky, and began measures to decommunize and professionalize public functions. All of this was done by a cascade of decrees previously prepared in the Russian Council of Ministers. Thus, although all constitutional forms were preserved by restoring Gorbachev to power, and indeed using him to validate the new decrees, in fact a counter-coup had been carried out disestablishing the Communist system. This behavior was criticized abroad at the time as "autocratic." But there could be no democracy in Russia without first dismantling the Leninist system. It would have been absurd to try to pass Yeltsin's measures through the "due process" of a Communist legislature. The only feasible course was to seize the opportunity provided by the post-coup vacuum and to act swiftly, while the momentum of victory was still strong.

So began the third and most radical stage of what had become an open revolution against Leninism. And this third stage will be the most difficult in the exit from communism. For getting rid, at last, of the system also means provoking the final collapse of all its components: the economy, the administrative system, the state structure itself. Nor were the democrats ready for these problems. Their clear adversary, the Party, had evaporated. Thrust into power far sooner than they had anticipated, the new government floundered in its first six weeks, eroding the trust of a public bewildered by Yeltsin's lack of follow-through and panicked as full realization of the economic disaster at last hit them. The president disappeared to the Crimea for two weeks, whether to recuperate after a grueling year or to let his contentious followers sort themselves out back in Moscow, it is still not clear. For there was—and still is—a real problem of the coherence of the Yeltsin coalition.

Who constitutes this coalition? Among Yeltsin's supporters there is first the Democratic Russia Movement, whose president is Afanasiev, an alliance of various parties and lobbies going back to March 1990, which put Yeltsin, Sobchak, Popov, and other democrats into office. But this is a broad movement, like Solidarity, not a cohesive political party; and once *the* Party was no longer in the field, "Dem Russia" began to splinter, just as Solidarity did. Second, there is the Interregional Group of Deputies, which has given Yeltsin crucial members of his Advisory Council, such as Stankevich and the radical democrat Galina Staravoitova. Quite different is the Urals group of old Yeltsin aides, prominent among whom is his de facto prime minister, Gennadi Burbulis, a 45-year-old ex-professor of "scientific communism." These men are provincials, often from the old apparat and with links to the military-industrial complex so dominant in the Urals, though they are now fiercely anti-Communist.

Then there are the liberal deputies of the Russian Parliament, associated with that body's chairman, Ruslan Khasbulatov, who is, however, still a defender of socialism. Yeltsin acquired this dubious ally for his first election as president in 1990, and Khasbulatov, as well as most of the Parliament, is now opposing Yeltsin's liberalization by refusing to name a new, non-Communist director of the State Bank. Beyond this circle, there is General Alexander Rutskoi, Afghan War hero, leader of "Communists for Democracy," and vice president. This ally Yeltsin acquired in March 1991 in order to split the Communist majority in Parliament, so as to survive impeachment by Gorbachev's Communists, and he took him in June as vice president. Rutskoi is also outspoken against liberalization, so there is a growing chance of constitutional conflict between Yeltsin and Parliament. Then there is Yeltsin's still solid clientele in the army, which voted heavily for him in June, led by Marshal Shaposhnikov; and with these, most of the intelligentsia of Moscow and St. Petersburg, who abandoned Gorbachev for Yeltsin. Such a heterogeneous group obviously could not live in harmony for long after August: choices both of policy and of personnel would have to be made. It was only in late October that these choices began to emerge, and it was not until late November that a new government was formed to implement them.

After August two great issues faced the new government: how to effect the unavoidable shift to the market and private property, and what to do about the "Union." And these two were closely linked: economic reform within the Union as a whole could only be based on com-

promise and hence would be by steps; economic reform in Russia alone would mean a sharp plunge, and hence meant destroying the Union framework. On both issues the radical option was finally chosen—but only after four months of struggle within the democratic coalition, and between Russia and the other republics.

In August a special committee under the Russian prime minister, Ivan Silayev, and Yavlinsky was put in charge of the economy and made into a Union body. This approach led by October 1 to the signing of an economic Union at a meeting of most of the republics in Alma-Ata. A month after Alma-Ata, however, further talks failed to give life to the new economic Union because of a deep divergence of Russia's interests from the other republics'. The conflict was due above all to the fact that Russia—unlike all the others except the Baltic states and Caucasian republics—had made an anti-Communist revolution. In Ukraine, Belarus, Kazakhstan, and Central Asia, the Party of Leonid Kravchuk, Ivan Shushkevich, and Nursultan Nazarbayev is still in power. All had behaved ambiguously during the coup. Most were neither ready nor eager for rapid marketization.

In late October the Yeltsin government therefore opted for a radical "Russia first" program, which the republics could follow as they might. In an address on October 28, Yeltsin announced that most prices would be freed by year's end, without wage indexation; privatization would also begin. He also called for accompanying emergency political measures. First, he had elections suspended for a year. Public opinion surveys made by the government had shown that if elections were held, the democrats would be in trouble. The Russians had also noted that recent elections to the Polish Sejm had returned a fragmented, unmanageable legislature. Yeltsin thus received power to rule by decree, subject to some parliamentary supervision. Finally, he assumed direct responsibility by taking the post of premier himself. He declared that if his new government did not begin to produce results within a year, he would step down.

When things had shaken down by November, it turned out that the August government of Prime Minister Silayev, and yesteryear's economic innovator, Yavlinsky, who advocated an all-Union, phased approach, had lost out to a more junior group of economists, mostly under 35, led by Yegor Gaidar, who favored a "Russia first" program of shock therapy. It is Burbulis, the allegedly benighted professor of scientific communism, who persuaded Yeltsin (obviously no expert in economics) to adopt this radical program, and to form the new ministry around the "Young Turks," or the "Boys in Reeboks," as they are known.

Accordingly, at the end of November Burbulis became first deputy prime minister, Gaidar deputy prime minister for the economy and finances, and Alexander Shokhin deputy prime minister for labor and employment. In the words of Mikhail Berger, the highly regarded economic expert of *Izvestia*, these men and their colleagues are the first group of real economists ever to be put in charge of the Russian economy. Basically pragmatic, they have also worked with the International Monetary Fund and the World Bank to make sure their program meets international standards, and with such Western economists as Jeffrey Sachs of Harvard and Anders Aslund, the Swedish economist and Soviet expert, who have been given offices near the Kremlin and have worked actively in preparing Gaidar's reform.

This reform proposes the most far-reaching change since Stalin built socialism. In December the country was opened to almost unrestricted foreign investment, with a right to repatriate profits. On January 2 came the liberation of prices except for basic food staples, energy, and transportation, where prices are to be increased three- or fourfold. Still to come are control of the budget deficit and inflation, stabilization of the currency, and internal convertibility of the ruble. Privatization of 70 percent of retail commerce and services has been targeted for the end of 1992. At the same time, measures of "social defense" have been adopted by Labor Minister Shokhin to tide the country over what can only be a painful transition for the majority of the population, some 50 percent of which lives below the official poverty line.

In addition, major decisions have at long last been made about agriculture, the greatest scandal of the Soviet economy. At the end of the year Yeltsin decreed that land would be given to peasants as private property, with resale subject only to minimal restrictions. This measure was to take effect immediately to permit results before spring sowing. Moreover, Russia's state and collective farms are to be dissolved. Gorbachev never contemplated anything more than long-term leasing of land to peasants, a precarious tenure they were never willing to accept. Yeltsin's decision is truly revolutionary, the surest sign that the new government is in earnest. Though many criticisms can be made of this program, Russia at last *has* a program, and Yeltsin must act while he still enjoys public confidence. The program is risky, but it is less risky than doing nothing.

This choice of a radical economic program was also a major factor in condemning the Union. Gaidar and his "boys" had always wished to get rid of the dead weight of the republics and their conservatism. When in December the latter tried to postpone the date of price liberalization from December 15 to late January, Russia unilaterally fixed the date at January 2. Most of the republics followed. If the former empire is to modernize its economy rapidly, clearly Russia will have to be the locomotive of the transformation.

Other forces worked to condemn the Union. Nationalism is one of these, but it acts in a special way under Soviet conditions. Most of the fifteen former republics are not real nations. With the exception of Georgia, Armenia, and the Baltic states, none has existed as a historic nation within its present borders or ever had an independent state. These republics were administrative subdivisions, created by the "center" to neutralize national feeling and, in Asia, Islamic internationalism, by giving them a purely formal statehood. Russia is a case apart, because it is a real historic nation with a genuine state. But it was never simply a *russkii*, national state. It was a *rossiiskii*, imperial state, that included other nations as protected, if not equal, subjects of the czar. The USSR was not a Russian national state either, though it used the Russian language and culture to cement the empire. The Soviet empire was a Party-empire, in which Communist, not national, loyalty was what counted.

Moreover, neither under the old regime nor under the new had the present Russian Federation existed as a separate entity; like all the other republics, it was a Soviet administrative creation. And, strange as it may seem to foreigners, the Russians have long considered themselves to be especially oppressed by Sovietism. Their standard of living was lower than that of the other republics. Their republic had been accorded none of the external trappings of nationhood, such as a separate Communist Party or Academy of Sciences. Rather, their culture was expropriated by the "center" for socialist purposes, and Russian values denigrated as reactionary. Hence, Russian nationalism could be even more virulently anti-Soviet than that of the non-Russian republics.

When the Union's crash came last year, it was propelled by two forces: ethnic nationalism and a strong movement for local control against the Party-center. This drive for local power explains why even Russian areas of the Federation, from St. Petersburg to the Far East, and even districts within the city of Moscow, sought autonomy. And it explains the iconoclastic passion with which all Bolshevik symbols, from the name of Leningrad to the Red Flag itself, have been repudiated. Finally, it tells why the apparently reasonable device of the federal Union framework, so convenient to foreign powers and so potentially handy for negotiating the transition to democracy, could not in the end be preserved.

What emerged was Yeltsin's Commonwealth, no analogue to the European Community, and no body capable of coordinating the ex-Soviet "economic space." But neither is it simply a device for creating a new Russian hegemony in the East: Yeltsin's sponsorship of Baltic independence and his willingness to let the Asian republics go show he is no traditional "Great Russian chauvinist." What the Commonwealth comes down to is the best available compromise to keep Russia and the republics cooperating, to negotiate their real and many conflicts of interest.

For Russia, the first of these interests is the 25 million nationals beyond its frontiers, especially in Ukraine and Kazakhstan. The members of this diaspora are Yeltsin's constituents; they are, after the Armenians, the ethnic group most threatened by violence; and the Russians at home expect their government to protect those now abroad. And Ukraine, though wary of Russia's intentions, has in fact taken account of these concerns by extending citizenship to all who live on Ukrainian territory, recognizing the official use of Russian where its speakers are the majority, and reassuring the Jewish population that their rights will be respected. So far, that permanent diplomatic conference that is the Commonwealth—and the caution of its leaders—has kept the former Soviet Union from going the way of Yugoslavia.

Moreover, the Russian nationalism that we have so far seen is a positive one. The horrors of World War II have given national sentiment such a bad name that it is now often considered the antichamber of fascism—except in the Third World. This is a shallow judgment: a sense of communal cohesion, of common values, all founded on a minimally "usable past"— in short, of patriotism—is necessary for the healthy functioning of any nation. And humanity does come in national units.

The nationalism of Yeltsin and the Russian democrats is in the lineage of the national democrats of the European revolutions of 1848. Moreover, it is not so much directed against other ex-Soviet peoples as against the spurious internationalism of communism. In its most dignified and cultural form it is represented by the medieval historian Dmitri Likhachev, advocating the return to traditional spiritual values. In its more practical and predominant form, as represented by Yeltsin and his Young Turks, it is a "Westernizing" nationalism, in the tradition of Peter the Great or the reformist prime minister of 1906–11, Piotr Stolypin. Its aim is to modernize Russia along European, and especially American, lines so as to realize her national potential.

So what can we in the West reasonably expect as the outcome of this revolution? It would be wholly misplaced to assess the Yeltsinian wager through the prism of our own Jeffersonian democracy. Attaining such standards is not in the cards; insisting on them would simply play into the hands of the many losers, East and West, of the August revolution, who have a vested interest in its failure, so as to salvage belief in the allegedly unrealized potential of the Soviet experiment. For what the Yeltsin democrats are building now in Russia is capitalism, and building capitalism is not a goal that inspires lyrical engagement, or one that people of generosity readily take to. Yet it is only if Russia succeeds in building a market economy that the higher refinements of democracy will eventually be added onto it. Thus Yeltsin's economic effort is far more important than the attempt to contract a Commonwealth. Yeltsin and his partisans also know that they have only the narrowest margin of error, and that if they fail, some rougher modernizer, on the model of General Pinochet, will take over and resort to much more brutal methods.

What we will have for at least one more year, therefore, will be an emergency executive government trying, from one crisis and improvisation to another, to navigate its way out of what is the most appalling national collapse in history. This crisis is often described as a deeper version of the Great Depression in America. In fact, the ex-Soviet Union is in much worse condition, nearer to that of post-World War II Germany and Japan. Its infrastructure is crumbling. Aeroflot no longer has adequate fuel, its planes decrepit and disintegrating; the collapse of the railroads is not far off; the oil industry is a similar shambles. At the same time, factories now function mainly through barter. This is a situation that in any country leads to emergency government. We should not forget that Franklin Roosevelt in 1933 governed largely by decree, and with the aid of Young Turks known as a "braintrust," or that the Mother of the Parliaments in 1940 suspended elections during the war, with the result that Britain went ten years without a vote. Lincoln's Emancipation Proclamation was an executive decree. Perhaps we should be prepared to allow "Czar" Boris a similar leeway, as well as the margin to make a number of mistakes.

For the task in Russia now is difficult beyond anything the privileged West has ever known. Not only must a modern society be built out of the unprecedented wreckage of the late Soviet economy and polity, but this building must be done by a population that until 1991 was molded and deformed by the Leninist lie. As the matter was put, on the day the Union died, by one longtime party member who always knew the system was a fraud: "And we must now try to produce good out of all that evil."

■ INTERVIEW WITH 'SOVIETICUS'

What's Really Happening in Russia?

STEPHEN F. COHEN

Stephen F. Cohen is a professor of politics and director of Russian studies at Princeton University. He is author of, among other books, Rethinking the Soviet Experience *and (with Katrina vanden Heuvel)* Voices of Glasnost.

Recently returned from Russia, Stephen F. Cohen responded to a series of questions from Nation *editors on developments there. A transcript of his replies follows.* —The Editors

Q: *The longstanding discrepancy between American media perceptions and Soviet realities was a constant concern in your* Nation *column in the 1980s ["Sovieticus"]. Given all the changes in the Soviet Union, and the end of Russian censorship, is there no longer a discrepancy?*
SFC: We have a thousandfold more information about Soviet, and particularly Russian, affairs than we had before Mikhail Gorbachev came to power in 1985, and American reporting from the scene is far better—less simplistic and more detailed. But new stereotypes, myths and misconceptions have emerged in our mass media—especially in what passes for commentary—and in our political discourse. And though they are the opposite of cold war misperceptions, they too obscure much more than they reveal. Indeed, I worry that it may become just as difficult to have an informed, dispassionate discussion of Russia in the United States today as it was during the cold war years.

The basic problem, as always, is the American habit of interpreting Russia through the prism of our own ideology—of finding there only what we seek, and seeking only what we find comforting. For decades, it was an alien "Communism" and "totalitarianism." Now it's an American-style "free-market democracy" and "civil society." Many commentators, and some correspondents, are functioning less as journalists than as cheerleaders for "free-market" capitalism, which they can't distinguish from corrupt black-marketeering. Some base their accounts on self-described Moscow democrats, who aren't always objective sources and whose radical views may be no less self-destructive than those of Russia's pre-Soviet intelligentsia. Even eminent professors have entered the fray. A Berkeley historian tells us in *The New Republic* that we shouldn't hold Boris Yeltsin to high democratic standards, because of the good things he is trying to achieve. Yeltsin deserves our support, but didn't American apologists for the Bolsheviks, and even for Stalin, offer the same excuses?

Each of us has the right to hope that Russia will become what we think it should be. But the ideological perspectives of the American right and left can't make analytical sense of that country's defiantly complex history and politics. As always, they only distort our political discourse and policies toward Russia.

Q: *You speak of new myths about Russia. Give us an example.*
SFC: Myths may not be entirely false. Usually, they inflate a partial truth into an overwhelming one that obscures other truths. Take, for example, the current notion that a "civil society," eager for a democratic market system, has emerged as the driving force in Russian political life, even defeating the coup last August. For many observers of Russia who consider themselves to be right-minded—scholars, journalists and democratic activists alike—this has become a new orthodoxy. Everything used to be attributed to a "totalitarian Kremlin." Now we have another extreme of simplistic analysis.

"Civil society" isn't even a very meaningful or useful concept in this context. Borrowed from the history of Western democratic theory, it's another attempt to squeeze Russia's traditions and realities into our ideological constructs. Indeed, the idea of a civil society is more philosophical than sociological because it is assumed to be democratic by nature. If so, how to explain Nazi Germany, which had some kind of civil society? Nor is it a valid empirical generalization about Russia's 150 million people. Opinion polls tell us that a great many of them don't understand or don't want markets or democracy. Some Russian sociologists worry that much of their country is more akin to a "*lumpen* society," the opposite of civil society. Anyway, to explain everything in terms of a surging civil society is bad analysis and history. Several hundred thousand Russians may have actively opposed the coup; the rest were passive or silent.

Myths popularized by the failed coup, which remains a mystery in important respects, would matter less if they did not focus on partial truths. A struggle for markets and democracy is part of the Russian political story today, though that saga began under Gorbachev, not under Yeltsin after the coup. But consider two other large developments.

In most of the former Soviet republics, notably in Russia itself, leaders are calling for radical political and economic reform in the name of society. Even leaving aside how much of this may be designed to win American support, most of these leaders were Communist Party functionaries in the Soviet system—members of Soviet elites that fragmented during the Gorbachev years—now engaged in a zealous struggle over vast property and power formerly controlled by the Soviet state: factories, banks, land, shops, television networks, publishing houses, apartments, transportation and, of course, military property. Like yesterday's Marxists, today's anti-Communists understand that property is power, so the struggle is raging everywhere, from the capitals to the provinces. Some of these people, perhaps many of them, are sincere converts to marketization and democratization. But it is foolish to ignore the politics of confiscation unfolding since late 1991 and its dangerous echoes of politically motivated expropriations earlier in Soviet history. It helps to explain the revival of some authoritarian traditions around governments in the former republics professing to be democratic, including Yeltsin's.

The second development is related. Our attention is riveted on Yeltsin's government in Moscow. But in Russia and several other republics, considerable real power has migrated from the capital to the provinces. The process began under Gorbachev as central political authority weakened and elections made provincial officials more dependent on local constituencies. But it's now being driven and intensified by the economic situation. The scarcity of goods and the breakdown of distribution have put enormous power in the hands of producers. That means the country's large state factories and farms are still run by the old elites or *nomenklatura* and are located mainly in the provinces. Neither Yeltsin nor any other Moscow leader can govern, much less reform, Russia today without at least the tacit support of these powerful provincial elites. Real power—to produce and deliver goods—is in their hands. They could, for example, starve the large cities, the bastions of whatever democracy now exists, while bartering among themselves. Many of these economic elites want to take more direct control of their enterprises by "privatizing" them, but is that real marketization? Most of them now profess to be anti-Communists, but does that make them democrats? And what about their close ties to provincial military commanders? Whatever the case, while our diplomats and journalists seek Russia's destiny in Moscow, it is being determined largely in the vast and remote provinces.

Q: *For someone who always argued that fundamental change was possible in the Soviet system, you don't seem to be impressed by the dramatic changes that have occurred.*

SFC: Despite prevailing scholarly and media views to the contrary in the 1970s and early 1980s, it was easy to understand that significant changes would eventually come in the Soviet system. Nothing in history or politics is immutable, and factors favoring reform were already observable. It is much harder today to be certain about what has actually changed irrevocably and what has not, and to weigh what has passed against what remains. Take, for example, the prevailing conclusion, which has become so axiomatic that hardly anyone disputes it: "The Soviet system has collapsed."

Certainly, this is so in important ways, but also not so in important ways. It's a mistake to equate the Soviet system over the years so completely with the Communist Party—or Communism with what we might call "sovietism." The party was a very important part of it, but far from all of it. For example, the party controlled the state, but the state—the "administrative-command system," as it became known—primarily controlled society, at least the economy. So what happened? The Communist Party actually lost its monopoly on politics as early as 1989—in that fundamental respect, the Leninist system was already disintegrating as a result of Gorbachev's reforms—but the state administration continued to function. After the 1991 coup attempt, the party collapsed, but has the Soviet state system? We shouldn't be misled by surface changes, however dramatic. Many links in the system have been ruptured, especially between Russia and the republics and in economic distribution. The names of lots of cities, institutions and streets have been changed.

But consider some fundamental continuities in Russia itself. The economy—at least 95 percent of it—remains in the hands of the state. No new elites, as I said before, have emerged. At the regional and local levels, the old authorities are largely still in place, having fled from the party to other power structures. And class relations are as they were. A new class of entrepreneurs is emerging, but it remains tiny and weak. Many popular attitudes do not seem to have changed greatly. Most citizens still expect the kind of cradle-to-grave welfare state that was a defining component of latter-day Soviet Communism.

In all these fundamental respects, no new revolution has occurred in Russia, although it is fashionable to speak of one. And if we ask more correctly about the prospects of further reforms in the system, the towering question that faced and undermined Gorbachev also remains: How do you actually implement marketization and democratization in a system where large segments of local officialdom—which evolved over decades into an entrenched caste of political, economic and military power-holders—and of the populace are opposed? It can be done, I think, but not easily or quickly.

There's an even larger interpretive question here. Was Communism or sovietism really something entirely alien to and imposed upon Russia, as many Western and Russian commentators now insist? If so, we could imagine a quick escape from the past. We could believe Yeltsin when he tells us he is president of "another country." But if to a significant degree

Soviet Communism grew out of and perpetuated Russia's authoritarian traditions, as I think was the case, we need a different perspective. Despite the modernizing and Westernizing changes that have occurred over the years, Russia cannot jump out of its skin—certainly not into ours.

I even have some doubts about another prevailing certainty in the media—that we've seen the last of something like the Soviet Union. The union has collapsed politically. All fifteen former republics say they are fully independent states. Some have gained diplomatic recognition and some are moving toward separate militaries and currencies. But here too we have to think about continuities and factors that may favor some kind of new union of several or most of the former republics.

Think of these pro-union factors as grids that stretch across and bind the entire territory. There is, of course, a single energy and economic grid. Few essential industrial enterprises can produce without components made in other republics. There is a single military grid. For all the rival claims to military property, the Soviet Army is still garrisoned in most of the republics and largely under Moscow's command. And there is a human grid—75 million former Soviet citizens who live outside their ethnic territories, including 25 million Russians; millions of ethnic intermarriages; millions of non-Russians who speak only Russian and Russians who live elsewhere but can't speak the native language. Not surprisingly, in a referendum only last March, 77 percent voted for preserving the Soviet Union.

These ties that bind now seem less important than nationalist politics in the newly proclaimed states, but here we have to think further. Most nationalist leaders are ex-Communists engaged in political struggles at home. If their conversion to nationalism is less than sincere or complete, how long and fully will they play the nationalist card on territorial space that has been dominated by Russia's size and power for centuries? Meanwhile, Yeltsin insists that the imperial "center" ended with the Soviet government. But Russia, or Moscow, was the center of the Soviet Union. And though Yeltsin has renamed those Soviet ministries "Russian," they still exist. Some are being reduced, but others are being consolidated, including the security ministries. Moreover, Russian nationalism, the strongest ideological force in Moscow today, won't disregard its 25 million compatriots living elsewhere, or easily concede the Soviet Union's former economic and military property, as we see in the dispute over armed forces in Ukraine.

I'm not predicting a new Soviet Union, only arguing that here too there are more good questions than answers. One is whether Gorbachev was right in insisting that marketization and democratization stood a better chance in a reformed Soviet Union rather than without a union.

Q: *So you don't put much credence in the Commonwealth of Independent States, which was created in December by abolishing the Soviet Union and Gorbachev's government?*

SFC: We should wish it well, because it's a fine idea. But it's a paper idea unlikely to withstand all the factors I've already mentioned, from the struggle over property to the enduring union grids. In fact, republic leaders who joined the commonwealth had conflicting reasons for doing so. Some hoped it would become a reformed union along the lines proposed by Gorbachev, others a way station to total independence. Not surprisingly, there's been more conflict than consensus ever since the documents were signed. Moreover, it's not possible to create a new state or commonwealth overnight, just by declaring it. Even the best such political intentions require decades, and not all the intentions leading to the commonwealth were of the highest political order. Much of the process was based on a chain of political betrayal. Gorbachev's own ministers—by the way, they were chiefly men of the state, not the party—betrayed him by staging a coup. Gorbachev returned to Moscow and reached a series of political arrangements with Yeltsin, who then betrayed him and all the leaders of the non-Slav republics by going to Belarus with the Ukrainian leader Leonid Kravchuk. Kravchuk then betrayed Yeltsin and the Russian Parliament by reneging on several military and financial agreements. And so it goes. How much that is good or durable can be built on the politics of betrayal?

Q: *Most of the changes we now see are results of Gorbachev's almost seven years in power. As one of the few American scholars who argued from the beginning that he was an authentic reformer, can you now evaluate his years as a leader?*
SFC: It's not a simple matter. Political obituaries published since Gorbachev left office differ greatly. Western commentators tend to agree, and rightly, that his role in international affairs has earned him a great and positive place in history. More than anyone else, he deserves credit for ending the cold war, liberating Eastern Europe, reuniting Germany and ending Russia's long isolation from the West. On the other hand, many people, particularly in Russia, insist that no leader who presided over the disintegration of his own country, the crisis of its economy and the collapse of his own party can be called successful. Others try to strike a balance: Gorbachev brought freedom but eliminated sausage.

So, many complex factors and outcomes have to be taken into account. A full scholarly evaluation of Gorbachev's leadership won't be possible for many years, for several reasons. First, Sovietologists who denied for decades that change was possible in the system now lack useful concepts for even defining the success or failure of such reforms. Second, Gorbachev attempted something unprecedented in history: simultaneous transformations to democracy, a market economy and real federalism. Comparisons with lesser reforms in other societies are therefore partial or seriously misleading. Third, we still do not know how much freedom of decision making Gorbachev had during his years in power, and thus how many unwise decisions were actually of his own making. For this, we need memoirs and archives. Fourth, it's not impossible that Gorbachev will have some kind of political afterlife that will alter our judgment.

But mainly, much depends on how the great transformations he set into motion turn out in the years and decades ahead. If Russia becomes a predominantly democratic state with a flourishing market economy, coexisting benignly with the former Soviet republics, historians may conclude that

Gorbachev was the twentieth century's greatest leader, having launched the transformation of its largest country. But if Russia plunges into a new despotism, with a rapacious state economy and imperialism, he's more likely to be viewed as another tragic leader in Russia's long history of failed reform.

Q: *Fair enough. But surely you can make a tentative evaluation today.*

SFC: On an interim basis, I would rank Gorbachev among this century's greatest reformers and as the greatest reformer in Russian history. Setting himself against centuries of Russian and Soviet experience, he consciously set out to liberate his society from the state's political and economic domination, and he succeeded far beyond what anyone could have imagined. Incidentally, many of the people who today criticize Gorbachev's domestic reforms as inadequate are those who previously said he would change nothing. Moreover, along the way, Gorbachev led Russia closer to a real democratic process than it had ever had before. He persuaded even the country's conservative elites of the need for substantial marketization and privatization. And the dogma of a monopolistic state economy was only one of the orthodoxies he shattered, a feat that bequeathed political capital to new reformers for years to come. Still more, unlike any previous czarist or Soviet leader, Gorbachev offered to negotiate Russia's empire with its constituent nations. And in doing all this, he caused remarkably little bloodshed, which is a great tribute to his belief that radical purposes had to rely on centrist tactics and consensual approaches. Finally, Gorbachev achieved all this despite far greater opposition than is generally known. Pop analysts fault him for not moving more quickly and taking even bolder steps. But leaders must be judged in light of the obstacles they face. And there is plenty of evidence that Gorbachev's reforms—from overhauling the political and economic system to negotiating with the United States and withdrawing from Afghanistan—were actively opposed, even sabotaged, by political forces at high levels in the party and the state.

Q: *You credit Gorbachev with moving the Soviet Union toward democracy and suggest that Russia's future political development will strongly influence the fate of the other republics. What are the prospects for democracy in Russia?*

SFC: Democracy may still have its best chance ever in Russia, but it's a slim chance for the near future. The mythology of the failed coup generated the illusion that big obstacles to democratic development had been swept away. Some antidemocratic institutions were crushed or weakened, but many authoritarian obstacles remain, as I've already pointed out. Nor is it true that all the anti-Communists who call themselves democrats are actually democratic, as I know from firsthand observations. In addition, Russia still lacks many aspects of a functioning democracy, even leaving aside the absence of markets and a consensual democratic culture. It's a long list: a parliament and judiciary comparable to the traditions of executive power; a multiparty system; regularly scheduled elections; a nationwide and self-sustaining free press; and more. Russia doesn't even have a real constitution yet.

Still worse, antidemocratic developments have grown stronger and more numerous since the failed coup. These include not just the deteriorating economic situation—scarcity, rampant inflation and unemployment have never fostered democracy—but other less noted factors. The military has been politicized in unprecedented ways. It began in 1989 when Gorbachev had to allow active officers to stand for the new Parliament. During their final showdown, both Gorbachev and Yeltsin had to plead openly for the military's support. Yeltsin won because he could make budgetary promises, though dubious ones. Since then, the military has been drawn even more deeply and clamorously into politics, as its top leaders protest the country's disintegration and the efforts in several former republics to defy their authority and seize their property. They've marched onto the political stage, as we saw in January when a large assembly of wrathful officers convened in the Kremlin. They are only a step from center stage. Wildcat acts by district commanders may be no less a threat—in the Baltics, for example, where large Russian garrisons are feeling increasingly disfranchised; in the Transcaucasus, where civil wars could incite them; or in the Russian provinces, where garrison elites are part of the military-industrial-agricultural complex. Even if traditional generals have no stomach for taking power, don't overlook colonels and captains, who are closer to the woeful economic plight of junior officers.

Yeltsin is relying on the czarist and Soviet tradition of centralizing authority.

We ought to take notice of other antidemocratic factors as well. Before the coup, a progressive conservatism was emerging in Soviet political debates. It was discredited by the coup, unfairly I think, and the result is even greater polarization between self-professed radical democrats and militant reactionaries, who have found new adherents among disemployed Communist officials and disadvantaged workers. Add here increasingly assertive "national-patriotic" movements, one of the strongest of which is indignantly called "Ours." Russian nationalism may turn out to be liberal and democratic, but it's hard to see how, in present circumstances. It is already menacing the Chechens, Tatars and other large non-Russian minorities that want more independence within Russia. And a retrograde nationalism, yet another legacy of both czarism and Stalinism, is also likely to be fed by an indignant backlash against Westernization, which is becoming excessive and primitive. Have a look at all the Western advisers swarming over Russia and at the amount of imported rock videos and soft porn on government-run television.

Q: *Are you saying that Russia has not moved closer to democracy since the coup and the disintegration of the Soviet Union?*

SFC: It depends on your understanding of democracy. Russia has a popularly elected President and Parliament. That's very important. But as a process, there may be less democracy now than before. Yeltsin is ruling primarily by decree, an old Russian tradition, rather than through constitutional process or parliamentary legislation. Some of his decrees are of dubious legality. Banning a political party and confiscating property, even the Communist Party and Soviet property, doesn't set democratic precedents. More generally, there's Yeltsin's campaign to build "presidential power," which already involved postponing regional elections last December and establishing an apparatus of personal envoys to oversee provincial officials. Real Russian democratization must move toward political decentralization and representative government at all levels. Yeltsin's campaign seems to be relying on the czarist and Soviet tradition of centralizing authority in Moscow and imposing it on the rest of the country.

To be fair, a case might be made that these measures are necessary to cope with an emergency situation and to implement reforms. In fact, Yeltsin's people are saying that some of them are only temporary. But it's a mistake to pretend they are democratic; that will only distort or discredit the democratic idea in Russia. And don't forget that temporary emergency measures have a habit of becoming permanent in Russia.

On the other hand, I don't share the widely held view, which began in Moscow and spread to the American media, that the only choice now is between democracy and fascism. Both possibilities exist, but there's a large spectrum of authoritarian outcomes in between them that seem more likely. Nor do I share the widespread notion, which also originated in Moscow, that a popular upheaval from below is lurking in the wings. It's a very remote possibility exaggerated by the lingering spell of 1917. Russia is no longer the country it was in 1917. If large-scale disorders break out in the streets, some segments of the political class probably will be behind them, most likely forces associated with the security apparatus or the military-industrial complex.

Q: *Speaking of the political class, you spoke earlier of its growing polarization. Is there no consensus about the country's future?*

SFC: Russian politics has often revolved around two questions: What is to be done, and who's guilty? Part of the problem today is that because so many people don't know what to do, they demand to know who's guilty. Therein lies the danger of another political witch hunt, actually encouraged by Westerners who advise putting former Communist officials on trial in a country that had 20 million party members.

I don't think Russia can move toward a stable system, much less a democratic one, until the political class openly discusses and resolves on some consensual basis three fundamental questions. First, should everything created during the Soviet period be rejected as criminal or unworthy, and therefore everything built from scratch? Or should important aspects of the existing system be retained? Second, what kind of system is best for Russia: one that tries to imitate a Western model or one that borrows from Western experiences but is equally reliant on Russian traditions and circumstances? And third, how fast should the country move toward a new system? In a leap through "shock therapy" or gradually and incrementally? (In thinking about such questions, it's important to understand that Russia's need in the foreseeable future is not to produce an American-style excess of goods but to eliminate scarcity of those goods necessary for a comfortable life.) Gorbachev generally preached moderate answers to these questions. The danger inherent in a very radical approach, which may now be ascendant, is that it could plunge Russia into another Bolshevik-like experiment, further polarize the country and produce a system that is neither stable nor democratic.

Q: *Now that Yeltsin has launched his own economic program by liberalizing prices, which approach has he embraced?*

SFC: In economic policy, the conflict is between those who want to dismantle the state economy and build on a free market and those who want to combine large parts of the state sector with a market economy—to walk on both legs, so to speak. Yeltsin's government includes advocates of both approaches. His present economic team, headed by Yegor Gaidar, is preaching radical abolitionism and market "shock therapy," while his Vice President, Aleksandr Rutskoi, advocates policies similar to Gorbachev's. Rutskoi, a relatively young and very substantial political figure, is increasingly nationalistic and critical of the Gaidar team for practicing "economic genocide." He has been excluded from Yeltsin's inner circle but hardly from the political scene.

Yeltsin has espoused both views. Politically, he has rejected virtually the entire Soviet experience and suggested the need for a Western-style system. But economically, he is promising to retain large parts of the state and welfare system, which were the bedrock of Soviet "socialism." Having risen to power by assailing Communism, Yeltsin may now be finding that there are few social constituencies and circumstances favoring its opposite, capitalism. If so, he'll probably have to act even less democratically and make more inflationary concessions to public opinion in order to maintain stability. Eventually he may have to form a coalition with the Rutskoi forces.

It's not clear what Yeltsin really hopes to achieve by letting prices soar, as was done in Poland two years ago with very mixed results. Yeltsin says it will cause hard times but also generate many more goods and trigger extensive marketization. He says prices, and the general economic situation, will stabilize by year's end. Let's hope so. But Russia is not Poland, a small homogeneous country where private farming and a rudimentary market infrastructure already existed. No substantial demonopolization, denationalization or privatization of Russian industry, agriculture or even trade has yet taken place. The process is scheduled to begin this year, but first and primarily in the areas of shops and housing, not the productive sectors. And no one knows if newly adopted land reform legislation will actually create a sizable number of productive private farmers.

So where is the incentive for large monopolistic producers to respond to liberalized prices (which was an administrative and not a market decision) by putting more goods in the stores? They may wait for still higher prices. Or factory managers, who as in the past must supply their work force, and collective-farm chairmen, who need industrial goods, may not care about acquiring more rubles of dubious value. They can continue to barter among themselves, leaving state shops without goods and cities without provisions. The result would be hyperinflation and a mass victimization of millions of urban citizens who depend on state stores (the elderly, the young and almost everyone who's not a secure part of the industrial-agricultural work force or black market) without real marketization or privatization. Russian economists who foresee this outcome call it "shock without therapy."

Yeltsin may also have less-publicized reasons for liberalizing prices so soon. One could be to skim off the excessive rubles in consumer hands, the "ruble overhang" that economists complain is inflationary but that represents people's life savings. Another could be to reduce the state's enormous budget deficit by sharply cutting subsidies for essential consumer goods. And yet another, to entice more foreign aid by convincing Western governments and banks that he is acting on their advice. But it is hard to imagine anything except an even deeper economic and political crisis, perhaps as early as April, if people have been deprived—some say "robbed"—of their everyday necessities, savings and possibly jobs. At worst, such policies could vaporize already weak constituencies for reform and bring reactionary forces to power in Moscow or in the provinces. At best, they would create a situation compelling Yeltsin, or another leader, to try to revive a gradual, incremental approach, if it's not too late.

Q: *What should or could the United States do about all these changes and dangers in the former Soviet Union? Has the Bush Administration adopted the right policies toward Russia?*

SFC: What policies? There are no clear ones except for desperately trying to safeguard Soviet nuclear weapons and hoping for good political outcomes in fifteen former republics. We claim to be leading an international economic assistance program, but we've given less than 7 percent of the total, mainly in credits to buy our agricultural surplus and that must be repaid, while Europeans have contributed more than 75 percent. We promised to help Russia and the others through a potentially destabilizing winter but held a midwinter conference on the problem, and none of the food aid promised in November had reached Soviet territory by early February. We are giving lots of "technical advice," but much of it is dubious. Meanwhile, we rushed to recognize the independence of several republics on the assumption that the proclaimed Commonwealth of Independent States was a divorce, when actually it was only a separation. Now they're fighting over a final settlement, and we've squandered diplomatic influence.

To be fair, these are complex questions without easy answers. The Bush Administration has good intentions, but will it act on them? After all, it never came to Gorbachev's financial aid in ways that might have prevented the coup. There may also be some bad intentions in or close to the Administration. One occasionally hears triumphalist suggestions that the Unit-ed States should exploit Russia's weakness to prevent it from becoming such a great power again—by preventing Russia from regaining strong influence over the former republics, as Henry Kissinger seems to be urging, or by imposing a unilateral disarmament on it. Great powers don't disappear and great countries don't stay in crisis. If we act on these unwise and dangerous proposals, what kind of Russia will then confront us?

Post-Communist Russia must find its own, native future, or it will never be stable.

But I'm even more worried about the consensus emerging among people inside and outside the Administration, conservatives and liberals alike. It assumes that U.S. aid should be conditioned on Russia following our economic and political advice, which means replicating our system and having a large American presence in Russia: economic advisers to the government, business advisers to enterprises, political advisers to parties, guardians against black-market corruption, inspectors to gather and dismantle their weapons, and more. In short, a great crusade to convert Russia to our way of life.

Almost everything is wrong with this kind of missionary and exceedingly intrusive American policy. It presumes that a political-economic-social system can be artificially and firmly implanted in a different, much older civilization, that we can intervene wisely in a seething caldron of rival Russian ideas and movements, and that in the end Russia will be grateful. In reality, it means blatantly allying ourselves with one extreme program, "free-market shock therapy," and with the enormous social pain it will cause. And remember, political pendulums always swing. Anti-Westernism remains a powerful Russian tradition. When the natural backlash against excessive Westernization comes, hordes of Americans perceived to be engineering everyday pain, Klondike capitalism and the exploitation of the country can only make it worse and direct it against us. Similarly, the Bush Administration's plan to import Russian nuclear scientists may be a virtuous effort to prevent proliferation, but how will Russians eventually react to this Alaska-like purchase of their best and brightest?

Many well-intentioned Russians want this kind of American policy, but we lack the wisdom, power and right to intervene so directly and deeply. Post-Communist Russia must find its own, native future, or it will never be stable. Why presume there can be no good third—or fourth and fifth—way? The West began with markets and moved toward state regulation and welfare. Russia begins instead with a statist system. Let it resolve the duality in its own way. Where is our fabled open mind and pluralism?

Q: *Are you saying that the United States should do nothing? Have a policy of benign neglect toward Russia?*

SFC: I want a much more generous American policy of helping Russia reform, but a far less smug, conditional and intrusive one. Most Russian elites and movements now accept the need for marketization and privatization. They disagree over how much, how fast and how to do it. So long as the general direction is toward reform, under Yeltsin or other leaders, let us give generously from afar and let them decide. Plenty of Russian economists understand the problems and possibilities better than do itinerant ones from Harvard, Hoover, Heritage and world banks who know little or nothing about Russia.

The United States ought to mobilize economic assistance comparable to the Marshall Plan but, alas, that isn't going to happen. Given our own economic problems and presidential-year politics, there's no sufficient constituency or leadership, and won't be. But at a minimum, we must do several large things immediately, without any more excuses about aid going into "black holes" and black markets, for the sake of our national security and national honor.

Massive humanitarian relief has to be given, not for one winter but several, to citizens most imperiled by marketization—the very young and very old. Why are none of our vaunted elder statesmen leading a supplementary private aid mission, as Herbert Hoover did in the early 1920s? A very large, long-term, low-interest credit program is needed so Russia can import essential goods and technology. Similarly, existing debt has to be restructured and interest considerably deferred or even forgiven. If Western private capital is really a large part of the solution, a stabilization fund, as was done for the Polish zloty, is required to make the ruble convertible. And surely it's time to abolish U.S. cold war laws and regulations discriminating against the Russian economy.

All this is a bare minimum, but far more than we're now doing. It's said we can't afford even the few billion dollars a year that would be the U.S. contribution to such an international effort. Of course we could, simply by reducing defense spending in degrees truly responsive to cuts now under way in Russia. But such reductions are unlikely, even for the sake of our own pressing economic needs.

Clearly, a larger problem is at work: Four decades of cold war have so militarized our thinking that we can't think politically about our real national interests at home or abroad. For example, the post–cold war world may be even more dangerous than the cold war era if only because thousands of Soviet nuclear weapons, particularly battlefield ones, are scattered across that enormous, unstable territory. Only political solutions can bring security, but the only one proposed is to convert fifteen independent states, most of them with barely any democratic experience, into replicas of America. It's a conceit, not a policy. As for Russia itself, a Eurasian country, perhaps Europeans should bear the brunt of economic assistance. But if a reformed Russia moves closer to Europe—to Germany, for example—than to us, will we accept that natural political development? We should, but imagine our indignant outrage when we take time from bashing Japan to notice.

What's needed is new political thinking about ourselves and the world, not the new weapons we continue to develop. Indeed, future historians of the late twentieth century may wonder why so many unorthodox political ideas germinated in the old authoritarian Soviet system and so few in democratic America—why there were so few, for example, in our presidential campaigns.

The Third World: Diversity in Development

The Third World is an umbrella term for a disparate group of states, often called developing or less developed countries (LCDs). The most important shared characteristic may well be what these countries have not become—namely, modern industrial societies. Otherwise they differ considerably in terms of both history and politics as well as present socioeconomic conditions and prospects. Moreover, the designation Third World has been used so variously that it is dismissed by some critical observers as a category that offers plenty of cognitive confusion and ideological symbolism but lacks much analytical rigor or insight. Their objections should at least make us cautious when speaking about the Third World.

Most of the Third World nations also share the problems of poverty and rapid population growth. However, their present economic situation and potential for development vary considerably, as a simple alphabetical juxtaposition of countries such as Angola and the Argentines, Bangladesh and Brazil, or Chad and China illustrates. An additional term, Fourth World, has therefore been proposed to designate countries that are so desperately short of resources that they appear to have little or no prospect for a self-sustained economic improvement. Adding to the terminological inflation and confusion, the Third World countries are now often referred to collectively as the South and contrasted with the largely industrialized North. Most of them, in fact, are located in the southern latitudes of the planet—in Latin America, Africa, Asia, and the Middle East.

In studying the attempts by Third World countries to create institutions and policies that will promote their socioeconomic development, it is important not to leave out the international context. The political and intellectual leaders of these countries have often drawn upon some version of what is called dependency theory to explain their plight, often combining it with demands for special treatment or compensation of various kinds. Dependency theory is itself an outgrowth of the Marxist theory of imperialism, according to which advanced capitalist countries have established exploitative relationships toward the weaker economic systems of the Third World.

Much attention has been given to the success of the new industrial countries or NICs, a small group of former Third World countries that have succeeded in breaking out of the cycle of chronic poverty and low productivity. It is not fully clear what lessons we can draw from the impressive records of the four or five tigers or dragons—Singapore, Hong Kong, South Korea, Taiwan, and possibly Thailand or Malaysia. Some observers have suggested that the combination of authoritarian politics and market economics have provided a successful mix of discipline and incentives that have made the economic takeoff possible. Others stress special cultural factors in these countries, which supposedly encourage rational forms of economic behavior.

Sometimes called the Group of 77, but now consisting of some 120 countries, the Third World states once linked themselves together in the United Nations to promote whatever interests they may have had in common. In their demand for a New International Economic Order, they focused on promoting changes designed to improve their relative commercial position vis-à-vis the affluent industrialized nations of the North. This common front, however, has turned out to be more rhetorical than real.

Outside the United Nations, some of these same countries have tried to increase and control the price of industrially important primary exports through the building of cartel agreements among themselves. The result has sometimes been detrimental to other Third World nations. The most successful of these cartels, the Organization of Petroleum Exporting Countries (OPEC), was established in 1960 and reigned for almost a decade. Its cohesion has since eroded, resulting in drastic reductions in oil prices. While this development has been welcomed in the oil-importing industrial world as well as in many developing countries, it left some oil-producing nations, such as Mexico, in economic disarray.

The problems of poverty, hunger, and malnutrition are socially and politically explosive. In their fear of revolution and their opposition to meaningful reform, the privileged classes often resort to brutal repression as a means to preserve a status quo favorable to themselves. In Latin America, this led to a politicalization of many laypersons and clergy of the Roman Catholic church, who demanded social reform in the name of what was called liberation theology. For them, some variant of the dependency theory filled a very practical ideological function by providing a relatively simple analytical and moral explanation of a complex reality. It also gave some strategical guidance for political activists who were determined to change this state of affairs. Their views on the inevitability of class struggle, and the need to take an active part in it, often clashed with the Vatican's outlook.

The collapse of Communist rule in Europe is bound to have some impact on the ideological explanation of Third World poverty and on the resulting strategies to overcome it. The Soviet model of modernization, which fascinated some Third World leaders until recently, now appears to have very little of practical value to offer these countries. The fact that even the Communists who remain in power in China have been willing to experiment with market reforms, including the private profit motive, has added to the general discredit of the centrally planned economy. Perhaps even more important, countries in Africa and Latin America that have pursued more market-oriented strategies of development appear on the whole to have performed better than some of their more statist neighbors.

Today the cultural explanation appears to be less valid than it did a few years ago for the simple reason that one after the other dictatorship in Latin America has been replaced by an elected government. The negative experience with authoritarian rulers may well be one of the strongest cards held by their democratic successors. But unless they also meet the pragmatic test, by becoming legitimated through social and economic progress, the new democracies in Latin America and elsewhere in the Third World will also be in trouble shortly. They may yet turn out to have been short interludes between authoritarian regimes that excel at achieving order through repression.

In much of Latin America there has been a turn toward a greater emphasis on market economics, replacing the traditional commitment to strategies that favored statist interventions. In one article, five of the leaders in the continent's economic modernization are compared with two of the laggards. Of particular interest to Americans is the attempt by President Carlos Salinas of Mexico to move his country toward a more competitive form of market enterprise. At the same time, he has been hesitant to move from economic to political reform. His reluctance is understandable, since such a move could reduce the hegemony of his own long-ruling party, the PRI, and give new outlets for protest in a time of enormous socioeconomic dislocations.

It is not possible within the confines of this anthology to explore thoroughly all areas of the Third World. However, many articles will introduce you to some examples of the problems that face many of these countries. *The Economist* reports on the spread of popular government and market economics in many African states, but it also points out that there continues to be a dire need for good government, that is, for competence and expertise in the public sector.

South Africa faces the monumental task of introducing democracy in a multiracial society where the ruling white minority has never shared political or economic power with black Africans or Asian immigrants. President F. W. de Klerk will be challenged from all sides as he attempts to implement reforms that go too far and too fast for a privileged minority, and not nearly far or quickly enough for many more who demand political equality and social improvement. Yet there has been amazing progress in the last couple of years. In March 1992 almost 70 percent of the white voters endorsed de Klerk's plans to move on to some form of power sharing with the other races. A conservative attempt to block such plans received surprisingly little support from the white voters, who presumably could be said to have had something to lose by supporting reform.

The last two subsections deal with the world's most populous countries, China and India. China is the homeland of over a billion people, or more than one-fifth of the world's population. Here the reform Communists, who took power after Mao Zedong's death in 1976, began much earlier than their Soviet counterparts to steer the country toward a relatively decontrolled market economy. They also introduced some political relaxation, by putting an end to the recurrent ideological campaigns to mobilize the masses. In their place came a domestic tranquility such as China had not known for over half a century. But the regime encountered a basic dilemma: it wished to maintain tight controls over politics and society while reforming the economy. When a new openness developed in Chinese society, comparable in some ways to the pluralism encouraged more actively by Gorbachev's glasnost policy, it ran into determined opposition among hard-line Communist leaders. The aging reform leader, Deng Xiaoping, presided over a bloody crackdown on student demonstrations in Beijing's Tiananmen Square in May 1989.

In the article "Preparing for the Succession" on China, the author discusses the important question of who will replace the aging leadership headed by Xiaoping. One group to watch is made up of the university trained, middle-aged governmental leaders. They have important operational functions but rank below the present ultimate powerholders. The former's life experience is very different from that of the octogenarian rulers, who were steeled in the long civil war that preceded the establishment of Communist power in 1949. In the next article, Daniel Southerland tries to answer the question of why the repressive Chinese rulers were able to introduce economic reforms that appear to work, while Gorbachev's formula of perestroika plus glasnost resulted in economic chaos and political disintegration for the Soviet state. A still unanswered question is whether a well-developed industrial society can long coexist with a repressive political system. China is still in an early stage of modernization, but the issue is likely to present itself more acutely in the future.

The final subsection introduces another important region, namely the subcontinent of India. With its almost 800 million people, India is more populous than Latin America and Africa combined. It is deeply divided by ethnic, religious, and regional differences, and its struggling economy has been hampered by a long tradition of what entrepreneurs perceive as bureaucratic meddling. The potential for social and economic crisis looms over the country, and last year the national elections were marred by the assassination of Rajiv Gandhi, the former prime minister and leader of the Congress party. Prime Minister P. V. Narasimha Rao, the political veteran who took charge of a tenuous minority government after the election, has followed in the steps of other reform governments in the Third World by adopting more market-oriented policies. The attempt to bring India, with its long tradition of heavy state regulation and protectionism, into the world economy bears careful watching. More than 40 decades after independence, India continues to disprove the standard forecast of political and economic disaster.

Looking Ahead: Challenge Questions

Why is the term Third World of little analytical value? What have these countries in common, and how are they diverse? What is meant by the term Fourth World?

How do explanations of Third World poverty and slow development differ in assigning responsibility for these conditions to external (foreign) and internal (domestic) factors? Why can theories of development be important factors in shaping strategies of modernization?

What is the dependency theory, and why has it had so much appeal, especially in Latin America? How do you explain the current wave of market-oriented reforms?

Why do economic development and representative government run into such difficulties in most of Latin America and much of Africa? How do you explain the strong white vote in favor of President de Klerk's reform plans? What are some of the major political, economic, and social problems that South Africa still has to face in overcoming the legacy of apartheid?

Why has the succession question become so acute in contemporary China? How do you explain China's relative success in turning toward market reforms for the economy, as compared to the Soviet Union? What is the likelihood that pluralist tendencies will again seek to find political expression in China?

How has India managed to maintain itself as a parliamentary democracy, given all the economic, social, and cultural conflicts that divide this multiethnic society?

Third World Embracing Reforms To Encourage Economic Growth

Sylvia Nasar

A powerful new economic pragmatism is sweeping third world capitals from Brasilia to Bangkok, and countries that were once proud economic nationalists are now trying to forge closer ties with the rest of the world.

The broad changes are the subject of the World Bank's annual World Economic Development Report, which was made public this morning. And in interviews last week, government officials and economists from third world nations said they were committed to allowing market forces to flourish free of government restraints, abandoning fiscal and monetary policies that were politically motivated but economically unsound and opening borders to foreign goods and investment.

'Time for Fresh Thinking'

"Everybody is convinced it is time for fresh thinking," India's Finance Minister Manmohan Singh said in an interview last week.

And Sebastian Edwards, a Chilean economist at the University of California at Los Angeles, said, "For Chile, there is no turning back."

Argentina, for example, has caught tax-reform fever. Mexico is selling its Government-owned businesses. Peru is cutting its budget deficit. Turkey has thrown off its decades-old protectionist blanket. Thailand kept its budget balanced and held inflation to a modest 3 percent. Ghana and a handful of other African nations no longer tax their farmers out of producing.

"The change in thinking is really remarkably pervasive," said Stanley Fischer, former chief economist at the World Bank and now a professor at the Massachusetts Institute of Technology. "Ten years ago, for example, Mexicans insisted that their main job was to protect themselves from the imperialist U.S."

If the nascent economic changes take root and spread, the four billion people who live in the developing world could enjoy a better standard of living.

The changes could also provide a wealth of opportunities to businesses and investors in the United States and other rich countries.

What started the revolution? For one thing, the stunning growth of South Korea, Taiwan, Singapore and other Asian economies. For another, the collapse of socialism in Eastern Europe.

The belief that this revolution is an enduring one is strongest among early reformers who have already reaped the rewards of faster growth. Hasan L. Ersel, deputy governor of Turkey's central bank, said, "If Turkey doesn't experience an enormous external shock, it is highly unlikely that these policies will be reversed."

Certainly, the road to economic reform is lined with ruts. Steps toward reforms in Argentina and Brazil have been derailed by a repeated failure to control inflation. Despite progress on trade and liberalizing financial markets, Turkey has not brought its budget under control. Ghana's far-reaching reforms have not yet persuaded many investors to come aboard. And Eastern European political leaders have found that their commitment to market-driven economies—with the layoffs and higher prices these bring in the short run—have brought strikes, protests and challenges to incumbent officials.

But it now seems clear that in many development nations there is a new sense of realism, much of it inspired by the hardships of the last decade.

'Nothing Inevitable About Stagnation'

"The enormous differences in performance among developing countries in the 80's suggests that there is nothing inevitable about stagnation" said Lawrence H. Summers, chief economist at the World Bank. While many economies in Africa and Latin America shrank during the decade, Botswana, Chile, Indonesia and Thailand, among others, expanded.

"The key," Professor Fischer of M.I.T. said, "is moving away from saying that world is unfair to saying however unfair it is, we want to make the best use of it."

Comparing the World's Economies

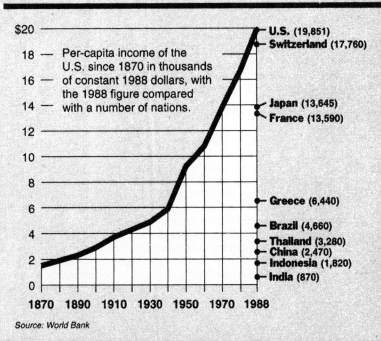

Per-capita income of the U.S. since 1870 in thousands of constant 1988 dollars, with the 1988 figure compared with a number of nations.

- U.S. (19,851)
- Switzerland (17,760)
- Japan (13,645)
- France (13,590)
- Greece (6,440)
- Brazil (4,660)
- Thailand (3,280)
- China (2,470)
- Indonesia (1,820)
- India (870)

Source: World Bank

The New York Times

From *The New York Times*, July 8, 1991, pp. A1, C3. Copyright © 1991 by The New York Times Company. Reprinted by permission.

The international economy is widely expected to hold modest expansions among the wealthier countries, continued high interest rates, weak commodity prices and persistent debt problems.

So the poorer nations, already starved for investment, are likely to have to compete for scarce capital.

The good news, the World Bank says, is that reform is sufficiently widespread that the economies of the developing countries should grow, on average, 5 percent a year, faster than in the 1980's. That is also faster than the 3 percent rate the bank expects for rich countries.

Countries that have adopted economic reforms, the bank says, include Chile, Ghana, India, Indonesia, South Korea, Mexico, Morocco and Turkey. Even China, which doubled its growth rate in the 1980's by allowing some farmland to be privately owned, is on the list. "You can see reasons for optimism in what developing countries are doing in almost every part of the world," Mr. Summers said.

Countries Will Lag Without Reforms

Those reformers that succeed could narrow the gap between their standards of living and those of rich countries at a rapid pace. But countries that continue to mismanage their economies—tolerating inefficiency for political ends, squandering precious resources on wars, investing too little in education—may be doomed to fall further behind. "It no longer makes sense to think of the third world as one group," Mr. Summers said.

The old strategy for transforming a poor country into a rich one, advocated from the 1930's through the 1960's, called for rapid government-led industrialization at the expense of agriculture, protecting infant industries from foreign competition and replacing imports with domestic production for the local market.

At the nub of this philosophy was the notion that government should guide economic development. Thus came a tight web of licensing requirements, restrictions on who could enter or leave industries, constraints on bankruptcy filing and layoffs, and price controls.

"These views have not stood test of time," the World Bank says bluntly. The institution is bankrolled by rich nations that dispense aid, loans and advice to poor countries.

And seemingly small steps toward deregulation have often produced great spurts of economic activity. Ghana, for instance, used to levy confiscatory taxes of 50 percent or more on cocoa, and some farmers left crops to rot in the fields or smuggled them out. When it sharply lowered the taxes, cocoa production and exports soared. When South Korea lifted interest rates on bank deposits in the 1970's, the size of its banking system quadrupled in less than four years. Morgan Stanley & Company estimates that the United States exports to the third world have lately grown at three times the rate of sales to other rich countries. And third world stock markets from Mexico City to Taipei have been booming.

Many developing countries also tried to build up local industries by shielding them from competition. The result was often that inefficient companies turned out shoddy goods that cost too much. Many Argentines drive cars that Detroit might have been proud of in, say, 1960, and Indians buy homemade steel that costs more than the imported kind. In disastrous cases—Tanzanian shoe companies, Polish shipyards, Chinese car companies—the products have been worth less than the cost of the raw materials used to make them.

An Avalanche of Borrowing

Many third world countries also saw foreign ownership as a greater threat to sovereignty than borrowing. After an avalanche of borrowing, many countries had more debt than they could carry, and they lost control of their economies.

Mexico, Brazil, South Korea, Poland and Ghana, among others, borrowed half a trillion dollars—most of it from commercial banks—and put the money into government sponsored projects. But many borrowers found they could not pay their debts.

Some countries tried to renegotiate the terms of their loans, stretching them out over longer periods to reduce payments, or seeking lower interest rates. If the banks balked, the borrowers threatened to halt debt payments. Brazil and Argentina eventually negotiated more favorable terms on their huge foreign debt. Peru, on the other hand, simply announced that it would no longer pay its debts, and lost its ability to borrow abroad, with calamitous consequences for its economy.

In the last three years, the United States offered what came to be known as the Brady plan, for Treasury Secretary Nicholas F. Brady, which encouraged banks to forgive some of the debt in return for promises of economic reforms that improve the climate for private investment. Other industrial nations supported the Brady plan, which has had at least one notable success—Mexico.

Mexico obtained relief of roughly a fifth of its $60 billion outstanding private debt. That, along with Mexico's economic reforms, gave a big boost to investor confidence.

Argentina, on the other hand, is still trying to qualify for debt reduction. Its President twice signed an agreement with the International Monetary Fund, only to have Parliament reject it. The result has been that Argentina has been unable to get new loans.

Foreign Investment Needed for Growth

Many of these countries that preferred to borrow now see foreign direct investment as a catalyst to growth. Chile, for example, laid out the welcome mat to overseas investors, many from the Pacific Rim.

Private investment has doubled since its low in the mid-1980's, according to Guy Pfeffermann, an economist at the International Finance Corporation, with most of the increase in East Asia, Latin America and, to a lesser extent, Africa. It is rising fastest in countries like Morocco, Chile, Mexico, Botswana and Thailand, where the business climate is improving.

Many countries have also learned the dangers of a boom-bust economy. The old populist prescription was to take windfall gains—from a surge in commodities prices, say, or oil—and throw a party. After oil prices surged in 1973, Nigeria tripled its public payroll to 1.5 million. After the 1979 jump in oil prices, Mexico's budget deficit soared to 17 percent of G.N.P.

But today Mexico has slashed its budget deficit to 4 percent of gross national product, which compares favorably with the United States. And it has cut tax rates and ended the practice of taxing dividends twice, which discourages investment. At the same time, the Mexican Government has beefed up tax collection by closing loopholes and prosecuting corporate tax dodgers in record numbers.

It has taken to heart a notion that has won converts in Eastern Europe: when it comes to government, smaller is better. Since 1982, Mexico has sold 875 of 1,155 Government-owned companies, including giants like TelMex, the national phone company; Mexicana, the airline, and Cannanea Copper. Banamex, Mexico's largest bank, will soon go on the block.

The payoff has been three years of 3 to 4 percent growth and an inflation rate that is less than 20 percent—low by Latin standards. Even more promising, an estimated $10 billion that had been taken overseas has returned, as investors' confidence in the stability of Mexico's economy has grown.

A New Discipline in Economics Brings Change to Latin America

Balanced Budgets and Free Markets Take Hold

Nathaniel C. Nash

Special to The New York Times

SANTIAGO, Chile—Suddenly, a look at the economic map of Latin America shows a startling change. After a decade of no growth, crippling inflation, rising foreign debt, protectionism and bloated state payrolls, governments—at least for now—have found a new economic religion.

Balanced budgets are in, as is privatization, the buzzword for selling off government enterprises. Negotiations to reduce foreign debt have been successful in some countries, especially Mexico, and are continuing in others. Stabilization and discipline have become winning political slogans. The free market, open economies and deregulation are now part of the vocabulary of taxi drivers and laborers.

In Latin American cities there are signs of change everywhere.

In Concepción, two hundred miles south of here, three new paper plants costing more than $1.3 billion are opening. In Buenos Aires, the Park Plaza Hotel is overrun with investment bankers from New York, London, Bonn and Paris looking for deals. In Lima, adventurous business executives talk with the Peruvian Government about its plans to sell off state-run enterprises.

'Committed to Free Enterprise'

"We have a country committed to free enterprise, where there are established rules, a central bank you can deal with and zero bribery," said Vincent A. Russo, general manager of Santa Fe Forestal y Industria, a $460 million pulp plant in Nacimiento, Chile, that is owned by Shell Oil, Scott Paper and Citicorp. "There's not a lot more you can ask for."

Driving this new-found optimism and economic activity are profound policy changes that run from the Rio Grande to Tierra del Fuego. The new consensus says that inflation is bad, particularly for the poor, that governments do not know how to run businesses, that printing money is political suicide and that tax evasion, a time-honored sport here, should be punished severely.

Also, in the face of democracy's growing popularity, Marxism has all but disappeared. All of Latin America, except for Cuba and Haiti, have democratically elected governments. In early 1979, Argentina, Bolivia, Brazil, Chile, Ecuador, Paraguay, Peru and Uruguay were all run by military dictatorships. Military governments—except in Chile—have been unable to run stable economies. Huge amounts of unpaid debt borrowed over the last decade or so underscore the insolvency of those governments and their inability to meet social needs. Now, the only alternative seems to be to generate jobs through internal growth.

There has been a psychological lift for several countries, including Mexico and Venezuela, from the Bush Administration's debt reduction plan. Especially in Mexico, the negotiation of a successful debt plan lowered the level and cost of billions of dollars in foreign commercial bank loans and eased the economic burden on a new Mexican administration. With the added imprimatur of aid from the International Monetary Fund and World Bank, a successful debt reduction agreement has made Mexico and some other countries more attractive to foreign investors.

Even though both Argentina and Brazil have yet to frame a debt reduction agreement, the mere prospect of one has been a spur to foreign investor interest.

Country by Country

In Argentina, President Carlos Saúl Menem has announced a vast deregulation of his country's economy, reversing decades of protection for industries. In Chile, a prospering free-market economy generated by Gen. August Pinochet, who stepped down from office 18 months ago, has been maintained by a coalition of his successors. In Bolivia, the poorest country on the continent, a general and his leftist opponent have teamed up to impose tight monetary discipline and promote growth. And even in peru, long plagued by poverty, President Alberto Fujimori has instituted a severe package of economic restrictions that are unpopular but accepted as necessary.

Growth rates of major economies in Latin America, in percent.			
	'89	'90	'91*
Venezuela	−8.3	4.4	10.0
Mexico	3.1	3.9	5.3
Chile	10.0	2.1	4.1
Paraguay	5.8	3.1	3.5
Colombia	3.2	3.8	3.0
Argentina	−4.4	−0.5	3.0
Bolivia	2.8	2.6	n.a.
Uruguay	1.5	0.9	1.6
Ecuador	0.2	1.5	1.5
Brazil	3.3	−4.6	−0.7
Peru	−11.2	−3.9	−4.8

Figures are for gross domestic product. *Estimates based on first six months. n.a.–Not available.

Sources: Inter-American Development Bank; United Nations Economic Commission on Latin America

From *The New York Times*, November 13, 1991, pp. A1, C18. Copyright © 1991 by The New York Times Company. Reprinted by permission.

Changing Economies in Latin America

THE LEADERS

Argentina

Inflation	'89	'90	'91*
	3,079.2	2,314.0	26.0

Efforts to stabilize the currency, toughen tax collection and stop printing money to cover the deficit have cut inflation and given Argentina a reputation as the next emerging economy. President Carlos Saúl Menem, using executive power, has decreed the deregulation of almost all industry. He is seeking to renegotiate $60 billion debt.

Chile

Inflation	'89	'90	'91*
	17.0	26.1	18.0

The new Government retained most open-market policies left by Gen. Augusto Pinochet, but has raised some taxes for social programs. After a bout with inflation in 1990, the central bank has restricted money growth. Foreign investment is pouring in.

Colombia

Inflation	'89	'90	'91*
	25.8	29.1	30.6

Years of sound money and fiscal policies have made this country one of the continent's most stable. Broad reductions in tariff barriers have forced protected industries to compete or close. Austerity has limited domestic growth and consumer demand. Also, the continued flow of drug dollars has stymied real industrial development and the fight against drug trafficking has drained resources.

Mexico

Inflation	'89	'90	'91*
	20.0	26.7	20.0

The three-year-old Government of Carlos Salinas de Gortari has sold off 150 state-owned companies in an aggressive privatization program, stabilizing the economy and resulting in almost $7 billion in foreign capital this year.

Venezuela

Inflation	'89	'90	'91*
	84.2	40.8	32.9

A cut in taxes and tariffs by President Carlos Andrés Pérez returned economy to growth last year after a drop of 8 percent in 1989. The Gulf crisis and the rise in oil prices also helped, but added to Venezuela's perennial problem of excessive inflation.

THE LAGGARDS

Brazil

Inflation	'89	'90	'91*
	1,287.0	2,968.0	366.5

The Latin American giant is struggling to end the days of excessive state employment and the habit of paying for government deficits by printing money. A freeze on bank accounts and wage and price control failed to halt inflation. A privatization program is struggling. Loss of confidence in President Fernando Collor de Mello could cause severe inflation.

Peru

Inflation	'89	'90	'91*
	3,398.9	7,481.7	143.6

Despite tight monetary controls, a refusal to raise Government salaries, layoffs of thousands of workers and broad deregulation, Peru is still struggling with recession, which is worsened by terrorism and drug trafficking. President Alberto Fujimori is trying to gain investor confidence by settling disputes with three U.S. companies.

*Figures for 1991 inflation are estimates based on the first six months of the year except for Argentina; its figure is for the most recent six months.

Sources: Inter-American Development Bank; United Nations Economic Commission on Latin America

In the last two months three respected organizations—the International Monetary Fund, the International Bank for Development and the United Nations—have all issued cautious reports predicting a new era of vigorous, through sporadic, economic growth.

But none of these new policies have been able to wipe out poverty. In 1980, 40 percent of the Latin American population was considered living in poverty. By last year, that had risen to 44 percent. In Peru, where the minimum wage is $50 a month, 90 percent of the people are considered to be either unemployed or underemployed. In Chile, five million people, or a third of its population, is considered to live in poverty.

What astounds economists and analysts is that the tough economic medicine continues to be popularly supported even though it has resulted in large government layoffs a precipitous drop in the buying power of the average

Balanced budgets and open markets are in; inflation is out.

citizen and less spending on public needs like housing, water and electricity. In both Mexico and Argentina the incumbent political parties won large midterm elections because of economic stability.

Brazil Plans Frustrated

Brazil is the only country still struggling to produce a plan to stop perennial inflation. President Fernando Collor de Mello has been frustrated by an opposition Congress and has failed to persuade the public that with the dole and a relaxed life on the beach, Brazil will remain in the past.

In other Latin nations, results are more impressive. In Chile, inflation is under 20 percent and foreign investment this year, at $3 billion, is triple what it was in 1990. Mexico will record 20 percent inflation for the third year in a row, and its economy will grow close to 5 percent. Venezuela, an oil importer that benefited from last year's oil run-up, has scored 10 percent growth so far this year, with higher levels of inflation, around 35 percent, but far less than the 90 percent inflation in 1989. Argentina, after 1,000 percent inflation in 1990 and 6,000 percent in 1989, imposed a stringent economic policy earlier this year, and has had an annual inflation rate of less than 20 percent in the last three months. Colombia is also generating about 20 percent inflation and 2.2 percent growth.

The new governments defy old Latin stereotypes. Parties that promoted highly nationalistic, isolationist policies in the past, like President Menem's Peronist Party in Argentina, are now seeking friendship with the United States for economic and political reasons.

"We can't wait for anybody to help other than ourselves," said Oscar Imbellone, president of CPC International in Buenos Aires. "We need to use our own management know-how, capitalist structure, innovation and research and development. We have to do the things all civilized countries do."

A Risky Game

Still, politicians know they are playing a risky game—just how long will people endure the pain of unemployment for the sake of future prosperity? That worry has generated efforts to add some social spending to the economic plans, without risking their effectiveness. Chile has doubled business taxes to 10 percent, and used the new funds on education, medical care and housing.

"The thinking here is that there will be stability as long as the poor see the Government is making an effort," said Oscar Altimir, director of the Economic Development division in the United Nations Economic Commission for Latin America, based in Santiago.

But while the rich continue to get richer, the gap between them and the middle and lower classes widens.

In Bogotá, Colombia, Pilar Barco, a language professor, and her husband, Francisco Garcia, a fine arts professor and commercial artist, together make about $500 a month, which is four times the minimum wage, "and still we never buy clothes and we live a minimum existence," she said.

One response in the attempt to spur economies is to get government out of business and privatize everything from state oil companies to railroads to park maintenance, with the hope of creating an industrial sector that generates jobs. This both cuts government employment and stops the flow of red ink most of the state-owned companies are producing.

Chile was long the leader of the privatization movement under General Pinochet. More recently, Mexico has led the way with the privatization of its telephone company, which raised $2.3 billion in foreign capital from a stock sale.

Some countries seem in a race to privatize before the public get tired of seeing its patrimony on the auction block. President Menem of Argentina has ordered his Economy Minister to finish all such sales in 1992.

A second self-help response is the formation of alliances aimed at creating more competitive economies. Brazil, Argentina, Uruguay and Paraguay are trying to create a free-trade zone by 1994 called Mercosur. Mexico and Chile have signed a free-trade agreement. Colombia and Venezuela are trying to integrate their economies.

"When they sign that, we are going to be the next ones knocking at the door," said Guido Di Tella, Argentina's Foreign Minister.

In all this, the trouble spot is still Brazil, a vast country of 125 million people, the largest debtor in Latin America and so large that troubles there will always threaten to spill into other countries."

While President Collor de Mello was easily elected in 1990, and seemed poised to revamp the economy, he has failed so far. A bank account freeze followed by wage and price controls eventually collapsed. Recent attempts to privatize the state's crown jewel, a big steel plant, were nearly undone by protesting union workers.

Since then, a loss of confidence in the President has pushed the country close to hyperinflation.

MEXICO: PROGRESS AND PROMISE
National Agenda

Mexico is radically shifting its economy and ideology. The nationalist, state-run model is out. The free market is in. But there are costs.

Marjorie Miller and Juanita Darling

Times Staff Writers

Mexico City—A decade ago, when the Perisur shopping center opened its glitzy doors in southern Mexico City, consumers marveled at the state-of-the-art mall with multilevel parking, three department stores and dozens of pricey specialty shops. Here was the best that Mexico had to offer in clothing, furniture and appliances.

That was the problem.

Under the bright lights and modern displays were made-in-Mexico clothes, many copied from international designs, second-rate Mexican toasters and televisions and Mabe-brand kitchen appliances—maybe they worked and maybe they didn't, consumers quipped. Mexico's best was mediocre.

Today the upscale, stucco-and-glass Polanco Pavilion that opened across town in December offers an altogether different fare: Benetton for clothes, Nintendo for games and McDonald's for lunch.

An import grocer in the pavilion sells everything from American breakfast cereals to microwave dinners. Electronics stores are stocked floor-to-ceiling with Japanese stereos, Korean televisions and U.S. kitchen appliances. They even sell Mabe refrigerators, which now compare favorably with their foreign competitors.

Polanco Pavilion is a monument to the radical transformation of Mexico's economy and official ideology. The government has abandoned the nationalist model that came with the 1910 Mexican Revolution—a protected, state-run economy where imports and foreign investment were blocked—to embrace a competitive, free-market system.

Casting aside its historic fear of foreign domination, Mexico is trying to forge a free-trade agreement with the United States and Canada. The rest of Latin America is watching closely, hoping Mexico will pave the way to open borders throughout the Western Hemisphere.

These momentous shifts, begun in 1985 by President Miguel de la Madrid, have gained force under his Harvard-trained successor. Taking office three years ago, President Carlos Salinas de Gortari promised to modernize not just Mexico's ailing economy but also its stifling system of one-party rule.

Midway through Salinas' term, Mexico is awash in the cross-currents of change—with hopeful progress, painful dislocation and unfulfilled promise. Aspiring to greatness, it is weighed down by a volatile past.

Half of Mexico's 82 million people live in poverty. The country lost half its territory in a war with [the] United States and millions of lives in the revolution. Presidents come in promising and go out plundering. An oil boom went bust in the early 1980s, leaving an unpayable foreign debt and an unhappy irony—a nation that exports some of its hardest workers as well as petroleum.

Today, for the first time in a decade, Mexicans have a clear sense of where their president is leading them. But his mission is fraught with controversy and uncertainty.

Salinas has shrunk the state dramatically, shedding its huge deficit and restoring economic growth after a "lost decade" of stagnation. But the massive sale of state-owned factories, withdrawal of subsidies for small farmers and depressed salaries have left millions of Mexicans behind, widening the gap between rich and poor.

The president is counting on the free-trade agreement to attract investment and sustain growth. But his critics argue that the proposed treaty could backfire—making Mexico too dependent on the United States without creating enough jobs, spurring more migration over the border and drawing more industries that pollute the environment.

While economic change has come quickly, political reform has lagged. The Institutional Revolutionary Party's 62-year dominance of Mexico is unshaken. Instead of encouraging debate on his economic program, Salinas has mustered his near-monarchical powers to push it through. Heavy-handed management of the press has fed expectations of prosperity. But if those hopes are dashed, he risks a political backlash.

From *Los Angeles Times*, October 22, 1991, pp. 1, 2. Copyright © 1991 by Los Angeles Times.

"The political system is proving inadequate to accommodate such a thorough economic liberalization," said economist Rogelio Ramirez de la O. "Either there is steady progress on all fronts, or a society is disrupted as we saw in the Soviet Union."

Fear that the political system would topple prompted the government to change its economic model in the first place. Since its founding in 1929, the PRI had been a social welfare machine that distributed the benefits of continuous growth to its constituencies—mainly peasants, workers and bureaucrats—in exchange for political support.

When international oil prices fell and Mexico's debt-ridden economy collapsed in 1982, the resources of this patronage system dried up. Confronted by the demands of a youthful population for 800,000 new jobs a year, Mexican leaders realized there was an urgent need to grow.

De la Madrid tried to revive the economy with government spending but failed. In 1985, he decided to join the General Agreement on Tariffs and Trade, initiating the switch to a free-market model. He picked Salinas, his budget and planning secretary, to succeed him as president.

Identified as the architect of De la Madrid's reforms, Salinas was elected with the lowest vote percentage ever for a PRI presidential candidate amid widespread charges that the election was stolen. Union workers and government bureaucrats who were squeezed by the economic crisis had abandoned the ruling party.

Salinas started his term by negotiating a reduction of Mexico's $104-billion foreign debt and a $1.8-billion reduction in annual debt service payments. The accord began to restore international confidence in Mexico and bring down the federal deficit.

At home, the president attacked opponents of economic reform: He jailed the corrupt leader of the vast oil workers union, Joaquin Hernandez Galicia, then streamlined the state-run oil monopoly, eliminating jobs and contracts for union-owned companies.

But still foreign investors were reluctant. They wanted guarantees that the reforms would continue. And with the emergence of capitalism in Eastern Europe, Mexico faced unexpected competition for resources. Salinas reversed his campaign position, announcing that he would negotiate a free-trade pact. Then he began to privatize the banks.

Today the government owns only about a quarter of the 1,228 enterprises it did a decade ago, having sold mines, mills, airlines and the telephone company. Salinas has relaxed franchise laws, stopped requiring import permits and cut tariffs once as high as 200% to an average of 9%.

The payoffs have been remarkable. Mexico's 5% annual growth rate has a solid economic foundation: The public deficit, once 16% of gross national product, has been virtually eliminated; inflation is down from 159% a year to an estimated 19%, and foreign reserves are a record $16.3 billion. More than $10 billion in new foreign investment has flowed into the country, along with the plethora of imported goods.

"I can assure you that the Mexican economy is entering a virtuous circle of growth with price stability," Secretary of Finance Pedro Aspe told bankers in Acapulco this month. "If we persevere in the adjustment and adoption of structural change measures, that virtuous circle should become permanent."

In the course of restructuring, Salinas has redefined official language. The word *revolutionary*, which used to mean putting the interests of workers and peasants first, now means favoring free enterprise. *Sovereignty* once encompassed the ideal of strong national industrial base; now it means competing successfully in international trade. In essence, the government has shifted alliances from workers and peasants to business and the United States.

Nonetheless, Salinas has won sweeping popular support. In a Times poll finished this month, 83% of Mexicans surveyed gave him a positive job rating and 77% said they approved of his handling of the economy—even though most people said the economy is weak and identified economic issues as their primary concern. Only 36% said they are better off today than when Salinas took office—a reflection of the fact that Mexicans' purchasing power has been cut by about one quarter.

Analysts offer a variety of explanations for these seemingly contradictory opinions—from media manipulation to the popularity of Solidarity, the president's multibillion-dollar social welfare program. Financed from the sale of state-owned companies, Solidarity has mitigated the economic squeeze by delivering public services to poor communities. Half the people who told The Times that they support Salinas cited Solidarity as one of the reasons.

Cuauhtemoc Cardenas, champion of Mexico's old nationalism and Salinas' leading rival in the 1988 election, lost ground; his 50% approval rating in a Times survey two years ago fell to 39%.

Salinas' popularity has risen in spite of his reluctance to deliver political reform. The president has not separated the PRI from the state or the electoral process from the government. The PRI-dominated Congress limits itself to rubber-stamping presidential proposals, rather than initiating its own.

Even some who agree with his economic reforms worry about the way Salinas is imposing them.

"The Mexican presidency has always resembled the enlightened despotism of late 18th-Century Europe," said Enrique Krauze, one of Mexico's foremost historians. "The 18th-Century despots made many changes in the right direction without the participation of the people. That is exactly the case [in Mexico] today."

By way of warning, Krauze compares the Salinas administration to that of President Porfirio Diaz, who ruled for 34 years before he was toppled by the 1910 Mexican Revolution. Diaz made a success of the Mexican economy, beefing up exports and integrating Mexico into international markets. He attracted foreign investment. But his government was a dictatorship.

"In 1991, nobody can sell a hegemonic, one-party system in the world. You have to put makeup on it and say we are gearing towards democracy. But Mexico is not Mars and one-party systems do not work. The only way to modernize is to modernize in both the economy and politics," Krauze said.

In an interview last month with The Times, Salinas defended his record on political reform, citing a new electoral code and a $300-million voter registry. "I would say that we have engaged in both economic and political reform simultaneously," he said.

But his hopes that the new law and registry would restore credibility to the election process were dampened in the Aug. 18 midterm vote. The new Federal Electoral Institute failed to count the congressional votes quickly, leading to public suspicions of tampering.

The PRI swept the congressional elections and claimed victory in all six governorships at stake. But mass opposition protests against fraud forced the government to give up the two most-contested state-houses, in Guanajuato and San Luis Potosi.

Rather than recognize irregularities in either state, Salinas simply replaced the declared winners with interim governors. His solution demonstrated what some critics and business people describe as their main concern about the system—its arbitrary and often illegal behavior.

Mexicans routinely call the courts "lousy" and "corrupt." International human rights groups accuse the police of torturing prisoners. Traffic police decide whether to apply the law or take a bribe. Bureaucrats want their cut too.

Investors want legal guarantees.

"A lot of our clients are concerned that what the law says is not always what it means," said Cheryl Schechter, an American lawyer whose Mexican firm represents foreign companies. "That gives rise to a lot of insecurity."

Their opinion matters greatly. Under the neo-liberal model, sustained growth depends more on foreign investment and less on government spending.

Such dependence is one of many criticisms of the reforms: Free trade makes the country more vulnerable to fluctuations in the U.S. economy, as Mexican firms become export-oriented and multinationals produce a greater share of exports.

Economists caution that the government is losing control over the economy to the private sector and foreign capital. As the government sells off key industries, it has fewer tools to fix problems such as lingering inflation.

That point was driven home last month in the government's response to a credit crunch. Officials blamed bankers for overlending in August and announced that they would do nothing to alleviate the problem. But a week later, they caved in to pressure from bankers and dropped the reserve requirement that had forced banks to invest $1 in government securities for every $3 in deposits.

Optimism about the economic program is evident in companies that believe they can compete in a world market. The Visa Brewery, which produces Tecate, Carta Blanca, Superior and Bohemia, already exports to the United States and is planning its regional strategy in anticipation of a free-trade agreement.

"We used to say we sold 52% of the beer in Mexico," said Edgardo Reyes, special projects director at Visa. "Now we say we sell 7% of the beer in North America."

At Polanco Pavilion, businessman Jorge Troop said he had owned two J. Troop clothing stores when Salinas took office. Now he has four stores under his name and five franchises of the Italian designer Benetton.

"I am investing and taking risks because of my confidence in the current policies," said Troop, 47. "I believe in what is happening."

While joining in the import boom, Troop also stocks Mexican-made clothing because he believes that Mexican manufacturers are beginning to match the quality of foreign producers now that they are allowed to import materials such as linings, buttons and shoulder pads.

"They aren't Armani suits, but they are excellent quality. The best Mexican suit costs about $400 and competes with $600 to $700 suits from other countries that are not significantly better," he said.

The Mexican government insists that producers are becoming more efficient and competitive. The manufactured goods sector is growing at a rate of 10% per year. But critics note that the growth is primarily in automobiles, pharmaceuticals and petrochemicals, sectors that are dominated by multinational firms. In other words, Mexican exports by foreign companies.

Not all businessmen are confident that Mexican firms will make it in the world market. Salvador Garcia, of the Mexican Institute of Small and Medium Enterprise, said he believes most of his colleagues are unprepared for open borders.

Garcia estimates that there are 325,000 small and medium businesses in the formal economy and another 200,000 mom-and-pop operations in the so-called informal or underground economy. Most don't produce enough volume to export and have no knowledge of export markets, he said. He expects half of them to fold.

"I think a free-trade agreement can be good for the country, but not immediately," he said. "Mexican business is not ready to compete with American companies. They have never worried about investing in technology. They don't look ahead. . . . They don't speak English. Their businesses are undercapitalized.

"They copy models from abroad. For example, a Mexican clothier buys an Italian fashion magazine and copies a design with a few changes. Instead of having a unique product that's exportable, he has a poor copy that nobody will buy," he said.

Small business is not the only group unprepared for free trade.

Under Mexico's old system, pro-government unions commanded wages that kept up with inflation and offered job security. But Salinas has kept wages low to control inflation and will continue to do so to attract foreign companies. Low wages and the sale and closure of state-run companies have forced hundreds of thousands of people into the informal or underground economy. Once a major pillar of the PRI, organized labor's power has been broken.

Union member Salvador Perez, 55, was laid off from the government's bankrupt Zacatepec sugar mill in August after 38 years of working at the plant. But under bankruptcy law, the severance pay called for in his contract was reduced.

"Salinas is to blame," Perez said. "His idea is to put everything in private hands. Perhaps this is correct, but our rights ought to be protected. If I enslaved myself to this plant, it was to earn a good retirement and pension."

Salinas' changes have upset the ruling party's other traditional ally—farmers. He has eliminated price supports for most crops, reduced government lending and cut subsidies for seeds and fertilizers.

Even the *ejido*, a kind of communal farm that once enjoyed special status as a symbol of the revolution, is being forced to change. Subsidies have been cut and credit withheld from unproductive farms. When *ejido* members protest that they need capital, the administration suggests that they join the 70 farms that have formed partnerships with private industry.

"Salinas' policy is to force the *ejido* farmers into a desperate situation, to oblige us to accept any investment scheme," complained Jesus Leyva, head of the National Agricultural Credit Union, one of Mexico's largest independent farmers' groups with 100,000 members. "On some *ejidos*, the profits won't be much more than minimum wage. The farmers will become salaried workers of their partners."

Agriculture Secretary Carlos Hank Gonzalez said the government can no longer afford to prop up the countryside or maintain protective trade barriers in agriculture. His goal is to make the country self-sufficient in basic foods, and to that end he is channeling credit and technical assistance to the production of corn, beans, wheat, rice and milk—much of which is now imported.

Like Salvador Garcia in the business world, Leyva believes the shift in agricultural policy is too abrupt. He argues for continued subsidies, saying they failed in the past because corrupt officials stole much of the money. "Mexican farmers need 20 years to catch up with farmers in the United States and Canada," he said.

While they worry that changes are coming too quickly, some business people fear the system is not adapting swiftly enough. They bemoan the lack of infrastructure—roads, railroads and working telephones—and insidious red tape.

The government hails its reduction of bureaucracy. Previously, securing a permit for foreign investment could take years. Now, if the government doesn't respond within 45 days, the investment is automatically approved.

But business people say that is not enough.

"We have two employees whose only job is the paperwork involved in exporting," said Eduardo Garza, chairman of Frisa, a Monterrey-based manufacturer of machine tools that exports 80% of its production. "That means more people. It offsets the advantage of cheaper labor."

Business also complains about continued corruption. The government has attacked several well-known rip-off operations, such as international customs and the port of Veracruz. Last summer, the government confiscated the union-run company that operated the port and reformed the PRI-affiliated unions, which had commanded huge bribes to unload ships.

Still, 41% of the respondents in the Times Poll said bribery had increased in the last three years compared to 17% who said it had decreased. About a third of the people said it was business as usual.

What most preoccupies business people is the permanence of the current economic policies. While noting a historical swing of the pendulum between populist and pro-business administrations—President Venustiano Carranza confiscated the banks in 1915, President Alvaro Obregon returned them in 1921 and President Jose Lopez Portillo nationalized them again in 1982—they tend to view Salinas' reform program as permanent.

"I don't think you can call this a swing of the pendulum," said Mexican economist Jonathan Heath. "There have been basic policy changes."

Just to be sure, the businessmen want a free-trade agreement, to inscribe Mexico's neo-liberal identity in stone.

Times staff writer Richard Boudreaux contributed to this report.

DEMOCRACY IN AFRICA

Lighter continent

Black Africa, like Latin America and Eastern Europe before it, is turning away from autocracy and state domination of the economy. That is a big step. The next one will be harder still: ensuring good government

A FUNDAMENTAL shift in the way western aid donors treat Africa is in train. Witness a meeting held in Paris late last November, when 12 donor governments and international aid agencies, chaired by the World Bank, discussed aid to Kenya. In the past, such a meeting would have ended with an announcement of new aid and polite recommendations for economic-policy improvements. Not this time.

Instead, the donors called for "early implementation of political reform to reinforce the benefits of economic structural change". That meant "greater pluralism, respect for human rights and firm action to deal with corruption". Then came the bombshell. No new aid would be approved for six months. Meanwhile, the donors said, they would "review progress".

Never before had donors been so forceful—and so political. It worked. Kenya's President Daniel arap Moi, who had been denouncing multi-party democracy as an invitation to tribalism, hooliganism, banditry and treason, heard the message from Paris loud and clear. On December 3rd he accepted a shift toward a multi-party system; grumbling, maybe, but he did it .

The message was not addressed just to Kenya. Malawi's president-for-life, Kamuzu Banda, has been warned by EC governments that a donors' meeting this spring may treat his country like Kenya if he fails to meet their expectations. Britain has already cut its aid programme for Malawi from £10m ($18m) to £5m this year, in protest against Dr Banda's disregard of human rights and his tolerance of waste in government. With still better reason, France and Belgium have cut off aid to Zaire.

Something new

Five years ago, dictatorships proclaiming socialist theories, and applying the centralist part of them, prevailed in Africa, while donors pumped out conscience-saving loans without bothering too much what happened to the money. No longer. Africans have shown that they want multi-party democracy and are beginning to achieve it. Many African governments have decided that free-market policies are their most likely salvation. And western donors are demanding open politics and open markets in return for continued aid.

It all comes not before time—and the blame for what went wrong in Africa does not lie only there. The success of independence movements in the late 1950s and 1960s was accompanied by high hopes for democracy. But democracy is a late-grown and tender plant even in its European home. It formed little part of the colonial heritage. Rule in Africa was "essentially one-party rule by the administering authority," says the Nigerian secretary-general of the (ex-British) Commonwealth, Emeka Anyaoku. Colonial officials had little use for the notion of "loyal opposition". Nor, remarks Mr Anyaoku, did Africa. "I do not know of any African language whose political lexicon includes the concept of a 'leader of the loyal opposition'. Instead there is a clear concept of a political enemy."

To make things worse, one bit of European culture that had taken firm root among the elite of the new Africa was socialism, 1950s-style: the conviction—not unknown, either, to far-from-socialist colonial officials—that governments must have their hands on the levers of economic power. Bad in itself, a collective hand on the levers also meant opportunities for individual fingers in the till. The stage was set for the mismanagement of the past 30 years.

Most of the might-have-been democracies soon fell under the unchallenged rule either of those who had led the fight against colonialism—leaders such as Ghana's Kwame (The Saviour) Nkrumah, an able man corrupted by power, or Tanzania's Julius (The Teacher) Nyerere, an honest one led astray by potty economic ideas—or of ambitious soldiers. Many rulers were neither able nor honest. Barely anywhere (Botswana and Mauritius are long-established exceptions) did democracy take root.

The slide of the strongmen

Now it is doing so. Opposition leaders last year won elections in two former Portuguese colonies, the **Cape Verde Islands** and **Sao Tome and Principe**. In ex-British **Zambia's** presidential election last November, Kenneth Kaunda, who had ruled since 1964, lost to the opposition leader, Frederick Chiluba, and handed over gracefully.

In ex-French **Senegal**, the incumbent president won a fairly free election. The party of **Gabon's** President Omar Bongo, despite some ballot-stuffing, won only 59 of 120 seats in its election, but Mr Bongo obtained a majority by doing a deal with a small party. In many other former French colonies, however, one-time strongmen have lost power. **Benin's** Mathieu Kérékou lost an election to an opposition reformer, Nicéphore Soglo. In **Niger**, the opposition obliged General Ali Saibou to hold a "national conference" on the country's future, and to transfer power to a prime minister from its own ranks until elections are held. **Madagascar's** President Didier Ratsiraka, facing mass demonstrations, accepted a coalition with the opposition—and the opposition leader as effective head of government—until an election is held, supposedly by the end of this year. In **Mali**, General Moussa Traoré was deposed, after 23 years in power; elections are due on March 26th.

In **Togo**, however, there was a backlash. Soldiers tried last month to oust Joseph Koffigoh, a democrat who had been appointed prime minister by a national conference convened to decide the country's future, and who had taken executive power from the unloved General Gnassingbé Eyadéma. Mr Koffigoh had to make concessions, but has hung on. He now heads a coalition in which the general wields influence. And in ex-French **Congo**, after General Denis Sassou-Nguesso, a repentant Marxist, had been eased out of power by a national conference, the prime minister, André Milongo, faced an army mutiny. He too survived.

More good news to come

Prospects for democracy this year look fairly bright. **Nigeria's** ruler, General Ibrahim Babangida, has held state elections with fair success (though electoral hanky-panky led to some being annulled). Primaries for a presidential election are due in August, the election itself in December. **Ghana's** ruler, Flight-Lieutenant Jerry Rawlings, has set up a committee to write a new constitution, which is due to be put to a referendum in April. Presidential and parliamentary elections are to be held near the end of this year.

Sierra Leone has approved, in a referendum, a return to multi-party democracy and is due to hold elections soon, though the country's ruler, General Joseph Momoh, has not yet set a date. He will probably be a candidate and be challenged by an opposition leader, Sallia Jusu. **Tanzania's** President Ali Mwinyi, observing what was happening next door in Kenya, has switched deftly from insisting on a one-party state to calling for multi-partyism. This will be approved by the rubber-stamp parliament in April, and elections due in 1995 may be brought forward. The president of **Gambia**, Sir Dawda Jawara, in office for 26 years, has announced that multi-party elections will be held in April. He will be a candidate, and will probably win, but the election will be strongly contested.

Cameroon's President Paul Biya has had to retreat in the face of 13 opposition parties demanding a national conference, but so far has conceded only the appointment of a commission to propose constitutional changes. However, a parliamentary election may be held this spring. **Angola's** first presidential and parliamentary elections are promised this year, probably in September, pitting President Jose Eduardo dos Santos against the rebel leader, Jonas Savimbi. **Guinea-Bissau** is seeing the start of a multi-party system. **Burundi** is to vote on a new democratic constitution in March, though progress will be slow if recent tribal violence continues. A transitional regime is meant to lead to multi-party democracy in **Rwanda**. But it too faces a long-running civil war in part of the country.

Not everywhere, though

So far, so good, more or less. But strongmen rarely give up without a fight. Some are holding on to power with devious skill.

In **Mauritania** President Ould Taya was predictably declared the winner of a presidential election last month. Opposition parties claimed they had been robbed, and refused to take part in legislative elections due shortly. In **Côte d'Ivoire** Félix Houphouet-Boigny, the wily patriarch of black Africa, deployed all the power of the state last year to win 163 of 175 seats in parliament. In the remote **Central African Republic**, General André Kolingba is putting off demands for a national conference by evading meetings with the opposition. In **Burkina Faso** (formerly Upper Volta), Captain Blaise Compaoré announced on November 5th a presidential election on De-

Good intentions

	IMF agreement	Contested election in past five years	Contested election likely soon
Angola			●
Benin	●	●	
Botswana		●	
Burkina Faso	●		
Burundi	●		
Cameroon	●		●
Cape Verde Islands		●	
Central African Rep.			
Chad			
Congo	●		●
Côte d'Ivoire	●	●	
Equatorial Guinea			
Ethiopia			
Gabon	●	●	
Gambia	●		●
Ghana	●		
Guinea	●		
Guinea-Bissau			
Kenya			●
Lesotho			
Liberia			
Madagascar	●		●
Malawi	●		
Mali			●
Mauritania	●	●	
Mozambique	●		
Namibia		●	
Niger			●
Nigeria	●		●
Rwanda	●		
Sao Tome & Principe		●	
Senegal	●	●	
Sierra Leone			●
Somalia			
Swaziland			
Tanzania	●		?
Togo	●		
Uganda	●		
Zaire			
Zambia		●	
Zimbabwe	●		

cember 1st. His rivals refused to take part. Mr Compaoré was duly "elected".

Zimbabwe's President Robert Mugabe has stepped back from imposing a one-party state, but his way of government looks curiously like one. In **Zaire** wealthy President Mobutu Sese Seko, by encouraging the formation of several dozen parties, has done his best to divide his opponents. Finding that not enough, he recently suppressed the national conference which they had organised, and the latest demonstration against him in Kinshasa was put down last Sunday by troops, with many deaths.

And, alas, in **Chad**, **Liberia**, **Ethiopia** and wretched **Somalia**, the only real arbiter of power is the gun.

Fed up

Why the new trend? Africans have at last lost patience with their rulers. They are particularly angry about declining living standards, but also about arbitrary and bad government, corruption and a breakdown of law and order. Many members of the small middle class are government officials. Since most governments are short of cash, having been told by the IMF and World Bank to cut spending, these officials are underpaid or paid late. Unhappy and articulate—and often represented by militant trade unions—they demonstrate, they go on strike and they oblige the strongmen to convene national conferences. Among the demonstrators are people from the countryside who have been flooding into towns seeking (but rarely finding) a better life.

The strongmen were vulnerable. They could no longer blame the colonialists, who had gone home two or three decades ago. The blame lay close to home. Nor, after the collapse of communism, could any African leader say with a straight face that he favoured Marxism or state control of the economy. The collapse of communism affected the aid donors too. They were embarrassed to be seen backing freedom in Eastern Europe, while hobnobbing with dictators in Africa. And it freed them from the illusion that countries such as Zaire were strategic assets whose mineral wealth had to be saved from falling into communist hands. Mr Mobutu and his like became dispensable.

So the donors, already "totally fed up" with Africa's performance, according to a senior aid official, changed their tune. Britain's foreign secretary, Douglas Hurd, laid the new approach on the line in mid-1990:

> Countries which tend towards pluralism, public accountability, respect for the rule of law, human rights and market principles should be encouraged. Governments which persist with repressive policies, corrupt management and wasteful, discredited economic systems should not expect us to support their folly with scarce aid resources which could be used better elsewhere.

President François Mitterrand, speaking after a Franco-African summit in his country at about the same time, sent the same message. France would go on giving help, but

> This traditional aid will be more tepid for regimes that behave in an authoritarian manner, without accepting the evolution toward democracy, and more enthusiastic for those who take this step bravely and go as far as they can.

There are limits to this change, however. Aid donors are now rightly emphasising the need for "good government" in a continent where government is often a shambles. They, and foreign investors, are inclined to overlook dictatorial tendencies in the rare regimes that can show economic success. Well-performing Ghana has for several years been the darling of the World Bank and western donors (though not of investors). All have turned a blind eye to Mr Rawlings's strongman act. Some sceptics indeed murmur that things might not be so great if the democrats ever got back: the last time, they were a disaster.

The other half of the story

The familiar trouble is that, though free politics and free-market economics go most happily together, one does not necessarily lead to the other, nor guarantee its success. Africa has as much work to do getting rid of—often well-intentioned—economic interventionism as in chasing out dictators.

The IMF has loan agreements with 23 African governments. None has been carried through to completion and economic take-off. The structural reforms that are needed, says the fund's managing director, Michel Camdessus, are "as far-reaching in economic culture as anything that is being undertaken in Eastern Europe or Latin America". They are indeed. Africa's list of "things to do" is daunting. For example: balance the budget; make the docks, airports and public utilities work; close corrupt (and bankrupt) state banks and encourage private ones; privatise state enterprises; get rid of needless controls and licences; make the currency competitive; liberalise markets and labour laws; make it easy to set up a company; encourage the "informal sector"; go for export-led growth; don't treat investors, domestic or foreign, as predators, but allies, and go out and woo them.

That is a big adjustment. Yet it is one that must be made rapidly, says Mr Camdessus:

Good economics is good politics, and vice versa. A newly established democracy needs to establish, as quickly as possible, the basic framework for a viable economic system, and for this it needs very strong policies in its early days. Only in this way can a country create, in the minds of both the domestic population and the international community, confidence in its stability and long-term prospects.

Zambia's new President Chiluba has followed this advice and abolished subsidies. Will such daring democrats survive? If Latin American experience is any guide, they will have a bumpy ride, at best. People tend to accept painful policies more readily from elected governments than from dictators. But they also want results. And it takes time for adjustment programmes to work, still longer for foreign investment to start arriving. Even then, market forces or world economic conditions can upset high hopes. When Ghana and Côte d'Ivoire, urged on by aid donors, boosted their cocoa exports, prices collapsed. Tanzania's push into cotton exports suffered much the same fate last year. And, increasingly important, rich countries are far from opening their doors freely to third-world manufactures.

Governments that follow Mr Camdessus's advice may well be booted out of office before their policies have borne fruit.

Other countries apply much the same policies. If eventually the country concerned acquires a good economic record, and establishes a stable business environment, investment will start coming in, households will begin to feel slightly better off and voters will start reelecting their

governments. That takes time. But it has been done in Latin America.

An ethnic solution

The difficulty will be in getting from "here" to "there". There will be plenty of setbacks. And democracy—majority rule, but also fairness to minorities—is not a natural concept. Oligarchy is (yes, in Africa too: do not imagine the whole continent used to be run by warm-hearted conclaves of village elders). So is tribalism, and Africa (not alone) has plenty of it. It shapes politics everywhere in black Africa, and democracy could make it worse, so long as parties have a tribal basis.

That is why Kenya's President Moi would really prefer a one-party state, in the form of a carefully constructed tribal mosaic. As the leader of a small tribe, he fears domination by the more numerous Kikuyu and Luo. Nigeria's President Babangida has a different answer: a two-party state, with one party to the left of centre and the other to the right. These have been formed and seem to be multi-tribal. Whether such a tidy, soldierly arrangement can last is another matter. A better version might be a constitution allowing any number of parties but requiring them to demonstrate significant support in most regions of the country.

Yet Africa's journey towards democracy and sound economic policies has achieved a remarkable momentum. A historic opportunity is being seized. The remaining autocrats will be shifted only by the continued bravery of their opponents and some pushing by aid donors. Yet shifted they may well be. Then the really hard part will start: achieving widespread good government.

'Today We Have Closed the Books on Apartheid'

South Africa gives de Klerk the go-ahead

David S. Ottaway and Paul Taylor

Washington Post Foreign Service

CAPE TOWN, South Africa—President Frederik W. de Klerk received a massive vote of confidence last week from white South Africans in his leadership and negotiations for a new nonracial constitution, winning nearly 70 percent of the vote in a historic whites-only referendum.

The margin of victory, far greater than had been predicted here, means that he will be able to go ahead with an almost completed agreement with black groups to set up an interim, multi-racial government in the next few months without again seeking white approval.

"Today we have closed the books on apartheid," de Klerk said on March 18, referring to South Africa's system of racial separation.

The final results showed that 1.9 million whites, or 68.6 percent, voted yes and 875,619, or 31.2 percent, no. The overall turnout of registered voters was 85 percent, one of the highest in white South Africa's electoral history.

The overwhelming victory for de Klerk also means that the threat of violence from white right-wing groups opposed to his plan for power-sharing with blacks has most likely been reduced.

Both white and black leaders had predicted "unprecedented political turmoil" and renewed international sanctions and isolation if the opposition Conservative Party succeeded in defeating the referendum. That prospect has now been averted and the way apparently opened for a far smoother transition from white-minority rule to a black-dominated government.

De Klerk, who had promised to resign if he lost the referendum, emerges with a far stronger hand to deal both with the white right wing that has been seeking to sink the negotiation process

and with militant blacks demanding immediate control of the government.

The vote is likely to weaken the Conservative Party, which led an alliance of right-wing groups in opposition to the referendum. De Klerk predicts a shattering of conservative ranks in the coming weeks, with one faction finally joining the constitutional talks and a smaller one likely resorting to violence.

De Klerk was clearly delighted with the results, which exceeded the wildest expectations of all local analysts and his own campaign strategists, who had predicted at most a 60 percent victory.

"Today will be written up in our history as one of the most fundamental turning points," he said last week, addressing a small crowd of well-wishers and supporters on the back lawn of the presidential office here. "It doesn't often happen that in one generation a nation gets an opportunity to rise above itself. The white electorate has risen above itself in this referendum."

There was "an element of justice," the president added, that "those who started this long chapter in our history were called upon to close the book on apartheid."

De Klerk called the outcome "a landslide win" and "the real birthday of the real New South Africa."

It was also his own 56th birthday.

Also clearly relieved by the outcome is African National Congress President Nelson Mandela, who says he had called de Klerk that morning to wish him a happy birthday and the best of luck in the vote counting, which began March 18 after March 17's all-day voting.

Mandela says the big yes vote means that the peace process is "definitely on course."

"The possibility of a no vote was a source of great concern to blacks as well as whites," he says, adding that

there has been no "great relief" across the country at the outcome.

"Apartheid is still very much alive. I still cannot vote in my own country," the Associated Press quoted Mandela as saying. He also has warned that this should be the "absolute last" all-white vote.

The radical black Pan-Africanist Congress, which has refused to take part in the constitutional negotiations, calls the referendum "an obscenity and an insult to the dispossessed masses of our country."

Most analysts credit the huge white turnout and margin of victory to a well-orchestrated campaign by government, business, civic, media and sports leaders that hammered home the dire consequences of being once again expelled from the family of nations.

South Africa is a sports-crazed nation and in the closing days of the referendum campaign, voters were paying almost as much attention to the fortunes of its national cricket team competing in the World Cup for the first time in two decades. The team reached the semifinals, but the cricket board threatened to pull it out of the competition in Sydney if a no vote prevailed.

Several European nations, including Germany and Switzerland, had threatened to reimpose sanctions if the referendum was not approved. The threats came at a time when South Africa is struggling to emerge from a three-year recession.

In Washington, President Bush's spokesman, Marlin Fitzwater, praises the vote "for a just and democratic future" and says that "the United States firmly and fully supports" the constitutional negotiations here.

British Prime Minister John Major says the referendum "will bring South Africa back into the international community." U.N. Secretary General

From *The Washington Post National Weekly Edition*, March 23-29, 1992, p. 9. Copyright © 1992, The Washington Post. Reprinted by permission.

Boutros Boutros-Ghali says the results "constitute a new factor for peace and development throughout Africa."

Another factor in the victory was thought to be the fear of more violence—perhaps even civil war—if the referendum were defeated. De Klerk's National Party blanketed the country with posters raising the specter of white terrorism, fascism and neo-Nazism if the Conservative Party and its allies won.

De Klerk was pressed into calling the referendum after his party lost by-elections to the Conservatives over the past two years. But as he noted, white voters had "divorced their grievances" over rising crime, taxes and joblessness to focus on the larger question of the nation's destiny.

De Klerk dismissed suggestions that he had taken a huge risk in calling a referendum. "I am not a gambling man," he said, adding that from the outset, opinion polls had given him "the basic assurance" of victory. But he admitted that he had been aware that "sometimes things can go wrong."

The Conservative Party managed to win in only one of the nation's 15 electoral regions, small, far-northern Pietersburg. Even there in the heartland of white right-wing farmer resistance, it only won 57 percent of the vote.

It lost in four other conservative strongholds—Pretoria, Roodepoort, Bloemfontein and Kroonstad—even though three of those regions have elected far more members of Parliament from the Conservative Party than from the ruling National Party.

Conservative Party leader Andries Treurnicht ascribes the surprisingly meager show of support for a no vote to the "hysterical claims" made by the National Party during the three-week campaign.

"Whites have now voted for power-sharing," he says. "They will find out what it means to lose power and not to have power of your own to protect your own freedom," he says. "Black-majority rule must still come."

Treurnicht says that despite the right-wing defeat, "the struggle for freedom and survival is now continuing in even greater earnestness than before." But he denies that his party would resort to violence "as long as there is any constitutional way or door open."

One well-known political analyst here, Frederik van Zyl Slabbert, says the referendum was probably the last hurrah for white politics in this country.

"This vote signals the end of parliamentary politics as we have known it," he remarked over the state-run television.

The present constitution excludes blacks from South Africa's tricameral Parliament representing whites, Indians and mixed-raced Coloreds.

At a press conference after the referendum results, the president said he felt he now had a strong mandate to negotiate a new constitution and that it was "improbable" he would again call a white referendum to approve a final agreement.

But he made clear that "an important gap" remains in the negotiations between the National Party and the ANC over the structure of an interim government expected to be created shortly.

"Some tough negotiations lie ahead" over power-sharing, he said, because the National Party believes that "if you have 51 percent of the vote, you should not have 100 percent of the power," referring to majority rule. Mandela, he said, apparently feels strongly that the majority, whatever its percentage of the vote, should rule.

Such "winner-take-all" political systems might be "marvelous" for Britain, but "not for our society," de Klerk said, because of its political and ethnic diversity.

De Klerk warned in his victory speech that there was a risk now of "radicalism from both the [black] left and the [white] right" and called upon the "90 to 95 percent" of all South Africans to join hands and "stand firm."

On the question of potential right-wing terrorism, de Klerk said he would not act to disband the neo-Nazi National Resistance Movement of Eugene Terre'Blanche so long as it did not engage in illegal activities.

De Klerk also said there was "no factual basis whatsoever" to reports that he planned "a purge" of the security forces if he won the referendum. There have been widespread allegations from black groups that these forces are partly responsible for stirring violence in the black townships.

Before and during the referendum campaign, there were reports that

right-wing elements within the security forces were contemplating a coup because of their dissatisfaction with de Klerk's handling of the constitutional talks.

De Klerk said he has "a very good relationship" with the top echelons of the military and police.

Here on the streets of Cape Town, where the yes vote piled up a whopping 85 percent to 15 percent margin, the mood is more somber and subdued than celebratory. A coalition of anti-apartheid groups staged a rally in front of Parliament around the time the results came in—but it was to protest a new government budget. Marchers merely shrugged at the news of the lopsided referendum vote.

"You can't get excited when it was an illegitimate, whites-only vote," says Hans Moeti, 26, a Colored student at the University of Cape Town. "And you know it will still be ages before any new democratically elected government addresses all the discrepancies we have between the races on wealth, land distribution, education and all the rest."

Among whites here, there is a mix of quiet dread and cautious hope.

Frederick Lombaard, a middle-aged white attorney, says he is "pleased" with the vote but not optimistic about the future of South Africa. "The yes vote was the best of two very bad possibilities," he says. "But when you look at what has happened in the rest of Africa when blacks take over, it puts you in a kind of a panic."

Lombaard estimates that a black-dominated government would be running the country within two years. "I'm not going to pull up stakes and leave," he says, "but I doubt very much my children will still be here in 10 or 15 years."

On the other hand, Anna Breytenbach, 23, a junior marketing executive for a computer company, says she had had her "passport ready" and was prepared to leave the country if the no vote won.

"Today is a great day for my country, especially for the young people," she says. "Our generation believes that apartheid was immoral. The older generation merely believed it was unworkable. That is a big difference, and that is why I think the young of South Africa will lead the country to true racial reconciliation."

A Mandate for Change

For South Africa, Pace Is Now Issue

Christopher S. Wren

Special to The New York Times

CAPE TOWN, March 19—Despite the overwhelming mandate that whites gave President F. W. de Klerk to end their monopoly on political power, South Africa has a distance to travel before blacks inherit the vote and other basic rights flowing from it.

The ringing approval of 68.7 percent of the whites who voted in Tuesday's referendum left little doubt that Mr. de Klerk has their support to negotiate power sharing with blacks.

"The referendum result is close to being unique in the annals of politics," Hermann Giliomee, a political scientist at the University of Cape Town, wrote in The Cape Times newspaper today. "Here the South African whites, who have become a byword in the world for myopic bigotry, endorse a process which is most likely to reduce their political representation in a year or two to a minority in an elected legislature."

"To make it even more exceptional," Professor Giliomee said, "whites have done this from a position of relative strength and in the absence of any sense of imminent defeat."

Timetable for Change

Mr. de Klerk, who repealed the basic laws underpinning apartheid last year, has insisted that basic change must be negotiated and enshrined in a new constitution that will replace the present racially biased one. The time that he expects this to take is more than his foremost opponent, the African National Congress, is prepared to spend.

"When you get to the fundamentals, there's no quick fix," President de Klerk told a news conference in Cape Town yesterday afternoon.

Mr. de Klerk proposed interim measures like the inclusion of blacks in the current Cabinet, which Nelson Mandela and other black leaders have rejected as tokenism. In turn, Mr. Mandela's recent suggestion that some seats be set aside for whites in the new Parliament was rejected by the National Party.

Though the final outline of a settlement remains murky, both sides have agreed upon the need for an interim government with a multiracial executive body and for the existing Parliament or a subsequent one-chamber legislature to approve legal changes to the present constitution. This scenario has emerged as the likeliest route to a democracy beyond apartheid, which the congress has proposed be covered within 15 months.

The negotiators from the Congress and the Government have also reportedly agreed upon a final two-chamber legislature elected by proportional representation, an independent judicial system and a bill of rights, as key features of the proposed constitution.

In return for Mr. de Klerk's acceptance in principle of an interim government, the congress has muted its opposition to the Government's proposal to shift certain powers from Federal to regional authority. The effect of such transfers would be to allow white areas to gain political prerogatives while blacks established an electoral majority at the national level.

'Sunset Clause' Proposed

In addition the Congress has proposed "sunset clauses" that would phase out the preferential rights that whites currently enjoy and would mandate a coali-

Toward Change In South Africa: What Happens Next

NEGOTIATIONS

President F. W. de Klerk's National Party and the African National Congress are among 19 groups that have been negotiating a new constitution since December. There could be agreement soon on the general principles, but the actual document is likely to take many months.

POSSIBLE ROADBLOCKS

Mr. de Klerk wants strong protections for minorities, but the A.N.C. objects to special privileges for whites. Also, right-wing white groups and militant black organizations are not participating in the negotiations and will almost certainly object to any agreements.

INTERIM GOVERNMENT

If the constitutional talks go well, there could be an interim government this year that would include blacks for the first time. But Mr. de Klerk has stressed that he will still be in control.

MULTIRACIAL ELECTIONS

Mr. de Klerk does not have to call an election until 1994 and considers that year his deadline for having a new constitution.

Source: Associated Press

SOUTH AFRICA

The New York Times

From *The New York Times*, March 20, 1992, pp. A1, A6. Copyright © 1992 by The New York Times Company. Reprinted by permission.

tion government for the first years of multiparty rule.

Disagreements abound over how or when all this is to be achieved, but the overwhelming approval by whites of the referendum is expected to accelerate the talks that are under way at the Convention for a Democratic South Africa, as the negotiating forum is called.

"I think that the referendum will give us just the impetus that is required," said Helen Suzman, a veteran human rights campaigner who is a delegate for the liberal Democratic Party at the negotiations.

Mr. de Klerk has emerged strengthened by his referendum's success and could consequently take a harder line at the talks. He has promised whites that he would insist upon a new constitution incorporating sufficient guarantees to protect the white minority from majority—meaning black—domination. Unless he could achieve this, he said, fundamental changes would have to be referred back to his white constituency in another referendum.

Bridge to Democracy

"I like to use the image of a bridge, which must contain enough steel to withstand the worst possible scenario of floods and heavy vehicles," Mr. de Klerk explained last Thursday.

"Just so, this constitution must have enough steel—that is what we mean by checks and balances—to handle the complexities of our situation," Mr. de Klerk said.

And campaigning for his referendum earlier this month, Mr. de Klerk assured whites that negotiation did not mean surrender.

At a news conference today, Mr. Mandela, the president of the African National Congress, said Mr. de Klerk must move faster now that he had defused the political threat from the right. Mr. Mandela reiterated the congress's insistence upon an interim government, which he said would "supervise the transition from an apartheid to a democratic state."

"Our demand is that the interim government must be introduced this year and we think that is possible," Mr. Mandela told reporters.

Retention of Sanctions

Until then, Mr. Mandela urged that foreign economic sanctions remain in place, despite the willingness of more countries to lift them as a gesture to Mr. de Klerk's successful referendum.

"Sanctions were introduced for the purpose of inducing the ruling party to dismantle apartheid and to extend the vote to all South Africans," Mr. Mandela said. "Neither of these have been achieved."

International pressure played a role in persuading the majority of whites to break with apartheid, although not always in ways commonly assumed in the West. Few whites have felt directly threatened by the disinvestment of foreign companies, for example, because it has been mostly blacks who lost jobs. South Africa has grown adroit at sidestepping sanctions. It buys its oil through shadowy middlemen overseas and has built a formidable domestic arms industry.

A Sense of Isolation

But whites have been embarrassed to have to pass themselves off as Australians or Britons overseas, to see their sports heroes and cultural performers barred from international arenas where they might have excelled, all for the sake of a legalized system of racial discrimination policies that has proven unworkable.

The whites sent a clear message that they want to become part of the world again rather than live hunkered down in the isolation brought on by apartheid. At the same time, many of them have been terrified at the prospect of surrendering their privileges.

The referendum coincided with the international success of South Africa's cricket team, which is the first national team to tour overseas since an international sports boycott was lifted last year. The team rose to the semifinals of cricket's World Cup matches, only to find that it might have to withdraw if the referendum was defeated. That was enough to convince many sports-happy whites to vote yes.

"While the sports issue was undoubtedly significant in its own right," said David Welsh, Professor of Southern African Studies at the University of Cape Town, "it was symptomatic of some-

Mandate in hand, de Klerk still faces many obstacles.

thing deeper: a widespread sense of relief that South African whites were no longer being regarded as lepers in the international community."

Other forces encouraged the high turnout. White business, which normally stays clear of partisan politics, went all out for the referendum's approval donating over $1 million for newspaper and radio advertisements. Some executives urged white employees to vote yes, warning that sanctions could otherwise threaten their jobs.

The South African press, with little pretense of objectivity, also threw its support unabashedly behind the referendum. Newspapers published passionate front-page editorials warning of the disasters inherent in a no vote and ran political advertising at discount rates.

Many whites apparently voted for what they regarded as the lesser of two evils, though it was seldom evident in the good-natured tolerance that prevailed in the long lines at most polling stations.

"People are not reacting to the referendum as if we were standing on the brink of a precipice," said Laurie Schlemmer, a veteran political analyst as the returns trickled in yesterday.

Deng Struggles to Set Reform Back on Track

Facing the worst succession crisis since Mao's death, Beijing's hard-line leaders are caught between the demands of modernization and political control

Ann Scott Tyson and James L. Tyson

Staff writers of The Christian Science Monitor

BEIJING

One day last month while touring China's prosperous south to promote his market-oriented reforms, Chinese leader Deng Xiaoping came upon a jade tree in a lush botanical garden.

To the cheers of his entourage, Mr. Deng reached out and felt the smooth bark of the tree, believed to bring riches to whoever touches it.

The gesture symbolizes a major, if simplistic, tenet of Dengism: Unabashedly encouraging 1.1 billion Chinese to become rich is the best way to modernize China and sustain Communist Party rule.

Nearly three years after the June 4, 1989 massacre of protesters in Beijing unleashed a conservative backlash, Deng is campaigning hard to revive reforms at this year's pivotal 14th party congress.

"Reform and opening are the only way out. Not reforming is a dead end," Deng was quoted as saying in south China. Opposition, he said, will not be tolerated.

Echoing Deng, Chinese leaders and the state-run media are calling for "urgent" reform, an end to ideological "dogmatism," and even the development of "a capitalist economy . . . as a useful supplement to the socialist economy."

Yet even if Deng manages to overcome strong opposition and put economic reforms back on track, his effort may be too little, too late, Beijing-based diplomats and scholars say.

Deng's vision of China's modernization is marred, they say, by a fundamental contradiction: A market-driven economy is ultimately incompatible with Marxism and harsh political control. According to Deng, both are needed to keep the Communist Party in power.

The dilemma is perpetuated by the refusal of Deng and a handful of other revolutionary veterans to give up power. A weak successor generation will find it harder to break with the old guard's legacy, they say.

"There is a basic contradiction between the goals of economic construction and those of political control. But the party will continue to pursue this contradiction to try to stay in power," an Asian diplomat says.

With no immediate alternative to the Communist Party, China will probably undergo several years of political stagnation, diplomats and scholars say.

Chinese are unlikely to rise up if the current regime can sustain economic growth. Instead, central authority will slowly erode as provincial officials, wealthy private businessmen, and other groups empowered by reform disregard Beijing's dictates, they say.

"There is no clear policy that the leadership can follow to restore its control over wayward provinces and regions," a Western diplomat says.

Deng's tour last month of China's thriving Guangdong Province illustrates both the achievements and contradictions of his 14 year old rule, as well as the emerging succession crisis.

Nowhere in China has Deng seemed to have a Midas touch more than along the booming southern coast of Guangdong. The brash Cantonese have risen from backwardness to become China's richest citizens since 1980, when Beijing began dismantling Mao Zedong's communes and reviving family farming and private enterprise.

Despite clear successes, uncertainty continues to overshadow the reforms.

Deng's support for Marxist precepts like state ownership puts reform on a weak theoretical footing. Reform is a blind, trial-and-error process, like "groping for stones while crossing a river," Deng says.

As a result, vital experiments with stock markets, price deregulation, and bankruptcy are vulnerable to attack by party ideologues.

Similarly, Deng's backing for one-party dictatorship has undermined efforts to build a less corrupt and more efficient system of rule by law. Without such institutional guarantees, Chinese can neither fully

184   Reprinted by permission from *The Christian Science Monitor,* February 26, 1992, pp. 9, 12. Copyright © 1992 by The Christian Science Publishing Society. All rights reserved.

trust the free market nor adequately protect their new hard-won wealth.

All Deng can do to assure Chinese that his reforms endure is to personally reiterate his policies, as he did in Guangdong last month. Yet even this gesture underscores a weakness of his regime: "Men rule, not the law," as the Chinese saying goes.

Deng's decision to step out of official retirement and into the limelight to bolster his reforms also demonstrates why China faces its worst succession crisis since Mao's death in 1976.

The final arbiters of power in Beijing today are a handful of revolutionary veterans, with Deng a tentative first among equals.

The veterans include President Yang Shangkun, conservative economist Chen Yun, and hard-liners such as Vice President Wang Zhen, Bo Yibo, Peng Zhen, and Li Xiannian.

Jealous of each other's power and accustomed to lifetime rule, these veterans are reluctant to yield to the younger technocrats who now manage China's day-to-day affairs.

The younger leaders, obliged to defer to their elder patrons, face difficulty building the independent power bases in the party, government, and military that are vital to securing their positions.

Even Deng's annointed successor, party chief Jiang Zemin, has failed to muster significant backing and is likely to prove a transitory figure in Chinese politics.

As veterans compete to promote protégés from within their factions, independent-minded leaders are unlikely to emerge at this year's 14th party congress.

Instead, compromise figures like economic planner Zou Jiahua are expected to outnumber controversial reformers like Vice Premier Zhu Rongji, who is backed by Deng.

Potentially the most important outcome of the congress would be the promotion to the party Central Committee of several offspring of China's elder leaders, diplomats and Chinese sources say. Many veterans seek to ensure their legacy by installing relatives.

Known to many Chinese as "crown princes," the offspring include: central banker Chen Yuan (son of Chen Yun), Beijing tourism chief Bo Xicheng (son of Bo Yibo), corporate manager Wang Jun (son of Wang Zhen), and Fuzhou party secretary Xi Jinping (son of Xi Zhongxun).

Thanks to their family connections, the "crown princes" already enjoy political influence and prestige that extends well beyond their current positions.

"The older generation basically trusts them. These people have more than a little power," one Chinese source familiar with the crown princes says. The princes use family ties to advance policies they favor and participate in decisions on a wide range of issues including foreign affairs, says the source.

The up-and-coming offspring are known to have ideas that differ substantially from the orthodox Marxism of their elders. None, however, is believed to oppose strong-arm party rule.

Chen Yuan is linked to a group of neo-conservative intellectuals who advocate replacing the party's revolutionary creed with a combination of nationalism, Confucianism, and Western philosophy. Yet this unorthodox theory, like the "new authoritarianism" promoted in 1988 by then-party chief Zhao Ziyang, would maintain dictatorial powers for party leaders.

Facing no evident revolt from within its 50 million-strong ranks, the party also confronts no well-organized outside opposition.

Chinese people have tolerated political repression for centuries. In the near term, as long as the economy remains afloat, a repeat of the nationwide protests of spring 1989 is improbable.

Even Chinese intellectuals jailed for months for their role in the democracy movement say they see no ready substitute today for party rule.

"Democracy must begin from within the party," a released Chinese political prisoner says.

Instead, many analysts believe the party's authority will gradually wither, or be transformed, as new interest groups and private aspirations unleashed by Deng's reforms continue their irreversible rise.

"Chinese people over 40 all went through [Mao's radical 1966–76] cultural revolution. They suffered so much from social chaos; they all want stability," says a middle-aged Chinese official who sympathizes with the 1989 protests. "It doesn't mean the people don't want democracy, but it must come step by step."

"Deng Xiaoping's successor will likely be someone who responds to events rather than shaping them, someone who manages the Chinese ship of state rather than steering it in bold new directions, and someone who spends most of his time bargaining with important domestic groups rather than formulating a clear-cut ideology."

Preparing for the Succession

DAVID BACHMAN

DAVID BACHMAN *is associate professor of international studies at the Henry M. Jackson School of International Studies at the University of Washington. He is the author of* Bureaucracy, Economy, and Leadership in China *(New York: Cambridge University Press, 1991),* Chen Yun and the Chinese Political System *(Armonk, N.Y.: M.E. Sharpe, 1985), and coeditor and cotranslator of* Yan Jiaqi and China's Struggle for Democracy *(Armonk, N.Y.: M.E. Sharpe, 1991).*

A deceptive calm has descended over China. Overt power struggles are rare, and there have been few dramatic political developments. The Chinese leadership has attempted to put the democracy movement of 1989 and its bloody suppression behind it by projecting an image of progress, control, and—to use its favorite post-June 4, 1989, phrase—stability and unity.[1] No mass demonstrations have taken place, and social tensions have subsided. Stability and unity seem to reign in China.

But the depth of elite unity and social stability should not be overestimated. Political tension did not disappear simply because the leadership suggested that all was healthy in the Chinese body politic. The question of who would succeed paramount leader Deng Xiaoping, although it was addressed only covertly, dominated Chinese politics over the last year. To an increasing degree, the actions of all major Chinese political figures revolved around this issue.

China is currently ruled by two different sets of leaders. The members of one set are in their fifties and sixties. Most are college educated and many have spent time abroad, usually in the Soviet Union. They exercise operational authority over the Chinese state, making routine policy decisions and determining policy implementation. The highest-ranking members of this group are contenders for the ultimate succession, aspiring to gain full authority in the areas of policy and power.

The winner of the succession contest will try to replace with his own people the second set of leaders, a group of men in their eighties who are the final arbiters of power and policy in China, although few of them hold formal positions in the government or the Communist party apparatus. The leaders of this group are Deng Xiaoping, who turned 87 in August 1991, and the conservative economist Chen Yun, who recently turned 86. They and the group's approximately half-dozen other veterans of the Chinese Communist party's struggle for power in the 1920s, 1930s, and 1940s are reluctant to allow the younger generation any real authority. To some extent, this hesitation to retire is natural; the revolutionary veterans believe they are tougher and more experienced than their putative heirs. Chinese culture in general and Chinese Communist party culture in particular are ambivalent about retirement: The true Communist fights to his dying breath for the cause; the true Chinese works for his country to the last day of his life. But in fact these octogenarians are reluctant to retire because they do not want to give up power.

The older generation's refusal to relinquish power exacerbates the uncertainties surrounding succession in China. Potential successors are inexperienced, and older leaders will not cede greater powers to them until they are more experienced. But the older leaders have made it impossible for younger leaders to gain the needed experience, creating a vicious circle.

SUCCESSION POLITICS

In any one-party political system, succession is a critical and noninstitutionalized political process. In China the pressure to win and to employ all available strategies and tactics is especially pronounced because the rules of the game are not formalized and the costs of failure may include political oblivion and, as in the past, loss of life.

Reprinted with permission from *Current History* magazine, September 1991. Copyright © 1991 by Current History, Inc.

Then there is the recurring dilemma of the successor in China: To maintain his position as designated successor, the leader-to-be must maintain the trust of the top leader, the person who anointed him as heir apparent.[2] Yet the successor inevitably lacks some of his patron's resources, and thus must develop independent power bases. The dilemma arises from the fact that it is all but impossible for the successor to maintain the trust of the top leader and build independent power bases at the same time.

China's modern political history is filled with examples of the importance of the political succession question. In 1953 two leading regional officials, Gao Gang and Rao Shushi, were removed from office because they tried to reduce the influence of potential successors to Chairman Mao Zedong, who may have been ill at the time. The early phases of the Cultural Revolution (1966–1968) involved attacks on Mao's apparent successor, Liu Shaoqi, then president of China. In the late 1960s and early 1970s, Mao turned on his newly designated successor, Lin Biao, the commander of the Chinese army, who seemed overly anxious to secure his succession. (Lin died in a mysterious airplane crash in 1971.) From 1973 to 1976, radical and moderate factions battled to determine who would succeed the Chairman after he finally died. The moderates won the battle, but the struggle among them continued until 1978, when Deng Xiaoping finally became China's top leader.

Deng had not been in power long before he tried to manage his own succession in order to avoid a recurrence of past disruption. But Deng's attempts to manipulate his own succession have fared no better than Mao's. In the early 1980s, Deng first tried to establish Hu Yaobang, an old ally and the party's new general secretary, as his successor. After student demonstrations and calls for fundamental political change by many of China's leading intellectuals in 1986, however, Hu was forced from power in early 1987; a few months later Zhao Ziyang, then prime minister, was made general secretary. Deng thus tried to designate Zhao as successor, but Zhao was ousted after he refused to suppress the 1989 demonstrations. After the crackdown on the demonstrators, Deng elevated Jiang Zemin, then party secretary of Shanghai, to the general secretaryship, making him the heir apparent.

A complicating factor in the current succession is that not only will the top leader be replaced, but a new generation of leaders will finally replace China's remaining revolutionary veterans. It is not merely that one fifty- or sixty-year-old will replace one octogenarian, but that all the octogenarians will soon die. This imminent generational transition has apparently increased the older leaders' distrust of their potential successors and has made them even less willing to relinquish power completely. This lack of trust is perceived by everyone in the political system, further weakening the already limited authority of the younger leaders. Moreover, the revolutionary generation's failure to leave the stage may lead the "younger" generation to repeat the older generation's example by holding on to power until their own deaths; this would create a new backlog of even younger, more educated leaders who are frozen out of power as the once "young" leaders age.

CANDIDATES FOR SUCCESSION

In addition to Deng Xiaoping and Chen Yun, probably the two most powerful leaders in China, the other elder leaders include Yang Shangkun, who is president of the People's Republic; Vice President Wang Zhen; Deng Yingchao, Zhou Enlai's widow; and hard-line revolutionary veterans Li Xiannian, Peng Zhen, and Bo Yibo, all of whom are in their eighties. Yang Shangkun and Wang Zhen appear to be in relatively good health, but the mental acuity and physical strength of the others are questionable. Chen Yun, Yang Shangkun, and Wang Zhen are often seen as conservative, though this varies from issue to issue.

Obvious contenders for the succession are the members of the Chinese Communist party Politburo standing committee, officially the highest institution in the party. This group comprises General Secretary Jiang Zemin, Prime Minister Li Peng, law and security expert Qiao Shi, propaganda chief Li Ruihuan, party organization head Song Ping, and economic overseer Yao Yilin (who is thought to be in poor health).

Other possible candidates for the succession include Yang Baibing, Yang Shangkun's younger half-brother and secretary general of the party's central military commission; Zhu Rongji, formerly mayor of Shanghai, who was recently appointed deputy prime minister of the State Council; Ye Xuanping, the son of Ye Jianying (one of China's most famous military leaders) and former leader of Guangdong province; and Zou Jiahua, chairman of the State Planning Commission, newly appointed deputy prime minister, and Ye Xuanping's brother-in-law. Several seventy-year-old leaders may also play a role, including ideologues Hu Qiaomu and Deng Liqun, and Zhao Ziyang, who may retain some following in the party.

Each of the elder leaders supports a coterie of younger leaders. Deng has lent his patronage to Jiang Zemin, Li Ruihuan, and Zhu Rongji on occasion. Chen Yun tends to support Li Peng and, to a lesser extent, Yao Yilin and Song Ping (both Yao and Song are in their seventies and neither is seen as a long-term successor). Yang Shangkun aids Li Peng and Yang Baibing.

Of obvious importance to the succession is the order in which the party elders die. Leaders who count on Deng Xiaoping as their patron cannot expect much success if Deng is the first elder to die. Similarly, the more conservative younger leaders cannot expect much help if Chen Yun or Yang Shangkun dies first. At present a loose consensus among the elders gives Jiang Zemin and Li Peng the edge. But the death of even one of the elders may destroy this consensus, so the situation remains fluid.

In addition to clientelism, the elders managing the succession must consider factors such as "stability and unity," and the contenders' military support, "image," and political skills. The emphasis on "stability and unity" reflects the party's desire to avoid unchecked power struggles that would weaken its rule and disturb the current succession order. An overt power struggle could split the party, bring the people out into the street as in the spring of 1989, and threaten party rule. Thus there is a bias against anyone who initiates a struggle for supreme power; his career will be short if he loses the battle. This situation also gives the incumbents Jiang Zemin and Li Peng an advantage.

Military support is an obvious necessity for the successor. Which leader can call on the military and other forces of coercion to defend his position (or use force to seize power) if necessary? In this respect, Yang Baibing seems to be in the strongest position, but Jiang Zemin, Ye Xuanping, Zou Jiahua, and perhaps Qiao Shi can also rely on some military support. Zou currently heads the State Planning Commission, but before he held that position he was in charge of the defense industry, giving him important contacts with military professionals (Jiang Zemin also has experience in the military-industrial complex). All this makes Zou a dark horse candidate for the top leadership position.

The importance of image means that the best candidate is someone who was not intimately involved in the crackdown and suppression that began in June 1989. Selecting a leader without connection to the Tiananmen incident is intended to give confidence to observers abroad and to Chinese at home that reform will continue and expand; such a selection will implicitly acknowledge the leadership's errors in the crisis of 1989. This reasoning benefits Zhu Rongji, Ye Xuanping, and, to a lesser extent, Jiang Zemin.

Finally, political skills, intelligence, and other personal attributes will play an important role in the outcome of the succession struggle. It is difficult to assess the political skills of most contenders because they have lived so long in the shadow of their elders. But their instincts and political savoir faire will be of greater importance after the elders die.

THE LIMITS TO LEADERSHIP

Succession, however, is less significant today than it was five years ago because the direction of policy is so firmly established that who is in charge in China is no longer as important as it once was. Moreover, China's new leader will no longer command the authority that Chinese leaders did in the past, and he will have little leeway to execute bold new initiatives.

It is instructive to examine how the Chinese leadership has responded to domestic issues since June 4, 1989. In the Western and Hong Kong media, the leadership is portrayed as "hard-line." The leadership's rhetoric—and actions—in 1989 were harsh, casting doubt on the future of reform. But actual policy has changed much less than the rhetoric and actions would suggest, and many important economic reforms continue.*

For example, both Jiang Zemin and Li Peng criticized rural and collective industry in 1989. Yet this sector remains the fastest growing part of the Chinese economy. Hard-line leaders threatened to reinstitute central planning and reduce the influence of market forces. But even Li Peng has conceded the need to allow the market to regulate most production. Conservative leaders wanted to pursue a tight monetary policy, but credit has gradually been loosened (in a likely attempt by Li Peng to try to build support for his succession). Ad hoc price reform is under way, and capital markets are being introduced informally. The "open door" continues, with the coastal provinces still reaping most of the benefits.[3] In fact, the Chinese state currently controls only about one-third of China's gross national product (GNP), a level no higher than that of many capitalist countries of Western Europe, such as France and Italy.[4] In spite of the political climate, China's economic problems and the dynamics of economic reform have pushed economic reform forward, even if the Chinese media has not made the fact widely known.

Political reform is not proceeding, but subterranean currents may be creating the conditions for future change. The leadership at all levels is increasingly educated and technocratic; while this does not necessarily mean support for democracy and an end to one-party rule, it suggests that traditional ideology and the thought of Marx, Lenin, and Mao will be less useful to the new leaders than the ability to solve practical problems.[5]

Moreover, the central government has lost a great deal of its influence over the provinces, especially the coastal provinces. Before the Cultural Revolution (1966-1976), the Chinese state resembled the archetypal totalitarian state; it was extremely hierarchical, with the central government imposing its will on lower levels of government and on the public. The factional violence and chaos that wracked China during the Cultural Revolution left the party and the government unable to control much of the country.

Beginning in 1978, reforms were instituted without a full recentralization of authority; power was explicitly devolved to provincial and lower-level governments, enabling them to resist demands from the central government. The central government and the party now have to bargain with important provincial leaders.

*Editor's note: For a fuller discussion of the economy, see "The Economy Emerges from a Rough Patch," by Barry Naughton in *Current History*, September 1991.

Guangdong and Jiangsu provinces in particular have been so successful as a result of the economic reforms that the central government has found it difficult to obtain their compliance with central policies.

A successor therefore faces entrenched regional interests that are not inclined to sacrifice their hard-won autonomy. No matter who the successor is, he will find it even more difficult than Deng Xiaoping did to impose central authority over the provinces.

PREDICTING THE OUTCOME

Deng Xiaoping's successor will likely be someone who responds to events rather than shaping them, someone who manages the Chinese ship of state rather than steering it in bold new directions, and someone who spends most of his time bargaining with important domestic groups rather than formulating a clear-cut ideology. This profile of a future leader reflects Deng's partial success in moving away from Mao's revolutionary leadership. Deng may have institutionalized the process of economic change, but in the realm of political reform his imagination, will, and political skill have failed him.

This legacy of failed political reform will prove the most troublesome issue for the successor generation. The party continues to strive to maintain its Leninist heritage, but in doing so it has become divorced from society at large. Chinese society is growing increasingly autonomous, diverse, and assertive as a result of economic growth, urbanization, growing literacy, and higher levels of education, and the old mechanisms of party rule cannot accommodate the change. This does not mean that the Communist party is in danger of imminent collapse. Many one-party states have survived a series of crises and continued to exist for extended periods. The cleavage between a growing economy and a corrupt dominant political party is by no means unique in Asia.

Predicting the outcome of China's forthcoming succession struggle is problematic at best because of the possibility of unforeseen developments, new actors, and the appearance of heretofore unknown qualities of various Chinese politicians. But at least one scenario is highly unlikely when Deng dies: a repeat of the 1989 mass protests in Tiananmen Square.

First, the Communist party will undoubtedly dispatch large security and military forces to the square before a public announcement of Deng's death. After dramatic demonstrations in Tiananmen in 1976 opposing the Gang of Four and favoring Deng's succession, and in those in 1989 that called for Deng's and Li Peng's removal from power, the symbolic importance of Tiananmen is so great that every Chinese official has an interest in keeping the people out of the square. The leadership will attempt to resolve the succession crisis without allowing the people a voice, and in the short run it will succeed.

Second, it is not clear whom the Chinese people would favor in a succession struggle (although most urban Chinese, especially Beijing residents, dislike Li Peng). Moreover, any attempts at promoting a people's choice must be set against the events of the past two years. The regime has learned that protests must be quickly crushed, and with many of China's most famous dissidents abroad, it is unclear who would lead any anti-government activities.

The Chinese government will have to relax its vigilance at some point, and a contender for power who is in desperate straits may try to appeal to the people for support. It is unlikely that the immediate successors will be faced with another democracy movement. Nor is it likely that a leader comparable to Soviet President Mikhail Gorbachev will emerge in China, since none of the Chinese contenders for Deng's position possesses Gorbachev's political vision, energy, or youth.

But the lack of identifiable popular leaders and the state's efforts to avoid street demonstrations on the death of the octogenarians will not necessarily result in a perpetual public silence. The public will make its views known through its cooperation or lack of cooperation with the leadership's policies. Chinese intellectuals and others will press against the boundaries of state-defined orthodoxy whenever they perceive some cracks in the state's armor. The state must reach out to the key elements of the population whose support is required for economic development and modernization. The Chinese people will thus have their say in the choice of China's top leadership.

---

[1] For discussion of the suppression of the democracy movement and the aftermath, see articles by the author, "Retrogression in Chinese Politics," *Current History*, September 1989, and "China's Politics: Conservatism Prevails," *Current History*, September 1990.

[2] See Lowell Dittmer, "Bases of Power in Chinese Politics," *World Politics*, vol. 31, no. 1 (October 1978), pp. 26–60, especially pp. 48–49.

[3] On these points see Nicholas R. Lardy, "Redefining US-China Economic Relations," *NBR Analysis*, no. 5 (Seattle: National Bureau of Asian and Soviet Research, June 1991).

[4] Personal conversation with Nicholas R. Lardy, April 18, 1991.

[5] See Cheng Li, "The Rise of Technocracy: Elite Transformation and Ideological Change in Post-Mao China," doctoral dissertation in progress, Princeton University, Department of Politics.

How China's Economy Left Its Comrade Behind

The Soviets could take notes on the value of pragmatism and flexibility

Daniel Southerland

Daniel Southerland, The Post's Beijing correspondent from 1985 to 1990, is on leave. He is a fellow at the Council on Foreign Relations in New York.

The dramatic victory for Soviet democracy stands in stunning contrast to China's bloody crackdown on protesters two years ago. But China's economy, despite worldwide criticism of Beijing's repressive politics, is considered by many experts to be in far better shape than that of the increasingly democratic Soviet Union.

In the two years since the Tiananmen Square bloodshed, the Chinese have dampened inflation, expanded production and exports, swelled their foreign exchange reserves, resumed normal business ties with most nations and revitalized several stalled reforms.

Prof. Nicholas R. Lardy of the University of Washington notes that China is the only reforming socialist economy to become an increasingly significant participant in world trade. China's $10 billion trade surplus with the United States in 1990 startled many Americans. Analysts doubt that the Soviet Union will enjoy a trade surplus with any major Western nation any time soon.

This does not mean that repression is a formula for economic success. But it does make clear that economic pragmatism and flexibility are essential, whether or not a political system is becoming democratic.

When China's top leader, Den Xiaoping, launched his economic reforms in 1978–79, government-owned enterprises contributed 80 percent of China's industrial output. Though such state industries remain the backbone of the Chinese economy, their share of total industrial output has fallen to about 50 percent, according to official estimates. It is the nongovernmental sector, made up of private businesses and collective farms, that has led the country's economic growth. The output of foreign investment enterprises grew more than 50 percent in 1990.

The gap between the financial fortunes of China and the Soviet Union is no accident, most observers agree. The longstanding ability of the Chinese to wheel, to deal and to reform their economic system has given China, regardless of its besmirched name, a high growth rate and made it a better business bet for foreigners than the Soviet Union.

In reforms of agriculture, exchange controls and foreign trade, the Chinese left the Soviets behind several years ago. Most of China's progress can be attributed to the Chinese themselves. Unlike the Soviet Union's tentative reforms, which have been imposed from the top down, many of China's have been driven from the bottom up.

Their progress is hardly without problems. China's government-run industries still suffer from gross inefficiencies, overstaffing and corruption. Inflationary pressures are building again. Tens of millions of Chinese farmers are unemployed or underemployed. Many Chinese workers labor in unsafe and heavily polluted factories.

Hong Kong trade unions have documented the tragic case of a fire that broke out in May of this year in a poorly equipped factory lacking fire exits and using migrant workers to produce raincoats for export in the southern Chinese province of Guangdong. Workers had been locked in dormitories near flammable materials and could not escape the fire. More than 80 died and about 40 were seriously injured. The Hong Kong-based owner was not made to shoulder any responsibility and those injured were given no clear pledges of compensation.

But compared to the Soviet Union, observers see the Chinese economy as a triumph in many ways. Since the late 1970s, the Chinese have been implementing reforms with which the Soviets are only beginning to experiment: contracting land, allowing free markets, permitting limited private enterprise and opening the economy to joint ventures with foreign capitalists.

Beijing's economy also has had the special advantages of geography and the overseas Chinese. Chinese

From *The Washington Post National Weekly Edition*, September 2-8, 1991. Copyright © 1991, The Washington Post. Reprinted by permission.

investors and traders from prospering nearby Asian nations have brought capital and new ideas to the China mainland. The Chinese of Singapore and Taiwan and the South Koreans have set examples for the Chinese leadership of how authoritarian regimes can prosper economically. China is negotiating a trade agreement with South Korea even though the two nations lack diplomatic relations.

Chinese living overseas, particularly those in Hong Kong but also an increasing number in Taiwan, have taken advantage of China's cheap labor to start thousands of new factories along the Chinese coast, turning out highly competitive products for the export trade. Hong Kong capital has been critical to the development of Guangdong province, which leads China in exports.

China's rising trade surplus with the United States has been ascribed by U.S. officials to unfair trade practices, such as foreign exchange controls and import quotas. But it also results from the shift to mainland China of small industries from Hong Kong and Taiwan producing exports such as shoes and cosmetics. South Korea has now shifted some of its low-value factories to China.

Paradoxically, the Soviet Union, which has developed a more open political system in recent years, has as yet been unable to produce an entrepreneurial class to match China's. There, despite hard-line political leaders, the entrepreneurs have taken the lead in economic growth.

In China, the chaos and ideological fanaticism of the Cultural Revolution of 1966–76 made many Chinese distrust ideology and inclined them to pursue their own self-interest in a practical way. Those "lost" years of the Cultural Revolution were not entirely wasted. They succeeded in reducing bureaucratic resistance and clearing the way for reform and the rise of the entrepreneurs.

Economic statistics for the decade of the Cultural Revolution, when radicals and Red Guards held sway, show that the period nearly wrecked the Chinese economy. So Deng Xiaoping's program to invigorate the economy gained widespread support from the start, particularly in the rural areas.

Then there is the Japan factor. Japan has been reluctant to undertake large-scale investment or loans in the Soviet Union. But Japan still carries a burden of guilt toward China as a result of atrocities committed in China in the 1930s and 1940s. Japan not only wants a stable Chinese neighbor but also covets China's business potential, and, given its record in World War II, is hardly in a position to lecture the Chinese on human rights issues.

Japan's Prime Minister Toshiki Kaifu visited China in August and began releasing more of the $6 billion in Japanese credits promised to China before the Tiananmen crackdown. It was the first top-level visit since Tiananmen by a representative of one of the leading industrialized nations. Britain's Prime Minister John Major and Italy's Prime Minister Giulio Andreotti are to follow Kaifu's path to Beijing.

But the roots of China's progress can be attributed not to foreign assistance but to experimental reforms brought about by the Chinese people. The first in the countryside came more than a decade ago when farmers in Anhui province took matters into their own hands and began experimenting with decontrolled, free-market sales of crops.

Deng Xiaoping and his reformist colleagues saw the results and began breaking up farm communes and loosening central controls. They gave farmers a chance to make their own decisions when it came to opening rural enterprises and determining what crops to grow.

In late 1989 and early 1990, when hard-liners in the central government began cutting loans to rural entrepreneurs, there was a rebellion among the provincial authorities whose governments benefited from the growth of the rural entrepreneurs' private and collective enterprises. They resisted, or avoided, orders coming down from Beijing. In the end, the central planners in Beijing realized that they were creating a growing unemployment problem by squeezing the entrepreneurs. They had to back off.

As Crosby Securities Ltd. pointed out in a report in June, the small stock markets that grew up in the Chinese cities of Shanghai and Shenzhen were the product of local reforms, which have only since been endorsed by the central authorities. There is nothing remotely comparable in the Soviet Union.

Whether or not Deng Xiaoping realizes it, his reforms have unleashed forces that are difficult to control and have momentum of their own. The Chinese, moreover, have a pragmatic ability to call an enterprise "socialist," while quietly transforming it into something else.

There are areas where the more highly industrialized Soviet Union is economically superior to China, such as the development of hydroelectric power.

But China has surged ahead of the Soviets in modifying a Stalinist economic structure, decentralizing economic power and allowing individual economic activities free of state control.

Deng Xiaoping's greatest success may have been in China's countryside, where seven out of 10 Chinese live and the results of economic reform were most dramatic.

At first, he concentrated on agriculture, but in the post-Mao Zedong decade of reconstruction, he aimed more broadly at transforming the entire inefficient, centralized, state-controlled economy into one that reacted to market demands and used capitalist-style management techniques, while retaining some of its socialist characteristics.

In the late 1970s and early 1980s, the results were dramatic. But by the mid-1980s, inflation, inequality and corruption in the Communist Party took a toll on the party's prestige and authority. Success was easier to achieve in rural China than in cities, where bureaucrats, party cadres and factory workers resisted change.

China's economy remains only half reformed. A. Doak Barnett of the Johns Hopkins School of Advanced International Studies in Washington said in congressional testimony in June that the biggest challenges in the reform process are still ahead.

Barnett mentioned the need for comprehensive price reform, monetary and fiscal reform, and basic reform in large state industrial enterprises. He believes that China "will move to attack these problems, under post-Deng leaders if not before."

The Tiananmen crisis complicated matters for China's economic reformers. The reformist party chief Zhao Ziyang was ousted, and conservative ideologues tried to recentralize and reduce the growth of government-owned enterprises. But they were not able to produce a workable economic plan of their own. This is partly because the popular consensus favoring change in China remains strong.

Despite shifting attitudes toward entrepreneurs in China's leadership, the Chinese, since the early 1980s, have allowed markets to develop outside the state-controlled system where entrepreneurs can purchase raw materials and machinery for their new enterprises at prices set by supply and demand.

The contrast between the Soviet and Chinese systems is evident on the Sino-Soviet border, where trade has grown rapidly with the decrease in tensions between the two countries. The main constraint on such trade appears to be the rigidity of the Soviet system, where barter is the main form of trade and everything has to be laboriously planned by the Soviet side. The Chinese side enjoys greater flexibility.

When this writer paid a 1989 visit to Heihe, a border town on the Chinese side of the Heilong River, a Soviet trader admitted that he and his colleagues were "just going through the motions of doing business."

"It's in the Chinese blood to do business," said another Soviet trader. "They've got the businessman's mentality. . . . Seventy years of socialism have wiped that out in the Soviet Union."

"After the 1989 elections, Indian politics came to be seen as following what might be called, rather loosely, an Italian model or, less benignly, an Indian version of the French Fourth Republic—a situation in which no single party commands a parliamentary majority and, punctuated by periodic crises, governments are formed in a pattern of shifting coalitions."

After the Dynasty:

Politics in India

Robert L. Hardgrave, Jr.

Robert L. Hardgrave, Jr., *is the Temple Professor of Humanities in Government and Asian Studies at the University of Texas at Austin. He is, with Stanley A. Kochanek, the coauthor of* India: Government and Politics in a New Nation, *5th ed. (Fort Worth, Tex.: Harcourt Brace Jovanovich, forthcoming).*

The assassination of Rajiv Gandhi in May 1991 brought an end to the dynasty that had dominated the politics of "the world's largest democracy" for nearly half a century.* Rajiv Gandhi, at the age of 40, had succeeded his mother, Indira, as prime minister after she was assassinated in October 1984 by two Sikh bodyguards. Indira Gandhi's murder was in retaliation for the Indian army's storming of a Sikh shrine, the Golden Temple at Amritsar, in an attempt to remove Sikh terrorists who had made the site their headquarters.

Less than two months after assuming office, Gandhi's leadership was confirmed in December 1984 when his Congress (I) party won parliamentary elections with 49 percent of the vote—its highest percentage ever—capturing 79 percent of the seats in the Lok Sabha, the lower house of Parliament.

Gandhi had been an Indian Airlines pilot and had only reluctantly entered politics in the early 1980s after the death of his younger brother Sanjay (who had been groomed to succeed Indira). But in his first year as prime minister he demonstrated considerable political skill and vision in reaching accords in the states of Punjab and Assam, where terrorism and insurgencies posed serious challenges, and in replacing the rhetoric of socialism with a commitment to economic liberalization. In seeking to free the Congress (I) party from cor-

*With only two short breaks, Jawaharlal Nehru, his daughter Indira Gandhi, and her son Rajiv led India for all but five years since independence in 1947.

ruption, he was portrayed as "Mr. Clean." However, the accords were unfulfilled, liberalization was half-hearted, and the party's old guard reasserted itself. Revelations of kickbacks in a major Indian arms purchase from the Swedish firm Bofors implicated the prime minister's office, and the term "Bofors" came to symbolize widespread corruption. On the defensive, Gandhi withdrew deeper into his coterie and lashed out at his opponents. The Indian press attacked him as immature, indecisive, and isolated.

In his own party Gandhi faced growing factionalism and dissidence. Congress (I) was organizationally in disarray, and its base of support had begun to erode, particularly among Muslims and the "untouchables," groups that often made the critical margin of difference in Congress (I) electoral victories.** The party lost a succession of state assembly elections, bringing nearly half of India's 25 states under opposition party control. But Congress (I) remained the only all-India party, and the opposition was divided among several fractious and contending groups whose strength was regionally concentrated.

THE OPPOSITION'S UNIFICATION

The opposition had united against Indira Gandhi in 1977 to defeat Congress (I), but its government, headed by Prime Minister Morarji Desai, collapsed in 1980

**Editor's note: Increasingly, the term "scheduled caste" has replaced "untouchable" in referring to the 400 castes that were placed on a list, or "schedule," by the government beginning in 1935 to receive special benefits because of their historical deprivation, including the reservation of legislative seats, government posts, and places in educational institutions (a program similar to affirmative action in the United States). See Eleanor Zelliott, "Dalit: New Perspectives on India's Untouchables," in Philip Oldenburg, ed., *India Briefing, 1991* (Boulder, Col.: Westview Press, 1991).

Reprinted with permission from *Current History* magazine, March 1992, pp. 106-112. Copyright © 1992 by Current History, Inc.

because of petty feuds and personal rivalries. Subsequent attempts to forge a united opposition involved a series of mergers and splits, but efforts to unite were continually frustrated by the mutual hostility of the Hindu nationalist Bharatiya Janata party (BJP) on the right and the two Communist parties and their allies on the left, and by ambitious personalities in centrist parties who were unwilling to yield leadership to any rival. But in 1988, V. P. Singh emerged as the catalyst of opposition unity.

Singh, a former Congress (I) chief minister of Uttar Pradesh, had served under Rajiv Gandhi as the minister of finance and later as minister of defense. There his efforts to ferret out evidence of kickbacks for foreign defense contracts (including the Bofors scandal) led to his dismissal from the Cabinet and, soon after, expulsion from Congress (I). Joined by others who had been expelled for "anti-party" activity (including Arun Nehru, Gandhi's cousin and once his closest adviser), Singh formed the People's Front to challenge Gandhi's leadership. Attracting large crowds wherever he went, Singh gained national visibility and was projected to become the next prime minister if the opposition could unite behind him.

With elections to be held no later than December 1989, seven opposition parties—four centrist national parties and three regional parties—met in July 1988 to hammer out a coordinated strategy. In an atmosphere of confusion and interparty conflict, the four national parties—the Janata party, the Lok Dal, the Congress-Socialist (S) party, and Jan Morcha—merged to form the new Janata Dal under Singh's leadership. The regional parties—the Telegu Desam in Andhra Pradesh, the Dravida Munnetra Kazhagam (DMK) in Tamil Nadu, and the Asom Gana Parishad in Assam—kept their separate identities, but joined with the Janata Dal to form the National Front.[1]

The National Front reflected the regional strengths of its constituent parties, and support for Janata Dal, though "national" in name, was largely concentrated in north India. On its own, the National Front would be unable to secure a parliamentary majority, and a divided opposition would likely ensure, as it had so many times before, a Congress (I) majority. However, the BJP and the Left Front, although regarding each other as unacceptable allies, were prepared to enter separately into electoral adjustments with the National Front on a constituency-by-constituency basis.

This strategy was possible because the BJP's strength was mainly in the states of Madhya Pradesh, Himachal Pradesh, Rajasthan, and Gujarat, while the Left Front was largely confined to its strongholds of Kerala and West Bengal, where the Communist party of India-Marxist (CPI-M) was the ruling party. Thus when elections were called for November 1989, the National Front, the BJP, and the Left entered into negotiations in some 400 constituencies to select one opposition candidate (usually from the locally strongest party) to face the Congress (I) candidate in a straight fight.

Facing a largely united opposition, Congress (I) was at a structural disadvantage. Moreover, Rajiv Gandhi had lost the appeal he had in 1984 and was beleaguered by charges of corruption. The opposition portrayed him as pro-rich, pro-urban, and, with a Westernized life-style and a foreign-born wife (Italian-born Sonia), out of touch with the people. At the national level, the elections were fought as a referendum on Gandhi, but voters were influenced by a range of local factors and by ethnic and religious considerations.

The election results did not render a clear verdict. For the first time, no party won a majority of Lok Sabha seats. Congress (I), with 40.3 percent of the vote, emerged with the largest number, 193, but the opposition parties arrayed against Gandhi commanded enough seats to form a government. On December 2, 1989, V. P. Singh was sworn in as prime minister, heading a minority coalition government of the four parties that had contested the elections as the National Front alliance: Janata Dal, which had 141 seats, and the three regional parties, which won only 2 seats. Lacking a parliamentary majority, the National Front government depended on the outside support of the 88 seats held by the BJP and the 52 seats held by the Left Front. These two groups chose not to join Singh's Cabinet to avoid the taint of direct association with each other.[2]

THE V. P. SINGH GOVERNMENT

Janata Dal, the principal constituent of the National Front coalition, was heir to the Congress culture, and all its leaders had been at one time or another in the Congress party. Its ideological embrace included market capitalists, Gandhians, and unreconstructed socialists, but its essential thrust, like that of the Congress party, was centrist and pragmatic, and this was the orientation of the new prime minister. Even before taking office, Singh was under siege from within his own party, and during the 11 months of his tenure his government was immobilized as he struggled for political survival.

Singh's Janata Dal was a party of clashing personalities that included Chandra Shekhar, a self-styled socialist who had sought the prime ministership for himself; a bitterly disappointed claimant, he was excluded even from the Cabinet. Another contender for power, Devi Lal, the leader of the peasant "backward castes"[†] and political boss of Haryana state, struck a last-minute deal with Singh and became deputy prime minister and minister of agriculture. But in mid-March, less than four months after the government had been formed, Devi Lal precipitated a crisis in response to opponents' attacks against him and his son, Om Prakash Chautala, the chief

[†]*Editor's note*: "Backward classes" refers to historically disadvantaged groups, such as the scheduled castes, scheduled tribes, and other non-scheduled castes.

minister of Haryana, for violence and vote fraud in the Haryana assembly elections. The confrontation and events that followed, culminating in July with Singh's removal of Devi Lal from the Cabinet, were farcical, but they underscored the fragility of the government and of Janata Dal itself.

Devi Lal now joined with Chandra Shekhar to bring down the government. Both had factional support among Janata Dal members of Parliament, but the 1985 anti-defection law helped secure the party against the splits that were once the bane of Indian legislative politics.[3] Moreover, at this point Singh was the only leader who could hold the National Front together and keep its outside support. But as head of a minority government, the prime minister was vulnerable. Both the Bharatiya Janata party and the Left Front had given him a vote of confidence in Parliament, but if either group were to withdraw its support, the government would likely fall.

SEPARATISM IN PUNJAB, ASSAM, AND KASHMIR

With his government in place, Singh turned to the regional demands for autonomy. These demands were not new—as a multiethnic country with distinct regional identities, India has long faced demands for increased regional autonomy. But the centralization of authority under Indira Gandhi had sharpened them. Nowhere was this more dramatic than in Punjab, Assam, and Kashmir, where separatist movements have posed major challenges to India's unity.

In Punjab, the Sikh Akali Dal movement for greater state autonomy and for protection of the Sikh religion was eclipsed by Sikh militants, who had turned to terrorism in a struggle for an independent nation of Khalistan. In one of his first acts as prime minister, Singh reached out to Sikh moderates by visiting the Golden Temple and by establishing special courts to try those involved in the anti-Sikh riots after Indira Gandhi's assassination. But the government's early initiative was soon replaced by indecision and drift, and efforts to find a political solution in Punjab were frustrated by divisions among Sikh leaders and continued violence.

Assam, in India's northeast, faced heightened violence because of demands by tribal groups for special protection through the creation of an autonomous region within the state. But the more serious challenge to the government was posed by the United Liberation Front of Assam (ULFA). This group, with a vaguely Maoist ideology, launched an insurgency for Assam's secession from the Indian union.

Singh faced his most pressing problem in Kashmir, India's only state with a Muslim majority. The Jammu and Kashmir Liberation Front and an assortment of separatist and fundamentalist groups initiated a wave of strikes, bombings, and assassinations in 1988, and the state government lost effective control to the separatists. When the National Front took power, turmoil in Kashmir increased, and the central government dismissed the

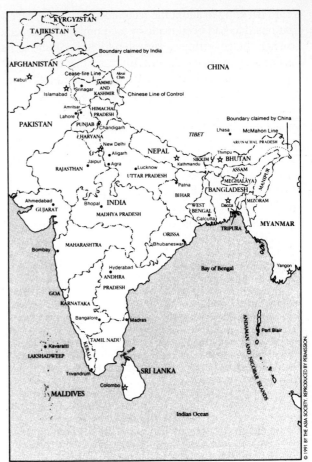

I N D I A

state government and imposed direct rule, only to face widespread resistance and a mounting death toll.

But Kashmir was more than a domestic problem: Indian charges that Pakistan was arming and training the insurgents brought the two countries to the brink of war. The government's approach was schizophrenic, reflecting divisions in Janata Dal and its external support. Elements of the government, backed by the Left Front, favored negotiation with the Kashmiri separatists for a political solution; hard-liners, buttressed by the BJP, pushed for a military solution.

THE RESERVATION ISSUE

In supporting the National Front government, the BJP assumed the role of watchdog in what party leader L. K. Advani called a "process of consultation." But Advani was not consulted when Prime Minister Singh decided in August 1990 to reserve 27 percent of all central government jobs for backward castes in addition to the 22.5 percent already reserved for scheduled castes and tribes. The announcement brought widespread press criticism and strong opposition from members of higher castes, especially students. In New Delhi and other urban areas in north India, violent protests, acts of self-immolation, and police shootings raised the specter of a "caste war" and deepened social conflict.

In deciding to adopt the recommendations for reservations that had been made by a commission a decade earlier, the government appealed directly to one of its major constituencies, the peasant castes that make up 52 percent of the Indian population. The National Front platform had supported the reservations as a commitment to equity and social justice, but the timing and haste with which Singh made the decision—immediately after the expulsion of Devi Lal from the Cabinet—suggested that the prime minister sought to undercut his Janata Dal rival's base of support among the backward castes. The Left Front and the BJP expressed displeasure at not having been consulted and indicated, each for its own reasons, that education and income, rather than caste, should be the criteria for job reservation.

THE AYODHYA AFFAIR

The BJP also believed that the reservation issue divided the Hindu community. To galvanize Hindu sentiment behind it, party president Advani launched a *rath yatra* (chariot rally), a 10,000-kilometer journey in a van fashioned to look like a mythological chariot across the heartland of north India to Ayodhya in Uttar Pradesh. It was here at the supposed birthplace of Lord Rama that construction of a new temple was to begin.

The site had long been disputed between Hindus and Muslims; in the sixteenth century the Mughal emperor Babur built a mosque on the site where Hindus claim a temple stood marking the birthplace of Rama. In 1989, before the elections, efforts by the Vishwa Hindu Parishad and other Hindu revivalist groups to demolish the mosque at Ayodhya and "to recapture injured Hindu pride" through the construction of a new temple precipitated perhaps the most serious Hindu-Muslim rioting since the partition of India in 1947.

The BJP supported the temple movement; Janata Dal, courting Muslim support, sought a mediated settlement. In the wake of violence and as the 1989 elections approached, the Vishwa Hindu Parishad—probably at the behest of the BJP—canceled a march in Ayodhya, but then set October 30, 1990, as the day to begin construction. As that date neared, tens of thousands of Hindu militants, led by Advani, converged on Ayodhya.

The prime minister warned that an interim order by the Indian high court to secure the status quo at the disputed site would be enforced and that the mosque at Ayodhya would be protected "at all costs." On October 23, as they were about to enter Uttar Pradesh in the drive to Ayodhya, Advani and other BJP leaders were arrested, and the party withdrew its parliamentary support from the national government. At the same time, the arrests and clashes in Ayodhya between paramilitary forces and Hindus intent on destroying the mosque sparked a wave of Hindu-Muslim violence that left more than 300 people dead. Hindu militants withdrew from Ayodhya with the promise to return.

In Parliament, as the vote of no confidence approached, Chandra Shekhar engineered a split in Janata Dal, denying Singh support from a substantial portion of his own party. With only the backing of the Left Front and what was left of the National Front, Singh lost the vote, 142 to 346, and submitted his resignation.

THE CHANDRA SHEKHAR GOVERNMENT

President R. Venkataraman, in accordance with parliamentary custom, invited Rajiv Gandhi, as the leader of the largest party in the lower house, to form a government. As expected Gandhi declined, preferring to build his party's strength for an election at a time of his own choosing, and gave his support to Chandra Shekhar. With a majority in Parliament behind him, Chandra Shekhar was sworn in as prime minister on November 10, and six days later won his vote of confidence, 280 to 214 (with 11 abstentions and 17 absentees). Devi Lal became deputy prime minister, the position he had held in the National Front government.

Chandra Shekhar, a firebrand socialist from Uttar Pradesh, had been one of the founders of the Janata party and later became its president. He only grudgingly yielded leadership of the new Janata Dal to Singh. After losing his December 1989 bid to head the National Front government, he began efforts to undermine Singh. In this he was allegedly financed by firms that Singh had investigated for tax fraud while he was finance minister under Rajiv Gandhi. Chandra Shekhar, an ardent opponent of multinational corporations and foreign investment, also cultivated the support of business interests seeking to secure their protected markets and sheltered inefficiencies.

A strident critic of Gandhi's economic liberalization (of which Singh, as finance minister, had been a chief architect), Chandra Shekhar found himself as prime minister dependent on Gandhi and Congress (I) for survival. That he was on a short tether and exercised power at Gandhi's sufferance was underscored by the statement of a Congress (I) spokesman: "I do not expect any problems to arise because we do not expect Mr. Chandra Shekhar to do anything that is inconsistent with Congress ideology and policies."

There were problems from the very beginning, first over the formation of the Cabinet (which took 11 days) and Chandra Shekhar's inclusion of people, such as Rajiv Gandhi's estranged sister-in-law Maneka Gandhi, who were anathema to Congress (I). With Congress (I) unwilling to participate in the government, Chandra Shekhar had a limited array of prospective ministers to draw on. His lackluster Cabinet was soon diminished by a ruling of the speaker in the Lok Sabha that eight Janata Dal (Socialist) members of Parliament, including five who were members of the Cabinet, had violated the terms of the antidefection law and thus forfeited their membership in Parliament. This reduced the number of Janata Dal (Socialist) seats to 54.

On Ayodhya, Chandra Shekhar called for a "healing

touch and cooling down of tempers," and tried to bring the Hindu and Muslim adversaries together to negotiate. He called for direct talks with Muslim separatists in Jammu and Kashmir, and took the initiative in opening talks with Sikh militants in Punjab—drawing fire from Gandhi for his action. Chandra Shekhar permitted United States planes to refuel in India as they flew from bases in the Philippines to Saudi Arabia during the Persian Gulf war in early 1991. But after Gandhi (courting Muslim voters sympathetic to Iraq) denounced the decision as a violation of India's nonalignment and threatened to withdraw Congress (I) support, Chandra Shekhar rescinded the permission.

Chandra Shekhar's attempts to define his own policies were fundamentally constrained by his dependence on Congress (I). On economic policy, abandoning his earlier position in clear deference to Congress (I) policies, Chandra Shekhar said that he would "welcome" liberalization and foreign investment, and he accepted the terms set by the International Monetary Fund (IMF) for a major loan. Under pressure from Congress (I), Chandra Shekhar moved against National Front regional parties in Assam and Tamil Nadu, dismissing their governments and imposing direct rule.

The situation in Assam had clearly deteriorated, and the state government was unable to cope with the heightened violence and insurgency. In Tamil Nadu, across the Palk Strait from Sri Lanka, direct rule was imposed allegedly because the ruling Dravida Munnetra Kazhagam government had permitted Sri Lankan Tamil guerrillas to operate with impunity, contributing to a breakdown of law and order in the state. That the DMK government had ties to the guerrillas was clear, but the state experienced far less disorder than north Indian states such as Bihar and Uttar Pradesh. The opposition called a nationwide strike to protest what they said was an unconstitutional and politically motivated act.

Chandra Shekhar and Gandhi deeply distrusted each other, since they both knew it was only a matter of time before Gandhi would withdraw support, forcing elections that he believed would return Congress (I) to power. Chandra Shekhar was not prepared to relinquish power so easily. Even before taking office, he had established contact with Congress (I) dissidents and was believed to be engineering a revolt against Gandhi that would enable him to merge his party with Congress (I) and to assume leadership of a new Congress party. For his part, Gandhi was in contact with dissidents in both Janata Dal (Socialist) and Janata Dal, and it was rumored in February 1991 that Gandhi had met with Venkataraman to discuss the possibility of forming, without new elections, a Congress (I)-led coalition government.

On March 5, 1991, Congress (I) members of Parliament walked out to protest the surveillance of Gandhi by plainclothes police officers from the Haryana state government (which was under the control of Deputy Prime Minister Devi Lal). Their assignment, denounced by Congress (I) as "political espionage," was to note which Janata Dal (Socialist) members of Parliament Gandhi was seeing. The next day, Chandra Shekhar, informing Parliament that he was no longer able to function as prime minister, resigned and asked the president to call elections. Venkataraman in turn asked Chandra Shekhar to continue as head of a caretaker government until elections could be held.

THE 1991 ELECTIONS

Three rounds of parliamentary elections were scheduled for May, with simultaneous elections in five states (Haryana, Uttar Pradesh, Bihar, West Bengal, and Kerala) and one union territory (Pondicherry). The troubled states of Assam and Punjab were to conduct polling separately in June for both Parliament and state assemblies. Jammu and Kashmir, paralyzed by insurgency, would not hold elections. Facing an electorate of 521 million voters, more than 9,000 candidates filed for 537 seats in the Lok Sabha and 20,000 for the 1,456 assembly seats up for election.

The pattern of electoral confrontation varied from state to state, but overall, with Chandra Shekhar's Samajvadi Janata party—the new name of the Janata Dal (Socialist)—having only limited support, the contest for power was essentially triangular—Janata Dal and its regional and Left allies (forming the National Front); the BJP; and Congress (I). The National Front under V. P. Singh emphasized social justice, with Janata Dal's particular appeal directed to the backward castes (the intended beneficiaries of the job reservations program) and Muslims (for whom Singh's "secular" stand on Ayodhya had special appeal). The BJP, with the symbol of Ayodhya, appealed to Hindu sentiment and challenged what it portrayed as the "privileges" accorded Muslims and other minorities under India's secular state. Congress (I), led by Gandhi, promised political stability and offered itself as the only party that could provide a workable government.

No party was expected to secure a clear majority, but public opinion polls pointed to Congress (I) as likely to win the largest number of seats and thus give Gandhi the chance of forming a coalition government. But on May 21, having taken his campaign to Tamil Nadu after the first round of voting, Gandhi, along with 17 bystanders, was killed in a powerful explosion. Forensic experts determined that the assassin was a woman who had detonated a bomb strapped to her body when she bent forward to touch Gandhi's feet in a traditional act of homage. Further clues identified her as part of a conspiracy by Sri Lankan Tamil guerrillas to assassinate Gandhi, probably in retaliation for his role in sending Indian troops to Sri Lanka in 1987 to try to end a guerrilla war there and in pushing for a crackdown on Tamil guerrilla operations from Tamil Nadu.

The government feared widespread violence after the assassination and postponed the second and third rounds of voting until June 12 and 15. Hoping to attract a sympathy vote and papering over deep divisions in the party, the

Congress (I) high command invited Sonia Gandhi to succeed her slain husband as party president. When she declined, the party turned to P. V. Narasimha Rao, a former foreign minister who at 69, in poor health, and without a political base, was perceived to be without ambition and thus an acceptable compromise.

With the non-Congress parties divided, Congress (I) was able to translate 38 percent of the vote into 225 parliamentary seats, an increase from its 196 seats in 1989 but still short of a majority in the Lok Sabha.[4] The results reflected what analysts saw as a sympathy vote in the second and third rounds, with an increase both in voter turnout and in support for Congress (I) accounting perhaps for as many as 30 to 40 seats. The shift was most notable in rural areas and among women and Muslims. As in 1989, the party's greatest strength was in the south, but while it picked up seats in the north, Congress (I) was virtually wiped out in Uttar Pradesh and Bihar. In state assembly elections, it won in Haryana, Kerala, and Assam, and its All-India Anna Dravida Munnetra Kazhagam ally took power in Tamil Nadu.

The BJP raised its strength in Parliament from 88 to 117 seats, and increased its share of the vote from 11 percent in 1989 to 20 percent. The party's gains were dramatic in Gujarat and Uttar Pradesh. In the latter, with support from upper-caste Hindus and the backward castes, the party rode the Ayodhya issue to power in assembly elections, forming the first BJP government in India's most populous state. But in a seeming judgment on poor government in the three states where the BJP had taken power in the 1990 assembly elections—Madhya Pradesh, Rajasthan, and Himachal Pradesh—the party lost parliamentary seats.

The National Front fared poorly, with Janata Dal reduced from 141 to 56 seats in Parliament and garnering only 11.6 percent of the vote, as compared with 17.6 percent of the vote in 1989. Janata Dal strength was concentrated in Bihar, where the Janata Dal chief minister, a backward-class leader, turned out the vote by appealing to the reservations proposal. The Left Front held its own, increasing from 44 to 48 seats, with about 9 percent of the vote. The CPI-M held its majority in the West Bengal assembly, but lost Kerala to Congress (I). Chandra Shekhar's Samajvadi Janata party won only 5 seats in Parliament.

As the results came in, Sharad Pawar, the powerful Congress (I) chief minister of Maharashtra, made a bid for the party leadership, but contending factions within the party, each unwilling to yield to the other, again compromised on Rao.[5] On June 21, Rao was sworn in as prime minister and given four weeks to prove in a vote of confidence that Congress (I) could command the parliamentary support necessary to govern as a minority government. Rao's Cabinet accommodated the party's various factions and included the three strongest contenders for party leadership.

The vote of confidence came on July 15. No party was prepared to face new elections, and none wanted to assume responsibility for bringing down the government. Congress (I) and its allies cast 241 votes in favor of the motion; the BJP, with 111 members present, voted against; and 112 of the National Front and Left Front members of Parliament abstained. Each of the opposition parties indicated its willingness to support the government selectively, "issue to issue," and Rao, reaching out to the BJP for support on one set of issues and to the National Front and Left Front on another, began a balancing act as he tackled issues that divided the parties: economic policy, job reservations, Ayodhya, and regional separatism.

RAO IN POWER

The new government's first actions were to correct India's pressing economic problems and the most serious balance of payments crisis since independence. Seeking loans from the IMF and adopting what Indian economists had increasingly prescribed, the government devalued the rupee and moved to reduce the budget deficit, cut subsidies, and liberalize the economy through a reduction of licensing requirements and allowing more foreign investment. The reforms, set out by Finance Minister Manmohan Singh, represented a dramatic reversal of the autarkic policies of "the license-permit raj" that were the hallmarks of India's commitment to socialism.

Deregulation has been generally welcomed, as has the opening to foreign investment, albeit more cautiously. The policy reforms—at this point still limited—have the tacit support of the BJP and a portion of the Janata Dal. In opposition are some protected industries; elements of the bureaucracy for whom licensing has been a source of power and personal profit; and the left, for whom socialism is both a matter of faith and the platform from which it appeals to the poor and dispossessed. Government spokesmen have declared the reforms "irreversible," and indeed, economic compulsions—together with the IMF—may give Rao's government little choice.

The budget has been more troublesome. Austerity measures to cut subsidies and reduce deficits immediately drew fire from within the Congress (I) party, for which populist programs had so long provided political succor. The proposed reduction in fertilizer subsidies touched an especially sensitive area. In response to direct protests by farmers, and to pressure from Congress (I) politicians who feared loss of support in their rural constituencies, the government backed down. The subsidy issue underscores the constraints under which Rao's government acts, and rising prices and potentially heightened urban discontent are likely to limit further the government's ability to control budget deficits.

Rao has had more success with his announcement that the government would implement the reservations program for backward castes, with preference for the poorer segments of the population, and an additional 10 percent of all central government jobs reserved for the disadvantaged in higher castes. The police were alerted for renewed demonstrations, but the announcement was greeted with a comparatively mild reaction from those who had earlier protested. With 52 percent of the Indian population designated as "backward," no political party was prepared to speak out in opposition, and Janata Dal was robbed of the issue that had become its virtual reason for existence.

Ayodhya was another matter. The Congress (I) government made common cause with three other parties against the BJP to secure passage of an act freezing the status of all religious shrines at the time of independence—except for the disputed Ayodhya site, whose case was before the court for adjudication. The BJP was committed to the construction of the Rama temple on the site where the mosque stands, and it was this issue that was its vehicle to power in Uttar Pradesh.

But in its control of the state government, the BJP faced a serious dilemma. It was under mounting pressure from the Vishwa Hindu Parishad to demolish and relocate the mosque, but to do so would bring it into confrontation with the central government and result, almost assuredly, in the dismissal of the BJP government for defiance of the court order protecting the mosque. Moreover, with aspirations for power at the national level, the party wanted to broaden its support, and it feared popular reaction against renewed turmoil over Ayodhya at a time when most Indians seemed to want nothing more than stability.

Unrest had surely not eased in Punjab, Kashmir, and Assam, and the government responded with continued force against terrorism and insurrection. In Assam, the new Congress (I) state government renewed efforts against the guerrilla ULFA. By December 1991 the guerrilla group had called a cease-fire, and on January 15, 1992, after a secret meeting in New Delhi with Rao, the guerrillas agreed to end attempts to set up an independent state and Rao ordered the Indian army to suspend its campaign against the guerrillas.

In Kashmir, with no prospect for political dialogue, the military engaged Kashmiri separatists as New Delhi, warning of dire consequences, denounced Pakistan for supporting them. In Punjab the situation deteriorated further, with more than 5,000 people killed in 1991 by either Sikh terrorists or government forces. Parliamentary and state assembly elections had been scheduled for June 22, but one day before the polling, the election commissioner—thought to be pressured by Congress (I)—canceled the elections, citing the unrest, and rescheduled them for September. These too were canceled, and with elections set for February 15, 1992, the government moved nine army divisions into Punjab, augmenting police and paramilitary forces, to ensure that elections are conducted with minimal violence and intimidation.

INSTITUTIONALIZED INSTABILITY?

After the 1989 elections, Indian politics came to be seen as following what might be called, rather loosely, an Ital-

ian model or, less benignly, an Indian version of the French Fourth Republic—a situation in which no single party commands a parliamentary majority and, punctuated by periodic crises, governments are formed in a pattern of shifting coalitions. The 1991 elections again failed to produce a parliamentary majority, and Rao oversees a minority government that depends for its survival, issue by issue, on at least tacit support from members of the opposition.

The inherently unstable nature of such government can be institutionalized—as it is in Italy—but it can also be transformed through party realignment. The rise of the BJP serves as a powerful force to consolidate at least the "secular" parties of the center. Beyond Congress (I) itself, these centrist parties and their leaders are splinters of the Congress party, alienated by Nehru or by Indira or Rajiv Gandhi, and they could well return to the fold.

India is evolving an essentially triangular alignment of forces at the national level, with variations among the states. With the left largely limited to its regional strongholds, the battle for power under conditions of realignment will be fought between the BJP and Congress—perhaps no longer with the "I" for Indira. The dynasty gone, Congress could well reemerge as the majority party.

---

[1]Portions of the discussion of the 1989 elections and the National Front government are adapted from Robert L. Hardgrave, Jr., "South Asian Internal Politics and Policies," in Robert A. Scalapino and Gennady I. Chufrin, eds., *Asia in the 1990s: American and Soviet Perspectives* (Berkeley, Cal.: Institute of East Asian Studies, University of California, 1991), pp. 196–197.

[2]For analyses of the 1989 elections, see Atul Kohli, "From Majority to Minority Rule: Making Sense of the 'New' Indian Politics," in Marshall M. Bouton and Philip Oldenburg, eds., *India Briefing, 1990* (Boulder, Col.: Westview Press, 1990); and Walter K. Andersen, "Election 1989 in India: The Dawn of Coalition Politics?" *Asian Survey*, vol. 30, no. 6 (June 1990).

[3]Under the law, legislators lose their seats if they break from their party, but splits are permitted, allowing potential defectors to retain their seats if such a split involves at least one-third of the party's members in the legislature.

[4]For analyses of the elections, see *India Today*, July 15, 1991, pp. 10–44; and Walter K. Andersen, "India's 1991 Elections: The Uncertain Verdict," *Asian Survey*, vol. 31, no. 10 (October 1991).

[5]Rao had not contested the elections, and he was thus named prime minister contingent on his election to the Lok Sabha within six months. In by-elections held in November, Rao won a "safe" Congress (I) seat in Andhra Pradesh.

Comparative Politics: Some Major Trends, Issues, and Prospects

- **The Democratic Trend: How Strong, Thorough, and Lasting? (Articles 53–55)**
- **The Turn to the Market? What Role for the State? (Articles 56–57)**
- **Tribal Threat to Pluralism? The Political Assertion of Group Identity (Articles 58–59)**

The articles in this unit deal with three major political trends or patterns of development that can be observed in much of the contemporary world. It is important at the outset to stress that, with the possible exception of Benjamin Barber, none of the authors suggest some form of global convergence, whereby all political systems are becoming alike everywhere. On closer examination, as we shall see, even Professor Barber argues that a strong tendency toward global homogenization is offset by a tendency toward intensified group differentiation.

The articles in the first subsection cover what has also been called democratization, that is, the enormous growth in the number of representative governments in recent years. Even if this trend is reversible, as many observers stress, we need to remember how remarkable it has been in the first place. Using very different criteria and data, skeptics on both right and left for a long time have expressed doubts about whether representative government is sufficiently stable, workable, representative, attractive, or, ultimately, legitimate to survive or spread in the modern world. It would be instructive to review their more recent discussion of the 1970s and early 1980s, not in order to refute the pessimists but to learn from both their insights and their oversights.

Samuel Huntington is one of the best-known observers of democratization, who in the past emphasized the cultural, social, economic, and political difficulties of both establishing and maintaining representative forms of government. In the aftermath of the collapse of Communist regimes in Eastern and Central Europe, he has identified a broader pattern of democratization that began in the mid-1970s, replacing the former dictatorships of Southern Europe (Greece, Portugal, and Spain). It spread to most of Latin America in the following decade, and has also reached some states in Africa.

In a widely adopted phrase, Huntington identifies this as the "third wave" of democratization in modern history. The first "long" wave began in the 1820s and lasted about a century, until 1926, a period during which the United States and 28 other countries established governments based on a wide and finally universal suffrage. In 1922, however, Benito Mussolini's capture of power in Italy began a period of reversal, lasting until the early 1940s. During these two decades, the number of democracies fell from 29 to 12, as many became victims of dictatorial takeovers or military conquests.

A "second wave" of democratization started with the Allied victory in World War II and continued in the early postwar years of decolonization. This wave lasted until about 1962 and resulted in the conversion of about two dozen previous dictatorships into democracies or quasi-democracies, sometimes of very short duration. During a second period of reversal, lasting from 1962 to 1973, the number of democracies fell from 36 to 30 and the number of nondemocracies increased from 75 to 95 as various former colonies or fresh democracies fell under military or other authoritarian forms of rule.

At the beginning of the 1990s, Huntington counted about 60 democracies in the world, which amounts to a doubling of their number in less than two decades. It is an impressive change, but he points out that the process is likely to be reversed once again in a number of the new democracies. His discussion supports the conclusion that democracy's advance has always been a "two steps forward, one step back" kind of process. The expectations associated with the coming of democracy are in some countries so high that disappointments are bound to follow. Already, the "third wave" democratic advances in countries like the Sudan, Nigeria, Haiti, and, most recently, Peru have been followed by authoritarian reversals.

Huntington and many other political scientists have tried to identify the general conditions that inhibit or encourage the spread and stabilization of democracy. There are some specific historical factors that seem to have contributed to the "third wave," including (1) the loss of legitimacy by both right- and left-wing authoritarian regimes, as they have become discredited by failures; (2) the expansion of an urban middle class in some Third World countries, which demands representative government and constitutional rule; (3) the influence of a more liberal Catholic church, especially in Latin America where most of the "third wave" democracies are located; (4) various forms of external influence by the United States and the European Community, as they have tried to promote a human rights agenda; and (5) the snowballing or demonstration effect of a successful early transition to democracy in a country like Spain or Poland, which served as a model for other countries in similar circumstances. A crucial instance of external influence took the form of Mikhail Gorbachev's shift toward nonintervention by the Soviet Union, when he abandoned the Brezhnev Doctrine's commitment to defend established Communist rulers in Eastern Europe and elsewhere against counterrevolution.

The problems facing the new democracies are enormous. Many of them have little experience with a democratic way of life. Where there has been such an experience, it may have been spotty and not very positive. There may be important cultural obstacles to democratization, according to Huntington, who discusses the Confucian and Islamic traditions as examples. Like most other observers, Huntington also sees poverty as a principal obstacle to democratization.

Nor does democratization come without some attendant problems. One of them concerns what people decide to do with their new popular governments. As Raymond D. Gastil reminds us, there continue to be two major and distinctive possibilities. One emphasizes the rights of the group to self-determination, while the other emphasizes the rights and liberties of the individual or minority group within such a self-governing community.

Such a discussion may appear to be far too steeped in Western assumptions for the comparativist, who wishes to avoid cultural bias in studying other countries. But Gastil's argument points to a dilemma that also faces people in established democracies of North America and Western Europe. When some of the Founders and, later, Alexis de Tocqueville worried about the possibility of "majority tyranny" in the United States, they were thinking about the sometimes illiberal qualities or propensities of popular rule. There is, in any case, considerable evidence in the past and present to support Gastil's observation that people often end up using their democratic rights to self-determination in a manner that is not liberal or democratic.

Huntington's rule of thumb is that a democracy can be considered to have become stable when a country has had at least two peaceful turnovers of power. It took two decades before that point had been reached in West Germany, and we know from other evidence that it did indeed take about that long for democratic values to become internalized among the country's elites and population at large. Yet German democracy, discredited by critics in the 1920s and early 1930s as responsible for the country's enormous economic, social, and political problems, fortuitously became linked after 1949 to an amazing record of economic prosperity and social harmony.

The second subsection covers the trend toward capitalism or, better, market economics. Here Gabriel Almond explores the connections between capitalism and democracy in an article that draws upon both theory and empirical studies. His systematic discussion shows that there are ways in which capitalism and democracy support each other, and ways in which they tend to undermine each other.

A related theme is explored by Lester Thurow. He points out that the economic competition between capitalism and socialism, in its Communist form of state ownership and centralized planning, has become a largely closed chapter in history. The central question now is which form of capitalism or market economy will be more successful. His argument resembles that of such European theorists as Michel Albert, who has distinguished between the neo-American and Rhenish models of capitalism. The former, which Thurow calls the Anglo-Saxon or British-American form, is individualistic, antigovernmental, and characterized by such traits as high employee turnovers and short-term profit-maximizing. Thurow contrasts it with what he calls the communitarian model of capitalism in Japan and Germany or, using the German label, the social market economy.

The third subsection deals with the revival of the ethnic and cultural factor in politics. Few observers foresaw how this element would play such a fractious role in the contemporary world. There were forewarnings, such as the ethnonationalist stirrings in the late 1960s and early 1970s in peripheral areas of such countries as Great Britain or Spain. Many of the conflicts in the newly independent countries of the Third World are also influenced by this element. But most Western observers seem to have been poorly prepared for the task of anticipating or understanding the resurgence of politicized religious, ethnic, or other cultural forces. Many others were taken by surprise as well.

The last two articles deal with this element in contemporary politics. Robin Wright discusses the politicization of religion in many parts of the world, using as a starting point the recent political conflict in Algeria, where a coalition of political moderates and the army moved to forestall an Islamic victory in parliamentary elections. Had the Islamic Salvation Front won overwhelmingly, as appeared certain shortly before the planned final election round, its opponents feared that it would impose a repressive fundamentalist order on the country. The article goes on to show how religious groups in Latin America, Asia, sub-Saharan Africa, and Europe have variously set out on the political road in the name of their faith. As Max Weber warned in a classic lecture shortly before his death, it can be dangerous to seek "the salvation of souls" along the path of politics. Religious conviction need not fully determine or direct a person's or group's politics. When it does, it can add an element of fervor and an unwillingness to compromise that make it difficult to live harmoniously with people who believe differently. Pluralist democracy requires an element of tolerance, which for many takes the form of a casual "live and let live" attitude, rather than a well-intentioned determination to make others conform to one's central beliefs.

Benjamin Barber brings a much broader perspective to the discussion of identity politics in the contemporary world. He sees two major tendencies that threaten democracy. One is the centripetal or homogenizing force of globalism, brought about by modern technology, communications, and commerce. Its logical end station is what he calls a "McWorld," in which human diversity, individuality, and meaningful identity are erased. The second tendency works in the opposite direction. It is the centrifugal or heterogenizing force of tribalism, which drives human beings to exacerbate their group differences, become intolerant, and engage in holy wars or "jihads" against each other.

Looking Ahead: Challenge Questions

What is meant by the "first," "second," and "third" waves of democratization? Describe the reversals that followed the first two.

Where are most of the countries affected by the "third wave" located? What factors appear to have contributed to their democratization?

Would you call Samuel Huntington optimistic, realistic, or pessimistic in his assessment of the prospects of democratization? Why?

Why does a nation's practice of the democratic right to self-determination not always bring about a liberal democratic society? Is there a possible tension between the values of liberal democracy and those of majoritarian or community democracy? Explain with reference to some new democracies.

In what ways can market capitalism and liberal democracy be said to be mutually supportive? How may they undermine each other? What solution does Gabriel Almond propose? Explain.

What is the difference between the British-American model of individualistic, laissez-faire capitalism and the more continental European model of communitarian or social capitalism?

Why is it so difficult to resolve political conflicts that arise from the political assertion of an exclusive religious or ethnic identity? Give examples from contemporary politics.

Democracy Takes Hold —Sort of

The collapse of communism in Eastern Europe is the latest boost. But while more open political systems are on the rise, it is easy to exaggerate their health.

Stanley Meisler

Times Staff Writer

UNITED NATIONS—Is democracy rising like a phoenix out of the ashes and disgrace of communism? Is democracy on a relentless roll? Some optimists often paint the world that way.

But it is a simplistic look at a complex notion. In his speech to the United Nations in mid-September, for example, President Bush extolled the Western Hemisphere as a vast sea of democracy. Fidel Castro, the President insisted, was "the lone holdout in an otherwise democratic hemisphere."

In less than a week, however, Cuba was no longer standing alone. Mutinous soldiers overthrew popularly elected President Jean-Bertrand Aristide of Haiti in a bloody and outrageous coup. Shocked by this usurpation of power, Bush pledged that the United States is "committed to the restoration of democracy" in that hapless, impoverished republic.

Yet many Latin America specialists have a far more complex view of democracy in the hemisphere than Bush. To them, Aristide's Haiti was never a democracy—although it had taken a significant democratic step with the U.N.-supervised elections that he won in December, 1990. Moreover, many academics believe that Cuba has lots more undemocratic company. Few specialists would accept Bush's contention that every state in the Western hemisphere save Cuba and Haiti is democratic.

"No, I don't agree with him," said Robert A. Dahl, professor-emeritus of political science at Yale University, one of America's foremost analysts of democratic theory. He described Bush's U.N. speech as "a very generous appraisal" of democracy in Latin America.

"There are a lot of people in the White House and the State Department," Dahl went on, "who say if you have elections without too much interference, well, that's it, that's democracy. That's not it, in my opinion. That's a pretty narrow view of democracy."

Carl Gershman, president of the National Endowment for Democracy, however, insisted that Bush's singling out of Cuba has validity "in the sense that you have had democratic movement all over the hemisphere, while Cuba remains a totalitarian state with no movement to democracy."

But Gershman acknowledged: "Clearly, there are many countries in the Western Hemisphere that you would not consider real democracies. . . . Just an election doesn't a democracy make."

It is often easy to confuse the form of democracy for its substance. In 1962, for example, this correspondent attended a session of the Western House of Assembly in Ibadan, Nigeria.

An African sergeant-at-arms in blue knee breeches and red stockings, carrying the ceremonial mace upon a pillow, strode into the chamber, bellowing out, "The Speak-uhhhh!" The Speaker, an enormous Nigerian in white wig and black robes, followed his sergeant-at-arms majestically.

A visitor could not help marveling how the pomp and tradition of Westminster had taken hold in the young, independent, former British colony of Nigeria, so far away from London and the mother of parliaments.

But, moments after the Speaker called the chamber to order, an assemblyman leaped up on his chair and cried out, as a signal: "Snake! Fire! Snake!"

Chairs cascaded across the floor as the members of the assembly chased each other in and out. One snatched the mace and tried to smash it down upon the Speaker. The fearful Speaker fled for his life while troops stormed into the building firing tear gas into every crevice.

It was a feverish turn in Nigerian history. The federal government used the riot as a pretext to declare a state of emergency. This infuriated a generation of young Nigerians and provoked coup and countercoup and finally the Nigerian Civil War, the greatest scourge in Africa since the slave trade.

More coups followed and a procession of short-lived attempts at civilian rule. The army still runs Nigeria these days, with the reigning general promising, like other dictators before him, democracy when the time is ripe.

The Nigerian experience reflects the elusive nature of democracy. Democracy is definitely on the rise throughout the world, but it is easy to exaggerate its health in the euphoria over the collapse of communism in Europe. A hard look at the worldwide status of democracy makes clear:

- Most people do not live in democratic countries. Democracy is entrenched in Western Europe and most of North America, strengthened in Latin America and incipient in Eastern Europe. But Africa and the Middle East are as inhospitable to democracy as ever. And Asia is still dominated by communism and authoritarianism.
- Many people who yearn for democracy do not understand much about it. Its difficulties and fragility are often glossed over.
- The current wave of democracy began long before the end of the Cold War and the collapse of East European communism.
- For the first time in history, democracy has no significant ideological competitors. But some rivals loom on the horizon—the most obvious, Islamic fundamentalism.
- The United States, the most powerful democracy on earth, has often failed

From *Los Angeles Times*, November 1, 1991, pp. A1, A16, A17. Copyright © 1991 by Los Angeles Times.

The Democracies

These are the countries classified "free" by Freedom House:

North America, English-speaking Caribbean

- United States
- Canada
- Barbados
- St. Kitts-Nevis
- Trinidad & Tobago
- Belize
- Dominica
- St. Lucia
- St. Vincent & Grenadines
- Grenada
- Jamaica
- Antigua & Barbuda
- Bahamas

Eastern Europe

- Czechoslovakia
- Hungary
- Poland

Asia

- Japan
- India
- South Korea
- Thailand*

Latin America

- Costa Rica
- Uruguay
- Argentina
- Chile
- Ecuador
- Venezuela
- Bolivia
- Brazil
- Dominican Republic
- Honduras

Australia, South Pacific

- Australia
- New Zealand
- Solomon Islands
- Tuvalu
- Kiribati
- Nauru
- Western Samoa
- Papua New Guinea
- Vanuatu

Africa

- Botswana
- Gambia
- Mauritius
- Namibia

Western Europe

- Austria
- Belgium
- Denmark
- Finland
- Iceland
- Ireland
- Italy
- Luxembourg
- Netherlands
- Norway
- Spain
- Sweden
- Switzerland
- France
- Germany
- Greece
- Portugal
- United Kingdom

Mediterranean, Middle East

- Greek-speaking Cyprus
- Turkish-speaking Cyprus
- Malta
- Israel

*Classified before recent coup.

Source: "Freedom in the World, 1990-91," Freedom House

Los Angeles Times

The ludicrous yet fearful coup attempt, in fact, served as a kind of inoculation for democracy in Spain. Its arrogance and madness convinced many Spaniards once and for all that no backpedaling from democracy was possible.

It is not yet clear whether the collapse of the foolish coup in the Soviet Union in August provided the same inoculation there. Democracy is still a weak reed in Eastern Europe. But there is little doubt that the popular resistance to the coup made almost everyone realize that, whether or not the Soviet people were heading to democracy, there was no going back to Communist dictatorship.

In assessing democracy, most experts look for a host of political and civil rights in addition to fair elections. Prof. Dahl, for example, says that a democracy must have fair and free elections of its top leaders; freedom of expression and the right to form all kinds of political associations; sources of news that are not monopolized by the government or powerful interests and a national electorate that includes almost everyone (and doesn't exclude blacks, as in South Africa, or women, as in the United States almost 75 years ago).

The snags of democracy and prospects for it differ from region to region throughout the world, and democracy can probably be understood best by looking at some of these differences in some detail.

to foster democracy even while trying to. In theory, the end of the Cold War should make it easier for the United States to shun dictators and embrace democracies, but there is a lot of evidence that this may not happen. Bush, after all, did not use the repercussions of the Persian Gulf War to try to encourage democratic government in Kuwait and Iraq.

Freedom House, a private organization in New York that monitors democracy throughout the world, ranked 65 of 165 countries, with 39% of the world's population, as "free" this year. In 1977, Freedom House classified only 41 countries, with 20% of the world's population, as free.

Samuel P. Huntington, professor of government at Harvard, believes that the world is now engaged in its third wave of democratization. Modern history's first wave lasted from the 1820s to the 1920s and carried democracy to almost 30 nations. After the defeat of Nazism and fascism in World War II, a second wave increased the number to 36. The third wave, which began with the Portuguese Revolution in 1974, has ballooned the number of democracies to more than 60.

But Huntington also points out that each wave of democracy in the past has been followed by a reverse whiplash that reduced the number of democracies before another wave increased them again.

Yet it is also true that the idea of democracy has a dynamic force in some areas of the world these days, infused with a power difficult to resist.

In 1981, a foolish colonel of the Spanish Civil Guard, backed by army generals with nostalgia for the fascist past, stormed into parliament and attempted a coup. Spain had been nurturing its young democracy for six years since the death of the dictator Fransisco France, and many Spaniards feared the worst.

But the coup collapsed, and now, a decade later, most Spaniards look on the attempt as a comic-opera interlude. Spaniards cannot now imagine what the colonel and the generals would have done even if they had taken over the country.

Latin America

Civilian governments predominate in Latin America today mainly because military governments have failed. The Argentine military, for example, withdrew in disgrace after the debacle of the Falklands War. The Chilean dictatorship of Gen. Augusto Pinochet submitted to plebiscite and lost.

This predominance of civilian rule, however, does not mean a predominance of democratic rule. Governments run roughshod over rights. Death squads strike with impunity. Presidents dare not offend generals. Coups are still a threat. As Abraham F. Lowenthal, professor of international relations at the University of Southern California, and Peter Hakim, staff director of the Inter-American Dialogue, put it in a recent article, "Latin American democracy today needs reinforcement, not premature celebration."

Elaborating on this later, Lowenthal said that those celebrating the supposed rush toward democracy ought to pause and take note that "the countries that have the strongest democracies now in South America had them 30 years ago." He cited Chile, Uruguay and Venezuela. Democracy, in short, was working best where it has roots, but it does not have roots in many countries of Latin America.

Nevertheless, there are healthy omens for democracy. "Fifteen years ago in Latin America," Lowenthal said, "both military guardians on the right and Leninist vanguards on the left argued the superiority of authoritarian formulas. That has really been undermined by the experience of the last 15 years."

Africa

In the last two years, 17 African despots, including President Mobutu Sese Seko of Zaire, have felt the need to legalize their opposition, but this has proven no more than a feeble step toward democracy.

The essence of the African political system was probably best described by President Daniel Arap Moi, who succeeded the late Jomo Kenyatta as the authoritarian ruler of Kenya 13 years ago. "I call on all Kenyans to sing like parrots," Moi told his countrymen in a political speech a few years ago, "During the Kenyatta time, I persistently sang the Kenyatta tune. I said I did not have any ideas of my own. Therefore, you should now sing the song I sing. This is how the country will move forward."

Almost all African countries came to independence with colonial-bequeathed democratic systems, but these did not last very long. They were probably not suitable to countries that were artificial creations with borders that paid no attention to tribal boundaries.

Before independence, African nationalists used to cry for "one man, one vote"—a slogan that demanded fair elections in which the African majorities could easily outvote the colonial settlers and bureaucrats. But, once these elections were held, producing an African government that led the country to independence, they were usually not repeated. The slogan should have been, according to one bitter joke, "one man, one vote, once."

Middle East

Either the State Department or Amnesty International or both cited almost every country in the Middle East last year for violations of human rights. In its survey of the Middle East, Freedom House ranks only Israel as free—although the Israeli-occupied territories are classified as "not free."

Some experts fear that the Islamic religion is simply incompatible with democracy. Gambia and the Turkish republic of northern Cyprus are the only Muslim entities in the world that are rated free by Freedom House.

In much of North Africa and the Middle East, the opposition to authoritarian governments comes not from democratic groups but from Islamic fundamentalists who believe that Koranic law should be the basic law of a state and that Islamic religious leaders should have the right to oversee the decisions of the government. Citing this dependence of the state upon religion, Prof. Huntington said, "Islamic concepts of politics differ from and contradict the premises of democratic politics."

But Michael Hudson, a leading Arab specialist at Georgetown University, insisted that this is an oversimplification. Pointing out that most of the Middle East emerged from colonialism only after World War II, Hudson said: "These post-independence governments tended to be wobbly affairs. But I wouldn't attribute that kind of instability to Islamic culture."

East Europe, Soviets

Democracy and multi-party politics are the new watchwords of the old Communist world of Eastern Europe and the Soviet Union. A recent poll by the Times Mirror Center for the People and the Press, for example, revealed that 60% of the Russians supported a multi-party system rather than a strong leader and that 55% believed that a democratic government was the best way to solve the country's problems. Majorities were even larger in the former Communist countries of Eastern Europe.

Yet the poll also revealed that support for some of the rudiments of democracy were fragile throughout the region and that there was deep suspicion of some of the new institutions. Most East Europeans looked on their elected parliaments as chambers of sound and fury and their political leaders as ineffectual windbags.

Asia

The collapse of communism in Europe may have evoked subversive ideas in the heads of Asian college students, but communism did not come crashing down in Asia. Although feeling isolated and defensive, North Korea, Vietnam and the world's most populous country, China, are all Communist. Asia, in fact, is now the heartland of communism.

Although Asia boasts the world's largest democracy in India, many of the non-Communist countries such as Burma and Indonesia are not democratic at all. In fact, despite the American belief that free markets and democracy go hand in hand, some Asian countries such as Singapore and Taiwan accomplished economic miracles with authoritarian regimes.

In a recent lecture, Robert A. Scalapino of the University of California, one of the leading Asian scholars in the country, argued that the enormous economic growth in several authoritarian Asian states is leading to a demand for more political freedom, a demand that has already forced more liberalization than ever before.

"An open economy and a closed polity cannot coexist for long," he said.

□

The nature of democracy is elusive and fragile and nettlesome. "Democracy is hard to do, period," said Lowenthal.

The collapse of democracy in Western Europe is now inconceivable to most of the world. Yet Greece, Portugal and Spain were dictatorships not so very long ago. And nazism and fascism ruled most of Europe only a half century ago. "We now think of Western Europe as unquestionably democratic," said Lowenthal. "But our parents, many of whom came from Europe, didn't have that experience of seeing firmly established democracies in Europe."

The caldron of recent events stirs both hope and caution in Prof. Dahl. "Democracy always competed with alternative and pretty credible belief systems: monarchy, aristocracy, Leninism, nazism, facism, Maoism," he said. "The astounding historical events that we are living in has changed this. All those competitors don't have much strength. . . .

"I don't know how long this is going to last. New competitors will begin to appear. My guess is that they will have a pseudo-democratic, populist component without the democratic institutions. But they can't any longer be elitist in character. It's impossible now for elites to say they can rule without regard to the wishes of the people."

A NEW ERA IN DEMOCRACY
DEMOCRACY'S THIRD WAVE

SAMUEL P. HUNTINGTON

Mr. Huntington is professor of government at Harvard University.

Between 1974 and 1990, at least 30 countries made transitions to democracy, just about doubling the number of democratic governments in the world. Were these democratizations part of a continuing and ever-expanding "global democratic revolution" that will reach virtually every country in the world? Or did they represent a limited expansion of democracy, involving for the most part its reintroduction into countries that had experienced it in the past?

The current era of democratic transitions constitutes the third wave of democratization in the history of the modern world. The first "long" wave of democratization began in the 1820s, with the widening of the suffrage to a large proportion of the male population in the United States, and continued for almost a century until 1926, bringing into being some 29 democracies. In 1922, however, the coming to power of Mussolini in Italy marked the beginning of a first "reverse wave" that by 1942 had reduced the number of democratic states in the world to 12. The triumph of the Allies in World War II initiated a second wave of democratization that reached its zenith in 1962 with 36 countries governed democratically, only to be followed by a second reverse wave (1960–1975) that brought the number of democracies back down to 30.

At what stage are we within the third wave? Early in a long wave, or at or near the end of a short one? And if the third wave comes to a halt, will it be followed by a significant third reverse wave eliminating many of democracy's gains in the 1970s and 1980s? Social science cannot provide reliable answers to these questions, nor can any social scientist. It may be possible, however, to identify some of the factors that will affect the future expansion or contraction of democracy in the world and to pose the questions that seem most relevant for the future of democratization.

One way to begin is to inquire whether the causes that gave rise to the third wave are likely to continue operating, to gain in strength, to weaken, or to be supplemented or replaced by new forces promoting democratization. Five major factors have contributed significantly to the occurrence and the timing of the third-wave transitions to democracy:

1. The deepening legitimacy problems of authoritarian regimes in a world where democratic values were widely accepted, the consequent dependence of these regimes on successful performance, and their inability to maintain "performance legitimacy" due to economic (and sometimes military) failure.

2. The unprecedented global economic growth of the 1960s, which raised living standards, increased education, and greatly expanded the urban middle class in many countries.

3. A striking shift in the doctrine and activities of the Catholic Church, manifested in the Second Vatican Council of 1963–65 and the transformation of national Catholic churches from defenders of the status quo to opponents of authoritarianism.

4. Changes in the policies of external actors, most notably the European Community, the United States, and the Soviet Union.

5. "Snowballing," or the demonstration effect of transitions earlier in the third wave in stimulating and providing models for subsequent efforts at democratization.

I will begin by addressing the latter three factors, returning to the first two later in this article.

Historically, there has been a strong correlation between Western Christianity and democracy. By the early 1970s, most of the Protestant countries in the world had already become democratic. The third wave of the 1970s and 1980s was overwhelmingly a Catholic wave. Beginning in Portugal and Spain, it swept through six South American and three

From *Current,* September 1991, pp. 27-39. From "Democracy's Third Wave," as it appeared in *Journal of Democracy,* Spring 1991, pp. 12-34.

Central American countries, moved on to the Philippines, doubled back to Mexico and Chile, and then burst through in the two Catholic countries of Eastern Europe, Poland and Hungary. Roughly three-quarters of the countries that transited to democracy between 1974 and 1989 were predominantly Catholic.

By 1990, however, the Catholic impetus to democratization had largely exhausted itself. Most Catholic countries had already democratized or, as in the case of Mexico, liberalized. The ability of Catholicism to promote further expansion of democracy (without expanding its own ranks) is limited to Paraguay, Cuba, and a few Francophone African countries. By 1990, sub-Saharan Africa was the only region of the world where substantial numbers of Catholics and Protestants lived under authoritarian regimes in a large number of countries.

THE ROLE OF EXTERNAL FORCES

During the third wave, the European Community (EC) played a key role in consolidating democracy in southern Europe. In Greece, Spain, and Portugal, the establishment of democracy was seen as necessary to secure the economic benefits of EC membership, while Community membership was in turn seen as a guarantee of the stability of democracy. In 1981, Greece became a full member of the Community, and five years later Spain and Portugal did as well.

In April 1987, Turkey applied for full EC membership. One incentive was the desire of Turkish leaders to reinforce modernizing and democratic tendencies in Turkey and to contain and isolate the forces in Turkey supporting Islamic fundamentalism. Within the Community, however, the prospect of Turkish membership met with little enthusiasm and even some hostility (mostly from Greece). In 1990, the liberation of Eastern Europe also raised the possibility of membership for Hungary, Czechoslovakia, and Poland. The Community thus faced two issues. First, should it give priority to broadening its membership or to "deepening" the existing Community by moving toward further economic and political union? Second, if it did decide to expand its membership, should priority go to European Free Trade Association members like Austria, Norway, and Sweden, to the East Europeans, or to Turkey? Presumably the Community can only absorb a limited number of countries in a given period of time. The answers to these questions will have significant implications for the stability of democracy in Turkey and in the East European countries.

The withdrawal of Soviet power made possible democratization in Eastern Europe. If the Soviet Union were to end or drastically curtail its support for Castro's regime, movement toward democracy might occur in Cuba. Apart from that, there seems little more the Soviet Union can do or is likely to do to promote democracy outside its borders. The key issue is what will happen within the Soviet Union itself. If Soviet control loosens, it seems likely that democracy could be reestablished in the Baltic states. Movements toward democracy also exist in other republics. Most important, of course, is Russia itself. The inauguration and consolidation of democracy in the Russian republic, if it occurs, would be the single most dramatic gain for democracy since the immediate post-World War II years. Democratic development in most of the Soviet republics, however, is greatly complicated by their ethnic heterogeneity and the unwillingness of the dominant nationality to allow equal rights to ethnic minorities. As Sir Ivor Jennings remarked years ago, "the people cannot decide until somebody decides who are the people." It may take years if not decades to resolve the latter issue in much of the Soviet Union.

During the 1970s and 1980s the United States was a major promoter of democratization. Whether the United States continues to play this role depends on its will, its capability, and its attractiveness as a model to other countries. Before the mid-1970s the promotion of democracy had not always been a high priority of American foreign policy. It could again subside in importance. The end of the Cold War and of the ideological competition with the Soviet Union could remove one rationale for propping up anti-communist dictators, but it could also reduce the incentives for any substantial American involvement in the Third World.

PROMOTION OF DEMOCRACY

American will to promote democracy may or may not be sustained. American ability to do so, on the other hand, is limited. The trade and budget deficits impose new limits on the resources that the United States can use to influence events in foreign countries. More important, the ability of the United States to promote democracy has in some measure run its course. The countries in Latin America, the Caribbean, Europe, and East Asia that were most susceptible to American influence have, with a few exceptions, already become democratic. The one major country where the United States can still exercise significant influence on behalf of democratization is Mexico. The undemocratic countries in Africa, the Middle East, and mainland Asia are less susceptible to American influence.

Apart from Central America and the Caribbean, the major area of the Third World where the United States has continued to have vitally important interests is the Persian Gulf. The Gulf War and the dispatch of 500,000 American troops to the region have stimulated demands for movement toward democracy in

Kuwait and Saudi Arabia and delegitimized Saddam Hussein's regime in Iraq. A large American military deployment in the Gulf, if sustained over time, would provide an external impetus toward liberalization if not democratization, and a large American military deployment probably could not be sustained over time unless some movement toward democracy occurred.

The U.S. contribution to democratization in the 1980s involved more than the conscious and direct exercise of American power and influence. Democratic movements around the world have been inspired by and have borrowed from the American example. What might happen, however, if the American model ceases to embody strength and success, no longer seems to be the winning model? At the end of the 1980s, many were arguing that "American decline" was the true reality. If people around the world come to see the United States as a fading power beset by political stagnation, economic inefficiency, and social chaos, its perceived failures will inevitably be seen as the failures of democracy, and the worldwide appeal of democracy will diminish.

SNOWBALLING

The impact of snowballing on democratization was clearly evident in 1990 in Bulgaria, Romania, Yugoslavia, Mongolia, Nepal, and Albania. It also affected movements toward liberalization in some Arab and African countries. In 1990, for instance, it was reported that the "upheaval in Eastern Europe" had "fueled demands for change in the Arab world" and prompted leaders in Egypt, Jordan, Tunisia, and Algeria to open up more political space for the expression of discontent.

The East European example had its principal effect on the leaders of authoritarian regimes, not on the people they ruled. President Mobutu Sese Seko of Zaire, for instance reacted with shocked horror to televised pictures of the execution by firing squad of his friend Romanian dictator Nicolae Ceausescu. A few months later, commenting that "You know what's happening across the world," he announced that he would allow two parties besides his own to compete in elections in 1993. In Tanzania, Julius Nyerere observed that "If changes take place in Eastern Europe then other countries with one-party systems and which profess socialism will also be affected." His country, he added, could learn a "lesson or two" from Eastern Europe. In Nepal in April 1990, the government announced that King Birendra was lifting the ban on political parties as a result of "the international situation" and "the rising expectations of the people."

If a country lacks favorable internal conditions, however, snowballing alone is unlikely to bring about democratization. The democratization of countries A and B is not a reason for democratization in country C, unless the conditions that favored it in the former also exist in the latter. Although the legitimacy of democratic government came to be accepted throughout the world in the 1980s, economic and social conditions favorable to democracy were not everywhere present. The "worldwide democratic revolution" may create an external environment conducive to democratization, but it cannot produce the conditions necessary for democratization within a particular country.

WORLDWIDE DEMOCRATIC REVOLUTION

In Eastern Europe the major obstacle to democratization was Soviet control; once it was removed, the movement to democracy spread rapidly. There is no comparable external obstacle to democratization in the Middle East, Africa, and Asia. If rulers in these areas chose authoritarianism before December 1989, why can they not continue to choose it thereafter? The snowballing effect would be real only to the extent that it led them to believe in the desirability or necessity of democratization. The events of 1989 in Eastern Europe undoubtedly encouraged democratic opposition groups and frightened authoritarian leaders elsewhere. Yet given the previous weakness of the former and the long-term repression imposed by the latter, it seems doubtful that the East European example will actually produce significant progress toward democracy in most other authoritarian countries.

By 1990, many of the original causes of the third wave had become significantly weaker, even exhausted. Neither the White House, the Kremlin, the European Community, nor the Vatican was in a strong position to promote democracy in places where it did not already exist (primarily in Asia, Africa, and the Middle East). It remains possible, however, for new forces favoring democratization to emerge. After all, who in 1985 could have foreseen that Mikhail Gorbachev would facilitate democratization in Eastern Europe?

In the 1990s the International Monetary Fund (IMF) and the World Bank could conceivably become much more forceful than they have heretofore been in making political democratization as well as economic liberalization a precondition for economic assistance. France might become more active in promoting democracy among its former African colonies, where its influence remains substantial. The Orthodox churches could emerge as a powerful influence for democracy in southeastern Europe and the Soviet Union. A Chinese proponent of *glasnost* could come to power in Beijing, or a new Jeffersonian-style Nasser could spread a democratic version of Pan-Arabism in the Middle East. Japan could use its growing economic clout to encourage human rights and democracy in the poor countries to which it makes loans and grants. In 1990, none of these possibilities seemed very likely, but after the surprises of 1989 it would be rash to rule anything out.

A THIRD REVERSE WAVE?

By 1990 at least two third-wave democracies, Sudan and Nigeria, had reverted to authoritarian rule; the difficulties of consolidation could lead to further reversions in countries with unfavorable conditions for sustaining democracy. The first and second democratic waves, however, were followed not merely by some backsliding but by major reverse waves during which most regime changes throughout the world were from democracy to authoritarianism. If the third wave of democratization slows down or comes to a halt, what factors might produce a third reverse wave?

Among the factors contributing to transitions away from democracy during the first and second reverse waves were:

1. the weakness of democratic values among key elite groups and the general public;

2. severe economic setbacks, which intensified social conflict and enhanced the popularity of remedies that could be imposed only by authoritarian governments;

3. social and political polarization, often produced by leftist governments seeking the rapid introduction of major social and economic reforms;

4. the determination of conservative middle-class and upper-class groups to exclude populist and leftist movements and lower-class groups from political power;

5. the breakdown of law and order resulting from terrorism or insurgency;

6. intervention or conquest by a nondemocratic foreign power;

7. "reverse snowballing" triggered by the collapse or overthrow of democratic systems in other countries.

Transitions from democracy to authoritarianism, apart from those produced by foreign actors, have almost always been produced by those in power or close to power in the democratic system. With only one or two possible exceptions, democratic systems have not been ended by popular vote or popular revolt. In Germany and Italy in the first reverse wave, antidemocratic movements with considerable popular backing came to power and established fascist dictatorships. In Spain in the first reverse wave and in Lebanon in the second, democracy ended in civil war.

The overwhelming majority of transitions from democracy, however, took the form either of military coups that ousted democratically elected leaders, or executive coups in which democratically chosen chief executives effectively ended democracy by concentrating power in their own hands, usually by declaring a state of emergency or martial law. In the first reverse wave, military coups ended democratic systems in the new countries of Eastern Europe and in Greece, Portugal, Argentina, and Japan. In the second reverse wave, military coups occurred in Indonesia, Pakistan, Greece, Nigeria, Turkey, and many Latin American countries. Executive coups occurred in the second reverse wave in Korea, India, and the Philippines. In Uruguay, the civilian and military leadership cooperated to end democracy through a mixed executive-military coup.

In both the first and second reverse waves, democratic systems were replaced in many cases by historically new forms of authoritarian rule. Fascism was distinguished from earlier forms of authoritarianism by its mass base, ideology, party organization, and efforts to penetrate and control most of society. Bureaucratic authoritarianism differed from earlier forms of military rule in Latin America with respect to its institutional character, its presumption of indefinite duration, and its economic policies. Italy and Germany in the 1920s and 1930s and Brazil and Argentina in the 1960s and 1970s were the lead countries in introducing these new forms of nondemocratic rule and furnished the examples that antidemocratic groups in other countries sought to emulate. Both these new forms of authoritarianism were, in effect, responses to social and economic development: the expansion of social mobilization and political participation in Europe, and the exhaustion of the import-substitution phase of economic development in Latin America.

Although the causes and forms of the first two reverse waves cannot generate reliable predictions concerning the causes and forms of a possible third reverse wave, prior experiences do suggest some potential causes of a new reverse wave.

First, systemic failures of democratic regimes to operate effectively could undermine their legitimacy. In the late twentieth century, the major nondemocratic ideological sources of legitimacy, most notably Marxism-Leninism, were discredited. The general acceptance of democratic norms meant that democratic governments were even less dependent on performance legitimacy than they had been in the past. Yet sustained inability to provide welfare, prosperity, equity, justice, domestic order, or external security could over time undermine the legitimacy even of democratic governments. As the memories of authoritarian failures fade, irritation with democratic failures is likely to increase. More specifically, a general international economic collapse on the 1929–30 model could undermine the legitimacy of democracy in many countries. Most democracies did survive the Great Depression of the 1930s; yet some succumbed, and presumably some would be likely to succumb in response to a comparable economic disaster in the future.

SHIFT TO AUTHORITAR-IANISM

Second, a shift to authoritarianism by any democratic or democratizing great power could trigger reverse snowballing. The reinvigoration of authoritarianism in Russia or the Soviet Union would have unsettling effects on democratization in other Soviet republics, Bulgaria, Romania, Yugoslavia, and Mongolia and possibly in Poland, Hungary, and Czechoslovakia as well. It could send the message to would-be despots elsewhere: "You too can go back into business." Similarly, the establishment of an authoritarian regime in India could have a significant demonstration effect on other Third World countries. Moreover, even if a major country does not revert to authoritarianism, a shift to dictatorship by several smaller newly democratic countries that lack many of the usual preconditions for democracy could have ramifying effects even on other countries where those preconditions are strong.

If a nondemocratic state greatly increased its power and began to expand beyond its borders, this too could stimulate authoritarian movements in other countries. This stimulus would be particularly strong if the expanding authoritarian state militarily defeated one or more democratic countries. In the past, all major powers that have developed economically have also tended to expand territorially. If China develops economically under authoritarian rule in the coming decades and expands its influence and control in East Asia, democratic regimes in the region will be significantly weakened.

Finally, as in the 1920s and the 1960s, various old and new forms of authoritarianism that seem appropriate to the needs of the times could emerge. Authoritarian nationalism could take hold in some Third World countries and also in Eastern Europe. Religious fundamentalism, which has been most dramatically prevalent in Iran, could come to power in other countries, especially in the Islamic world. Oligarchic authoritarianism could develop in both wealthy and poorer countries as a reaction to the leveling tendencies of democracy. Populist dictatorships could emerge in the future, as they have in the past, in response to democracy's protection of various forms of economic privilege, particularly in those countries where land tenancy is still an issue. Finally, communal dictatorships could be imposed in democracies with two or more distinct ethnic, racial, or religious groups, with one group trying to establish control over the entire society.

All of these forms of authoritarianism have existed in the past. It is not beyond the wit of humans to devise new ones in the future. One possibility might be a technocratic "electronic dictatorship," in which authoritarian rule is made possible and legitimated by the regime's ability to manipulate information, the media, and sophisticated means of communication. None of these old or new forms of authoritarianism is highly probable, but it is also hard to say that any one of them is totally impossible.

OBSTACLES TO DEMOCRATIZATION

Another approach to assessing democracy's prospects is to examine the obstacles to and opportunities for democratization where it has not yet taken hold. As of 1990, more than one hundred countries lacked democratic regimes. Most of these countries fell into four sometimes overlapping geocultural categories:

1. Home-grown Marxist-Leninist regimes, including the Soviet Union, where major liberalization occurred in the 1980s and democratic movements existed in many republics;
2. Sub-Saharan African countries, which, with a few exceptions, remained personal dictatorships, military regimes, one-party systems, or some combination of these three;
3. Islamic countries stretching from Morocco to Indonesia, which except for Turkey and perhaps Pakistan had nondemocratic regimes;
4. East Asian countries, from Burma through Southeast Asia to China and North Korea, which included communist systems, military regimes, personal dictatorships, and two semidemocracies (Thailand and Malaysia).

The obstacles to democratization in these groups of countries are political, cultural, and economic. One potentially significant political obstacle to future democratization is the virtual absence of experience with democracy in most countries that remained authoritarian in 1990. Twenty-three of 30 countries that democratized between 1974 and 1990 had had some history of democracy, while only a few countries that were nondemocratic in 1990 could claim such experience. These included a few third-wave backsliders (Sudan, Nigeria, Suriname, and possibly Pakistan), four second-wave backsliders that had not redemocratized in the third wave (Lebanon, Sri Lanka, Burma, Fiji), and three first-wave democratizers that had been prevented by Soviet occupation from redemocratizing at the end of World War II (Estonia, Latvia, and Lithuania). Virtually all the 90 or more other nondemocratic countries in 1990 lacked significant past experience with democratic rule. This obviously is not a decisive impediment to democratization—if it were, no countries would now be democratic—but it does make it more difficult.

Another obstacle to democratization is likely to disappear in a number of countries in the 1990s. Leaders who found authoritarian regimes or rule them for a long period tend to be-

LEADERSHIP CHANGE

come particularly staunch opponents of democratization. Hence some form of leadership change within the authoritarian system usually precedes movement toward democracy. Human mortality is likely to ensure such changes in the 1990s in some authoritarian regimes. In 1990, the long-term rulers in China, Côte d'Ivoire, and Malawi were in their eighties; those in Burma, Indonesia, North Korea, Lesotho, and Vietnam were in their seventies; and the leaders of Cuba, Morocco, Singapore, Somalia, Syria, Tanzania, Zaire, and Zambia were sixty or older. The death or departure from office of these leaders would remove one obstacle to democratization in their countries, but would not make it inevitable.

Between 1974 and 1990, democratization occurred in personal dictatorships, military regimes, and one-party systems. Full-scale democratization has not yet occurred, however, in communist one-party states that were the products of domestic revolution. Liberalization has taken place in the Soviet Union, which may or may not lead to full-scale democratization in Russia. In Yugoslavia, movements toward democracy are underway in Slovenia and Croatia. The Yugoslav communist revolution, however, was largely a Serbian revolution, and the prospects for democracy in Serbia appear dubious. In Cambodia, an extraordinarily brutal revolutionary communist regime was replaced by a less brutal communist regime imposed by outside force. In 1990, Albania appeared to be opening up, but in China, Vietnam, Laos, Cuba and Ethiopia, Marxist-Leninist regimes produced by home-grown revolutions seemed determined to remain in power. The revolutions in these countries had been nationalist as well as communist, and hence nationalism reinforced communism in a way that obviously was not true of Soviet-occupied Eastern Europe.

One serious impediment of democratization is the absence or weakness of real commitment to democratic values among political leaders in Asia, Africa, and the Middle East. When they are out of power, political leaders have good reason to advocate democracy. The test of their democratic commitment comes once they are in office. In Latin America, democratic regimes have generally been overthrown by military coups d'état. This has happened in Asia and the Middle East as well, but in these regions elected leaders themselves have also been responsible for ending democracy: Syngman Rhee and Park Chung Hee in Korea, Adnan Menderes in Turkey, Ferdinand Marcos in the Philippines, Lee Kwan Yew in Singapore, Indira Gandhi in India, and Sukarno in Indonesia. Having won power through the electoral system, these leaders then proceeded to undermine that system. They had little commitment to democratic values and practices.

Even when Asian, African, and Middle Eastern leaders have more or less abided by the rules of democracy, they often seemed to do so grudgingly. Many European, North American, and Latin American political leaders in the last half of the twentieth century were ardent and articulate advocates of democracy. Asian and African countries, in contrast, did not produce many heads of government who were also apostles of democracy. Who were the Asian, Arab, or African equivalents of Rómulo Betancourt, Alberto Llera Camargo, José Figueres, Eduardo Frei, Fernando Belaúnde Terry, Juan Bosch, José Napoleón Duarte, and Raúl Alfonsin? Jawaharlal Nehru and Corazon Aquino were, and there may have been others, but they were few in number. No Arab leader comes to mind, and it is hard to identify any Islamic leader who made a reputation as an advocate and supporter of democracy while in office. Why is this? This question inevitably leads to the issue of culture.

CULTURE

It has been argued that the world's great historic cultural traditions vary significantly in the extent to which their attitudes, values, beliefs, and related behavior patterns are conducive to the development of democracy. A profoundly antidemocratic culture would impede the spread of democratic norms in the society, deny legitimacy to democratic institutions, and thus greatly complicate if not prevent the emergence and effective functioning of those institutions. The cultural thesis comes in two forms. The more restrictive version states that only Western culture provides a suitable base for the development of democratic institutions and, consequently, that democracy is largely inappropriate for non-Western societies. In the early years of the third wave, this argument was explicitly set forth by George Kennan. Democracy, he said, was a form of government "which evolved in the eighteenth and nineteenth centuries in northwestern Europe, primarily among those countries that border on the English Channel and the North Sea (but with a certain extension into Central Europe), and which was then carried into other parts of the world, including North America, where peoples from that northwestern European area appeared as original settlers, or as colonialists, and laid down the prevailing patterns of civil government." Hence democracy has "a relatively narrow base both in time and in space, and the evidence has yet to be produced that it is the natural form of rule for peoples outside those narrow perimeters." The achievements of Mao, Salazar, and Castro demonstrated, according to Kennan, that authoritarian regimes "have been able to introduce reforms and to improve the lot of masses of people, where more diffuse forms of political authority had failed."

Democracy, in short, is appropriate only for northwestern and perhaps central European countries and their settler-colony offshoots.

The Western-culture thesis has immediate implications for democratization in the Balkans and the Soviet Union. Historically these areas were part of the Czarist and Ottoman empires; their prevailing religions were Orthodoxy and Islam, not Western Christianity. These areas did not have the same experiences as Western Europe with feudalism, the Renaissance, the Reformation, the Enlightenment, the French Revolution, and liberalism. As William Wallace has suggested, the end of the Cold War and the disappearance of the Iron Curtain may have shifted the critical political dividing line eastward to the centuries-old boundary between Eastern and Western Christendom. Beginning in the north, this line runs south roughly along the borders dividing Finland and the Baltic republics from Russia; through Byelorussia and the Ukraine, separating western Catholic Ukraine from eastern Orthodox Ukraine; south and then west in Romania, cutting off Transylvania from the rest of the country; and then through Yugoslavia roughly along the line separating Slovenia and Croatia from the other republics. This line may now separate those areas where democracy will take root from those where it will not.

WESTERN CULTURE THESIS

A less restrictive version of the cultural obstacle argument holds that certain non-Western cultures are peculiarly hostile to democracy. The two cultures most often cited in this regard are Confucianism and Islam. Three questions are relevant to determining whether these cultures now pose serious obstacles to democratization. First, to what extent are traditional Confucian and Islamic values and beliefs hostile to democracy? Second, if they are, to what extent have these cultures in fact hampered progress toward democracy? Third, if they have significantly retarded democratic progress in the past, to what extent are they likely to continue to do so in the future?

CONFUCIANISM

Almost no scholarly disagreement exists regarding the proposition that traditional Confucianism was either undemocratic or antidemocratic. The only mitigating factor was the extent to which the examination system in the classic Chinese polity opened careers to the talented without regard to social background. Even if this were the case, however, a merit system of promotion does not make a democracy. No one would describe a modern army as democratic because officers are promoted on the basis of their abilities. Classic Chinese Confucianism and its derivatives in Korea, Vietnam, Singapore, Taiwan, and (in diluted fashion) Japan emphasized the group over the individual, authority over liberty, and respon-

sibilities over rights. Confucian societies lacked a tradition of rights against the state; to the extent that individual rights did exist, they were created by the state. Harmony and cooperation were preferred over disagreement and competition. The maintenance of order and respect for hierarchy were central values. The conflict of ideas, groups, and parties was viewed as dangerous and illegitimate. Most important, Confucianism merged society and the state and provided no legitimacy for autonomous social institutions at the national level.

In practice Confucian or Confucian-influenced societies have been inhospitable to democracy. In East Asia only two countries, Japan and the Philippines, had sustained experience with democratic government prior to 1990. In both cases, democracy was the product of an American presence. The Philippines, moreover, is overwhelmingly a Catholic country. In Japan, Confucian values were reinterpreted and merged with autochthonous cultural traditions.

Mainland China has had no experience with democratic government, and democracy of the Western variety has been supported over the years only by relatively small groups of radical dissidents. "Mainstream" democratic critics have not broken with the key elements of the Confucian tradition. The modernizers of China have been (in Lucian Pye's phrase) the "Confucian Leninists" of the Nationalist and Communist parties. In the late 1980s, when rapid economic growth in China produced a new series of demands for political reform and democracy on the part of students, intellectuals, and urban middle-class groups, the Communist leadership responded in two ways. First, it articulated a theory of "new authoritarianism," based on the experience of Taiwan, Singapore, and Korea, which claimed that a country at China's stage of economic development needed authoritarian rule to achieve balanced economic growth and contain the unsettling consequences of development. Second, the leadership violently suppressed the democratic movement in Beijing and elsewhere in June of 1989.

In China, economics reinforced culture in holding back democracy. In Singapore, Taiwan, and Korea, on the other hand, spectacular growth created the economic basis for democracy by the late 1980s. In these countries, economics clashed with culture in shaping political development. In 1990, Singapore was the only non-oil-exporting "high-income" country (as defined by the World Bank) that did not have a democratic political system, and Singapore's leader was an articulate exponent of Confucian values as opposed to those of Western democracy. In the 1980s, Premier Lee Kwan Yew made the teaching and promulgation of Confucian values a high priority for his city-state and took vigorous measures to limit and suppress dissent and to prevent media criticism of the government and its policies. Singapore was thus an authoritarian Confucian anomaly among the wealthy countries of the world. The interesting question is whether it will remain so now that Lee, who created the state, appears to be partially withdrawing from the political scene.

TAIWAN AND KOREA In the late 1980s, both Taiwan and Korea moved in a democratic direction. Historically, Taiwan had always been a peripheral part of China. It was occupied by the Japanese for 50 years, and its inhabitants rebelled in 1947 against the imposition of Chinese control. The Nationalist government arrived in 1949 humiliated by its defeat by the Communists, a defeat that made it impossible "for most Nationalist leaders to uphold the posture of arrogance associated with traditional Confucian notions of authority." Rapid economic and social development further weakened the influence of traditional Confucianism. The emergence of a substantial entrepreneurial class, composed largely of native Taiwanese, created (in very un-Confucian fashion) a source of power and wealth independent of the mainlander-dominated state. This produced in Taiwan a "fundamental change in Chinese political culture, which has not occurred in China itself or in Korea or Vietnam—and never really existed in Japan." Taiwan's spectacular economic development thus overwhelmed a relatively weak Confucian legacy, and in the late 1980s Chiang Ching-kuo and Lee Teng-hui responded to the pressures produced by economic and social change and gradually moved to open up politics in their society.

In Korea, the classical culture included elements of mobility and egalitarianism along with Confucian components uncongenial to democracy, including a tradition of authoritarianism and strongman rule. As one Korean scholar put it, "people did not think of themselves as citizens with rights to exercise and responsibilities to perform, but they tended to look up to the top for direction and for favors in order to survive." In the late 1980s, urbanization, education, the development of a substantial middle class, and the impressive spread of Christianity all weakened Confucianism as an obstacle to democracy in Korea. Yet it remained unclear whether the struggle between the old culture and the new prosperity had been definitively resolved in favor of the latter.

THE EAST ASIAN MODEL

The interaction of economic progress and Asian culture appears to have generated a distinctly East Asian variety of democratic institutions. As of 1990, no East Asian country except the Philippines (which is, in many respects, more Latin American than East Asian in culture) had experienced a turnover from a popularly elected government of one party to a popularly elected government of a different party. The prototype was Japan, unquestionably a democracy, but one in which the ruling party has never been voted out of power. The Japanese model of dominant-party democracy, as Pye has pointed out, has spread elsewhere in East Asia. In 1990, two of the three opposition parties in Korea merged with the government party to form a political bloc that would effectively exclude the remaining opposition party, led by Kim Dae Jung and based on the Cholla region, from ever gaining power. In the late 1980s, democratic development in Taiwan seemed to be moving toward an electoral system in which the Kuomintang (KMT) was likely to remain the dominant party, with the Democratic Progressive Party confined to a permanent opposition role. In Malaysia, the coalition of the three leading parties from the Malay, Chinese, and Indian communities (first in the Alliance Party and then in the National Front) has controlled power in unbroken fashion against all competitors from the 1950s through the 1980s. In the mid-1980s, Lee Kwan Yew's deputy and successor Goh Chok Tong endorsed a similar type of party system for Singapore:

> I think a stable system is one where there is a mainstream political party representing a broad range of the population. Then you can have a few other parties on the periphery, very serious-minded parties. They are unable to have wider views but they nevertheless represent sectional interests. And the mainstream is returned all the time. I think that's good. And I would not apologize if we ended up in that situation in Singapore.

A primary criterion for democracy is equitable and open competition for votes between political parties without government harassment or restriction of opposition groups. Japan has clearly met this test for decades with its freedoms of speech, press, and assembly, and reasonably equitable conditions of electoral competition. In the other Asian dominant-party systems, the playing field has been tilted in favor of the government for many years. By the late 1980s, however, conditions were becoming more equal in some countries. In Korea, the government party was unable to win control of the legislature in 1989, and this failure presumably was a major factor in its subsequent merger with two of its opponents. In Taiwan, restrictions on the opposition were gradually lifted. It is thus conceivable that other East Asian countries could join Japan in providing a level playing field for a game that the government party always wins. In 1990 the East Asian dominant-party systems thus spanned a continuum between democracy and authoritarianism, with Japan at one extreme, Indonesia at the other, and Korea, Taiwan, Malaysia, and Singapore (more or less in that order) in between.

Such a system may meet the formal requisites of democracy, but it differs significantly from the democratic systems prevalent in the West, where it is assumed not only that political parties and coalitions will freely and equally compete for power but also that they are likely to alternate in power. By contrast, the East Asian dominant-party systems seem to involve competition for power but not alternation in power, and participation in elections for all, but participation in office only for those in the "mainstream" party. This type of political system offers democracy without turnover. It represents an adaptation of Western democratic practices to serve not Western values of competition and change, but Asian values of consensus and stability.

Western democratic systems are less dependent on performance legitimacy than authoritarian systems because failure is blamed on the incumbents instead of the system, and the ouster and replacement of the incumbents help to renew the system. The East Asian societies that have adopted or appear to be adopting the dominant-party model had unequalled records of economic success from the 1960s to the 1980s. What happens, however, if and when their 8-percent growth rates plummet; unemployment, inflation, and other forms of economic distress escalate; or social and economic conflicts intensify? In a Western democracy the response would be to turn the incumbents out. In a dominant-party democracy, however, that would represent a revolutionary change. If the structure of political competition does not allow that to happen, unhappiness with the government could well lead to demonstrations, protests, riots, and efforts to mobilize popular support to overthrow the government. The government then would be tempted to respond by suppressing dissent and imposing authoritarian controls. The key question, then, is to what extent the East Asian dominant-party system presupposes uninterrupted and substantial economic growth. Can this system survive prolonged economic downturn or stagnation?

ISLAM

"Confucian democracy" is clearly a contradiction in terms. It is unclear whether "Islamic democracy" also is. Egalitarianism and voluntarism are central themes in Islam. The "high culture form of Islam," Ernest Gellner has argued, is "endowed with a number of features—unitarianism, a rule-ethic, individualism, scripturalism, puritanism, an egalitarian aversion to mediation and hierarchy, a fairly small load of magic—that are congruent, presumably, with requirements of modernity or modernization." They are also generally congruent with the requirements of democracy. Islam, however, also rejects any distinction between the religious community and the political community. Hence there is no equipoise between Caesar and God, and political participation is linked to religious affiliation. Fundamentalist Islam demands that in a Muslim country the political rulers should be practicing Muslims, *shari'a* should be the basic law, and *ulema* should have a "decisive vote in articulating, or at least reviewing and ratifying, all governmental policy." To the extent that governmental legitimacy and policy flow from religious doctrine and religious expertise, Islamic concepts of politics differ from and contradict the premises of democratic politics.

Islamic doctrine thus contains elements that may be both congenial and uncongenial to democracy. In practice, however, the only Islamic country that has sustained a fully democratic political system for any length of time is Turkey, where Mustafa Kemal Ataturk explicitly rejected Islamic concepts of society and politics and vigorously attempted to create a secular, modern, Western nation-state. And Turkey's experience with democracy has not been an unmitigated success. Elsewhere in the Islamic world, Pakistan has made three attempts at democracy, none of which lasted long. While Turkey has had democracy interrupted by occasional military interventions, Pakistan has had bureaucratic and military rule interrupted by occasional elections.

The only Arab country to sustain a form of democracy (albeit of the consociational variety) for a significant period of time was Lebanon. Its democracy, however, really amounted to consociational oligarchy, and 40 to 50 percent of its population was Christian. Once Muslims became a majority in Lebanon and began to assert themselves, Lebanese democracy collapsed. Between 1981 and 1990, only two of 37 countries in the world with Muslim majorities were ever rated "Free" by Freedom House in its annual surveys: the Gambia for two years and the Turkish Republic of Northern Cyprus for four. Whatever the compatibility of Islam and democracy in theory, in practice they have rarely gone together.

Opposition movements to authoritarian regimes in southern and eastern Europe, in Latin America, and in East Asia almost universally have espoused Western democratic values and proclaimed their desire to establish democracy. This does not mean that they invariably would introduce democratic institutions if they had the opportunity to do so, but at least they articulated the rhetoric of democracy. In authoritarian Islamic societies, by contrast, movements explicitly campaigning for democratic politics have been relatively weak, and the most powerful opposition has come from Islamic fundamentalists.

ECONOMIC PROBLEMS   In the late 1980s, domestic economic problems combined with the snowballing effects of democratization elsewhere led the governments of several Islamic countries to relax their controls on the opposition and to attempt to renew their legitimacy through elections. The principal initial beneficiaries of these openings were Islamic fundamentalist groups. In Algeria, the Islamic Salvation Front swept the June 1990 local elections, the first free elections since the country became independent in 1962. In the 1989 Jordanian elections, Islamic fundamentalists won 36 of 80 seats in parliament. In Egypt, many candidates associated with the Muslim Brotherhood were elected to parliament in 1987. In several countries, Islamic fundamentalist groups were reportedly plotting insurrections. The strong electoral showings of the Islamic groups partly reflected the absence of other opposition parties, some because they were under government proscription, others because they were boycotting the elections. Nonetheless, fundamentalism seemed to be gaining strength in Middle Eastern countries, particularly among younger people. The strength of this tendency induced secular heads of government in Tunisia, Turkey, and elsewhere to adopt policies advocated by the fundamentalists and to make political gestures demonstrating their own commitment to Islam.

Liberalization in Islamic countries thus enhanced the power of important social and political movements whose commitment to democracy was uncertain. In some respects, the position of fundamentalist parties in Islamic societies in the early 1990s raised questions analogous to those posed by communist parties in Western Europe in the 1940s and again in the 1970s. Would the existing governments continue to open up their politics and hold elections in which Islamic groups could compete freely and equally? Would the Islamic groups gain majority support in those elections? If they did win the elections, would the military, which in many Islamic societies (e.g., Algeria, Turkey, Pakistan, and Indonesia) is strongly secular, allow them to form a government? If they did form a government, would it pursue radical Islamic policies that would undermine democracy and alienate the modern and Western-oriented elements in society?

THE LIMITS OF CULTURAL OBSTACLES

Strong cultural obstacles to democratization thus appear to exist in Confucian and Islamic societies. There are, nonetheless, reasons to doubt whether these must necessarily prevent democratic development. First, similar cultural arguments have not held up in the past. At one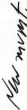

point many scholars argued that Catholicism was an obstacle to democracy. Others, in the Weberian tradition, contended that Catholic countries were unlikely to develop economically in the same manner as Protestant countries. Yet in the 1960s, 1970s, and 1980s Catholic countries became democratic and, on average, had higher rates of economic growth than Protestant countries. Similarly, at one point Weber and others argued that countries with Confucian cultures would not achieve successful capitalist development. By the 1980s, however, a new generation of scholars saw Confucianism as a major cause of the spectacular economic growth of East Asian societies. In the longer run, will the thesis that Confucianism prevents democratic development be any more viable than the thesis that Confucianism prevents economic development? Arguments that particular cultures are permanent obstacles to change should be viewed with a certain skepticism.

Second, great cultural traditions like Islam and Confucianism are highly complex bodies of ideas, beliefs, doctrines, assumptions, and behavior patterns. Any major culture, including Confucianism, has some elements that are compatible with democracy, just as both Protestantism and Catholicism have elements that are clearly undemocratic. Confucian democracy may be a contradiction in terms, but democracy in a Confucian society need not be. The real question is which elements in Islam and Confucianism are favorable to democracy, and how and under what circumstances these can supersede the undemocratic aspects of those cultural traditions.

Third, cultures historically are dynamic, not stagnant. The dominant beliefs and attitudes in a society change. While maintaining elements of continuity, the prevailing culture of a society in one generation may differ significantly from what it was one or two generations earlier. In the 1950s, Spanish culture was typically described as traditional, authoritarian, hierarchical, deeply religious, and honor-and-status oriented. By the 1970s and 1980s, these words had little place in a description of Spanish attitudes and values. Cultures evolve and, as in Spain, the most important force bringing about cultural changes is often economic development itself.

ECONOMICS

Few relationships between social, economic, and political phenomena are stronger than that between the level of economic development and the existence of democratic politics. Most wealthy countries are democratic, and most democratic countries—India is the most dramatic exception—are wealthy. The correlation between wealth and democracy implies that transitions to democracy should occur primarily in countries at the mid-level of economic development. In poor countries democratization is unlikely; in rich countries it usually has already occurred. In between there is a "political transition zone": countries in this middle economic stratum are those most likely to transit to democracy, and most countries that transit to democracy will be in this stratum. As countries develop economically and move into the transition zone, they become good prospects for democratization.

In fact, shifts from authoritarianism to democracy during the third wave were heavily concentrated in this transition zone, especially at its upper reaches. The conclusion seems clear. Poverty is a principal—probably *the* principal—obstacle to democratic development. The future of democracy depends on the future of economic development. Obstacles to economic development are obstacles to the expansion of democracy.

The third wave of democratization was propelled forward by the extraordinary global economic growth of the 1950s and 1960s. That era of growth came to an end with the oil price increases of 1973–74. Between 1974 and 1990, democratization accelerated around the world, but global economic growth slowed down. There were, however, substantial differences in growth rates among regions. East Asian rates remained high throughout the 1970s and 1980s, and overall rates of growth in South Asia increased. On the other hand, growth rates in the Middle East, North Africa, Latin America, and the Caribbean declined sharply from the 1970s to the 1980s. Those in sub-Saharan Africa plummeted. Per capita GNP in Africa was stagnant during the late 1970s and declined at an annual rate of 2.2 percent during the 1980s. The economic obstacles to democratization in Africa thus clearly grew during the 1980s. The prospects for the 1990s are not encouraging. Even if economic reforms, debt relief, and economic assistance materialize, the World Bank has predicted an average annual rate of growth in per capita GDP for Africa of only 0.5 percent for the remainder of the century. If this prediction is accurate, the economic obstacles to democratization in sub-Saharan Africa will remain overwhelming well into the twenty-first century.

The World Bank was more optimistic in its predictions of economic growth for China and the nondemocratic countries of South Asia. The current low levels of wealth in those countries, however, generally mean that even with annual per capita growth rates of 3 to 5 percent, the economic conditions favorable to democratization would still be long in coming.

In the 1990s, the majority of countries where the economic conditions for democratization are already present or rapidly emerging are in the Middle East and North Africa (see Table 1). The economies of many of these countries (United Arab Emirates, Kuwait, Saudi Arabia, Iraq, Iran, Libya, Oman) depend heavily on oil exports, which enhances the control of the state bureaucracy. This does not, however, make democratization impossible. The state bureaucracies of Eastern Europe had far more power than do those of the oil exporters. Thus at some point that power could collapse among the latter as dramatically as it did among the former.

In 1988 among the other states of the Middle East and North Africa, Algeria had already reached a level conducive to democratization; Syria was approaching it; and Jordan, Tunisia, Morocco, Egypt, and North Yemen were well below the transition zone, but had grown rapidly during the 1980s. Middle Eastern economies and societies are approaching the point where they will become too wealthy and too complex for their various traditional, military, and one-party systems of authoritarian rule to sustain themselves. The wave of democratization that swept the world in the 1970s and 1980s could become a dominant feature of Middle Eastern and North African politics in the 1990s. The issue of economics versus culture would then be joined: What forms of politics might emerge in these countries when economic prosperity begins to interact with Islamic values and traditions?

ECONOMICS VERSUS CULTURE

In China, the obstacles to democratization are political, economic, and cultural; in Africa they are overwhelmingly economic; and in the rapidly developing countries of East Asia and in many Islamic countries, they are primarily cultural.

ECONOMIC DEVELOPMENT AND POLITICAL LEADERSHIP

History has proved both optimists and pessimists wrong about democracy. Future events will probably do the same. Formidable obstacles to the expansion of democracy exist in many societies. The third wave, the "global democratic revolution" of the late twentieth century, will not last forever. It may be followed by a new surge of authoritarianism sustained enough to constitute a third reverse wave. That, however, would not preclude a fourth wave of democratization developing some time in the twenty-first century. Judging by the record of the past, the two most decisive factors affecting the future consolidation and expansion of democracy will be economic development and political leadership.

Most poor societies will remain undemocratic so long as they remain poor. Poverty, however, is not inevitable. In the past, nations such as South Korea, which were assumed to be mired in economic backwardness, have as-

TABLE 1. *Upper and Middle Income Nondemocratic Countries—GNP Per Capita (1988)*

Income level	Arab-Middle East	Southeast Asia	Africa	Other
Upper income (>$6,000)	UAE[a] Kuwait[a] Saudi Arabia[a]	Singapore		
Upper middle income ($2,000–5,500)	Iraq[a] Iran[a] Libya[a] Oman[a,b] Algeria[b]		(Gabon)	Yugoslavia
Lower middle income ($500–2,200)	Syria Jordan[b] Tunisia[b]	Malaysia[b] Thailand[b]	Cameroon[b]	Paraguay
$1,000 --------	Morocco[b] Egypt[b] Yemen[b] Lebanon[b]		Congo[b] Côte d'Ivoire Zimbabwe Senegal[b] Angola	

Source: World Bank, *World Bank Development Report 1990* (New York: Oxford University Press, 1990), 178–181.

[a]Major oil exporter.
[b]Average annual GDP growth rate 1980–1988 > 3.0%.

tonished the world by rapidly attaining prosperity. In the 1980s, a new consensus emerged among developmental economists on the ways to promote economic growth. The consensus of the 1980s may or may not prove more lasting and productive than the very different consensus among economists that prevailed in the 1950s and 1960s. The new orthodoxy of neoorthodoxy, however, already seems to have produced significant results in many countries.

Yet there are two reasons to temper our hopes with caution. First, economic development for the late, late, late developing countries—meaning largely Africa—may well be more difficult than it was for earlier developers because the advantages of backwardness come to be outweighed by the widening and historically unprecedented gap between rich and poor countries. Second, new forms of authoritarianism could emerge in wealthy, information-dominated, technology-based societies. If unhappy possibilities such as these do not materialize, economic development should create the conditions for the progressive replacement of authoritarian political systems by democratic ones. Time is on the side of democracy.

Economic development makes democracy possible; political leadership makes it real. For democracies to come into being, future political elites will have to believe, at a minimum, that democracy is the least bad form of government for their societies and for themselves. They will also need the skills to bring about the transition to democracy while facing both radical oppositionists and authoritarian hard-liners who inevitably will attempt to undermine their efforts. Democracy will spread to the extent that those who exercise power in the world and in individual countries want it to spread. For a century and a half after Tocqueville observed the emergence of modern democracy in America, successive waves of democratization have washed over the shore of dictatorship. Buoyed by a rising tide of economic progress, each wave advanced further—and receded less—than its predecessor. History, to shift the metaphor, does not sail ahead in a straight line, but when skilled and determined leaders are at the helm, it does move forward.

As the world moves toward more democratic governments,
we should consider how much emphasis is on the rights of the group and
how much on the rights of the individual

WHAT KIND OF DEMOCRACY?

RAYMOND D. GASTIL

Raymond D. Gastil is a social analyst and writer. His books
include Social Humanities: Toward an Integrative Discipline
of Science and Values *(1977) and the annual* Freedom in the
World: Political Rights and Civil Liberties *(1978–1989).*

AS WE CONGRATULATE OURSELVES ON A WORLD
becoming increasingly democratic, we should
recall that several times before in the past century it seemed that democracy had won universal acceptance, but the acceptance was much less trust-
worthy than had been imagined. In 1900–1901 leading
newspapers announced the good news that the twentieth
century was to be the century of democracy; in 1920 a
prominent authority on political systems could write that
democracy no longer had any challengers.

A society is generally said to be a full democracy if it
has a political system that guarantees both the civil and
political liberties of its people. In other words, a democracy must not only allow its people to choose freely who
will govern them but also guarantee the freedoms of expression and organization, which make possible effective
oppositions that can compete for, and eventually attain,
office. Unfortunately, in most historical treatments of the
growth of democracy the emphasis tends to be on the existence of electoral or legislative mechanisms that allow
for choice, with less attention paid to those civil liberties
that make that choice effectively free.

It is easy, and probably fundamentally wrong, to assume that the most important characteristics of democracy are the political rights that the word "democracy"
most clearly implies. Let me use personal experience to
explain this. Annually from 1973 until last year I produced the Comparative Survey of Freedom, which
placed countries on a continuum of freedom. I tried to
balance aspects of democracy by using a rating system
that included both political rights and civil liberties in the
final score. During the first few years of the survey I considered that when the final scores of two countries tied, I
would give the rating for political freedom—that is, for
the extent to which there were free elections and those
elected gained power—the greater weight. Perhaps I
made this choice because it was much easier to get information on elections and legislators than on the state of
civil liberties in a country. However, as time went on and
experience accumulated, I dropped this largely theoreti-

cal distinction in weighting. In the past few years I have
come to believe that if one thinks of freedom, or in this
case democracy, in time periods longer than a year, civil
liberties will be seen as the more important of the two
kinds of democratic freedom. I came to realize that political rights without civil freedoms would offer few of
the values that I cherish in democratic societies, while
civil freedoms without political rights (insofar as this is
conceivable) would offer the major values that I understand democracy to promote. The primacy of civil
freedoms becomes even more apparent in societies
whose governments appear to respond to the popular will
as expressed by the communications media, demonstrations, and other informal channels with more alacrity
than they do to the often indeterminate results at the
polling station.

DEMOCRACY AS WE KNOW IT HAS TWO QUITE DIF-
ferent roots. The first is the universal desire of
people to manage their own affairs, or at least to
have a say in who manages their affairs. In the primitive
band all adults, or sometimes all heads of families, tended to have a say in the affairs of the band. This tribal or
village democracy can be traced down through all of history. The democracy of ancient Athens is no doubt the
most famous example of a community ruling itself—a
community of relatively large scale. Of course, women,
slaves, and other outsiders were excluded. But a substantial part of the population took an active role in the decisions of the society; when "the people," thus defined,
changed their minds, society moved in the direction of
the change. When we speak of the democracy of the medieval Swiss cantons, or of the units of the Iroquois con-
federacy, this is also the democracy we have in mind.
The democracy of the New England towns of the seventeenth century and the democracy of the Swiss communities of Rousseau's day, including his native Geneva,
were essentially successive expressions of the tribal or
community democracy of primitive society. Though for
limited purposes these might form together in larger
"leagues," they were little more than alliances among independent units whose interrelationships might be no
more democratic than those in nondemocratic leagues.
The second root of modern democracy is liberalism,

From *The Atlantic*, June 1990, pp. 92–94, 96. Copyright © 1990 by Raymond D. Gastil. Reprinted by permission.

defined as that set of social and political beliefs, attitudes, and values which assumes the universal and equal application of the law and the existence of basic human rights superior to those of state or community. As used here, the term "liberal" is not meant to suggest any particular economic doctrine, or doctrine regarding the state's economic role; nor is it meant to be an antonym of "conservative." It does imply that the state's interests cannot override those of the citizenry. Derived from a variety of secular and religious tenets, liberalism affirms the basic worth of individuals, their thoughts, and their desires. In the liberal canon no one, whether king or majority, has the right to tell people how to think, or even act (except in instances of imminent threat to social well-being). Although it has ancient foundations, liberalism is primarily the outgrowth of the efforts of political and social philosophers since the seventeenth century to free humanity from the fetters of unchecked state power and imposed religious dogma. Before the eighteenth century, liberal democracy's role in history was much less important than tribal democracy's.

It was liberal democracy that abolished political censorship, that eventually found it impossible to justify slavery of any kind, or torture for any reason, or the unequal position of women and minority races and ethnic groups. It is liberal democracy that is always teetering on the edge of denying that the individual has any substantial duty to sacrifice himself for the community if he chooses not to. It was liberal democracy that fascism and similar ideologies sought to destroy utterly. It was liberal democracy that the Marxist-Leninist regimes now dissolving in Eastern Europe found so repugnant in its individualism and inherent tendency to sacrifice group interests to individual interests.

The international human-rights movement is based on the tenets of liberal democracy, and is a natural product of this political system. Everywhere, these rights have become the hope of the oppressed, and the societies that support these rights become the natural allies of all peoples.

WHEN THE CURRENT DEMOCRATIC REVOLUTION IS discussed, we should remember that we are referring to changes that represent the legacy of both these traditions, the tribal democratic and the liberal democratic. We must remember that their conjunction in modern democracies is the result of a long historical process, and far from automatic. Historically, democracies have tended to be more tribal than liberal. Regardless of the Constitution and the Bill of Rights and the values of the Founding Fathers, acceptance of liberal democracy came slowly to the American public. Even in recent years the United States has had periods in which tribal democracy rode roughshod over liberal democracy, as in the expulsion of the Japanese from the West Coast in the Second World War. Public-opinion polls continue to show that the tenets of liberal democracy may not be as thoroughly accepted in the United States and other democracies as we would like.

The slow pace of the liberalization of democracy, even in recent years, explains why as we go further back in history, the association of democracy and peace becomes more and more tenuous. Although the political systems of Athens and Sparta were far apart, both states were warlike; indeed, Athens became a specialist in imperial wars. The democratic Swiss cantons produced the mercenaries of Europe for several centuries. At the same time that democracy was being perfected in the West, its military forces conquered most of the world. Yet gradually the record has improved, as democracies have become more liberal. War became unfashionable in the democratic West after the First World War. Colonies became unfashionable after the Second World War. But if there is to be a "peace dividend" from the democratic revolution, it will occur only to the extent that tribal democracy has been overcome by liberal democratic attitudes that respect the rights of all peoples.

Today, as we contemplate a democratizing world, we must ask ourselves how strong the tribal and liberal elements actually are in the new democratic movements. We should recall that fascism in Italy, Japan, and Germany grew to maturity in democratizing societies, societies that provided the tools for free discussion and mobilization of small groups. Those groups were then able to use these privileges to overthrow the democratic system by capturing the attention and perhaps the majority of support of peoples in whom the assumptions of liberal democracy were only weakly rooted.

Outside the West democracy is beset with the problem of incorporating basically illiberal peoples and movements into the democratic framework. In the recent Indian election the third most powerful party was a Hindu party dedicated to advancing the cause of the Hindu majority at the expense of both the rights of Muslims and the concept of the secular state. In some parts of India many Sikhs and Muslims and members of other groups are equally intolerant of those whose beliefs or backgrounds are different from their own. Pakistan's emergence as a democracy has been repeatedly delayed by the claims of Muslim movements against the rights of others, and these claims may again cause the collapse of democracy in Pakistan.

The clash of tribal democracy and liberal democracy has been particularly acute in the Middle East. It is either the case or feared to be the case that a really open electoral process in most Middle Eastern states would result in the establishment of an oppressive Muslim fundamentalism in place of the less oppressive current regimes. Sudan's most recent attempt at democracy was ultimately torn apart by tribalism, which made democracy as we know it impossible. We should note that Iran, under Islamic guidance, has had several contested elections with fair voting procedures since 1980. From the political-rights viewpoint it can be argued that Iran is now ruled by an elected democratic government, a government more democratic than most in the Third World. But its oppression of individuals or groups that lie beyond the boundaries of tribal morality or acceptance has been persistent. Its initial unwillingness, for example, to allow the Bahais any place in Iranian society, and its equally vicious destruction of the radical left, represented tribalisms that an elected parliament could overwhelmingly endorse. Despite the panoply of Western political institutions in Iran, it remains outside the democratic world that requires a commitment to civil liberties as well as political rights.

From one perspective, the demand for self-determination is a demand for freedom. From another, it is a demand for independence unrelated to the maintenance of those freedoms basic to liberal democracy. Too often the demand for self-determination is a tribalist demand that ends by narrowing rather than broadening the sphere of human rights. It is the demand that has torn Sri Lanka apart, destroying what was a functioning democratic system. It is the demand that came very close on several occasions to arresting the development of democracy in our own South. In itself, self-determination is a legitimate right, and should be recognized insofar as it does not threaten other rights. But his right should not be confused with those basic civil rights fundamental to liberal democracy, nor is it as important as they are.

It is with this consciousness that we must consider the prospects for democracy in those areas of the world that remain nondemocratic but may soon institute full political democracies if current trends continue. We must ask particularly what values we hold most dear. Do we want the establishment of democratic regimes that will soon come to deny those liberal, humanistic values we see as essential to a full human life? Do we want, for example, a politically more democratic but also more fundamentalist Egypt? Would we really want a "free Afghanistan" whose political system put women back in the Middle Ages? Would we still endorse the democracy of an India that ended up exacerbating religious or ethnic tensions to the point of new and endemic slaughter?

If we are lucky, we may be able to avoid facing such questions. But if the development of democracy in the Soviet Union, for example, proceeds as it has, with an increasing emphasis on self-determination at the popular level, will we not find larger and larger sections of the population developing independent political systems in which the desires and opinions and interests of the majority allow for the suppression of all those who disagree, or all those who belong to other "tribes"? Some years ago I regarded descriptions of the danger of the highly nationalistic Pamyat movement in the USSR as little more than the scare-mongering of scholars or anti-Soviets. Today I wonder if "pamyats" might not break out all over the Soviet world, fueled by the frustrations of failure in other sectors of life, much as fascism was fueled between the wars.

WHAT DO WE BRING AWAY FROM THIS DISCUSSION? Certainly we should not conclude that because democratic movements are often less than thoroughly imbued with modern liberal ideals, we should

stop pushing for the democratization of the world. We should continue the effort for several reasons. First, people do have democratic rights to self-determination, even if we do not like what they do with these rights. Second, the continued rolling of the democratic bandwagon may bring us closer to our overall goals. Third, nondemocratic regimes are often as illiberal as democratic ones. Fourth, since democratic systems are often initially more tribal than liberal, by denying the right of tribal democracy we may end up denying the right of a people to any democracy at all.

But the discussion suggests some dangers, and perhaps some changes in direction, in the pursuit of the millennium. It suggests that the campaign for liberal democracy, represented in part by the human-rights movement, should be continued and enhances even as states become democratic in form. Also, we should develop educational programs that teach liberal values to broader and broader segments of the population in new democracies or states that have not yet become politically democratic. To avoid the arrest of this educational process we should in particular instances and for particular countries avoid pressing for the establishment of political democracy so long as the system in power takes an active role in developing and teaching the concepts of a liberal society.

I suspect that one reason for the collapse of communist systems in the Soviet sphere is that they appeared increasingly estranged from the world culture that has penetrated nearly everywhere since the Second World War. This culture simply no longer accepts the controls on movement and thought that characterized most of the world until recently. It no longer accepts discrimination for reasons of ideology, religion, gender, or ethnicity. It no longer accepts rulers that are not freely elected by their peoples. This culture has come upon the world rapidly, and may ultimately be destructive of essential values. But for now it advances the cause of the assumptions basic to liberal democracy, and therefore becomes an important aspect of the struggle for the extension of democracy.

In promoting democracy, governments and private organizations should place at least as much stress on the liberal underpinnings of modern democracy as on the forms of political democracy. The emphasis should be on the absolute value of the individual and the universal applicability of basic rights. We should support movements that undercut tribal thinking. We should refrain from insisting on rapid transitions to the political forms of democracy when establishing these forms appears likely to threaten the eventual attainment of the freedoms due every individual, and not just every group. We should be careful not to confuse the demand for self-determination with the demand for democracy. Thus the campaign for democracy, the campaign for human rights, and the campaign against war and armaments must become ever more closely identified with one another as we press on, both publicly and privately, toward a world of peace and freedom.

Capitalism and Democracy*

Gabriel A. Almond

Gabriel A. Almond, professor of political science emeritus at Stanford University, is a former president of the American Political Science Association.

Joseph Schumpeter, a great economist and social scientist of the last generation, whose career was almost equally divided between Central European and American universities, and who lived close to the crises of the 1930s and '40s, published a book in 1942 under the title, *Capitalism, Socialism, and Democracy.* The book has had great influence, and can be read today with profit. It was written in the aftergloom of the great depression, during the early triumphs of Fascism and Nazism in 1940 and 1941, when the future of capitalism, socialism, and democracy all were in doubt. Schumpeter projected a future of declining capitalism, and rising socialism. He thought that democracy under socialism might be no more impaired and problematic than it was under capitalism.

He wrote a concluding chapter in the second edition which appeared in 1946, and which took into account

*Lecture presented at Seminar on the Market, sponsored by The Ford Foundation and the Research Institute on International Change of Columbia University, Moscow, October 29–November 2.

the political-economic situation at the end of the war, with the Soviet Union then astride a devastated Europe. In this last chapter he argues that we should not identify the future of socialism with that of the Soviet Union, that what we had observed and were observing in the first three decades of Soviet existence was not a necessary expression of socialism. There was a lot of Czarist Russia in the mix. If Schumpeter were writing today, I don't believe he would argue that socialism has a brighter future than capitalism. The relationship be-

> *The economy and the polity are the main problem solving mechanisms of human society. They each have their distinctive means, and they each have their "goods" or ends. They necessarily interact with each other, and transform each other in the process.*

tween the two has turned out to be a good deal more complex and intertwined than Schumpeter anticipated. But I am sure that he would still urge us to separate the future of socialism from that of Soviet and Eastern European Communism.

Unlike Schumpeter I do not include Socialism in my title, since its future as a distinct ideology and program of action is unclear at best. Western Marxism and the moderate socialist movements seem to have settled for social democratic solutions, for adaptations of both capitalism and democracy producing acceptable mixes of market competition, political pluralism, participation, and welfare. I deal with these modifications of capitalism, as a consequence of the impact of democracy on capitalism in the last half century.

At the time that Adam Smith wrote *The Wealth of Nations,* the world of government, politics and the state that he knew—pre-Reform Act England, the French government of Louis XV and XVI—was riddled with special privileges, monopolies, interferences with trade. With my tongue only half way in my cheek I believe the discipline of economics may have been traumatized by this condition of political life at its birth. Typically, economists speak of the state and government instrumentally,

Reprinted from *PS: Political Science and Politics*, September 1991, pp. 467–474. Copyright © 1991 by the American Political Science Association.

as a kind of secondary service mechanism.

I do not believe that politics can be treated in this purely instrumental and reductive way without losing our analytic grip on the social and historical process. The economy and the polity are the main problem solving mechanisms of human society. They each have their distinctive means, and they each have their "goods" or ends. They necessarily interact with each other, and transform each other in the process. Democracy in particular generates goals and programs. You cannot give people the suffrage, and let them form organizations, run for office, and the like, without their developing all kinds of ideas as to how to improve things. And sometimes some of these ideas are adopted, implemented and are productive, and improve our lives, although many economists are reluctant to concede this much to the state.

My lecture deals with this interaction of politics and economics in the Western World in the course of the last couple of centuries, in the era during which capitalism and democracy emerged as the dominant problem solving institutions of modern civilization. I am going to discuss some of the theoretical and empirical literature dealing with the themes of the positive and negative interaction between capitalism and democracy. There are those who say that capitalism supports democracy, and those who say that capitalism subverts democracy. And there are those who say that democracy subverts capitalism, and those who say that it supports it.

The relation between capitalism and democracy dominates the political theory of the last two centuries. All the logically possible points of view are represented in a rich literature. It is this ambivalence and dialectic, this tension between the two major problem solving sectors of modern society—the political and the economic—that is the topic of my lecture.

Capitalism Supports Democracy

Let me begin with the argument that capitalism is positively linked with democracy, shares its values and culture, and facilitates its development. This case has been made in historical, logical, and statistical terms.

Albert Hirschman in his *Rival Views of Market Society* (1986) examines the values, manners and morals of capitalism, and their effects on the larger society and culture as these have been described by the philosophers of the 17th, 18th, and 19th centuries. He shows how the interpretation of the impact of capitalism has changed from the enlightenment view of Montesquieu, Condorcet, Adam Smith and others, who stressed the *douceur* of commerce, its "gentling," civilizing effect on behavior and interpersonal relations, to that of the 19th and 20th century conservative and radical writers who described the culture of capitalism as crassly materialistic, destructively competitive, corrosive of morality, and hence self-destructive. This sharp almost 180-degree shift in point of view among political theorists is partly explained by the transformation from the commerce and small-scale industry of early capitalism, to the smoke blackened industrial districts, the demonic and exploitive entrepreneurs, and exploited laboring classes of the second half of the nineteenth century. Unfortunately for our purposes, Hirschman doesn't deal explicitly with the capitalism–democracy connection, but rather with culture and with manners. His argument, however, implies an early positive connection and a later negative one.

Joseph Schumpeter in *Capitalism, Socialism, and Democracy* (1942) states flatly, "History clearly confirms . . . [that] . . . modern democracy rose along with capitalism, and in causal connection with it . . . modern democracy is a product of the capitalist process." He has a whole chapter entitled "The Civilization of Capitalism," democracy being a part of that civilization. Schumpeter also makes the point that democracy was historically supportive of capitalism. He states, ". . . the bourgeoisie reshaped, and from its own point of view rationalized, the social and political structure that preceded its ascendancy. . ." (that is to say, feudalism). "The

democratic method was the political tool of that reconstruction." According to Schumpeter capitalism and democracy were mutually causal historically, mutually supportive parts of a rising modern civilization, although as we shall show below, he also recognized their antagonisms.

Barrington Moore's historical investigation (1966) with its long

The relation between capitalism and democracy dominates the political theory of the last two centuries.

title, *The Social Origins of Dictatorship and Democracy; Lord and Peasant in the Making of the Modern World,* argues that there have been three historical routes to industrial modernization. The first of these followed by Britain, France, and the United States, involved the subordination and transformation of the agricultural sector by the rising commercial bourgeoisie, producing the democratic capitalism of the 19th and 20th centuries. The second route followed by Germany and Japan, where the landed aristocracy was able to contain and dominate the rising commercial classes, produced an authoritarian and fascist version of industrial modernization, a system of capitalism encased in a feudal authoritarian framework, dominated by a military aristocracy, and an authoritarian monarchy. The third route, followed in Russia where the commercial bourgeoisie was too weak to give content and direction to the modernizing process, took the form of a revolutionary process drawing on the frustration and resources of the peasantry, and created a mobilized authoritarian Communist regime along with a state-controlled industrialized economy. Successful capitalism dominating and transforming the rural agricultural sector, according to Barrington Moore, is the creator and sustainer of the emerging democracies of the nineteenth century.

5. COMPARATIVE POLITICS: Turn to the Market

Robert A. Dahl, the leading American democratic theorist, in the new edition of his book (1990) *After the Revolution? Authority in a Good Society,* has included a new chapter entitled "Democracy and Markets." In the opening paragraph of that chapter, he says:

It is an historical fact that modern democratic institutions . . . have existed only in countries with predominantly privately owned, market-oriented economies, or capitalism if you prefer that name. It is also a fact that all "socialist" countries with predominantly state-owned centrally directed economic orders—command economies—have not enjoyed democratic governments, but have in fact been ruled by authoritarian dictatorships. It is also an historical fact that some "capitalist" countries have also been, and are, ruled by authoritarian dictatorships.

To put it more formally, it looks to be the case that market-oriented economies are necessary (in the logical sense) to democratic institutions, though they are certainly not sufficient. And it looks to be the case that state-owned centrally directed economic orders are strictly associated with authoritarian regimes, though authoritarianism definitely does not require them. We have something very much like an historical experiment, so it would appear, that leaves these conclusions in no great doubt. (Dahl 1990)

Peter Berger in his book *The Capitalist Revolution* (1986) presents four propositions on the relations between capitalism and democracy:

Capitalism is a necessary but not sufficient condition of democracy under modern conditions.

If a capitalist economy is subjected to increasing degrees of state control, a point (not precisely specifiable at this time) will be reached at which democratic governance becomes impossible.

If a socialist economy is opened up to increasing degrees of market forces, a point (not precisely specifiable at this time) will be reached at which democratic governance becomes a possibility.

If capitalist development is successful in generating economic growth from which a sizable proportion of the population benefits, pressures toward democracy are likely to appear.

This positive relationship between capitalism and democracy has also been sustained by statistical studies. The "Social Mobilization" theorists of the 1950s and 1960s which included Daniel Lerner (1958), Karl Deutsch (1961), S. M. Lipset (1959) among others, demonstrated a strong statistical association between GNP per capita and democratic political institutions. This is more than simple statistical association. There is a logic in the relation between level of economic development and democratic institutions. Level of economic development has been shown to be associated with education and literacy, exposure to mass media, and democratic psychological propensities such as subjective efficacy, participatory aspirations and skills. In a major investigation of the social psychology of industrialization and modernization, a research team led by the sociologist Alex Inkeles (1974) interviewed several thousand workers in the modern industrial and the traditional economic sectors of six countries of differing culture. Inkeles found empathetic, efficacious, participatory and activist propensities much more frequently among the modern industrial workers, and to a much lesser extent in the traditional sector in each one of these countries regardless of cultural differences.

The historical, the logical, and the statistical evidence for this positive relation between capitalism and democracy is quite persuasive.

Capitalism Subverts Democracy

But the opposite case is also made, that capitalism subverts or undermines democracy. Already in John Stuart Mill (1848) we encounter a view of existing systems of private property as unjust, and of the free market as destructively competitive—aesthetically and morally repugnant. The case he was making was a normative rather than a political one. He wanted a less competitive society, ultimately socialist, which would still respect individuality. He advocated limitations on the inheritance of property and the improvement of the property system so that everyone shared in its benefits, the limitation of population growth, and the im-

provement of the quality of the labor force through the provision of high quality education for all by the state. On the eve of the emergence of the modern democratic capitalist order John Stuart Mill wanted to control the excesses of both the market economy and the majoritarian polity, by the education of consumers and producers, citizens and politicians, in the interest of producing morally improved free market and democratic orders. But in contrast to Marx, he did not thoroughly discount the possibilities of improving the capitalist and democratic order.

Marx argued that as long as capitalism and private property existed there could be no genuine democracy, that democracy under capitalism was bourgeois democracy, which is to say not democracy at all. While it would be in the interest of the working classes to enter a coalition with the bourgeoisie in supporting this form of democracy in order

---

There is a logic in the relation between level of economic development and democratic institutions.

---

to eliminate feudalism, this would be a tactical maneuver. Capitalist democracy could only result in the increasing exploitation of the working classes. Only the elimination of capitalism and private property could result in the emancipation of the working classes and the attainment of true democracy. Once socialism was attained the basic political problems of humanity would have been solved through the elimination of classes. Under socialism there would be no distinctive democratic organization, no need for institutions to resolve conflicts, since there would be no conflicts. There is not much democratic or political theory to be found in Marx's writings. The basic reality is the mode of economic production and the consequent class structure from which other institutions follow.

For the followers of Marx up to the present day there continues to be a negative tension between capitalism, however reformed, and democracy. But the integral Marxist and Leninist rejection of the possibility of an autonomous, bourgeois democratic state has been left behind for most Western Marxists. In the thinking of Poulantzas, Offe, Bobbio, Habermas and others, the bourgeois democratic state is now viewed as a class struggle state, rather than an unambiguously bourgeois state. The working class has access to it; it can struggle for its interests, and can attain partial benefits from it. The state is now viewed as autonomous, or as relatively autonomous, and it can be reformed in a progressive direction by working class and other popular movements. The bourgeois democratic state can be moved in the direction of a socialist state by political action short of violence and institutional destruction.

Schumpeter (1942) appreciated the tension between capitalism and democracy. While he saw a causal connection between competition in the economic and the political order, he points out ". . . that there are some deviations from the principle of democracy which link up with the presence of organized capitalist interests. . . . [T]he statement is true both from the standpoint of the classical and from the standpoint of our own theory of democracy. From the first standpoint, the result reads that the means at the disposal of private interests are often used in order to thwart the will of the people. From the second standpoint, the result reads that those private means are often used in order to interfere with the working of the mechanism of competitive leadership." He refers to some countries and situations in which ". . . political life all but resolved itself into a struggle of pressure groups and in many cases practices that failed to conform to the spirit of the democratic method." But he rejects the notion that there cannot be political democracy in a capitalist society. For Schumpeter full democracy in the sense of the informed participation of all adults in the selection of political leaders and consequently the making of public policy, was an impossibility

because of the number and complexity of the issues confronting modern electorates. The democracy which was realistically possible was one in which people could choose among competing leaders, and consequently exercise some direction over political decisions. This kind of democracy was possible in a capitalist society, though some of its propensities impaired its performance. Writing in the early years of World War II, when the future of democracy and of capitalism were uncertain, he leaves unresolved the questions of ". . . Whether or not democracy is one of those products of capitalism which are to die out with it. . ." or ". . . how well or ill capitalist society qualifies for the task of working the democratic method it evolved."

Non-Marxist political theorists have contributed to this questioning of the reconcilability of capitalism and democracy. Robert A. Dahl, who makes the point that capitalism historically has been a necessary precondition of democracy, views contemporary democracy in the United States as seriously compromised, impaired by the inequality in resources among the citizens. But Dahl stresses the variety in distributive patterns, and in politico-economic relations among contemporary democracies. "The category of capitalist democracies" he writes, "includes an extraordinary variety . . . from nineteenth century, laissez faire, early industrial systems to twentieth century, highly regulated, social welfare, late or postindustrial systems. Even late twentieth century 'welfare state' orders vary all the way from the Scandinavian systems, which are redistributive, heavily taxed, comprehensive in their social security, and neocorporatist in their collective bargaining arrangements to the faintly redistributive, moderately taxed, limited social security, weak collective bargaining systems of the United States and Japan" (1989).

In *Democracy and Its Critics* (1989) Dahl argues that the normative growth of democracy to what he calls its "third transformation" (the first being the direct city-state democracy of classic times, and the second, the indirect, representative inegalitarian democracy of the contemporary world) will require democ-

Robert A. Dahl, who makes the point that capitalism historically has been a necessary precondition of democracy, views contemporary democracy in the United States as seriously compromised, impaired by the inequality in resources among the citizens.

ratization of the economic order. In other words, modern corporate capitalism needs to be transformed. Since government control and/or ownership of the economy would be destructive of the pluralism which is an essential requirement of democracy, his preferred solution to the problem of the mega-corporation is employee control of corporate industry. An economy so organized, according to Dahl, would improve the distribution of political resources without at the same time destroying the pluralism which democratic competition requires. To those who question the realism of Dahl's solution to the problem of inequality, he replies that history is full of surprises.

Charles E. Lindblom in his book, *Politics and Markets* (1977), concludes his comparative analysis of the political economy of modern capitalism and socialism, with an essentially pessimistic conclusion about contemporary market-oriented democracy. He says

> We therefore come back to the corporation. It is possible that the rise of the corporation has offset or more than offset the decline of class as an instrument of indoctrination. . . . That it creates a new core of wealth and power for a newly constructed upper class, as well as an overpowering loud voice, is also reasonably clear. The executive of the large corporation is, on many counts, the contemporary counterpart to the landed gentry of an earlier era, his voice

amplified by the technology of mass communication. . . . [T]he major institutional barrier to fuller democracy may therefore be the autonomy of the private corporation.

Lindblom concludes, "The large private corporation fits oddly into democratic theory and vision. Indeed it does not fit."

There is then a widely shared agreement, from the Marxists and neo-Marxists, to Schumpeter, Dahl, Lindblom, and other liberal political theorists, that modern capitalism with the dominance of the large corporation, produces a defective or an impaired form of democracy.

Democracy Subverts Capitalism

If we change our perspective now and look at the way democracy is said to affect capitalism, one of the dominant traditions of economics from Adam Smith until the present day stresses the importance for productivity and welfare of an economy that is relatively free of intervention by the state. In this doctrine of minimal government there is still a place for a framework of rules and services essential to the productive and efficient performance of the economy. In part the government has to protect the market from itself. Left to their own devices, according to Smith, businessmen were prone to corner the market in order to exact the highest possible price. And according to Smith businessmen were prone to bribe public officials in order to gain special privileges, and legal monopolies. For Smith good capitalism was competitive capitalism, and good government provided just those goods and services which the market needed to flourish, could not itself provide, or would not provide. A good government according to Adam Smith was a minimal government, providing for the national defense, and domestic order. Particularly important for the economy were the rules pertaining to commercial life such as the regulation of weights and measures, setting and enforcing building standards, providing for the protection of persons and property, and the like.

For Milton Friedman (1961, 1981), the leading contemporary advocate of the free market and free government, and of the interdependence of the two, the principal threat to the survival of capitalism and democracy is the assumption of the responsibility for welfare on the part of the modern democratic state. He lays down a set of functions appropriate to government in the positive interplay between economy and polity, and then enumerates many of the ways in which the modern welfare, regulatory state has deviated from these criteria.

A good Friedmanesque, democratic government would be one ". . . which maintained law and order, defended property rights, served as a means whereby we could modify property rights and other rules of the economic game, adjudicated disputes about the interpretation of the rules, enforced contracts, promoted competition, provided a monetary framework, engaged in activities to counter technical monopolies and to overcome neighborhood effects widely regarded as sufficiently important to justify government intervention, and which supplemented private charity and the private family in protecting the irresponsible, whether madman or child. . . ." Against this list of proper activities for a free government, Friedman pinpointed more than a dozen activities of contemporary democratic governments which might better be performed through the private sector, or

---

. . . one of the dominant traditions of economics from Adam Smith until the present day stresses the importance for productivity and welfare of an economy that is relatively free of intervention by the state.

---

not at all. These included setting and maintaining price supports, tariffs, import and export quotas and controls, rents, interest rates, wage rates, and the like, regulating industries and banking, radio and television, licensing professions and occupations, providing social security and medical care programs, providing public housing, national parks, guaranteeing mortgages, and much else.

Friedman concludes that this steady encroachment on the private sector has been slowly but surely converting our free government and market system into a collective monster, compromising both freedom and productivity in the outcome. The tax and expenditure revolts and regulatory rebellions of the 1980s have temporarily stemmed this trend, but the threat continues. "It is the internal threat coming from men of good intentions and good will who wish to reform us. Impatient with the slowness of persuasion and example to achieve the great social changes they envision, they are anxious to use the power of the state to achieve their ends, and confident of their own ability to do so." The threat to political and economic freedom, according to Milton Friedman and others who argue the same position, arises out of democratic politics. It may only be defeated by political action.

In the last decades a school, or rather several schools, of economists and political scientists have turned the theoretical models of economics to use in analyzing political processes. Variously called public choice theorists, rational choice theorists, or positive political theorists, and employing such models as market exchange and bargaining, rational self interest, game theory, and the like, these theorists have produced a substantial literature throwing new and often controversial light on democratic political phenomena such as elections, decisions of political party leaders, interest group behavior, legislative and committee decisions, bureaucratic, and judicial behavior, lobbying activity, and substantive public policy areas such as constitutional arrangements, health and environment policy, regulatory policy, national security and foreign policy, and the like. Hardly a field of politics and public policy has been left untouched by this inventive and productive group of scholars.

The institutions and names with which this movement is associated in the United States include Virginia State University, the University of Virginia, the George Mason University, the University of Rochester, the University of Chicago, the California Institute of Technology, the Carnegie Mellon University, among others. And the most prominent names are those of the leaders of the two principal schools: James Buchanan, the Nobel Laureate leader of the Virginia "Public Choice" school, and William Riker, the leader of the Rochester "Positive Theory" school. Other prominent scholars associated with this work are Gary Becker of the University of Chicago, Kenneth Shepsle and Morris Fiorina of Harvard, John Ferejohn of Stanford, Charles Plott of the California Institute of Technology, and many others.

One writer summarizing the ideological bent of much of this work, but by no means all of it (William Mitchell of the University of Washington), describes it as fiscally conservative, sharing a conviction that the ". . . private economy is far more robust, efficient, and perhaps, equitable than other economies, and much more successful than political processes in efficiently allocating resources. . . ." Much of what has been produced ". . . by James Buchanan and the leaders of this school can best be described as contributions to a theory of the failure of political processes." These failures of political performance are said to be inherent properties of the democratic political process. "Inequity, inefficiency, and coercion are the most general results of democratic policy formation." In a democracy the demand for publicly provided services seems to be insatiable. It ultimately turns into a special interest, "rent seeking" society. Their remedies take the form of proposed constitutional limits on spending power and checks and balances to limit legislative majorities.

One of the most visible products of this pessimistic economic analysis of democratic politics is the book by Mancur Olson, *The Rise and Decline of Nations* (1982). He makes a strong argument for the negative democracy–capitalism connection. His thesis is that the behavior of individuals and firms in stable socie-

ties inevitably leads to the formation of dense networks of collusive, cartelistic, and lobbying organizations that make economies less efficient and dynamic and polities less governable. "The longer a society goes without an upheaval, the more powerful such organizations become and the more they slow down economic expansion. Societies in which these narrow interest groups have been destroyed, by war or revolution, for example, enjoy the greatest gains in growth." His prize cases are Britain on the one hand and Germany and Japan on the other.

The logic of the argument implies that countries that have had democratic freedom of organization without upheaval or invasion the longest will suffer the most from growth-repressing organizations and combinations. This helps explain why Great Britain, the major nation with the longest immunity from dictatorship, invasion, and revolution, has had in this century a lower rate of growth than other large, developed democracies. Britain has precisely the powerful network of special interest organization that the argument developed here would lead us to expect in a country with its record of military security and democratic stability. The number and power of its trade unions need no description. The venerability and power of its professional associations is also striking. . . . In short, with age British society has acquired so many strong organizations and collusions that it suffers from an institutional sclerosis that slows its adaptation to changing circumstances and technologies. (Olson 1982)

By contrast, post-World War II Germany and Japan started organizationally from scratch. The organizations that led them to defeat were all dissolved, and under the occupation inclusive organizations like the general trade union movement and general organizations of the industrial and commercial community were first formed. These inclusive organizations had more regard for the general national interest and exercised some discipline on the narrower interest organizations. And both countries in the post-war decades experienced "miracles" of economic growth under democratic conditions.

The Olson theory of the subversion of capitalism through the pro-

pensities of democratic societies to foster special interest groups has not gone without challenge. There can be little question that there is logic in his argument. But empirical research testing this pressure group hypothesis thus far has produced mixed findings. Olson has hopes that a public educated to the harmful consequences of special interests to economic growth, full employment,

---

Olson has hopes that a public educated to the harmful consequences of special interests to economic growth, full employment, coherent government, equal opportunity, and social mobility will resist special interest behavior, and enact legislation imposing anti-trust, and anti-monopoly controls to mitigate and contain these threats.

---

coherent government, equal opportunity, and social mobility will resist special interest behavior, and enact legislation imposing anti-trust, and anti-monopoly controls to mitigate and contain these threats. It is somewhat of an irony that the solution to this special interest disease of democracy, according to Olson, is a democratic state with sufficient regulatory authority to control the growth of special interest organizations.

Democracy Fosters Capitalism

My fourth theme, democracy as fostering and sustaining capitalism, is not as straightforward as the first three. Historically there can be little doubt that as the suffrage was extended in the last century, and as mass political parties developed, democratic development impinged significantly on capitalist institutions and practices. Since successful capitalism requires risk-taking entrepreneurs with access to investment capital, the democratic propensity for redistributive and regulative policy tends to reduce the incentives and the resources available for risk-taking and creativity. Thus it can be argued that propensities inevitably resulting from democratic politics, as Friedman, Olson and many others argue, tend to reduce productivity, and hence welfare.

But precisely the opposite argument can be made on the basis of the historical experience of literally all of the advanced capitalist democracies in existence. All of them without exception are now welfare states with some form and degree of social insurance, health and welfare nets, and regulatory frameworks designed to mitigate the harmful impacts and shortfalls of capitalism. Indeed, the welfare state is accepted all across the political spectrum. Controversy takes place around the edges. One might make the argument that had capitalism not been modified in this welfare direction, it is doubtful that it would have survived.

This history of the interplay between democracy and capitalism is clearly laid out in a major study involving European and American scholars, entitled *The Development of Welfare States in Western Europe and America* (Flora and Heidenheimer 1981). The book lays out the relationship between the development and spread of capitalist industry, democratization in the sense of an expanding suffrage and the emergence of trade unions and left-wing political parties, and the gradual introduction of the institutions and practices of the welfare state. The early adoption of the institutions of the welfare state in Bismarck Germany, Sweden, and Great Britain were all associated with the rise of trade unions and socialist parties in those countries. The decisions made by the upper and middle class leaders and political movements to introduce welfare measures such as accident, old age, and unemployment insurance, were strategic decisions. They were increasingly confronted by trade union movements with the capacity

of bringing industrial production to a halt, and by political parties with growing parliamentary representation favoring fundamental modifications in, or the abolition of capitalism. As the calculations of the upper and middle class leaders led them to conclude that the costs of suppression exceeded the costs of concession, the various parts of the welfare state began to be put in place—accident, sickness, unemployment insurance, old age insurance, and the like. The problem of maintaining the loyalty of the working classes through two world wars resulted in additional concessions to working class demands: the filling out of the social security system, free public education to higher levels, family allowances, housing benefits, and the like.

Social conditions, historical factors, political processes and decisions produced different versions of the welfare state. In the United States, manhood suffrage came quite early, the later bargaining process emphasized free land and free education to the secondary level, an equality of opportunity version of the welfare state. The Disraeli bargain in Britain resulted in relatively early manhood suffrage and the full attainment of parliamentary government, while the Lloyd George bargain on the eve of World War I brought the beginnings of a welfare system to Britain. The Bismarck bargain in Germany produced an early welfare state, a postponement of electoral equality and parliamentary government. While there were all of these differences in historical encounters with democratization and "welfarization," the important outcome was that little more than a century after the process began all of the advanced capitalist democracies had similar versions of the welfare state, smaller in scale in the case of the United States and Japan, more substantial in Britain and the continental European countries.

We can consequently make out a strong case for the argument that democracy has been supportive of capitalism in this strategic sense. Without this welfare adaptation it is doubtful that capitalism would have survived, or rather, its survival, "unwelfarized," would have required a substantial repressive apparatus.

The choice then would seem to have been between democratic welfare capitalism, and repressive undemocratic capitalism. I am inclined to believe that capitalism as such thrives more with the democratic welfare adaptation than with the repressive one. It is in that sense that we can argue that there is a clear positive impact of democracy on capitalism.

* * *

We have to recognize, in conclusion, that democracy and capitalism are both positively and negatively related, that they both support and subvert each other. My colleague, Moses Abramovitz, described this dialectic more surely than most in his presidential address to the American Economic Association in 1980, on the eve of the "Reagan Revolution." Noting the decline in productivity in the American economy during the latter 1960s and '70s, and recognizing that this decline might in part be attributable to the "tax, transfer, and regulatory" tendencies of the welfare state, he observes,

> The rationale supporting the development of our mixed economy sees it as a pragmatic compromise between the competing virtues and defects of decentralized market capitalism and encompassing socialism. Its goal is to obtain a measure of distributive justice, security, and social guidance of economic life without losing too much of the allocative efficiency and dynamism of private enterprise and market organization. And it is a pragmatic compromise in another sense. It seeks to retain for most people that measure of personal protection from the state which private property and a private job market confer, while obtaining for the disadvantaged minority of people through the state that measure of support without which their lack of property or personal endowment would amount to a denial of individual freedom and capacity to function as full members of the community. (Abramovitz, 1981)

Democratic welfare capitalism produces that reconciliation of opposing and complementary elements which makes possible the survival, even enhancement of both of these sets of institutions. It is not a static accommodation, but rather one which fluctuates over time, with capitalism being compromised by the tax-transfer-regulatory action of the state at one point, and then correcting in the direction of the reduction of the intervention of the state at another point, and with a learning process over time that may reduce the amplitude of the curves.

The case for this resolution of the capitalism-democracy quandary is made quite movingly by Jacob Viner who is quoted in the concluding paragraph of Abramovitz's paper, ". . . If . . . I nevertheless conclude that I believe that the welfare state, like old Siwash, is really worth fighting for and even dying for as compared to any rival system, it is because, despite its imperfection in theory and practice, in the aggregate it provides more promise of preserving and enlarging human freedoms, temporal prosperity, the extinction of mass misery, and the dignity of man and his moral improvement than any other social system which has previously prevailed, which prevails elsewhere today or which outside Utopia, the mind of man has been able to provide a blueprint for" (Abramovitz, 1981).

References

Abramovitz, Moses. 1981. "Welfare Quandaries and Productivity Concerns." *American Economic Review,* March.

Berger, Peter. 1986. *The Capitalist Revolution.* New York: Basic Books.

Dahl, Robert A. 1989. *Democracy and Its Critics.* New Haven: Yale University Press.

———. 1990. *After the Revolution: Authority in a Good Society.* New Haven: Yale University Press.

Deutsch, Karl. 1961. "Social Mobilization and Political Development." *American Political Science Review,* 55 (Sept.).

Flora, Peter, and Arnold Heidenheimer. 1981. *The Development of Welfare States in Western Europe and America.* New Brunswick, NJ: Transaction Press.

Friedman, Milton. 1981. *Capitalism and Freedom.* Chicago: University of Chicago Press.

Hirschman, Albert. 1986. *Rival Views of Market Society.* New York: Viking.

Inkeles, Alex, and David Smith. 1974. *Becoming Modern: Individual Change in Six Developing Countries.* Cambridge, MA: Harvard University Press.

Lerner, Daniel. *The Passing of Traditional Society.* New York: Free Press.

Lindblom, Charles E. 1977. *Politics and Markets.* New York: Basic Books.

Lipset, Seymour M. 1959. "Some Social Requisites of Democracy." *American Political Science Review,* 53 (September).

Mill, John Stuart. 1848, 1965. *Principles of Political Economy,* 2 vols. Toronto: University of Toronto Press.

Mitchell, William. 1988. "Virginia, Rochester, and Bloomington: Twenty-Five Years of Public Choice and Political Science." *Public Choice,* 56: 101-119.

Moore, Barrington. 1966. *The Social Origins of Dictatorship and Democracy.* New York: Beacon Press.

Olson, Mancur. 1982. *The Rise and Decline of Nations.* New Haven: Yale University Press.

Schumpeter, Joseph. 1946. *Capitalism, Socialism, and Democracy.* New York: Harper.

Communitarian vs. Individualistic Capitalism

Lester Thurow

Dean of MIT's Sloan School of Management, Lester Thurow has just completed a book on global competition entitled Head to Head *(William Morrow, 1992).*

In March 1990 the two biggest business groups in the world, Japan's Mitsubishi and Germany's Daimler Benz-Deutsche Bank, held a secret meeting in Singapore to talk about a global alliance. Among other things, both were interested in discussing how to expand their market share in civilian aircraft production.

From an American perspective, everything about that Singapore meeting was highly illegal, violating both antitrust and banking laws. In the U.S., banks cannot own industrial firms and businesses cannot sit down behind closed doors to plan joint strategies. Those doing so get thrown in jail for extended periods of time. Yet today Americans cannot force the rest of the world to play the economic game as they think it should be played. The game will be played under international, not American, rules.

With economic competition between communism and capitalism over, this other competition —between two different forms of capitalism— has quickly taken over the economic playing field. Using a distinction first made by Harvard's George C. Lodge, the individualistic, Anglo-Saxon, British-American form of capitalism is going to face off against the communitarian German and Japanese variants of capitalism: The "I" of America or the United Kingdom versus "Das Volk" and "Japan Inc." The essential difference

Today Americans cannot force the rest of the world to play the economic game as they think it should be played. The game will be played under international, not American, rules.

between the two is the relative stress placed on communitarian and individualistic values as the best route to economic success.

Shareholders and Stakeholders | America and Britain champion individualistic values: the brilliant entrepreneur, Nobel Prize winners, large wage differentials, individual responsibility for skills, easy-to-fire-easy-to-quit, profit maximization, hostile mergers and takeovers. Their hero is the Lone Ranger.

In contrast, Germany and Japan trumpet communitarian values: business groups, social responsibility for skills, team work, firm loyalty, growth-promoting industry and government strategies. Anglo-Saxon firms are profit maximizers; Japanese and German business firms play a game best termed "strategic conquest." Americans believe in "consumer economics"; Japanese believe in "producer economics."

In the Anglo-Saxon variant of capitalism, the individual is supposed to have a personal economic strategy for success, while the business firm is to have an economic strategy reflecting the wishes of its individual shareholders. Since shareholders want income to maximize their lifetime consumption, their firms must be profit maximizers. For the profit-maximizing firm, customer and employee relations are merely a means of achieving higher profits for the shareholders. Using this formula, lower wages equal higher profits—and wages are to be beaten down where possible. When not needed, employees are to be laid off. For their part, workers in the Anglo-Saxon system are expected to

From *New Perspectives Quarterly*, Winter 1992, pp. 41-45. Reprinted with permission.

change employers whenever opportunities exist to earn higher wages elsewhere.

Whereas in Anglo-Saxon firms the shareholder is the only stakeholder, in Japanese business firms employees are seen as the No. 1 stakeholder, customers No. 2, and the shareholders a distant No. 3, whose dividend pay-outs are low. Because employees are the prime stakeholders, higher employee wages are a central goal of the firm in Japan. The firm can be seen as a "value-added maximizer" rather than as a "profit maximizer." Profits will be sacrificed to maintain either wages or employment.

Workers in the communitarian system join a company team and are then considered successful as part of that team. The key decision in an individual's personal strategy is to join the "right" team.

In the United States or Great Britain, employee turnover rates are viewed positively. Firms are getting rid of unneeded labor when they fire workers, and individuals are moving to higher wage opportunities when they quit. Job switching, voluntary or involuntary, is almost a synonym for efficiency. In both Germany and Japan job switching is far less prevalent. In fact, many Japanese firms still refer to voluntary quits as "treason."

Coalesce for Success | Beyond personal and firm strategies, communitarian capitalists believe in having strategies at two additional levels. Business groups such as Japan's Mitsui Group or Germany's Deutsche Bank Group are expected to have a collective strategy in which companies are financially interlocked and work together to strengthen each other's activities. At the top of the pyramid of Japanese business groups are the major *zaibatsu* (Mitsui group, 23 member firms; Mitsubishi group, 28 member firms; Sumatomo group, 21 member firms; Fuji group, 29 member firms; Sanwa group, 39 member firms; Dai-Ichi Kangyo group, 45 member firms.) The members of each group will own a controlling block of shares in each of the firms in the group. In addition, each member firm will in turn have a group of smaller customers and suppliers, the *keiretsu*, grouped around it. Hitachi has 688 firms in its family; Toyota has 175 primary members and 4,000 secondary members.

Similar patterns exist in Germany. The Deutsche Bank directly owns 10 percent or more of the shares in 70 companies: It owns 28 percent of Germany's largest company Daimler-Benz; 10 percent of Europe's largest reinsurance company Munich Rai; 25 percent of Europe's largest department store chain, Karstady; 30 percent of Germany's largest construction company, Philipp Holzmann; and 21 percent of Europe's largest sugar producer, Sudzucker. Through its trust department, Deutsche Bank indirectly controls many more shares that don't have to be publicly disclosed.

When the Arabs threatened to buy a controlling interest in Mercedes Benz a few years ago, the Deutsche Bank intervened on behalf of the German economy to buy a controlling interest. Now the bank protects the managers of Mercedes Benz from the raids of the financial Vikings: it frees the managers from the tyranny of the stock market, with its emphasis on quarterly profits; and it helps plan corporate strategies and raise the money to carry out these strategies. But it also fires the managers if Mercedes Benz slips in the auto market and prevents the managers from engaging in self-serving activities such as poison pills or golden parachutes, which do not enhance the company's long-term prospects.

Government's Role in Economic Growth | Both Europe and Japan believe that government has a role to play in economic growth. An example of this philosophy put into practice is the pan-European project called Airbus Industries, a civilian aircraft manufacturer owned by the British, French, German and Spanish governments, designed to break the American monopoly and get Europe back into civilian aircraft manufacturing. Today it is a success, with 20 percent of the aircraft market and announced plans to double production and capture one-third of the worldwide market by the mid-1990s.

Airbus' penetration into the aircraft manufacturing industry has severely affected U.S. manufacturers. In 1990 Boeing's market share of new orders dropped to 45 percent — the first time in decades it had been below 50 percent. McDonnell Douglas' market share has been reduced from 30 percent to 15 percent. In this particular industry, a greater European share can only mean a smaller market share for Boeing and the demise of McDonnell Douglas.

The Europeans now have a number of pan-European strategic efforts underway to catch up

> Whereas in Anglo-Saxon firms the shareholder is the only stakeholder, in Japanese business firms employees are seen as the No. 1 stakeholder, customers No. 2, and the shareholders a distant No. 3.

with America and Japan. Each is designed to help European firms compete in some major industry. European governments spend from 5¹/₂ percent (Italy) to 1³/₄ percent (Britain) of the GNP aiding industry. If the U.S. had spent what Germany spends (2¹/₂ percent of GNP), $140 billion would have gone to help U.S. industries in 1991. In Spain, where the economy grew more rapidly than any other in Europe in the 1980s, government-owned firms produce at least half of the GDP. In France and Italy, the state sector accounts for one-third of the GNP.

"Social Market" vs. "Market" Economy | Germany, the dominant European economic power, sees itself as having a "social market" economy and not just a "market" economy. State and federal governments in Germany own more shares in more industries — airlines, autos, steel, chemicals, electric power, transportation — than any non-communist country on the face of the globe. Public investments such as Airbus Industries are not controversial political issues. Privatization is not sweeping Germany as it did Great Britain.

In Germany, government is believed to have an important role to play in insuring that everyone has the skills necessary to participate in the market. Its socially financed apprenticeship system is the envy of the world. Social welfare policies are seen as a necessary part of a market economy. Unfettered capitalism is believed to generate levels of income inequality that are unacceptable.

The U.S., by contrast, sees social welfare programs as a regrettable necessity brought about by people who will not provide for their own old age, unemployment or ill health. Continual public discussions remind everyone that the higher taxes required to pay for social welfare systems reduce work incentives for those paying taxes and that social welfare benefits undercut work incentives for those that get them. In the ideal Anglo-Saxon market economy social welfare policies would not be necessary.

Administrative Guidance | In Japan, industry representatives working with the Ministry of International Trade and Industry present "visions" as to where the economy should be going. In the past these visions served as guides to the allocation of scarce foreign exchange or capital flows. Today what the Japanese know as "admin-

> State and federal governments in Germany own more shares in more industries — airlines, autos, steel, chemicals, electric power, transportation — than any non-communist country on the face of the globe.

istrative guidance" is a way of life, and it is used to aim R&D funding at key industries.

An example of this can be found in the Japanese strategy toward semiconductor chips, which was similar to Europe's Airbus plan in that it was lengthy, expensive and eventually successful in breaking the dominance of American firms. The government-financed "very-large-integrated-circuit-chip" research project was just part of a much larger effort, where a combination of patience, large investments and American mistakes (a reluctance to expand capacity during cyclical downturns) paid off in the end.

The idea of administrative guidance could not be more foreign to the minds of American officials. According to the politically correct language of the Bush administration, the U.S. government has no role in investment funding and a "legitimate" R&D role only in "precompetitive, generic, enabling technologies." These rules are sometimes violated in practice, but the principle is clear: Governments should protect private property rights, then get out of the way and let individuals do their thing. Capitalism will spontaneously combust.

History as Destiny | These different conceptions of capitalism flow from very different histories. In the formative years of British capitalism during the 19th century, Great Britain did not have to play "catch up" with anyone. As the initiator of the industrial revolution, Great Britain was the most powerful country in the world.

The U.S. similarly had a head start in its industrial revolution. Protected by two great oceans, the U.S. did not feel militarily threatened by Britain's early economic lead. In the last half of the 19th century, when it was moving faster than Great Britain, Americans could see that they were going to catch up without deliberate government efforts to throw more coal into the American economic steam engines.

On the other hand, 19th-century Germany had to catch up with Great Britain if it was not to be overrun in the wars of Europe. The rulers of German states were expected by their subjects to take an active part in fostering the economic growth of their territories. To have its rightful place at the European table, Prussia had to have a modern industrial economy. German capitalism needed help to catch up.

The Japanese system similarly did not occur by accident. Admiral Perry arrived in the mid-1800s and with a few cannon balls forced Japan to begin trading with the rest of the world. But the mid-19th century was the height of colonialism. If Japan did not quickly develop, it would become a colony of the British, French, Dutch, Germans or Americans. Economic development was part of national defense — perhaps a more important part than the army itself, for a modern army could not be built without a modern economy.

In both Germany and Japan, economic strategies were important elements of military strategies for remaining independent and becoming powerful. Governments pushed actively to insure that the economic combustion took place. They had to up the intensity of that combustion so that the economic gaps, and hence military gaps, between themselves and their potential enemies could be cut in the shortest possible time. Under these circumstances, it was not surprising that firms were organized along military lines or that the line between public and private disappeared. Government and industry had to work together to design the national economic strategies necessary for national independence. In a very real sense, business firms became the front line of national defense.

American history is very different. Government's first significant economic act — the Interstate Commerce Commission — was enacted to prevent the railroads from using their monopoly power to set freight rates that would rip off everyone else. A few decades later, its second significant act — the antitrust laws — was to prevent Mr. Rockefeller from using his control over the supply of lighting oil to extract everyone else's income. The third major source of government economic activity flowed from the collapse of capitalism in the 1930s, when government had to pick up the resultant mess.

As a result adversarial relations and deep suspicions of each other's motives are deeply embedded in American history. While very different histories have led to very different systems, today those very different systems face off in the same world economy.

Let me suggest that the military metaphors now so widely used should be replaced with the language of football. Despite the desire to win, football has a cooperative as well as a competitive element. Everyone has to agree on the rules of the game, the referees, and how to split the proceeds. One can want to win yet remain friends both during and after the game. But what the rest of the world knows as football is known as soccer in America. What Americans like about American football — frequent time outs, lots of huddles, and unlimited substitutions — are not present in world football. It has no time outs, no huddles and very limited substitutions. It is a faster game.

> In both Germany and Japan, economic strategies were important elements of military strategies for remaining independent and becoming powerful. In a very real sense, business firms became the front line of national defense.

World View

Faith Comes in From Political Fringe

Religion is taking a central role in dozens of governments around the globe.

Robin Wright

Times Staff Writer

WASHINGTON—This week, the world was expected to witness the birth of a new form of government—the first Islamic democracy—when Algerians went to the polls for the second round of their parliamentary elections.

The Islamic Salvation Front was poised to win decisively—as it did in the stunning first round on Dec. 26—and in the process formally secure the two-thirds control needed to change the constitution and override presidential vetoes. The outcome appeared so certain—and the ramifications of a fundamentalist victory so fearsome to political moderates and the army in the North African country—that a newly proclaimed High Security Council moved over the weekend to abort the electoral process.

It now appears that President Chadli Bendjedid, Algeria's head of state since 1979, was forced to resign because the government and the military so feared the Islamic tide. The events have left angry Muslim leaders accusing the authorities of treason, thrown the future of the Islamic party into doubt and raised fears of widespread unrest in the nation of 25 million people.

In a larger sense, however, developments in Algeria are not an aberration.

The growing role of religion in politics, a trend that took root in the 1980s, has now become a global phenomenon affecting most major faiths and dozens of otherwise disparate governments.

Under growing pressure from the religious right, Israel passed a new budget two weeks ago providing $75 million for roads, schools and 5,500 new settlement homes in the occupied territories—in defiance of international pressure to suspend settlements during peace talks.

"The ultra-Orthodox and the extreme right, the very religious, have never been so powerful in Israeli politics," said Ehud Sprinzak, a Hebrew University political scientist and author of "The Ascendance of Israel's Radical Right."

"Because of their audacity and the *chutzpah* of the religious settlers, [Prime Minister Yitzhak] Shamir may soon have to make a decision about whether he is prime minister of a state that has settlers or head of a religious fundamentalist movement which has a state."

After openly criticizing the government of President Fernando Collor de Mello for "gradual impoverishment" of the electorate, Brazil's Roman Catholic Church last year endorsed national strikes and the takeover of factories by workers. The Catholic bishops' "Brotherhood Campaign" openly declared its intent to "provoke in the people a rage and indignation" to fight poverty where government efforts have failed.

In Mongolia, where the Communist stranglehold has loosened, Buddhism is making a comeback arm-in-arm with Mongolian nationalism.

And in Cambodia, the new peace pact opened the way for restoration of Buddhism as the state religion, ending years of persecution and murder of religious activists by the Khmer Rouge and the Vietnamese-backed government. Prime Minister Hun Sen's tolerance of the Buddhist resurgence and the restoration of Buddhist temples has helped foster rapprochement with former rival Prince Norodom Sihanouk.

With the demise of communism in Eastern Europe, Orthodox Christianity has emerged as a powerful alternative source of national identity and, indirectly, political direction. Protestant evangelical groups have gained ground in the former Soviet-aligned East Bloc as well as in Central America, in the process redefining the traditional political culture.

Among Muslims, Pakistan last year introduced Sharia, or Islamic law, as the supreme law of the land. Although authority remains in the hands of secular officials, school curricula, banking and penal codes, and the judiciary must, in theory, conform to Islamic standards.

From *Los Angeles Times*, January 14, 1992, pp. 1, 4. Copyright © 1992 by Los Angeles Times.

In Tunisia, which neighbors Algeria, the most serious opposition group today is the outlawed Islamic Renaissance Party. In the former Soviet Asian republics, Islam is also one of the most powerful new political forces, despite the fact that Muslim political groups are outlawed in all but two republics.

Western democracies appear to be least affected. A 1991 poll in Western Europe revealed that religion is considered less important than family, work, friends and leisure time. The European Values Study reported that traditional religious belief was declining, as was the influence of the church in daily life.

Yet religion is still a defining factor in many of the nascent right-wing movements in Europe—ranging from France's National Front to the neo-Nazi groups in Germany and Austria—that oppose integration of foreign ethnic groups and religions in their own societies.

Even in tolerant Denmark, major protests erupted last year against plans to build an Islamic Cultural Center and mosque in Copenhagen for the 60,000 resident Muslims. Although polls indicate that only 2% of Danes regularly attend the national Lutheran church, 55% opposed the project and only 23% favored it, according to local press reports.

One of the most noticeable differences from the trend in the 1980s is that religious movements are no longer limited to the political fringe; religious parties are prominent not only in radical states such as Iran or anarchic environments like Lebanon.

In India, the world's most populous democracy, a militant right-wing Hindu movement became the official opposition in elections last year. In 1984, the Bharatiya Janata Party (BJP) won only two seats in the 545-member Parliament; last year, it rose to 119. The saffron banner, a symbol of Hinduism, is now a trademark of Indian Politics.

One common denominator among the diverse movements is the troubled environments in which they grow. They are often more a reaction to the weakness or outright failure of the traditional political forces than a new display of piety. Alienated by political malaise or corruption and economic decline that has reached crisis proportions, electorates are looking for viable or visible alternatives.

"Religion is subject to being used politically in the search for a rationale or for identity during times of change, whenever there is a cultural vacuum or when the old order is falling apart," said James Turner Johnson, a Rutgers University political science professor who specializes in religious movements.

"Religion is always there in the subculture and relatively easy to grab onto for political use."

The Islamic Salvation Front's sweep of Algeria's first-round parliamentary elections was widely considered as much a rejection of the National Liberation Front (FLN), which has ruled since the 1962 independence from France, as a popular embrace of Islam. It came at a time when at least one in four Algerians is unemployed, inflation is running about 100%, and the budget deficit exceeds $2 billion.

Once famed throughout the Third World for taking on the French and forcing their retreat in 1962 after more than a century of colonial rule, the FLN was humiliated in the first round of voting. It came in third, winning only 16 of 232 seats. The Islamic front won 188.

The fundamentalists were expected to win most of the 199 additional seats up for grabs in a second round of voting that was to take place this Thursday, thus insuring its majority. The Islamic party advocates strict adherence to Muslim tenets, including a ban on alcohol, separation of the sexes at school and "protection of the family," a position widely interpreted as denying jobs to women.

The new High Security Council has called for new elections to replace Bendjedid within 45 days, as required by Algeria's constitution. But that is widely seen in Algiers as a ruse meant to provide time for the military to devise some method to politically cripple the fundamentalists.

The rise of the Hindu BJP in India has coincided with disarray and divisiveness within the Congress Party, which has ruled for most of the 45 years since independence from Britain. India's economy is also deeply troubled, while growing Sikh and Muslim insurgencies are challenging the Hindu-dominated central government for control of rich Punjab and Kashmir provinces.

Another common denominator is the reaction against the prevalent themes of modern times. "Secular civilization, with its guided missiles and broken moral compass, its good life and bad faith, has never had more doubters," wrote editor Nathan Gardels in an issue of New Perspectives Quarterly that focused on the activist religions.

"The yearning for old certitudes and new revelations abound. From ethnic revivals to Islamic fundamentalism, from Catholic conservatism to New Age holism and Japanese traditionalism, the quest is on for a way to fill the hollow where God and community dwelt."

Many U.S. analysts expect the trend to grow in the years ahead.

"With modern nationalism called into question in so many places, the large-scale trend will be toward tribalism or massive convulsive in-gatherings of peoples who consider themselves to have mythic and historic roots that radically separate them from all others," said Martin Marty, University of Chicago professor and head of an international project on religion in politics.

"Religion comes into the political picture here because it's almost always the reinforcer of the tribal habit and ethos."

5. COMPARATIVE POLITICS: Tribal Threat to Pluralism?

In the short-term, religion could increasingly become a defining force in conflict, as it has already in pitting Christian Armenians against Muslim Azerbaijanis, in those two former Soviet republics, and Catholic Croats against Orthodox Serbs in Yugoslavia.

The greatest threat to Nigeria's return to civilian rule, scheduled for later this year, is tension between the Christian south and the Muslim north. Twice last year, sectarian clashes left hundreds dead in Africa's most populous state.

Some Places Where Religion and Politics Meet

ALGERIA: Moderates and the army move over weekend to halt a certain Islamic victory in parliamentary elections.

ISRAEL: Religious right with hard line on Mideast peace enjoys unprecedented political power.

INDIA: Militant Hindu movement becomes leading opposition party in 1991 general elections.

ARMENIA AND AZERBAIJAN: Religion becomes defining force in conflict between Christian Armenians and Muslim Azerbaijanis in these former Soviet republics.

BRAZIL: Activist Roman Catholic Church endorses strikes, factory takeovers in protest over failed anti-poverty programs.

The rivalry played a major role in the demise of Nigeria's two previous civilian governments in 1966 and 1983, but African experts say the political division along religious lines has never been as intense as it is now. In the north, one group of Muslims is now demanding the creation of an Islamic state. In the south, Christian military officers were behind a failed 1990 coup attempt to overthrow the long-dominant Muslim leadership.

U.S. specialists say the most destructive influence of India's BJP is on the Kashmir crisis, which was twice responsible for wars with neighboring Pakistan. In 1990, the Third World witnessed its first nuclear scare when India and Pakistan, both believed to have nuclear arms capabilities, went on full alert because the long-simmering insurgency had turned into a full-fledged rebellion.

"The BJP is basically immobilizing the government on the Kashmir issue, preventing a flexible sensible position that would allow that mess to be resolved," said Sig Harrison, an Asian expert at the Carnegie Endowment for International Peace. "India is engaging in human rights violation and repression in Kashmir and is not moving toward a settlement that could be achieved by granting maximum autonomy" to the Muslim-dominated province.

Later this month the BJP has scheduled a march from southern India to Srinagar, the Kashmiri capital, to show opposition to a compromise. "In this climate, there's a real danger of a war," Harrison added.

Although the interim may be turbulent, U.S. analysts predict that, in most cases, politicized religious forces either will be tempered by having to deal with practical political and economic crises or they will not survive.

The growing pragmatism of Iran's 13-year-old Islamic revolution, symbolized by the release last month of the last American hostages held by pro-Iranian extremists in Lebanon, is widely viewed as a by-product of its need to get access to Western aid to reconstruct its troubled economy.

"The overall tide of history will take societies where religion is now being used in politics beyond this," said Rutgers' Johnson. "We in the West used to have religions used in this way. In some ways, what we're seeing in other regions in the world is a repeat of a process that Western societies have already gone through."

The case of the Catholic Church's role in Poland is another example. "A decade ago in Poland, religion was a driving force, the thorn in the side of the Communist regime and instrumental in supporting Solidarity," said Jeffrey Hadden, a University of Virginia sociologist and author of several works on religion in politics.

"But no sooner had the transition to democracy taken place when religion took a very different role." Based on a tour of Poland last year, he added, "it's hard to find many people, who have anything nice to say about the church, which is now seen as asserting a conservative agenda on the country."

Indeed, although the country is more than 90% Catholic, the Polish Parliament last year refused to pass a restrictive anti-abortion bill that had been endorsed by Pope John Paul II, a Pole and a pivotal supporter of Solidarity. And a call last year by Poland's Catholic bishops to end the constitutional separation of church and state has been basically ignored.

"Over the long run," Johnson concluded, "what will have to happen is an acceptance of pluralism by everyone to be able to carry on meaningful relationships beyond their own religio-cultural frameworks."

*The two axial principles of our age—tribalism and globalism—clash at every point
except one: they may both be threatening to democracy*

JIHAD VS. MCWORLD

BENJAMIN R. BARBER

*Benjamin R. Barber is the Whitman Professor of Political
Science at Rutgers University. Barber's most recent books
are* Strong Democracy *(1984) and* The Conquest of Politics
(1988); his new book, An Aristocracy of Everyone, *will be
published in the fall of 1992.*

Just beyond the horizon of current events lie two possible political figures—both bleak, neither democratic. The first is a retribalization of large swaths of humankind by war and bloodshed: a threatened Lebanonization of national states in which culture is pitted against culture, people against people, tribe against tribe—a Jihad in the name of a hundred narrowly conceived faiths against every kind of interdependence, every kind of artificial social cooperation and civic mutuality. The second is being borne in on us by the onrush of economic and ecological forces that demand integration and uniformity and that mesmerize the world with fast music, fast computers, and fast food—with MTV, Macintosh, and McDonald's, pressing nations into one commercially homogenous global network: one McWorld tied together by technology, ecology, communications, and commerce. The planet is falling precipitantly apart *and* coming reluctantly together at the very same moment.

These two tendencies are sometimes visible in the same countries at the same instant: thus Yugoslavia, clamoring just recently to join the New Europe, is exploding into fragments; India is trying to live up to its reputation as the world's largest integral democracy while powerful new fundamentalist parties like the Hindu nationalist Bharatiya Janata Party, along with nationalist assassins, are imperiling its hard-won unity. States are breaking up or joining up: the Soviet Union has disappeared almost overnight, its parts forming new unions with one another or with like-minded nationalities in neighboring states. The old interwar national state based on territory and political sovereignty looks to be a mere transitional development.

The tendencies of what I am here calling the forces of Jihad and the forces of McWorld operate with equal strength in opposite directions, the one driven by parochial hatreds, the other by universalizing markets, the one re-creating ancient subnational and ethnic borders from within, the other making national borders porous from without. They have

one thing in common: neither offers much hope to citizens looking for practical ways to govern themselves democratically. If the global future is to put Jihad's centrifugal whirlwind against McWorld's centripetal black hole, the outcome is unlikely to be democratic—or so I will argue.

McWorld, or the Globalization of Politics

FOUR IMPERATIVES MAKE UP THE DYNAMIC OF McWorld: a market imperative, a resource imperative, an information-technology imperative, and an ecological imperative. By shrinking the world and diminishing the salience of national borders, these imperatives have in combination achieved a considerable victory over factiousness and particularism, and not least of all over their most virulent traditional form—nationalism. It is the realists who are now Europeans, the utopians who dream nostalgically of a resurgent England or Germany, perhaps even a resurgent Wales or Saxony. Yesterday's wishful cry for one world has yielded to the reality of McWorld.

The market imperative. Marxist and Leninist theories of imperialism assumed that the quest for ever-expanding markets would in time compel nation-based capitalist economies to push against national boundaries in search of an international economic imperium. Whatever else has happened to the scientistic predictions of Marxism, in this domain they have proved farsighted. All national economies are now vulnerable to the inroads of larger, transnational markets within which trade is free, currencies are convertible, access to banking is open, and contracts are enforceable under law. In Europe, Asia, Africa, the South Pacific, and the Americas such markets are eroding national sovereignty and giving rise to entities—international banks, trade associations, transnational lobbies like OPEC and Greenpeace, world news services like CNN and the BBC, and multinational corporations that increasingly lack a meaningful national identity—that neither reflect nor respect nationhood as an organizing or regulative principle.

The market imperative has also reinforced the quest

for international peace and stability, requisites of an efficient international economy. Markets are enemies of parochialism, isolation, fractiousness, war. Market psychology attenuates the psychology of ideological and religious cleavages and assumes a concord among producers and consumers—categories that ill fit narrowly conceived national or religious cultures. Shopping has little tolerance for blue laws, whether dictated by pub-closing British paternalism, Sabbath-observing Jewish Orthodox fundamentalism, or no-Sunday-liquor-sales Massachusetts puritanism. In the context of common markets, international law ceases to be a vision of justice and becomes a workaday framework for getting things done—enforcing contracts, ensuring that governments abide by deals, regulating trade and currency relations, and so forth.

Common markets demand a common language, as well as a common currency, and they produce common behaviors of the kind bred by cosmopolitan city life everywhere. Commercial pilots, computer programmers, international bankers, media specialists, oil riggers, entertainment celebrities, ecology experts, demographers, accountants, professors, athletes—these compose a new breed of men and women for whom religion, culture, and nationality can seem only marginal elements in a working identity. Although sociologists of everyday life will no doubt continue to distinguish a Japanese from an American mode, shopping has a common signature throughout the world. Cynics might even say that some of the recent revolutions in Eastern Europe have had as their true goal not liberty and the right to vote but well-paying jobs and the right to shop (although the vote is proving easier to acquire than consumer goods). The market imperative is, then, plenty powerful; but, notwithstanding some of the claims made for "democratic capitalism," it is not identical with the democratic imperative.

The resource imperative. Democrats once dreamed of societies whose political autonomy rested firmly on economic independence. The Athenians idealized what they called autarky, and tried for a while to create a way of life simple and austere enough to make the polis genuinely self-sufficient. To be free meant to be independent of any other community or polis. Not even the Athenians were able to achieve autarky, however: human nature, it turns out, is dependency. By the time of Pericles, Athenian politics was inextricably bound up with a flowering empire held together by naval power and commerce—an empire that, even as it appeared to enhance Athenian might, ate away at Athenian independence and autarky. Master and slave, it turned out, were bound together by mutual insufficiency.

The dream of autarky briefly engrossed nineteenth-century America as well, for the underpopulated, endlessly bountiful land, the cornucopia of natural resources, and the natural barriers of a continent walled in by two great seas led many to believe that America could be a world unto itself. Given this past, it has been harder for Americans than for most to accept the inevitability of in-

terdependence. But the rapid depletion of resources even in a country like ours, where they once seemed inexhaustible, and the maldistribution of arable soil and mineral resources on the planet, leave even the wealthiest societies ever more resource-dependent and many other nations in permanently desperate straits.

Every nation, it turns out, needs something another nation has; some nations have almost nothing they need.

The information-technology imperative. Enlightenment science and the technologies derived from it are inherently universalizing. They entail a quest for descriptive principles of general application, a search for universal solutions to particular problems, and an unswerving embrace of objectivity and impartiality.

Scientific progress embodies and depends on open communication, a common discourse rooted in rationality, collaboration, and an easy and regular flow and exchange of information. Such ideals can be hypocritical covers for power-mongering by elites, and they may be shown to be wanting in many other ways, but they are entailed by the very idea of science and they make science and globalization practical allies.

Business, banking, and commerce all depend on information flow and are facilitated by new communication technologies. The hardware of these technologies tends to be systemic and integrated—computer, television, cable, satellite, laser, fiber-optic, and microchip technologies combining to create a vast interactive communications and information network that can potentially give every person on earth access to every other person, and make every datum, every byte, available to every set of eyes. If the automobile was, as George Ball once said (when he gave his blessing to a Fiat factory in the Soviet Union during the Cold War), "an ideology on four wheels," then electronic telecommunication and information systems are an ideology at 186,000 miles per second—which makes for a very small planet in a very big hurry. Individual cultures speak particular languages; commerce and science increasingly speak English; the whole world speaks logarithms and binary mathematics.

Moreover, the pursuit of science and technology asks for, even compels, open societies. Satellite footprints do not respect national borders; telephone wires penetrate the most closed societies. With photocopying and then fax machines having infiltrated Soviet universities and *samizdat* literary circles in the eighties, and computer modems having multiplied like rabbits in communism's bureaucratic warrens thereafter, *glasnost* could not be far behind. In their social requisites, secrecy and science are enemies.

The new technology's software is perhaps even more globalizing than its hardware. The information arm of international commerce's sprawling body reaches out and touches distinct nations and parochial cultures, and gives them a common face chiseled in Hollywood, on Madison Avenue, and in Silicon Valley. Throughout the 1980s one of the most-watched television programs in South Africa was *The Cosby Show*. The demise of apartheid was already in production. Exhibitors at the 1991 Cannes film festival expressed growing anxiety over the "homogenization" and "Americanization" of the global film industry when, for the third year running, American films dominated the awards ceremonies. America has dominated the world's popular culture for much longer, and much more decisively. In November of 1991 Switzerland's once insular culture boasted best-seller lists featuring *Terminator 2* as the No. 1 movie, *Scarlett* as the No. 1 book, and Prince's *Diamonds and Pearls* as the No. 1 record album. No wonder the Japanese are buying Hollywood film studios even faster than Americans are buying Japanese television sets. This kind of software supremacy may in the long term be far more important than hardware superiority, because culture has become more potent than armaments. What is the power of the Pentagon compared with Disneyland? Can the Sixth Fleet keep up with CNN? McDonald's in Moscow and Coke in China will do more to create a global culture than military colonization ever could. It is less the goods than the brand names that do the work, for they convey life-style images that alter perception and challenge behavior. They make up the seductive software of McWorld's common (at times much too common) soul.

Yet in all this high-tech commercial world there is nothing that looks particularly democratic. It lends itself to surveillance as well as liberty, to new forms of manipulation and covert control as well as new kinds of participation, to skewed, unjust market outcomes as well as greater productivity. The consumer society and the open society are not quite synonymous. Capitalism and democracy have a relationship, but it is something less than a marriage. An efficient free market after all requires that consumers be free to vote their dollars on competing goods, not that citizens be free to vote their values and beliefs on competing political candidates and programs. The free market flourished in junta-run Chile, in military-governed Taiwan and Korea, and, earlier, in a variety of autocratic European empires as well as their colonial possessions.

The ecological imperative. The impact of globalization on ecology is a cliché even to world leaders who ignore it. We know well enough that the German forests can be destroyed by Swiss and Italians driving gas-guzzlers fueled by leaded gas. We also know that the planet can be asphyxiated by greenhouse gases because Brazilian farmers want to be part of the twentieth century and are burning down tropical rain forests to clear a little land to plough, and because Indonesians make a living out of converting their lush jungle into toothpicks for fastidious Japanese diners, upsetting the delicate oxygen balance and in effect puncturing our global lungs. Yet this ecological consciousness has meant not only greater awareness but also greater inequality, as modernized nations try to slam the door behind them, saying to developing nations, "The world cannot afford *your* modernization; ours has wrung it dry!"

Each of the four imperatives just cited is transnational,

transideological, and transcultural. Each applies impartially to Catholics, Jews, Muslims, Hindus, and Buddhists; to democrats and totalitarians; to capitalists and socialists. The Enlightenment dream of a universal rational society has to a remarkable degree been realized—but in a form that is commercialized, homogenized, depoliticized, bureaucratized, and, of course, radically incomplete, for the movement toward McWorld is in competition with forces of global breakdown, national dissolution, and centrifugal corruption. These forces, working in the opposite direction, are the essence of what I call Jihad.

Jihad, or the Lebanonization of the World

OPEC, THE WORLD BANK, THE UNITED NATIONS, the International Red Cross, the multinational corporation . . . there are scores of institutions that reflect globalization. But they often appear as ineffective reactors to the world's real actors: national states and, to an ever greater degree, subnational factions in permanent rebellion against uniformity and integration—even the kind represented by universal law and justice. The headlines feature these players regularly: they are cultures, not countries; parts, not wholes; sects, not religions; rebellious factions and dissenting minorities at war not just with globalism but with the traditional nation-state. Kurds, Basques, Puerto Ricans, Ossetians, East Timoreans, Quebecois, the Catholics of Northern Ireland, Abkhasians, Kurile Islander Japanese, the Zulus of Inkatha, Catalonians, Tamils, and, of course, Palestinians—people without countries, inhabiting nations not their own, seeking smaller worlds within borders that will seal them off from modernity.

A powerful irony is at work here. Nationalism was once a force of integration and unification, a movement aimed at bringing together disparate clans, tribes, and cultural fragments under new, assimilationist flags. But as Ortega y Gasset noted more than sixty years ago, having won its victories, nationalism changed its strategy. In the 1920s, and again today, it is more often a reactionary and divisive force, pulverizing the very nations it once helped cement together. The force that creates nations is "inclusive," Ortega wrote in *The Revolt of the Masses*. "In periods of consolidation, nationalism has a positive value, and is a lofty standard. But in Europe everything is more than consolidated, and nationalism is nothing but a mania. . . ."

This mania has left the post–Cold War world smoldering with hot wars; the international scene is little more unified than it was at the end of the Great War, in Ortega's own time. There were more than thirty wars in progress last year, most of them ethnic, racial, tribal, or religious in character, and the list of unsafe regions doesn't seem to be getting any shorter. Some new world order!

The aim of many of these small-scale wars is to redraw boundaries, to implode states and resecure parochial identities: to escape McWorld's dully insistent imperatives. The mood is that of Jihad: war not as an instrument of policy but as an emblem of identity, an expression of community, an end in itself. Even where there is no shooting war, there is fractiousness, secession, and the quest for ever smaller communities. Add to the list of dangerous countries those at risk: In Switzerland and Spain, Jurassian and Basque separatists still argue the virtues of ancient identities, sometimes in the language of bombs. Hyperdisintegration in the former Soviet Union may well continue unabated—not just a Ukraine independent from the Soviet Union but a Bessarabian Ukraine independent from the Ukrainian republic; not just Russia severed from the defunct union but Tatarstan severed from Russia. Yugoslavia makes even the disunited, ex-Soviet, nonsocialist republics that were once the Soviet Union look integrated, its sectarian fatherlands springing up within factional motherlands like weeds within weeds within weeds. Kurdish independence would threaten the territorial integrity of four Middle Eastern nations. Well before the current cataclysm Soviet Georgia made a claim for autonomy from the Soviet Union, only to be faced with its Ossetians (164,000 in a republic of 5.5 million) demanding their own self-determination within Georgia. The Abkhasian minority in Georgia has followed suit. Even the good will established by Canada's once promising Meech Lake protocols is in danger, with Francophone Quebec again threatening the dissolution of the federation. In South Africa the emergence from apartheid was hardly achieved when friction between Inkatha's Zulus and the African National Congress's tribally identified members threatened to replace Europeans' racism with an indigenous tribal war. After thirty years of attempted integration using the colonial language (English) as a unifier, Nigeria is now playing with the idea of linguistic multiculturalism—which could mean the cultural breakup of the nation into hundreds of tribal fragments. Even Saddam Hussein has benefited from the threat of internal Jihad, having used renewed tribal and religious warfare to turn last season's mortal enemies into reluctant allies of an Iraqi nationhood that he nearly destroyed.

The passing of communism has torn away the thin veneer of internationalism (workers of the world unite!) to reveal ethnic prejudices that are not only ugly and deep-seated but increasingly murderous. Europe's old scourge, anti-Semitism, is back with a vengeance, but it is only one of many antagonisms. It appears all too easy to throw the historical gears into reverse and pass from a Communist dictatorship back into a tribal state.

Among the tribes, religion is also a battlefield. ("Jihad" is a rich word whose generic meaning is "struggle"—usually the struggle of the soul to avert evil. Strictly applied to religious war, it is used only in reference to battles where the faith is under assault, or battles against a government that denies the practice of Islam. My use here is rhetorical, but does follow both journalistic practice and history.) Remember the Thirty Years War? Whatever forms of Enlightenment universalism might once have come to grace such historically related forms of monotheism as Judaism, Christianity, and Islam, in many of their modern incarnations they are parochial rather than cosmopolitan, angry rather than loving, proselytizing rather than ecumenical, zealous rather than rationalist, sectarian rather than deistic, ethnocentric rather than universalizing. As a result, like the new forms of hypernationalism, the new expressions of religious fundamentalism are fractious and pulverizing, never integrating. This is religion as the Crusaders knew it: a battle to the death for souls that if not saved will be forever lost.

The atmospherics of Jihad have resulted in a breakdown of civility in the name of identity, of comity in the name of community. International relations have sometimes taken on the aspect of gang war—cultural turf battles featuring tribal factions that were supposed to be sublimated as integral parts of large national, economic, postcolonial, and constitutional entities.

The Darkening Future of Democracy

THESE RATHER MELODRAMATIC TABLEAUX VIvants do not tell the whole story, however. For all their defects, Jihad and McWorld have their attractions. Yet, to repeat and insist, the attractions are unrelated to democracy. Neither McWorld nor Jihad is remotely democratic in impulse. Neither needs democracy; neither promotes democracy.

McWorld does manage to look pretty seductive in a world obsessed with Jihad. It delivers peace, prosperity, and relative unity—if at the cost of independence, community, and identity (which is generally based on difference). The primary political values required by the global market are order and tranquillity, and freedom—as in the phrases "free trade," "free press," and "free love." Human rights are needed to a degree, but not citizenship or participation—and no more social justice and equality than are necessary to promote efficient economic production and consumption. Multinational corporations sometimes seem to prefer doing business with local oligarchs, inasmuch as they can take confidence from dealing with the boss on all crucial matters. Despots who slaughter their own populations are no problem, so long as they leave markets in place and refrain from making war on their neighbors (Saddam Hussein's fatal mistake). In trading partners, predictability is of more value than justice.

The Eastern European revolutions that seemed to arise out of concern for global democratic values quickly deteriorated into a stampede in the general direction of free markets and their ubiquitous, television-promoted shopping malls. East Germany's Neues Forum, that courageous gathering of intellectuals, students, and workers which overturned the Stalinist regime in Berlin in 1989, lasted only six months in Germany's mini-version of McWorld. Then it gave way to money and markets and monopolies from the West. By the time of the first all-German elections, it could scarcely manage to secure three percent of the vote. Elsewhere there is growing evidence that *glasnost* will go and *perestroika*—defined as privatization and an opening of markets to Western bidders—will stay. So understandably anxious are the new rulers of Eastern Europe and whatever entities are forged from the residues of the Soviet Union to gain access to credit and markets and technology—McWorld's flourishing new currencies—that they have shown themselves willing to trade away democratic prospects in pursuit of them: not just old totalitarian ideologies and command-economy production models but some possible indigenous experiments with a third way between capitalism and socialism, such as economic cooperatives and employee stock-ownership plans, both of which have their ardent supporters in the East.

Jihad delivers a different set of virtues: a vibrant local identity, a sense of community, solidarity among kinsmen, neighbors, and countrymen, narrowly conceived. But it also guarantees parochialism and is grounded in exclusion. Solidarity is secured through war against outsiders. And solidarity often means obedience to a hierarchy in governance, fanaticism in beliefs, and the obliteration of individual selves in the name of the group. Deference to leaders and intolerance toward outsiders (and toward "enemies within") are hallmarks of tribalism—hardly the attitudes required for the cultivation of new democratic women and men capable of governing themselves. Where new democratic experiments have been conducted in retribalizing societies, in both Europe and the Third World, the result has often been anarchy, repression, persecution, and the coming of new, noncommunist forms of very old kinds of despotism. During the past year, Havel's velvet revolution in Czechoslovakia was imperiled by partisans of "Czechland" and of Slovakia as independent entities. India seemed little less rent by Sikh, Hindu, Muslim, and Tamil infighting than it was immediately after the British pulled out, more than forty years ago.

To the extent that either McWorld or Jihad has a *natural* politics, it has turned out to be more of an antipolitics. For McWorld, it is the antipolitics of globalism: bureaucratic, technocratic, and meritocratic, focused (as Marx predicted it would be) on the administration of things—with people, however, among the chief things to be administered. In its politico-economic imperatives McWorld has been guided by laissez-faire market principles that privilege efficiency, productivity, and beneficence at the expense of civic liberty and self-government.

For Jihad, the antipolitics of tribalization has been explicitly antidemocratic: one-party dictatorship, government by military junta, theocratic fundamentalism—often associated with a version of the *Führerprinzip* that empowers an individual to rule on behalf of a people. Even the government of India, struggling for decades to model democracy for a people who will soon number a billion, longs for great leaders; and for every Mahatma Gandhi, Indira Gandhi, or Rajiv Gandhi taken from them

by zealous assassins, the Indians appear to seek a replacement who will deliver them from the lengthy travail of their freedom.

The Confederal Option

HOW CAN DEMOCRACY BE SECURED AND SPREAD in a world whose primary tendencies are at best indifferent to it (McWorld) and at worst deeply antithetical to it (Jihad)? My guess is that globalization will eventually vanquish retribalization. The ethos of material "civilization" has not yet encountered an obstacle it has been unable to thrust aside. Ortega may have grasped in the 1920s a clue to our own future in the coming millennium.

> Everyone sees the need of a new principle of life. But as always happens in similar crises—some people attempt to save the situation by an artificial intensification of the very principle which has led to decay. This is the meaning of the "nationalist" outburst of recent years. . . . things have always gone that way. The last flare, the longest; the last sigh, the deepest. On the very eve of their disappearance there is an intensification of frontiers—military and economic.

Jihad may be a last deep sigh before the eternal yawn of McWorld. On the other hand, Ortega was not exactly prescient; his prophecy of peace and internationalism came just before blitzkrieg, world war, and the Holocaust tore the old order to bits. Yet democracy is how we remonstrate with reality, the rebuke our aspirations offer to history. And if retribalization is inhospitable to democracy, there is nonetheless a form of democratic government that can accommodate parochialism and communitarianism, one that can even save them from their defects and make them more tolerant and participatory: decentralized participatory democracy. And if McWorld is indifferent to democracy, there is nonetheless a form of democratic government that suits global markets passably well—representative government in its federal or, better still, confederal variation.

With its concern for accountability, the protection of minorities, and the universal rule of law, a confederalized representative system would serve the political needs of McWorld as well as oligarchic bureaucratism or meritocratic elitism is currently doing. As we are already beginning to see, many nations may survive in the long term only as confederations that afford local regions smaller than "nations" extensive jurisdiction. Recommended reading for democrats of the twenty-first century is not the U.S. Constitution or the French Declaration of Rights of Man and Citizen but the Articles of Confederation, that suddenly pertinent document that stitched together the thirteen American colonies into what then seemed a too loose confederation of independent states but now appears a new form of political realism, as veterans of Yeltsin's new Russia and the new Europe created at Maastricht will attest.

5. COMPARATIVE POLITICS: Tribal Threat to Pluralism?

By the same token, the participatory and direct form of democracy that engages citizens in civic activity and civic judgment and goes well beyond just voting and accountability—the system I have called "strong democracy"—suits the political needs of decentralized communities as well as theocratic and nationalist party dictatorships have done. Local neighborhoods need not be democratic, but they can be. Real democracy has flourished in diminutive settings: the spirit of liberty, Tocqueville said, is local. Participatory democracy, if not naturally apposite to tribalism, has an undeniable attractiveness under conditions of parochialism.

Democracy in any of these variations will, however, continue to be obstructed by the undemocratic and antidemocratic trends toward uniformitarian globalism and intolerant retribalization which I have portrayed here. For democracy to persist in our brave new McWorld, we will have to commit acts of conscious political will—a possibility, but hardly a probability, under these conditions. Political will requires much more than the quick fix of the transfer of institutions. Like technology transfer, institution transfer rests on foolish assumptions about a uniform world of the kind that once fired the imagination of colonial administrators. Spread English justice to the colonies by exporting wigs. Let an East Indian trading company act as the vanguard to Britain's free parliamentary institutions. Today's well-intentioned quick-fixers in the National Endowment for Democracy and the Kennedy School of Government, in the unions and foundations and universities zealously nurturing contacts in Eastern Europe and the Third World, are hoping to democratize by long distance. Post Bulgaria a parliament by first-class mail. Fed Ex the Bill of Rights to Sri Lanka. Cable Cambodia some common law.

Yet Eastern Europe has already demonstrated that importing free political parties, parliaments, and presses cannot establish a democratic civil society; imposing a free market may even have the opposite effect. Democracy grows from the bottom up and cannot be imposed from the top down. Civil society has to be built from the inside out. The institutional superstructure comes last.

Poland may become democratic, but then again it may heed the Pope, and prefer to found its politics on its Catholicism, with uncertain consequences for democracy. Bulgaria may become democratic, but it may prefer tribal war. The former Soviet Union may become a democratic confederation, or it may just grow into an anarchic and weak conglomeration of markets for other nations' goods and services.

Democrats need to seek out indigenous democratic impulses. There is always a desire for self-government, always some expression of participation, accountability, consent, and representation, even in traditional hierarchical societies. These need to be identified, tapped, modified, and incorporated into new democratic practices with an indigenous flavor. The tortoises among the democratizers may ultimately outlive or outpace the hares, for they will have the time and patience to explore conditions along the way, and to adapt their gait to changing circumstances. Tragically, democracy in a hurry often looks something like France in 1794 or China in 1989.

It certainly seems possible that the most attractive democratic ideal in the face of the brutal realities of Jihad and the dull realities of McWorld will be a confederal union of semi-autonomous communities smaller than nation-states, tied together into regional economic associations and markets larger than nation-states—participatory and self-determining in local matters at the bottom, representative and accountable at the top. The nation-state would play a diminished role, and sovereignty would lose some of its political potency. The Green movement adage "Think globally, act locally" would actually come to describe the conduct of politics.

This vision reflects only an ideal, however—one that is not terribly likely to be realized. Freedom, Jean-Jacques Rousseau once wrote, is a food easy to eat but hard to digest. Still, democracy has always played itself out against the odds. And democracy remains both a form of coherence as binding as McWorld and a secular faith potentially as inspiriting as Jihad.

Credits/
Acknowledgments

Cover design by Charles Vitelli

1. Country Overviews
Facing overview—*The Christian Science Monitor* photo by R. Norman Matheny.

2. Factors in the Political Process
Facing overview—AP/Wide World Photos.

3. Europe—West, Center, and East
Facing overview—United Nations photo.

4. Third World
Facing overview—United Nations photo by T. Sennett.

5. Comparative Politics
Facing overview—United Nations photo by J. Isaac.

PHOTOCOPY THIS PAGE!!!*

ANNUAL EDITIONS ARTICLE REVIEW FORM

■ NAME: _____ DATE: _____

■ TITLE AND NUMBER OF ARTICLE: _____

■ BRIEFLY STATE THE MAIN IDEA OF THIS ARTICLE: _____

_____

_____

_____

_____

■ LIST THREE IMPORTANT FACTS THAT THE AUTHOR USES TO SUPPORT THE MAIN IDEA:

_____

_____

_____

_____

_____

■ WHAT INFORMATION OR IDEAS DISCUSSED IN THIS ARTICLE ARE ALSO DISCUSSED IN YOUR TEXTBOOK OR OTHER READING YOU HAVE DONE? LIST THE TEXTBOOK CHAPTERS AND PAGE NUMBERS:

_____

_____

_____

_____

_____

_____

■ LIST ANY EXAMPLES OF BIAS OR FAULTY REASONING THAT YOU FOUND IN THE ARTICLE:

_____

_____

_____

_____

_____

■ LIST ANY NEW TERMS/CONCEPTS THAT WERE DISCUSSED IN THE ARTICLE AND WRITE A SHORT DEFINITION:

_____

_____

_____

_____

_____

*Your instructor may require you to use this Annual Editions Article Review Form in any number of ways: for articles that are assigned, for extra credit, as a tool to assist in developing assigned papers, or simply for your own reference. Even if it is not required, we encourage you to photocopy and use this page; you'll find that reflecting on the articles will greatly enhance the information from your text.

ANNUAL EDITIONS: COMPARATIVE POLITICS 92/93
Article Rating Form

Here is an opportunity for you to have direct input into the next revision of this volume. We would like you to rate each of the 59 articles listed below, using the following scale:

1. **Excellent: should definitely be retained**
2. **Above average: should probably be retained**
3. **Below average: should probably be deleted**
4. **Poor: should definitely be deleted**

Your ratings will play a vital part in the next revision. So please mail this prepaid form to us just as soon as you complete it.
Thanks for your help!

Annual Editions revisions depend on two major opinion sources: one is our Advisory Board, listed in the front of this volume, which works with us in scanning the thousands of articles published in the public press each year; the other is you—the person actually using the book. Please help us and the users of the next edition by completing the prepaid article rating form on this page and returning it to us. Thank you.

Rating	Article	Rating	Article
	1. The End of an Era in British Politics		28. Europe: My Country, Right . . . or What?
	2. Having Outwitted the Seers, Tories Wax Conciliatory		29. As the World Turns Democatic, Federalism Finds Favor
	3. British Election of 1992: How and Why the Votes Were Cast		30. Staging Post on the Path to Federalism
	4. Britain's Constitutional Question		31. A Divided Continent Sees Shared Destiny
	5. The Myths Are Dead—So Let's Get Down to Business		32. My, How You've Grown
			33. Neither a State Nor International Organization
	6. Despite Integration, Britain Remains an Island Unto Itself		34. EC Girds Itself for Inevitable Expansion
			35. Europe's Open Future
	7. First Year Hangover		36. Eastern Europe After the Revolutions
	8. The New Germany		37. The Soviet State, Born of a Dream, Dies
	9. Germany: Power and the Left		38. Left With a Kingdom of Air
	10. Germany: Such Long Sorrow		39. Tumbling Back to the Future
	11. Germany: Too Right		40. Yeltsin Mystery: True Democrat or Tyrant?
	12. The New France		41. The Yeltsin Revolution
	13. France: The State Gives Way		42. What's Really Happening in Russia?
	14. Deep Changes in French Society Unsettle Socialist Leadership		43. Third World Embracing Reforms to Encourage Economic Growth
	15. The Lame Duck with a Long, Long Way to Waddle		44. A New Discipline in Economics Brings Change to Latin America
	16. The Real Japan		45. Mexico: Progress and Promise
	17. Poor, Honest, and Out of a Job		46. Democracy in Africa
	18. Trading in Mistrust: The U.S. and Japan: A Romance Turning to Ashes		47. 'Today We Have Closed the Books on Apartheid'
			48. A Mandate for Change
	19. For the Japanese: A Growing Sense of Disillusionment		49. Deng Struggles to Set Reform Back on Track
			50. Preparing for the Succession
	20. A Tale of Two Families		51. How China's Economy Left Its Comrade Behind
	21. Europe's Christian Democrats: Hello, Caesar, This Is God		52. After the Dynasty: Politics in India
	22. Europe: Right-Wing Parties Gain		53. Democracy Takes Hold—Sort Of
	23. Women, Power, and Politics: The Norwegian Experience		54. A New Era in Democracy: Democracy's Third Wave
	24. Europe's Women: How the Other Half Works		55. What Kind of Democracy?
	25. We the Peoples: A Checklist for New Constitution Writers		56. Capitalism and Democracy
			57. Communitarian vs. Individualistic Capitalism
	26. Parliament and Congress: Is the Grass Greener on the Other Side?		58. Faith Comes in From Political Fringe
	27. Presidents and Prime Ministers		59. Jihad vs. McWorld

(Continued on next page)

ABOUT YOU

Name_____ Date_____

Are you a teacher? ☐ Or student? ☐

Your School Name _____

Department _____

Address _____

City _____ State _____ Zip _____

School Telephone # _____

YOUR COMMENTS ARE IMPORTANT TO US!

Please fill in the following information:

For which course did you use this book? _____

Did you use a text with this Annual Edition? ☐ yes ☐ no

The title of the text? _____

What are your general reactions to the Annual Editions concept?

Have you read any particular articles recently that you think should be included in the next edition?

Are there any articles you feel should be replaced in the next edition? Why?

Are there other areas that you feel would utilize an Annual Edition?

May we contact you for editorial input?

May we quote you from above?

‖‖‖‖

No Postage
Necessary
if Mailed
in the
United States

ANNUAL EDITIONS: COMPARATIVE POLITICS 92/93

BUSINESS REPLY MAIL

First Class   Permit No. 84   Guilford, CT

Postage will be paid by addressee

The Dushkin Publishing Group, Inc.
Sluice Dock
DPG **Guilford, Connecticut 06437**

‖‖‖‖‖‖‖‖‖‖‖‖‖‖‖‖‖‖‖‖‖‖‖‖‖‖‖‖‖‖‖